Ch

MW00710605

# BUSINESS

D. C. HEATH AND COMPANY · LEXINGTON, MASSACHUSETTS · TORONTO

# BUSINESS

## Leon C. Megginson
Mobile College

## Lyle R. Trueblood
University of Tulsa

## Gayle M. Ross
Copiah-Lincoln Junior College

*To Our Families*

Bill, Peggy, and William, and
Jay and John

Wyn, Steve, and Mike

Tom and Arwen

*Cover:* Houston, Texas, 1984. Bill Ross/West Light

Published simultaneously in Canada.

Printed in the United States of America.

International Standard Book Number: 0-669-05878-5

Library of Congress Catalog Card Number: 84-81087

# Preface

"How to succeed in business without really trying" would be a catchy theme for a book like this. The only problem is, it isn't true! We know that the only way to succeed in this field is by trying harder than anyone else. So we've brought to this project a combined three-quarters of a century of business experience, a very real concern for the needs of our users, and seven years of hard work. We believe in what we've produced, and we hope that you will, too.

We wrote this book because we feel that a first course in business should be of immediate, practical use to all students—both first-time college students and adults returning to school. And the best use of such a book lies in preparing readers to be informed consumers and readers of business literature, as well as to hold careers in the business world. As a result, our approach in this text and package has been one of learning and application. We've provided students with the basic business concepts they need in order to become "business literate," and we've made these concepts meaningful through application to real examples from the world of business and to the student's own experience.

Since all three of us have worked in business and have taught the introduction to business course, we bring to this project our knowledge of both how business works and how to teach it. Our publisher, D. C. Heath, brought additional insight from the experts—those on staff who know how to publish successful textbooks, those who teach the introduction to business course, and those who currently work in business. D. C. Heath conducted over one hundred interviews with course instructors across the country; in August 1983, directed a focus group with six course instructors; and had the manuscript and supplements evaluated by thirty teachers and business professionals. The result, we feel, is a perfect fit of teaching package to classroom reality.

The *Business* package is a four-part instructional system, featuring the following components:

1. *Text content.* Exceptionally well-explained coverage of all key business concepts.
2. *Text pedagogy.* Extensive pedagogical features integrated throughout the text.
3. *Student supplements.* A variety of study aids designed for flexibility within any course structure.
4. *Instructor's supplements.* A complete teaching package fully coordinated with the text, for both full- and part-time instructors.

## TEXT CONTENT

The content of this text will adapt smoothly to any introduction to business syllabus. Instructors need not be concerned about integrating appendixes and supplemental chapters into their individual course organizations, since our text contains full chapters covering all topics they will need. At the same time, however, we've devoted extra space to those emerging topics that are affecting the world of business more than ever before. For instance, Part I includes a full chapter each on Small Business and on Opportunities in Franchising. Since productivity and quality control are of growing

concern, Chapter 8 covers Production and Operations Management, with special concentration on the role of computers and robotics.

The text is divided into seven parts: (1) Business and Its Environment, (2) Managing and Organizing a Business, (3) Managing Human Resources, (4) Marketing, (5) Tools of Business, (6) Finance, and (7) The World of Business. Since it is important that students get a sense of the interaction among the various functional areas of business and a feeling for how business really works, each of the part opening sections previews the chapters in that part, emphasizing the interlocking of those chapters, and at the same time refers back to the concepts discussed in the previous part. Similarly, each chapter's opening paragraphs refer back to previous chapters.

## TEXT PEDAGOGY

*Business* includes an outstanding array of pedagogical features. Learning objectives, vocabulary mastery, and real-world examples, among other features, combine with an informal writing style that facilitates understanding and encourages student enthusiasm.

### Learning Objectives

Since we believe in the meaningful use of learning objectives, we've structured each chapter's content around them. Each chapter begins with a concise list of objectives that summarizes exactly what students can expect to learn while reading the chapter. These objectives are repeated in the text margins throughout the chapter, for guided study. The chapter summary (Learning Objectives Revisited) clearly relates each objective to the content just covered. End-of-chapter questions thoroughly test students' mastery of the major topics highlighted in the objectives.

### In This Chapter

A brief review of the chapter's main topics is positioned adjacent to the first presentation of the learning objectives, for easy comparison and preview of the chapter.

### Chapter Opening Cases

Each chapter opens with a real-world situation closely related to the chapter content. Frequent text references back to the opening case and to other boxed features encourage students to relate the chapter content to the world of business.

### Important Terms

Since a key goal of the introduction to business course is building a business vocabulary, all important terms are boldfaced and clearly defined at their first appearance in the chapter. At the end of the chapter, an Important Terms exercise tests the student on all terms, with page references for further review. The terms are also listed and defined in the Glossary at the end of the book.

### Boxed Questions

Every chapter includes questions boxed within the running text, to encourage students to pause, reflect, and apply what they are learning to real-world business situations or to their own experience.

### Boxed Features

FYIs, Profiles, Business Debates, and Quizzes are used liberally throughout the text to bring key ideas to life.

FYIs ("For Your Information") focus on topics such as music videos, Levi Strauss from the Gold Rush to the 1984 Olympics, and the Cabbage Patch Kids. Profiles of well-known, and not as well-known (but equally important), businesspeople add a

human touch to the chapter's major topics. Business Debates are used, when appropriate, to inspire students to take a stand on controversial issues. Quizzes allow students to test themselves while reading.

### Real-World Examples

Each chapter includes an average of sixteen real-world examples within running text. These vignettes further bring the world of business to life.

### Readability

To ensure accessibility for students, the reading level of this text has been carefully monitored by the editors and course instructors who have reviewed it.

### Design

Introduction to business students of the 1980s are part of a visually oriented society and need a textbook that will hold their interest. To that end, we have a colorful, yet professional, design with the look of today's business magazines.

### Chapter-End Materials

A carefully graded set of chapter review materials is provided at the end of each chapter. First, the Important Terms exercise reviews vocabulary. From ten to twenty review questions follow, providing a rote review of the chapter's major topics and paralleling the learning objectives. Five or more Discussion Questions encourage students to stretch their learning beyond the chapter content. Finally, two or three short cases (80 percent real-world) challenge students to apply their knowledge to new situations. A list of current, relevant, and easily available supplementary readings is also included. The result? Business literacy.

### Careers Guidance

The last chapter, Your Future in Business, is an important part of our three-tiered approach to careers guidance, covering such topics as plotting a career strategy, the career life cycle (appropriate for students of any age), and choosing a first company and first job. In addition, both long-range and short-term career guidance is provided at the end of each part. Digging Deeper sections, thumb-indexed for handy reference, include tables of careers students are likely to pursue, popular salary ranges for those jobs, and employment prospects for the future.

## SUPPLEMENTS

Throughout the development of the text and supplements, we've tried to create a total package that will be interesting, easy to use, and well integrated. In providing the widest variety of supplements available for an introduction to business textbook, we hope to enable teachers to pick and choose the best mix for their particular style. To ensure coordination of the text package with the course, each supplement has been prepared by a text coauthor or by an experienced teacher of the introduction to business course.

### Student Supplements

Available for students are the (1) Study Guide, (2) Stock Market Practice Set, and (3) software.

**Study Guide.** Prepared by John W. Warner of the University of New Mexico and Michelle L. Slagle of George Washington University, the *Study Guide* has been designed as a five-step learning program that allows students:

1. To learn how to study for *all* college courses, in a unique section on "Becoming a More Successful Student."
2. To briefly review each chapter's contents in more depth, using a chapter review written especially for the *Study Guide.*
3. To review the chapter contents in more depth, simultaneously testing knowledge with a fill-in-the-blanks Chapter Outline.
4. To test knowledge more thoroughly in each chapter's Self-Test section. The Self-Test includes an Important Terms matching exercise, True/False Questions, and Multiple-Choice Questions.
5. To extend learning beyond the chapter content by reading and responding to real-world minicases, exercises, and projects in each chapter's Applying Terms and Concepts section.

All answers are supplied at the end of the *Study Guide.*

**Stock Market Practice Set.** The object of the Practice Set is for students to "invest" in several corporations, follow their stock purchases through published quotes in *The Wall Street Journal* or local newspapers, and keep track of their investments on a complete set of worksheets.

**Software.** The software package for *Business* consists of floppy disks with tutorial modules on each disk. The six tutorial modules supplement and reinforce concepts discussed in the textbook by requiring frequent input from students.

The software runs on Apple II+, Apple IIe, IBM Personal Computer, and IBM PCjr microcomputers and is menu driven and completely user friendly. Color and graphics are used wherever appropriate.

## Instructor's Supplements

The supplements designed for instructors include the (1) Instructor's Guide, (2) Test Bank, (3) User's Guide, (4) Audiovisual Guide, (5) Instructor's Resources, (6) Supplemental Topics Manual, (7) Profiles, (8) Business Papers, (9) Transparencies, and (10) Stepsavers.

**Instructor's Guide.** *The Instructor's Guide* is the most diverse of the instructor's supplements. It is divided into three parts, each of which can be used independently. Part I, Course Mechanics, includes much of the "nuts and bolts" of teaching preparation: grading suggestions, course syllabi, suggested term projects, and possible course sequences by semester and quarter. We also provide a chapter-by-chapter comparison of our text with those of other authors.

The bulk of the *Instructor's Guide,* Part II, is devoted to chapter-by-chapter teaching suggestions. Included are learning objectives; ten to twelve classroom projects; a detailed, four- to eight-page teaching outline; a section on the integration of the other supplements (transparencies, supplemental readings and lectures, profiles, and business papers); and brief answers to all chapter questions.

The final part of the *Instructor's Guide,* Part III, is a teaching guide for the *Stock Market Practice Set.*

**Test Bank.** The *Test Bank* includes over 2,000 possible test questions: 40 percent true/false, 50 percent multiple choice, and 10 percent matching. *Archive,* a computerized test bank for the Apple IIe microcomputer, is also available.

Since reliable test items are crucial, we've had sample items class-tested at St. Louis Community College at Meramec.

**User's Guide.** The *User's Guide* presents an overview of the entire supplemental package. The first part of the *User's Guide* describes and cross-references all of the

supplements. Part II is a good first step in preparing for teaching. The chapter teaching outline from the *Instructor's Guide* is presented here in abridged form, with keyed references to supplemental readings and lectures, transparencies, profiles, and business papers for each chapter. The final part of the guide pulls together every major topic included into a master index.

**Supplemental Topics Manual.** The purpose of the *Supplemental Topics Manual* is to help supplement lectures with important topics not covered in the text or to expand on topics introduced there.

Each chapter includes at least one Additional Lecture, on detailed subjects, and as many as twelve Related Readings—summaries of current articles from newspapers, magazines, and journals.

All supplemental readings and lectures are keyed to chapter content in the *User's Guide* and the *Instructor's Guide*.

**Audiovisual Guide.** In researching audiovisuals to use with this course, we found an astounding number and diversity of available films. The *Audiovisual Guide* presents these films, with the distributors' descriptions, for each chapter. An index of distributors and addresses is also provided.

**Instructor's Resources.** This booklet lists the addresses of organizations and associations that can provide instructors with free teaching materials. A brief section of toll-free numbers is provided.

**Profiles.** The *Profiles* include twenty-eight profiles, with photos, of key business-people. They can be used as lecture supplements or as class handouts. All profiles are keyed to chapter content in the *User's Guide* and the *Instructor's Guide*.

**Business Papers.** The *Business Papers* portfolio includes thirty-six widely used business papers and forms, ranging from a labor union contract to an Equal Employment Opportunity Reporting form. All business papers are keyed to chapter content in the *User's Guide* and the *Instructor's Guide*.

**Transparencies.** The transparency pack includes over 180 transparency acetates. About half are from the text; others are not included in the text but are directly related to the text or the *Supplemental Topics Manual*. Twenty-six transparencies are full-color. All transparencies are keyed to chapter content in the *User's Guide* and the *Instructor's Guide*.

**Stepsavers.** The *Stepsavers*—*unique* in the introduction to business field—are intended to fill a need in multisection courses with little time for class preparation. Each *Stepsaver* consolidates, in one handy booklet, the *User's Guide, Instructor's Guide, Supplemental Topics Manual, Profiles, Audiovisual Guide*, and *Business Papers* materials for each chapter. The entire set of Stepsavers consists of twenty-four booklets—one for each chapter. Each booklet has been punched for storage in a three-ring binder.

## ACKNOWLEDGMENTS

It takes so many people to develop and publish a book of this nature that it's impossible to thank all of them. We are grateful to a large number of professors and other professional colleagues for their suggestions for improving the package for *Business*. Many of their names appear on the following pages.

Special thanks to Charles R. Scott, Jr., formerly of the University of Alabama, and Curtis E. Tate, Jr., University of Georgia, for their help with the original manuscript.

Our thanks also go to the hundreds of businesspeople and government agencies who provided us with information, photographs, and visuals.

Suzanne S. Barnhill did a superb job of editing, typing, and proofreading various drafts of the text manuscript and was creative in suggesting examples, illustrations, and general improvements. Without her assistance and cooperation, it would have been much more difficult to produce *Business*.

And Joclaire Waldorf, secretary of the Management Department at the University of South Alabama, did an excellent job of typing much of the original draft and did many of the original drawings.

Finally, the book could not have been published without the help of Harry Briggs, Susan Gleason, Marret McCorkle, Mark Fowler, Mike O'Dea, Sharon Donahue, and the others at D. C. Heath and Company.

L. C. M.
L. R. T.
G. M. R.

# ACKNOWLEDGMENTS

For their reviews of
manuscript materials:

Ray Attner
Brookhaven College

Barbara Barrett
Saint Louis Community College at
Meramec

Carlyle Carter
Developmental Editor
Boston, Massachusetts

Joseph Cebula
Community College of Philadelphia

Melvin Choate
North Seattle Community College

Craig Christopherson
Richland College

Charles Clark
South Oklahoma City Junior College

Benjamin J. Cutler
Bronx Community College

Danny Dykes
Systems Analyst
Copiah-Lincoln Junior College

Frank M. Falcetta
Middlesex Community College

Robert M. Fishco
Middlesex County College

Douglas C. Gordon
Arapahoe Community College

Kenneth Graham
Rochester Institute of Technology

David E. Grainger
Oakland Community College

Joseph Grissom
Tarrant County Junior College

Charles Hart
CPA and Bookstore Manager
Copiah-Lincoln Junior College

Kathryn Hegar
Mountain View College

Jimmie Henslee
El Centro College

Clayton Hock
Miami University

Dale A. Johnson
University of South Florida

Steven D. Kapplin
University of South Florida

Linn Litkenhous
Vice President, Investments
A. G. Edwards and Sons, Inc.

Paul J. Londrigan
Charles Stewart Mott Community
College

Michael D. McIntyre
Copiah-Lincoln Junior College

Joseph Platts
Miami-Dade Community College

Thomas A. Ross, Jr.
CPA
Jackson, Mississippi

Perry Rothstein
Oakton Community College

David E. Shepard
Virginia Western Community College

Bea Smith
Eastfield College

Heidi Vernon Wortzel
Northeastern University


For their cooperation with
in-person interviews:

Deborah Alston
National Business College

John Beem
College of Du Page

Leonard Bethards
Miami-Dade Community College

Alan Bures
Radford University

Kent Claussen
Parkland College

Carol Cowan
Middlesex Community College

Gordon Fidler
Illinois State University

Roy Grundy
College of Du Page

Arthur Guiness
Manchester Community College

Robert Hardig
Parkland College

Jagdish Kapoor
College of Du Page

Mason Linkous
National Business College

Stuart Mandell
University of Lowell

Timothy Mescon
University of Miami

James Mitchell
Virginia Western Community College

Philip Phillips
University of Akron

John Rich
Illinois State University

Jean Saunders
Virginia Western Community College

Richard Shapiro
Cuyahoga Community College

Donna Silverman
University of Miami

Lee Sutherland
Suffolk University

Britt Turner
Shelton State Community College

John Vacek
Triton College

Richard Vizard
Manchester Community College

Lowell Watkins
Cuyahoga Community College

Geri Welch
Saint Louis Community College at
Meramec

# About the Authors

## LEON C. MEGGINSON

Dr. Megginson brings considerable management and international expertise to *Business*. He has served as consultant for such major U.S. and foreign firms as Exxon, Texaco, Crown-Zellerbach, and the National Rural Electric Cooperative Association.

Dr. Megginson, Fulbright Research Scholar, is currently J. L. Bedsole Professor of Business Studies, and Chairman of the Division of Business Administration and Computer Sciences at Mobile College. He has been Research Professor of Management at the University of South Alabama and is Professor Emeritus at Louisiana State University. He received his MBA and Ph.D. from LSU and did postdoctoral study at Louisiana State University, the University of Madrid, the U.S. Military Academy, and Harvard Business School.

While teaching at LSU from 1947 to 1977, Dr. Megginson studied management development in Europe as a Fulbright Research Scholar at Madrid from 1961 to 1962. From 1968 to 1970, he was a Ford Foundation Resident Adviser on management and case development in Pakistan. Those experiences, plus research in over fifty other countries, resulted in his being chosen as a U.S. representative to the 1971 UNIDO conference in Chile, on introducing consultancy in South America.

Dr. Megginson's research has resulted in about one hundred business cases and fifty journal articles. In addition, he is the author or coauthor of eleven books. One of those, *Personnel Management*, currently going into its fifth edition with Richard D. Irwin, won the Academy of Management Book Award in 1967. Another, *Management: Concepts and Applications*, with Donald Mosely and Paul Pietri, published in 1983 by Harper & Row, has been adopted by over one hundred schools.

Active in his profession, Dr. Megginson has been president of the Southwestern Social Science Association, the Southern Management Association, and the Case Research Association. He has also served in many capacities in the Academy of Management and other professional organizations. Dr. Megginson is a member of several honor societies, including Phi Kappa Phi, Beta Gamma Sigma, and Pi Gamma Mu. He was selected as the first Phi Kappa Phi Scholar at the University of South Alabama in 1982. Listed in *International Who's Who in Community Service*, *Men and Women of Distinction*, *Notable Americans*, and *Who's Who in the South and Southwest*, he also was selected as an Outstanding Educator of America in 1972 and won the Louisiana State University Alumni Foundation Distinguished Faculty Service Award in 1971.

## LYLE R. TRUEBLOOD

Dr. Trueblood is currently Professor of Management at the University of Tulsa and has been a faculty member at the University of Oregon. He received degrees in Business Administration and Economics from the University of Missouri and his doctorate from Indiana University. He did post-doctoral study at two Carnegie-Mellon Programs, Harvard Business School, and the University of California at Los Angeles.

He is coauthor of four textbooks: *Successful Small Business Management,* Fourth Edition, Business Publications, Inc.; *A Complete Guide for Your Own Business* and *Dow Jones Business Papers* for Dow Jones-Irwin; and *Managing for Profits* for Dow Jones-Irwin. He has also published articles and cases in such journals as *American Journal of Small Business* and *Review of Insurance Studies, The Case Research Journal,* and several books in business policy.

Also active in his profession, Dr. Trueblood brings strengths in small business management and entrepreneurship to this textbook. He is currently Project Director of the Small Business Institute Program at The University of Tulsa and Vice President for Research, Case Research Association and is a past president of the Southwest Division, Academy of Management. Dr. Trueblood is active in the Academy of Management, its Southern Management Association and its Southwest Division; the Small Business Institute Directors Association; the International Council for Small Business; the Case Research Association; and the Southwest Small Business Institute Association. He is a member of the honorary society, Beta Gamma Sigma.

## GAYLE M. ROSS

Professor Ross brings to *Business* five years of teaching experience at Copiah-Lincoln Junior College in Wesson, Mississippi. Four of those years have been devoted to teaching the introduction to business course, as well as consumer finance and introduction to computers and data processing.

Professor Ross received her undergraduate and MBA degrees from Mississippi College. While teaching and studying for her MBA, she won first place in the statewide Phi Beta Lambda economics competition and went on to win fifth place in the national competition.

Professor Ross has contributed her energy and teaching experience not only to the textbook, but also to developing the instructor's supplements package for *Business.* She also prepared the Study Guide, Test Bank, and Instructor's Manual to accompany *Management: Concepts and Applications,* by Megginson, Mosley, and Pietri.

# Contents in Brief

# Contents

## 3 *Forms of Business Ownership*                                       58

## 4 Small Business 88

## 5 Opportunities in Franchising 112

**Profile:** Charles Kemmons Wilson 120

**FYI:** Kentucky Fried Chicken 122

**FYI:** D'Lites of America 125

**Quiz** 131

## ⑥ Managing a Business — 142

**FYI:** Gulf Coast Construction Company 150

**Business Debate:** Which Leadership Style Is Best for You? 153

FYI: Tips for Managers 300

**Business Debate:** In the Public Interest: Should Public Employees Strike? 304

---

**PART IV**  **MARKETING** 315

# 12 *The Marketing Process: Satisfying Customer Needs* 316

**Business Debate:** Is Marketing Good for the U.S. Economy? 322

FYI: Where You Live Affects the Kind of Goods You Buy 329

# 13   *Product and Price*   342

# 14 *Promoting, Advertising, and Selling* 368

# 15 *Channels and Distribution* 394

**PART V TOOLS OF BUSINESS 425**

## 16 *Computers and Data Processing* 426

## 17 *Accounting for the Firm's Resources* 452

Profile: Sidney Kess 458

FYI: United American Bank 461

FYI: How to Read an Annual Report 471

Business Debate: Does Corporate Financial Reporting Represent Reality or Illusion? 474

---

**PART VI**    **FINANCE** 483

## 18 *The American Financial System* 484

FYI: Goldsmith Banking 488

FYI: The Fall of the Franklin National Bank 490

Profile: Paul A. Volcker 494

## 21   *Risk Management and Insurance*     558

**PART VII**   THE WORLD OF BUSINESS                                   591

22  *International Business*                                           592

23  *The Legal and Governmental
    Environment*                                                      616

**FYI:** The Fateful Decision of Exxon
Corporation and China Light & Power
Company 597

**Profile:** Sam Ayoub 601

**Business Debate:** Should We Have
a Protectionist Industrial Policy? 610

# 24   *Your Future in Business*    642

**Digging Deeper:** CAREERS IN INTERNATIONAL BUSINESS AND
                    BUSINESS LAW          668

# PART I

## BUSINESS AND ITS ENVIRONMENT

Welcome to the exciting world of business! Regardless of your reasons for studying this material, you have chosen wisely. You may want to become directly involved in business, or merely increase your knowledge of business and its workings in order to be a more intelligent and productive citizen and informed consumer. Whichever is your primary goal, the material in this part will help you understand the environment in which stimulating, challenging, and rewarding business activities occur.

Chapter 1 explains what business is, how it operates, and how you're constantly involved with it. Particular emphasis is given to the role of the free enterprise system, entrepreneurs, and the profit motive.

In Chapter 2, the rationale for social responsibility is presented, along with some areas requiring action by enlightened businesspeople. These areas include equal employment opportunity, pollution control, conservation, product safety, and business ethics.

The more popular forms of business ownership—proprietorships, partnerships, corporations, trusts, and cooperatives—are discussed in Chapter 3.

Some characteristics of small business are covered in Chapter 4, as are some traits often found in successful small business owner-managers.

Chapter 5 emphasizes the role of a specific type of small business—the franchise—and evaluates some opportunities in franchising.

**1**

# The U.S. Business System

*The chief business of the American people is business.*

Calvin Coolidge

*Our concept of a free-enterprise system is not a fixed ideology. It can't be. Our marketplace must continually adapt to meet the realities of the age we live in.*

Lee Iacocca

**Learning Objectives**

After studying the material in this chapter, you will understand:

1. The nature and importance of business.
2. The role of business, profits, and entrepreneurs in a free enterprise system.
3. The four economic resources—land, labor, capital, and entrepreneurship—and their prices.
4. How demand and supply interact in the economic environment.
5. The characteristics of the two major economic systems: capitalism and communism.
6. The current economic issues of recession, inflation, and productivity and their effects on business.
7. Why there is so much current interest in studying and entering business.
8. How business activities affect you directly.

**In This Chapter**

What Is Business?
Business in a Free Enterprise System
Business in the U.S. Economic Environment
Different Economic Environments
The U.S. Economic Environment Today
Current Emphasis on Business

# CONESTOGA I
*Space-Age Entrepreneurs*

"Long live free enterprise!" shouted some 300 observers as the thirty-seven-foot-long Conestoga I rocket lifted off from a makeshift launch pad on the Texas Gulf Coast in September 1982. And David Hannah, Jr., chairman of Space Services, Inc. (SSI), said to his fellow investors, "I think we're going to make a lot of money with this."

By 1986, this privately financed rocket venture is expected to serve the needs of business with a fleet of private telecommunications and earth-scanning satellites launched monthly (at $5 million a shot) from a Hawaiian site. At least a dozen energy companies have expressed interest in doing business with SSI, especially to monitor oil flows at untended offshore wells and to conduct geological surveys from space.

The Conestoga, aptly named for the covered wagons used by early American pioneers, was essentially built from spare rocket parts. SSI first bought a 1960s-vintage Minuteman I solid-fuel engine from the National Aeronautics and Space Administration (NASA) for around $350,000 and built an aluminum missile around it. But in 1981 it blew up while being tested the week before launch. The firm then hired a California contractor who had built twenty-two rockets for the government to build another rocket—the Conestoga I—and brought former astronaut "Deke" Slayton on board as flight director for the launch. With the help of a $2.5 million investment, these two and six other full-time employees succeeded where less experienced personnel had failed the year before.

After spending $6 million just to achieve one successful launch, the investors backing SSI must now raise at least $15 million more before the venture can hope to earn a profit. The firm's strategy for beating NASA at its own game of providing space transportation is simple: keep costs down by using existing technology more effectively. The competition at NASA wished the firm well, even though its success might mean less commercial business for NASA's space shuttle.

From Cabbage Patch dolls and tanning parlors to Conestoga I, when there's a demand for a new product or service, U.S. business will step in to provide it as quickly and as profitably as possible. This couldn't happen without the basic ingredients of the U.S. economy: entrepreneurs, the profit motive, and the free enterprise system.

Ask the person on the street what business means and you'll get no two answers alike. Most of us get some or all of our living from business, so some of your answers will come from an employee's point of view: "Business pays my bills." "Business has given me a raw deal." "I'm thinking of going into business for myself." Business is also the complex system of producers and distributors that provides us with our goods and services. So some answers will come out as consumer responses: "Well, my home is being remodeled by a business." "I bought my Apple IIe from a business." "My broker sure is a good business." In fact, all the equipment, materials, services, and supplies needed by such diverse groups as schools, hospitals, churches, and government agencies are provided by business. And business can be where we invest our extra cash with the hope of making a profit. Thus business may be seen from the viewpoint of an employee, a customer or receiver of some type of service, or an investor.

Business has become an important part of all the world's cultures, since services and products touch everyone's life, even in remote nations. But business is especially booming in the United States. People here spend more time in activities affected by business than in any other environment, since business firms not only loom as economic entities like IBM and General Motors but also touch most aspects of our lives in one way or another. Everyone, whether MBA graduate or unemployed steel worker, has an interest in seeing that business remains economically sound, productive, and socially responsible. For example, Kenneth Clark, the noted black psychologist, said, "Business and industry are our last hope because they are the most realistic elements in our society."[1] Realistic or not, business is the only institution that has the technology, skills, and resources to really deal with the urgent issues of our times: education, unemployment, the environment, hunger, and productivity. In fact, companies like IBM, Johnson & Johnson, Mobil, Du Pont, Xerox, and Pfizer are committed to a corporate goal of improving the quality of life for their customers and employees.

## WHAT IS BUSINESS?

**Objective 1**

**The nature and importance of business.**

Just what is business? It isn't just buildings, machinery, or money. Business is people—not only people who voluntarily come together because they can do much more working together than they could working alone, but also people who do work on their own, as entrepreneurs. **Business,** then, can be defined as the activities of individuals or groups that are involved in developing, producing, and distributing the goods and services needed to satisfy other people's needs or desires.

Naturally, this is a broad definition. We've alluded to the fact that businesses can differ widely in size, in type of product, and in degree of profitability. But Disney's Epcot Center and the local exercise club are both in business to provide for consumers' needs and to make some money in the process.

## BUSINESS IN A FREE ENTERPRISE SYSTEM

**Objective 2**

The role of business, profits, and entrepreneurs in a free enterprise system.

In a **free enterprise system,** businesses are organized, owned, operated, and controlled by private individuals who have the right to a profit (or must suffer the loss) from operations. The system results from the free association of people in a free society. Under this system, you can organize any business the law allows, produce whatever you wish, charge whatever you want, or even sell your interest in the firm. In reality, however, a business can succeed only if it produces a product or service that the public wants, sells it at a price people are willing to pay, does the job somehow better than the competition, and makes a profit for its efforts. In addition, government regulations and the legal system set limits on certain types of products, businesses, and pricing. These limits will be discussed in more detail in the following section and in Chapter 23.

### The Role of Profit

The most common motive for entering business is the **profit motive,** the desire to make a profit as a reward for taking the risks of running a business. **Profit** is a term we've been using freely so far, in the same breath with *business.* It is income received, minus the costs of operating the business. Profit serves both as a reward for undertaking the risks of business and as a yardstick of one's success at it. Simple as it is, though, a profit isn't always made. Sometimes there are losses.

There's a lot of misunderstanding about how much profit business makes. Some people think profits are entirely too high, as discussed in the Business Debate on page 6. After reading the debate, answer the following questions:

1. How much of their sales dollar do you think manufacturers *should be able* to keep as profit after all their expenses and taxes have been paid? ____ percent
2. How about supermarkets? ____ percent
3. How much do you think manufacturers *are actually able* to keep in a typical year? ____ percent[2]
4. Supermarkets? ____ percent[2]

### Entrepreneurs

Of course, things don't just happen by themselves in any economic endeavor, especially in the world of free enterprise and profit. Someone has to make them happen. **Entrepreneurs** are the innovative owner-managers who create some new product or service or suggest a better way of using existing products or services. They are the first risk takers to see that the public wants a new product or service and to try to provide it. Entrepreneurs think up ways to satisfy people's needs. They invest money, time, and effort in organizing and managing a firm; run the risk of failure; and reap the rewards of success.

Fortunes are being made or lost in business ventures by those willing to take the risk—people like Barrie Bergman, who started Record Bar, the second-largest U.S. retail record company, on a shoestring in the late 1950s. The

# Business Debate

## Are Profits Too High?

Are profits too high? Do they cause high prices? Are they "stolen from the poor" or "sweated out of workers who don't get their fair share"? These are some of the claims that have been made about the profits of U.S. businesses. Alternatively, should profits be of vital concern to everyone, since they benefit employees and consumers as much as owners?

Some of the arguments that *profits are too high* are:

1. Firms put up with waste and inefficiency that would be intolerable if profits were lower.
2. Workers are paid low wages because so much in the way of profit goes to owners that little is left over for workers' wages.
3. Price supports inflate prices, leading to higher profits.
4. Firms build an excessive inflation rate into their prices in order to earn exorbitant profits.
5. Companies are using their excess profits to buy up other firms instead of investing in additional productive facilities.

6. High profits lead to greed and avarice.

Arguments that *profits aren't too high* are:

1. Without high profits, there's no incentive for a business to produce goods and services needed by consumers.
2. Profits aren't as high as some claim because of recurring inflation and the decreasing value of the dollar.
3. Since risk must be rewarded, profits are needed to stimulate research and development of new products and new businesses.
4. If profits really are too high, they will lead new producers to enter the field, thereby increasing the supply of goods and services and lowering prices.
5. Low profits would make investors sell their stocks and discourage others from investing.
6. Profits protect free choice, personal savings, and independence from complete government control.

*What do you think?*

flamboyant young entrepreneur is now a multimillionaire, and the firm's 138 outlets have annual sales of over $80 million. He says he likes to take risks.[3] Frederick Smith, thirty-seven, risked his entire $3.5 million fortune to found Federal Express in 1972. It was based on an idea he developed in a term paper while in college over six years earlier. Although the term paper got a poor grade, the firm is now a leader in fast freight-carrying.[4]

Figure 1-1 gives you a roadmap of the entrepreneurial process. It begins when a person has an idea for a new product or service to meet consumer needs. He or she organizes the business; puts up the money for buildings, such as a plant, office, or store; buys the necessary equipment and materials; hires and trains employees; and begins production or operations. The sales resulting from operations bring in revenue, which is used to pay expenses. What's left over is either profit or loss, the reward or penalty for the owner's risk taking. Ted Turner (see the Profile on page 8) is one such entrepreneur.

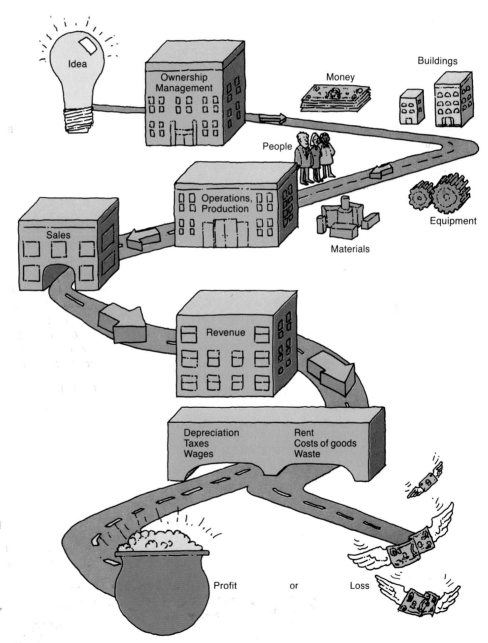

**Figure 1-1** How a business is formed and operates. [Adapted from Curtis E. Tate, Jr., Leon C. Megginson, Charles R. Scott, Jr., and Lyle R. Trueblood, *Successful Small Business Management*, 3rd ed. (Plano, Tex.: Business Publications, Inc., 1982), pp. 224–225. © 1982 Business Publications, Inc.]

## *Profile*

### Ted Turner: Super-Entrepreneur

In 1981, Ted Turner owned the Atlanta Braves baseball team, the Atlanta Hawks basketball team, the Atlanta Chiefs soccer team, and Atlanta's TV superstation, WTBS. He had skippered the yacht *Courageous* to its 1977 victory in the prestigious America's Cup races, and his net worth was estimated at over $100 million. You might think he'd be satisfied to rest on his laurels. But he wasn't. He believed the time had come for a fourth—and unusual—television news alternative. So he conceived and organized the pioneering Cable News Network (CNN) to feed news around the clock to nationwide cable systems.

CNN started operating in June 1980. During its first year, it was largely responsible for a 4 percent drop in the news audience of the "big three" networks. In 1981, Turner sued the White House and the three major networks for leaving his CNN reporters out of the White House press pool—and won! By early 1984, CNN was reaching 25 million households (31 percent of USA's TV homes).

Ironically, this super-entrepreneur's phenomenal career began with tragedy. In 1963, his father's suicide left Turner, then only twenty-four, with a failing outdoor advertising business so overextended that his father had been selling the firm's properties to pay debts. Turner sold two of the family plantations to pay real estate and estate taxes. Then, through involved and delicate financing, he started regaining the parts of the business his father had sold. He bought Channel 17, an independent UHF station, and, after initially losing $2 million, overcame local competition to corner Atlanta's sports, situation comedy, and movie rerun market.

Turner was one of the first people to see the potential business frontiers in cable television (CATV) resulting from changes in the legal environment. In 1975, the FCC's relaxed rules permitted independents access to the cable system, and RCA launched its first satellite into orbit 22,300 miles over the equator. Turner took advantage of these events to expand WTBS, a regional station, into a national station that is now the flagship of the Turner Broadcasting System. National sponsors compete—at very high rates—to advertise on the station. It now serves over 30 million homes, reaches 35 percent of the national TV audience, and earned $7 million in 1983.

Why does he run so hard? Turner is a self-proclaimed workaholic—competitive (with over 200 yachting trophies on his mantel), energetic, egoistic, and public-spirited. (He bought the Braves, Hawks, and Chiefs partly to prevent their leaving Atlanta.) Georgetown University named him its Business Man of the Year in 1982.

Is Ted Turner slowing down? If anything, he's speeding up. In 1982, he formed Cable News Network Headline News, which is now providing programs to other stations. CNN and CNN Headline News were expected to earn a profit during 1984.

Sources: Based on various sources including David Shaw, "Captain Courageous Loves Rocking the Boat," *TV Guide,* August 22, 1981, pp. 26–28; Jim Montgomery, "Ted Turner Expects Firm to Break Even or Post Profit in '82," *Wall Street Journal,* June 21, 1982, p. 22; "The Man from Atlanta," Channel 17, February 27, 1983; Andrew Mallison, "Ted Turner Puts Playboy on His 'List'," *Jackson Daily News,* July 3, 1983, p. 9A; and Ben Brown, "The Cable King's Coffers Need Filling," *USA Today,* January 5, 1984, p. 5D.

How do Ted Turner's operations fit into this description of the activities of an entrepreneur?

As you've probably noticed, entrepreneurs may stay in business even though their firms only break even, or even lose money, because they hope to make sufficient profit in the long run to more than cover their losses. Thus, in the short run, entrepreneurs may work without direct compensation.

Do you suppose that the backers of Conestoga I will continue to operate if they don't make a profit? Why did they continue after the first rocket blew up in 1981?

Some of the risks to watch for in starting and operating a business are competition, lack of consumer acceptance of the product or service, changing government rules and regulations, lack of competent employees, scarce or high-priced materials and supplies, poor management, and adverse weather. For instance, a sharp-witted entrepreneur would have the foresight *not* to open a car wash in a town with a population of 6,500. Assuming a car for every two people (an optimistic thought at best) and not even allowing for Boy Scout car washes and people washing their own cars, the owner might have to wash every car in town twice a week just to break even.

What trends did Ted Turner see before other communications people saw them? What did he do to take advantage of the opportunities these new developments offered? Would he have taken the risks he did without hope of a profit?

### Results of the Free Enterprise System

The free enterprise system has done an outstanding job of providing for people's basic needs. Even critics admit that businesses operating under the system in the United States have been a powerful force for economic good. They've been largely responsible for our high standard of living. Our **gross national product (GNP)**, which is the monetary value of all the final goods and services produced by a nation in one year, is rapidly approaching the $3 trillion ($3,000,000,000,000) level—over $12,000 for every man, woman, and child in the nation. Three trillion dollars in one-dollar bills would fill a warehouse twenty feet high, forty-seven feet wide, and twenty-four miles long. No other economic system comes close to that output.

## BUSINESS IN THE U.S. ECONOMIC ENVIRONMENT

Business is carried on in and is an inseparable part of an economic environment. And economics is basically about people's behavior in producing, exchanging, and consuming the material goods and services they want. It focuses on how economic resources are combined to satisfy human wants, under free enterprise as well as other systems. In sum, then, **economics** is the study of how scarce resources are allocated to satisfy human wants. Because human wants are unlimited, scarce economic resources are used to provide the maximum satisfaction possible.

Consider diamonds, for example. If they were freely available, we'd all wear them as jewelry or give them to someone else. But since diamonds were formed billions of years ago when carbon was subjected to great heat and pressure, their supply is quite limited. Less than 40,000 pounds of diamonds were mined in the entire world in 1981. This limited supply was cut, polished, and sold for premium prices to satisfy the great demand. Then, because of worldwide recession, the demand for diamonds declined so that the price of a one-carat prime diamond fell from $80,000 to $16,000.[5]

Levi Strauss & Company is another example. Levi's is now the largest manufacturer of branded apparel in the world, with 48,000 people working in seventy plants and distribution centers in North America and thirty-seven in Asia, Latin America, and Europe. It remains a dramatic example of the economics of free enterprise. Levi's jeans weathered not only the storms of gold rush–era California, but also the forces of supply, demand, scarce resources, and competition (see FYI on page 11).

### What Are Economic Resources?

**Objective 3**

The four economic resources—land, labor, capital, and entrepreneurship—and their prices.

Like diamonds, **economic resources** are scarce. These resources, which are the means businesses use to produce goods and services, are sometimes called the **factors of production** because they are inputs into the production process. The factors of production can be grouped into four broad types: land, labor, capital, and entrepreneurship resources.

▲ **Land** Land resources include all the natural resources occurring on, in, and under the earth's surface, such as timber, petroleum, water, iron ore, sand, and gravel. Some, such as petroleum, coal, and diamond deposits, may run out in the next few decades, but others, such as air and water, may last almost indefinitely.

Since land resources are limited, choices must be made as to how they will be used. Should crops be planted, or should a factory be built? Perhaps a shopping mall should be constructed or a forest planted for future generations. Someone must make these choices—usually business owners or managers, within guidelines set by government agencies. Because resources are scarce while human desires for them are unlimited, some reward must be offered in order to attract resources for a particular use. Therefore, each of the resources has its price. The price of using land is **rent**. Even if we own the land and its natural resources we pay an implicit price for its use, for by using the land ourselves we give up the opportunity to rent it to someone else.

## *FYI*

### Levi Strauss & Company: A Perfect Economic Fit

In 1847, seventeen-year-old Levi Strauss emigrated from Bavaria to America. For three years he made a scant living peddling clothing and household items door to door through towns and villages in rural New England and Kentucky. The lure of prosperity led Strauss to go by clipper ship to California in 1850 to peddle dry goods—especially canvas for tents—to gold miners. There was little demand for tents but great demand for durable work clothes, so the ever-adaptable Strauss had a tailor make the unsold cloth into waist-high overalls. The pants were so popular that the miners called them "Levi's," and Strauss was in business. Later, they also became favorites of farmers, cowboys, and lumberjacks. Since the material was ironically guaranteed to "shrink, wrinkle, and fade," owners would jump into water with the new jeans on. When they dried, they fit like a second skin!

Eventually Strauss switched to a tough cotton fabric called *serge de Nîmes* (later Americanized to "denim"), as it was woven in Nîmes, France. Similar cloth was also imported from the Italian town of Genoa, called "Gênes" in French (later Americanized to "jeans").

In 1873, the pants were made more durable with the help of a Nevada tailor, Jacob Davis, who put copper rivets at all points of strain, including the crotch. The company's famous logo, a double arc of orange thread stitched on the back pockets, has been in use longer than any other apparel trademark in America and is known worldwide as the sign of authentic Levi's® jeans. The original model "501 Double-X blue denim waist overalls" is the only item of wearing apparel whose style has remained basically the same for well over a century. One notable change was made in 1933, after the firm's president, Walter Haas, Sr., suffered "hot rivet syndrome" while camping out—the crotch rivet was removed.

The firm has operated in an enlightened manner since its founding. After the 1906 earthquake and fire destroyed the firm's premises, along with most of the rest of the business district, ads told the 350 employees that their salaries

were guaranteed. And the firm's retail merchants were offered low- or no-interest loans to rebuild.

During World War II, Levi's jeans were declared an "essential commodity" and were sold only to people doing defense work. Demand was so overwhelming and the supply so limited that the jeans had to be rationed for two years after the war was over. Production facilities were finally expanded to meet demand in 1950.

By the late 1960s, Levi's jeans had become the standard uniform of the youth culture. Later, the firm successfully anticipated the shift in demand to designer jeans. In 1968, Strauss introduced "Levi's for Gals," a snug, hip-hugging version of the original 501 style. And Levi's has continued to adjust its product line and its advertising and marketing strategies to meet changing market forces. The firm has branched out from jeans into many other areas, such as men's and women's wear, boots and shoes, belts, and hats. In fact, Levi's warmup suits, ceremonial wear, and uniforms were worn by the 1984 U.S. Olympic team, staff, and employees.

Sources: Based on material furnished by Levi Strauss & Co. See also Irving Wallace, David Wallechinsky, and Amy Wallace, "The Blue Jeaniuses," *Parade,* May 16, 1982, p. 20; Milton Moskowitz, Michael Katz, and Robert Levering, "Levi's," *Everybody's Business: An Almanac* (New York: Harper & Row, 1980), pp. 152–56; and "Going for the Gold," *Time,* March 14, 1983, p. 66.

▲ **Labor** Natural resources are of little economic use if they remain in the ground. So a second type of resource is needed: labor. **Labor** is all human physical and mental effort. The farmer who plants cotton, the secretary who types a letter, the carrier who delivers the paper, and the worker on the automobile assembly line all provide a needed productive resource. The term *labor* refers not only to hourly workers but to managers as well. Even the top managers of a large corporation like Levi Strauss provide mental and physical effort for the benefit of the enterprise. The only human element not considered a labor resource is owners or entrepreneurs, for, as you will see, they play a unique role in the productive process. The price of labor is **wages,** the compensation employees are paid for their effort. If no compensation is given, they'll withhold their labor or sell it to another business.

▲ **Capital** The third economic resource is **capital,** which is all the human-produced items, such as tools, machinery, and buildings, used to produce and distribute other goods and services. For example, tractors used by farmers, typewriters used by secretaries, bicycles and cars used by paper carriers, and assembly line equipment in automobile plants are devised and produced by humans to enable other humans to be more productive. Otherwise, these activities would have to be done by hand—an unproductive method. Most of our increased standard of living is due to advances in technology that have made the U.S. economy more productive.

In an economic sense, capital doesn't mean money. Money by itself isn't productive; it becomes productive only when it's used to purchase other economic resources. A million dollars stacked in a bank vault produces no new goods or services. Money is transformed into productive resources when it's used to purchase a site for an office building (land) or a lathe or drill press (capital), which produces goods, or when it's used to hire workers and managers (labor) to staff a sales outlet, which produces services.

When capital goods are acquired, someone must supply the money to pay for them. The money suppliers expect to be compensated for tying up their funds instead of using them themselves. For instance, whenever a business obtains a bank loan to purchase a new computer, the bank charges interest on the money it provides. **Interest,** then, is the price of capital.

▲ **Entrepreneurship** The three resources examined so far—land, labor, and capital—become productive only when combined in a rational way for some creative or gainful purpose. This is the function of the fourth economic resource, familiar to you by now: entrepreneurship. Entrepreneurs combine the other three economic resources in a new or different way to produce goods or services, as shown in Figure 1-2. Just as a car engine will remain motionless

**Figure 1-2** The entrepreneur combines the factors of production to produce goods and services.

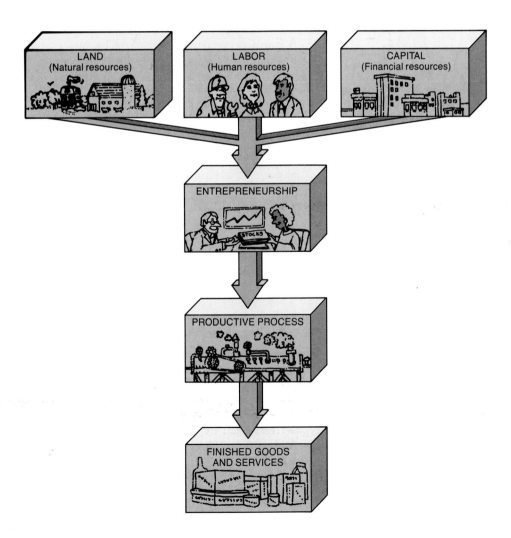

until the spark ignites the combined gasoline and air, which then moves the piston, so an entrepreneur provides the spark that combines land, labor, and capital into products and services.

Since land and its natural resources have now been paid for, labor has been compensated, and the capital providers have been paid interest, what about the entrepreneur? The price expected by the owner-entrepreneur for providing the idea or spark, taking the risk, and operating the business is *profit*. However, entrepreneurs aren't guaranteed a return for providing their services. Profits, as we've pointed out, may not occur.

## Demand and Supply

**Objective 4**

**How demand and supply interact in the economic environment.**

"Teach a parrot to say 'demand and supply' and you'll have an economist." While this is an obvious exaggeration, it does contain a grain of truth. It is the interaction of the economic forces of supply and demand that determines the price paid for a given product or service. In turn, the price determines how that product or service will be distributed and used in a free enterprise economy.

**Demand** is more than just the desire for some product or service. It also involves the ability to buy. True demand exists when people not only desire a good or service, but also have the buying power to purchase it and are willing to part with some of that buying power in order to purchase it.

Common sense tells us that if the price of a product, such as a sports car, were $5,000, more people would be willing to buy it than if the price were $25,000. This is the **law of demand**, as shown in Figure 1-3: as price goes up,

**Figure 1-3** The law of demand.

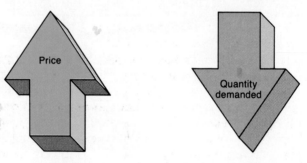

As price goes up, the quantity demanded goes down.

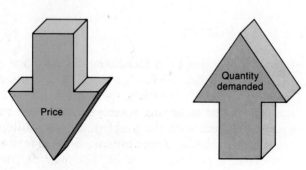

As price goes down, the quantity demanded goes up.

**Figure 1-4**  The law of supply.

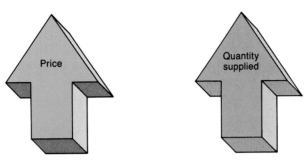

As price goes up, the quantity supplied goes up.

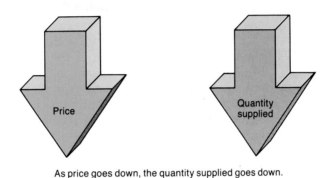

As price goes down, the quantity supplied goes down.

the quantity demanded goes down.  The reverse is also true: if price goes down, the quantity demanded goes up.

**Supply** results from the desire and effort of producers to satisfy consumer demands.  Just as consumers' desires and willingness to spend affect demand, so producers' and suppliers' willingness and ability to provide goods and services affect supply.  The **law of supply** says: as price goes up, the quantity supplied goes up, and as price goes down, the quantity supplied goes down (see Figure 1-4).  Obviously, as the price of a product goes down, producers become less willing to supply the product and the quantity supplied decreases.

## DIFFERENT ECONOMIC ENVIRONMENTS

**Objective 5**

**The characteristics of the two major economic systems: capitalism and communism.**

Every society has been faced with the problem posed by the two basic economic facts of life: society's material wants are unlimited, but the economic resources needed to satisfy them are scarce.  Every economic system is a framework for satisfying society's wants, but the methods used by various systems to deal with the problem are very different.

Without doubt, Americans need to understand their own economic system better, for 37 percent of the public can't think of *any* way their personal lives are affected by the rise and fall of the general level of profits in business.[6]

When asked to define *private enterprise,* 24 percent of the general population said they don't know what it is. As Americans, we believe our economic system is the best and worth preserving. But in order to do so, we must first understand how that system functions, as compared with the other most popular systems, communism and socialism.

## Capitalism

In 1776, the publication of a book entitled *An Inquiry into the Nature and Causes of the Wealth of Nations* caused an economic revolution that coincided, in time and magnitude, with the American Revolution. Its author, Adam Smith, was a Scottish professor of moral philosophy and the world's first economist. Smith believed that the best possible economic system would be one in which individuals were free to engage in commerce without undue restraint, in the pursuit of their own self-interest. In this pursuit, people would be guided by the competition of the marketplace, as by an "invisible hand" ultimately serving the common good. The resulting business activity would increase everyone's wealth and expand the nation's well-being. Smith did believe that there were certain things that governments should do for their people, such as providing for the national defense. However, he felt that business activity should be free of government restraint, as any interference by government with free competition was almost certain to be harmful.

Another term for Smith's philosophy is **laissez faire,** a French term loosely translated as "leave it alone," referring to government's ideal role in business. This philosophy is the basis of capitalism.

**Capitalism** is an economic system based on the private ownership of resources, in which individuals have the right to make choices about how they will use their resources. The resulting concepts—free enterprise and competition—are so basic to capitalism that capitalism is synonymous with the free enterprise system. The major characteristics of capitalism are:

- Private enterprise and freedom of choice. **Private enterprise** means private ownership of resources and of the businesses that use them. Individuals have the right to acquire, use, and sell property as they see fit.

- Freedom to compete. **Competition** is the rivalry among similar businesses for a share of the same consumer dollars. As Adam Smith stated, competition benefits society when people are free to compete with others to sell their resources as they see fit.

- Limited role of government. Under pure capitalism, the government doesn't interfere at all with the functioning of the economic system. Its role is only to provide basic public services.

- Prices set by the interaction of the economic forces of supply and demand. Because there is limited interference by government, the price set by these forces is a true indication of the desires of both suppliers and buyers.

Of course, pure capitalism has never actually existed. The U.S. system comes close, but it contains forces that restrict competition and free enterprise. At best, the system can be described as one of **mixed capitalism,** a system based on the principles of pure capitalism but limited by government involvement.

## Communism

The second major economic system, communism, is very different from capitalism. Yet it has the same basic economic purpose: to provide a system or framework for satisfying human wants. Communism's roots go back to the middle of the nineteenth century, when German philosopher Karl Marx wrote *Das Kapital.* The book described how contradictions within capitalism would cause the system to break down. Marx advocated a new political and economic system based on the forces of change. In 1848, he and Friedrich Engels wrote the *Communist Manifesto,* amplifying these theories.

Communism is based on the concept that every person should be treated equally. The poor should be given clothing, the sick should be given medical care, and the strong should work to provide these services. **Communism,** then, is founded on the two principles that (1) all factors of production, including labor, are either owned or controlled by the state, and (2) each person produces according to ability but shares in the economic benefits according to need. Under communism, the individual is less important than the system, and there is no private property. Marx emphasized that the government would dictate how resources should be used, at least until perfect communism evolved. The market forces of supply, demand, and competition have no influence in communism. Instead, government planners set economic goals and make all the economic decisions about production and allocation of resources.

In summary, then, communism has the following characteristics:

- State ownership of economic resources
- Social and economic equality
- Central planning for economic and social activities
- No freedom of competition

## Socialism

Countries with socialist economies believe that there are certain products and services, such as steel, utilities, transportation, and medicine, to which everyone is entitled. Such goods are also available in a capitalist system, but only to those who have the money to pay for them. Under **socialism,** however, the government owns, operates, and controls these industries, and it makes economic decisions for the good of the nation as a whole. Unlike communism, socialism allows those industries not considered essential to continue operating in a relatively free market.

In Britain, for example, the government owns the steel, transportation, shipbuilding, and aerospace industries and large portions of the oil and auto industries. And in France, the government has undertaken a program of nationalization, or government takeover, of the banking system and other essential industries.

## Modern Modifications of These Systems

Today, there are no pure capitalistic or communistic systems. Instead, the systems are modifications of the two extremes, as shown in Figure 1-5. Until recently, Hungary's economy was very close to pure communism. But now even Hungary has begun to experiment with such radical ideas as limited free

**Figure 1-5** Continuum of economic environments. Distribution of selected countries on the basis of their perceived emphasis on communism and capitalism.

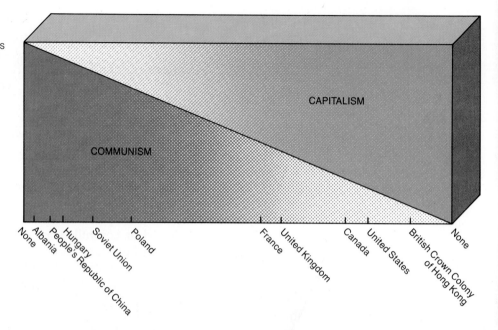

CAPITALISM

COMMUNISM

None
Albania
Hungary
People's Republic of China
Soviet Union
Poland
France
United Kingdom
Canada
United States
British Crown Colony of Hong Kong
None

enterprise, competitive pricing, and profits. For example, managers of the nation's 130 state-owned farms must follow official production guidelines. But chairpersons of the 1,360 cooperative farms, which cultivate 80 percent of the farmland, operate under a system of loose controls unlike any other system in the communist world. They operate the farms to make a profit for their members. In fact, many cooperatives have diversified into light industry to increase profits. The result? Hungary's agricultural products make up nearly a fourth of its exports, while other Eastern European countries must import food.[7]

Most Hungarian cooperatives now make a profit for their members.

Farmers in the Soviet Union are permitted to operate a one-acre tract for their own purposes while also working on a state-owned or collective farm. These farms, worked by 34 million households, use only 3 percent of the farmland yet provide 24 percent of total farm output.[8]

China's expanding private businesses (called "cooperative and individual economic undertakings") are openly credited with meeting some of the nation's needs much better than state-operated enterprises do. Individual vendors and crafts workers are being encouraged to create their own jobs—even to compete with state-run shops and services.[9] Joint ventures are now permitted with outsiders. And one food processing and marketing company is raising $25 million by selling 49 percent of its stock to foreigners.[10]

## THE U.S. ECONOMIC ENVIRONMENT TODAY

**Objective 6**

The current economic issues of recession, inflation, and productivity and their effects on business.

The economic theories we have discussed provide the foundation for business activity. Only by understanding these theories can we understand such business functions as management, operations, marketing, and finance. Production is closely tied to the concept of scarce resources, and entrepreneurship explains why small businesses are so vital. These concepts have operated throughout our history to shape events which in turn have shaped the economy (see Figure 1-6).

Whenever we talk of the economy as a whole, it's important to keep some basic relationships in mind. This economy is made up of thousands of business firms, which provide needed goods and services; millions of individuals, who provide their resources and purchase their finished products; and various levels of government, which provide direction and support. Anything that affects one part of the system affects the other parts. Changes in the business cycle, inflation, and productivity have great effects on the overall economy.

### The Business Cycle

Throughout its history, the U.S. economy has had times of spectacular growth, followed by periods of declining economic activity and unemployment. These swings have tended to follow a pattern, or cycle. Each period of growth has been followed by a period of decline, then a period of recovery. This roller-coaster pattern, called a **business cycle,** is composed of the stages shown in Figure 1-7.

At the low point of the cycle, the economy is in a **recession.** Consumers buy less of the products produced by businesses. Businesses cut back on output and lay off workers, creating unemployment. These workers can then buy fewer products, further slowing the economy. In order to sell the products they've produced, most suppliers hold prices steady, or even lower them. The overall mood of the economy is pessimistic.

For various reasons, at some point the economy begins to pick up. This *recovery* can be due to a change in consumer attitudes, a tax cut, or one of several other causes. For whatever reason, businesses find that more products are being demanded, so they step up production. More workers and raw materials are needed, and so unemployment is eased. Economic activity gradually

**Figure 1-6** Events that shaped the U.S. economy. [Adapted from "Events that Shaped the U.S. Economy," *U.S.News & World Report,* April 26, 1982, pp. 34–35. Reprinted from "U.S.News & World Report." Copyright, 1982, U.S.News & World Report, Inc.]

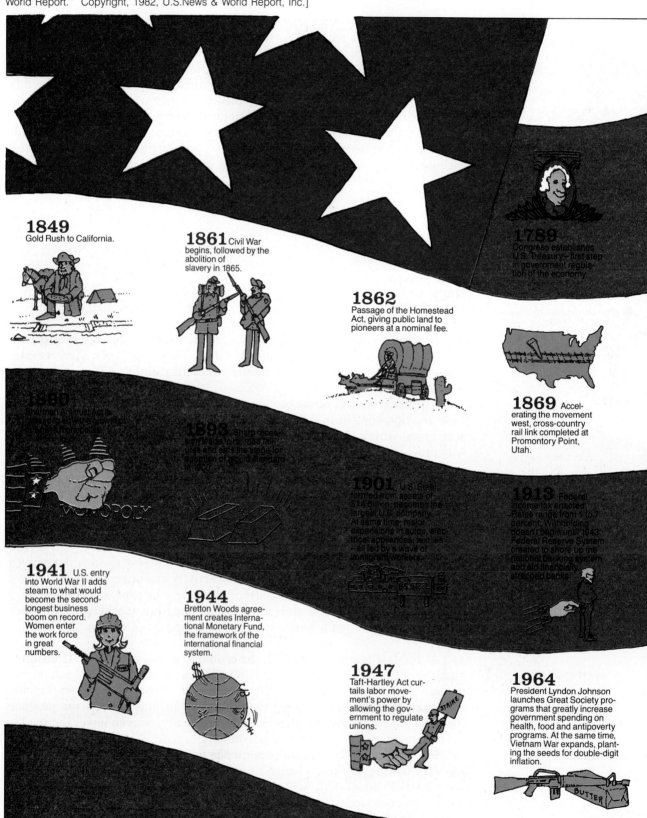

**1849** Gold Rush to California.

**1861** Civil War begins, followed by the abolition of slavery in 1865.

**1862** Passage of the Homestead Act, giving public land to pioneers at a nominal fee.

**1789** Congress establishes U.S. treasury—first step in government regulation of the economy.

**1869** Accelerating the movement west, cross-country rail link completed at Promontory Point, Utah.

**1880** Sherman Antitrust Act is passed to prevent growth of large monopolies.

**1893** Sharp recession leads to railroad failure and sets the stage for adoption of gold standard in 1900.

**1901** U.S. Steel formed from assets of $1.4 billion; becomes the largest U.S. company. At same time, major expansions in autos, electrical appliances, textiles—all fed by a wave of immigrant workers.

**1913** Federal income tax enacted. Rates range from 1 to 7 percent. Withholding doesn't begin until 1943. Federal Reserve System created to shore up the national banking system and aid financially strapped banks.

**1941** U.S. entry into World War II adds steam to what would become the second-longest business boom on record. Women enter the work force in great numbers.

**1944** Bretton Woods agreement creates International Monetary Fund, the framework of the international financial system.

**1947** Taft-Hartley Act curtails labor movement's power by allowing the government to regulate unions.

**1964** President Lyndon Johnson launches Great Society programs that greatly increase government spending on health, food and antipoverty programs. At the same time, Vietnam War expands, planting the seeds for double-digit inflation.

20

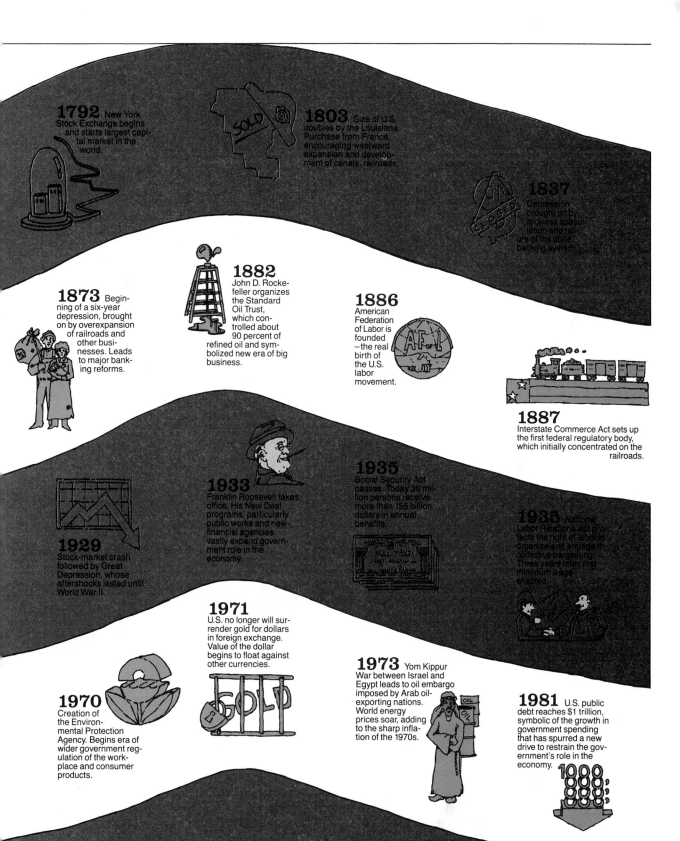

**1792** New York Stock Exchange begins and starts largest capital market in the world.

**1803** Size of U.S. doubles by the Louisiana Purchase from France, encouraging westward expansion and development of canals, railroads.

**1837** Depression brought on by reckless speculation and failure of the state banking system.

**1873** Beginning of a six-year depression, brought on by overexpansion of railroads and other businesses. Leads to major banking reforms.

**1882** John D. Rockefeller organizes the Standard Oil Trust, which controlled about 90 percent of refined oil and symbolized new era of big business.

**1886** American Federation of Labor is founded — the real birth of the U.S. labor movement.

**1887** Interstate Commerce Act sets up the first federal regulatory body, which initially concentrated on the railroads.

**1929** Stock-market crash followed by Great Depression, whose aftershocks lasted until World War II.

**1933** Franklin Roosevelt takes office. His New Deal programs, particularly public works and new financial agencies, vastly expand government role in the economy.

**1935** Social Security Act passes. Today 36 million persons receive more than 155 billion dollars in annual benefits.

**1935** National Labor Relations Act protects the right of labor to organize and engage in collective bargaining. Three years later first minimum wage enacted.

**1970** Creation of the Environmental Protection Agency. Begins era of wider government regulation of the workplace and consumer products.

**1971** U.S. no longer will surrender gold for dollars in foreign exchange. Value of the dollar begins to float against other currencies.

**1973** Yom Kippur War between Israel and Egypt leads to oil embargo imposed by Arab oil-exporting nations. World energy prices soar, adding to the sharp inflation of the 1970s.

**1981** U.S. public debt reaches $1 trillion, symbolic of the growth in government spending that has spurred a new drive to restrain the government's role in the economy.

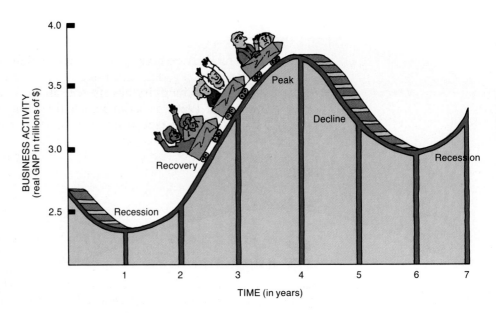

**Figure 1-7** The roller coaster of the business cycle.

slips into high gear. As the economy rises to a *peak*, optimism reigns. Businesses operate at top capacity. Consumers buy the available output and demand more. As demand races ahead of supply, prices soar, creating a classic example of inflation. But this rate of growth cannot be sustained for long, and strains begin to be felt. The roller coaster starts to turn down. Consumers begin to worry about the future and buy less. Businesses react by producing less, and the cycle begins again. These *declines* have been less severe in the United States since World War II, as compared to earlier periods.

## Inflation

Simply stated, **inflation** is an increase in prices over a period of time, usually occurring during a peak in the business cycle. Over the last two decades, our economy has experienced long stretches of high inflation, especially during the 1970s. But the only period of *sustained* falling prices during the last century occurred during the Great Depression of the 1930s. Some inflation is necessary to keep the economy growing. Too much inflation, however, can undermine our economic foundations. High inflation strikes especially hard at retirees and others on fixed incomes, who cannot pay the higher prices without lowering their living standards. Also, employed people must work longer for the same amount of goods and services. Over time, we come to expect higher prices; so, rather than save money to buy later, we buy now. This inflationary psychology further fuels inflation.

During the last decade, the inflation experienced has been different than ever before. It has continued even into recessions, when the old economic logic would have dictated falling prices. Thus a new creature of the 1970s was **stagflation,** or stagnant economic growth coupled with inflation—the worst of both worlds. Recently, though, the annual inflation rate has dropped to below 4 percent, the prime rate has dropped to about 12 percent, and there are 100 million employed people (though unemployment is still 8 percent).

### Low Productivity

Another problem area involves **productivity,** which is the ability of a nation's work force to produce goods, as measured in units of work per unit of time. Historically, U.S. productivity has risen at about 3 percent per year. Yet, beginning in the mid-1960s, it began a gradual decline; by the late 1970s, it was dropping alarmingly. In fact, from 1970 to 1980, the U.S. increase was less than that of any other industrial nation except Great Britain. In 1982, productivity began to increase, and it's now rising at close to the historical 3 percent rate.

## CURRENT EMPHASIS ON BUSINESS

**Objective 7**

**Why there is so much current interest in studying and entering business.**

There's no question that this is a frustrating time for businesspeople and consumers alike. Consumers must deal with unpredictable inflation and products that aren't made the way they used to be. Businesses have to struggle with shortages of energy and other resources, foreign competition, low productivity, labor unrest, government regulation, image problems caused by some colleagues' unethical practices, shortages of skilled personnel, and antibusiness feelings. In fact, business seems to be included in the public's general dissatisfaction with institutions such as governments, schools, and unions. To top it all off, there seems to be an antibusiness bias in much that appears in the media. For example, the Media Institute, in a recent survey of prime-time TV series, found that half the fictional corporate chiefs in TV dramas committed illegal acts. Another study found that 60 percent of the 226 businesspeople portrayed in prime time were shown in a negative light and only 28 percent were shown positively.[11] In other words, the heroes of "Dallas" and "Dynasty" were the bad guys of prime time.

These issues are covered throughout this text. For example, inflation and scarce resources have been discussed in this chapter. Unethical practices and government regulation are covered in Chapters 2 and 23. Chapter 9 deals with trying to attract more capable and skilled personnel, and Chapter 11 discusses

"Make the teeth a little sharper and it's perfect for TV!"

dealing with unions. Foreign competition is covered in Chapter 22. We don't deny that these problems exist, but they shouldn't cause anyone to reject the study of business. Instead, these problems represent challenging opportunities for you to become involved with business and help make it work.

## Renewed Interest in Business

While there are some defects in the U.S. business system, it is generating more interest now than ever before. For instance, Enterprise Square, Oklahoma City's Disney-style center, endeavors to teach about private enterprise via video displays and computer games. Also, an increasing number of students are majoring in business or seeking MBAs and hunting for jobs within the system. Finally, new businesses are springing up at a dizzying rate.

▲ **Student Interest** The number of students enrolled in schools of business administration more than doubled during the 1970s. Only 15 percent of all students in the United States were enrolled in business schools in 1966; by 1982 that figure had increased to 21 percent.[12] One out of eight American adults had gone back to school in 1983, and business courses were their top choices.[13] During the 1970s, average undergraduate business enrollment per school increased 52 percent, while that of MBA candidates jumped 145 percent.[14] Business is now one of the preferred areas of study at U.S. colleges.[15] There are many reasons for this trend, including the more realistic and practical orientation of students today. Former students from the idealistic 1960s are now joining establishment ranks as entrepreneurs and managers and eyeing the new crop of serious undergraduates with a mixture of awe and trepidation.

Enterprise Square, Oklahoma. The student is taking a computer test on loans and interest rates.

A survey by the Council of Education in 1980 found that freshman students are becoming much more materialistic. "Being well off financially" was considered an "important" or "essential" goal by 28 percent more men and 77 percent more women than in 1970. Over 15 percent of the women and 18 percent of the men planned business careers, as compared to 4 percent and 17 percent in 1970.[16] Although a glut of business graduates is hitting the job market, career opportunities are still great for students with business education and training. One out of every ten employees is a manager. Also, firms hire business graduates as trainees for management and related positions.

▲ **Increase in New Businesses** New businesses are always being started. About 50,000 new firms are incorporated each month, or around 600,000 each year. Not all new businesses succeed. In fact, almost half of all new firms will ultimately fail. Bankruptcies and failures increase drastically during business downturns, such as the 1981–1982 recession. In spite of the large number of business failures during the recession year 1982, nine new firms were formed for every one that failed.[17] This trend indicates the faith of new entrepreneurs in the U.S. business system and their willingness to invest in it.

## How Business Affects You

**Objective 8**

**How business activities affect you directly.**

Before picking up this book, you may have thought that business was mainly impersonal, giant corporations trying to maximize profits. But that isn't true. Most businesses are small, and most owners and managers are ethical in their relationships with their customers, employees, and the general interests of society. Whatever you may decide to do with your future, the world of business is going to affect you. If you were to ignore the realities of business, you would be not only blindfolding yourself but also seriously limiting your chances of success. You're surrounded by business activities. Business is going to be involved in almost everything you do, from keeping up your end of a conversation at lunch to simply getting through a normal day. You, in turn, affect business, for it varies its strategy with changing times—and you affect those changes (see FYI on page 26).

Consider this book. It was published by a firm located in Lexington, Massachusetts, typeset by a company in York, Pennsylvania, delivered by one or more freight services, and sold by a bookstore. The paper came from a paper mill, which made it from pulp obtained from trees cut by a timber company, which probably paid a landowner for it. The ink, machinery, and other supplies came from many other sources.

## Changes in Today's Business

Now is a time of great and rapid changes in all aspects of business. Some old, established, and well-known products (such as fountain pens and bow ties) and services (such as home delivery of dairy products) are disappearing in many areas. Entirely new ones are emerging to take their place. New businesses both add to those already in existence and replace those that are declining or disappearing. Drive-in movies, for example, which were so popular from the 1940s through the 1960s, are now disappearing. Their place is being taken by new entertainment media like cable TV, video discs and cassettes, video game

## FYI

### New Discs Click with TV Flicks

After declining for four years, sales of tapes and records are now heading back up. From 1978 to 1982, factors such as competition from video games, rising prices, fewer hits, limited radio station play, and home taping caused a 13 percent decline in sales. Then variables such as more economically priced records and declining video game activity led to a comeback.

But the most important new source of record support comes from cable TV. MTV, owned by American Express and Warner Communications, beams rock music to 13 million households, twenty-four hours a day. The station has a cozy relationship with the record companies, which provide it with eye-catching videotapes of artists performing their latest songs in exchange for free air time. The arrangement works fine for both parties—it sells both records and advertising—and also makes superstars of unknowns.

For instance, the unknown group Men at Work appeared in 1982 (see the accompanying photo). Now, thanks to TV support, it has had two albums in the Top Ten, and its first one, *Business as Usual,* was on the best seller charts for a year.

Source: Alexander L. Taylor III, "New Discs Click with TV Flicks," *Time,* May 23, 1983, p. 42.

arcades and home video games, and satellite dish receivers for TV. To be an informed consumer, you need to stay in touch with changes in the business world around you.

Businesspeople are changing their attitudes, practices, and life patterns to meet the changing demands of customers, employees, and society. New and improved management techniques are resulting from a better understanding of how and why people act as they do. These changes have provided a great challenge to people like Ted Turner, Barrie Bergman, and Frederick Smith. The challenge leads them (and you?) to try new things, to change careers, and to aspire to new and higher positions.

In essence, many opportunities do exist for adventurous, capable, educated, and highly motivated people. You may be one of those who will have a bright future in the world of business.

## ⚎ LEARNING OBJECTIVES REVISITED

1. *The nature and importance of business.*

   Although it can mean different things to different people, business is all the activities that are involved in developing, producing, and distributing the goods and services people need to satisfy their needs or desires.

2. *The role of business, profits, and entrepreneurs in a free enterprise system.*

   In a free enterprise system, businesses are organized, owned, operated, and controlled by private individuals. Customers have relative freedom of action, and there is much competition for their trade. Entrepreneurs take the risks of starting and running businesses, for which they expect to receive a profit as their reward. The profit motive is the usual reason for entering business. The free enterprise system, which recognizes this motive, is responsible for greater productivity and a higher standard of living, even in socialist countries.

3. *The four economic resources—land, labor, capital, and entrepreneurship—and their prices.*

   While real human needs in an economic environment are few, human wants are unlimited. But the economic resources—land, labor, capital, and entrepreneurship—are limited and expensive. Therefore, economics attempts to understand how scarce resources are allocated to satisfy unlimited human wants. The economic price of land is rent, the economic price of labor is wages and salaries, and the return on capital is interest.

   The other three resources are relatively useless without the fourth one: entrepreneurship. This is the economic service performed by the entrepreneur, who functions as a catalyst and risk taker in combining the other factors to produce goods and services. Entrepreneurs hope to receive a profit for performing their function.

4. *How demand and supply interact in the economic environment.*

   The economic forces of supply and demand determine the price of resources and of the finished products and goods resulting from the economic process. The law of demand states that as price goes up, the quantity demanded goes down, and as price goes down, the quantity demanded goes up. The law of supply states that as price goes up, the quantity supplied goes up, and as price goes down, the quantity supplied goes down.

5. *The characteristics of the two major economic systems: capitalism and communism.*

   All economic systems have the same purpose: to satisfy unlimited human wants with limited resources. The United States has an economic system that can be called mixed capitalism. It has private ownership of the productive resources and relative freedom of enterprise, choice, and competition. Yet government modifies the price system with its ability to tax and spend.

Communism is based on the principle of each person sharing in the economic resources according to need and producing according to ability. Hence there is state ownership of economic resources, social and economic equality, central planning of social and economic activities, and little or no competition.

In socialist economies, the state owns and controls the primary industries so that everyone who needs their services can have them, regardless of ability to pay. Nonessential industries operate in a relatively free environment.

6. *The current economic issues of recession, inflation, and productivity and their effects on business.*

   Business cycles and inflation greatly influence the operation of the U.S. economy. Throughout its history, the U.S. economy has had periods of spectacular growth, followed by declines in business activity and employment. These business cycles, as they are called, have well-defined stages: recession, recovery, peak, and decline.

   During the last two decades, there have been long stretches of inflation, or increases in prices over time. Usually inflation occurs during peaks in the business cycle. In the 1970s, however, a new economic creature evolved: stagflation, or stagnant economic growth combined with inflation. During recent decades, productivity declined, but it is now increasing at about 3 percent per year.

7. *Why there is so much current interest in studying and entering business.*

   Student interest in business is increasing, as evidenced by the increase in college enrollments and degrees granted in that area. The number of new businesses is increasing rapidly in spite of many failures, which indicates that many people are still succeeding in business and continue to be willing to take the risks of entrepreneurship.

8. *How business activities affect you directly.*

   When you consider your reading, school, and work, you can understand the many ways that business affects you.

## ⏏ IMPORTANT TERMS

As an extra review of the chapter, try defining the following terms. If you have trouble with any of them, refer to the page listed.

business  *4*

free enterprise system  *5*

profit motive  *5*

profit  *5*

entrepreneurs  *5*

gross national product
(GNP)  *5*

economics  *10*

economic resources  *10*

factors of production  *10*

land  *10*

rent  *10*

labor  *12*

wages  *12*

capital  *12*

interest  *13*

demand  *14*

law of demand  *14*

supply  *15*

law of supply  *15*

## REVIEW QUESTIONS

1. In what ways does business mean different things to different people?
2. Describe the functions and characteristics of the free enterprise system.
3. What role does profit play in the free enterprise system?
4. What steps does an entrepreneur follow in forming and operating a business?
5. What are the four economic resources? What price does each command?
6. How do the economic forces of supply and demand function to set price?
7. What is the purpose of an economic system, regardless of type?
8. Discuss the four characteristics of capitalism.
9. How does pure capitalism differ from mixed capitalism? Which one best describes the U.S. economic system?
10. Differentiate pure communism from socialism.
11. Describe how the economy moves through the phases of the business cycle.
12. What is inflation, and what are some problems with it?
13. How do you explain the renewed interest in business being shown by students?
14. How do you explain the increasing number of new businesses?

## DISCUSSION QUESTIONS

1. Comment on Kenneth Clark's statement that "Business and industry are our last hope because they are the most realistic elements in our society."
2. Can business exist (a) without profit? (b) without entrepreneurs? (c) without competition? Think carefully about your answers and explain fully.
3. Do you think profits are too high? Explain.
4. How would you explain the fact that nearly half of all new businesses will ultimately fail?
5. Do you think the free enterprise system is the best for the United States at this time? Why or why not?
6. Do you think entrepreneurship is more or less common today than in the past? Why?
7. Assume that you own an office building with a manually operated elevator. The operator works eight hours a day and five days per week. Including wages and benefits, she receives $10 per hour, which she is paid even during her two-week vacation. A replacement for her is then hired at the same cost. The elevator manufacturer offers to install an automatic eleva-

tor at a total cost to you of $18,000 per year, including electricity, maintenance, repair, and monthly payments. Would you accept the offer? Why or why not?

8. What is the relationship between risk and free enterprise?
9. Could entrepreneurship play a role in a pure communist system? Why or why not?
10. Do you think inflation is good or bad? Explain.

## ⛰ CASE 1-1    Hurricane Frederic: Where Was Business When the Lights Went Out?

When Hurricane Frederic hit the Gulf Coast in 1979, the entire area was devastated, and for the next few days economic activities were limited. Power stations were knocked out and transmission lines were down, so there was practically no electricity. Telephone lines, water mains, and sewer lines were damaged too. There were no newspapers or TV. One radio station was able to broadcast the news, but only people with battery-powered radios could receive it. Preparing meals was next to impossible without gas or electricity. Without refrigeration, frozen and chilled foods spoiled, and fresh food wasn't available for days.

Virtually all businesses were closed, since they were experiencing the same problems as households. The few stores that did allow patrons into their lamp- and candle-lit interiors had to use hand-held calculators to add up the bills, and boxes served as cash registers. The most desirable item was ice, but there was virtually none available. When it was finally trucked in from the outside, the demand was so great that armed guards were needed to prevent rioting and price gouging.

Money was scarce, since the banks couldn't operate. Even after the banks opened, there was a shortage of dimes, which were needed for the few working pay phones. Some bank branches opened without power, but withdrawals were impossible because computers couldn't be consulted to find out account balances. Chain saws were used to cut away the trees that had fallen on houses and cars, but there was little gasoline to run them. Portable generators could produce electricity, if you could find the fuel—and shrug off the neighbors' resentment!

For several days, people were reduced to the subsistence level.

### Case Questions

1. What does this case explain about the role of business?
2. How do you think entrepreneurs dealt with the devastation?
3. If you'd been the regional manager of the electric power or telephone company, what would you have done? Why?

## ⛰ CASE 1-2    Americans in Moscow: Riding in Style

Late one spring afternoon, two American tourists in Moscow left their tour group to venture out on their own for a walking tour of the Kremlin area. A young student from the humanities division of nearby Moscow University, hearing them speak English, joined them as their guide-interpreter. (He said he'd learned English from listening to U.S. jazz and swing music on records and short-wave radio.)

Around 5 in the afternoon, they tried to find a taxi to take them back to their outlying hotel. Several taxis were parked, but when their drivers, who were reading or talking, were approached, they refused to take another fare, claiming that they'd reached their earnings quota for the day.

The tired tourists then tried flagging down taxis that were cruising around empty, but those drivers ignored them too. Finally, a big black

chauffeur-driven limousine pulled up to the curb in answer to their wave. The young Russian student became quite agitated and physically tried to restrain them from entering the car. The driver just as vigorously insisted that they get in. Throughout the drive, the young man was a nervous wreck and translated the driver's sightseeing lecture reluctantly.

After the requested fare—plus a sizable tip—had been paid and the driver had left the hotel, the student explained, "That car belongs to a top government official. His driver was just earning some extra money!"

### Case Questions

1. What does this case show about the nature of the Soviet economy?
2. What does it say about the profit motive?
3. What does the refusal of the regular taxi drivers tell about the role of wages?

# 2

# Social Responsibility

*It is a fallacy to think that business can prosper—
or, indeed, even exist—without regard to broader
social concerns.*

S. Prakash Sethi

*Business has a soul, and management has social
responsibilities as a major partner in the
community, alongside capital and labour.*

Oliver Sheldon

**Learning Objectives**

After studying the material in this chapter, you will understand:

1. What social responsibility is.
2. The need to balance social responsibility and profits.
3. How the concept of social responsibility has evolved.
4. How to set up action plans to fulfill a company's social responsibility.
5. What business ethics are, and some aspects of business in which they are involved.

**In This Chapter**

What Is Social Responsibility?
The Evolution of Social Responsibility
A Social Responsibility Action Plan
Business Ethics

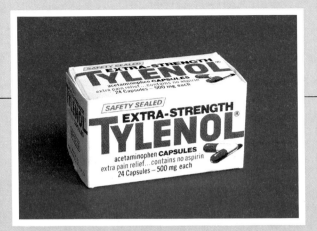

## TYLENOL
*Social Responsibility in Action*

In September 1982, Americans were gobbling up over 130 million painkilling tablets, pills, or capsules daily, at a cost of over $1.2 billion a year. Makers of the five major brands—Tylenol, Anacin, Bayer, Bufferin, and Excedrin—were spending over $130 million every year on advertising. It was worth that much, though, for a 1 percent increase in their market share meant more than $7 million in extra sales.

In 1955, McNeil Consumer Products Company, a subsidiary of Johnson & Johnson (J&J), the brilliant marketing company, had introduced Tylenol as a prescription drug when aspirin was found to be potentially harmful. In the mid-1960s, J&J's marketing experts transformed Tylenol into a consumer product to compete with Anacin, Bufferin, and Bayer. It had 7 to 8 percent of the market by 1975, when Datril, a copycat product, was introduced—at a lower cost—by Bristol-Myers. J&J retaliated by reducing prices, increasing advertising, and resorting to knuckle-dusting lawsuits to beat down competition. In three years, Tylenol had captured another 25 percent of the market and become the best seller. After spending over $85 million on advertising from 1978 to 1982, J&J had 37 percent of the market and was increasing that share 2 to 3 percent each year.

Then, in October 1982, seven people in Chicago died from cyanide-laced Extra-Strength Tylenol capsules. Although it was proven that the tampering was done on retail store shelves and not at the factory, Tylenol's sales dropped 80 percent, and its share of the market dropped to 12 percent in November 1982. J&J immediately stopped production, recalled 22 million bottles of capsules, offered a $100,000 reward for information leading to the arrest of the guilty party or parties, and opened up toll-free lines to answer customer concerns. Since 80 percent of its customers bought Tylenol on the recommendation of their doctors, J&J also used telegrams, telephone calls, and visits by sales representatives to reassure physicians and pharmacists all over the country.

J&J had three alternatives: do nothing and hope that people would buy the product again after the crisis was over, bring the product out under another name, or do everything possible to protect the brand and recover its lost customers. Since sales totaled $500 million a year and profits were $80 million, 17 percent of J&J's earnings, the company made an absolute commitment to rebuilding Tylenol's name.

A three-way tamperproof package was designed. Then the chairmen of McNeil and J&J demonstrated to the public at news conferences and on TV talk shows how safe and secure the new product was. They explained that Tylenol would cost no more because of the new packaging, and that the U.S. Food and Drug Administration had cleared J&J of any negligence or wrongdoing. Retailers and customers were reimbursed for any capsules thrown away, and a 25 percent discount was given to retailers for Tylenol purchases at or above pre-crisis levels. Also, $1.00 customer coupons for purchasing the new safety-sealed capsules appeared in newspapers, magazines, and mailboxes. These coupons went out before customers had had a chance to replace their discarded Tylenol with a competing brand. The company paid the entire cost of these activities—over $100 million—but the effort paid off. Tylenol had recaptured over 30 percent of the total market by early 1984.

The Tylenol example vividly illustrates that the profit motive does have restraints imposed by society—and by managers themselves. And companies can benefit from a socially responsible approach to those constraints, as Johnson & Johnson did.

Companies have exercised social responsibility for a long time. For example, Carnegie Foundation, with resources from Carnegie Steel, has endowed libraries and made numerous grants to colleges and universities. The Ford Foundation, with resources from Ford Motor Company, has provided consulting assistance for agricultural and management development programs in many developing countries.

But the meaning of the term *social responsibility*, as well as its importance to those owning and managing companies, has changed significantly in recent years. Historically, business firms have been asked by society to use their resources efficiently to produce goods and services that consumers wanted and to sell them at prices customers were willing and able to pay. It was felt that if this was done well, profits would be made and the economic well-being of society would be greatest. This view meant that managers were permitted to maximize profits within the rules of the game set up by custom and the law. Now the view is changing, as we'll see.

## WHAT IS SOCIAL RESPONSIBILITY?

**Objective 1**

**What social responsibility is.**

There are widely differing explanations of what is meant by the term **social responsibility.** Essentially, however, it means a firm's obligation to set policies, make decisions, and follow courses of action that are desirable in terms of the values and objectives of society. Many businesspeople don't care for the term *social responsibility* and prefer to use terms such as *social action, public affairs, community activities, social challenges,* and *social concern.* But, no matter what term they use, most owners and managers have adapted to the change in thinking about business's responsibility to society. In fact, many corporations have set up committees, special offices, or departments for this purpose. Probably the best known is General Electric's Public Issues Committee of the Board, set up in the late 1960s. Aetna Life & Casualty has a Corporate Social Responsibility Department; Allied Corporation has a senior vice-president to oversee public and government affairs; INA, a major insurance firm, has the position of Executive Vice-President, Legal and Government Affairs; and GM has appointed a full-time executive just to handle environmental and safety problems (see the Profile on page 35).

In addition, many firms have unique programs. Sperry Rand, for example, has taken steps to encourage operating managers to help the community with social development. Allied Corporation includes managers' community service in performance evaluations for bonuses. Procter & Gamble encourages its executives to participate in student groups such as Junior Achievement. IBM sponsors a management training program for executives of not-for-profit organizations. The five-day program, taught by IBM's own management development personnel, tries to improve skills in people management and leadership, planning, and finance. More than 800 representatives of small community

# *Profile*

## Betsy Ancker-Johnson: Guardian of the Environment and Safety

Dr. Betsy Ancker-Johnson, a vice-president in charge of environmental activities at General Motors, and her husband, Harold, chairman of the mathematics department of Trinity College near Chicago, live in suburban Detroit. When she first joined GM in 1978, she commuted from Chicago, where the family lived, to Detroit, where she worked. Now, because of the pressure of her work, Harold commutes to Chicago.

This living arrangement isn't the only unique characteristic of Dr. Ancker-Johnson. She has a B.A. in physics (with high honors) from Wellesley College and a Ph.D. (magna cum laude) from the University of Tübingen in Germany. She was an American Association of University Women Fellow in 1950–1951 and has been a National Science Foundation grantee, a Fellow of the American Physical Society, and a member of Phi Beta Kappa.

Dr. Ancker-Johnson taught at the University of California and at the University of Washington, was a member of the staff of Inter-Varsity Christian Fellowship, and served as Trustee of Wellesley College. She also served as Assistant Secretary of Science and Technology in the U.S. Commerce Department—the first female Assistant Secretary of Commerce—and was a member of an advisory committee on the Soviet Union and East Europe for the National Academy of Sciences.

She worked for the Sylvania Microwave Physics Laboratory and RCA Labs and was a research specialist at Boeing Company. In 1970, she shocked her bosses at Boeing by saying she wanted to change careers and go into management instead of continuing her highly successful electronics research. After serving as an executive at Boeing for three years, and elsewhere for five, she joined GM as its first woman vice-president. Her job involves ensuring that GM not only conforms to all environmental protection laws but goes beyond that to break new ground in protecting the environment.

---

Sources: Based on communications with GM and *Who's Who in America,* 41st ed., 1980–81, Vol. 1, p. 67; *Who's Who in Government,* 3rd ed., 1977, p. 11; and "Three Who Made It to the Top," *Newsweek,* September 14, 1981, p. 67.

Business training program led by Junior Achievement.

programs and national groups, such as the American Red Cross and the National Urban League, attended the Community Executive Program '82.[1]

## The Rationale of Social Responsibility

There are four basic reasons for assuming social responsibility. First, since corporations are separate entities, just like individuals, under the law (see Chapter 3), they are assumed to have the same responsibilities as individuals. Since companies operate at the pleasure of society, the people can take away a business's right to operate if it isn't responsive to society's needs. This can be done by revoking the firm's charter, which is its right to do business in the state. Or, as more often happens, a law can be passed prohibiting the offending product or activity. For instance, when it was determined that urea-formaldehyde foam insulation was potentially harmful when blown into walls, it was outlawed in schools and residences until it could be made safe. (In 1983, a U.S. appeals court lifted the ban because of insufficient evidence.) The harmful effects of asbestos led to its abandonment as a building material.

Second, it is in the long-term self-interest of a firm to promote the public welfare in a positive way. If not, the firm may be boycotted by an aroused public. For example, recruiters for Dow Chemical were practically run off college campuses when one of its products, napalm, was used in flamethrowers against the Vietnamese in the 1960s. Nestlé products were boycotted worldwide when its baby-formula marketing strategy was thought to be inappropriate for developing nations (see Chapter 22 for more details).

Third, by assuming social responsibilities, businesspeople reduce the pressure for government regulation. This means that owners may avoid the high costs of regulation and retain more flexibility and freedom in making decisions.

> Do you think these ideas occurred to Johnson & Johnson in the Tylenol case? If it and other drug firms hadn't voluntarily gone to tamperproof packaging, what do you think the government would have done? Were the firms better off doing what they did?

Finally, such actions will help businesses maintain credibility with the public. J&J was able to maintain its status and prestige with the public, especially physicians and pharmacists, because of the way its management acted in the crisis.

## Social Responsibility and Profits

**Objective 2**

**The need to balance social responsibility and profits.**

Many people, including managers, think that being socially responsible will reduce short-range and perhaps even long-range profits, but this isn't necessarily so (see the Business Debate on page 38). Is a firm only being socially responsible in replacing a dangerous machine with a newer and safer one, or may the action also improve productivity, profits, and taxes? For example, air pollution regulations have provided economic benefits that far outweigh the costs of compliance, according to the White House Council on Environmental Quality.[2] It was estimated that the cost of meeting pollution standards for a year was about $13.1 billion, but about $22 billion in environmental damage was being prevented. The panel also showed that air and water pollution was diminishing.

> While the management of Johnson & Johnson acted quite responsibly in the Tylenol crisis, wasn't it also acting to protect profits by minimizing losses? Did it have to choose between acting profitably and acting responsibly?

Of course, some social programs may reduce profits. For example, if a firm installs expensive antipollution devices and the costs can't be passed on to consumers, its profits will probably be lower than before. Another example is investment companies that create funds to put investors' money into securities of companies that promote environmental protection, equal employment opportunity, and smooth labor-management relations. Experience has shown that the desire for profit, rather than for social responsibility, has produced better results. A research firm, Lippert Analytical Services, Inc., found that three "do-gooding" funds, Dreyfus Third Century, Pax World, and Foursquare, ranked in the bottom third of all mutual funds on performance in 1982. However, this doesn't seem to have discouraged Shearson/American Express, Inc. and the Calvert Group from creating mutual funds to invest in socially responsible companies.[3]

Not everyone agrees that businesses have social responsibilities beyond the traditional ones. Milton Friedman, a Nobel Prize–winning economist,

# Business Debate

## Does Social Responsibility Reduce Profits?

Does a company have to pay for social responsibility in reduced profits? Or does social responsibility ultimately benefit the firm and make it more profitable? The advantages and disadvantages of a management orientation that emphasizes profits and one that concentrates on social responsibility are presented in the tables below.

### ADVANTAGES

| *Profit* | *Social Responsibility* |
| --- | --- |
| Higher return on investment | Better social and political climate |
| Expansion and growth | Ethical policy decisions |
| Financial strength | Knowledge of quality-of-life trends |
| Better price/earnings ratio | Better life for community surrounding, or affected by, business |
| Evidence of skill of current management team | Protection of right to privacy of individuals |
| Higher market (book) value of company | Improved community understanding of business's goals and place in society |
| Increased financial leverage | Discouragement of added government regulation |
| Economic prestige, good performance record | Increased openness toward and awareness of new ideas |
| Financial rewards to individuals involved in the management process | Responsiveness to employees' needs |
| Stockholders'/owners' satisfaction | Consumer loyalty |
| Larger share of market | Increased long-range profitability of business |
| | Higher per-employee output because of positive work environment |
| | Word-of-mouth endorsement in the public sphere |

### DISADVANTAGES

| *Profit* | *Social Responsibility* |
| --- | --- |
| Narrow point of view, goals | Cost and distraction of having to take remedial action |
| Lack of foresight in terms of changing social climate | Expense of public relations |
| Risk of product/service failure due to concentration on profit margin only, with less product quality and safety | Cost of internal and external programs |
| | Personnel time involved |

| *Profit* | *Social Responsibility* |
|---|---|
| Secondary or expendable role of people when profit is the only consideration | Opening Pandora's box in terms of social expectations |
| Inceased performance and growth stress on personnel | Diffusion of business's primary purpose |
| Small margin of social accountability, leading to increased government regulation | Risk of closing or bankruptcy due to environmental and personnel requirements |
| Pressure on community or economy to keep supplies and labor as cheap as possible—the firm's way or no way | Higher product cost, with possible negative effects on international balance of trade |
| Lack of employee/community goodwill when their needs are being ignored or used against them | Decreased ability to compete with competitors who don't play by the same rules (e.g., overseas competition in the area of cheap and unskilled nonunion labor) |

After you've weighed the advantages and disadvantages, try to answer the following questions:

1. Which alternative—profit or social responsibility—seems more logical?

2. How would you resolve the dilemma posed by these advantages and disadvantages?

says that managers are employees of the owners, not the public, and so should act for the owners. Moreover, the costs of social responsibility are passed on to consumers as higher prices, and this is "taxation without representation."[4]

### Social Responsibility's Current Acceptance

For all practical purposes, the issue of whether businesses have social obligations is settled. To survive, business must act responsibly, and most managers do, in spite of the costs involved. As an example, General Motors spent nearly $2 billion in 1978 just to comply with government environmental and work safety regulations.

## THE EVOLUTION OF SOCIAL RESPONSIBILITY

**Objective 3**

**How the concept of social responsibility has evolved.**

Because large businesses are such major power centers, it's assumed that they have an obligation to see that employees, consumers, and the general public—as well as the owners—are treated fairly, for "stockholders have no special priority."[5] This is quite a change from the philosophy held by the Supreme Court of Michigan in 1919. Henry Ford wanted to use his large profits to reduce the price of his cars so that more people could buy them. The Court ruled against him, saying that "a business corporation is organized and carried on primarily for the profit of the stockholders."[6]

As you can see, the acceptance of social responsiveness has increased not only in business but in the judicial system and government as well. In general, though, the emphasis has been on government's forcing business to act responsibly.

### The Early Period[7]

Nearly 5,000 years ago, in Sumer (present-day Iraq), the government enforced minimum wages and controlled employee working conditions. Nearly 4,000 years ago, the Code of Hammurabi (king of Babylon) contained several laws relating to business, especially liability and minimum wages for workers.[8]

During the Industrial Revolution, outside restrictions on business declined, especially in England. The guiding principles were John Locke's philosophy of ownership of private property, which was to be protected by government, and Adam Smith's belief that the well-being of society was enhanced when business acted on its own, guided by the "invisible hand" of the marketplace. These principles were later incorporated into the U.S. Constitution.

These principles, plus the **work ethic,** which emphasized hard and diligent work, thrift, frugality, and productivity, dominated U.S. business from about 1800 to the early 1930s. Entrepreneurs like John D. Rockefeller, Andrew Carnegie, and Henry Ford concentrated on increasing efficiency to lower prices and maximize profits. Profits were then used to foster economic growth. These three capitalists were later enlightened to the point of improving products, working conditions, and wages. Ford doubled his workers' wages in 1914—from $2.50 to $5.00 per day—in order to improve productivity.

But other owners, known as robber barons, weren't so socially aware. Many of them believed that employees, like other resources, were to be bought, exploited, and then discarded when no longer productive. They felt they were accountable only to themselves and not to anyone else, especially consumers. Railroad tycoon William H. Vanderbilt expressed this thought in 1882 when he said, "The public be damned. I'm working for my stockholders."[9]

The actions of these robber barons led to a concentration of wealth and power, which in turn led the public to demand government regulation. The Interstate Commerce Act (1887) prohibited unjust and unreasonable shipping rates, as well as rebates and favorable rates to favored customers. The Sherman Antitrust Act (1890) restricted combinations and conspiracies to monopolize and restrict trade. The Pure Food and Drug Law (1906) was a direct result of Upton Sinclair's book *The Jungle,* which vividly described the filthy and dangerous conditions in the meat-packing industry.[10]

### The Modern Period

Two management scholars have classified management styles into three historic phases: profit maximization, trusteeship, and quality of life.[11] The first phase, profit maximization, was discussed in the previous section. The second phase, trusteeship management, in which managers began to be concerned for employees, customers, and the community, as well as stockholders, began in the 1930s with the Great Depression.

Just a few of the laws passed at that time to protect employees were the Wagner Act (1935), which gave employees the right to join unions and bargain collectively against management; the Social Security Act (1935), which provided for unemployment insurance, old-age pensions, and disability and health insurance; and the Wage and Hour Law (1938), which set minimum wages and maximum hours to be worked.

Among the laws passed to protect consumers were the Wheeler-Lea Act (1938), which enlarged the power of the Federal Trade Commission (FTC) to prevent unfair competition and false advertising, and amendments to the Pure Food and Drug Act (1938), which added cosmetics to the list of products covered. The Securities Act (1933) and Securities Exchange Act (1934) gave a measure of protection to investors.

## Period of Activism

The third phase of management, quality-of-life management, began with the activism of the early 1960s. There were several streams of activities, or movements, during this period that drastically and permanently changed the way businesses operate. The main movements were in the areas of equal employment opportunity, environmental protection, and consumerism.

▲ **Equal Employment Opportunity** The civil rights marches of blacks in the early 1960s were reinforced by the Civil Rights Act (1964), as amended, and a series of other remedial laws. These resulted in **equal employment opportunity,** which meant that all employment opportunities were available to minorities, women, Vietnam veterans, and older and disabled workers. The Equal Employment Opportunity Commission (EEOC) is the primary guardian of these rights.

▲ **Environmental Protection** The Clean Air Act (1963) really started the movement toward environmental control, although there were environmental laws as far back as 1899 (the Refuse Act). Although this first act only covered air, later all aspects of the environment—air, solid waste, toxic substances, nuclear energy, and water—would be included. The National Environmental Policy Act (1969) set up the Environmental Protection Agency (EPA) to guard the public's interest.

▲ **Consumerism** Ralph Nader's book *Unsafe at Any Speed* (1966), which named the dangerous defects of Chevrolet's Corvair, really started the consumer movement. **Consumerism** is the organized efforts of independent, government, and business groups to protect consumers from undesirable effects resulting from poorly designed and produced products.

In 1966, Congress passed the Traffic and Motor Vehicle Safety Act, which is administered by the National Highway Traffic Safety Administration (NHTSA). The act required manufacturers to notify new car purchasers of safety defects discovered after manufacture and delivery. Probably the most renowned case under this law was the Ford Pinto trial (see FYI on page 42). Next came the Child Protection and Toy Safety Act (1969), which provided greater protection from children's toys with dangerous mechanical or electrical hazards. Probably the crowning point of the movement was the passage of the Consumer Product Safety Act (1972). The resulting Consumer Product Safety Commission (CPSC) is empowered to set safety standards, require warning labels on potentially unsafe products, and order recalls of hazardous products.

# FYI

## The Pinto Trial: Corporate Manslaughter?

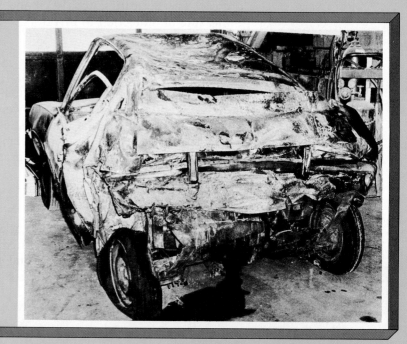

In 1980, Ford Motor Company was tried in Indiana on three extraordinary charges of reckless homicide as a result of the death of three girls in the wreck of a 1973 Ford Pinto. In August 1978, the subcompact erupted in flames near Goshen, Indiana, when rammed from behind by a van. The prosecutor charged that Ford officials knew that the Pinto's gas tank tended to explode upon impact but had knowingly built and sold a car with such a safety hazard. He urged the jury to "send a message that would be heard in board rooms across the country." Ford officials claimed that the Pinto was as safe as any comparable car on the road.

During the early 1970s, Ford had paid several million dollars in damages for several less severe cases in which the company had been found liable for passengers' injuries. This case was different, though, for it went beyond the generally accepted legal concept that a company is liable for injuries caused by defects in its products, and assumed it could be guilty of homicide.

In 1978, the National Highway Traffic Safety Administration had determined that more than a million and a half Pintos produced from 1971 to 1977 had improperly designed fuel systems. The systems were likely to spill fuel and catch fire in rear-end crashes. Ford had then recalled those Pintos in order to correct the defect. But the three girls died two months later, before all the defects had been corrected.

It's ironic that Ford might have saved itself time, money, and embarrassment if it had listened to one of the engineers who helped design the original car. It was alleged at the trial that he had repeatedly claimed that the car's design was not only faulty but dangerous. He was demoted for his criticisms.

Still, after eight weeks of testimony and twenty-five hours of deliberation, the jury found Ford "not guilty."

Sources: Andy Pasztor, "Pinto Criminal Trial of Ford Motor Co. Opens Up Broad Issues," *Wall Street Journal,* January 4, 1980, pp. 1 and 23; Alice L. Priest, "When Employees Think Their Company Is Wrong," *Business Week,* November 24, 1980, p. 8; and "Ford's Pinto: Not Guilty," *Newsweek,* March 24, 1980, p. 74.

## A SOCIAL RESPONSIBILITY ACTION PLAN

**Objective 4**

How to set up action plans to fulfill a company's social responsibility.

Social responsibility can best be explained in terms of specific action programs that a firm undertakes. These programs usually include activities in such areas as employee relations, environmental protection, consumerism, public service, educational assistance, urban renewal and development, and culture, arts, and recreation. The first three are so important and interesting that we'll look at them in greater depth. The others, while also important, will be discussed only briefly.

### Employee Relations

In general, management is much more employee-oriented now than before the 1960s. There is a growing interest in and concern for employee rights, especially as concerns employment, promotions, pay, and safety.

▲ **Equal Employment Opportunity** Employees' rights are now protected by the Equal Employment Opportunity Commission (EEOC) and the U.S. Department of Labor. Current Equal Employment Opportunity (EEO) regulations make it unlawful for any employer to discriminate against any person because of race, religion, color, creed, sex, national origin, age, or disability. These laws cover all aspects of employment from recruiting to termination. Now firms must do more than just *not* discriminate; they must also set up **affirmative action programs (AAPs),** which means actively seeking out members of these protected groups, hiring them, training and developing them, and moving them into better positions in the firm. AAPs also involve setting up goals and timetables for recruiting and promoting these protected groups.

▲ **Women and Minorities** The laws requiring equal opportunity for women and minorities are the Civil Rights Act of 1964 (CRA), the Equal Employment Opportunities Act of 1972 (EEOA), and various presidential executive orders. Much progress has been made, especially in employment of women, but much more is needed. More than half the women in the United States are now working or looking for work outside the home. During the last two decades, two out of three new jobs have been filled by women; seven out of every ten new openings in the 1980s will go to women.[12] But women are still concentrated in sex-stereotyped jobs. For example, 96 percent of registered nurses, 88 percent of hairdressers, and 75 percent of grade-school teachers are women. Although only 14 percent of lawyers and 13 percent of physicians are women, this is an improvement over 1970, when only 5 percent of lawyers and 9 percent of physicians were women.

For blacks, the figures are also mixed. Nearly 14 percent of blacks in the work force (as compared to 17 percent of whites) are in professional and technical jobs. But only 6 percent of blacks are managers (12 percent for whites). And only 4 percent of all corporate officials and managers are black.[13] Yet it has been nearly fifteen years since the Reverend Leon H. Sullivan became the first black member of GM's board of directors in 1971.

Although discrimination still exists (see FYI on page 46), most firms now accept and implement EEO. For instance, twenty-three of Coca-Cola's 4,000 fountain wholesalers were black in 1982, up from the number the year before.

The number of black professionals and managers is much lower than that of whites, although gains are being made.

Also, in 1983, Coca-Cola sold part of its stock in its New York bottling company to Bruce Lloweyn, a black businessman. And it was negotiating to sell more of its stock to entertainer Bill Cosby and Philadelphia 76ers forward Julius Erving.[14] Coca-Cola is also targeting its advertising to blacks, as a result of a "moral covenant" between the company and Operation PUSH (People United to Save Humanity). And Seven-Up has committed itself to PUSH to raise minority employment and service contracts to minority firms to 15 percent.

▲ **The Handicapped** In 1973, the Vocational Rehabilitation Act was passed to prevent discrimination against the handicapped. A **handicapped person** is anyone with a physical or mental disability that substantially restricts major normal activities such as walking, seeing, speaking, working, or learning.

The more progressive firms are responding positively. For example, Eastman Kodak has over seventy-five deaf employees in its apparatus-manufacturing arm. There is also at least one deaf tool-and-die maker in its U.S. Equipment Division. Du Pont assigns a colleague to inform each deaf worker if there is warning to evacuate the building.[15] ABC Television network spends $629,000 annually to caption programs for the hearing impaired.

▲ **Older Workers** During the 1960s, there was a decline in hiring and an increase in firing and early retirement of older workers to make room for younger ones. The Age Discrimination in Employment Act was passed in 1967 to

Coke is one of relatively few firms to target black consumers.

prevent discrimination against people between the ages of thirty-nine and seventy.

▲ **Maintaining Health and Safety**  An important aspect of employee relations is maintaining employee health and safety.  While business has been active in this area, the Occupational Safety and Health Act (1970) has forced even speedier action.  It is enforced by the Occupational Safety and Health Administration (OSHA), which concentrates inspections in those industries with the highest accident rates.

▲ **Equal Pay**  The Equal Pay Act (1963) says that men and women must receive equal pay for jobs requiring substantially the same skill, effort, responsibility, and working conditions.  Yet women are still receiving, on the average, only about 60 percent as much in wages as men.

## Public Service

IBM won the 1982 award from the National Industries for the Blind for its efforts to employ blind people through its subcontracting work.  NCR Corporation, of Dayton, Ohio, and Armco, Inc., of Middletown, Ohio, funded research on the use of computers to assist paraplegics to walk.  The result was that paraplegic Nan Davis rose from her wheelchair and walked ten feet to receive her diploma from Wright State University in Dayton.

# FYI

## TV Anchor Women Never Die, They Get Replaced by the Young

Christine Craft, 37, was the first woman to anchor the evening news at KMBC-TV in Kansas City, Missouri. After she'd been on the job eight months, the station's evening newscasts took the lead in the local ratings. But viewer response in a market survey didn't reflect favorably on her appearance. Her wholesome, outdoorsy look was evidently too rugged for some viewers.

The station did what it could to improve Ms. Craft's appearance. Her hair was cut, her chin was "minimized," and one eye was "enlarged" with cosmetics. She was provided with a new several-thousand-dollar wardrobe, which was organized on a daily calendar and coordinated down to the proper bracelets for each outfit. But research didn't show much improvement. At that point, Ms. Craft claims, the station's news director told her she was too old and too unattractive for the anchor job. She was given a choice of leaving the station or staying on as a reporter.

Instead, she went back to anchoring the news on KEYT-TV, a much smaller Santa Barbara, California, sta-

tion, and filed a $1 million sex-discrimination suit against Metromedia, Inc., then the owner of KMBC. She charged that there was a double standard for judging male and female newscasters. The jury found Metromedia and KMBC-TV guilty of demoting Ms. Craft because they valued appearance more than ability. A federal judge later upheld the $500,000 award to her. She has since resigned from KEYT-TV and plans to write a book and go on a lecture tour. An appellate court threw out the award. In 1984, the case was retried, and she won a $325,000 award from the jury—$225,000 in compensatory damages and $100,000 in punitive damages. Many viewed this case as a graphic example of the cosmetic side of TV news, as well as a test of the unspoken precept that old anchor women never die, they are merely replaced by younger faces.

Source: Jane Mayer, "TV Anchor Women Never Die, They Get Replaced by the Young," *Wall Street Journal,* May 25, 1983, p. 1; and reports of the trial in the *Mobile Register,* from July 26, 1983 to March 1984.

## Environmental Protection

Environmental protection essentially deals with maintaining a healthy balance in the **ecology,** which is the relationship between living things—especially people—and their environment. These relationships are complex

and often fragile. Almost everyone believes that they should be maintained. But the real problem is how to maintain the balance between the use of our natural resources now and conservation for future generations.

Unfortunately, we don't always know when we're upsetting that balance. For example, a generation ago, no one realized that lead in gasoline and paint was so harmful. And scientists now tell us that the carbon dioxide generated by burning fossil fuels—coal, gas, oil, and wood—may be causing polar ice caps and glaciers to melt by holding in the earth's heat.

Even when we become aware of problems, it's difficult to balance economic needs with ecological ones. For instance, coal is a relatively cheap energy source. But there are two problems. First, much of the eastern coal is high in sulfur, and burning it can result in acid rain. Western coal is purer, but the best way to extract it is through strip mining, which destroys terrain that can then be replaced only at a high cost. As another example, irrigation of rich but arid lands in California, Arizona, and Texas has provided abundant, cheap agricultural products but lowered the water table to a dangerous level, so that future generations may have to ration water.

A socially responsible action program involves two steps: conserving natural resources and preventing pollution. But such programs may be difficult and expensive to implement. For instance, Dow Chemical spent $7.2 million to build twenty-eight cooling towers to reduce by half the amount of heat returned to the Tittabawassee River, which runs through its Midland, Michigan, production complex. The towers reduced potential harm to the river's ecology and the firm's water intake by 100 million gallons a day. Dow also built "zero discharge" plants that recycle chemical wastes, cutting its costs and helping the community.[16] Yet a preliminary study by the EPA in 1983 indicated that up to thirty-five pounds of toxic chemicals, including a highly toxic form of dioxin, were being released daily by Dow into the Tittabawassee River. Dow said part of the pollution came from natural sources.[17]

▲ **Conservation** **Conservation** involves practicing the most effective use of resources, considering society's present and future needs. One way of conserving is by limiting use of scarce resources. We are now trying to do this with energy sources. Because of legislation and competition, automakers are now producing more fuel-efficient cars, and we are using them less; thus petroleum use is increasing only slightly. Another aspect of conservation is **recycling,** which is reprocessing used items for further use. Many companies use stationery printed on recycled paper. Alcoa and Reynolds Aluminum pay for used cans, from which new aluminum products can be made more cheaply than from raw materials.

The U.S. Department of the Interior has the overall responsibility for conserving our natural resources. The U.S. Forestry Service protects our forests by preventing unwise cutting of timber lands and extraction of minerals from government forests.

▲ **Pollution Control** **Pollution,** which is the destruction or contamination of the natural environment, is one of our greatest problems. Efforts to prevent or control air, land, noise, and water pollution are major goals of responsible companies. The Environmental Protection Agency (EPA) is responsible for overall protection of the air and water. It is also responsible for regulating chemical and toxic waste disposal and seeing that these wastes are cleaned up when accidents or violations occur.

The Nuclear Regulatory Commission (NRC) licenses nuclear power plants and sets standards for their construction and use. When there is an accident, such as that at Three Mile Island, where radioactive matter was released, the NRC sees that it is cleaned up and that action is taken to prevent a recurrence. Even potential accidents and ways to handle them are of concern to the NRC. For example, in 1983, the NRC prevented Long Island Lighting Company from opening its $3.2 billion plant on Long Island Sound because there was no feasible emergency evacuation plan.[18]

Companies and governments have taken actions to reduce pollution. For instance, Dow Chemical announced in mid-1983 that it would spend nearly $3 million on new studies of the environmental and health effects of dioxin in and around its Midland operations.[19] Mobil Oil Corporation spent $25 million on a state-of-the-art water treatment system, and now the water returned to the Delaware River is of better quality than the water entering Mobil's Paulsboro, New Jersey, refinery.[20]

## Consumerism

The cliché that "the customer is always right" may not be true, but at least business is now truly concerned about consumers. The movement to protect the interests of consumers is a major force in the world of business and government. Many groups have sprung up around the nation to speak for—and support legislation to protect—consumers. In fact, there are over 500 such state and local groups, as well as over 100 national ones.

Probably the most famous such group is headed by Ralph Nader. His Center for the Study of Responsive Law is the home of research teams, often referred to as Nader's Raiders, that study such subjects as product safety and the quality and cost of health care.

Consumers now have more rights to know what is in products as well as more protection against mislabeling and false advertising. Warner-Lambert, for example, was forced to stop claiming that Listerine cured colds. You now have the right to know your true interest rate (APR) on loans. Also, you can see your credit rating and have factual errors corrected. Finally, consumers have more rights and protection against dangerous or contaminated food and drugs.

## Other Action Programs

Business continues to cooperate with educational institutions to set up new programs. For instance, a group of computer makers donated $2 million worth of equipment to the University of Massachusetts's Amherst campus to establish a computer science major for undergraduates. Some of the nation's largest computer-related firms, including Atari, Random House, and Warner Communications, joined together to donate a state-of-the-art computer center to Tulsa's South Regional Library. It included computers, support equipment, and expertise.[21] Corporations including Apple, Control Data, Data General, Digital Equipment (DEC), and IBM donated about $100 million worth of computer hardware to schools in one year.[22] Frequently, business assistance is in the form of expertise.

However, two aspects of this relationship between business and education—defense contracts and faculty working for the Department of Defense (DOD)—are causing reactions reminiscent of the 1960s protests. For instance, a group of University of Michigan students protesting the college's military research revived the 1960s chant "Hey, hey, ho, ho, DOD has got to go."[23]

Firms are also helping with urban renewal and development. For example, Ralston Purina Company, the giant agribusiness firm, spent $4.5 million to help the city of St. Louis rehabilitate the area around its headquarters, with favorable reaction from the community. However, Aetna Life & Casualty Company got into trouble when it decided to lend $20 million to a community redevelopment project in Chicago. It offered a low-interest loan to a landlord to improve an abandoned and decaying apartment building. But the area residents wanted the building torn down and the land made into a park. They accused Aetna of supporting a slumlord.[24]

Mobil Oil sponsors many cultural and news programs on public TV, and Texaco has sponsored the Metropolitan Opera on the air since the 1930s.

## BUSINESS ETHICS

**Objective 5**

What business ethics are, and some aspects of business in which they are involved.

Among students, interest in business ethics is increasing at a rapid rate. According to a Harvard Business School professor, business ethics courses are a "growth industry."[25] About five times as many schools have such courses now as did five years ago. Business executives are also displaying more interest in the study of ethics. There are few management development programs that don't cover the subject to some extent.

"O.K. Whose turn is it to set the moral tone?"

**Business ethics** are the standards used to judge the rightness or wrongness of a business's relations to others. Just a few of the aspects of business involving ethical decisions are bribery, industrial theft and espionage, conflict of interest, false and/or misleading advertising, collusion, reverse discrimination, and tax evasion.

### Bribery

**Bribery** is offering something of value to a person to influence his or her judgment or conduct. Such actions are considered illegal, or at least unethical, in the United States, though they may be part of the normal way of doing business in some foreign countries. Yet the distinction between bribery and gift giving is often blurred. For instance, a salesperson has the chance to get a big order from a large firm. The firm's buyer hints that he needs a new motor for his boat. The cost of the boat motor is hidden in the selling company's accounts. Is it bribery or a gift?

In 1975, it was disclosed that, in order to sell the TriStar jet to Japanese airlines, Lockheed paid out about $12 million, most of it in bribes. A $1.7 million secret payment was made to Japan's prime minister.[26] He was tried and convicted, but later reelected to Japan's Diet, or parliament. Boeing concealed $7.3 million in "commissions" to sell thirty-five airplanes to Spain, Honduras, Lebanon, and the Dominican Republic.[27]

The Foreign Corrupt Practices Act (1977) was passed to prevent U.S. firms from bribing foreign officials.

---

Suppose you were in the airport of a West African city with a paid-for reservation, and the airline clerk told you that no seat was available. Someone then calls you aside and says that there *are* seats available, and that for $10 the clerk will assign you one. There is an important company meeting the next afternoon in New Orleans, and that is the last plane that can get you there on time. What would you do?

---

### Industrial Theft and Espionage

In the past, corporate spies would break into an office or plant and steal blueprints or formulas for a new product or process. Now the process may be more subtle, such as hiring the victim's computer programmer away with a fabulous offer. But espionage is still a fact of business life. For instance, Hitachi Ltd. paid $612,000 to Glenmar Associates, a front company operated by the FBI, for allegedly stolen IBM trade secrets for transfer to Japan. In 1983, Hitachi and two of its employees pleaded guilty and paid a $24,000 fine. Mitsubishi Electric Corporation was also charged in the case.[28]

### Conflict of Interest

Conflict of interest is one of the most difficult ethical problems for business-people because it occurs so often and in so many forms. It is easy to rationalize

a conflict between company needs and personal or other needs. For instance, many companies now issue their own stock to their employees' pension fund in order to save cash. U.S. Steel, American Motors Corporation, and Reynolds Metals Company are some well-known examples. Harcourt Brace Jovanovich used $25.5 million of its employee pension fund to build its corporate headquarters in Orlando. The fund is administered by trustees who are all Harcourt executives.[29] It is legal for a firm to put up to 10 percent of its assets into such a fund. But the practice is questionable, for employees already rely heavily on the company for their pensions; yet the "least attractive asset a pension fund ought to hold is its own stock."[30] The companies rationalize their action by assuming the stock will grow in value and the pensions will benefit.

> Is it ethical for members of the U.S. Congress to accept fees and other benefits from companies, unions, environmental groups, and others with legislation pending before them?[31]

### Advertising

As will be discussed in Chapter 14, there is much concern about truth in advertising. Other questions involve the ethics of advertising to children, especially during Saturday morning cartoon shows. Also, is it really ethical for Bic to use John McEnroe's personality defects—his reputation for "ranting and raving and [being] out of control on the court"—to sell its razor blades?[32]

### Other Areas

Another worrisome area is collusion between companies to harm—or help—another one. In 1983, the U.S. Justice Department investigated charges that several U.S., British, West German, Dutch, Belgian, and Swiss airlines acted in collusion to drive Sir Freddie Laker's low-cost transatlantic airline out of business. They were accused of offering uneconomically low fares and blocking Laker's arrangements for refinancing. James McMillan, president of McDonnell Douglas Finance Corporation, said as much in a school report for his teenage daughter. He wrote that Laker "had . . . a worldwide list of . . . enemies who were . . . determined to see that Laker did not survive."[33]

> Was CBS producer George Crile acting ethically when he secretly taped a brief "off-the-record" phone interview with former Defense Secretary Robert S. McNamara for CBS's document, "The Uncounted Enemy: A Vietnam Deception"?[34]

Discrimination, which has already been discussed, is not only unethical but illegal. But what about **reverse discrimination,** in which it is charged that a more qualified (or senior) person is denied an opportunity because of guarantees given to members of a legally protected group who may not be as well qualified (or have as much seniority)? In *Bakke* v. *Regents of the University of California* (1978), the issue was whether the University of California Medical School at Davis could reserve sixteen places in its freshman class each year for minorities, when it meant refusing to accept Bakke, a white who had scored higher on admissions criteria. The Supreme Court ruled that Bakke had to be admitted, but that admission plans that used race as a factor were not illegal. In 1979, in *Kaiser Aluminum and Chemical Corporation* v. *Weber,* the Court ruled that voluntary apprentice programs could discriminate because of race to "eliminate traditional patterns of racial segregation."[35] But management must still balance the demands and needs of all groups.

### Social Audits and Codes of Ethics

Some progressive firms are using a **social audit,** which is a formal procedure for evaluating and reporting on actions with social implications. Subjects usually covered are equal employment and training, conservation and pollution control, educational assistance, and contributions to culture, the arts, and recreation.

A **code of ethics** is a formal statement that serves as a guide to action in problems involving ethical questions. There are many such codes for regulating the behavior of professions or occupational groups, business associations, advisory groups, and individual companies. They can be long and formal, like that of Dayton-Hudson Corporation (see Figure 2-1), or as short as that of the late J. C. Penney: "Do unto others as you would have them do unto you." Probably the best such code is Rotary International's Four-Way Test:[36]

1. Is it the truth?
2. Is it fair to all concerned?
3. Will it build goodwill and better relationships?
4. Will it be beneficial to all?

## ⏚ LEARNING OBJECTIVES REVISITED

1. *What social responsibility is.*

   When a firm acts in a socially responsible manner, it sets policies, makes decisions, and follows courses of action that are desirable in terms of the values and objectives of its customers, employees, and people in the community, as well as its stockholders. Companies act responsibly because (1) if they do not, the people will take away their right to operate; (2) it is in their long-run best interest to do so; (3) if they don't, adverse legislation may result; and (4) it helps them maintain their credibility with the public.

# DAYTON-HUDSON CORPORATION

## *Statement of Philosophy*

### Strategic Mission and Direction

Dayton-Hudson Corporation is a diversified retailing company whose business is to serve the American consumer through the retailing of fashion-oriented quality merchandise.

Serving the consumer over time requires skilled and motivated employees, healthy communities in which to operate and maximum long-range profit. We are committed to meaningful and comprehensive employee development, to serving the business, social and cultural needs of our communities, and to achieving levels of profitability equivalent to the leading firms in industry.

Thus, Dayton-Hudson Corporation serves four major constituencies: consumers, employees, shareholders, and communities. The common denominator in serving these constituencies is profit—our reward for serving society well. Long-range profit is thus our major responsibility so that we can continue to serve our constituencies in the future.

### Corporate Purposes

The corporation has specific purposes with regard to serving each of its four constituencies. These purposes and associated key objectives are as follows:

**A.** To serve as the consumers' purchasing agent in fulfilling their needs and expectations for merchandise and services.

1. To offer dominant assortments of quality and fashion merchandise.
2. To offer merchandise which represents true value to consumers.
3. To support merchandising activities with appropriate levels of service, creative yet informative advertising, and well-maintained stores.
4. To occupy preeminent competitive positions in each market we serve and within the merchandise lines we carry.
5. To maintain the highest levels of honesty, integrity and responsiveness in meeting merchandise and service needs of our customers.

**B.** To contribute to the personal and professional development of our employees.

1. To provide opportunity for all employees—regardless of age, race, color, sex, religion or national origin—to develop their full potential through education, training and work experience.

2. To provide employees opportunity to advance in position and responsibility consistent with proven performance.
3. To provide an atmosphere which encourages employee initiative and input and which fosters trust, creativity and economic security.
4. To support the concept of superior compensation for superior performance.

**C.** To provide an attractive financial return to our shareholders.

1. To be a premier investment as measured against the best in the retail industry and industry in general.
2. To provide shareholders with consistent growth in dividends per share as current income.
3. To provide shareholders with growth in share value over time, consistent with growth in earnings—ranking in the industry's top quartile in terms of Price Earnings multiple, Return on Investment and Return on Equity.
4. To achieve the following standards of financial performance.

**D.** To serve the communities in which we operate.

1. To demonstrate exemplary corporate citizenship in the conduct of our business and in the relationship of the corporation and its employees to all their constituencies.
2. To observe the highest legal, ethical and moral standards.
3. To work cooperatively with business, civic, and governmental agencies to improve the environments in which we operate.
4. To contribute annually 5% of federally taxable income to improve the quality of life in communities of which we are a part.

### Corporate Objective

Our primary objective is to be premier in every facet of our business. We aspire to be recognized as premier in fulfilling our obligations to all four constituencies—customers, employees, shareholders and communities. Further, we strive to be innovative and at the forefront of the retail industry in its continuing evolution.

Achievement of this objective assumes attaining premier status as a retail investment. While profit is our reward for serving society well, it is also a requisite for continuing to serve society at all. Thus, the task is to manage the corporation so that it is recognized as a premier investment in the retail field.

**Figure 2-1** Dayton-Hudson Corporation's "Statement of Philosophy." (Reprinted by permission of Dayton-Hudson Corporation, 777 Nicollet Mall, Minneapolis, Minn. 55402.)

2. *The need to balance social responsibility and profits.*

In many cases, social responsibility may even increase profits. In others, it may reduce them. But in still other cases, companies are able to balance gains from effective operation with the costs of social action so that there is no net loss to themselves.

While social responsibility is now generally accepted, some authorities think management's primary social responsibility is to make a profit for the owners. But the prevailing belief is that business must balance the interests of customers, employees, the public, and stockholders in order to survive.

3. *How the concept of social responsibility has evolved.*

Social responsibility has evolved through three phases. In earlier days, the government and religious groups tried to force business owners to act responsibly, but business was primarily operated for the benefit of owners. U.S. business grew and prospered as a result of applying the work ethic of hard work, thrift, and savings to the principles of private property and unfettered competition. And there is no doubt that these variables built a great nation. But abuses by some greedy and shortsighted owners near the close of the nineteenth century led to legislation to protect customers, too.

This period of profit maximization ended with the Depression, when trusteeship management began. It emphasized concern for all four groups and gave meaning to that concern through passage of many significant pieces of social legislation. However, primary emphasis was still on the owners.

The third phase, quality-of-life management, blossomed during the 1960s and 1970s. It was a period of activism, with movements fostering equal employment opportunity, environmental protection, and consumerism.

4. *How to set up action plans to fulfill a company's social responsibility.*

To have an effective employee relations plan, a company must provide equal employment opportunity for all, including minorities, women, older workers, and the handicapped. Also, occupational health and safety must be maintained and equal pay provided for women and men.

The physical environment must be protected from pollution, especially from toxic wastes and nuclear harm. Resources must be productively used but also conserved through recycling and more efficient use, particularly of energy.

Consumerism is designed to protect the interests of consumers, especially from unsafe transportation, faulty design and production of electrical and mechanical toys, unsafe food and drugs, and unfair packaging and deceptive advertising.

Business tries to help develop and provide quality education, as well as to encourage the arts, culture, and recreation.

5. *What business ethics are, and some aspects of business in which they are involved.*

Business ethics are the standards used to judge the rightness or wrongness of a business's relations to others. There is growing interest in this subject

among students, faculty, and business owners and managers. Many groups, including private companies, have developed formal codes of ethics. The primary areas requiring ethical consideration are bribery, industrial theft and espionage, conflict of interest, false and misleading advertising, collusion, discrimination (including reverse discrimination), and tax evasion.

## IMPORTANT TERMS

As an extra review of the chapter, try defining the following terms. If you have trouble with any of them, refer to the page listed.

| | |
|---|---|
| social responsibility  *34* | conservation  *47* |
| work ethic  *40* | recycling  *47* |
| equal employment opportunity  *41* | pollution  *47* |
| | business ethics  *50* |
| consumerism  *41* | bribery  *50* |
| affirmative action programs (AAPs)  *43* | reverse discrimination  *52* |
| | social audit  *52* |
| handicapped person  *44* | code of ethics  *52* |
| ecology  *46* | |

## REVIEW QUESTIONS

1. What is social responsibility?
2. What are some other terms used instead of *social responsibility*?
3. What does Milton Friedman think management's social responsibility is?
4. "Business must act socially responsibly to survive." What is meant by this statement?
5. What were the "robber barons"? What were their characteristics?
6. Name the three main movements during the period of "activism." What were some of the laws or events shaping each movement?
7. What are the main ingredients (or characteristics) of an effective equal employment opportunity action plan?
8. What are the main ingredients (or characteristics) of an environmental protection plan?
9. What are the main ingredients (or characteristics) of a consumerism action plan?

## DISCUSSION QUESTIONS

1. What is the rationale for social responsibility?
2. Can one really practice social responsibility and still make a profit for the owners? In other words, after studying the Business Debate on page 38, do you think the odds favor trying to earn a profit or maintaining social responsibility?

3. How can you explain the evolution of the three stages of managerial values: profit maximization, trusteeship, and quality of life?
4. Why do you think the jury found Ford Motor Company "not guilty" in the Pinto trial?
5. Your firm needs a new employee, and you have a friend who needs a job. You think the friend is qualified, but there are probably some better qualified people available if the firm keeps looking. What would you do? Why?

## ⏁ CASE 2-1   To Caption or Not to Caption TV Programs

In 1982, a group of about forty deaf people picketed WKRG-TV, the CBS-TV affiliate station in Mobile, Alabama, protesting the fact that CBS did not caption programs for the benefit of the hearing-impaired. According to one sign, "CBS is deaf—and dumb." NBC, ABC, and PBS had for four years carried some programs with closed captions, which are invisible to the general viewing public but can be seen by viewers who buy a decoder for about $280. CBS, however, refused to close-caption programs, claiming that the system would soon be obsolete. Instead, CBS was experimenting with another system. At the time an estimated 85 percent of the 14 million deaf citizens owned decoders.[37]

**Case Questions**

1. Was CBS acting in a socially responsible manner? Why or why not?
2. Were the protestors acting responsibly in picketing an affiliate station with very little control over what the network did?
3. If you were the manager of the local station, what would you have done? Why?

## ⏁ CASE 2-2   Seniority, Ability, or ?

Roger Crowell,[38] thirty-eight years old, with a bachelor's degree in chemical engineering from State University, had been employed by a large petrochemical company at one of its major plants in South Louisiana for fourteen years. In 1957, he had been a manager there for about twelve years. The company was known as one of the more progressive companies in the country and was among the top twenty-five in sales and profits.

Crowell had just been transferred to another department in the organization to replace a man who had recently retired after having been manager there for about fifteen years. The department had about twenty-five employees who did operating-type work. Because of economic conditions, management found it necessary to reduce the work force for the first time in nearly twenty years. All managers were asked to eliminate one person from their departments, but they could decide who it was to be. (There was no union and no government regulations as to who should be discharged.) Retirement could be taken only after age sixty, and severance benefits equaled about one week's pay for each year of service.

Crowell found that there were two people doing the same type of work, and he could possibly get by with just one of them. The first, Jack Allen, was fifty-three years old and had a high school education and twenty-five years with the firm. For fifteen years his efficiency ratings had consistently been "poor" or "fair." He had signed each of his rating sheets, but the previous managers hadn't discussed them with him. He was married, his wife was an invalid, his divorced daughter and her

child lived at home with him, and his son was overseas in the Army. The other, Nick Baker, was twenty-five years old and had a B.S. degree and three years of service. His efficiency ratings had been "very good" to "excellent." He was single.

Crowell knew that his decision, whatever it was, would be unpopular because no one had been involuntarily terminated in over twenty years. The workers were proud of the company and wore their name badges in the open where everyone could see them, even when shopping downtown.

Practically no one had been hired from 1945 to 1955, as the company had been reducing the work force, and those who quit or retired had not been replaced. But in 1955, hiring had resumed, so that there were several younger and several older workers.

### Case Questions

1. Which one would you terminate? Why?
2. How would you handle (a) the one you terminated and (b) the one you kept?
3. What do you think Crowell did? Why?
4. If this situation arose today, how would it probably be handled?

**3**

# Forms of Business Ownership

*Splitting up a partnership is just like a divorce, without the kids.*

Stephen G. Thomas

*A corporation is an artificial being, invisible, intangible, and existing only in contemplation of the law.*

Chief Justice John Marshall

## Learning Objectives

After studying the material in this chapter, you will understand:

1. The relative importance of the different forms of business.
2. Why some businesses are owned by private investors and some are publicly owned.
3. What a sole proprietorship is and why it is used.
4. The two basic types of partners.
5. Why a partnership is used.
6. What a corporation is and why it is used.
7. How a corporation is formed and governed.
8. The growth of corporations and how mergers have affected that growth.
9. Some of the other types of organizations, such as trusts and cooperatives.

## In This Chapter

# HENRY E. KLOSS
*Inventor-Entrepreneur*

Henry E. Kloss is often compared to Edwin Land, developer of the instant camera and founder of Polaroid, as one of a very rare group in U.S. industry—successful inventor-entrepreneurs. His first venture into business, as a young undergraduate at Massachusetts Institute of Technology, was designing, making, and selling cabinets for stereos. The money he earned put him through school.

After a stint in the U.S. Army, he returned to Cambridge, Massachusetts, where his skills as a cabinetmaker, combined with his interest in electronics and sound, led him to Edgar Villchur, who had an idea called the acoustic suspension system. In 1954, they formed a partnership, Acoustic Research, and pioneered in the production of acoustic suspension speakers, which have since made all other types of loudspeakers obsolete. Half the company went to the outsiders who put up the money, and equal shares went to Kloss, who brought in his cabinet proprietorship, and Villchur, who had the new idea. After three years, there was a rift over day-to-day management of the firm. Kloss and two top managers, Malcolm Low and Anton Hoffmann, were on one side and Villchur on the other.

Kloss, Low, and Hoffman were essentially forced out and sold their interest for about $56,000. They formed KLH Corporation to produce a low-cost, full-range speaker. They constantly expanded their product base, adding items such as the Dolby noise-reduction system. In fact, their sales doubled from $2 to $4 million in the year after they were the first to use transistors in a consumer product—a portable stereo. Kloss sold his interest to Singer for $1.2 million of Singer stock in 1964, after Low and Hoffmann left. (The next year, unfortunately, Singer stock was the next-to-the-biggest loser on the New York Stock Exchange.) Kloss ran KLH for Singer until 1967, but when Singer refused to build a large-screen TV set he had designed, Kloss sold his stock to Singer for $400,000 and started developing the set in the basement of his house. He spent two years developing a working model of the Videobeam. But by then he was out of money, so he founded Advent Corporation to produce high-quality, low-priced speakers and the Videobeam. Advent had constant financial problems because of the low price charged for the high-quality speakers and TV sets. Its bankers forced Advent to raise new capital in 1975, resulting in Kloss's being demoted from president to chief scientist.

After leaving Advent, Kloss spent the next two years perfecting a low-cost method for manufacturing the tubes for his large-screen TV. In 1979, he founded Kloss Video with $800,000 raised from friends and became its president and treasurer. Its two-piece, large-screen set, the Novabeam, which sells for about $3,300, has sharper and brighter images than its competitors. By 1983, his 60 percent share of Kloss Video was worth about $8 million at market.

If entrepreneurship is really as central to the U.S. business scene as we claimed in Chapter 1, where can an entrepreneur go with his or her dream? What's the next step after coming up with that idea for making a million? It's obvious that there are different options. Exxon, for instance, is a far cry from Jerome Milton, Inc., whose seventy-year-old owner makes and sells Shane toothpaste with the help of his college-junior granddaughter.

The options before the entrepreneur are basically the same three that Kloss faced when starting out: sole proprietorship, partnership, and corporation. These basic forms of legal ownership are the subject of this chapter. Each form is slightly more complex than the one before it, offering its own advantages and disadvantages to the fledgling business owner. The form of operation is basic to how a given business works. The choice of form is probably the most important decision you'll make if you go into business yourself.

## TYPES OF BUSINESS OWNERSHIP

**Objective 1**

**The relative importance of the different forms of business.**

As you can see from Figure 3-1, most U.S. businesses are sole proprietorships, with corporations and partnerships trailing them in numbers. Yet corporations take in by far the most in revenues and profits from the sale of goods and services. Proprietorships are second, with partnerships following a wobbly third.

### Private Ownership

In Chapter 1, you learned that in a free-enterprise system people, alone or in groups, can risk their money by going into business to try to make a profit. **Private ownership,** which is a basic part of our economic system, is a feature of

**Figure 3-1**   U.S. business: Who has which piece of the pie? [Adapted from U.S. Department of Commerce, Bureau of the Census, *Statistical Abstract of the United States* (Washington, D.C.: Government Printing Office, 1982–1983), p. 528.]

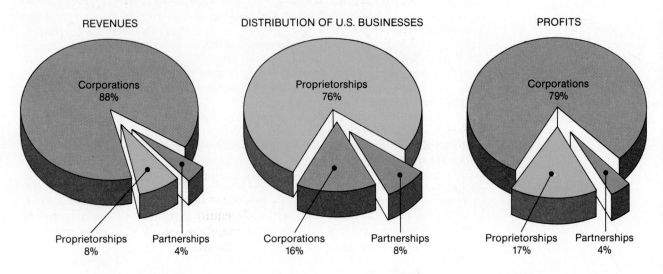

REVENUES

Corporations 88%

Proprietorships 8%  Partnerships 4%

DISTRIBUTION OF U.S. BUSINESSES

Proprietorships 76%

Corporations 16%  Partnerships 8%

PROFITS

Corporations 79%

Proprietorships 17%  Partnerships 4%

each of the three forms of business. In fact, with over 50 million Americans owning a direct share in some business, chances are good that you will join their ranks.

## Public Ownership

**Objective 2**

**Why some businesses are owned by private investors and some are publicly owned.**

Private ownership isn't the only form of ownership in our business system. **Public ownership,** in which some level of government owns and operates a company for the public's benefit, has grown rapidly in recent decades. The government in one form or another now buys more goods and services than any other institution in the world. And the federal government owns about a third of the land, and hires nearly one out of five employees, in the United States.

## SOLE PROPRIETORSHIPS

**Objective 3**

**What a sole proprietorship is and why it is used.**

An executive abandons the corporate lifestyle to run a general store in Vermont. A Chicago chemist invents and sells his own toothpaste in the very teeth of the competition from Procter & Gamble. A college graduate takes her degree in marketing and opens a boutique in her living room. What all these individuals have in common is their business role as sole proprietors.

As you might expect, a **sole proprietorship** is a business that's owned and operated by one person. It's the oldest and most common form of business ownership. In fact, there are over 12 million proprietorships in the United States. But, although nearly four out of five businesses are sole proprietorships, they do less than one-tenth of all business and receive only one-fifth of all profits (see Figure 3-1).

The proprietorship is the easiest type of business to enter, since it usually requires very little legal red tape. While this form of business is owned by only one person, it may have paid managers and employees. Sole proprietorships include small farms, retail stores, and service operations like hairdressers, repair shops, and restaurants.

Some characteristics of the sole proprietorship are (1) a single owner, or proprietor, who both owns and operates the business; (2) the owner's sole right to the firm's profits; and (3) the owner's authority to begin and end operations whenever he or she chooses.

### Advantages of Sole Proprietorships

The sole proprietorship is attractive because of its simplicity and relative freedom. Some of its advantages, shown in Figure 3-2, include:

1. *Ease of formation and dissolution.* Because there are no special laws affecting sole proprietorships, anyone can start a business without permission, and at relatively low cost, except in the case of businesses such as restaurants, health spas, and child care centers, which require a license. It's usually just as easy to close the business. The owner merely settles outstanding accounts and closes the doors, and the business is finished.

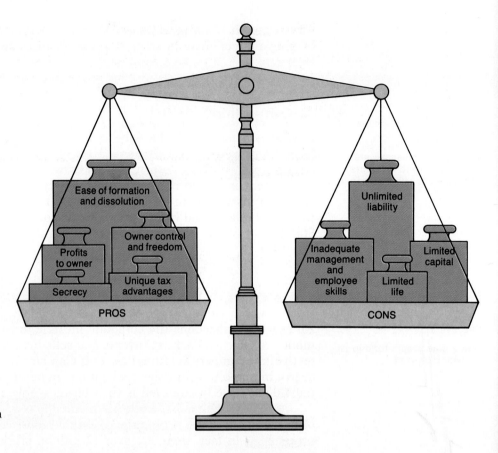

**Figure 3-2**  Pros and cons of a sole proprietorship.

Did you notice how easy it was for Henry Kloss to go into business? There was also little formality when he merged the business into a partnership with Edgar Villchur.

2. *Profits to owner.*  All profits from the business go straight to the owner's personal income—and are taxed accordingly.

3. *Owner control and freedom.*  This form of business appeals to the independent streak in all of us.  The sole proprietor has no one else to answer to in making decisions about how to run things, from working hours to hiring.

Did you note that Henry Kloss made his own decisions as a sole proprietor making stereo cabinets but lost that independence when he brought his firm into the partnership?

Sole proprietorship is a test of the owner's ambition and hard work.  Success or failure rests on the owner's shoulders alone.

4. *Secrecy.* Sole proprietors don't have to report or publicize their actions or the results of their activities to anyone. They're much less vulnerable to secret-stealing than are corporate giants.

5. *Unique tax advantages.* Since the owner's business and personal affairs are legally inseparable, there are no special taxes on a sole proprietorship. Instead, the owner just pays personal income tax on the profits and can deduct many household expenses. For example, people who operate out of their homes are allowed to deduct the part of their household expenses, such as transportation, rent, phone, electricity, gas, pest control, and repairs, that is business-related.

### Disadvantages of Sole Proprietorships

But a sole proprietorship has disadvantages as well. Since the business and its owner are considered one and the same, their activities can't be legally separated. Like Siamese twins, the business suffers if the owner makes a fatal blunder, and if the business founders the owner can go down with it. Some of the disadvantages of the sole proprietorship are the flip side of its advantages.

1. *Unlimited liability.* The owner of a sole proprietorship has **unlimited liability,** which means that he or she not only reaps all the profits but also is responsible for all debts, even if personal assets must be sold to pay creditors. As an unprofitable sole proprietor, you can lose not only your shirt but also your stereo, your car, and your home.

2. *Limited capital.* Although operating costs can be low, the fact of unlimited liability makes it hard for this type of business to attract sufficient capital, even if the owner is quite wealthy. Though personal assets are helpful in securing loans, they're also vulnerable to the firm's debts. Potential backers are reluctant to invest in such poor credit risks.

3. *Inadequate management and employee skills.* Blissfully independent owners, who usually manage all the firm's operations, don't always have the basic management skills and may be unable to attract or keep the highest quality employees. They have such an emotional investment in the business that they may resist delegation of work, new ideas, and shared decision making. As a result, they're often left with employees who are relatives, friends, or inexperienced newcomers to the business.

4. *Limited life.* Since a proprietorship relies on the abilities and resources of its owner, and since it's so easy to dissolve, it's also quite unstable. Anything, from injury to death, that removes the owner from the business causes its legal end. The business may be handed down to the owner's spouse or children, but in that case a new proprietorship must be formed.

## PARTNERSHIPS

On April 11, 1887, Richard W. Sears of Chicago placed an ad in the *Daily News* for a skilled watchmaker. When Alvah Roebuck answered the ad, one of the country's most successful partnerships was born. Whether it's Sears, Roebuck or Joe and Peggy's Record Shop, a **partnership** is a business run by two or more co-owners. It's similar to the sole proprietorship but more complex and more difficult to end, since its life is defined by the life of *all* its partners.

## Types of Partners

Objective 4

The two basic types of partners.

By definition, then, partnerships have two or more partners, one of whom must be a general partner. Any or all of the others may be limited partners. **General partners** have all the benefits of the partnership, including managerial authority and a share in the profits, but they also suffer all the shortcomings or liabilities of partnerships, including unlimited liability for debts. General partners are usually quite active in the management of the business.

The participation of **limited partners,** on the other hand, is usually restricted to certain agreed-upon aspects of the business, and the extent of their liability is limited to the amount they invest. Limited partnership is frequently used in new businesses with high risk but with an equally high potential income. It's often used in the breeding and racing of thoroughbred horses, Broadway shows and movie making, sports franchises, and real estate development projects for shopping malls, condominiums, and industrial parks. Partnerships can attract investors' capital by offering limited partners less financial risk and the tax advantage of being taxed only on personal income.

The Boston Red Sox baseball franchise is owned by three general partners, who run the team, and nine limited partners, who are primarily just investors. Yet the limited partners, with the controlling interest, joined with Buddy Le Roux, one of the general partners, in a move to replace the general manager. Later, a superior court judge ruled that they couldn't do it.[1]

A **joint venture** is a temporary partnership formed to carry out a specific business activity. For instance, CBS, Columbia Pictures Industries, and Home Box Office formed Nova, a new movie studio, to produce films financed by the partners.

## Advantages of Partnerships

Objective 5

Why a partnership is used.

Partnerships are usually formed to avoid some of the drawbacks of a sole proprietorship. For example, when the R. W. Sears Watch Company grew too large for Sears to handle alone, he added a partner. While partnerships share many of the advantages and disadvantages of sole proprietorships, they also have some different ones (see Figure 3-3). The primary advantages include:

1. *Ease of formation.* Like a sole proprietorship, a partnership is relatively easy to start. All that's needed is for the partners to agree on such matters as how profits will be shared, the circumstances under which new partners may be admitted, where to locate the business, and when and how the partnership is to cease. These agreements form the basis for the partnership contract, also called the **partnership agreement.**

2. *More capital.* Because it can draw on the savings of all partners, a partnership can obtain funds more easily than a proprietorship. The partners' combined personal wealth and talents also make them a better credit risk.

3. *More specialized management and skills.* A major reason for a partnership is to combine the different resources and skills of two or more people. In the Sears, Roebuck team, Sears' skills as a hyperactive salesman and promoter were balanced by Roebuck's reserved organizational abilities. Unlike the single-minded sole proprietor in our example, partners working together may make better decisons than they would have made individually.

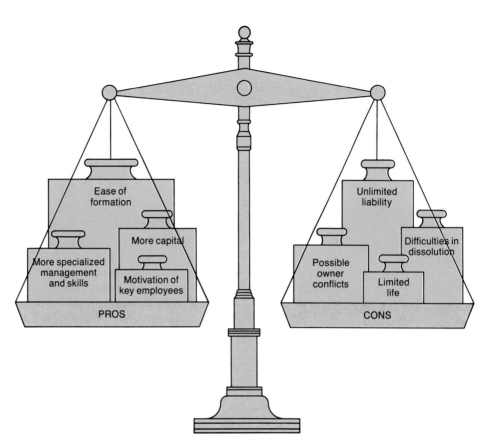

**Figure 3-3** Pros and cons of a partnership.

4. *Motivation of important employees.* If a partnership wishes to reward outstanding employees, it can make them partners in the firm. Unlike a sole proprietorship, in which there is no route upward, a partnership can attract and motivate good people. Many accounting and law firms use this method to reward performance. National accounting firms such as Ernst & Whinney and Deloitte, Haskins & Sells use this method.

## Disadvantages of Partnerships

The partnership overcomes some disadvantages of the proprietorship but magnifies others. Some of the more significant drawbacks include:

1. *Unlimited liability.* As in a sole proprietorship, in a partnership each *general partner* is personally liable for the obligations of the business. Furthermore, with each partner an equal agent of the firm, if one partner's decision costs the company money, it affects all the other partners, who may have to pay for losses out of their personal assets. All partners are also equally liable for lawsuits affecting one partner—a potentially disastrous situation for teams of accountants, doctors, and lawyers.

2. *Possible owner conflicts.* Richard Sears' aggressive advertising and marketing techniques made his partner Roebuck so nervous that, in 1895, Roebuck sold his one-third interest in the firm for $25,000.[2] Henry Kloss had

a rift with his partner over operating the business and had to leave the firm. Thus, whether it's Sears and Roebuck, Acoustic Research, or a rock group, the relationship between partners can sour, the partners can fail to agree on important issues, or one partner may need to leave in order to grow. In such cases, partners may dissolve an otherwise successful business because of their inability to resolve personal or business differences. Needless to say, this can be as wrenching an experience, emotionally and financially, as a divorce. For instance, the law partnership of Califano, Ross & Heineman suffered many of these pangs when it broke up (see the Profile on page 67).

3. *Difficulties in dissolution.* At times, though, a partnership isn't so easy to dissolve. Sometimes one partner wants out, but the other partners aren't willing to buy him or her out or can't agree on a replacement partner. Also, it may be difficult to withdraw if the partners can't agree on how to divide their accumulated assets. Finally, a partner can't withdraw if the partnership is in the middle of filling a contractual obligation.

4. *Limited life.* Partnerships can have an even shakier life than sole proprietorships. If the owner of a sole proprietorship dies, the business comes to an end. In a partnership, however, if *any one* of the *general partners* dies or becomes mentally or physically incapacitated, the partnership ends.

Only 8 percent of U.S. businesses are partnerships, doing only 5 percent of all business and earning only 5 percent of the profits. Given the hazards of partnership, it isn't hard to see the reasons for its lack of popularity!

## CORPORATIONS

**Objective 6**

**What a corporation is and why it is used.**

The corporation is a relatively new form of business ownership that didn't become really popular until about a century ago. Yet today it's the best known and most powerful form of business ownership in the country. Although less than 15 percent of all U.S. businesses are corporations (see Figure 3-1), they account for over 86 percent of revenues each year ($4.125 trillion out of a total of $4.790 trillion in 1980) and receive 75 percent of all profits ($219 billion out of $292 billion). This staggering financial record gives corporations tremendous economic and political clout. Corporations even influence election campaigns by forming political action committees (PACs) to contribute to favored candidates.

### Characteristics of Corporations

As indicated in the opening quotation from Chief Justice Marshall, a **corporation** is "an artificial being, invisible, intangible, and existing only in contemplation of the law." What that seemingly illogical statement means is that the corporate form of business is given many of the duties, rights, and powers of people who run a business, even though it is only a legal creation. This unique creature can form other businesses; borrow and lend money; pay taxes on its profits (even though the stockholders also pay taxes on their income from it); own property; sue and be sued, even by its own stockholders; hire and fire people; produce and sell goods and services; and do anything else an individual is legally permitted to do. In fact, this concept was recently pushed to its

## Profile

### Califano, Ross, and Heineman: Frustrated Partners

At the beginning of 1980, the law firm of Califano, Ross & Heineman opened the doors of its posh Washington, D.C., office with great expectations.

One of the founding partners, Joseph Califano (see photo), had some of the best political connections in Washington. He had served as White House special assistant to Lyndon Johnson and had been Secretary of Health, Education and Welfare (HEW) in the Carter administration. He also had close personal ties to House Speaker Tip O'Neill. Stanford Ross, the second founding partner, was a highly regarded expert on international taxation. His client list included the construction and engineering giant Flour Corporation, a number of international oil companies, and a large real estate development company. The third partner, Benjamin Heineman, was a brilliant lawyer specializing in corporate litigation. His credits included having been executive secretary to Califano at HEW and a strong corporate background by virtue of being the son of the president of Northwest Industries.

Through the next two years, the firm flourished, adding to its client list such groups as the Coca-Cola Company, the National Mortgage Association, the U.S. Postal Service, and the governor of New York State at that time, Hugh Carey. Business rolled in, and the firm expanded to fifteen lawyers. The dream of power was becoming a reality.

As 1982 drew to a close, however, so did the partnership. The reason behind the breakup wasn't economic but rather personality clashes and policy differences, especially over future growth. Apparently, Califano wanted a small political "boutique" that could specialize in political issues while remaining easy to manage. His hard-driving style and often uncompromising manner had a frustrating and disruptive effect on the other partners and associates. Ross and Heineman both wanted to expand the firm and broaden its corporate law practice, but were blocked in their recruitment efforts.

As the fragility of the balance of personalities became more pronounced, along with the differences over expansion, the stress of constant arguments led to one final effort at compromise in the summer of 1982. Ross and Heineman tried to settle the problems through concessions but were unsuccessful, so they declared that they were leaving the firm.

Stunned, Califano tried to keep the firm afloat by working with the remaining partners and, somewhat ironically, by considering new partners. Despite a series of frantic meetings of Califano and other members of the firm during the fall, the partnership was dissolved. The net result of the breakup was that all three original partners moved on to join other established law firms. The gross result went far deeper, though. In the wake of bitter feelings, many of the former firm's lawyers were barely on speaking terms with Califano.

Source: From William Carley, "Parting of the Ways, Law Firm Breakup Is Tale of Dashed Hopes and Bitter Feelings," The Wall Street Journal, June 8, 1983, pp. 1 and 16. Adapted by permission of The Wall Street Journal, © Dow Jones & Company, Inc., 1983. All Rights Reserved.

limits. In the case of the burning Pinto (see FYI on page 42), Ford Motor Company was charged with reckless homicide in the death of three girls. Although Ford was found not guilty, it was the first time a corporation had been tried as a real person. One wonders how Ford went about finding a "jury of its peers."

## Types of Corporations

Most talk about corporations revolves around giants like General Motors (GM), International Business Machines Corporation (IBM), and U.S. Steel. But there are many types and levels of corporations; some involve just individuals, and some have government backing.

**Public corporations** are large corporations, like AT&T and GM, whose stock is publicly bought and sold. These are perhaps the most familiar type of corporation. At the time of its breakup in 1984, AT&T had over 3 million stockholders. GM had over 1.3 million stockholders in 1984.

**Private corporations** are profit-seeking businesses with few owners, whose shares aren't traded on the open market. For example, the two founders of Amway Corporation, their wives, and two small foundations own all of the company's stock.

**Government-owned corporations,** such as the Tennessee Valley Authority (TVA), are federal, state, or local businesses operated for the public welfare. All shares are government-owned.

**Quasi-public corporations,** such as Amtrak, are businesses owned partly by the government and partly by private investors. These are usually high-risk ventures whose products or services are so important to society that the government takes a hand in their operation. Some, such as Chrysler Corporation (see FYI on page 72) and the Penn Central Railroad, are owned by private investors but are or were backed by the government.

**Nonprofit corporations,** among them hospitals and universities, are service institutions incorporated in order to gain limited liability.

**Professional corporations (P.C.)** and **service corporations (S.C.)** have become popular with doctors, lawyers, and other professionals as a means of limiting liability and reducing taxes. The abbreviation P.C. or S.C. attached to a professional group's name pinpoints corporations of this type.

## Advantages of Corporations

Some of the primary advantages of a corporation, as shown in Figure 3-4, include:

1. *Limited liability.* Because the corporation is a legal entity separate and distinct from its owners and their activities as individuals, the owners' liability for the firm's debts is limited to the amount they invest in its stock. Their private resources can't be touched except in rare situations, such as where a firm goes bankrupt and does not have enough money to pay Social Security taxes collected from employees but still owed to the government.

2. *Ease of raising capital.* Large amounts of capital can be raised relatively easily by issuing and selling stock, making it easy for a corporation to grow and diversify. Notice the large assets of the twenty-five largest U.S.

A Chicago wig shop, an example of a sole proprietorship.

These two women are partners in the ownership of a jewelry shop.

Members of the Board of Directors of a corporation.

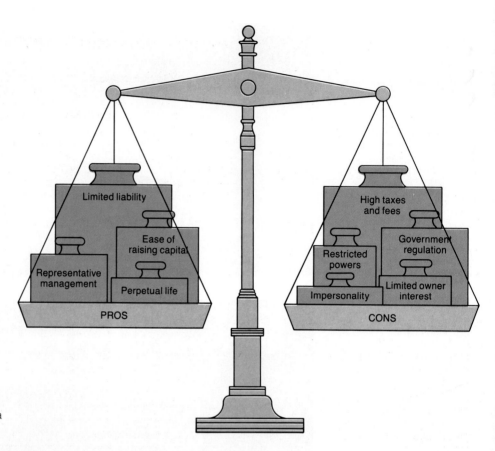

**Figure 3-4** Pros and cons of a corporation.

corporations, as shown in Table 3-1. Sums like these could not be raised by either a sole proprietorship or a partnership.

3. *Representative management.* If the owners lack knowledge of or interest in the business, the corporation can hire talented and experienced executives, who may not own an interest in the firm, to manage it. The corporation doesn't end if a manager leaves or is fired, so it gets the benefit of the best talent with no strings attached.

4. *Perpetual life.* The corporation offers relative permanence. If one owner dies or wishes to leave for any reason, his or her shares can be willed, sold, or transferred to others without affecting the legal life of the firm.

## Disadvantages of Corporations

Some disadvantages that might keep a business from incorporating are:

1. *High taxes and fees.* Not only must corporations pay higher income taxes than individuals, but their owners must also pay personal income taxes on their stock dividends. This requirement is called *double taxation.* As if that weren't costly enough, fees must be paid for corporate charters, lawyers, and public stock offerings. Most small firms simply can't afford the advantages of incorporation.

One way to lessen the tax burden on stockholders is to form a **Subchapter S corporation,** especially during startup of the firm. This type of corporation

**TABLE 3-1  The twenty-five largest U.S. industrial corporations (ranked by sales).**

| RANK | | COMPANY | SALES | ASSETS | | NET INCOME | | EMPLOYEES | |
|---|---|---|---|---|---|---|---|---|---|
| '83 | '82 | | $ Thous. | $ Thous. | Rank | $ Thous. | Rank | Number | Rank |
| 1 | 1 | **Exxon** (New York) | 88,561,134 | 62,962,990 | 1 | 4,977,957 | 2 | 156,000 | 9 |
| 2 | 2 | **General Motors** (Detroit) | 74,581,600 | 45,694,500 | 2 | 3,730,200 | 3 | 691,000 | 1 |
| 3 | 3 | **Mobil** (New York) | 54,607,000 | 35,072,000 | 4 | 1,503,000 | 11 | 178,100 | 7 |
| 4 | 5 | **Ford Motor** (Dearborn, Mich.) | 44,454,600 | 23,868,900 | 9 | 1,866,900 | 6 | 380,077 | 2 |
| 5 | 6 | **International Business Machines** (Armonk, N.Y.) | 40,180,000 | 37,243,000 | 3 | 5,485,000 | 1 | 369,545 | 3 |
| 6 | 4 | **Texaco** (Harrison, N.Y.) | 40,068,000 | 27,199,000 | 5 | 1,233,000 | 12 | 54,683 | 62 |
| 7 | 8 | **E.I. du Pont de Nemours** (Wilmington, Del.) | 35,378,000 | 24,432,000 | 7 | 1,127,000 | 13 | 159,231 | 8 |
| 8 | 10 | **Standard Oil (Indiana)** (Chicago) | 27,635,000 | 25,805,000 | 6 | 1,868,000 | 5 | 56,734 | 55 |
| 9 | 7 | **Standard Oil of California** (San Francisco) | 27,342,000 | 24,010,000 | 8 | 1,590,000 | 8 | 40,091 | 92 |
| 10 | 11 | **General Electric** (Fairfield, Conn.) | 26,797,000 | 23,288,000 | 10 | 2,024,000 | 4 | 340,000 | 4 |
| 11 | 9 | **Gulf Oil** (Pittsburgh) | 26,581,000 | 20,964,000 | 13 | 978,000 | 14 | 42,700 | 83 |
| 12 | 12 | **Atlantic Richfield** (Los Angeles) | 25,147,036 | 23,282,307 | 11 | 1,547,875 | 9 | 49,693 | 70 |
| 13 | 13 | **Shell Oil** (Houston) | 19,678,000 | 22,169,000 | 12 | 1,633,000 | 7 | 35,185 | 113 |
| 14 | 15 | **Occidental Petroleum** (Los Angeles) | 19,115,700 | 11,775,400 | 21 | 566,700 | 25 | 41,369 | 87 |
| 15 | 14 | **U.S. Steel** (Pittsburgh) | 16,869,000 | 19,314,000 | 14 | (1,161,000) | 489 | 98,722 | 19 |
| 16 | 17 | **Phillips Petroleum** (Bartlesville, Okla.) | 15,249,000 | 13,094,000 | 18 | 721,000 | 18 | 28,400 | 143 |
| 17 | 18 | **Sun** (Radnor, Pa.) | 14,730,000 | 12,466,000 | 19 | 453,000 | 34 | 37,804 | 104 |
| 18 | 20 | **United Technologies** (Hartford) | 14,669,265 | 8,720,059 | 32 | 509,173 | 28 | 193,700 | 6 |
| 19 | 19 | **Tenneco** (Houston) | 14,353,000 | 17,994,000 | 15 | 716,000 | 19 | 97,000 | 20 |
| 20 | 16 | **ITT** (New York) | 14,155,408 | 13,966,744 | 17 | 674,510 | 21 | 278,000 | 5 |
| 21 | 29 | **Chrysler** (Highland Park, Mich.) | 13,240,399 | 6,772,300 | 38 | 700,900 | 20 | 81,478 | 29 |
| 22 | 23 | **Procter & Gamble** (Cincinnati) | 12,452,000 | 8,135,000 | 34 | 866,000 | 17 | 61,700 | 50 |
| 23 | 25 | **R.J. Reynolds Industries** (Winston-Salem, N.C.) | 11,957,000 | 9,874,000 | 26 | 881,000 | 16 | 96,228 | 21 |
| 24 | 24 | **Getty Oil** (Los Angeles) | 11,600,024 | 10,385,050 | 23 | 494,314 | 29 | 19,440 | 192 |
| 25 | 21 | **Standard Oil (Ohio)** (Cleveland) | 11,599,000 | 16,362,000 | 16 | 1,512,000 | 10 | 44,000 | 77 |

has ~~twenty-five~~ thirty-five or fewer shareholders, and its corporate profits or losses can flow straight through it to the owners, who then pay income taxes at individual rates.

2. *Government regulation.* Government is much more restrictive of corporations than it is of either sole proprietorships or partnerships. Required procedures, reports, and statements, such as the incorporating procedure, annual reports, and ownership declarations, can become expensive and cumbersome. Also, because of their size and power, corporations are targets for criticism as well as regulation.

3. *Restricted powers.* The powers of the corporation are limited to those stated in its charter, and these aren't always easy to change. For example, a corporation can perform only the activities listed in its charter.

## FYI

### The Chrysler Bailout: Is Chrysler Corporation Really Private?

In August 1979, Chrysler Corporation was in trouble: inventories were piling up, sales were sagging, and losses were staggering. Top management tried to obtain help from private sources, but without success. The firm finally petitioned the U.S. government for $1 billion in cash to prevent bankruptcy.

After a bitter national debate, Congress agreed to bail Chrysler out with $1.2 billion in federal loan guarantees to private lenders. In turn, Chrysler agreed to allow the Secretary of the Treasury to approve the way the funds obtained under the guarantee were used. The government was also permitted to dictate many of Chrysler's operating policies, which included requiring that the head of the United Auto Workers union be put on the board of directors (see the Profile on page 288).

Chrysler proved it had ended the epic four-year struggle back from the brink of bankruptcy when it repaid a third of the government-backed rescue loans a full seven years ahead of schedule. While on a routine business trip to New York, on Friday, June 10, 1983, Chrysler treasurer Fred Zuckerman dropped off a check for $409.9 million (including $9.9 million interest) to U.S. Trust for distribution to holders of its notes. The balance of the guarantee was paid off in July 1983 by the chairman of Chrysler, Lee Iacocca.

Sources: Various sources, including John Koten, "Chrysler Repayment of Rescue Loan Goes into History Quietly," *Wall Street Journal*, June 17, 1983, p. 8; and "Chrysler's Speedy Payoff," *Business Week*, July 25, 1983, p. 34.

4. *Limited owner interest.* Owners may not be terribly interested or involved in the activities of the firm. Since owners tend to think of themselves not as entrepreneurs but as financiers, much of the smaller firm's enthusiasm and creative energy is hard to come by in a corporation.

5. *Impersonality.* When a corporation is very large and has many owners, it can become impersonal, with little or no contact among owners, managers, and employees. Employees can begin to feel uninvolved, like cogs in the corporate machinery.

### How Corporations Are Formed

**Objective 7**

**How a corporation is formed and governed.**

We've hinted at the complexity and expense involved in starting a corporation. To give you an idea of exactly how detailed the process is, let's walk through a sample incorporation.

FUNNY BUSINESS

A medium-sized digital sundial company decides, wisely, that it would be in its best interests to incorporate. The next wise step the company takes is to hire a lawyer to guide it through the tangled process. Next, since corporations are established under the protection of state governments, the company chooses a favorable state in which to incorporate. The requirements for forming a corporation vary greatly from state to state, and some states have more stringent requirements than others. For example, in spite of its size, Delaware charters or authorizes many more corporations than any other state simply because its requirements are lenient. One study found that Texas had fewer filing requirements and simpler forms than any other state; Tennessee was second.[3]

In a document called the **articles of incorporation,** filed with the state, the company gives its name (Sundesigns, Inc.), its address, its purpose, the number of shares of stock it will issue and how they will be issued, beginning capital requirements, tentative **bylaws** (rules governing the formation, management, and operations of Sundesigns, Inc.), and the names of its founders and directors. The state subsequently issues a **corporate charter,** an official document based on the information in the articles of incorporation and contingent on the payment of various corporate fees and taxes. At this point, an official meeting is held to adopt the bylaws and to elect the board of directors. The board, in turn, chooses a chief executive officer to run the corporation. Then Sundesigns, Inc. is in business.

## How Corporations Are Governed

Beyond the initial founders or incorporators of a business, there are several groups that share the responsibility for governing a corporation. As shown in Figure 3-5, they are the stockholders; the board of directors, acting as a group or

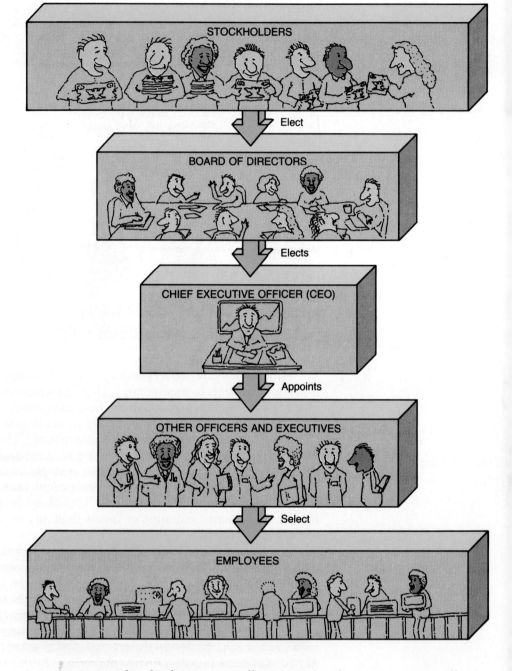

**Figure 3-5** Who governs a corporation?

in committees; the chief executive officer (CEO); other committees, officers, and executives; and, of course, the employees.

▲ **Legal Rights of Stockholders** The **stockholders** are the ultimate owners of a corporation, and their ownership is proportionate to the number of shares they have purchased in the company. Stockholders in very large corporations may have relatively little say about operations, but their rights are well defined.

One of these rights is, of course, to buy and sell stock. A corporation may issue many types of stock to its owners, but the most common types are pre-

Annual Gulf stockholders' meeting. The stockholders are the ultimate owners of a corporation.

ferred stock and common stock. **Preferred stock** is a certificate of ownership in a corporation that entitles its holder to receive a fixed dividend before any profits are paid to common stockholders. The owners of preferred stock are thus given priority over common stockholders when profits are distributed as dividends. They are also given preference over other stockholders in sharing assets if the firm is dissolved. Because of these privileges, the owners are given little control over running the business and usually have no voting rights. This type of stock is frequently used when one firm acquires another, in which case it is given in exchange for the stock or assets of the firm being acquired.

**Common stock** is a certificate of ownership in a corporation that generally entitles its owner to receive dividends and to vote on matters such as choice of company directors. One share is the equivalent of one vote on most matters, so that a stockholder with twenty-five shares is entitled to twenty-five votes. The shareholder may temporarily assign his or her voting right to someone else. This is done by means of a **proxy,** which is a document, signed by the stock's owner, that permits the person named on it to vote the owner's shares of stock. It may indicate how the person must vote, or it may permit the person to vote as he or she thinks best.

Common stockholders are the real owners of a corporation. They receive all the profits remaining after preferred stockholders have received their stated amount of dividend. They also receive all the assets when the corporation is dissolved—after the creditors and preferred stockholders have received their share. Most stockholders own some form of common stock, and most corporations issue no other kind.

▲ **Role of the Board of Directors** Elected by the stockholders, the **board of directors** serves as the stockholders' representative in overseeing the management of the business. The board is responsible for appointing the principal officers and watching after the stockholders' interests, but it doesn't usually become involved in the detailed operations of the firm. In fact, boards of directors often include **outside directors,** executives from other companies or nonprofit institutions who may serve on several corporate boards at once.

## *Profile*

### An Wang: Orient Express of Computers

They may be giants, but IBM and Xerox are no longer the leaders in introducing office machines. That position has increasingly been taken over by Wang Laboratories, Inc., a research- and development-based manufacturer of computers and word processing equipment, with headquar- ters in Lowell, Massachusetts. Wang dominates the market for integrated information systems—complex arrangements of computerized word and data processors, high-speed printers, telecommunications connections, and display terminals used by all levels of office personnel.

The authority and responsibilities of the board usually include at least:

1. Defining corporate objectives—the goals the corporation is trying to achieve.
2. Formulating corporate policies—the guidelines needed to achieve the stated objectives.
3. Determining major corporate strategies—the long-range plans for achieving objectives.
4. Electing and overseeing the corporate officers.
5. Reviewing the performance of the corporation and its officers.

▲ **Role of Corporate Officers** Selected by the board, the **corporate officers** are responsible for achieving the corporate objectives as defined by the directors. In addition, the officers are responsible, within limits set by the board, for directing day-to-day corporate activities in a manner that conforms to the policies and strategies established by the board. They select and supervise employees, obtain funds, oversee operations, and see that the firm's product or

Dr. An Wang, the firm's founder, was born in Shanghai. He received his B.S. degree from Chiao Tung University, Shanghai, in 1940 and a Ph.D. in applied physics from Harvard in 1948. Three years later, at age thirty-one, he invented the magnetic core memory, a key element in computer storage for almost twenty years (it was displaced by the semiconductor chip in the late 1960s), and founded Wang Labs in Boston.

Wang's company started small, in one room over a store, where he custom-made electronic equipment to fill specialized customer needs. Wang Labs gained attention and success in 1964 with the introduction of one of the first desk-top electronic calculators to use an adding machine–type keyboard. In 1972, when Texas Instruments became a leader in the hand-held calculator market, Wang quickly moved into large-scale office electronics, entering the word processing market and introducing the video terminal now almost universally used in word processing. Wang Laboratories now has 35 percent of the world market in word processors.

Because of its talented and versatile engineering staff and one of the best sales staffs in the industry, as well as continuous innovations in electronic instruments and systems, the company has averaged a 66 percent annual growth in profits over the past five years. It continues to grow and develop, although further growth is expected to be more difficult, with older firms (notably IBM) becoming more aggressive in going after the office market.

Yet An Wang isn't without further worlds to conquer. He's on the board of the First National Bank of Boston and the Massachusetts Board of Regents and is a trustee of Boston College, Northeastern University, Concord Academy, and Boston's Museum of Science. Dr. Wang is president and trustee of the fully accredited Wang Institute of Graduate Studies, which he founded in 1979 to grant graduate degrees in software engineering.

An Wang is also a financial genius. When high fixed costs, swollen inventories, and accounts receivable caused a need for prodigious amounts of cash during the last three years, Wang was able to raise $465 million, primarily through convertible debentures. Then, $200 million more was raised by converting those debentures into common stock. Also, his family now owns or controls 55 percent of the voting and nonvoting common stock.

"The doctor," as An Wang is affectionately called by his employees, says that he has no plans to retire. But he's gradually phasing himself out of day-to-day operations, which he's turning over to his son and heir apparent, Fred Wang, and a professional management committee. But neither his son nor a management committee can replace An Wang's entrepreneurial genius and ability to inspire fervent zeal and loyalty among his employees.

Source: Used by permission of Wang Industries, Inc. See also "The Guru of Gizmos," *Time*, November 17, 1980, p. 81; and "Wang Labs' Run for a Second Billion," *Business Week*, May 17, 1982, pp. 100 and 104.

service is marketed effectively. The most visible corporate officer is the **chief executive officer (CEO),** who may be the chairperson of the board, the company president, or both. Some well-known CEOs are Victor Kiam of Remington Products, Lee Iacocca of Chrysler, Walter Wriston of Citicorp, former astronaut Frank Borman of Eastern Airlines, and An Wang of Wang Laboratories (see Profile above).

## CORPORATE GROWTH

**Objective 8**

The growth of corporations and how mergers have affected that growth.

A corporation can expand in two ways: (1) by growing internally through greater efficiency of operation or (2) by acquiring other firms. Ford Motor Company, for instance, grew through internal expansion by constantly reinvesting its profits. General Motors, on the other hand, expanded by buying out competing firms, among them Chevrolet, and restructuring them as divisions of the parent company.

Company growth through acquisition of other firms occurs in many different ways and for many different reasons. Companies may acquire the resources of other firms in order to increase output faster, and at lower relative cost, than would be possible if they remained the same size. They may want to acquire the resources to assure themselves of a captive supplier or a customer for their product. An added division can help to balance out fluctuations in income; if one group suffers losses, the blow is softened by higher revenues elsewhere. Even during the greatest period of trial for Chrysler Corporation, its tank division was making money selling to the government. But the firm had to sell the division to General Dynamics in order to get enough cash to stay afloat. Buying out a competitor is one way to reduce competition.

Two types of growth that are gaining in significance are mergers and conglomerate mergers. A **merger** is the purchase of one business by a similar business, in which the purchasing company retains its independence and dominance. When most or all of one corporation's stock is owned by another corporation, it is a **subsidiary** of the other company. The owning corporation is the **parent company.** Usually, the parent company's chief executive, with board approval, selects the CEO of the subsidiary. Many well-known businesses are subsidiaries of equally renowned corporations. For instance, McNeil Consumer Products, the maker of Tylenol, is a subsidiary of Johnson & Johnson. Coca-Cola is the parent of Columbia Pictures.

A **conglomerate** results from the merging of two or more corporations that operate in entirely different and unrelated industries. For example, Mobil Corporation, an energy firm, bought Marcor, Inc. in 1974 in order to acquire its subsidiaries, Montgomery Ward & Company, a retailer, and Container Corporation of America.

## Mergers

Since 1975, there has been a tremendous increase in the number and dollar value of U.S. mergers and acquisitions. During the first nine months of 1981, for example, there were 1,807 acquisitions valued at $61 billion. In the process, some famous corporate names were swallowed up in a matter of months, as shown in Table 3-2. This was over a third more acquisitions than in the same period in 1980. Some believe that such a wave of mergers is harmful and should be restricted (see the Business Debate on page 79).

▲ **Horizontal Mergers** Mergers are nothing new. They've been taking place since the latter part of the nineteenth century. Aggressive financiers, such as J. P. Morgan, assisted and financed many **horizontal mergers** by buying up competing companies in the same industry in order to form such mammoth firms as Standard Oil and U.S. Steel. These mergers tended to reduce competition because larger firms bought up smaller competitors. The reduction in competition led to passage of the Sherman Antitrust Act, which prohibited such practices and resulted in the breakup of Standard Oil into thirty-four separate companies in 1911.

▲ **Vertical Mergers** The next merger movement, from about 1900 up through the depression of the 1930s, resulted in **vertical mergers,** whereby a company buys another firm that is either a supplier of or customer for materials or

# Business Debate

## Should "Dinosaur" Mergers Be Made Extinct?

The U.S. economy is in the midst of a major wave of mergers and merger proposals. Many people, including some members of Congress, are becoming concerned that this trend is hurting the economy by reducing needed competition. According to Arthur Burck, a business consultant, it is likely that by the year 2000 "several score multinational corporations will control most of the nation's industrial assets," and industry could be a stagnant swamp "dominated by many dinosaurs." Now some congressional committees are studying the possibility of restricting mergers.

The arguments *for* restricting mergers include the following:

1. If mergers continue at the present rate, a few large firms will eventually dominate the economy.
2. The result of this trend will be many quasi-nationalized firms that the government must subsidize to keep them from failing.
3. When companies get too big, they move into other firms' fields and hurt business.
4. Fighting a merger takeover is very costly and weakens the management of the firm that is to be taken over.
5. When a firm gets too big, it becomes bureaucratic and inflexible, losing the ability to take risks and develop new products.
6. Larger firms have too much economic and political power.

The arguments *against* restricting mergers include the following:

1. The Clayton Act has proven effective in preventing mergers that restrict competition in the same industry.
2. Figures show that the relative size of the nation's largest corporations has not been growing since the mergers. Instead, real growth has resulted from internal efficiencies in expanding fields such as chemicals, aerospace, and electronics.
3. The percentage of the nation's private employees working in the 1,300 largest companies has actually declined in the last decade.
4. The largest firms have grown more slowly than the overall economy during the last decade.
5. Many large firms are spinning off and divesting themselves of unprofitable subsidiaries almost as rapidly as mergers are occurring.
6. Merging is sometimes necessary to achieve the most effective performance and to obtain capital for technological development.

*What do you think?*

---

Sources: Based on several sources, including "Merger Boom Can Lead to 'Dinosaur' Companies," *U.S. News & World Report*, December 21, 1981, p. 64; Lawrence J. White, "The Merger Wave: Is It a Problem?" *Wall Street Journal*, December 11, 1981, p. 26; and "Quest for Ways to Run a Tighter Ship," *U.S. News & World Report*, November 30, 1981, pp. 58–59.

---

services. Many firms in the oil, steel, and automobile industries grew through this type of merger. When General Motors needed a reliable supplier of bodies for its vast line of automobiles, it acquired Fisher Body Company. And U.S. Steel acquired American Bridge Company, which used its steel to build bridges.

TABLE 3-2  Companies that have disappeared.

| These Well-Known Companies | Have Merged into These Companies |
|---|---|
| Conoco | Du Pont |
| Ethan Allen | Interco, Inc. |
| Franklin Mint | Warner Communications |
| Howard Johnson Co. | Imperial Group, Ltd. |
| Liggett Group, Inc. | Grand Metropolitan, Ltd. |
| Marathon Oil | U.S. Steel Corporation |
| Pullman, Inc. | Wheelabrator-Frye, Inc. |
| Warner & Swasey | Bendix Corporation |
| Bendix Corporation | Allied Corporation |
| Haagen-Dazs | Pillsbury |
| Getty Oil | Texaco |
| Gulf Oil | Socal |

### Conglomerates

In the 1950s, a new type of merger began to occur, the *conglomerate merger.* In order to grow and increase profits, while avoiding legislative restrictions on mergers, a company would buy up firms that weren't competitors, suppliers, or customers. Instead, the firms acquired were in entirely different industries, as in the Du Pont-Conoco merger (see FYI on page 82).

Some of the best-known conglomerates are Litton Industries, RCA, Ford, International Telephone and Telegraph (ITT), and Pepsico. ITT owns much of California's croplands, while Pepsico owns Pepsi Cola, Frito-Lay, Wilson Sporting Goods, and Pizza Hut.

## OTHER FORMS OF OWNERSHIP

**Objective 9**

Some of the other types of organization, such as trusts and cooperatives.

Other forms of ownership that are becoming important are the trust and the cooperative.

### Trusts

A **trust** is an arrangement that takes legal possession of personal assets and manages them for the benefit of those who created the trust or for some other designated person. For example, when Ronald Reagan became president, he and most of his tax aides set up trusts to handle their financial affairs. A trust differs from a corporation in that it is established for only a specific period of time, or until certain stated events have occurred (for example, until a minor reaches majority). The trust, which is administered by a trustee, receives specific assets from the persons establishing it and administers the assets for their benefit.

The Ford conglomerate is a leader in diverse technologies.

## Cooperatives

A **cooperative** is a business enterprise enjoying many of the advantages of both the sole proprietorship and the corporation. It is owned by and operated for the benefit of those it serves, and its income is distributed to shareholders according to their participation. Early cooperatives were loose, unincorporated business organizations in agriculture or retailing. For example, the San Francisco–based Tri/Valley Growers is the nation's largest fruit and vegetable cooperative. More recently, however, cooperatives have been incorporating in order to have the benefits of the corporate form, and they may be stock or nonstock corporations. Since cooperatives come under the laws of individual states, their nature and structure will vary from state to state.

The primary advantage of cooperatives is their tax advantage. For tax purposes, they are allowed to deduct from gross income all dividends paid to stockholders. A second advantage is cost, since the capital investment is usually limited to around $1,000. The principal disadvantage of cooperatives is that members tend not to participate in their management. Consequently, it is easy for management to become so self-serving that the cooperative fails to serve the interests of the membership for which it was established.

## FYI

### Du Pont Versus Seagram: To the Victor Belong the Spoils

In mid-1981, Seagram Company, a Canadian distiller, made a $2.55 billion offer to buy 41 percent of Conoco, Inc. It offered Conoco's stockholders $73 a share for their stock. Upon learning this, Du Pont Company made Conoco a $6.82 billion offer. It agreed to buy 40 percent of Conoco stock at $87.50 a share and give 1.6 Du Pont shares for each of the remaining Conoco shares.

After much negotiation and legal action, Conoco accepted Du Pont's last offer of $7.8 billion, which resulted in the largest such transaction in corporate history. The merger was approved by both Du Pont and Conoco stockholders. It was also approved by the U.S. Justice Department and the Federal Trade Commission after they had studied detailed reports on the firms' products, markets, and areas where their products competed. It was decided that, while the merger did have some aspects of a vertical merger (some of Conoco's petroleum and coal served as raw materials for Du Pont and its competitors), it was not a horizontal merger. The conclusion was that, although some of Du Pont's suppliers of petroleum-based raw materials would lose business, there would be little harmful effect on competition in the energy or chemical industries.

So Du Pont, the number one chemical company, acquired the larger Conoco, the ninth-largest oil company, to become the seventh-largest of the *Fortune* 500 firms. Du Pont, which had to borrow $3.9 million from a group of banks to finance the deal, continued to operate as Du Pont Company.

While the merger was a surprise to financial analysts, it was the result of two joint ventures in natural gas exploration in Texas and eight other states beginning in 1978. The price of the merger proved too steep, however, even for Du Pont, which had to borrow $3.9 million to swing the deal. In 1982, the parent company had to sell nearly 10 percent of its proved oil and gas reserves to reduce its indebtedness.

Sources: From "Du Pont Company Agrees to Buy Conoco, Inc. for Cash, Stock Totaling $6.82 Billion," *The Wall Street Journal*, July 7, 1981, pp. 3 and 18. Adapted by permission of *The Wall Street Journal*, © Dow Jones & Company, Inc., 1981. All Rights Reserved. Also based on John S. DeMott, "White Knights and Black Eyes," *Time*, February 14, 1983, pp. 56–57; Clements P. Work, "The Merger Drive Goes into Reverse," *U.S. News & World Report*, May 2, 1983, pp. 55–56; and "After the Merger, Du Pont Still Likes Conoco," *Business Week*, May 30, 1983, pp. 73–74.

Cooperatives are now quite important to U.S. business. They market about one-fourth of all U.S. farm produce and provide farmers with a fifth of their supplies, such as fertilizer, seed, and feed. Rural electric cooperatives supply more than half the electricity used in rural areas. Credit unions, with nearly 30 million members, have over $30 billion in assets. And there may be a cooperative even closer to home. Perhaps your bookstore, like the Harvard Coop in Cambridge, Massachusetts, is a cooperative.

## ⚠ LEARNING OBJECTIVES REVISITED

1. *The relative importance of the different forms of business.*

   The most common forms of legal ownership are the sole proprietorship, the partnership, and the corporation. Although proprietorships outnumber corporations more than five to one, corporations take in over nine times as much revenue and make nearly four times as much profit. Partnerships are a poor third in all three categories.

2. *Why some businesses are owned by private investors and some are publicly owned.*

   A business can be owned by one or more private individuals or by a government or public body. Most firms have private owners, but at times government must step in when private firms are unable to fulfill their mission of providing for consumer needs.

3. *What a sole proprietorship is and why it is used.*

   Most businesses are sole proprietorships, which are easy to enter and leave and have immediate profitability, satisfaction, and secrecy, as well as unique tax advantages. However, they also have unlimited liability, limited capital, sometimes inadequate management skills, and a limited life.

4. *The two basic types of partners.*

   General partners, who actively manage the firm, gain all the advantages and suffer all the disadvantages of a partnership. Limited partners are liable only for the amount they invest in the firm but have no say in its day-to-day operation.

5. *Why a partnership is used.*

   A partnership is a business run by two or more co-owners. Partnerships are easy to form, can have more capital and more specialized management, and can motivate key employees with the hope of being made partners. Yet they also have unlimited liability and limited life, and there may be conflicts between owners and difficulties in dissolution. A joint venture is a temporary partnership organized to perform a certain activity.

6. *What a corporation is and why it is used.*

   Corporations are artificial creations with the rights and responsibilities of running a business. They may be public, private, government-owned, quasi-public, nonprofit, or professional. As separate legal entities, corporations have limited liability, easy methods of raising capital, representative management, and permanence. But they also have high taxes and fees, heavy government regulation, restricted powers, limited owner interest, and a tendency to be impersonal.

7. *How a corporation is formed and governed.*

   Corporations are formed by receiving a charter from a state, preparing bylaws, and paying incorporation fees. They may issue preferred stock but must issue common stock, for common stockholders ultimately own the business and elect the board of directors. The board of directors selects a chief executive officer, who appoints other officers and executives, who in

turn select employees. A Subchapter S corporation can save on taxes by passing the profits straight through to the owners, who pay individual rates.

8. *The growth of corporations and how mergers have affected that growth.*

Companies can grow by operating efficiently and effectively or by acquiring other businesses. The latter method can take the form of a horizontal merger with competitors in the same industry, a vertical merger with the company's customers or suppliers, or a conglomerate merger with firms in unrelated industries.

9. *Some of the other types of organizations, such as trusts and cooperatives.*

A trust is set up so that the trustee can manage the assets of another person for that person's benefit. A cooperative is owned by and operated for the benefit of the people it serves.

## ⬦ IMPORTANT TERMS

As an extra review of the chapter, try defining the following terms. If you have trouble with any of them, refer to the page listed.

private ownership  *60*
public ownership  *61*
sole proprietorship  *61*
unlimited liability  *63*
partnership  *63*
general partners  *64*
limited partners  *64*
joint venture  *64*
partnership agreement  *64*
corporation  *66*
public corporations  *68*
private corporations  *68*
government-owned
   corporations  *68*
quasi-public corporations  *68*
nonprofit corporations  *68*
professional corporations
   (P.C.)  *68*
service corporations (S.C.)  *68*
Subchapter S corporation  *70*

articles of incorporation  *73*
bylaws  *73*
corporate charter  *73*
stockholders  *74*
preferred stock  *75*
common stock  *75*
proxy  *75*
board of directors  *75*
outside directors  *75*
corporate officers  *76*
chief executive officer
   (CEO)  *77*
merger  *78*
subsidiary  *78*
parent company  *78*
conglomerate  *78*
horizontal mergers  *78*
vertical mergers  *78*
trust  *80*
cooperative  *81*

## ⬦ REVIEW QUESTIONS

1. Why is it important to understand the three main forms of business?
2. What are the characteristics, advantages, and disadvantages of a sole proprietorship?
3. What are the characteristics, advantages, and disadvantages of a partnership?

4. What are the types, advantages, and disadvantages of corporations?
5. Describe the way a corporation is governed. Who is involved, and what are their duties and responsibilities?
6. What are the differences between common and preferred stock?
7. Explain the difference between a horizontal and a vertical merger.
8. Why are cooperatives increasing in popularity?
9. What is a Subchapter S corporation?
10. How does a conglomerate merger differ from horizontal and vertical mergers?

## DISCUSSION QUESTIONS

1. Why would a person want to become a limited partner in a partnership rather than a general partner? a general partner rather than a limited partner?
2. Why would a person choose to incorporate a business rather than be a sole proprietor or partner?
3. Why are partnerships relatively unpopular?
4. Which form of business would you personally find the hardest to handle? Why?
5. Discuss the differences in taxation for sole proprietorships, partnerships, and corporations.
6. If the present trend toward conglomerate mergers continues, what do you think it will do to the competitive position of business in the United States?
7. Jo Brown and Bob Green want to open a television repair shop. Which form of business would be to their best advantage? Why?

## CASE 3-1 Andrew Ponder: The Young Entrepreneur

Andrew Ponder,[4] a twenty-three-year-old senior at State College, has been an independent carrier for the *Morning News* for five years. His route, covering all of central Bay City, is about thirty miles from the college. From 2 A.M. to 6 A.M. each morning, he delivers about 900 papers. Andy is responsible for all aspects of his job. His duties, after buying the papers, are rolling, bagging (in wet weather), and stacking them for delivery; delivering them; keeping up with the new orders and stop orders; collecting payments; and keeping his two station wagons in running order. His net income of about $21,000 a year results from buying and selling papers and keeping expenses down.

His only part-time employee, who usually runs the route one or two days a week and when Andy is on vacation, is an older, retired man. His helper's work is in the very early hours, but Andy usually lets him choose his own work days. This unstructured, flexible system has been effective for Andy and for his present and past helpers. Since the job is at odd hours, Andy rewards accordingly. An unskilled retired person would usually have to work two to three times as long at another job to make the same amount of money.

Andy, who usually does the paperwork at his convenience, occasionally gets help from his wife. He bills his customers once a month, but some take two to five months to pay. Sometimes one will move without notifying him. Collections are important because every dollar Andy loses is a total loss to him; he still has to pay the same cost

for his papers, cars, and help whether he collects or not. Often it's difficult or awkward to collect. The greatest cost involved in running the business, though, is keeping the two cars running. On a paper route, transportation costs are very high, and the cars demand a lot of very regular maintenance. The cars need at least one brake job and new tires about every two months.

"I'd classify my business as a service operation," says Andy. "Sales are what bring in the money, but service is what makes the sales."

Since service industries are growing so fast, Andy thinks that his route has a lot of growth potential. His route has grown from 500 to over 900 papers a day in five years. Andy really enjoys his job and finds it very satisfying. His only problem with the job is lack of prestige. Many older people, friends, and relatives wonder when he's going to quit "playing paperboy" and get a "real job." Yet, to him, his job is very real, and he says that as long as he enjoys it and can earn a good living from it, he will continue to do his work.

### Case Questions

1. What are the advantages and disadvantages to Andy of remaining a sole proprietor?
2. As there are several other routes around him, and one occasionally becomes available, should Andy try to get another one? Why?
3. If he gets another route, what form of business would you suggest? Why?

## ⛰ CASE 3-2  U.S. Steel Corporation: "Buy American" in Trouble[5]

The U.S. steel industry is in trouble. The plants of the major companies are getting old and obsolete. In the past, the United Steelworkers union and the firms made cooperative agreements emphasizing the quality of work life in order to make it less unpleasant to work in hot, dirty, noisy mills. These agreements, which included sabbatical leaves of thirteen weeks' vacation after fifteen years of service, various other employee benefits, and restrictive work rules that reduced productivity, have driven up costs, as have many management practices. Government regulations, especially those of the Environmental Protection Agency, have also made costs skyrocket. The result is that one firm, U.S. Steel Corporation, can import raw steel from the British for $35 a ton less than it can produce it at the company's Fairless Works on the Delaware River near Philadelphia. It's estimated that renovating the plant would cost $1.5 billion.

U.S. steel mills face competition from firms within the United States as well. One source of competition is the new mini-mills. All they do is melt scrap into steel, so they don't require the costly equipment needed to smelt iron ore, coke, and limestone into raw steel. The firms operating these small mills are a fraction of the size of the integrated companies, and so is their cost. Their share of the U.S. steel market has increased from almost zero twenty years ago to 20 percent in 1983. The mini-mills tend to be nonunion, whereas the major firms are fully unionized. It's estimated that to operate at 85 percent of capacity, a recently closed integrated plant near Los Angeles used 1,100 employees. A new Nucor Corporation mini-mill at Plymouth, near Salt Lake City, Utah, requires only about 300. Thanks to the mini-mills and foreign imports, the integrated firms' market share declined from 93 percent to 60 percent from 1963 to 1983.

U.S. Steel is negotiating with British Steel Corporation (BSC) to buy about 3 million tons of semifinished steel annually from BSC. U.S. Steel would stop producing basic steel at its Fairless Works; instead, it would form a joint venture with BSC to finish steel there. BSC would invest $600 million in the renovation; the plant would be jointly owned, but operated by U.S. Steel. U.S. Steel would salvage the plant, which is scheduled to close in 1990; BSC would get an assured market for its steel, much of which is now surplus.

Other countries, such as Japan, several European countries, and many developing countries, also want to sell semifinished steel to U.S. Steel.

Brazil is building a new mill that can offer steel for half the British price. However, if U.S. Steel turns to foreign steel, it will antagonize the United Steelworkers, which has been cooperating with the U.S. industry in its efforts to retrench and become more economical.

Another option for U.S. Steel is to merge with another American firm, of which there are many ready to mate. But this option would have to be approved by the U.S. Department of Justice, as it would be a horizontal merger that would reduce competition.

Further complicating the problem is the reduced use of steel in U.S. autos. Not only are companies not making as many cars, but they're using about a quarter to a third less steel in each one.

There are no easy choices, but something has to be done, since the integrated mills are operating at only about 50 percent of capacity.

**Case Questions**

1. Which alternative would you choose? Why?
2. If you chose to go with British Steel, what form of business would you use? Why?
3. Would your answer be the same if you were to merge with one of the other U.S. firms? Why?
4. What would you suggest the steel companies do to survive?

# Small Business

*In battle or business, whatever the game,*
*In law or in love, it is ever the same;*
*In the struggle for power, or the scramble for pelf,*
*Let this be your motto—rely on yourself!*

John Godfrey Saxe

## Learning Objectives

After studying the material in this chapter, you will understand:

1. What small business is and the types of small business.
2. Some of the unique contributions of small business.
3. Some of the limitations of small business.
4. Motives of small business owners.
5. Formulas for success and failure in small business.
6. The importance of a business plan when starting a small business.
7. Sources of financing for small businesses.

## In This Chapter

What's Small?
Characteristics of Small Businesses
Unique Contributions of Small Business
Limitations of Small Business
Profile of a Small Business Owner
Developing a Business Plan
Financing Small Businesses

## THE PENTE® GAME
*Back to Basics*

Pente®, a board game like the ancient Japanese game of Gō, is played with colorful glass beads on a classic grid embellished with Grecian figures. Sound boring, in the age of Donkey Kong and Zaxxon? Not for Gary Gabrel, who designed the game in 1974.

After making a startup investment of $20,000, Gabrel sold his first games at a 1976 arts and crafts fair for $5 apiece. Now the selling price for game sets ranges from $5 to $100. By 1980, Pente® was being sold in retail outlets like Neiman-Marcus and Bloomingdale's, and sales volume hit $1 million. By 1981, sales had climbed to $3 million, and Gabrel's net income was a comfortable $300,000. Sales were $16 million in 1982. In March 1983, the millionth game was sold.

In the beginning, Pente® was played as a diversion in campus hangouts, but now it's marketed internationally. Gabrel once used a full-time sales representative who traveled nationwide and 140 independent commissioned sales reps who pushed the game. He also hosted tournaments around the country.

Gabrel's optimism for his brainchild's future isn't daunted by the competition from video games. "Video games will never replace the social interaction people enjoy with a board game. With video, it's always going to be man versus the machine," he says. "What's more, there's a void among traditional board games. Backgammon sales are slipping, and Pente® is the only one that looks like a winner." He may be right, as video and arcade games begin to hit a slump because of fierce competition.

How did it all happen? How did Gabrel's firm get to be worth $4 million, with an annual payroll of only $600,000 and thirty employees, seven of whom were among the first hired in 1977? Most employees are students and recent graduates of Oklahoma State University. Gabrel kept his initial overhead low by operating out of a 10,000-square-foot building in the downtown business district of Stillwater, Oklahoma. In 1982, Pente® headquarters moved to a new 15,000-square-foot facility located on a major highway. Financing was arranged by the County Industrial Authority through tax-exempt revenue bonds issued to a local bank at four percentage points below the prime interest rate.

Every day, Gabrel's secretary provides him with a report showing unit and dollar sales and the current cash balance. Gabrel says, "The money aspect is a curiosity to me. A way of keeping score." It's clear that, for Gary Gabrel, work is play. But he plays for profit.

Shortly after being honored at the White House as one of the nation's outstanding young businesspeople, Gary was named Bachelor of the Month in the September 1982 issue of *Cosmopolitan* magazine. Upset over the onslaught of letters Gabrel received from readers of *Cosmopolitan,* his fiancée, Nora Jo Rose, laid down the ultimatum "Wedding bells in five months or it's over." She noted that *pente* is the Greek word for five. The couple was married in late December 1982.

In July 1983, Gabrel signed an agreement to sell Pente® to Parker Brothers Game Company, the makers of Monopoly and a subsidiary of General Mills. Production will shift to Salem, Massachusetts, with the fate of the thirty-five local workers uncertain. Gabrel is test marketing a new game, Decipher.

89

The Gary Gabrel story may sound like just one more "small town boy makes it big" success yarn, but the fact is that Gabrel is one of a majority. Small businesses like Gabrel's make up about 97 percent of U.S. businesses and generate nearly half of our gross national product (GNP).[1] They are expected to create seven out of ten new jobs during the 1980s, after creating eight out of ten during the last decade.[2] Like the Pente® operation, they grow up from modest origins, both rely on and supply larger firms, and keep the spark of free enterprise glowing in a massive economic engine. And sometimes they fail.

Small business is one form of private ownership, one that is drawing so many entrepreneurs daily that a new crop of magazines has sprung up to support it, including *Inc., Small Business Journal, Venture,* and *Journal of Small Business Management.* Around 600,000 new firms are launched every year, half of which will meet untimely ends within five years. Yet, for all their hazards, small firms provide an outlet for creativity and independence in an era when the secure prestige of a corporate suite may yield only alienation and stress. For example, Thomas K. Hunt resigned from the computer products division of the billion-dollar Itel Corporation to go with Deltak, Inc., a small firm with sales of about $50 million. "I wanted a small firm," he said. "Here I can make my own decisions, and, right or wrong, see them carried out."[3]

Small businesses are more likely to hire women, older, younger, and part-time workers than larger firms, according to a 1984 Small Business Administration news item.

## WHAT'S SMALL?

**Objective 1**

What small business is and the types of small business.

One of the snags in trying to develop a usable definition of small business is simple relativity. For instance, it's clear that Amtrak, the top-ranked passenger railway, with $436 million in 1980 sales, isn't a small operation. But relative to Conrail's 1982 revenues of $3.6 billion, it's *small*. We know that a one-woman dog-walking service is small business, but what about the local kennel with twenty employees and revenues of $750,000? The answer is, of course, that neither Amtrak nor Conrail is a small business, and both canine companies are. How do we arrive at these distinctions?

Perhaps the best definition is the one used by Congress in the Small Business Act of 1953, when it said that a **small business** is one that's independently owned and operated and that isn't dominant in its field of operation.[4] Qualitative characteristics are also important in describing small businesses. The Committee for Economic Development stated that a small business is characterized by at least two of the following features:[5]

1. Management is independent, since the manager usually owns the firm.
2. Capital is supplied and ownership is held by an individual or a few individuals.
3. The area of operations is primarily local, although the market isn't necessarily local (as in the case of the Pente® game).
4. The firm is small in comparison with the largest competitors in its industry.

The definition currently used by the U.S. Small Business Administration (SBA) for reporting purposes is a business "having fewer than 500 employees."[6]

## Types of Small Business

The SBA, an agency of the federal government that provides advice, financial assistance, and other services to small businesses, classifies them as follows.

**Manufacturing firms** use raw materials and semifinished parts to produce finished goods. Since the initial investment—the plant, machines, and equipment—is great, and operating costs and risks are high, relatively few such firms are small. A small business is one with a maximum of 250 to 1,500 employees, depending on the type of industry. Small firms tend to provide parts and components to larger companies.

**General construction firms** build residences, both private and rental; commercial and industrial buildings; government offices and installations; and structures of other types. Small businesses are those with less than $9.5 million in annual sales. They often do subcontracting for larger contractors, such as installing doors, windows, and cabinets in buildings.

**Wholesalers** buy finished products from manufacturers and other producers and resell them to retailers for sale to the ultimate consumer. A small firm would have annual sales of $22 million or less.

**Retailers** obtain goods from wholesalers, brokers, and agents and sell them to customers for use. Small retailers have annual sales of $7.5 million or less. Grocery stores, drugstores, and food service establishments are examples.

**Service businesses** perform essential, specialized, and often technical services for customers, businesses, and institutions such as schools, governments, and hospitals. To be classified as small, they must have annual sales of $8 million or less. These services are usually those the customers are unable or unwilling to provide, such as consulting, custodial and janitorial, accounting and tax, and automotive and appliance repair services.

Small firms are most popular in wholesale and retail trade, services, and financial services (see Figure 4-1) and not so popular in manufacturing, mining,

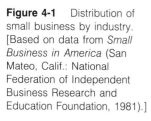

**Figure 4-1** Distribution of small business by industry. [Based on data from *Small Business in America* (San Mateo, Calif.: National Federation of Independent Business Research and Education Foundation, 1981).]

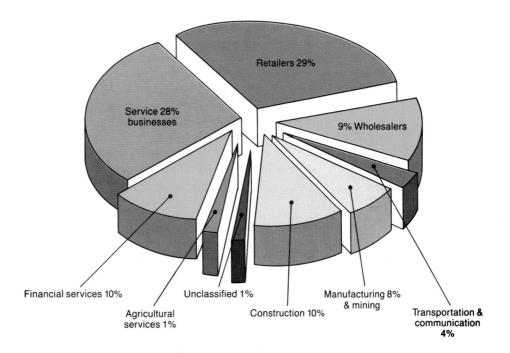

Retailers 29%

Service 28% businesses

9% Wholesalers

Financial services 10%

Agricultural services 1%

Unclassified 1%

Construction 10%

Manufacturing 8% & mining

Transportation & communication 4%

**TABLE 4-1  Some business options, classified into related groups.**

I. Retailing
  1. Food
    a. Grocery
    b. Fast-prepared
    c. Convenience
    d. Restaurant
    e. Lounges
    f. Specialty shops
  2. Appliance
  3. Hardware and building
    material
  4. Specialty
  5. Clothing

II. Service
  1. Service station
  2. Auto repair
  3. Appliance repair
  4. Building repair and
    renovation
  5. Janitorial
  6. Plumber
  7. Electrician
  8. Floor covering
  9. F.O.B. (fixed base
    operation-aircraft)
  10. Travel agencies

III. Wholesaling
  1. Jobbers
  2. Brokers
  3. Distributors
  4. Manufacturing agents

IV. Research and development
  1. Materials
  2. Products

  3. Software information
    systems
  4. Specialized machinery
  5. Manufacturing systems

V. Consulting
  1. Management
  2. Management information
    systems
  3. Financial
  4. Investment
  5. Marketing
  6. Risk management
  7. Land use and development
  8. Engineering
  9. Economic
  10. Government
  11. Various additional highly
    specialized areas

VI. Manufacturing
  1. Metals
    a. Sheet metal
    b. Machine shop
      (1) General
      (2) Special equipment
    c. Foundry
    d. Mini-steel mill
  2. Plastics
    a. Extrusion
    b. Applicators
    c. Formulators
  3. Food processing
    a. Meat
    b. Vegetables
    c. Bakery
    d. Specialty items

SOURCE: Reprinted by permission from Curtis E. Tate, Jr., Leon C. Megginson, Charles R. Scott, Jr., and Lyle R. Trueblood, *Successful Small Business Management*, 3rd ed. (Plano, Tex.: Business Publications, Inc., 1982), p. 63. © 1982 Business Publications, Inc.

and construction. Table 4-1 shows some of the opportunities in small business, classified into related groups.

### Size, Sales, and Employment

Although small businesses are clearly the majority of all U.S. firms, there's really little relationship between these numbers and their effect on total U.S. sales and assets. For example, Figure 4-2 shows that only 3 percent of all firms have annual sales of over $1 million; yet these firms account for 84 percent of all sales. And although only 7 percent of corporations have assets of $1 million or over, they own 94 percent of all assets. Small companies with sales of $100,000 or less (82 percent of all firms) have only 4 percent of all sales. And

**Figure 4-2** Percentage distribution of firms by business receipts and assets. (Based on data from *Statistical Abstract of the United States, 1982–1983,* p. 528.)

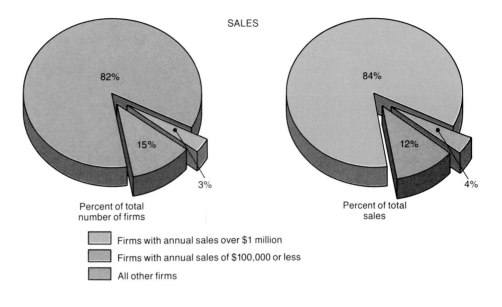

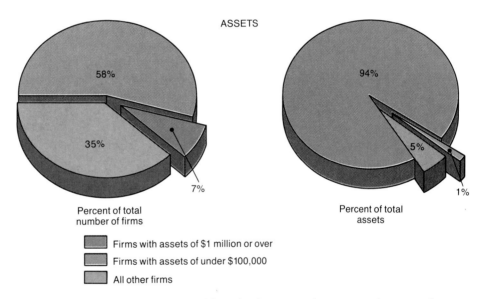

small corporations with assets of under $100,000 (58 percent) own only 1 percent of all assets.

As we'll see, one of the great assets of small business is its stimulation of employment. For instance, small businesses produced 11 million jobs (80 percent of all new jobs) during the last decade.[7] In 1976 alone, 65 percent of all newly created jobs were in firms with fewer than twenty employees.[8] And from 1979 to 1981, small firms accounted for 60 percent of the 2.8 million *new* jobs created. The majority of those were in services.[9] However, as indicated earlier, employment in large and small companies does differ according to industry. Most employees in wholesale trade, construction, and retail trade are in small firms. The reason for this concentration is that these firms are easy to start up and stop, are located near customers, and require relatively little initial investment. But most employees in manufacturing and services are in large companies, as these activities tend to be nationwide in coverage.

For instance, the "big eight" accounting firms do most of the accounting activities, and H&R Block does most of the tax work. These are technical and specialized services.

## CHARACTERISTICS OF SMALL BUSINESSES

Small businesses begin in almost as many ways as there are entrepreneurs. Some are started by people who are out of work or unhappy where they're working. Some are started on a part-time basis to bring in extra income for the owner. Still others are begun for the sheer challenge or creativity involved (see the Profile on page 95). Some of these part-time operations never grow beyond their simple beginnings. Owners may be content with small-scale operations and not want to get any bigger. Other businesses grow into full-time larger companies, sometimes becoming partnerships or corporations.

Richard Ross, for example, started his jelly bean business about halfway through high school. He broke into jelly beans by doing some purchasing for his mother's gift and candy shop and then moved up to distributing gourmet jelly beans to other candy shops. By the age of twenty, he had twenty-five wholesale customers in seven states, serviced via United Parcel Service. He plans to retire at age twenty-six.[10]

Other small businesses are started by people who've developed a product or service that can be produced and sold only in a new business set up for that purpose. Historically, many such businesses have evolved into large corporations, providing employment opportunities for many other people, as did the J. R. Simplot Company (see the Profile on page 96) and Apple Computer.

For many people, the chance to be out on their own becomes even more important than money or security. Cecil and Susan, for instance, fell in love with an old house in a declining urban neighborhood. They took a risk and bought, restored, and redecorated it. Their friends, seeing what could be done with a little imagination and effort, started to do the same—with advice and suggestions from them. The couple soon quit their better-paying jobs—he to organize a renovation firm and she to open an interior design shop.

Another enticement of small business is that the lines of communication are shorter and more personal. Owners don't have to seek approval from dozens of superiors. Also, the business is often located closer to material and supply sources and to markets, easing the burdens of transportation and time.

## UNIQUE CONTRIBUTIONS OF SMALL BUSINESS

**Objective 2**

Some of the unique contributions of small business.

Small businesses clearly have benefits that their larger competitors don't and can't have. Because of these advantages, smaller firms make a needed contribution to the economy. Imagine life without the twenty-four-hour store, the shoe repair and barber shops, and the tree doctor, and you'll have some idea of the needs small businesses fill so well.

### Innovation and Creativity

Small firms lead in innovation. As often as not, the small enterprise is a source of new materials, processes, ideas, services, and products that larger

## *Profile*

### Jerome M. Schulman: The Intrepid Entrepreneur

Since 1937, Jerome Milton Schulman has been making compounds that bakeries use to make breads and cakes pop out of pans more easily. At seventy, Schulman isn't exactly the type to be starting a new business, especially one that has to compete with such giants as Lever Bros. and Procter & Gamble.

About two years ago, bothered by canker sores, fever blisters, and other problems, he formulated his own toothpaste. He added aloe, a gel extracted from the aloe vera plant, to fluoride and other basic toothpaste ingredients. Aloe, a folk remedy for minor burns and pains, is now popular as a shampoo, soap, and lotion additive. When the toothpaste worked well for him, Schulman shared some samples with friends who had similar complaints. Encouraged by their favorable reactions, he ordered a large supply of pink-and-white tubes and cartons and hired a company to manufacture and package his unique product.

As owner and sole employee of Jerome Milton, Inc., he began to push his product to Chicago drug and food chains like Walgreen's, Osco, and Dominick's. Rebuffed—but undaunted—by wholesalers and retailers who were unwilling to stock a product that wasn't advertised, and dismayed by the high cost of clinical studies, Schulman pressed buyers for testimonial letters.

His radio spots for Shane (Hebrew for "tooth"), highlighted by the testimonials, began to bring the large company buyers around. At $5.95 for a 6.4 ounce tube, about three times the price of most other brands, Shane still had sales about equal to those of mint-flavored Crest.

Now, with over 700 drug and food outlets in Chicago stocking Shane, Schulman has begun to see profits on his $200,000 investment. With orders for over 150,000 tubes at $3.26 apiece, Schulman intends to expand his market area. He's also expanding his operation. His granddaughter, who will soon graduate from the University of Wisconsin, is going to go to work for Jerome Milton, Inc.

Source: From Bill Abrams, "A New Toothpaste Takes Off," *The Wall Street Journal*, May 26, 1983, p. 33. Adapted by permission of *The Wall Street Journal*, © Dow Jones & Company, Inc., 1983. All Rights Reserved.

firms are unable or unwilling to provide. The big company usually has a heavy investment in the tools, inventory, and personnel needed to produce the same product in large quantities or for long periods of time. Therefore, it isn't as interested in new products or processes as a smaller firm may be. As a matter of fact, much of the economic growth and development in the United States has as its source innovations that were born in small firms.

# *Profile*

## J. R. Simplot: French Fry King

At age thirteen, J. R. Simplot had a fight with his father, quit the eighth grade, and moved into a boardinghouse. He then worked on canals and sorted potatoes until he'd saved enough money to buy 700 hogs, which he traded in to buy some potato fields and machinery. Next came a newfangled electric potato sorter, which was to be the foundation of his business, the J. R. Simplot Company.

The family-owned business, which he controls, is now run by a management team that includes his four children and a son-in-law. The firm sells frozen french fries and other potato products to fast-food chains, and expected annual sales to top $1 billion.

According to Simplot, his success comes from guts, hustle, rugged individualism, and hanging on when things were tough. He still lives in what he calls a "comfortable old shack," although he has a posh high-rise office near Boise, Idaho. And his red Continental sports a license plate that reads "MR SPUD." This whole empire was founded on his personal motto, "When the time is right you got to *do* it." Simplot has a dashing style; he scorns formalities and embraces quick, decisive action. He avoids red tape and group decisions as if they were potato blight. (He says he never held a staff meeting when he was president of the firm, which was until 1973.) His first food-processing contract "was written on the back of an envelope with a guy I met while waiting to collect a debt in California." He used the same approach in the early 1960s to get a contract to sell frozen french fries, on which he held the patent, to Ray Kroc, who was just starting a hamburger chain. After spending the night at Kroc's California home, they shook hands and the deal was set—for Simplot to supply the first string of McDonald's restaurants.

Source: Adapted from Joanna Davidson, "Saga of a French-Fry King," in "Modern Tycoons—How They Made It, How They Live," *U.S. News & World Report*, May 31, 1982, pp. 58–59. Reprinted from "U.S.News & World Report." Copyright, 1982, U.S.News & World Report, Inc.

Small firms produce two-and-a-half times as many innovations as large firms relative to the number of people employed.[11] The first automobile, airplane, jet engine, helicopter, office copying machine, instant camera, and air conditioner were among the breakthroughs that sprang from the workshops of small businesses. Other important innovations include the aerosol can, foam

fire extinguishers, heart pacemakers, quick frozen foods, the safety razor, the vacuum tube, and the zipper.

In a smaller firm, there's more flexibility in what can and can't be done. This is especially true in the creative development and marketing of new products and services. There's simply less red tape involved for smaller firms. There are fewer channels to go through to get a decision, fewer reports are needed, and managers have greater leeway to make decisions. For example, in 1942, the owners of Smith's Bakery in Mobile read that vitamins and minerals were lacking in people's diet, so they were the first bakery to enrich their bread.[12] There was no red tape involved; they just did it.

The first full-scale commercial electronic computer, the Univac, was conceived and developed by a small firm—Univac Corporation—formed by Dr. John Mauchly and J. Presper Eckert. IBM, a giant firm, was reluctant to produce such a revolutionary product because of its heavy investment in punch-card equipment. It already controlled 97 percent of that business on a rental rather than a purchase basis, and it had little incentive to change. The development of the Univac ultimately led to the computer revolution.

## Competitiveness and Independence

Small firms have become a controlling factor in the American economy because they keep larger firms competitive. How do they manage to do this? By introducing new products, methods, and services, they help keep larger firms from becoming monopolies. Amerada Hess Corporation pioneered many now-common practices of gasoline marketing. Its stations never did repairs and didn't issue credit cards. The company concentrated on a relatively small number of high-volume outlets rather than many low-volume ones.[13]

Because small businesses are independent, they encourage competition in price as well as service and efficiency. Small firms also play a key role as suppliers of items that a large firm needs but can't be bothered with producing. Textile manufacturers, for instance, rely on "cottage" designers and sample weavers who work out of their homes.

## Development

Another unique advantage of small businesses is that they develop people as well as goods and services. Their freer, less specialized environment enables employees to strive for more balanced, well-rounded development than they could hope for in larger firms. People in small firms have to be more versatile and have a greater variety of work activities than if they were working in specialized jobs in larger companies. Instead of just being cogs in the corporate machine, employees have greater freedom to learn by making decisions and living with the results. This freedom, in turn, lends zest and interest to work, trains people to become better leaders, and encourages more effective use of individual talents and energies (see FYI on page 98).

## Opportunities

People who want to try to achieve success quickly, without spending years climbing the ranks of a large firm, can always start their own firm. This is

## *FYI*

### Korey, Kay & Partners: The Restless Ad Executives

As ad executives at Needham, Harper & Steers, Inc., Allan Kay and Lois Korey both earned salaries well into six digits (hers was $200,000 a year; his was $175,000). They had generous perquisites and walls glowing with mutually won prizes from such clients as Xerox, Exxon, Coca-Cola, Amtrak, and Frigidaire. Competing firms vied for them with offers as high as $300,000 a year and free houses. But neither the enticements of competitors nor the power of working for one of the top twenty advertising agencies in the country was enough to keep Kay and Korey happy.

Tired of the administrative demands and the constant dilution of creative ideas that are the norm in large ad agencies, Korey and Kay struck out on their own. Famed for being the team that had conceived of the Brother Dominic monk character, which Xerox used so successfully, and other equally successful campaigns, they opened for business in a friend's spare office space in the Empire State Building.

Success came far more slowly than Korey and Kay had expected. The new partners wrote, phoned, and met over 1,000 prospective clients, only to be told that their agency was either too small or too new.

Large agencies rarely have to advertise for business. But Korey, Kay did. The agency wanted to promote itself as an agency for risk takers. The attrition rate for new ad companies is so high that the ad agency association, to avoid excessive turnover, will not accept new agencies until they've finished their second profitable year.

Risk they knew about, but, as Kay put it, "it takes a pretty thick skin" not to collapse every time a rejection comes in. Reading and running newspaper ads for potential clients wasn't bringing in the type of business they needed fast enough. In a daring move that bespoke their creativity, they landed a $3 million account with WCBS-TV of New York City by sending its nearly unapproachable communications director a mock ransom note using letters clipped from newspapers. The message, accompanied by a videotape of commercials the two had made, read: "We've got your dog. See our reel if you want to see him again."

Korey, Kay's ads are no more conventional than its approach to new accounts. They have done an ad for neckties in French with English subtitles and one showing a competing casino's clients as cave men. They hope their style won't just move merchandise for clients but will also attract attention to Korey, Kay.

From a two-person operation, Korey, Kay has grown to a staff of sixteen, with an ad budget of $10 million, a new partner, and offices in an Upper East Side townhouse. Needless to say, they are already running out of working space. Other signs of growth are the new time logs that employees have to fill out and the employee manual in the works. Such is the price of success.

Source: From Bill Abrams, "Pair of Ad Executives, Pampered But Restless, Set Out on Their Own," *The Wall Street Journal,* June 9, 1983, pp. 1 and 25. Adapted by permission of *The Wall Street Journal,* © Dow Jones & Company, Inc., 1983. All Rights Reserved.

particularly true for women and minorities, whom the corporate culture may implicitly hold back. Owning a firm permits one unlimited flexibility and control over its size and operations.

For example, Kathleen Bowers, who started K. E. Bowers & Associates, a personnel consulting and employment service in Washington, D.C., says:

> I started my business to make money and to provide myself with a more lucrative alternative than the long climb up the corporate ladder. . . . Certainly, the entrepreneurial route is a high-risk and a lonely venture. But that is where the dollars are. And the desire to become an entrepreneur needs an ego that only wants to start one way, and that is at the top. So be your own boss.[14]

Small firms provide opportunities for women and minorities. According to the Small Business Administration, employment in the small firms to which it gave assistance in 1979 jumped nearly 10 percent, while total national employment increased only 3.2 percent.[15] More to the point, these firms increased minority employment by 16 percent and female employment by 11 percent. According to the Bureau of Labor Statistics, the numbers of the self-employed have grown at a faster rate in recent years than the ranks of those who work for someone else. In 1972, women accounted for 20 percent of the self-employed; in 1979, they accounted for 25 percent. During this same period, blacks accounted for a steady 5.5 percent of those working for themselves.[16]

## LIMITATIONS OF SMALL BUSINESS

**Objective 3**

**Some of the limitations of small business.**

Lest you begin to think there's no reason not to jump into small business, just remember that for every three new ventures started at any one time, two will go out of business (see the Business Debate on page 101).[17] And read on!

### Poor Management

Many small businesses rely on one-person management. These managers tend to guard their positions jealously and may not select effective subordinates. And even if they do, they may fail to give them enough authority and responsibility to work well. Also, managers of small firms can't afford to specialize in one area of management, as they might if they had stayed in the corporate world. They must make a wide variety of decisions and live with their choices. They're caught in a bind. Because of limited resources, they can't afford to make costly mistakes, but they also can't afford to hire capable assistants. As a result, poor performance of the managerial functions covered in Chapters 6 and 7 accounts for most failures of small businesses.

### Shortages

The most obvious difference between small and large businesses is in the amount of resources available to them. Larger firms usually start operating with larger amounts of capital and find it easier to raise additional capital. In today's economic environment, most larger firms are able to generate funds

internally, through profits, to finance their capital needs. Also, the cost of capital is less for larger firms than it is for smaller ones, since they're usually able to borrow at a lower rate of interest.

Smaller firms generally set out with limited financial resources, a strike against them in taking advantage of new opportunities. The shortage of working capital in small firms also prevents them from keeping up with larger competitors. **Working capital** is a firm's investment in short-term assets, such as cash, short-term securities, accounts receivable, and inventories. A meagerly financed firm also may have trouble finding willing investors—a catch-22, indeed. And the lack of financial resources, as well as the feeling that personal development and advancement are limited, prevents the small firm from attracting and keeping a staff of competent people. It simply can't recruit and train the professionals it may need.

Since the key to continued success in firms is the ability to develop new products, new applications, and new methods, limited funds may also restrict the development of an adequate research and development (R&D) capacity in smaller firms. However, figures from the federal Office of Management and Budget (OMB) showed that, while small businesses receive only about 3.5 percent of all federal research and development funds, they account for more than half of all scientific developments. A National Science Foundation study found evidence that small firms are producing four times as many innovations per R&D dollar as medium-sized firms and twenty-four times as many as the largest firms.[18]

### Imbalances

Another disadvantage of small business is the problem of coordination between production and marketing. It's often difficult to balance the amount of goods produced with the amount of goods sold. A small business has to struggle to keep a balance between having so few products that orders can't be filled and sales are lost and having so many that inventory costs skyrocket.

### Paperwork

Because of limited time and lack of personnel, the small business owner often isn't prepared to cope with the problems caused by complex government and tax regulations. The National Federation of Independent Business (NFIB) found that in a group of small firms with less than forty employees each had to employ an accountant just to keep up with federal, state, and local forms.[19] The records that are needed to prepare the required reports and to pay the business tax liability often aren't kept because of lack of time or ability or both. This situation may lead to conflict between the owner and federal or state agencies. Small wonder, then, that the burden of paperwork dampens the ardor of many entrepreneurs. Until the early 1960s, state and federal governments usually exempted small companies from laws, rules, and regulations, but since then small companies have become more regulated. Small businesses still do get help, however, from agencies like the Occupational Safety and Health Administration (OSHA) and the Equal Employment Opportunity Commission (EEOC). For example, OSHA compliance officers don't routinely inspect smaller firms unless they're in hazardous industries, and the EEOC doesn't require as many or as detailed reports from small businesses.

# *Business Debate*

## Small Business: Success? Survival? Failure?

In 1953, it was decided that small businesses needed help from the federal government to survive. The U.S. Small Business Administration was established to provide management, finance, procurement, and other forms of assistance.

However, small businesses today still face the same questions: Will they be able to deal effectively with external environmental pressures and demographic trends? Will they have the appropriate internal resources—human, physical, and financial—necessary to succeed, or will they just barely survive or even fail?

### Survival or Failure?

1. In 1982, there were 65,800 bankruptcies, 38 percent more than in 1981. The major reasons were inflation, severe debt burdens, high interest rates, and the length of the recession. Half of the firms going bankrupt in 1981–1982 were less than five years old, 30 percent were six to ten years old, and the others were more than ten years old. Nearly 75 percent of these companies had fewer than twenty employees.

2. Almost 90 percent of businesses that close do so without going into bankruptcy.

3. About 600,000 new ventures are started every year, and about 400,000 are discontinued. This tremendous failure rate among new ventures has a major personal impact on the entrepreneurs concerned.

4. Poor management and incompetence in performing the business functions—marketing, operations, and financing—are the principal causes of small business failures.

5. Many small firms have been badly hurt financially or have even had to close because of tough environmental regulations.

6. Many small companies have a very difficult time meeting occupational safety rules, product safety regulations, and high minimum wages.

7. Many small businesses find it difficult to raise capital, arrange stable supply sources, and remain competitively strong. The cost and scarcity of capital are among their major problems.

8. Small firms often find that many of their vendors will not give them fixed prices for any length of time and some even price "at time of delivery." On the other hand, these firms must give their customers longer commitments and then often find it difficult to collect.

9. Small businesses often have trouble raising prices in inflationary times for fear higher prices will lead to a loss of sales.

### Success?

1. Small businesses weathered the 1980–1982 recession better than large businesses, laid off fewer people, are now in a better position to hire, and are expected to be a major force in the current economic recovery. The services sector, dominated by small firms, gained 528,000 jobs, while 90 percent of the 2.7 million job losses were in mining and manufacturing, dominated by big businesses. Of about 560,000 new business incorporations in 1982, almost all were small firms.

2. The contributions of small business are needed in our economy. In the service industry, they render unique, personalized services that appeal to particular customers, and they are able to perform better than large firms. In manufacturing, they produce and sell customized, special-order products and can surpass larger competitors, who tend to emphasize standardized products and economies of scale.

3. Many young people begin their careers in small businesses because they feel that their talents will be used better and sooner than in larger firms.

4. Most new jobs are created by small business. For example, 60 percent of the 2.8 million new jobs in 1979–1981 were in firms with under 500 employees. Most new jobs occurred in the service sector, a stronghold of small business.

5. Of the approximately 13.3 million nonfarm businesses, about 97 percent are small.

6. Small business leads in innovations.

7. A pool of about $7 billion in venture capital is now available to small firms. More capital is becoming available to small firms because of innovations in the financial service industry and increased competition among financial institutions, a result of the deregulation of the financial industry.

8. Recently enacted legislation has benefited small businesses. This includes (a) reduction of tax barriers to the formation of and investment in small firms, (b) reductions in individual tax rates (most small firms are sole proprietorships and partnerships), (c) reform of Subchapter S incorporation, making it easier for small firms to adopt this form of organization, (d) reform of estate tax law, making it easier for small business owners to build and maintain their operations, (e) passage of the Export Trading Company Act, which enables small firms to better compete in foreign markets, and (f) passage of the Prompt Payment Act, which requires the federal government to pay its bills on time or face interest penalties.

*What do you think are the prospects for small business? Failure? Survival? Success?*

Source: *The State of Small Business: A Report of the President* (Washington, D.C.: Government Printing Office, March 1983).

## PROFILE OF A SMALL BUSINESS OWNER

If you tried to sketch a portrait of the successful small business owner, you'd have a hard time of it. That person could be black or white, male or female, and of almost any age. But there are several traits that all would have in common. Since the skills, abilities, and personal traits of owner-managers have a greater influence on the fortunes of small companies than they do on those of larger firms, it's fairly important to know what these traits are. It's doubtful that any one person will have all of these keys to success, but the qualities named in the following sections are most frequently found in successful owner-managers of smaller firms.[20]

### Motives

**Objective 4**

**Motives of small business owners.**

To begin with, the motives of small business owners are different from those of large business owners. The owners (stockholders) of big businesses usually aren't active in managing the firms' activities. Instead, they select professional managers to run the business for them. These managers are really highly paid, high-level employees. Professional managers think like, and identify with, the narrower interests of employees, whereas the owner-managers of small firms tend to think like independent entrepreneurs.[21]

Although the motives of large business managers are many and varied, they can be summarized as the desire for job security; the desire for power,

position, and prestige; and the desire for high income. People who become managers in order to pull down a high income admit that managing a large company has its load of responsibilities and worries. But they're willing to accept those drawbacks in order to have power, high income, and executive perks like expense accounts and the free use of company facilities.

While those same desires might motivate some people to become owners of small businesses, the vast difference in motives can be summed up in one word—independence. The goal of most entrepreneurs is freedom from interference or control by anyone (see the Profile on page 96). They essentially want the freedom to exercise their own initiative, ambition, and creativity.

## A Formula for Success

**Objective 5**

Formulas for success and failure in small business.

Given that basic motivation for freedom, anyone could start out in a small business and either succeed or fail resoundingly. What are the other ingredients in a formula for success?

▲ **Independence** Do you like to be your own boss? As we've said, successful small business managers have a well-developed sense of independence and tend to fight any restraints on their actions. In general, they're the rebels of the business world, who enjoy the feeling of freedom that comes from being in control of their own fate. They tend to be rugged individualists who are willing to take risks and who have the determination and perseverance to exploit those risks.

> Which of these characteristics did you notice in J. R. Simplot (in the Profile on page 96)? Do you think he could successfully move into a structured situation? Why or why not?

▲ **Enterprise** Are you resourceful? Most small business managers have a strong sense of enterprise, the ability and willingness to take bold and daring action. They're self-starters who are able to come up with new ideas, plan them, carry them out, and profit from the results (see FYI on page 104). In larger firms, different specialists do different phases of the work and often don't see a project carried out from beginning to end.

▲ **Commitment** Are you willing to put in the time necessary to make your business a success? Another trait usually found in people working in small business is a single-minded drive for achievement and the willingness to commit long, hard hours of work in order to reach their goal. J. R. Simplot often starts as early as 3:30 A.M. on whirlwind tours of his farms on horseback, in one of the company's five planes, or in a helicopter.

▲ **Family Concerns** Are ties to a family business important to you? Managers of small firms tend to be highly motivated by family considerations. Our students often tell us they are returning home to take over the family business

## *FYI*

### The Snugli: Look, Ma, No Hands!

When Ann and Michael Moore were in the Peace Corps in West Africa, it seemed to them that the local mothers had stumbled on a great idea. Their infants and children seemed to bask in an unusual peacefulness, mainly because they were carried in pouches, snuggled close to their mothers' bodies. The mothers were able to carry on everyday activities because their hands were completely free. Ann Moore adopted the idea for her own baby, and a million-dollar business was born.

At home, the Moores started making the same kind of cloth pouch, appropriately christened the Snugli. The baby sits in a pouch, which the adult wears by slipping straps over the shoulders and around the waist. Parents usually wear a Snugli on the front for infants and switch it to the back when the child gets older and heavier.

Today, thousands of adults worldwide are carrying their offspring in Snuglis. Sales of Snugli, Inc., in 1981 were about $4.5 million. The home-sewn version of Snugli retails for $50 to $60, while the factory-made item is priced at about half that amount.

Source: From Eric Morgenthaler, "Snuggling Business Booms as Babes in Pouches Proliferate," *The Wall Street Journal*, April 23, 1982, pp. 1 and 29. Adapted by permission of *The Wall Street Journal*, © Dow Jones & Company, Inc. 1982. All Rights Reserved.

rather than go somewhere else and work for another company. Frequently this is done as much for family reasons as for profit. Jimmy Carter came home to Plains, Georgia, from the U.S. Navy to run the family peanut business when his father died.

▲ **Time Management** Are you good at budgeting your time? Time is at a premium for managers of small businesses. Unlike managers of large firms, who are expected to give much of their time to public relations and who can delegate their duties to someone else, small business managers have to do

everything themselves. As a result, they're forced to become experts at budgeting their time effectively.

### A Formula for Failure

Just as there's a formula for success, there's one for failure. The following inadequacies will almost certainly ensure failure as an entrepreneur.[22]

▲ **Low Aspirations** Do you have the driving force to achieve what you desire in life? If not, you probably won't be willing to expend the effort required to succeed.

▲ **Unwillingness to Accept Responsibility** Are you willing to accept responsibility for your actions and those of others to whom you have delegated authority? Are you willing to make difficult decisions promptly? Two of the greatest causes of failure are indecisiveness and the tendency to shift responsibility to others.

▲ **Lack of Self-Discipline** Are you able to exercise discipline over yourself and your affairs? Can you control your temper, accept uncertainty and ambiguity, and be mentally and emotionally controlled? Can you control money? If not, how can you succeed on your own?

▲ **Unwillingness to Take Risks** Do you seek only sure things in life, or are you willing to chance losing your shirt in order to gain what you desire? Your answer makes the difference between success and failure.

▲ **Inadequate Commitment** Are you willing to endure the trials, tribulations, and personal and family sacrifices needed to achieve your ambitions? Lack of perseverance has caused many small business failures.

The FYI on page 106 is a checklist for you to use to see if you have the potential for being the owner of a small business.

## DEVELOPING A BUSINESS PLAN

**Objective 6**

The importance of a business plan when starting a small business.

A business begins as an entrepreneurial idea that is converted into a business plan, which is prepared by the one(s) responsible for starting and operating the company. The **business plan** is a document covering all aspects of the business, beginning with the objective of the business—which usually is to produce a good or service that the public wants, at a cost of production that will return a profit to the owner. The plan then describes the steps needed to achieve that objective.

Preparation of the plan usually involves assistance from others, such as one's banker, lawyer, investors, accountant, and suppliers, as well as representatives of government agencies. These people are involved because they will be affected by the business. The most important aspects of such a plan are shown in Table 4-2.

## FYI

### To Be or Not To Be a Small Business Owner

The following checklist is designed to help you assess your potential for being the owner of a small business. Why don't you complete it and compare results with others who have used it?

ARE YOU A SELF-STARTER?

____ I do things on my own. Nobody has to tell me to get going.

____ If someone gets me started, I keep going all right.

____ Easy does it. I don't put myself out until I have to.

HOW DO YOU FEEL ABOUT OTHER PEOPLE?

____ I like people. I can get along with just about anybody.

____ I have plenty of friends—I don't need anyone else.

____ Most people irritate me.

CAN YOU LEAD OTHERS?

____ I can get most people to go along when I start something.

____ I can give the orders if someone tells me what we should do.

____ I let someone else get things moving. Then I go along if I feel like it.

CAN YOU TAKE RESPONSIBILITY?

____ I like to take charge of things and see them through.

____ I'll take over if I have to, but I'd rather let someone else be responsible.

____ There's always some eager beaver around wanting to show how smart he is. I say let him.

## FINANCING SMALL BUSINESSES

**Objective 7**

**Sources of financing for small businesses.**

Most small businesses are launched with funds provided by the owner and his or her family and friends. These resources can come from a salary the owner earned working for someone else while getting the business established. Or the owner and others may use their savings or even sell or mortgage their homes or property.

While Steven Jobs designed video games for Atari, his friend Stephen Wozniak was designing a small, easy-to-use computer to help families and small businesses. They raised $1,500 by selling Jobs' VW microbus and Wozniak's Hewlett-Packard scientific calculator. In 1976 they opened a makeshift production line in Jobs' garage. This was the beginning of Apple Computer.

HOW GOOD AN ORGANIZER ARE YOU?

____ I like to have a plan before I start. I'm usually the one to get things lined up when the group wants to do something.

____ I do all right unless things get too confused. Then I quit.

____ You get all set and then something comes along and presents too many problems. So I just take things as they come.

HOW GOOD A WORKER ARE YOU?

____ I can keep going as long as I need to. I don't mind working hard for something I want.

____ I'll work hard for a while, but when I've had enough, that's it.

____ I can't see that hard work gets you anywhere.

CAN YOU MAKE DECISIONS?

____ I can make up my mind in a hurry if I have to. It usually turns out OK, too.

____ I can if I have plenty of time. If I have to make up my mind fast, I think later I should have decided the other way.

____ I don't like to be the one who has to decide things.

CAN PEOPLE TRUST WHAT YOU SAY?

____ You bet they can. I don't say things I don't mean.

____ I try to be on the level most of the time, but sometimes I just say what's easiest.

____ Why bother if the other fellow doesn't know the difference?

CAN YOU STICK WITH IT?

____ If I make up my mind to do something, I don't let anything stop me.

____ I usually finish what I start—if it goes well.

____ If it doesn't go right away, I quit. Why beat your brains out?

HOW GOOD IS YOUR HEALTH?

____ I *never* run down!

____ I have enough energy for most things I want to do.

____ I run out of energy sooner than most of my friends seem to.

Well, how did you do? If most of your checks were beside the first answer, you probably have what it takes to run a business successfully. If not, you are likely to have more trouble than you can handle. If most of your checks were beside the third answer, not even a good partner will likely overcome the indicated deficiencies.

Source: Reprinted by permission from "Checklist for Going into Business," Management Aid No. 2016 (Washington, D.C.: U.S. Small Business Administration, Management Assistance, 1977).

> Do you remember how Kloss (Chapter 3) used the $400,000 he received from the sale of KLH when he was developing his big-screen TV in his basement? Later, he raised $800,000 from friends to found Kloss Video to produce another big-screen set.

## Credit

Capital may also be obtained from banks by means of a secured or unsecured loan, from equipment supplied by manufacturers on the installment plan, from goods and operating supplies on open credit from vendors, or from other private sources.

### TABLE 4-2 Ingredients of a typical business plan.

1. Brief description of business, including operating history, if any.
2. Directors, including names and corporate affiliations.
3. Management team—brief resumes covering qualifications for attaining company objectives.
4. Management compensation and incentives.
5. Outside professional assistance; e.g., attorney, CPA.
6. Organization chart.
7. Capital required and its specific uses.
8. Company's current financial condition.
9. Major products:
   a. Detailed description, including photographs and/or drawings.
   b. Uses.
   c. Unique characteristics.
   d. Warranties.
   e. Profit margins.
   f. Costs.
   g. Patent protection.
   h. Technological advantages.
   i. Research and development.
   j. Product liability.
10. Market served:
    a. Overall market.
    b. Market studies.
    c. Ease of entry.
    d. Overall growth rate.
    e. Names of potential customers.
    f. Names of competitors.
    g. Expectations concerning percentage market share.
11. Market strategy:
    a. Market segments.
    b. Channels of distribution.
    c. Advertising plan.
    d. Methods of financing sales.
    e. Pricing.
    f. Sales organization.
12. Manufacturing:
    a. Assembly characteristics.
    b. Vertical integration.
    c. Product cost breakdown.
    d. Tooling cost.
    e. Special or general-purpose equipment.
    f. Economies of scale.
    g. Supplier relationships.
    h. Availability of raw materials.
13. Appendixes:
    a. Pro-forma projections for three to five years.
    b. Legal structure of business.
    c. Founders' resumes and financial statements.
    d. Founders' compensation.
    e. Market surveys.

SOURCE: Extracted from Donald M. Dible, *How to Plan and Finance a Growing Business* (Reston, Va.: Reston Publishing Company, 1980), pp. 87–110. Reprinted with permission of Reston Publishing Co., a Prentice-Hall Co., 11480 Sunset Hills Rd., Reston, Va. 22090.

## Venture Capital

**Venture capital** is money invested in risky new or struggling companies by investment specialists who expect to receive a fast, above-average rate of return. These individuals or groups don't lend money to the owner but provide capital in return for a piece of the action. With this source of funds, then, the owner experiences a certain loss of control, as the capitalist may ask for up to a 50 percent interest in very risky ventures. If the venture is profitable but appears to be stabilizing, the outsider may sell the shares at a tremendous profit when the firm begins to sell shares to the public. There is now a pool of about $7 billion in venture capital available to small firms.[23]

When Apple Computer needed financing to start commercial operations, Mike Markkula, a millionaire marketing genius, helped finance the budding

business. His financial contribution and marketing skills helped the firm to reach the $600 million sales level in 1983.[24]

### SBA Loans and Guarantees

The Small Business Administration (SBA) helps small businesses in two ways: by making direct loans to them and by helping them obtain bank loans by guaranteeing repayment if the firms fail. The SBA also licenses, regulates, and provides financial aid to privately owned and operated Small Business Investment Corporations (SBICs). These groups then invest in small companies that meet their investment criteria. The financial terms are arranged directly with the business owner and may be either a secured loan or the purchase of an ownership interest in the firm. However, the interest can't be a controlling one. The SBICs also provide counsel and guidance. SBICs had a pool of $1.1 billion in 1982.[25]

## LEARNING OBJECTIVES REVISITED

1. *What small business is and the types of small business.*

   Although small businesses vary in size from very small, part-time operations to medium-sized corporations, true small businesses can be defined as those that are independently owned and operated and not dominant in their field. They fall into the categories of manufacturing, general construction, wholesale, retail, and service businesses.

2. *Some of the unique contributions of small business.*

   Much of the economic growth and development in the United States has come from small enterprises. They serve as a source of innovation and creativity, both supply larger firms and keep them competitive, develop employees, and provide opportunities not available elsewhere, especially for women and minorities.

3. *Some of the limitations of small business.*

   The limitations of owning and operating a small firm include inadequate managers and managerial ability, shortages of financial and human resources which put the firm in a poor competitive position, imbalances in production and marketing, and burdensome paperwork.

4. *Motives of small business owners.*

   The motives of managers of larger companies differ from those of smaller firms' managers. Small business owners tend to seek opportunity, freedom, and a chance to be innovative and creative. Managers in larger firms tend to seek financial security and power.

5. *Formulas for success and failure in small business.*

   The formula for a successful owner-manager is a strong sense of independence, enterprise, commitment to working hard for long periods of time, a tendency to enter business for family reasons, and a good sense of time management.

   The formula for failure as a small business entrepreneur includes low aspirations, unwillingness to accept responsibility, lack of self-discipline, unwillingness to take risks, and inadequate commitment.

6. *The importance of a business plan when starting a small business.*

Successful small business owners prepare and follow a business plan, which gives the steps needed to reach objectives. The plan deals with such topics as the organization of the firm, the products or services it will provide, production and marketing processes, relations with customers and employees, and sources of capital.

7. *Sources of financing for small businesses.*

Financing for small firms is obtained from the owner's income or savings, friends or relatives, banks, suppliers, venture capitalists, and the Small Business Administration and Small Business Investment Corporations.

## ▲ IMPORTANT TERMS

As an extra review of the chapter, try defining the following terms. If you have trouble with any of them, refer to the page listed.

small business  *90*
manufacturing firms  *91*
general construction firms  *91*
wholesalers  *91*
retailers  *91*

service businesses  *91*
working capital  *100*
business plan  *105*
venture capital  *108*

## ▲ REVIEW QUESTIONS

1. How is a small business defined (by at least two sources)?
2. How are the sales and assets of small firms related to the number of such firms? How does employment relate to size?
3. What are the five types of small businesses?
4. What are some of the unique products (and even industries) developed by smaller enterprises?
5. What are some of the unique contributions of small firms?
6. What are the primary limitations of small businesses?
7. What are some of the reasons why people start a small business?
8. What are some of the essential personal traits needed to operate one's own business successfully?
9. Why do many small businesses fail?
10. Outline the ingredients of a sound business plan.
11. What are some of the sources of small business financing?

## ▲ DISCUSSION QUESTIONS

1. Make a list of some of the small businesses you deal with in a typical week. Categorize them by type (retail, wholesale, and so on), and describe how you would cope without them.
2. Why do you think small businesses are able to create twice as many jobs each year as large firms do?
3. Why are smaller firms more effective in their use of research funds?

4. What are some of the current economic factors that seem to offer a favorable opportunity to entrepreneurs organizing new businesses? Is this a danger to larger firms? Explain.

5. From your experience as a customer, employee, or owner, what do you think are some specific problems facing small business managers? What would you suggest doing to overcome these problems? The next time you are in contact with a small business, ask the owner-manager these same questions and compare your answers with his or hers.

## ⬡ CASE 4-1 The College Band: Blossoming Entrepreneurs

Charlie Overton,[26] an engineering major, began having financial problems during the early part of his second year at college. Since he was a good trumpet player, he relaxed by playing at night and on weekends with several of his friends. Needing money badly, he suggested to his fellow musicians that they try to book engagements playing for college social events for a small fee. Although his friends didn't need the money, they enjoyed playing together so much that they agreed. They called themselves the Bengal Jazz, bought posters and flyers, set rates, and were in business.

The group became so popular with student, faculty, and local social organizations that they were soon booked every weekend, both on and off campus. Still, they turned down more offers than they could accept. They continued to play until they graduated.

Not only were they able to pay their way through school this way, but they even saved enough to help them enter business following their graduation.

### Case Questions

1. What characteristics of small business owners did Charlie have? Explain.
2. What were his friends' reasons for going into business? Explain.
3. What do you think were some problems and limitations of this small business?

## ⬡ CASE 4-2 Jan and Olga Erteszek: Idealistic Owners

In 1941, Jan and Olga Erteszek founded the Olga Company in Van Nuys, California, with a $10 investment. Jan was the sales force, and his wife Olga, who had immigrated from Poland earlier that year, was the designer. They started their business to achieve the objective of "helping people meet their physical, psychological, and spiritual needs." This creed, plus hard work, succeeded. In 1978, the firm had annual sales of over $42 million in women's lingerie and employed 1,500 people.

Employees are encouraged to make suggestions for improving operations and the quality of work life. There are lines of communication to ensure that employees know what's going on and are provided opportunities to make their wishes known. Each year, 25 percent of before-tax profits goes to employees through profit-sharing and stock option plans.[27]

### Case Questions

1. Do you think their business objective was too idealistic? Why?
2. What do you think primarily motivates the employees—the owners' objective or the 25 percent profit sharing?
3. Do you think it unusual that this husband-wife combination, with her as the leader, was successful a quarter of a century before the emphasis on equal rights? Explain.

# 5

# Opportunities in Franchising

*Buying a franchise is probably the quickest, easiest, and most successful way of becoming an entrepreneur.*

Colonel Harland Sanders

**Learning Objectives**

After studying the material in this chapter, you will understand:

1. What a franchise is, and why it is such an important part of American business.
2. The types of franchising arrangements.
3. The benefits of a franchise for both customers and owners.
4. Franchise requirements and controls.
5. How one of the more popular franchises operates.
6. How to evaluate a franchise opportunity.
7. The future of franchising.

**In This Chapter**

What Are Franchises?
Why Are Franchises So Popular?
Franchisors' Requirements and Controls
What's Involved in Opening a Franchise?
Evaluating Franchise Opportunities
The Future of Franchising

If you haven't tried Pan Pizza...
you don't know what you're missing.

Aaahh!

## PIZZA HUT
### *No Flash in the Pan*

How would you turn around a business with an 80 percent management turnover rate every year, a fast-food product that takes over fifteen minutes to cook, inconsistent and often poor-quality food sold at high prices, shabby restaurants, and slow service? Donald N. Smith, who revolutionized the fast-food industry by bringing breakfast to McDonald's and sandwiches to Burger King, did it for Pizza Hut, Inc.

Pizza Hut, Inc., founded in 1958, was purchased in 1977 for over $340 million by PepsiCo, a conglomerate. Until then, Pizza Hut had been very profitable; it had tripled in size from 1972 to 1977. But then its profit margin slipped from about 15 percent in 1976 to 4 percent in 1979. Management's reaction was to increase prices, but operating profits went on dropping, from $56 million in 1977 to $43.7 million in 1978 and $26.4 million in 1979.

In 1980, PepsiCo lured Smith away from Burger King with a one-third increase in salary (rumored to be over $350,000 a year) and made him head of its food service division. He in turn hired Arthur G. Gunther away from Jerrico, Inc., whose Long John Silver's Seafood Shoppes represent one of the fastest-growing franchises in the country.

Smith and Gunther donned aprons and put in time cooking pizzas and serving tables to evaluate the firm's strengths and problems. After six months of poking around in over 300 outlets, nibbling soggy pizzas and oily breadsticks, the two introduced some sweeping changes. First, they moved to change the stores from fast-food outlets to family restaurants, "somewhere between fast food and white tablecloth." They brightened up the stores with more pleasing booths—as well as carpeting, silverware, improved lighting, landscaping, and sidewalks. Even Pizza Hut's red roof was replaced with more sedate brown shingles. And management turnover was reduced from 80 percent to 50 percent a year by increasing salaries and cutting paperwork from twenty-seven to twelve hours a week.

Marketing methods were changed, too. The menu was expanded to include a salad bar and pan pizza, a tantalizing, thick-crusted concoction cooked in a deep pan, which now accounts for well over half of all Pizza Hut pizzas sold. Operations were also improved, with new kitchen equipment that reduced pizza-cooking time to about five minutes. These changes have attracted new customers—young and middle-aged adults instead of just teenagers—and have made Pizza Hut more appealing to the time-conscious lunchtime crowd.

There's new competition from pizza chains like Pizza Time Theatres, which offer floor shows and video games, but Pizza Hut intends to keep concentrating on quality pizza. So far, the strategy seems to be working. Sales per outlet are up from about $250,000 a year in 1979 to about $350,000, and total sales are up to over $1 billion from $532 million in 1979. Pizza Hut's market share has increased from 18 percent to around 23 percent.

Pizza Hut is, of course, a franchise operation, and this case is just an example of one of the fastest-growing and most significant segments of U.S. business. Accounting for nearly a third of all retail sales, franchises provide the organizational structure for the businesses with which you are probably most familiar and for which you may already have worked. Every day, you drive or walk past dozens of businesses that operate under a franchise agreement. Yet you may not always be aware that these businesses are franchised and are linked in a long, nationwide chain of such businesses. You may have heard of franchises without really knowing what such an arrangement is. Table 5-1 lists a number of franchises, some of which may surprise you. In addition to these, most automobile dealerships and many gasoline service stations and tire dealerships are franchised.

## WHAT ARE FRANCHISES?

**Objective 1**

What a franchise is, and why it is such an important part of American business.

A **franchise** is an exclusive arrangement that enables a private owner (franchisee) to conduct business using the name, operating guidelines, and distinguishing features of the parent company (franchisor). The franchisee often receives operating, marketing, and management assistance from the franchisor. A **franchisor** is the national or regional company that owns a franchise's name; distinguishing features such as its building, sign, and symbols; and operating rights. A **franchisee** is the local independent businessperson who contracts with a franchise owner to operate the franchise locally or regionally.

### Types of Franchise Arrangements

**Objective 2**

The types of franchising arrangements.

In general, there are two types of franchise arrangements: the franchising of a product and the franchising of an entire business enterprise. Under the first arrangement, the franchisee receives the franchise's products and sells them through one or more independent outlets. A familiar illustration is an automobile dealership, where little control is exercised by the franchisor. What control there is has to do with the product, not with the franchisee's business operations. But even this arrangement is changing. In the past, franchise agreements with auto manufacturers made the dealer the sole sales outlet for domestic cars, with the power to negotiate the final price and supply arrangements with customers. Yet manufacturers are now negotiating deals with fleet owners such as Avis and Hertz in which the dealers "merely deliver the cars for a small fee." Some dealers complain, "It makes my franchise worth nothing."[1]

Under the second arrangement, the enterprise's appearance, merchandise, business operations, and operating procedures are all determined by the franchisor. Red Lobster is an example of this type of franchise, where everything from signs to silverware is standardized. Even the furniture and layout of the interior are exactly duplicated in all stores.

Because franchises can be highly profitable, it's no surprise that a lot of people want one. Therefore, franchisors also have different policies for assignment of outlets. Most franchisors operate some of their franchises themselves as company-owned units and sell other units to franchisees. Some companies assign units on the basis of franchisee merit. In other companies, the policy

**TABLE 5-1  Selected franchise companies.**

**AUTOMOTIVE**
AAMCO Automatic Transmissions, Inc.
ABC Mobile Systems
Bernardi Bros., Inc.
Firestone Stores and Service Centers
B. F. Goodrich Stores and Service Centers
Goodyear Stores and Service Centers
Grease Monkey International
Insta-Tune, Inc.
Jiffy Lube
Johnson Auto Wash & Wax Systems
Mechanical Man Car Wash Factory, Inc.
Midas International Corp.
Milex, Inc.
OTASCO
Parts, Inc.
Scotti Muffler Centers, Inc.
Triex
Tunex, Inc.
Western Auto
White Stores, Inc.

**AUTO/TRAILER RENTALS**
Budget Rent a Car Corporation
Dollar Rent a Car Systems, Inc.
Econo-Car International, Inc.
Hertz Corporation
National Car Rental System, Inc.
Payless Car Rental System, Inc.
Thrifty Rent-A-Car System

**COMPUTERS**
The Program Store of Washington, D.C.

**DOUGHNUTS**
Dunkin Donuts of America, Inc.
Mister Donut of America, Inc.

**FOOD SPECIALTY STORES**
Convenient Food Marts, Inc.
Cookie Factory of America
Hickory Farms of Ohio, Inc.
Majik Market
The Southland Corporation (7-Eleven)
Swiss Colony Stores, Inc.
Tiffany's Bakeries, Inc.

**GENERAL MERCHANDISE RETAIL**
Ben Franklin

Coast to Coast Stores
Gamble-Skogmo, Inc.

**GUARD DOGS**
Western Metro Guard Dogs, Inc.

**HEALTH CLUBS**
Gloria Stevens
Gymboree
Nautilus
Vic Tanny

**HOME FURNISHINGS—RETAIL, REPAIR, AND SERVICES**
Crossland Furniture Restoration Studios
Decorating Den
Deihi Chemicals, Inc.
Rug Crafters
Spring Crest Company
Steamatic Incorporated

**ICE CREAM**
Baskin-Robbins, Inc.
Bresler's 33 Flavors, Inc.
Haagen-Dazs
Mister Softee, Inc.
Swift Dairy & Poultry Company

**LAUNDRY/DRY CLEANING**
A Cleaner World
Comet International Corporation
Dutch Girl Continental Cleaners "Martinizing"

**MAINTENANCE/JANITORIAL SERVICE**
ABC Maintenance Development Corp.
Mini Maid Services
National Surface Cleaning Corp.
Port-O-Let Company, Inc.
Roto-Rooter Corporation
Servicemaster Industries, Inc.
Servpro Industries, Inc.

**MOTELS**
Admiral Benbow Inns, Inc.
Best Western
Econo-Travel Motor Hotel Corp.
Holiday Inns, Inc.
Howard Johnson's Motor Lodge
Quality Inns, Inc.
Ramada Inns, Inc.
Rodeway Inns of America
Sheraton Inns, Inc.
Travelodge International, Inc.

**TABLE 5-1  Selected franchise companies (continued).**

**PAINT**
Davis Paint Company
Mary Carter Industries, Inc.

**PRINTING**
Big Red Q Quickprint Centers
Insty-Prints, Inc.
Kopy Kat, Inc.
Kwik-Kopy Corporation
Postal Instant Press

**REAL ESTATE**
Century 21 Real Estate Corp.
E.R.A. Real Estate, Inc.
Gallery of Homes, Inc.
Realty World, Inc.
Red Carpet Corporation of America

**RECREATION/TRAVEL**
Empress Travel Franchise Corp.
Flagstaff Camp Grounds, Inc.
Billie Jean King Tennis Centers, Inc.
KOA Campground
Putt-Putt Golf Courses of America, Inc.

**RESTAURANTS/FAST FOOD**
A & W International, Inc.
Brown's Chicken
Burger King Corporation
Captain D's
Church's Fried Chicken, Inc.
Country Kitchen International, Inc.
Craig Food Industries
Dari-International, Inc.
Denny's
Der Wienerschnitzel Int'l, Inc.
Dino's, Inc.
El Taco Restaurants, Inc.
Hardee's Food System, Inc.
International Blimpie Corporation
International Dairy Queen, Inc.
Judy's Foods, Inc.
KFC Corporation
Le Chateau Great Steaks
Lum's Restaurant Corporation
McDonald's Corporation
Mr. Steak, Inc.
The Peddler, Inc.
Pizza Hut, Inc.
The Pizza Inn, Inc.
Ponderosa Steaks
Red Lobster
Shakey's Incorporated

Sizzler Family Steak Houses
Stuckey's, Inc.
Tastee Freez Big T Family
  Restaurant Systems
Wendy's Old Fashioned Hamburgers
Wiener King Corporation

**RETAILING, MISCELLANEOUS**
Edward's Shoes, Inc.
Fayva
Flower World of America, Inc.
Lafayette Electronics Sales, Inc.
Radio Shack
The Tinder Box International, Ltd.
World Bazaar

**SECURITY SYSTEMS**
Dictograph Security Systems
Guardsman Corporation—Sovereign
  Corp.
Rampart Corporation

**SOFT DRINKS/BOTTLED WATER**
Coca-Cola
Double-Cola Company
Mission of California
Mountain Valley Spring Company
Pepsi Cola
7UP

**SWIMMING POOLS**
Blue Dolphin Pools, Inc.
Cascade Industries, Inc.
Fort Wayne Pool Equipment, Inc.
Sylvan Pools

**TELEVISION**
Video Connection of America

**TOOLS, HARDWARE**
Ace Hardware
American Hardware
Mac Tools, Inc.
Snap-On Tools Corporation
True Value Hardware
Vulcan Tools

**TRANSIT SERVICE**
Aero Mayflower Transit Company, Inc.

**WATER CONDITIONING**
Culligan International Company
Edodyne Corporation
Rainsoft Water Conditioning
  Company
Water Refining Company

**TABLE 5-1  Selected franchise companies (continued).**

| | |
|---|---|
| **MISCELLANEOUS** | Mr. Build International |
| A-Z Rental | Nationwide Exterminating, Inc. |
| Coloramic Tile Company, Inc. | Tepco, Inc. |
| First Interstate Bancorp | Terminix International, Inc. |
| Key Korner Systems, Inc. | United Air Specialists, Inc. |
| Magic Fingers, Inc. | VR Business Brokers |
| Meistergram | |

may be mixed; in some cases units are assigned on an individual local basis, and in others the franchisee is assigned a geographic area in which he or she has the exclusive right to obtain all franchises. There are still other franchisors who think it best to distribute their franchises *only* in a group, or geographic, package. Their reasoning is that success breeds success; therefore, the successful franchisee is given priority in obtaining additional franchises. For example, Wendy's concentrates on selling franchise territories to experienced fast-food operators rather than selling single-unit franchises to newcomers. Jack C. Massey, a co-founder of Kentucky Fried Chicken, owns the right to open Wendy's stores in Louisiana, southern California, South Carolina, and Massachusetts.[2]

Some franchisors believe it isn't desirable for franchisees to have had experience in their particular type of business. Instead, they prefer inexperienced operators, who come with no preconceived notions or biases that may conflict with the way the franchisor wants things run.

## Quality

There's a wide range of quality among franchises, too. Some franchises are well developed and planned for long, continued success. If one of these can be had, success is practically guaranteed. On the other hand, some franchises seem destined to fail from the start. They've often been planned for short-run profit to the franchisor, at the expense of the franchisee. These franchisors seek out greenhorns with money and good credit but little business sense. They hope to persuade the unlucky fledgling to part with money or credit in exchange for grandiose but mythical visions of success and profits.

Franchisors can also exploit franchisees by overexpanding in the area, so that none of the units can make a profit; concealing legal or financial problems the franchisor has; having termination or renewal clauses that make it difficult for the franchisee to renew the agreement if successful or terminate it if unsuccessful; and not providing promised services. For example, a majority of Arthur Treacher's fast-food franchisees refused to make monthly royalty payments for over two years. They claimed the parent company failed to service its outlets. The franchise was then sold to Lumara Foods.[3]

Some examples of franchise areas with poor prospects for success are vending machines, services, swimming pool sales, fast-food franchises without adequate support programs, and, of course, any franchise with a history of failure.

Before reading any further, consider some of the franchises you're familiar with that seem to be successful—like McDonald's, Wendy's, Pizza Hut, and Holiday Inn. Why do you think they're succeeding? Is it because of their location, product or service offered, personnel, or condition?

Next, have you noticed a franchise that appears to have failed or to be in danger of failure? If so, why do you think that it is failing?

## WHY ARE FRANCHISES SO POPULAR?

**Objective 3**

**The benefits of a franchise for both customers and owners.**

During the past decade or so, franchising has been one of the fastest-growing areas of American business. From 1969 to 1980, the number of establishments grew from 384,000 to 466,000, and their sales ballooned from $116 billion to $437 billion.[4] Figure 5-1 shows that this trend continued through 1982. Over a third of all retail sales in 1982 were made by franchises.

**Figure 5-1**   More franchises have booming sales. [Based on data from U.S. Department of Commerce, Bureau of Industrial Economics, *Franchising in the Economy, 1980–1982* (Washington, D.C.: Government Printing Office, 1982), pp. 1–12; and "A Franchise Investment in Every Pot," *Business Week*, April 12, 1982, pp. 113–14.]

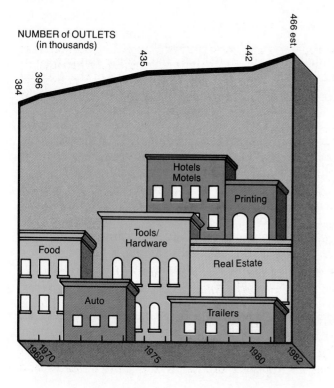

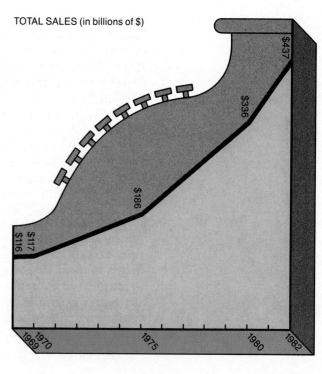

Professional services such as dentistry are being franchised in shopping malls.

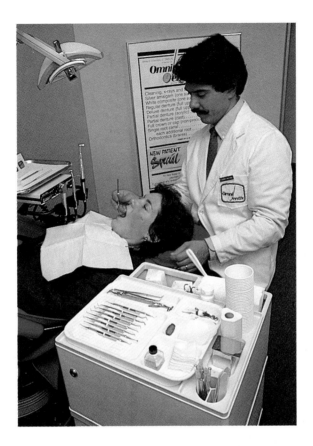

## They Satisfy Customers' Needs

The outstanding success of some franchises is entirely due to the fact that they're designed to identify the needs of consumers, to create a product or service, to convert the consumers' need into demand for their product or service, and to get that product or service to a spot where consumers can obtain it conveniently.

The U.S. population continues to be on the move. When people travel, they want the comfort and convenience of a well-designed and comfortably furnished motel with ready access to a pool, a restaurant, and parking. This is what Holiday Inns (see the Profile on page 120) attempt to provide.

Many people don't want to spend a lot of time fixing food or eating it. Today, around 50 percent of all meals are eaten away from home. In single-parent or dual-career homes, who has the time to cook a three-course dinner? And since most people operate on a limited budget, when they feel they "deserve a break today," they'll head out to a fast-food franchise.

Other franchises that satisfy a customer need include the following: Midas Muffler Shops, H&R Block, Omnidentix Systems, and Mini Maid Services. Omnidentix Systems Corp. offers dentists a ready-to-use facility, complete with equipment, furnishings, and staff, for a $50,000 fee and about $1,000 a week for advertising and management support. Mini Maid Services was started in 1973 by Leone Ackerly of Marietta, Georgia, who cleaned the houses herself. Now Ackerly has thirty-seven offices in the United States and

# *Profile*

## Charles Kemmons Wilson: The Nation's Innkeeper

In 1951, Charles Kemmons Wilson, World War II veteran and seasoned entrepreneur, took his wife and five children in a station wagon from Memphis, Tennessee, to Washington, D.C., and the motel industry was changed forever. He was appalled at the astonishingly primitive lodgings they had to put up with. They charged him $2 a head for each of his children, even though they stayed in the room with him and his wife. "This isn't fair! I'm going back and build a chain of motels, and we'll *never* charge extra for children," he promised his wife. And he did. And they haven't.

Within a year, he'd built the first Holiday Inn, named after the Bing Crosby film featuring the hit songs "Easter Parade" and "White Christmas." It was family-oriented, with air conditioning, a private bath, a Bible, a dog kennel, a swimming pool, phone service in every room, free ice and parking, soft-drink machines in the halls, and babysitters, clergy, dentists, and doctors on call. Children under twelve could stay in their parents' room free. Needless to say, the 120 rooms were fully booked within a week, and Wilson was on the way to achieving his goal of "building a chain of motels." Within eighteen months, he had built three more Inns on the other three highways leading into Memphis.

At that point, he teamed up with his friend Wallace E. Johnson, devout Baptist layman and former vice-president of the National Association of Homebuilders, who had the financial savvy—and contacts—to build a national franchise. They invited a group of home builders from around the United States to hear their sales pitch, and they were in business. And they haven't hesitated since. Now there are over 1,700 establishments in fifty states and fifty-three nations, including a $50 million, 600-room joint venture with Tak How Investment Company in Hong Kong. Holiday Inn has also changed its old sign, which looked cheap and old-fashioned, to a simpler, sleeker one that is cheaper to build and operate and looks more modern.

Wilson became an entrepreneur the hard way. After his father died when he was nine months old, his mother supported him with a series of low-paying jobs. When she became unable to work, Wilson dropped out of high school, bought a popcorn machine on credit, installed it in a theater, and started bringing home $30 a week. After succeeding as a pinball machine and jukebox distributor and then as an Air Force pilot flying in India and Burma, he became a successful builder. Then he founded Holiday Inn and served as its chairman until he retired in 1979.

Sources: Based on correspondence with Holiday Inns, Inc., and published sources, including "Holiday Inns Agrees to Manage 10% of Hong Kong Hotel," *Wall Street Journal,* May 8, 1979, p. 6; Milton Moskowitz, Michael Katz, and Robert Levering, *Everybody's Business: An Almanac* (New York: Harper & Row, 1980), pp. 720–22; "Charles Kemmons Wilson (born 1913)," *Fortune,* March 22, 1982, p. 105; and Bill Abrams, "Holiday Inns Plans to Replace Its Kitschy Old Roadside Signs," *Wall Street Journal,* October 7, 1982, p. 35.

twenty-seven in Canada. The franchise requires only a modest investment ($10,500 plus a $200 per month flat fee), since operators can work out of their own homes and supplies are cheap.[5] Kentucky Fried Chicken (see FYI on page 122) is a classic example of a franchise that succeeded when it satisfied customers' needs but got into financial hot water when it began to ignore them.

### They Cater to Changing Lifestyles

Since franchises are in the business of lightning-fast response to changing demand, they're usually at the cutting edge of the latest lifestyle trends. From the addition of salad bars in fast-food outlets to the development of running-shoe chains like Athlete's Foot, franchises have picked up on the health craze of the eighties. D'Lites of America, Inc. (see the FYI on page 125) is another example of a franchise picking up on a changing lifestyle.

The abundance of leisure time has provided an opportunity for a variety of businesses designed to meet leisure-time needs. Hence the boom in franchises for crafts, video games, tanning parlors, roller rinks, time-share vacation resorts, health spas, racquetball courts, and tennis clubs.

If you're one of the millions of Americans on wheels, you're acutely aware of the problem of having a car serviced and repaired properly. Recent articles in various publications indicate that U.S. automobile dealers haven't expanded their service department facilities and trained personnel to accommodate the ever-increasing automobile population. This fact has been recognized by a growing number of companies that have established regional or national franchises to serve drivers' needs. These companies tend to provide a specialized

Nautilus Club, a franchise devoted to physical fitness and body building.

## FYI

### Kentucky Fried Chicken: A Classic Turnaround Story

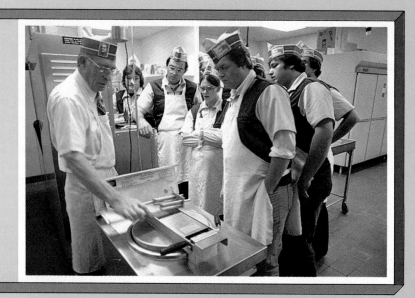

In 1956, at an age when most people are well on the road to retirement, Colonel Harland Sanders started a fried chicken franchising business. He had dropped out of school in the seventh grade to start a career that took him into many fields, including operating a successful motel and restaurant in Corbin, Kentucky.

He experimented until he came up with a seasoning mix and a revolutionary pressure-cooking method for fried chicken. In 1956, he took his ideas on the road to persuade restaurant owners to sell his chicken.

In 1964, a group of businessmen headed by another Kentuckian, John Y. Brown Jr., bought the business, which now had 600 Kentucky Fried Chicken stores, from Colonel Sanders for $2 million and built it into a $250-million-a-year business.

The colonel stayed on as a $200,000-a-year consult-

service, like AAMCO Automatic Transmissions, Inc., or more general services, like B. F. Goodrich Stores and Service Centers.

The founding of Holiday Inns (see the Profile on page 120) was only the beginning for the motel franchise industry. With tourism and job requirements now taking thousands of people away from home for a night or longer, the market for rooms of moderate cost and uniform quality is a sizable one. The Best Western, with well over 2,000 units, is the largest motel chain. Others are Marriott, Motel 6, and Intercontinental Hotels.

Catering to the remodeling trend, Mr. Build International has signed on 400 builders in the United States and Canada to remodel old homes, at a fee of $7,900, 7 percent of annual gross, and $300 a month for advertising. Mr. Build offers customers a guarantee of up to $100,000 (backed by a performance bond) that the job will be completed to specifications.[6]

ant to KFC. Entitled Goodwill Ambassador, his function included making commercials and public appearances at the company's outlets. He also continued his role as KFC's chief quality control expert, visiting KFC stores and teaching employees how to cook his chicken.

Under Sanders and Brown, KFC was an entrepreneurial business with highly motivated owners and employees. At one point, there were 21 millionaires working for Brown.

In 1971, Heublein, a conglomerate with interests as diverse as liquor and steak sauce, acquired KFC for $285 million.

Heublein's president admitted that many of his managers didn't understand the operations of the new business. In the wine and liquor business, it doesn't matter so much what stores look like, and product quality can be controlled at the factory. But in the fast-food outlets, the appearances and quality of the store are very important. The president conceded, "We had actually bought a chain of 5,000 little factories all over the world, and we simply didn't have experience in handling that kind of operation."

Michael Miles, then KFC chairman and CEO, set about to correct the situation. He stressed quality, service, and cleanliness and used inspectors to assure that these goals were achieved. A new store design was developed and implemented. A corporate training center was established in Louisville. KFC advertising began to promote quality instead of discount prices.

At the end of 1983, KFC had more than 50 percent of the fast-food chicken market but was running into stiff competition, especially from Church's Fried Chicken, Inc., and regional chains such as Sisters, Mrs. Winners, Grandy's, and Popeye's.

Colonel Sanders had declared, "Quality is all I'm living for. It's paid off to my great satisfaction." He died in 1980.

In 1982, Heublein, Inc., was acquired by R. J. Reynolds Industries, Inc., the 23rd largest corporation in the U.S., and KFC became a separate operating company under RJRI.

In 1984, Kentucky Fried Chicken had more than 6,000 restaurants worldwide, including almost 4,500 in the United States and 1,500 in 50 countries overseas. Systemwide sales for 1983 were $2.6 billion.

The company was embarked on the most ambitious expansion program in its history, announced in May 1983, with plans to build about 2,200 additional stores worldwide within five years.

---

Sources: Based on various sources, including Mitchell C. Lynch, "Playing Chicken: Gray Flannel Crowd at Heublein Bones Up on Fast-Food Business," *Wall Street Journal*, January 8, 1979, pp. 1, 21; David P. Garino, "At Kentucky Fried Chicken, It's Time to Set Itself Apart," *Wall Street Journal*, March 19, 1981, p. 29; Harold Seneker, "We Took Our Eye off the Ball," *Forbes*, August 6, 1979, pp. 56–57; "Col. Sanders Turns 89," *New York Times*, September 10, 1979, p. D-2; "The Japanese Market: Views from Within," *Fortune*, August 10, 1981, pp. 58–60; and David P. Garino, "Fried Chicken Competition Is Heating Up," *Wall Street Journal*, December 21, 1982, pp. 29, 45.

## They Encourage Entrepreneurship

Although it's bad for small business in general, the limited amount of venture capital available (see Chapter 4) offers an opportunity for well-recognized, reputable franchises. Individuals often find it easier to get financing for a new franchise than to obtain financing for an independent project. A franchise provides an entrepreneur with an instant market because of its easily recognized name, sign, building, and other unique features. The individual franchise unit can benefit from the franchisor's regional or national advertising programs and management savvy.

Some believe that the best way to succeed in small business is to purchase a franchise from an established company, since the failure rate for franchises is far lower than for other small businesses. For example, while the SBA esti-

**TABLE 5-2  How franchising benefits both franchisee and franchisor.**

| Selected Benefits to the Franchisee | Selected Benefits to the Franchisor |
|---|---|
| 1. Brand recognition | 1. Faster expansion and market penetration |
| 2. Management training and/or assistance | 2. Franchisee motivation |
| 3. Economies of large-scale buying | 3. Franchisee attention to detail |
| 4. Financial assistance | 4. Lower operating costs |
| 5. Share in national promotion | |

mates that two-thirds of all small businesses fail within five years, fewer than 5 percent of franchised outlets have failed each year since 1971.[7]

### They Provide Managerial Support

Unlike independent owners bogged down in the morass of unfamiliar business procedures and paperwork, franchisees of competent franchisors get the support of an established management, accounting, and control system. A regular reporting system is set up for the franchisee to use in submitting operating information to the franchisor. In return, the franchisor can send back information drawn from similar franchise units, which lets the franchisee compare notes with other franchisees. Corrective suggestions concerning operations are sometimes included in the reports. Another service provided by better franchisors is regular visits by trained personnel to monitor and review operations and to offer appropriate suggestions for improvement.

Instead of floundering alone, the franchisee can get help with management problems. A management consulting service is usually available—sometimes without cost—as part of a franchise arrangement.

The franchisee can also obtain financial assistance from the franchisor. Sometimes franchisors lend money to franchisees and don't require repayment until the firm is operating effectively. And, as mentioned previously, since banks and other financial institutions see a franchise as less risky than a nonfranchised small business, capital is easier to come by.

Table 5-2 shows some of the benefits of a franchise to the franchisee. It also shows that the franchisor benefits from selling new franchises.

## FRANCHISOR'S REQUIREMENTS AND CONTROLS

**Objective 4**

Franchise requirements and controls.

During the early days of franchising, franchisees were more like sharecroppers than like independent businesspeople. Franchisors sometimes offered low initial contract prices designed to lure new buyers. Then the franchisees were required, among other things, to purchase only those products supplied by the franchisor. They were a perfect captive market. Franchisors usually claimed that their restrictions were necessary to maintain uniformly high standards of quality. Yet congressional testimony in 1970 revealed that many franchisors added outrageously high mark-ups to the products sold to independent own-

## FYI

## D'Lites of America: Calorie Watchers Eating on the Run

"We want to be to the fast-food industry what Miller Lite is to the beer industry," said Douglas N. Sheley. His Atlanta-based franchise, D'Lites of America, has as its promotional slogan "More of a good thing. And less." Sheley has combined the marketability of high-quality and fitness-related products with our mobile society's need to eat on the run.

Sheley, who formerly owned eighteen Wendy's restaurants and several health clubs, says D'Lites, a healthier, better-quality burger, is a product of his own lifestyle and that of today's American society. We are a mobile, health- and youth-oriented group that sometimes has to eat at fast-food restaurants. D'Lites outlets offer a dual menu for those who are weight- and calorie-conscious and those who just want a good meal. The typical fast-food meal of cheeseburger, fries, and soft drink contains 1,066 calories, while D'Lites's cheeseburger, baked potato, and sugar-free drink contain 498 calories. Or customers can opt for a vegetarian sandwich, or soup or the salad bar, in lieu of the burger. Extra-lean meats, which cost more, are used, but in that way taste, which sells the new product, is saved.

In 1983, there were two D'Lites restaurants operating in Atlanta, and others were being built in Atlanta, Tampa, St. Petersburg, and Orlando. The firm's strategy is to have a slow, methodical growth to 1,000 units nationwide by 1993. A Chicago venture capital group, William Blair Venture Partners, invested $2.3 million in the new franchise, and Sheley increased that to $5 million through an Atlanta bank. Franchisees must have a minimum $150,000 equity in each unit, of which $15,000 goes to D'Lites of America as a franchise license. The franchisor also gets 3 percent of each unit's first-year gross revenue.

New Jersey General's running back, Herschel Walker, opened his first franchised D'Lites in Atlanta in April 1984. He has the rights to open twelve more in Georgia and Tennessee.

Sheley's objective is not to be the biggest fast-food franchise, but to be the best.

Source: Kevin Higgins, "D'Lites Goes After Calorie Watchers Eating on Run," *Marketing News*, April 29, 1983, p. 5.

ers. For example, one franchisor bought a spice blend for $3.00 and wholesaled it to franchisees for $21.50. For the most part, though, economies of scale can be obtained by buying in large quantities. This practice permits the sellers to share savings from reduced selling and handling costs with the franchisees.

### Quality Standards

Since 1970, the courts have generally held that franchisees should be free to purchase their materials and supplies from whomever they choose, as long as product quality isn't affected. Sometimes franchisors are permitted to be the

sole provider of principal products—such as coffee and baked goods for the Chock Full O' Nuts franchise—but franchisees can buy other products elsewhere. These court decisions have provided a real marketing boost for many small businesses that are independent suppliers of items such as milk, bread, and paper products.

Many franchisors let their franchisees buy from any supplier whose products meet quality standards established by the franchisor. They sometimes develop a list of approved suppliers whose products the franchisor has reviewed and found reliable.[8]

### Financial and Legal Arrangements

Because of the contractual nature of franchising, a franchisor can dictate every aspect of the business: wall colors, employees' uniforms, lighting, signs, types of shrubbery, and minute operating details. For example, Insty-Prints's contract obligates the franchisee to produce printing to its quality standards. If those standards aren't met, and if there's no improvement after fair warning, the franchisor can end the franchise. Insty-Prints is then obligated to buy the franchisee's equipment at fair value. But the franchisee can't collect anything for the going business value of the franchise when the contract expires after ten years or if it is terminated by the franchisor.

Franchisees usually pay a one-time franchise fee and continuing royalties and advertising fees, often collected as a percentage of sales. For instance, Insty-Prints collects a nonrefundable $8,000 franchise fee, a royalty of 3 percent of gross sales, payable monthly, and an additional 2 percent of sales for advertising materials.

The Program Store, which sells software for personal computers, was one of the first franchises in the high-tech field. Begun in 1978 in Washington, D.C., it now has outlets in the Washington-Baltimore area; Columbus, Ohio; and Boston. A franchise costs a fee of $15,000, plus $70,000 for the initial inventory, basic fixtures, and a training course.[9]

The sale of a franchise to a third party can usually be made only after a first offer to the franchisor. If the latter refuses to make a bid, the sale to the third party can then proceed.

Sometimes a franchise pays off so well that the franchisor moves in other outlets to take part of the volume. A Dunkin Donuts spokesman states flatly that his company gives no geographical protection to its franchisees and is free to move in on them at any time.[10]

## WHAT'S INVOLVED IN OPENING A FRANCHISE?

**Objective 5**

How one of the more popular franchises operates.

Now that you understand what franchising is, know what some of the most popular franchises are, and are aware of their benefits and potential problems, let's look at how you obtain a franchise and begin operating it. The internal activities of one of the more successful franchise operations—McDonald's—are explained below in some detail as an illustration. Most other companies have about the same activities and guidelines.

Everyone knows the golden arches, almost a logo for U.S. popular culture for over twenty years. There are twice as many McDonald's as there are Bur-

McDonald's efficient layout and production system have contributed to its success.

ger Kings. McDonald's has even been given the stamp of sound nutrition by no less than The French Chef, Julia Child. It's a good example of a fast-food franchise for these and other reasons, including its record of success; its rise to the top in fast-food sales and number of franchise units; its thoroughly planned, developed, and maintained management program for franchisees; and its attractiveness to most untrained prospective franchisees.

### Obtaining a Franchise

McDonald's' success has led to long lines of would-be franchisees waiting to obtain a franchise. A license costs the franchise owner $275,000 and up, which covers the cost of the original license, together with site selection charges and other fees, and provides the necessary working capital. In addition to the original cost, the franchisee pays 11½ percent of gross receipts to cover rent and royalties on the McDonald's name. Franchisees also pay property taxes, buy insurance, are responsible for maintenance, buy food from company-approved suppliers, and pay wages. In any event, each franchise has a life of only twenty years, at the end of which ownership reverts to the company.

### Operating the Franchise

Before the franchise opens, the franchisee and sometimes the assistant manager spend two weeks at McDonald's' Hamburger University for a required management training program in "hamburgerology." The program stresses McDonald's' system of management to ensure success. At the same time, the franchisee is instilled with experience-based expertise in making all the decisions involved in operating the franchise. For example, McDonald's has found

that high school students make the best sales and kitchen help. Also, since McDonald's has discovered that franchises run more smoothly when the owner is present, franchisees are required to spend a minimum of four hours each day in the store.

McDonald's' efficient production system is designed for easy maintenance of a sanitary environment with a minimum of wasted motion. In addition to its efficient layout, McDonald's has an inventory control and supply system that helps the franchisee to requisition necessary materials and supplies from approved sources.

## EVALUATING FRANCHISE OPPORTUNITIES

**Objective 6**

**How to evaluate a franchise opportunity.**

Prospective franchisees should follow certain basic steps in evaluating a franchise operation and determining its worth. As a bare minimum, hopeful entrepreneurs should (1) identify and investigate franchising opportunities, (2) investigate the advantages and disadvantages of the prospective franchisor, and (3) obtain professional assistance.[11]

### Sources of Information

Reliable sources of information about franchising opportunities include newspapers such as *The Wall Street Journal* and trade journals such as *Marketing News,* which carry advertisements for new opportunities. The exhibitions and trade shows periodically held by franchisors in various cities are another source of information. Finally, of course, franchisors can always be contacted directly for information on specific opportunities.

As much information as possible should be gathered about the franchisor. One clear warning flag is a franchisor who seems too eager to sell franchises. Reputable franchisors normally investigate prospective franchisees carefully before making a deal in order to assess their ability to operate a franchise successfully.

### Types of Information Needed

Information about investment requirements, costs, and profits for a few selected franchises should be obtained before any specific franchise is considered. If you're still interested in a franchise after obtaining this kind of financial information about franchises in general, you should proceed to ask yourself questions like those shown in the Quiz on page 131.

If a franchisor seems to be a desirable and reasonably profitable firm to work with and offers a franchise contract, the prospective franchisee should arrange for an attorney to review it. Contract provisions related to cancellation and renewal of the franchise and the degree of control the franchisor will have over operations are particularly important. Other vital contract clauses have to do with the franchise fee, percentage of gross revenues, training, territorial limits, and the supplying of materials. The prospective franchisee

**TABLE 5-3  Checklist for potential franchise buyers.**

*Have you checked out the franchisor?*
- Does the company have a solid business reputation and credit rating?
- Have you contacted other franchisees for their opinions?
- For how many years has the firm offering you a franchise been in operation?
- Will the firm assist you in finding a good location for your new business?
- Is the franchising firm adequately financed to carry out its stated plan of financial assistance and expansion?
- Has the franchisor shown you any certified figures indicating exact net profits of one or more going operations? Have you had the figures analyzed by your accountant and other franchisees?
- Have you had any negative feedback from the franchisor's operating franchisees you have contacted?
- Are training and continuing supervision a myth or a reality?

*What about the franchise contract?*
- Did your lawyer approve the franchise contract after studying it paragraph by paragraph?
- Does the franchise give you an exclusive territory for the length of the franchise or can the franchisor sell a second or third franchise in your territory?
- If you sell your franchise or your contract is terminated, will you be compensated for your goodwill or will the goodwill you have built into the business be lost by you?
- Are you prepared to give up some independence of action to secure the advantages offered by the franchise?
- Are you required to buy your merchandise exclusively from the franchisor? If so, are the prices competitive?
- Can you sell, trade, or invest the franchise?
- Are royalty or other financing charges exorbitantly out of proportion to sales volume?
- Is your territory protected?
- Is the franchise fee worth it? What exactly is the fee for? If the fee includes costs for equipment or supplies, are they reasonable?

SOURCE: National Association of Franchised Businessmen, 1404 New York Avenue NW, Washington, D.C. 20005.

should also consult with a banker and an accountant concerning the contract. Table 5-3 suggests some penetrating questions to ask before signing the contract.

# THE FUTURE OF FRANCHISING

**Objective 7**

**The future of franchising.**

It's anticipated that the number of franchises in this country will continue to grow. The U.S. economy has become more service-oriented, and many franchise systems perform much-needed services. Opportunities for franchises catering to those needs should indeed abound.

Probably the greatest new opportunity for franchising, however, is outside the United States. The success achieved by some of the franchises in America

Kentucky Fried Chicken's
Japanese operation.

has resulted in international interest and opportunity. As early as 1980, 279 U.S. franchisors operated 27,428 outlets abroad—this was a sixfold increase over 1971. Three of the best-known franchises that have gone abroad have already been discussed in this chapter—Holiday Inns, Kentucky Fried Chicken, and McDonald's. KFC now operates in over fifty countries, including Japan.

Foreign firms are beginning to franchise outlets in the United States. For instance, Descamps STD, Inc., a French firm selling linens and tablecloths, and the Canadian company Holiday Rent-A-Car have already entered the U.S. market.

It's also reasonable to expect that there will be a significant increase in the number of franchisee associations both within and across franchise systems, such as the National Association of Franchised Businessmen. These associations perform such functions as establishing procedures for mediating franchisee-franchisor disputes, providing information to franchisors on franchisee problems, and increasing security for franchisees.

More legislation regulating franchising also is expected over the next decade. Certainly more laws are needed to protect franchisees from unfair practices by a few unscrupulous franchisors.

Since retailing is becoming more complex, changes will come in product/service mix, store design, and layout. These marketing moves will be geared to fulfilling customers' needs more effectively. Already, Pizza Time Theatres, gourmet popcorn stands, and phone-in, drive-through grocery stores are stepping in to fill the marketing gaps left open by Pizza Hut, Jolly Time, and 7-Eleven.

# *Quiz*

Ask yourself these questions.

1. What type of franchise appeals to me most?
2. What type of franchise appeals to me least?
3. What type of franchise will best help me achieve my objectives?
4. What type will give me the best opportunity to use my skills and talents?
5. What type would provide me with satisfaction as I operate it on a daily basis?
6. What type seems to be within my financial means?
7. Does there seem to be room for another outlet of this franchise in my area?
8. If not, are other franchise locations available?
9. Am I really willing to take the risks (financial and others) involved in operating that franchise?

## LEARNING OBJECTIVES REVISITED

1. *What a franchise is, and why it is such an important part of American business.*

   Franchises are now an important segment of business, especially at the retail level. The growth of these exclusive arrangements between private owners (franchisees) and parent companies (franchisors) has resulted in rapidly expanding business opportunities for potential entrepreneurs.

2. *The types of franchising arrangements.*

   There are two general types of franchising arrangements: (1) the franchising of a product and (2) the franchising of an entire business enterprise. Within these types, there are policies providing for individually owned, company-owned, and geographically owned franchises.

3. *The benefits of a franchise for both customers and owners.*

   Franchises are growing in popularity because they satisfy customers' needs, cater to changing lifestyles, encourage entrepreneurship, and provide managerial support for franchisees.

4. *Franchise requirements and controls.*

   Franchisors usually set quality standards for materials and supplies used

by franchisees and sometimes specify approved suppliers. They also dictate most aspects of the business, require payment of a franchise fee, and receive ongoing percentages of sales.

5. *How one of the more popular franchises operates.*

McDonald's is an example of a typical franchising arrangement, designed for high efficiency and quality.

6. *How to evaluate a franchise opportunity.*

In evaluating a franchise opportunity, one should research the sources of information on existing franchises, evaluate the quality of those available, and seek professional guidance.

7. *The future of franchising.*

The future of franchising encompasses penetration of international markets, increased numbers of franchisee associations, improved legislation, and new marketing methods.

## ▲ IMPORTANT TERMS

As an extra review of the chapter, try defining the following terms. If you have trouble with any of them, refer to the page listed.

franchise *114*
franchisor *114*
franchisee *114*

## ▲ REVIEW QUESTIONS

1. What percentage of retail operations is represented by franchises?
2. What are some of the differences in the types of franchise arrangements?
3. What are some of the factors that have contributed to the growth of franchising in America?
4. What are some common forms of assistance provided by franchisors to franchisees?
5. What are some of the abuses practiced by franchisors in the past?
6. What types of franchises have generally poor prospects?
7. What are the usual arrangements for a franchisee to pay for a franchise?
8. What rules and regulations must a franchisee abide by?
9. In general, what are the steps involved in acquiring and opening a McDonald's franchise?
10. What are some questions that a prospective franchisee should ask before determining whether a specific franchise is appealing?
11. What steps should be followed by the prospective franchisee in evaluating a franchise operation and determining its worth?

## ▲ DISCUSSION QUESTIONS

1. What changes in the U.S. work force, consumer habits, and customs have led to the rapid growth of the fast-food industry?
2. How has the shortage of venture capital led to the growth of franchising?

3. Are franchises really such good investments? Why or why not?

4. Do you think you would like to own a McDonald's franchise? Why or why not?

5. Why do you suppose a major corporation would choose to go the route of selling franchises?

6. Do you think that franchises are exploitative? If so, how?

7. Call one of your favorite franchises and ask for an interview with the owner as part of your course work. During the interview, ask the following questions, along with any others you can think of. Then decide whether you would like to own one of these franchises.

    a. When did you buy this franchise? Is it only a single outlet, or do you have the right to open other outlets in a given area?

    b. Why did you buy it? What were you looking for in this franchise? Have you achieved what you sought?

    c. What was your background and prior experience? How do they help (or hinder) you in operating the franchise?

    d. What is your territory? Is it exclusive?

    e. What is your personal work schedule in the outlet? Does it vary much from day to day? How rewarding do you find it? What are the busiest periods for the store?

    f. What products and services does your franchisor supply? Is the delivery timely? Are the prices competitive?

    g. Are you considering buying another franchise? Why or why not?

8. Giving your imagination free rein, think up two ideas for franchises of the future. Discuss them with your instructor—you may have a salable idea or two!

## ⌂ CASE 5-1 Pepsi Tastes Better at Burger King[12]

Burger King, with its 3,200 restaurants in the United States, is second only to McDonald's in its industry; Pepsi Cola is second to Coca-Cola in its field. Yet, until mid-1983, Burger King served Coke as its cola drink, and so did McDonald's. As early as 1979, Burger King authorized its franchises to sell Diet Pepsi, and Pepsi's Mountain Dew was authorized in 1980. From 1979 on, Pepsi's goal was to dislodge Coke from the fast-food franchise.

On June 13, 1983, it was announced that Burger King was going to serve Pepsi in its fountains rather than Coke. Pepsi's price to the burger franchise was $4.25 a gallon, slightly less than Coke's. But it wasn't price that turned the trick. Instead, it was the similarity of the two firms' marketing strategies. For a long time, Pepsi had used the "Pepsi Challenge" in its ads against Coke. It had become increasingly competitive in selling fountain syrup to restaurants, a market long dominated by Coke.

In late 1982, Burger King started its famous "Battle of the Burgers" campaign, which emphasized that "broiling is better" than frying. Apparently, the two fighting franchises—Pepsi against Coca-Cola and Burger King against McDonald's—thought they should team up. Thus the number twos joined together against the number ones. The similarity in strategies should help the two franchises develop cooperative advertising campaigns. Pepsi will gain $30 million in additional sales each year. And Burger King will differentiate itself from its arch-rival, McDonald's.

**Case Questions**

1. Why do you think Burger King really decided to go with Pepsi instead of Coke? Explain.

2. Do you think Pepsi might lose some fast-food franchises to Coca-Cola if it starts cooperative advertising with Burger King? Explain.
3. What actions, if any, do you think Coca-Cola will now take? Explain.

## ⬙ CASE 5-2   VR BUSINESS BROKERS[13]

According to former Kentucky Fried Chicken franchise owner George A. Naddaff, the future of franchising is in service-type franchises. Thus he thinks there is a great future in a franchise to link up business brokers nationwide. The result: VR Business Brokers (VRBB), of which he is founder and chairman. He founded VRBB in 1979 to sell franchises to people who wanted to bring together owners interested in selling their ongoing business and prospective entrepreneurs. In early 1982, the chain had 239 franchised outlets finding buyers for such small businesses as accounting services, computer stores, and convenience food stores. It expected to have 600 offices by the end of 1983. In 1981, the ninety franchisees masterminded the sale of about 900 small businesses.

The franchisee must pay a one-time licensing fee of around $10,000, plus minimum monthly payments of $400 the first year and $1,000 thereafter. Since the franchise doesn't require an elaborate building and equipment, the initial investment can be as low as $50,000. Franchisees must find their own office space and pay franchising expenses. The commission on each sale is 12 percent of the sales price, with 8 percent of the receipts going to the franchisor and 4 percent to the franchisee.

VRBB has a computerized list of some 35,000 businesses for sale around the country. Thus it is easy to match buyers with these sellers. VRBB is a franchisor's franchisor; that is, it sells franchises for franchise companies such as John R. Powers modeling agencies and 1-Hour Martinizing dry cleaners. It also provides many accounting, tax, management, and other financial services for small businesses.

### Case Questions

1. Would you be interested in buying one of these franchises (if you could afford it)? Why or why not?
2. If you were to buy one, where would you try to find office space? Why?
3. What do you see as VRBB's strengths?
4. What do you see as its weaknesses?
5. Do you think service-type franchises are the wave of the future? Explain.

# DIGGING DEEPER

## Careers in Business

Now that you've finished this first part, have you decided to have a career in business? Or are you merely considering such a choice? For many of you, career options may not really matter much at this time. But eventually you will have to make one or more career decisions. In fact, career authorities say that you may make as many as seven fundamental job changes during your working life.

Considerable assistance is available to you in making career decisions. Career planning is popular, and many books, pamphlets, and other materials that have been published by federal agencies and private publishers are available in libraries and college placement offices. Also, vocational counselors, employed by schools or other agencies, are anxious to give you a hand.

Useful career materials are found in three places in this book. First, there is this overview of general business opportunities. Second, descriptions of careers in various functional fields of business are listed at the end of each major part of the book. Third, a good portion of the last chapter is designed to help you find your niche in business. You can use these materials in any way you want. However, if you're undecided on how to approach them, we suggest reading this discussion first, then reading about careers in the last chapter, and then looking for career opportunities in the functional areas of greatest interest to you.

### Job Opportunities During This Decade

Competition for careers in business is going to be intense during the late 1980s and early 1990s. However, there should be plenty of opportunities for those who plan and implement a sound career strategy. Employers no longer want to hire people who just think; they want employees who can think *and* do.

### *Opportunities for College Graduates*

By 1990, there will be more people with a college education than higher-level jobs available for them. In fact, as Figure I-1 (p. 136) shows, only 10.2 million job openings will be available for 13.5 million new college graduates entering the work force up to 1990. Thus, not all graduates—even those with business degrees—will be assured of getting a good professional job. You'll be competing with a large group of people born during the postwar baby boom who are now holding supervisory and management positions. You should therefore prepare yourself for alternative job opportunities and occupations.

Still, as you can see from Figure I-2 (p. 136), students with a college degree won't suffer as much as other workers because they'll have entry-level skills to offer and because they'll be able to work in such a wide variety of fields.

### *Specific Career Opportunities*

In choosing a career, you should ask yourself questions such as: Which industries are growing and creating job opportunities? Which occupations provide opportunities for advancement? What are the salary opportunities in various positions? In what part of the country do I want to work (and live)? The following discussion should help you in making these decisions.

● FAVORABLE INDUSTRIES. By 1990, 75 percent of employed persons will be in service-performing industries, especially the information, health care, and computer-related fields. Most job openings will be in those fields. Teaching, farming, and household service, as well as the smokestack industries, such as autos, steel, and textiles, won't generate many job openings.

● FAVORABLE OCCUPATIONS. The U.S. Department of Labor estimates that nearly 25 million jobs will open up by 1990. But the job opportunities will vary according to occupation; for example, around 55 percent of all employees will be in white-collar jobs. Table I-1 (page 137) shows that the fastest-growing occupations are services,

135

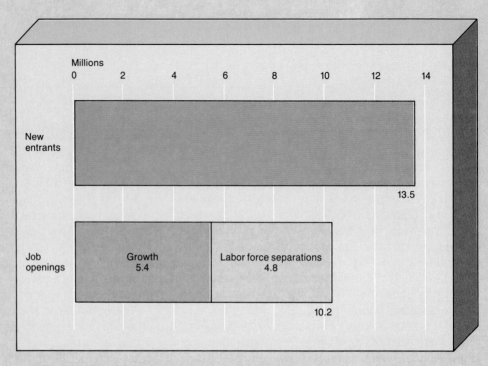

**Figure I-1**   College graduates entering the labor force are expected to exceed openings in jobs traditionally filled by graduates by 3.3 million by 1990.   [Adapted from "Tomorrow's Jobs for College Graduates," *Occupational Outlook for College Graduates* (Washington, D.C.: Government Printing Office, 1982), p. 23.]

**Figure I-2**   Requirements for college graduates are expected to grow faster than requirements for all workers.   [Adapted from "Tomorrow's Jobs for College Graduates," *Occupational Outlook for College Graduates* (Washington, D.C.: Government Printing Office, 1982), p. 20.]

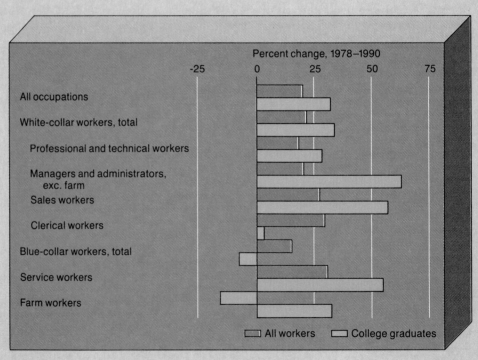

**TABLE I-1. Expected employment in selected occupations in 1990.**

| Occupation | Percentage Change | Expected Number of Jobs (in millions) |
|---|---|---|
| Service | +32 | 19.2 |
| Sales | +28 | 8.8 |
| Clerical | +27 | 24.0 |
| Professional and technical | +26 | 20.7 |
| Transport | +26 | 4.4 |
| Production workers | +23 | 13.2 |
| Unskilled laborers | +22 | 7.1 |
| Managers and administrators | +21 | 11.3 |
| Farm | −18 | 2.2 |

SOURCE: U.S. Department of Labor, Bureau of Labor Statistics.

**TABLE I-2. Some occupations that are growing and some that are not.**

| | Job Growth, 1980–90 |
|---|---|
| Secretaries | 700,000 |
| Sales clerks | 479,000 |
| Cashiers | 452,000 |
| Fast-food restaurant workers | 400,000 |
| General office clerks | 377,000 |
| Waiters, waitresses | 360,000 |
| Elementary-school teachers | 251,000 |
| Accountants, auditors | 221,000 |
| Building-trades helpers | 212,000 |
| Automobile mechanics | 206,000 |
| Blue-collar supervisors | 206,000 |
| Typists | 187,000 |
| Carpenters | 173,000 |
| Bookkeepers | 167,000 |
| Guards, doorkeepers | 153,000 |
| Stock clerks (warehouse) | 142,000 |
| Computer-systems analysts | 139,000 |
| Store managers | 139,000 |
| Physicians | 135,000 |
| Utility repairers | 134,000 |
| Computer operators | 132,000 |
| Child-care workers | 125,000 |
| Welders | 123,000 |
| Stock clerks (sales floor) | 120,000 |
| Electrical engineers | 115,000 |
| Computer programmers | 112,000 |
| Electricians | 109,000 |
| Bank tellers | 108,000 |
| Electrical, electronic technicians | 107,000 |
| Lawyers | 107,000 |
| Real-estate agents | 102,000 |

| | Job Reductions, 1980–90 |
|---|---|
| Secondary-school teachers | 173,000 |
| College, university teachers | 55,000 |
| Graduate assistants | 24,000 |
| Compositors, typesetters | 13,000 |
| Clergy | 9,000 |
| Postal clerks | 6,000 |
| Central-office repairers | 3,000 |
| Ticket agents | 2,000 |
| Taxi drivers | 2,000 |

SOURCE: "Where New Jobs Will Be in the 1980s," *U.S.News & World Report,* February 7, 1983, p. 73. Reprinted from "U.S.News & World Report." Copyright, 1983, U.S.News & World Report, Inc.

sales, clerical, professional and technical, and transport; the slower-growing ones are production workers, unskilled labor, managers and administrators, and farm workers (which will actually decline). Table I-2 gives a more detailed listing of the increase in the number of specific occupations. Notice the large number of clerical job openings, new health care jobs, and sales jobs.

● JOB CONCENTRATION. Figure I-3 shows you where the jobs are concentrated in the United States, by job category, industry, and geographic region. Once you've decided what industry and occupation you prefer, this map should help you select the region of the country in which you may want to start your career.

● FAVORABLE SALARY OPPORTUNITIES. Sound financial, as well as nonfinancial, reasons exist for getting at least a bachelor's degree, whether in business or in some other area. According to the U.S. Bureau of the Census, a bachelor's degree is worth more than $300,000 in extra lifetime earnings for a young man and $142,000 for a young woman.[1] A male college graduate is expected to earn $1.4 million, a high school graduate $1 million, and a dropout $845,000. There are few opportunities that offer that high a return on investment.

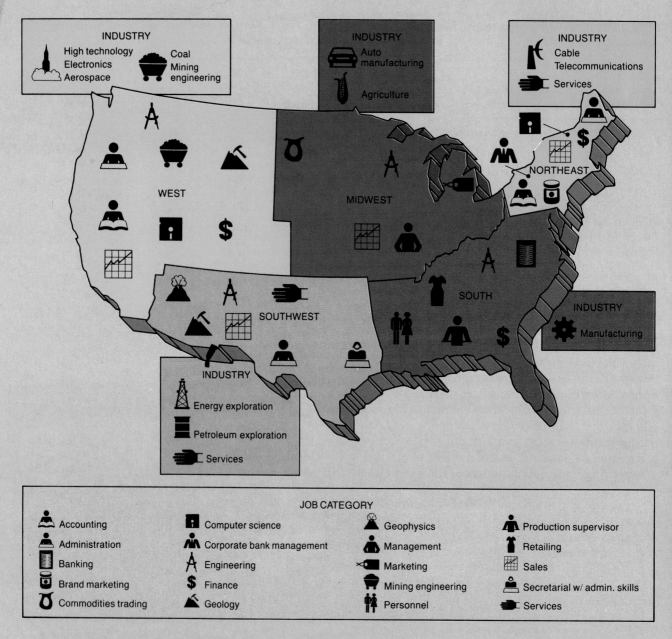

**INDUSTRY**
High technology — Coal
Electronics — Mining
Aerospace — engineering

**INDUSTRY**
Auto manufacturing

Agriculture

**INDUSTRY**
Cable
Telecommunications
Services

WEST

MIDWEST

NORTHEAST

SOUTHWEST

SOUTH

**INDUSTRY**
Energy exploration

Petroleum exploration

Services

**INDUSTRY**
Manufacturing

**JOB CATEGORY**

| | | | |
|---|---|---|---|
| Accounting | Computer science | Geophysics | Production supervisor |
| Administration | Corporate bank management | Management | Retailing |
| Banking | Engineering | Marketing | Sales |
| Brand marketing | Finance | Mining engineering | Secretarial w/ admin. skills |
| Commodities trading | Geology | Personnel | Services |

**Figure I-3**  Job concentration by region.  (Reprinted by permission from Patrice Johnson, "Where the Jobs Are," *Black Enterprise*, February 1981, pp. 40–41.  Copyright The Earl G. Graves Publishing Co. Inc., 295 Madison Avenue, New York, NY 10017.  All rights reserved.)

## Career Option

Among the most challenging career options are small business ownership and management. However, beginners shouldn't choose it.  Only after gaining management experience in a given line should one buy an existing firm or establish a new venture.  A rule-of-thumb is three years' experience, with some of that preferably being managerial in nature.

Why should you want to own or manage a small business? Probably the only way most people are ever going to become wealthy is by starting their own business.  Also, the idea of being

independent—being one's own boss—has tremendous appeal.

Small businesses can range in size from a one-person, at-home, part-time venture to one involving a number of employees, perhaps up to 250 employees in, say, a manufacturing firm. Most entrepreneurs start out as the owner, manager, and employee. People running a small business wind up being everything from the chief executive officer to the custodian. They do the planning, financing, accounting, purchasing, producing, marketing, and managing. To be able to do all this requires knowledge, experience, and certain personal characteristics, such as a willingness to assume risk, to work long hours, to tolerate the uncertainty of success during the early stages of the firm, and to keep thorough records. Capital should be sufficient to start up the firm, operate it until the business passes the breakeven point, and support the owner-manager and his or her family in the meantime.

Franchises have been found effective in many instances in minimizing risk, because of the management and operations training and assistance provided, a nationally known name and a tested product, cooperative buying power, and financial assistance provided by the franchisor.

# PART II

## MANAGING AND ORGANIZING A BUSINESS

Now that you're familiar with the overall environment of business, it's time to see how a business is managed and organized inside its walls. Chapter 4 showed that the failure of owner-managers to give attention to the various management functions is the cause of the vast majority of small business failures. The same is true of companies of other sizes. While management basically involves getting things done through people, it's also much more. Managers make decisions and allocate scarce resources so that the firm will achieve its objectives efficiently and effectively. Five basic functions—planning, organizing, staffing, leading, and controlling—are performed by all managers. If they're performed well, the business succeeds; if they're performed poorly, it will fail. That's what this part is all about.

Chapter 6 discusses the levels of management, the functions performed by managers, basic skills required of them, and the role of decision making.

In Chapter 7, various aspects of organizing a business—the overall organizing process, departmentation, delegating authority, and span of management—are discussed.

Production and operations management—including production planning, production facilities and their layout, materials management, and production control—are covered in Chapter 8.

# 6

# Managing a Business

*You manage things; you lead people.*

Grace Hopper

*Labor can do nothing without capital, capital nothing without labor, and neither labor nor capital can do anything without the guiding genius of management.*

W. L. Mackenzie King

## Learning Objectives

After studying the material in this chapter, you will understand:

1. What management is.
2. The role of each of the three levels of management: top, middle, and supervisory.
3. Each of the basic managerial functions: planning, organizing, staffing, leading, and controlling.
4. The role of organizational mission and objectives in strategic planning.
5. The conceptual, human relations, technical, and administrative skills that managers need.
6. The nature of managerial decision making.

## In This Chapter

# LEE IACOCCA
*Turnaround Specialist*

At a fund-raiser for a hospital in mid-1982, Lido Anthony (Lee) Iacocca, chairman of Chrysler Corporation, was honored as Detroit's man of the year. George Steinbrenner, the controversial owner of the New York Yankees, introduced Iacocca by saying, "I can't think of anyone I'd rather follow . . . as president . . . of the United States." Illinois admirers set up an "Iacocca for President" committee. Lee Iacocca responded to such political overtures by jokingly saying, "I could handle the economy in six months. . . . Running Chrysler these last few years has been bigger than running the country."

At age fifty-seven, Iacocca was considered a miracle worker who overcame apparently insurmountable odds, including a depressed economy and the auto industry's worst recession ever, to save and rehabilitate Chrysler. His story shows how a brilliant financial analyst and marketing genius persuaded some of the country's strongest and most influential bankers, some of the toughest and most powerful union leaders, and some hard-nosed and skeptical politicians—as well as the company's endangered managers and employees—to save an essentially bankrupt corporation.

Iacocca started at Ford Motor Company as a salesman. Leaping quickly up the corporate ladder, he became president in 1970. He was responsible for introducing the Pinto, one of the first truly small cars produced by a U.S. manufacturer, as well as the Mustang, one of the most successful new products in modern industrial history.

Then, in 1978, he was fired as president by Henry Ford II. Legend has it that Ford said, "I just don't like you," but Iacocca says it was because he believed in small cars and Ford didn't. Iacocca was banished to a distant warehouse with an office and a secretary and was shunned by Ford personnel. Yet he was hired four months later as president and later as chief operating officer by the failing Chrysler Corporation's board. He was given the mission of saving the firm, regardless of the cost.

His first decision was not to file for bankruptcy; next, he arranged for a $1.2 billion loan guarantee from a skeptical Congress, converted creditors into preferred stockholders, and arranged new credit sources. Then he had to dismiss half the firm's managers and white-collar employees, reduce by nearly half its productive capacity, and lay off thousands of production workers—many of them permanently. The remaining unionized workers gave up nearly $1 billion in wages and benefits. Finally, Iacocca became Chrysler's star salesman. TV commercials featuring the tough-talking executive were amazingly successful in building the company's image as a quality producer. He was also a remarkable morale builder for Chrysler's remaining people.

The charismatic chairman had apparently turned the firm around by 1984. He'd built a solid management team, reduced costs, increased Chrysler's domestic market share from 10 to 12 percent, and restored the confidence of financial markets. The firm's stock was a leading performer in 1982, rising 425 percent in value. In July 1983, Iacocca unexpectedly paid off the entire loan, seven years ahead of schedule, thereby saving the company $392 million in interest and winning a bet with New York City mayor Ed Koch over which of their organizations would be the first to get out of debt!

Iacocca couldn't have achieved the desired results with only his financial and marketing skills—as formidable as they were. Instead, it took that abstract and intangible quality we know as management expertise to reverse Chrysler's plunge.

Management can mean any number of things, depending on your perspective. To a union organizer at Caterpillar Tractor Company, management is the other side of the fence in a 205-day walkout. To a programmer for Digital Equipment Corporation (DEC), it's an unattainable Olympus where pinstriped executives gather to determine the future—at least for the next five years. To a Holiday Inns franchisee, it's the place in Memphis that calls the shots and takes the royalties. To a university professor, it's everyone from the department chairperson on up to the university president. To a linebacker for the Dallas Cowboys, it's the quarterback or the general manager. To a church social group member, it's the person who organizes the Holiday Bazaar. In short, management can be found on many levels of any organization, wherever and whenever people are organized to work together toward a common goal.

## WHAT IS MANAGEMENT

**Objective 1**

**What management is.**

Some authorities refer to the basic resources of a company as the five M's: manpower, money, machinery, materials, and minutes (time). Management itself, though, is the linchpin, since its task is to use these and other resources efficiently and effectively to achieve the enterprise's objectives.

**Management** is an economic concept—basically it is the process of working through people to achieve objectives by means of effective decision making and efficient allocation of scarce resources. **Effectiveness** is doing whatever needs to be done to achieve objectives. **Efficiency** is doing something in the best possible way, so that there are minimal wasted resources. The word *management* itself has at least four meanings. It can be used to refer to (1) an individual who performs managerial activities (from the university president to the bazaar organizer in the previous examples), (2) an occupational group consisting of all the people who supervise and direct the activities of others (the Cowboys' chain of command, or a franchisor), (3) a discipline (the management curriculum), or (4) the process of performing managerial activities (the five-year plan of DEC). In this chapter, the word will usually refer to the *process* of managing.

You've probably sat in on informal meetings where the agenda disintegrated into irrelevant meanderings, painful silences, and little sense of anything getting done. Without someone to take charge of the squabbles, sidetracks, and wasted talent in such get-togethers, nothing *can* be done effectively and efficiently. Without management, a lot of effort can be wasted. And larger, more complex enterprises simply could not exist without managers performing their functions.

## LEVELS OF MANAGEMENT

**Objective 2**

**The role of each of the three levels of management: top, middle, and supervisory.**

Except in very small businesses, there are usually several different levels of management. These managers have varying amounts of **authority,** which is the right to do something or to have someone else do it, and **responsibility,** which is accountability for performance of assigned duties, by oneself or by

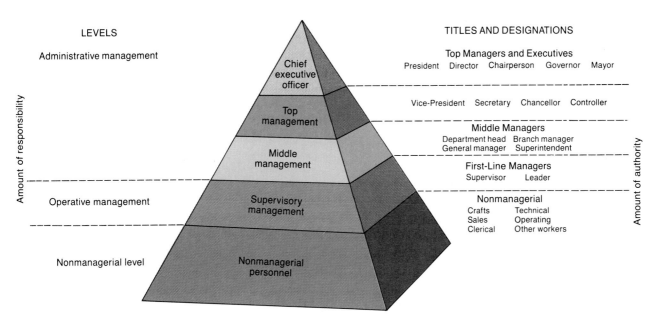

**Figure 6-1** The levels of management.

subordinates. In large organizations, there are usually at least three levels of management: (1) top, or administrative, management; (2) middle, or intermediate, management; and (3) supervisory, or first-line, management.

**Top,** or administrative, **management** has overall responsibility for the whole organization and also has the authority to run it. At the pinnacle of a company's management team is the president or chairperson of the board, who serves as the chief executive officer (CEO). Next in rank come the vice-presidents, who coordinate the performance of such major operating functions as production, finance, marketing, and personnel. All of these officers are top, or administrative, management. Examples are the president of the United States, the pope in the Roman Catholic Church, the general manager of a football team, and the CEO of Exxon.

**Middle,** or intermediate, **management** is still in upper-level management circles but is responsible for a lower level of the firm, such as a department within a division. The chief of cardiology in a hospital, the head coach of a football team, the director of advertising within a marketing division, and bishops of the Roman Catholic Church are examples of middle managers.

**Supervisory,** or first-line, **management** has control over the operations of the narrowest organizational units (offices, labs, assembly lines for specific parts). They are the bosses most of us come in contact with every day.

Notice in Figure 6-1 that, although authority and responsibility increase as one rises in the organizational hierarchy, the number of managers decreases—until there is finally only one person at the top: the CEO.

## FUNCTIONS PERFORMED BY MANAGERS

You've probably heard the complaint "Managers don't *do* anything! Why should they make so much more money than someone who *produces* something?" That's a compelling argument, but the fact is that managers do *do*

**Objective 3**

Each of the basic managerial functions: planning, organizing, staffing, leading, and controlling.

something. It's just harder to measure in units produced. In fact, there are at least five separate, but overlapping, basic managerial functions—planning, organizing, staffing, leading, and controlling—that must be performed by anyone in a managerial position. Managers who are considered successful, whether at the top, the middle, or the supervisory level, perform these functions efficiently and effectively. Unsuccessful ones don't. Figure 6-2 shows that although these functions can be seen as separate and distinct, they're really related. The functions usually are performed in the sequence shown.

## Planning

**Planning** can be defined as selecting, and deciding how to achieve, future courses of action for the organization as a whole and for each subunit that's involved in attaining objectives. It's the keystone management function be-

**Figure 6-2** What managers do. [Based on Figure 2.4 (page 31) from *Management: Concepts and Applications,* by Leon C. Megginson, Donald C. Mosley, and Paul H. Pietri, Jr. Copyright © 1983 by Harper & Row Publishers, Inc. Reprinted by permission of the publisher.]

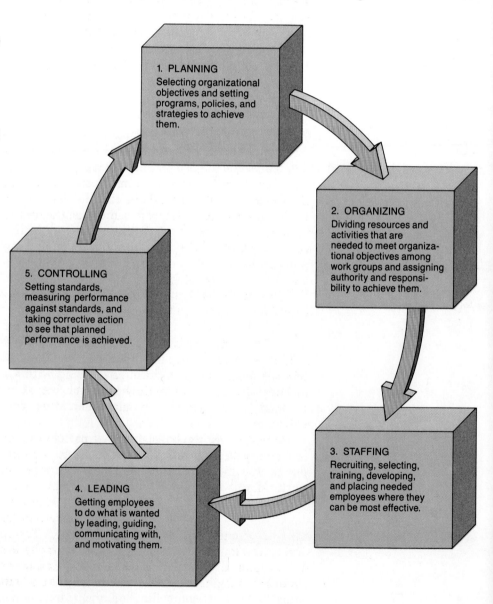

1. PLANNING
Selecting organizational objectives and setting programs, policies, and strategies to achieve them.

2. ORGANIZING
Dividing resources and activities that are needed to meet organizational objectives among work groups and assigning authority and responsibility to achieve them.

3. STAFFING
Recruiting, selecting, training, developing, and placing needed employees where they can be most effective.

4. LEADING
Getting employees to do what is wanted by leading, guiding, communicating with, and motivating them.

5. CONTROLLING
Setting standards, measuring performance against standards, and taking corrective action to see that planned performance is achieved.

cause organizing, staffing, leading, and controlling all carry out the decisions made at the planning stage and would have nowhere to go without it.

▲ **Strategic Planning** **Strategic planning** involves identifying the long-range mission of an organization and determining objectives and appropriate strategies for achieving it. This type of planning is usually done by top management, but there's a direct link between it and the shorter-range planning done by middle managers and supervisors. All middle-management plans are derived from strategic plans made at higher levels. But at the same time, supervisors' plans go back up the organizational ladder to strategic plans. An experience of one of the nation's largest paper companies shows how important this is. The company installed a new five-year program based on motivating production workers to increase output. The strategies and goals were worked out with the general managers at the division, district, and plant levels. Even the production supervisors were briefed on the improved procedures, but somehow the plant maintenance manager and his people weren't told. Production increased 5 percent the first year, and profits increased 7 percent. But the added output put such a strain on machines and equipment that the plan was jettisoned after eighteen months to prevent machine failure.

**Objective 4**

The role of organizational mission and objectives in strategic planning.

▲ **The Organization's Mission** The **mission** of an organization is a long-term vision of what the organization is trying to become. The basic questions answered by a company mission are: What is our business? and What should it be? Simple as it may seem, the inability to ask and answer questions like these has been one of the most important causes of business failure. For example, although Sir Freddie Laker claimed that collusion by other airlines put him out of business, some analysts think his low-cost transatlantic line failed because it forgot its mission. Laker started out with a lean, no frills, cash-and-carry operation. When he started adding space and staff to take advanced bookings, serve meals, and otherwise compete with full-service lines, his overhead became so great that he failed.[1]

Three important considerations in formulating an organization's mission are:

1. *The organization's environment.* What will the technological, economic, political and legal, and sociocultural environment be like in the future? For example, the projected decline in numbers of college-aged people during the 1980s has certainly been considered in the plans of college and university administrators, manufacturers of school equipment, and textbook publishers.

In many managerial jobs, there's pressure to ignore the past, concentrate on the present, and "let tomorrow take care of itself." Many ignore the future because it's a realm of uncertainty. Yet managers need to plan for tomorrow.

2. *The organization's distinctive competence.* What does the organization do especially well? What gives it an advantage over similar organizations? This advantage is based on human resources, financial resources, location, distribution network, and so forth. For instance, Eastman Kodak Company's long dominance of still photography has been based on its expertise in chemical processes. But now Sony Corporation's new developments in electronic imaging may give it a competitive advantage.

3. *The organization's clients.* What are the clients' needs? The mission should focus on the broad class of needs that the organization is attempting to satisfy (external focus), not on the product or service that the organization wishes to sell (internal focus). In other words, the organization can't survive in an ivory tower. Texas Instruments (TI), a leader first in pocket calculators and later in home computers, had to address the declining need for home computers when the market became glutted with price-slashing competitors. IBM's top management has long believed that the company is in the problem-solving business—helping solve administrative, scientific, and human problems—rather than just the business of manufacturing and selling computers. Certain publishers see themselves as managers, not of books, but of intellectual ideas.

▲ **Organizational Objectives** Organizational **objectives** (also called goals, purposes, targets, or results) translate the firm's mission into workable day-to-day goals. Statements of organizational objectives can be quite elaborate or as simple as that of ServiceMaster, a housekeeping and maintenance firm with contracts with over 800 U.S. health care institutions (see Figure 6-3). Well-managed organizations usually share the following objectives.[2]

1. *Profitability.* This objective is usually expressed not only in terms of profit but also in terms of how that profit relates to the firm's assets and the owner's investment. For some reason, people get apologetic about profit as a primary objective of a business. They shouldn't, for, as shown in Chapter 1, profits are a necessary part of the game of business survival. Firms must be profitable to provide owners with a satisfactory rate of return, considering the degree of risk they're assuming in the first place. Also, there must be profits to attract additional capital from investors.

2. *Competitiveness.* Objectives are set in terms of specific rates of increase in sales and market share.

3. *Efficiency.* Measures of efficiency relate to how well the organization's resources are being used. Human resource objectives are often set concerning the quality of management, its succession, numbers of key personnel, and rate of employee turnover. Objectives are also set concerning the use of plant and equipment. Production costs can be cut simply by anticipating operating needs, thinking about the best sequence of operations, and making sure that the right materials and personnel are there when they're needed (see FYI on page 150).

4. *Flexibility.* One objective that a company might have would be to develop and deliver new products at the right time. This may be difficult for many companies. As they grow in size and complexity, they resist change and begin to freeze up with rules, regulations, and pigeonholes. It's up to intelligent planning to keep things flexible.

Other objectives are important, too. For example, unless a company provides a service to its customers through the marketing and production of needed products and services, there won't be profits. Social objectives, such as providing meaningful jobs, a good working environment, and job training for the disadvantaged and establishing good corporate relations with the community, are also vital.

It is best to have business objectives put in writing. This practice can be beneficial to all concerned—management, employees, customers, suppliers,

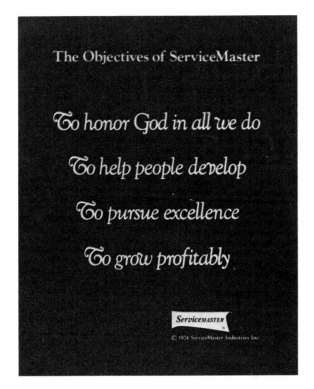

The Objectives of ServiceMaster

*To honor God in all we do*

*To help people develop*

*To pursue excellence*

*To grow profitably*

ServiceMASTER
© 1974 ServiceMaster Industries Inc.

**Figure 6-3** The four corporate objectives of ServiceMaster Industries, Inc. (Reprinted by permission.)

and the community. Just the act of getting the objectives on paper can help to clarify them in the minds of management. Setting specific, written objectives is the basis of the established **management by objectives (MBO)** technique. In this technique, managers and their subordinates jointly set objectives, which they then are motivated to achieve. Based on the concept that we try harder to reach goals we set for ourselves, this technique is a good procedure for planning, motivating, and controlling.

Did you notice the objective the Chrysler board set for Lee Iacocca? Then he set himself an even tougher objective. To what extent do you think these objectives motivated him?

### Organizing

Once a manager has planned the specific activities that are necessary to reach the organization's objectives, the next step is figuring out how to get them done. This step is **organizing**—dividing tasks among work groups and assigning each group to a manager who has been delegated the necessary authority and responsibility to carry out the tasks and reach the objectives. In essence, organizing is bringing together the physical, financial, and human resources needed to achieve the organization's objectives. It's a function most often performed by top management.

## FYI

## Gulf Coast Construction Company: The Best-Laid Plans

When Professor Wiley* decided it was time to get a locked home office for his consulting, it seemed a simple enough matter to call in professionals to design and construct one in his attic. He had no idea of the steps involved and just wanted the thing done efficiently and well. He rang up Paul Pardue, president of Gulf Coast Construction Company, a small new firm that had advertised in a local newspaper. Pardue estimated the job at $2,000 (allowing for $700 gross profit) and said it would be finished in five days. No problem!

Bob and Joe were assigned to the job. They arrived at Professor Wiley's home bright and early, ready to go. All they needed was an extension cord for their electric saw. "No problem," said Joe, who returned to the firm's office for the cord while Bob waited. Checking in early that afternoon, the professor was thrilled with the progress. The subflooring was already in place. Being curious, he asked what type of insulation they'd used under the subflooring. "Insulation? You wanted insulation? Well, no problem," they drawled. After a phone call to Mr. Pardue, Bob and Joe took up the subflooring and left for the day.

Early the next afternoon, after installing the insulation and putting back the subflooring, they began paneling the inside of the office. Up to a point. They ran out of paneling; so both went to a building supply store to buy more and then quit early.

The next day, with an edge of justifiable homicide in his voice, Professor Wiley inquired about *wall* insulation. No problem. The panels came down, and Bob went out to buy insulation and more paneling to install. The air conditioning ducts were the next item to pose no problem for the intrepid builders. Another phone call, another trip to buy insulation.

And it was no real problem that the door was installed the wrong way, with the wrong doorknob (without a lock). Bob and Joe just removed both, bought new ones, and reinstalled them.

Three weeks later, the door still wouldn't lock, the office wasn't finished, the costs had risen to $2,300, and Paul Pardue couldn't understand what the problem was. Two months later he declared bankruptcy.

*All names have been changed.

As will be shown in the next chapter, organizing also involves drawing lines of authority, as well as showing departments and levels of management. The person with authority is responsible for reaching the organization's objectives. He or she may also delegate authority to someone else in order to achieve the objectives. **Delegation** is giving another person the right to use part of one's authority.

### Staffing

Even the most finely tuned plan and the best-charted organization aren't worth the paper they're drafted on without people. **Staffing** can be defined as the

process of recruiting, selecting, training, and developing people, and placing them in jobs that have been created by organizing. This function, which will be discussed in more detail in Chapter 9, is basically one of matching the right people with the right jobs. It's usually performed by middle and first-line managers.

## Leading

Once the people are in place, management's most familiar function comes into play. After all, how could the managers of an organization ensure that plans were being implemented without directing its employees? **Leading** is directing, guiding, supervising, and motivating subordinates to perform their duties and responsibilities in a way that will achieve the organization's objectives. There are many concepts of leadership, but they all boil down to one truth: if people follow you, you are a leader; if they don't, you aren't. In essence, **leaders** are those who inspire others to follow them to achieve agreed-upon goals. **Leadership** occurs when one person induces another person to work toward achieving some specific goal. As Grace Hopper, the Navy's computer expert, implied in the opening quotation, this is the "people" function of management. Middle managers and first-line supervisors are more heavily involved in leading than is top management.

The three most basic factors involved in managerial leadership are (1) the leader and his or her abilities, traits, and characteristics; (2) the subordinates and their abilities, traits, and characteristics; and (3) the situation.

▲ **The Leader**   Studies in leadership have often emphasized the leader's personality traits or personal characteristics such as height, appearance, intelligence, and dominance. For example, Dwight D. Eisenhower, a boy from a small Midwestern town, became a great war hero. Then he became president of a large university and later Supreme Commander of NATO. Finally, as president of the United States, he became a popular father figure who maintained peace and prosperity. He apparently had some indefinable trait that led to his success. John F. Kennedy, young, handsome, and articulate, gave the United States a national mission—to put a man on the moon in the 1960s. This challenge, plus his charisma, made him a widely admired leader, fired people's imagination, and stimulated their performance for years.

While this theory is interesting, it's not very useful, for most leaders have many other common talents and characteristics. People's individual characteristics may be either beneficial or harmful to them as leaders. The traits found more often in successful leaders than in nonleaders are supervisory ability, intelligence, and initiative.[3]

▲ **The Subordinates**   The abilities, traits, and characteristics of those being led also affect leadership. It's easier to lead capable employees who are educated, trained, and experienced than to manage incapable, untrained, and inexperienced ones. In general, the easiest employees to lead are those with a high need for independence, willingness to accept responsibility, interest in the task, an understanding of organizational goals, and high occupational status.

▲ **The Situation**   Different situations call for different leadership styles. For example, the entrepreneur in a new small business may need to be a promoter and a charismatic leader. Later, as the firm grows, the situation may call for

more objective and analytical leadership. People who are unable to adapt their leadership style to a given situation may have little success until they find themselves in a situation that suits their style. For instance, Winston Churchill was not very successful as undersecretary of the British Navy during World War I because his dynamic, aggressive, adventurous, risk-taking, abrasive, and colorful personality didn't fit the mood of the people—at that time. Yet, when it looked as if Hitler would conquer England at the beginning of World War II, Churchill was called upon to lead the country. Later, when the war had been successfully concluded, he was voted out of office and replaced by a more participative leader.

▲ **Styles of Leadership** Effective managers use differing styles of leadership with different followers, in different situations. Styles vary from the completely "boss-centered" style to the completely "subordinate-centered" method. As Figure 6-4 shows, the leader's use of authority declines and the subordinates have greater freedom as the leader's style shifts toward subordinate-centered leadership. Yet, in other situations, the leader must shift toward the boss-centered side and exercise greater authority. At least four leadership styles—autocratic, bureaucratic, democratic, and free-rein—have been identi-

**Figure 6-4** Leadership behavior varies from the boss-centered to the subordinate-centered. [Reprinted by permission of the Harvard Business Review. Exhibit from "How to Choose a Leadership Pattern," by Robert Tannenbaum and Warren H. Schmidt. (March/April 1958) Copyright © 1958 by the President and Fellows of Harvard College; all rights reserved.]

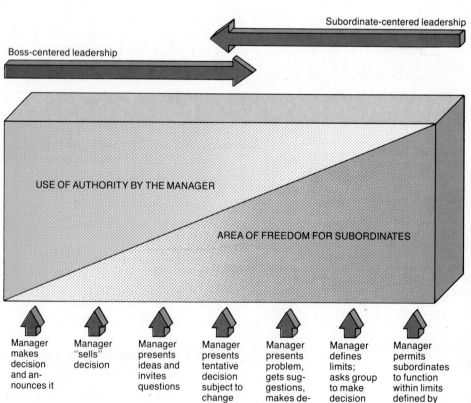

# Business Debate

## Which Leadership Style Is Best for You?

Here are the characteristics of the four most popular leadership styles. Study them to see which one would be most effective for you.

### The Autocratic Style

The autocratic style (also called authoritarian or dictatorial) stresses the use of the leader's authority and is task-oriented. An autocratic leader tells subordinates what to do and uses organizational and position authority and economic rewards to get them to perform. This style may be useful in situations where quick decisions and actions are needed, or where employees are relatively untrained, unskilled, and unmotivated. Its disadvantages are its emphasis on orders and discipline and its disregard for subordinates' ideas. It *can* be effective, however. One of the most frequently quoted comments of Vince Lombardi's players is "He treated us all the same—like dogs." Yet Lombardi was one of the winningest coaches in professional football, and his players look back on his leadership style with respect and admiration.

### The Bureaucratic Style

The bureaucratic style is guided by rules, regulations, and procedures from which there is little or no deviation. A bureaucratic leader operates by the book, doing exactly what higher authorities require. The term has fallen into disrepute because of some negative and arbitrary actions of some government bureaucrats. Yet the bureaucratic style can be used effectively to bring order and stability to a situation.

### The Democratic Style

The democratic, or participative, style is people-oriented and stresses employee participation in goal setting and decision making. A democratic leader uses the authority given by the group and encourages a free flow of communication within the group. One advantage of this style is that subordinates require little supervision because of their willingness to perform their assignments. Some disadvantages are slower decision making and limited control.

### The Free-Rein Style

Under the free-rein style (also called laissez-faire), the leader sets performance standards and then leaves people alone to do their work. The leader's role is that of an advisor, motivator, or cheerleader. One difficulty with this style is that the goals of group members must be the same as the organization's. Also, everyone must know what the goals are and actively seek to attain them. This style is commonly used in organizations emphasizing creativity, such as small advertising agencies, research laboratories, and university faculties.

Considering your own traits and characteristics, with which style would you be most comfortable as a manager? As a subordinate?

---

fied. The Business Debate above gives you a chance to evaluate the effectiveness of each from your own point of view.

None of the styles is always effective, for leadership varies with the people and situations involved. Instead, the appropriate answer to the question

"Which leadership style is best?" is "It all depends." The characteristics of the leader, the followers, and the situation all affect which leadership style will be best. When a problem situation requires immediate attention, the leader may have to handle it without consulting subordinates. When there is less time pressure, a manager may use participative decision making. And when appropriate, the democratic style of leadership is preferred. It enhances employees' job satisfaction, since human relationships are considered as well as output.

## Controlling

As shown in Figure 6-5, the controlling function feeds directly back into the planning function. How does this work? First, the planning phase sets standards of performance. The management team then organizes and sets into action resources, a staff, and leadership techniques for meeting those stand-

**Figure 6-5** Control feedback loop.

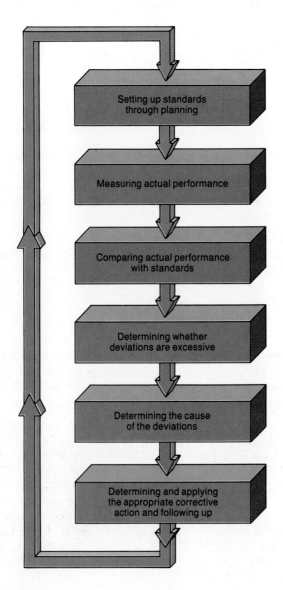

Setting up standards through planning

Measuring actual performance

Comparing actual performance with standards

Determining whether deviations are excessive

Determining the cause of the deviations

Determining and applying the appropriate corrective action and following up

ards. **Controlling**—usually performed by middle managers—involves following up on planned performance by measuring and correcting it to ensure that the company's objectives and plans have been achieved. Has the organization done what it set out to do in the first place?

The control process usually consists of at least six steps, as shown in Figure 6-5:

1. Setting up standards of performance during the planning phase.
2. Measuring actual performance, to the extent possible.
3. Comparing actual performance with the planned performance standards.
4. Determining whether deviations between actual and planned performance are excessive.
5. Determining the cause of the deviations.
6. Determining and applying the appropriate corrective action to bring planned and actual performance into balance.

Because the whole process is basically a big feedback loop, a final step must often be taken. After the results of corrective action have been checked, it may be necessary to go back to square one and replan, reorganize, restaff, and so on. This is essentially what happens in high-growth technological companies like Computervision or DEC, where major reorganizations seem as frequent as quarterly reports.

## BASIC SKILLS REQUIRED OF MANAGERS

**Objective 5**

The conceptual, human relations, technical, and administrative skills that managers need.

 A manager might be able to perform all five functions perfectly well and still not be an effective manager. The other needed ingredients are certain basic, but difficult to measure, skills. The most useful are conceptual, human relations, technical, and administrative skills.[4]

### Conceptual Skills

In order to see the big picture, managers need to know quite intimately the internal and external environments in which they operate. They also need to understand the ripple effects of changes in any part of the environment on their own business. Top managers, in particular, need strong conceptual skills. **Conceptual skills** involve one's mental ability to sift, analyze, and draw conclusions from information received from any number of sources, without becoming immersed in irrelevant details. For example, Norman Grossman, a brilliant technical man and chief engineer for Fairchild Republic, said his greatest mistake with the company was getting "too involved with details." After retiring as chairman, he said that he had become so involved solving the technical problems of the A10 Thunderbolt II attack plane for the U.S. Air Force that he didn't watch market changes. He missed the Air Force's need for a lightweight fighter. Fairchild got the $1 billion A10 contract but lost the $25 billion F16 contract to General Dynamics.[5]

### Human Relations Skills

It goes without saying that a manager who doesn't get along with anyone won't be a manager for long. **Human relations skills** consist of the ability to understand other people and to interact effectively with them. They include the ability to communicate clearly with, motivate, and lead others so that their work is done effectively. These skills are most necessary when one is performing the leading function.

### Technical Skills

Technical skills are needed to supervise the specific, detailed activities of the business. **Technical skills** include the ability to understand and perform effectively the processes, practices, procedures, or techniques appropriate to the industry, the company, and the job. Some examples are the ability to program a computer; operate a lathe, typewriter, or printing press; and prepare financial statements.

These skills are relatively more important for first-line supervisors than for top managers, because supervisors are closer to the actual work being done. They often have to show employees how to do the job and must know whether it is being done properly. Yet even top managers should have some of the technical skills appropriate to the activities they direct. Among the technical skills needed by the owner or manager of a clothing store would be the ability to select appropriate clothing styles, fabrics, and details. This skill could be acquired through experience as a buyer of such clothing.

On the other hand, technical skill can be a handicap if a manager remains too close to the work. One error commonly made in selecting managers is to promote an efficient operating employee to a supervisory position simply because he or she is highly skilled and has been able to perform technical jobs well. The assumption is that he or she has all that's required to supervise others doing these jobs. But a good producer isn't necessarily a good supervisor or executive. Technical expertise may keep managers from delegating well or seeing better ways to do the job.

### Administrative Skills

**Administrative skills** include the ability to establish and follow procedures, process paperwork in an orderly way, and manage expenditures in a budget. *Coordination, order,* and *movement* are terms that explain what these administrative skills are, for they invoke maintaining order. Although administrative skills are less important than the others, they require the use of all the skills discussed so far.

The relative importance of all these skills to specific managers varies according to the type of industry they're in, the organization to which they belong, their managerial level, the job being performed, and the employees being managed. Figure 6-6 shows how the need for these skills varies according to managerial level. Notice that lower-level managers use technical skills more than other managers. *All* managers require considerable human relations skills, however. At Ford Motor Company, many executives spend time working on the factory floor to better understand worker problems.[6]

Upper management.

Middle management.

First-line management.

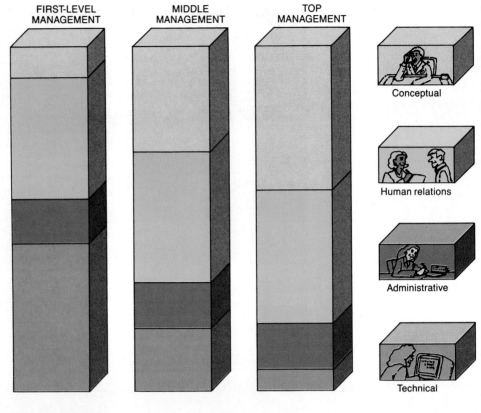

| FIRST-LEVEL MANAGEMENT | MIDDLE MANAGEMENT | TOP MANAGEMENT |

Conceptual

Human relations

Administrative

Technical

**Figure 6-6** The relative importance of managerial skills at different managerial levels. (Based on *The Nature of Managerial Work*, by Henry Mintzberg. Copyright © 1973 by Henry Mintzberg. Used by permission of Harper & Row Publishers, Inc.)

## DECISION MAKING

**Objective 6**

The nature of managerial decision making.

**Decision making** is the conscious selection of an effective course of action from among two or more available alternatives in order to reach an objective. If managers are anything, they're decision makers; the use of personal judgment to make decisions is the primary difference between managers and nonmanagers. Decision making isn't easy and can't be learned easily. It takes knowledge, effort, time, and experience. One of the greatest problems in business is managers who just can't make a decision.[7] In fact, a poor decision is often better than none at all. A manager's failure to decide confuses employees and marks the manager as weak, vague, uncertain, and indecisive—undesirable qualities in a leader, to say the least. Finally, decisions need to be timely—not made too quickly or too late. Knowing when to make a decision is almost as important as making the right one. Thomas A. Murphy, the chairman of General Motors, said that when there are differences of opinion and people are reluctant to move, someone has to say, "All right, this is what we're going to do."[8]

### Steps in Decision Making

Most managerial decisions involve certain well-defined steps. Those steps are

1. Recognizing that there's a problem to solve or an opportunity to seize,
2. Developing alternative courses of action,

3. Evaluating the advantages and disadvantages of each alternative,
4. Selecting the best alternative,
5. Implementing the decision, and
6. Following up to see that the decision was effective.

Figure 6-7 sums up how effective managers systematically follow these steps to solve a problem or make a decision. Each step involves gathering, interpreting, and evaluating information.

### How to Improve Decision Making

There are a few simple steps managers can take to improve their decision-making abilities. You may find these useful the next time you have to choose among different alternatives.

1. Effective decision making requires considerable time and effort. Be willing to invest both in important decisions—but without taking a year to come up with an answer.
2. Decision making requires mental effort. Be careful not to make a choice just to get it over with because you are fatigued.
3. Rarely is the first option the only or even the best choice. Similarly, decisions made alone are rarely as sound as those made by a group. Be patient, solicit other points of view, brainstorm, and list as many options as you can.

"My answer is 'maybe' . . . and that's final."

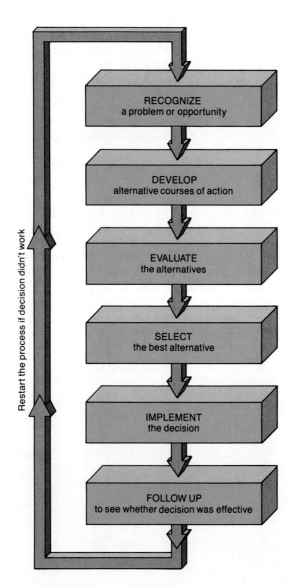

**Figure 6-7** Steps in decision making.

4. A decision tends to cause chain reactions as different people realize how they'll be affected by the decision. Be prepared not to please everyone, and brace yourself to respond to negative reactions from those who feel they'll be hurt.
5. Decisions aren't always carried out like clockwork. Set up a follow-up, or feedback, system.
6. Since practice makes perfect, you'll tend to improve as you make more and harder decisions.
7. Situations are never exactly the same, and neither are decisions. Modify your thinking according to changed circumstances.

The experience of two large retail chain stores are a classic example of the need to modify decision making with changing circumstances. Both Sears, Roebuck and Montgomery Ward, then about the same size, had government contracts that left them with large amounts of capital at the end of World War II. Up to that time, a depression had followed every major war, since demand for goods and employees decreased while returning veterans increased the supply of workers.

Sewell Avery, chief executive officer of Montgomery Ward, knew this sequence of events from experience and decided to conserve the organization's financial resources until the inevitable depression came. Then he could use them to build new stores and plants at a lower cost. The head of Sears, General Robert E. Wood (builder of the Panama Canal), knew the facts from experience, too. But he also realized that the G.I. Bill passed during the war would reduce the supply of workers by providing opportunities for millions of returning veterans to continue their education. Also, the funds available for loans to build or buy homes and to enter business would increase demand for goods and workers. Therefore, the chances of a depression were reduced, so Sears started building new stores and manufacturing plants in order to meet the increased demand.

The expected depression didn't materialize. In fact, the first real recession didn't come until four years after the war. Thanks to its flexibility, Sears gained in sales and profits at Ward's expense.

## ⏚ LEARNING OBJECTIVES REVISITED

1. *What management is.*

   There is a need for management whenever and wherever people are organized to work together toward a common goal. Management achieves a company's objectives through gathering, developing, and using scarce physical, financial, and human resources in an efficient and effective way. *Management* can refer to an individual, an occupational group, a discipline of study, or the process itself.

2. *The role of each of the three levels of management: top, middle, and supervisory.*

   There are three levels of management in large firms. Top, or administrative, management is responsible for the total organization. Middle, or intermediate, management is responsible for a lower-level division or department. And supervisory, or first-line, management controls smaller units or groups.

3. *Each of the basic managerial functions: planning, organizing, staffing, leading, and controlling.*

Planning, organizing, staffing, leading, and controlling are the five basic managerial functions. Planning is selecting, and deciding how to achieve, future courses of action for the firm as a whole and for each of its subunits. Organizing is dividing tasks among work groups and assigning each group to a manager who has the needed authority and responsibility. Staffing is the process of recruiting, selecting, training, and developing people to fill the jobs created through organizing. Leading is guiding, supervising, and motivating employees' performance. Controlling follows up on planned performance by measuring and correcting it as necessary.

4. *The role of organizational mission and objectives in strategic planning.*

Strategic planning involves identifying the long-range mission of an organization and determining objectives and appropriate strategies for achieving it.

5. *The conceptual, human relations, technical, and administrative skills that managers need.*

To perform the basic managerial functions effectively, managers need to use conceptual, human relations, technical, and administrative skills. Conceptual skills help a manager to understand the relationships between the parts of the firm and the whole system. Human relations skills involve understanding other people and interacting effectively with them. Technical skills consist of specialized knowledge and practices related to the industry, the company, and the job. Administrative skills provide for the orderly performance of the firm's activities.

6. *The nature of managerial decision making.*

Managers are decision makers who must select an effective course of action from two or more available alternatives in order to reach an objective.

## ▲ IMPORTANT TERMS

As an extra review of the chapter, try defining the following terms. If you have trouble with any of them, refer to the page listed.

## ◢ REVIEW QUESTIONS

1. Who needs management? Why is management needed in organizations?
2. Describe the three levels of management found in large organizations.
3. What needs to be taken into consideration when formulating an organization's mission?
4. In what areas of business should objectives be set, and how are they set?
5. What is meant by the statement "Objectives should be realistic"?
6. Often, phrases like *flying by the seat of your pants, expediency management, crisis management, day-by-day management,* and *fire fighting* are applied to the management of a firm. How do these relate to the performance of the planning function?
7. What are the three basic factors involved in the leadership process, and how are they related?
8. Describe the stages in the control feedback loop.
9. Describe how each level of management spends its time on the management functions.
10. What are the basic management skills?
11. What are the steps in the decision-making process?

## ◢ DISCUSSION QUESTIONS

1. Assume that you're the president of a club. How would you use the basic managerial functions while serving in that capacity?
2. Which levels of management could be safely left out of an organization? How would it function without them?
3. Do you know the objectives of your school? If so, what are they? How do you help the school achieve its objectives?
4. What is meant by the claim "Managers can delegate authority, but not responsibility?"
5. Are all of the five management functions really needed? Why or why not?
6. Under what circumstances would each of the four most popular leadership styles be used? Why?
7. Describe the steps in the decision-making process. Are all of the steps needed? Why or why not?
8. Specifically, how could a manager improve his or her decision-making ability? What aspects of your decision-making ability need improvement?

## ◢ CASE 6-1   Texas Instruments, Inc.

Texas Instruments, Inc. (TI) is known as one of the leading technological innovators in the country. Its developments in the industrial, commercial, and government markets made it quite profitable and established its reputation as a leader rather than a follower. Its semiconductor parts and government electronics business is still doing well. Yet there are some managerial flaws in the com-

pany. Its top managers, including the president and chairman, are primarily engineers and scientists with design, engineering, and operations skills; they are weak in consumer marketing skills. There is little fuel for the consumer markets. This was exhibited in early 1983 when Fred Bucy, the president, told stockholders at their annual meeting that, because of mismanagement, the firm hadn't produced the "right products" for the "right market" at the "right time." The result was a $100 million loss during the second quarter, with a resulting drop of nearly a third in the price of TI's stock. The losses were caused primarily by losses in TI's consumer electronics business, especially the TI 99/4A home computer. TI blamed the loss on a growing industry-wide inventory glut of low-priced computers. But others blamed it on TI's inept management in the consumer products division.

Earlier, TI had gone out of the digital watch business after helping to lower the price to around $10. History seemed to be repeating itself with the TI 99/4A. The 99/4A was one of the first truly low-cost home computers. Yet, in 1982, when competitors, especially Commodore International's VIC 20, began clobbering TI's computer, TI lowered the price from $250 to $150. This attracted customers who tended to use it primarily as a high-priced video game, which requires little of the more profitable supplemental equipment. This price reduction helped create a mass market for large retailers, such as K mart and Sears. Instead of developing a newer, lower-cost product, TI lowered the price to under $100 and flooded the market, hoping to make a profit on the sale of software. The price was below the cost of production, and the demand for the computer just wasn't there. And the money-making software business also dried up in mid-1983. Ironically, many customers feel that the 99/4A was the top of the line among cheap computers, but was incorrectly marketed as an expensive game.

From 1981 to mid-1983, TI reduced its payroll from 90,000 to 80,000. A large proportion of those laid off were white-collar workers. Then, TI announced it was going out of the home computer business and would concentrate on business computers.

### Case Questions

1. What do you think Texas Instrument's management's skills had to do with the mistakes it made?
2. What could have been done to prevent the losses?
3. Should TI have continued in the consumer electronics business? Explain your answer.
4. What could have been done to improve its competitive position?

### ⏚ CASE 6-2  Sears' Changing Strategy

Sears, Roebuck and Co. started out with a strategy of selling products of medium quality at a low price to the mass market, especially to those in rural areas, far from big-city department and specialty stores. During the late 1960s and early 1970s, with a change in top management, the strategy was changed. Sears began to upgrade its product line by selling high-quality products (such as fine jewelry and furs) at a high price, in an attempt to attract middle- and upper-income customers. Sears became known as one of the largest U.S. diamond and mink merchants. It did attract the more affluent customers, and the higher prices and profit margins led to higher profits—for a while. The company's image as a seller of low-priced, quality products evaporated, however, and it lost a large share of its market to K mart and others. Then the new customers started waiting for Sears' inevitable sales to buy the high-priced merchandise at lower prices—and profits fell. During the 1970s, Sears' share of the market remained the same while those of Penney's, K mart, and others increased.

In the late 1970s, the earlier strategy of selling to middle-class, homeowning families who wanted good value and reliable service was reintroduced. After that, Sears management decisions were built around that strategy—with success. The next move was to upgrade its stores to appeal to the upwardly mobile younger professionals, as well as the other group.

**Case Questions**

1. Why do you think the new management changed Sears' basic—and successful—strategy?
2. Why do you think the second strategy failed?
3. Do you think the third strategy will succeed? Why or why not?

# 7

# Organizing a Business

*The only things that evolve by themselves in an organization are disorder, friction, and malperformance.*

Peter Drucker

*Take away all our factories, our trade, our avenues of transportation, our money, but leave me our organization, and in four years, I will have reestablished myself.*

Andrew Carnegie

## Learning Objectives

After studying the material in this chapter, you will understand:

1. How the management function of organizing results in an organization.
2. The distinction between formal and informal organizations.
3. The steps involved in the organizing process.
4. The major means of departmentation.
5. How delegation of authority works.
6. The differences among line authority, staff authority, and functional authority.
7. The difference between centralization and decentralization of authority.
8. The concept of span of management.

## In This Chapter

What Is an Organization?
Formal and Informal Organizations
The Organizing Process
Departmentation
Delegating Authority
Span of Management

# THE LOS ANGELES DODGERS
*A Super Organization*

The Los Angeles Dodgers baseball team is one of the best and most profitable franchises in professional sports. Of course, some of the reasons for its enviable position are winning teams (the Dodgers won more games than they lost for twenty-one out of twenty-five seasons in Los Angeles), nonstop sunny weather, and a market area of over 10 million people to draw on for fans. But none of these would count for much without the organizing abilities of the owners, Walter O'Malley and his son Peter, who follow sound management principles. According to former baseball commissioner Bowie Kuhn, "They're just good businessmen. They could make money on widgets."

The O'Malleys run the team using fundamental organizational principles. First, they pour all their business energies into operating the team and don't have outside interests to distract them, as some other owners do (see the profile of Ted Turner in Chapter 1). They're usually among the first to arrive at the stadium every day.

Second, they have a top-down, integrated system. They own their own stadium and have a maintenance crew keeping it spotless year round. So there are no conflicts in scheduling, and the natural turf isn't damaged by teams from other sports. They also promote each game as if it were a special event, have plenty of parking space, and keep ticket prices low.

Third, they try to keep stable, loyal personnel by taking care of them with generous salaries and benefits, including a profit-sharing plan. Loyalty is rewarded; disloyalty is punished. Former manager Walt Alston operated for twenty-three years under a one-year contract; the vice-president of personnel has been with the team forty-three years; and the present manager, ebullient Tommy Lasorda, has been player, scout, coach, and manager for thirty-four years. On the other hand, one manager who had the nerve to demand a two-year contract was fired, and a player who sang in a night club after begging off from an exhibition tour was traded—in both cases the O'Malleys were reacting to disloyalty to the team. For loyal team members, though, the organization is one big, supportive family. The team has its own private jet, which is very convenient for the players and managers, as it lets them be home more.

Fourth, the organization is departmentalized for the most efficient possible operation. For example, while most teams have only one publicity manager, the Dodgers have separate managers for ticket sales, marketing, and concession sales, and the owners keep hands off the operations of the departments to which they've delegated authority.

Finally, operations are standardized and applied to both the main team and its minor league farm teams. The 1954 book *The Dodger Way to Play Baseball,* which tells how every player at every level should play his position, ensures standardized operations in all the Dodgers' teams. Last, but not least, the team has developed top-notch players through training and promotion from within.

167

There's no question that the O'Malleys exercise all of the management functions we've talked about: planning, organizing, staffing, directing, and controlling. But the real key to their success lies in one particular function: organizing. Professional sports teams need that function as much as the hierarchy of a conglomerate or the staff of a McDonald's restaurant. We've talked about *organizing* as dividing tasks among work groups and assigning each group to a manager who has the authority and responsibility needed to get the job done. The Dodgers' organization puts ultimate authority in the owners, who are responsible for nearly everything—from maintenance to souvenirs. At the same time, the Dodgers are departmentalized because the O'Malleys can't do everything. So they delegate tasks like coaching and sales to other managers. And the Dodgers' organization is so clear that everyone understands and follows the basic ground rules of quality and loyalty.

You know from Chapter 6 what the organizing function, authority, responsibility, and delegation are. When you put them all together, what do you get? An organization. This offspring of organizing activities takes the form of an overall structure or established set of relationships that is much more than the sum of its parts.

## WHAT IS AN ORGANIZATION

**Objective 1**

How the management function of organizing results in an organization.

An **organization** is basically a group of people striving together to achieve a common goal and bound together by a set of understood authority-responsibility relationships. Some important conclusions that can be drawn from this definition are that:

1. Organizations are made up of people. Machines, furniture, equipment, and other nonhuman elements are important, but they're useless without the human element. For instance, Hewlett-Packard Company is a leader in the high-tech electronics field. Yet its emphasis is on its people. It was a leader in introducing flexible work schedules and other innovative personnel policies. Employees share in the profits and they have job security: when semiconductor sales slumped in 1970, everyone in the company took a 10 percent pay cut, but no one was laid off. The company's philosophy that business should have meaning as well as make money has paid off in high productivity and top-quality products.[1]
2. Organizations result from attempts to reach common goals, objectives, programs, and plans. Businesses, hospitals, schools, governments, and other organizations do now what individuals or families did a century ago. They help us reach our objectives.[2]
3. Organizations are part of their cultural, political, social, economic, and technological environment. They must be dynamic and adapt to those surroundings if they're going to survive and fulfill their mission. For example, Bausch & Lomb, Inc. had roughly 90 percent of the soft contact lens market in the 1970s. But success blinded management to the fact that extended-wear soft lenses were the wave of the future. By 1982, the company's share of the contact lens market had fallen to about 55 percent. CooperVision, Inc. and Continuous Curve

Organizations are based on the principles of cooperation and coordination.

Contact Lenses, Inc. (a Revlon, Inc. subsidiary) now dominate the $50 million to $60 million extended-wear market.[3]

4. Organizations must have order, discipline, and control if they're to succeed. Therefore, delegation of authority and placement of responsibility must be well defined. An example of a well-organized business is Tandem Computer, Inc., which grew by 4,000 percent from 1976 to 1979. According to one of its founders, "We assume people are adults. We give them a lot of responsibility and tell them where we want them to go. The 1 percent who abuse the freedom, we fire. It's that simple."[4]

Since people are social creatures, they live, work, and play together. They learn to organize and to depend on groups that will get more done than any one of them could alone. Once organized into a group, though, people must specialize if the group is to function well. The principle of **specialization,** or **division of labor,** states that the most efficient way to do something is for each person to do only what he or she does best instead of doing everything. It's the basis of any organization.

There are benefits and disadvantages of using division of labor. Some of the more important benefits are that (1) less skill is required of workers, (2) employees can specialize in the part of the work they can do best, (3) it's easier to train workers to do their part if it's kept simple, and (4) time is saved. Division of labor does have its negative side, though. It tends to cause monotony, boredom, loss of motivation, and downright frustration when carried too far. Also, as specialization increases, so does the need for coordination to see

that each person's work fits with that of other employees. A more specialized company isn't necessarily more productive. Therefore, managers must make certain that individual interests, efforts, timing, and work methods mesh if the group's objectives are to be reached.

## FORMAL AND INFORMAL ORGANIZATIONS

**Objective 2**

**The distinction between formal and informal organizations.**

As we've seen, people form organizations to achieve goals that they can't reach alone. Yet the groups they join differ greatly. Some are quite formal, while others within the same organization may be very informal.

### Formal Organizations

**Formal organizations** are the sum of clearly defined relationships, channels of communication, and responsibilities resulting from the delegation of authority from one organizational level to another. When you read an organization chart, what you're really seeing is a graphic representation of a formal organization. The formal organization tends to:

1. Have a clearly defined structure of authority-responsibility relationships.
2. Have well-established formal communication systems, detailing who keeps whom informed, who approves whose actions, and so on.
3. Be relatively stable and permanent, at least until there's a formal reorganization.
4. Expand in size and become more complex.

The clearly defined structure of formal organizations is useful for both managers and nonmanagers. The roles of employees are usually explained in job descriptions that state the duties involved, job titles, responsibilities, and to whom people report.

Formal communication systems—downward, upward, and horizontal—are found in all formal organizations. Downward communications are illustrated by orders, requests for information from the ranks, and explanations of management decisions. Examples of upward communication are status reports, policy questions, warnings about potential problems, and complaints. A statement of procedures and methods of doing work is an example of horizontal communication.

To see how a formal organization works, let's look at an example. Jay is a senior systems analyst in the data processing department of a chemical firm near Baton Rouge, Louisiana. His duties are to supervise the work of nine junior analysts in the department and to work on complex systems assignments when called upon. His supervisor is Nancy Baker, the department manager, to whom he's accountable. While she's almost always available to Jay and his fellow managers, she also holds a staff meeting with them every Monday morning. At that time, subordinate managers receive formal job assignments, and Nancy makes formal plans. The managers also give her written reports concerning plans, progress, and new programs.

## Tools of Formal Organizations

Some of the tools that are used to build and maintain formal organizations are organization charts, policy manuals, and organization manuals.

**Organization charts** show graphically the authority-responsibility relationships among members of a formal organization. These charts let employees see how their work relates to that of other people in the company and where they stand in the hierarchy. The overall shape of most organization charts is a pyramid. The base is wide because most organization members are at the lowest organizational levels. The higher the level on the organization chart, the fewer people there are at that level, so that at the top of the pyramid there's only one person: the chief executive officer.

When you dig deeper into an organization chart, it begins to take on more meaning. In Figure 7-1, for instance, the lines connecting the individual boxes represent lines of authority and responsibility at International Harvester. They tell you that the manager of the manufacturing group reports to the president and chief operating officer, who reports to the chairman and chief executive officer. Reading in reverse, you can see who has authority over whom. The chairman has authority over the president, who has authority over the managers of the manufacturing, equipment, and truck groups. The manager of manufacturing, though, has no authority over equipment and trucks.

**Figure 7-1** Simplified organization chart for International Harvester.

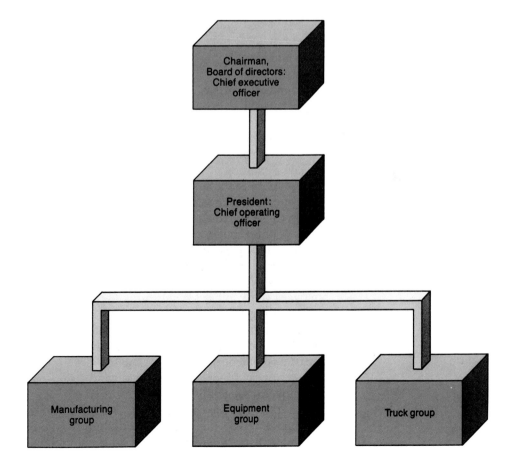

Chairman,
Board of directors:
Chief executive
officer

President:
Chief operating
officer

Manufacturing
group

Equipment
group

Truck group

Organization manuals and policy manuals also show organizational relationships, but in written rather than chart form. They're often put together in loose-leaf binders that are distributed to all operating units. The advantages of manuals are fewer misunderstandings, less working at cross-purposes, and improved morale. **Organization manuals** give descriptions of formal authority-responsibility relationships, the functions of operating units, and job procedures. **Policy manuals** explain basic personnel activities and company policies on working hours, absences, and so on.

## Informal Organizations

**Informal organizations** are spontaneous natural groups of employees who share channels of communication and personal relationships not shown in any formal organization chart or manual. Informal organizations or groups begin because people in structured, formal groups also need and develop looser, personal interactions.

> In the Profile on page 173, how did Sandy McDonnell use the informal organization to advantage when he was made CEO of McDonnell Douglas?

Informal groups also serve as communication systems, often more effectively than formal ones. These groups also tend to set and enforce work standards and norms of behavior. If a member violates the group's unwritten standards, he or she is punished by being ignored by the other work group members or even banished from the group. This type of system can put such pressure on workers that it can even hurt the employer's interests.

Two familiar examples of informal organizations in business are the grapevine and informal leaders. The **grapevine** is the communication system used by the informal organization to relay news outside and around formal communication channels. It may encourage rumors and incorrect information but it's often pretty accurate. **Informal leaders** are workers with no formal authority who nevertheless have great influence because their fellow workers respect them and look to them for leadership. Effective managers try to get the support of informal leaders because they can be very helpful in running a unit. And their opposition can ruin a manager's effectiveness with the work group. Jackie Johnson, a supervisor in a government office, had three informal leaders. One was effective in solving difficult work programs, and her fellow employees went to her for solutions to these problems. Another leader was good at handling personal problems, and he became the group's sounding board. The third person was the primary informal leader, who served as the group's spokesperson. Jackie wisely took advantage of the abilities of each of them without considering any a threat.

The effective use of formal authority depends heavily on its acceptance by employees, especially those in informal groups. Therefore, effective managers don't try to oppose these groups. They can't be destroyed, and if a boss tries to suppress an informal group, it will simply go underground. It isn't a question of choosing between formal and informal groups but of how managers can best

## *Profile*

### Sandy McDonnell: The Hands-On Leader

In 1948, twenty-six-year-old Sanford N. (Sandy) McDonnell tried to get a job with his uncle, who had founded the McDonnell Aircraft Corporation in 1939. He was offered a job as a floor sweeper, at the lowest wage rate. Sandy refused, since he thought a record that included a B.A. in economics from Princeton and a B.S. in mechanical engineering from the University of Colorado was worth somewhat more. After much haggling, they settled on $1.26 an hour, and Sandy's brilliant career was begun. He had to prove himself at each level—from a trainee in a company-wide program on up—before moving on to the next. But by 1972 he was elected chief executive officer of McDonnell Douglas Corporation (formed in 1967 when McDonnell, specializing in military equipment, merged with Douglas Aircraft company, a leader in commercial aircraft). In 1980, he also was named chairman.

Shortly after becoming CEO, McDonnell attended a monthly dinner meeting of the company's management club. He was led into a private room where the top managers were gathered. But he went on to mix with the hundreds of supervisors and middle managers in the main dining area, calling many of them by their first names. The episode was a perfect example of McDonnell's hands-on leadership approach and his emphasis on the informal organization. No shouting, overbearing, table-pounding tyrant, he believes a good executive can be firm and tough yet still be personable.

He views himself as someone putting together the best possible team of people and bringing out their potential to achieve common goals. His approach includes short, stand-up meetings as a basis for communication among different parts of the company. He not only believes in, but practices, delegation and decentralization. These qualities are essential in a firm that produces four main types of products: commercial aircraft, military aircraft, spacecraft, and computer products and services.

Sources: Correspondence with McDonnell Douglas and published sources, especially Karol White, "Profile: Sanford N. McDonnell, Chairman of the Board & CEO, McDonnell Douglas Corporation," *Sky*, March 1982, pp. 27–30; Milton Moskowitz, Michael Katz, and Robert Levering, eds., *Everybody's Business: An Almanac* (New York: Harper & Row, 1980), pp. 691–95; and Harlan S. Byrne, "Steady Climb: New Chairman Passes Early Tests with Ease at McDonnell Douglas," *Wall Street Journal*, August 25, 1983, pp. 1, 8.

work with and use both of them. Firms in California's Silicon Valley, such as Hewlett-Packard, Tandem, Advanced Micro Devices (AMD), and Signetics Corporation, wage constant war on bureaucracy and rigid organizational structure. They emphasize informal groups, with their instant communication, as the basis for quick decisions and action.[5]

Still, informal groups can damage an organization, as shown in FYI on page 176.

> How did the formal structuring of duties in FYI on page 176 lead to informal groups?

## THE ORGANIZING PROCESS

**Objective 3**

**The steps involved in the organizing process.**

The process of setting up formal organizations is relatively simple—at least in theory. Consider, for example, the true case of a group of students at a year-end picnic on the Mississippi River levee. Naturally enough, given the location, the conversation turned to the joys of floating down the river to New Orleans on a raft. The first step was taken when someone said, "Let's do it!"

After talking for a while about what they would need for the trip, they put Pam in charge of planning and carrying out the arrangements. She said, "Mike, you and some of the others can list the materials we need to build the raft, collect money, buy the stuff, and build the raft. Mary, you and Paul collect some more money and stock up on food, drinks, and other supplies. Joe, you and Shirley get the charts, maps, and radio equipment we'll need. I'll check with the authorities to see if we need permits."

They all did what they were supposed to and—with some mistakes and false starts—actually got to New Orleans.

### Steps in Organizing

The steps involved in organizing a simple activity like a trip down the Mississippi are found in a similar order in any organizing process. They are:

1. Set (or know) the group's objectives (getting to New Orleans via raft).
2. Determine the specific activities, duties, or tasks needed to reach the objectives (discussing all that would be needed to make the trip).
3. Divide the work into operating units on the basis of the similarity or importance of the work or the abilities and preferences of the workers (different groups for raft construction, supplies, equipment, and permits). This step is called the process of **departmentation.**
4. Assign the necessary authority to the managers who are to be held responsible for each of the units (Pam, Mike, Mary and Paul, and Joe and Shirley). This step is the delegation process.
5. Provide the needed financial and physical resources for each unit (in this case, hat passing and elbow grease).
6. Select qualified employees, or at least those who can be developed, for each unit (collecting group members for raft building).

## The Process Applied to Business

The process operates quite effectively in most situations. However, it has to have many practical modifications, especially in a new and growing small business. As shown in Figure 7-2, people starting new businesses may at first do all the work and other activities themselves (Stage 1). There's only one organizational level, and there are no real lines of authority or responsibility. Then, as the firm grows, the owner hires employees to help, thereby introducing the authority-responsibility problem (Stage 2). With additional growth, the owner obtains a manager or managers to whom day-to-day duties and responsibilities are assigned (Stage 3). Finally, the business reaches a point

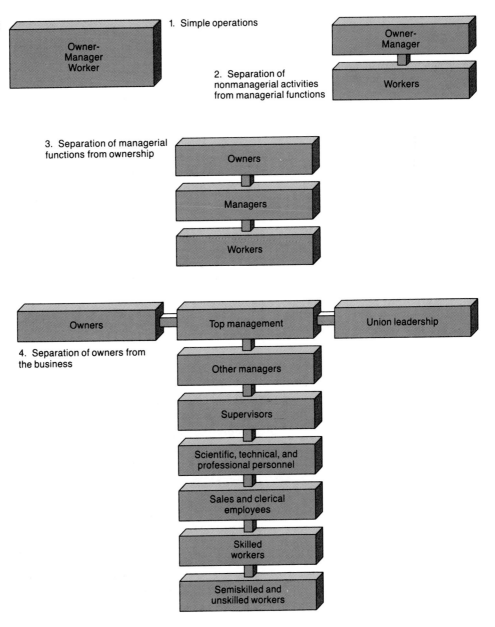

**Figure 7-2** Stages in the growth of a business.

## *FYI*

## The Partners: Informal Groups in Action

Joclaire Wilson,* an MBA student at the Harvard Business School, and Warren Brown, a computer science major at the Massachusetts Institute of Technology, were high-school friends. While attending college, they had dinner together, with their spouses, every weekend. Their favorite topic of conversation was going into business for themselves when they graduated.

In the meantime, they began looking into the possibility of renting computer time to sell to small businesses to maintain inventories, place purchase orders, and do bookkeeping. At first they operated out of Joclaire's basement. Soon there was so much business that they rented a building, hired sales and service representatives, and set up an office staff. Although there was no organization chart,

Joclaire was responsible for all selling and business activities. She and the sales and office personnel had a well-developed social system, with frequent dinners and parties. Warren, the computer science major, handled the technical and service activities with the help of several employees, who had a separate social system of their own.

Soon the partners were quarreling over who had authority for what activities. They began choosing sides with their employees, dropped the weekly family dinners, and almost stopped communicating with each other. The partnership was ultimately dissolved, and each of the partners formed a new corporation.

---

*All names have been changed.

where there are many levels of management and complex authority-responsibility relationships (Stage 4).

Although each of the six steps in the organizing process is important, only steps 3 (departmentation) and 4 (delegation of authority) will be discussed further in this chapter.

## DEPARTMENTATION

**Objective 4**

**The major means of departmentation.**

In dividing work and related activities into operating units, there are two main questions to ask: What activities, duties, and tasks are needed to reach the organization's objectives? and How will the activities be put together into workable groups?

There are many ways of dividing work into operating units. Most companies provide customers with products or services, so the business functions of *production* (or manufacturing, or operations) and *marketing* (or distribution)

are required. These activities require capital, so the *financing* function must also be performed. These three basic functions of production, marketing, and financing become the primary operating bases for dividing most firms into departments or units. For instance, while Chrysler was flirting with bankruptcy from 1979 to 1983, Lee Iacocca, its chairman, was intimately involved in most of management's day-to-day decision making. In mid-1983, he reorganized the firm by setting up a four-person "office of the chairman" so he could devote more time to broad strategic matters. Daily operations were to be divided among Gerald Greenwald—financial matters; Harold Sperlich—manufacturing; and Bennett Bidwell—sales and marketing.[6]

However, additional work divisions are usually needed. For example, the scope of marketing may be so broad that the work will be subdivided into such units as advertising, sales promotion, and selling. In the production area, the work may be subdivided into such units as engineering and research, manufacturing, and purchasing. The growth of a company may result in even more organizational subunits.

The most popular ways of grouping work into manageable units or departments are according to (1) functions, (2) products, (3) territories, and (4) processes. Newer methods are project and matrix departmentation.

### Functional Departmentation

**Functional departmentation** involves putting together in one unit those activities needed to perform the same business function. Functional grouping is frequently used to set up the highest operating units in a hierarchy, such as production, marketing, and finance. This was done by Chrysler in 1983. However, it may also be used at lower levels in the firm. For example, a company with many products may set up departments to produce and sell different products, and each of these divisions may then be organized on a functional basis.

### Product Departmentation

**Product departmentation** involves placing all work activities related to specific product lines in separate operating units. Department stores, for instance, are organized according to different products (housewares, children's clothing, shoes). Automobile manufacturers like Chrysler Corporation have divisions based on car make, such as the Chrysler, Plymouth, and Dodge divisions.

### Territorial Departmentation

**Territorial departmentation** means putting all the activities that take place in a certain geographic location in the same operating unit. Nationwide sales organizations, branch banks, and international operations are commonly organized by territorial grouping. Before its break-up in 1984, AT&T was a classic example of this type of departmentation. It had twenty-two geographic divisions. These are now incorporated into seven independent operating companies, still organized on a territorial basis, as shown in Figure 7-3.

### Process Departmentation

**Process departmentation** means putting together in one unit all activities involving the same operating process. Process grouping is found most frequently

**Figure 7-3** An example of territorial departmentation. (Reproduced with permission of AT&T.)

**Far West**
- Pacific Telephone
- Nevada Bell

**Mountains and Great Plains**
- Northwestern Bell
- Mountain Bell
- Pacific Northwest Bell

**Southwest**
- Southwestern Bell

**Midwest**
- Illinois Bell
- Indiana Bell
- Michigan Bell
- Ohio Bell
- Wisconsin Telephone

**Southeast**
- South Central Bell
- Southern Bell

**Mid-Atlantic**
- Bell of Pennsylvania
- Diamond State Telephone Company
- Chesapeake and Potomac Companies (4)
- New Jersey Bell

**Northeast**
- New England Telephone
- New York Telephone

Donald E. Guinn
Chairman,
Pacific Telephone

Jack A. MacAllister
Chairman,
Northwestern Bell

Zane E. Barnes
President,
Southwestern Bell

William L. Weiss
Chairman,
Illinois Bell

Wallace R. Bunn
Chairman,
South Central Bell

Thomas E. Bolger
Executive
Vice President,
AT&T

Delbert C. Staley
Chairman,
New York
Telephone

**Reorganizing the Bell Operating Companies**
After divestiture, the 22 Bell operating telephone companies will be grouped into seven regional companies, each independent of the others and of AT&T. Shown here are the Bell System officers who have been designated chief executive officers for each of the regional companies and the central services organization which these companies will jointly own.

**Central Services Organization**

Rocco J. Marano
Vice President,
AT&T

in production. Some familiar examples are a manufacturing plant that divides such processes as drilling, grinding, welding, and painting; a word processing center within a larger company; a computer service center; and a university registration procedure in which activities are grouped according to advising, scheduling, and fee payment.

### Project and Matrix Organizations

During the 1960s, when other methods of departmentation fell short of meeting NASA's needs, the project and matrix forms of organization were developed in the aerospace industry. These methods of departmentation are really unique blends of the other methods, modified to meet demands for special skills. Unconventional as they may seem, they do work. Project and matrix organizations designed, built, launched, and returned the space vehicles that put astronauts on the moon in 1969.

In a **project organization,** independent teams from different departments are brought together for a limited time, to complete a specific project. As shown in Figure 7-4(a), the project manager has authority over his or her team members during the life of the project. For example, a manufacturing plant sets up a project to improve its pollution control. A research chemist, a production engineer, a government affairs specialist, a computer analyst, a statistician, and an economist—all from different departments—are temporarily brought together under the project manager responsible for pollution control. During the life of the project, this manager has temporary authority over the employees, although their regular managers continue to have overriding authority and responsibility for paychecks, evaluations, and other routine personnel procedures. When the project is completed, the team is dissolved, the team members return to their original functional departments, and operations return to normal.

In a **matrix organization,** employees simultaneously report to their regular functional manager *and* to a project manager. Unlike project organizations, a matrix set-up is a way of life—not a temporary arrangement lasting only for the life of a project. As shown in Figure 7-4(b), this means always reporting to two bosses at the same time. To avoid the conflicts possible in such a situation, the project manager gives specialized instructions about project-related matters, while the functional manager supervises regular activities and administrative details. Both have equal authority, however.

The matrix organization provides an organizational structure that can respond quickly to changes in technology and the environment. Hence it is found in such technically oriented companies as TRW, General Dynamics, Dow Chemical, General Electric, Texas Instruments, and NASA.

## DELEGATING AUTHORITY

**Objective 5**

**How delegation of authority works.**

Step 4 in the organizing process is delegation of authority—in other words, giving managers the authority they need to run their units effectively. Four questions to ask about delegation are: Why should one delegate? How does one delegate? What type of authority is delegated? and How much authority is delegated?

**Figure 7-4** How project and matrix organizations work. [Part (b) adapted from Figure 8.9 (page 236) from *Management: Concepts and Applications*, by Leon C. Megginson, Donald C. Mosley, and Paul H. Pietri, Jr. Copyright © 1983 by Harper & Row Publishers, Inc. Reprinted by permission of the publisher.]

(a) Project organization

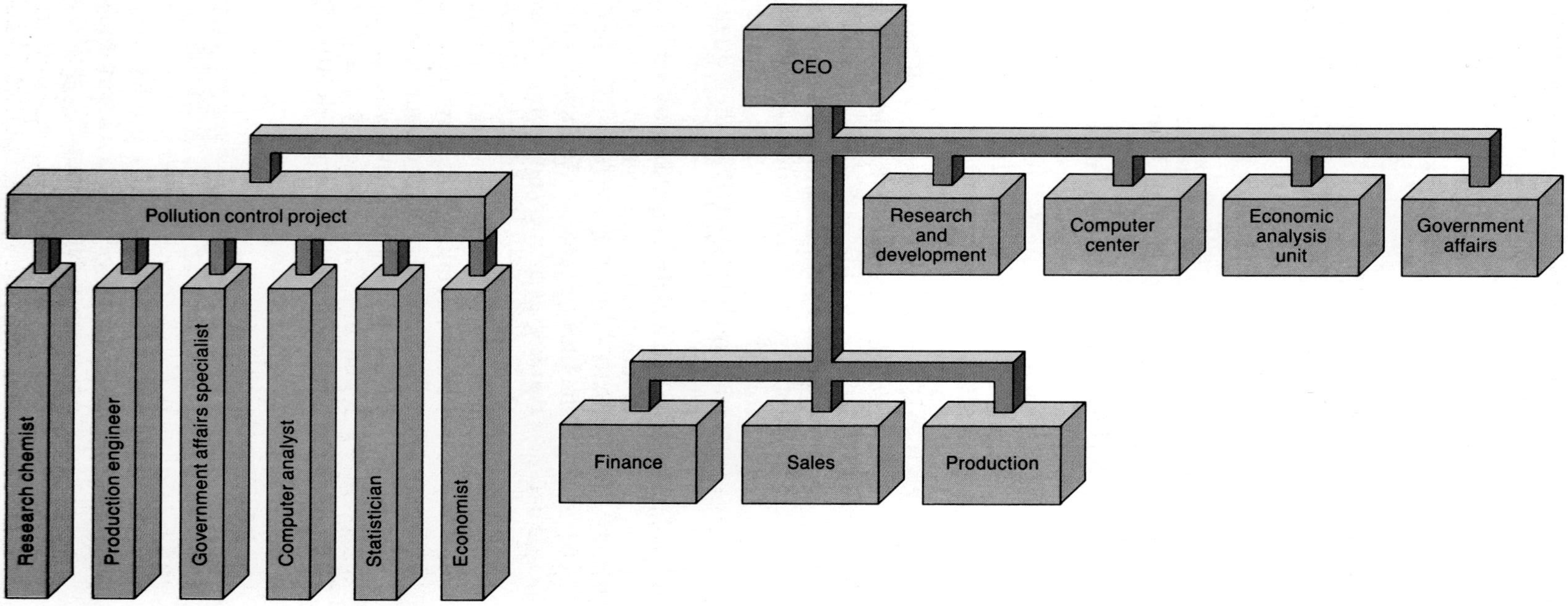

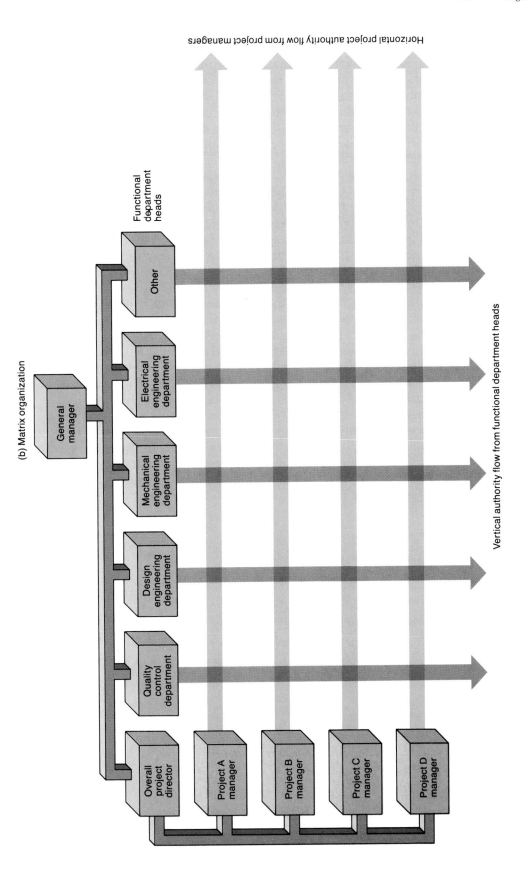

(b) Matrix organization

Horizontal project authority flow from project managers

Functional department heads

General manager

Other

Electrical engineering department

Mechanical engineering department

Design engineering department

Quality control department

Vertical authority flow from functional department heads

Overall project director

Project A manager

Project B manager

Project C manager

Project D manager

## Why Delegate?

Delegation is needed whenever there are two or more people on different levels in a business. It becomes even more necessary when there are two or more levels of managers, as shown in Figure 7-5. The principal reasons for delegation are (1) to relieve managers who are in charge of more work than they can do themselves, (2) to develop subordinates, and (3) to provide qualified back-up people to fill in in case of absences and of changes brought about by promotions, transfers, and resignations.

Delegation is essential in any formal organization. As a business grows, the responsibility and authority needed to manage the total business must be divided and subdivided. Take a look at Figure 7-5, for instance. Assume that you're sitting at the top of the pyramid and are responsible for all the activities performed beneath you. You delegate part of your authority to your top managers, but keep some, like the right to take the authority back and to supervise their activities. The top managers are now responsible to you for how they use their authority. They, in turn, delegate part of their authority to the middle managers, and so on all down the line. (See the Quiz on page 183 for an analysis of how you would delegate if you were an employer.)

Notice, however, that delegation doesn't mean throwing responsibility out the window. Instead, a manager who delegates some authority continues to have overall responsibility, including the authority to take back what has been delegated. That manager is now responsible not only for what he or she does but also for what the people receiving the delegated authority do. Therefore, managers don't delegate by allowing their subordinate managers to run organizational units however they see fit. Instead, superiors delegate specific authority, clearly explaining the rights and responsibilities of the person receiving it. Specific delegation not only keeps subordinate managers fully informed but also informs others who may work with them.

**Figure 7-5** How delegation works.

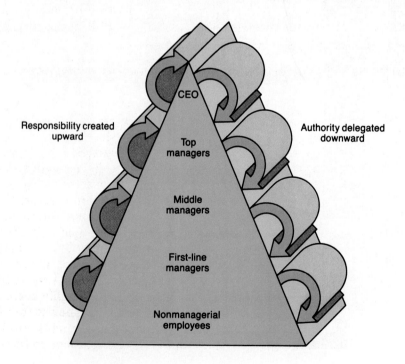

Responsibility created upward

Authority delegated downward

CEO

Top managers

Middle managers

First-line managers

Nonmanagerial employees

# Quiz

## A Delegation Self-Analysis

1. Do my employees and I agree on what results are expected of them?
2. Do my employees and I agree on measures of performance?
3. Does each of my employees feel that he or she has sufficient authority concerning personnel, finances, facilities, and other resources?
4. What additional authority does each of my employees think should be delegated to him or her?
5. What new authority have I delegated within the past six months?
6. Is accountability fixed for the authority I have conferred? Is my follow-up procedure adequate?
7. Am I accessible when an employee needs to see me?
8. Do any of my employees seek me out too frequently for decisions?
9. Do my employees fail to seek or accept additional responsibility?
10. Do I bypass employees by making decisions that are part of their jobs?
11. Do I do things my employees should do? Why?
12. What factors interfere with the effective use of my management time?
13. In what ways could I best improve my delegation? Am I willing to use them?
14. If I were incapacitated for six months, would someone be ready to take my place? Could he or she do it adequately? Why or why not?

All organizations have some problems with delegation, since delegation doesn't come naturally to everyone. In fact, many managers want to hang onto activities that should be delegated to others. If a manager is berated by the boss for work that subordinates have botched, that manager will probably want to do the work personally in the future, to be sure it's done right.

Some managers hate to delegate because holding onto authority makes them feel that the firm can't get along without them. They may also want to run their operations in an autocratic manner. For instance, National Semiconductor Corporation, the third-largest and lowest-cost producer of semiconductors, suffered an exodus of its most talented managers in 1981. Some of those leaving charged that the main problem was the red-tape-ridden organization structure. While Charles Sporck, the "highly autocratic" CEO, could accept decentralized decision making in theory, he had trouble carrying it out in practice.[7] In fact, he'd begun to tighten the reins on his organization. Another problem was the use of fiercely independent profit centers to create competi-

### How to Delegate

In delegating work to subordinates, a manager should try to arrange that *authority is equal to responsibility*. In other words, subordinates should be given enough authority to carry out their responsibilities, or they'll lack the means of performing their duties. This means that they shouldn't have to waste time in unnecessary consultation and cross-checking before they act. However, delegating more authority than subordinates need to fulfill their responsibilities is unwise, since they may use that authority to inappropriately take over someone else's decision-making power. Even firms in Silicon Valley, with their emphasis on informality and creativity, hold their employees—from the "most senior vice-president to the lowliest technician"—strictly responsible for their actions.[8]

Managers also have to remember to follow the organizational principle that *decisions are best made by those closest to the problem*. Lower-level supervisors usually know the situation better than anyone else, especially better than higher-level managers. Procter & Gamble, the gigantic and prosperous consumer packaged-goods conglomerate, has difficulty applying this principle. According to its critics, during the last thirty years it "has become increasingly centralized and bureaucratic . . . [and] too many decisions are being made by those farthest away from the market."[9]

A final caution to managers is to *delegate meaningful work*. It's tempting to have others do the things you prefer not to do yourself, but subordinates will sense this and resent it. It's much harder to allow them to do the things you'd rather do yourself, but this is the only way they can grow.

### What Type of Authority to Delegate

**Objective 6**

The differences among line authority, staff authority, and functional authority.

The next important issue is the type of authority that should be delegated to subordinates. Since managers of different types of operating units need different decision-making powers in order to reach their goals, the delegation of different types and amounts of authority is called for.

As shown in Figure 7-6, the types of authority most often used are line authority, staff authority, and functional authority.

## SALLY FORTH

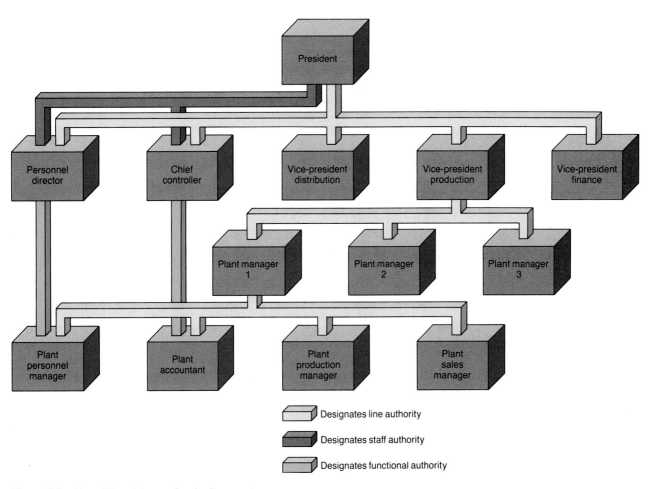

**Figure 7-6**   How different types of authority operate.

▲ **Line Authority**   The simplest of the three types of authority, **line authority** is the manager's right to tell subordinates what to do and then see that they do it.   Line managers are responsible for all the activities within their units. They are doers who accomplish such activities as scheduling work, hiring and training staff, computing costs, and checking quality.   Figure 7-6 shows that the superior delegates line authority, or the right to command others, to subordinates (see the yellow line).   They, in turn, delegate authority to other subordinates, and so on, forming a "line," or chain of command, from the top to the bottom level of the business.   For example, the vice-president of production has line authority over Plant Manager 1, who has line authority over the four managers below.

Line authority alone commonly is used in small businesses.   Needless to say, the manager using it must have a wide variety of abilities and knowledge.

▲ **Staff Authority**   Line managers often need specialized advice and counsel based on greater knowledge, technical competence, and expertise than they or their subordinates possess.   Therefore, line managers have specialists to provide them with information and counsel.   These experts are usually granted

only **staff,** or advisory, **authority,** which is the right to give advice to a superior. However, the specialist can't order anyone to carry out the advice.

Certain service units, such as legal, public relations, research and development, and personnel departments, employ specialists. Since such units primarily advise line managers, they are called *staff departments.* Most medium-sized and large firms rely on combined line and staff authority.

▲ **Functional Authority** Line-and-staff arrangements rarely work smoothly in actual practice, for there tends to be conflict between managers with line authority, who can command others, and those with staff authority, who can only advise—and hope they'll be listened to. A new form of authority has been developed to overcome this problem. Some staff specialists—in this case, the personnel director and chief controller—are given **functional authority** (see the green line in Figure 7-6), which is the right to oversee lower-level personnel involved in that specialty, regardless of the level or department where the personnel are located in the organization. These specialists have the right to say how and when something will be done, but not who will do it. For instance, the vice-president of human resources at GM has this right.

Controllers, personnel officers, research and development specialists, and safety inspectors usually have functional authority. In one company, a safety inspector touring a storage area of a large warehouse discovered water on the cement floor. As the workers were manually moving 100-pound containers to a conveyor belt, their feet were slipping. The inspector ordered the operation shut down until sawdust could be strewn on the floor to improve traction. The warehouse general manager was incensed because "the staff person was usurping my line authority." He was wrong, of course, because the staff person had functional authority.

## How Much Authority to Delegate

**Objective 7**

The difference between centralization and decentralization of authority.

Another important question in organizing is how much authority should be delegated to subordinates and how much should be retained by superiors. This problem involves centralization or decentralization of authority. **Centralization** is the concentration of authority in the hands of higher managers, who reserve the decision-making authority for themselves. **Decentralization** is the division and sharing of authority, through delegation, among managers at lower levels in the organization.

Some decentralization of authority exists in every business with one or more employees. Otherwise the firm couldn't operate, because top management would have all the authority and no one else could act independently. Likewise, managers can't delegate *all* their authority, because chaos would reign. As a result, you don't find either extreme in the real world.

✗ Figure 7-7 shows a highly centralized business. Notice that the managers of purchasing, R&D, engineering and standards, and personnel, as well as the four plant managers, all report to the vice-president for production. Authority is concentrated, or centralized, in that one executive's hands, and then in the president's. A similar action was taken by Warner Communications when sales of its subsidiary, Atari, plunged from $2 billion in 1982 to $1 billion in 1983. Warner pushed through a full-scale management shake-up at Atari that centralized operations of its home computer and video game division.[10] Fol-

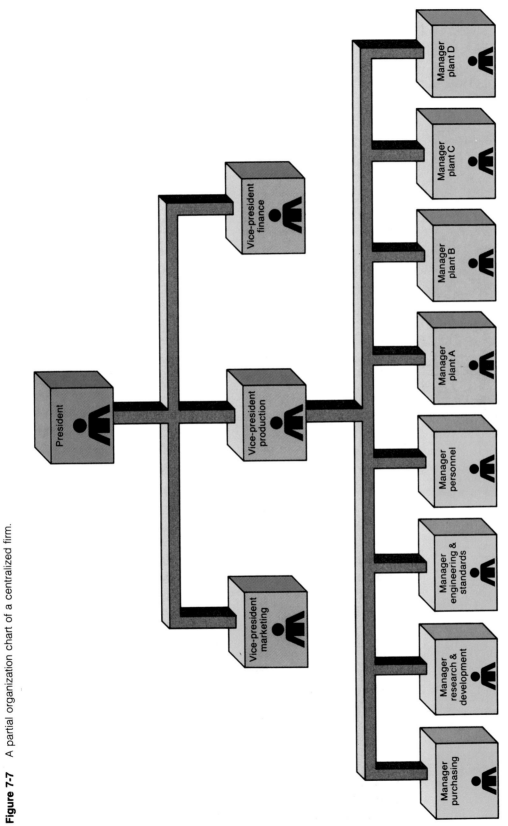

**Figure 7-7** A partial organization chart of a centralized firm.

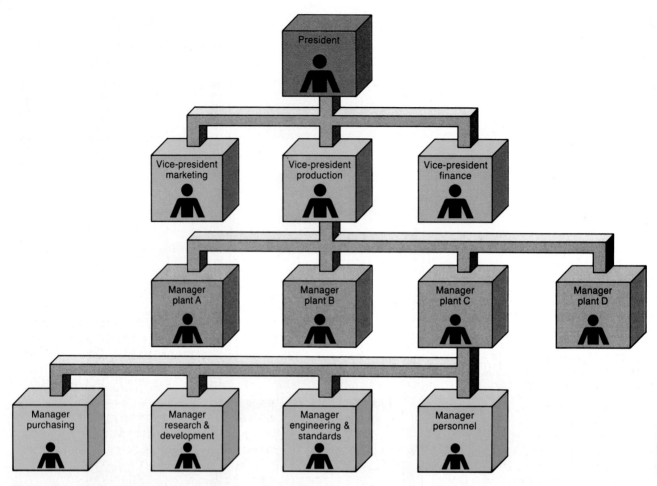

**Figure 7-8** A partial organization chart of a decentralized firm.

lowing severe losses during the 1974–1975 recession, R. J. Reynolds Industries, Inc. also moved from "loosely administered" to tighter corporate controls at the top.[11]

Figure 7-8 shows the same firm with decentralized authority. Notice that, again, only the three vice-presidents report to the president. In turn, though, four managers report to *each* of the plant managers. Under this decentralized structure, each manager is given greater freedom to operate. Whether the units of purchasing, R&D, engineering and standards, and personnel are centralized or decentralized should depend on how effectively and efficiently these activities can be performed at lower organizational levels. Exxon Corporation is an example of a highly decentralized organization. It's CEO, Clifton C. Garvin, Jr., says, "Exxon would continue to operate without missing a beat if I were to suddenly vanish from the scene."[12]

## SPAN OF MANAGEMENT

**Objective 8**

**The concept of span of management.**

Two other important aspects of organizing are span of management and the number of managerial levels. They're really so interrelated that they can't be separated; thus we'll consider them together. The **span of management** (often

# FYI

## Moses and Jethro: Span of Management in Action

In the Old Testament account of the Exodus from Egypt, the progress of the approximately 3½ million Israelites had ceased, and Moses, their leader, didn't know what to do about it. They were wallowing in the wilderness while the people stood around all day waiting for him to judge each one of them. At that point, the following discussion took place between Moses and his father-in-law, Jethro.

JETHRO: What is this that you are doing to the people? Why do you sit here alone, with all the people standing about you from morning till night?

MOSES: Because the people come to me to inquire of God. And when they have a dispute with their neighbors, they come to me and I decide between them.

JETHRO: What you are doing is not good for you or them. You and your people will wear yourselves out, for this burden is too heavy for you. You cannot do it alone. Choose able men from among the people, and place them over the people as rulers of tens, of fifties, of hundreds, and of thousands. And let them judge the people at all times. All small matters they shall decide themselves, but the great matters they shall bring to you. Thus it will be easier for you, and they will share the burden with you. If you do this, you will be able to endure, and the people also will go to their place in peace.

And so Moses chose able men and made them heads over the people, rulers of thousands, of hundreds, of fifties, and of tens, to judge the people at all times. The hard cases they brought to Moses, but the small ones they decided themselves. And they came out of the wilderness and reached their objective—the Promised Land.

Source: Adapted by permission *Exodus* 18:13–27 from the *Revised Standard Version of the Bible.* Copyrighted 1946, 1952, ©1971, 1973.

called span of control) is the number of people a given manager supervises directly. In Figures 7-7 and 7-8, the president's span of management is three vice-presidents. In Figure 7-7, however, the span for the vice-president for production is eight, while in Figure 7-8, the span for the vice-president and each plant manager is a more manageable four.

Obviously, an unlimited number of people shouldn't report to any one person (see FYI above). In general, the nearer managers are to the top of the business, the smaller the number of people reporting to them. Conversely, the lower managers are in the firm, the greater the number of subordinates reporting to them. The problem with decreasing the span of management is that expenses, such as costs of staff, coordination, office space, communication, and time, will increase. Too few managerial levels, however, will result in a wide span of management, which may also be costly. When managers are

spread too thin, they don't have enough time to make decisions, to help subordinates, or to confer with them.

> As the span of the vice-president for production decreased from eight in Figure 7-7 to four in Figure 7-8, what happened to the number of management levels? How do you explain this relationship?

There is no one best span of management. Instead, the best in any given situation depends on factors such as the manager's personal skill and leadership ability, the workers' skills and motivation, and the nature of the work. For example, a company president might have only three executives reporting directly to him or her: the vice-president for marketing, the vice-president for production, and the controller. This number would be appropriate if the required functions were complex, interdependent, and important for achieving an effective external balance for the company in the industry and the general economy. On the other hand, first-line supervisors in a textile plant might have fifteen to twenty employees reporting to them. The similarity or uniformity of the work done by textile workers and their low degree of job freedom permit an increased span of management.

## ▲ LEARNING OBJECTIVES REVISITED

1. *How the management function of organizing results in an organization.*

   Organizing involves deciding what activities, duties, and tasks are needed to reach the firm's objectives; dividing the tasks among employees in small working groups; and assigning each group to a manager with the authority and responsibility to get the job done. The result is an organization.

   As people become more interdependent, they come to depend more on organizations, which are based on the principle of specialization.

2. *The distinction between formal and informal organizations.*

   Most business organizations are formal in nature, but informal groups are found in all of them. Formal organizations, as shown in organization charts and manuals, have a clearly defined structure, formal communication systems, relative stability and permanence, and a tendency to expand. Informal organizations are spontaneous natural groups of employees. These groups have informal channels of communication, set and enforce norms of behavior and performance, and maintain many interpersonal contacts. Informal organizations create the grapevine and informal leaders.

3. *The steps involved in the organizing process.*

   The organizing process involves (1) setting up objectives, (2) determining the specific activities, duties, and tasks required to reach the objectives, (3) dividing the activities into operating units, (4) assigning the appropriate

authority and responsibility to managers for each unit, (5) providing the needed financial and physical resources, and (6) selecting, training, and developing qualified employees.

4. *The major means of departmentation.*

The most important means of departmentation are according to the functions, products, territories, or processes involved in the business. Newer and more intricate methods of departmentation are project and matrix organizations.

5. *How delegation of authority works.*

As a business grows, the responsibility and authority needed to run it effectively must be delegated appropriately.

6. *The differences among line authority, staff authority, and functional authority.*

The main types of delegated authority are line, staff, and functional. Line authority is command authority, while staff authority is advisory in nature. Most medium- and large-sized businesses use a combination of line and staff authority. Functional authority is given to certain specialists to say how and when a function is to be performed, regardless of where it occurs in the organization.

7. *The difference between centralization and decentralization of authority.*

Centralization of authority occurs when top managers keep most of the authority in their own hands. Decentralization is a sharing of authority with subordinates at lower levels through delegation.

8. *The concept of span of management.*

The span of management is the number of people a manager directly supervises. In general, fewer subordinates report to top managers and more report to supervisors.

## ▲ IMPORTANT TERMS

As an extra review of the chapter, try defining the following terms. If you have trouble with any of them, refer to the page listed.

organization  *168*
specialization (division of labor)  *169*
formal organizations  *170*
organization charts  *171*
organization manuals  *172*
policy manuals  *172*
informal organizations  *172*
grapevine  *172*
informal leaders  *172*
departmentation  *174*
functional departmentation  *177*

product departmentation  *177*
territorial departmentation  *177*
process departmentation  *177*
project organization  *179*
matrix organization  *179*
line authority  *185*
staff authority  *186*
functional authority  *186*
centralization  *186*
decentralization  *186*
span of management  *188*

# ⏏ REVIEW QUESTIONS

1. Describe how the organizing function results in an organization.
2. Upon what principle is organization based?
3. What are the differences between formal and informal organizations?
4. What are the differences between an organization chart, an organization manual, and a policy manual?
5. List and give examples of the six steps in the organizing process.
6. What are the four most popular methods of departmentation?
7. Explain project and matrix organizations.
8. What are the principal reasons for delegating?
9. Describe line, staff, and functional authority. Under what circumstances should each be used?
10. What is meant by centralization and decentralization of authority?
11. What is span of management?

# ⏏ DISCUSSION QUESTIONS

1. Why isn't a more specialized company necessarily more productive?
2. Assume that you have a part-time job on the assembly line in a local manufacturing company. What are some examples of informal organization that you might find in your department? How would you handle them?
3. After getting approval for a class picnic at the end of the semester, your fellow students have elected you to be in charge of organizing it. What steps would you take?
4. Is staff authority "real" authority? Why or why not?
5. What are some examples of informal communication in an organization? How do these differ from those in the formal structure?
6. Why should fewer subordinates report to the chief executive officer of a large company than to the supervisor of its typing pool?
7. What are some of the conflicts that occur between line, staff, and functional personnel in a firm? How can they be minimized?

# ⏏ CASE 7-1   GM Reorganizes

In addressing GM's 1982 annual stockholders' meeting, its chairman, Roger Smith, listed some of the things GM had done to become even more competitive. During the previous three years, the biggest manufacturer in the country had removed 27,000 salaried employees. During the two previous years, it had absorbed more than $1 billion of extraordinary expenses in order to introduce many new products. In fact, a third of GM's product line in the United States was new.

In other moves to remain competitive, or to improve its competitive position, GM had eliminated or consolidated many divisions, reassigned many employees, and realigned operating units. It had aligned itself with several foreign firms, setting up a joint venture with Fujitsu-Fanuc Company of Japan and purchasing a minority interest in other companies including Suzuki Motor Company of Japan. And there were many other joint agreements to improve its exports, which accounted for 39 percent of its total sales.

Finally, it had negotiated a new labor agreement with the United Auto Workers, providing for terms more favorable to the company and assuring job security for the workers.

**Case Questions**

1. What effects might these changes have on GM's organization structure?
2. How does an organization as large as GM remain responsive to customers? How could its organization be changed to make it more responsive?
3. How would you have introduced the organizational changes if you had been one of the managers involved?

## ⏷ CASE 7-2   Star Wars at Atari[13]

In the third quarter of 1982, Atari, a subsidiary of Warner Communications, Inc., was one of the premier companies in the video game and home computer industry. Sales had increased from $200 million in 1977 to $2 billion in 1982. And earnings had reversed from a $300 million loss to a profit of $320 million.

But something happened during 1982's fourth quarter—sales plummeted, inventories skyrocketed, and profits reverted to losses. There are many explanations of what happened, but one problem was organizational. As sales—and output—increased rapidly, CEO Raymond Kasser had to build a management team quickly. He turned from the engineers and researchers who had helped Atari prosper to consumer marketing specialists. Some managers were hired and fired within three months. The remaining executives had the good life, though. They traveled in style, flying first class, staying in swank hotels, and riding in chauffeur-driven limousines. Salaries and bonuses were very high.

Yet there was little relationship between earnings and performance. Video game designers who converted a game were given the same lavish bonuses as those who invented new ones. Technical personnel in other divisions felt like second-class citizens, as did the high-performance, creative people. So many engineers left that Atari had to bring in outsiders to produce its home games.

Communication broke down completely between the marketing specialists and the engineers and other technical people. In turn, the marketing people felt intimidated by the technical experts. There was little face-to-face communication, and top executives spent less than an hour and a half each week in meetings. There was a blizzard of memos, though. The result was that, while research and development continued, many proposals for new products wound up pigeonholed.

According to one source, the decline was a classic example of "inattention to management controls and communication." The company was so spread out in Silicon Valley that only two out of nine executives who reported to the CEO were housed in the same building with him. Also, when the mentality shifted from profits to sales, Atari hired "droves of people." In mid-1983, Steven J. Ross, Warner's CEO, added a new layer of vice-presidents at the corporate level to deal with specific divisional problems. This move still didn't solve the problem, and Atari was sold in July 1984 after a reported $539 million loss.

**Case Questions**

1. If you had been brought in to reorganize Atari in early 1983, how would you have approached it?
2. How would you have improved communications?
3. What relationship would you have between marketing and design and engineering?
4. Why do you think the new level of vice-presidents wasn't able to coordinate things successfully?

# 8

# Production and Operations Management

*Nothing can be produced out of nothing, any more than a thing can go back to nothing.*

Marcus Aurelius

*Quality is never an accident; it is always the result of intelligent effort.*

John Ruskin

## Learning Objectives

After studying the material in this chapter, you will understand:

1. What production is, as well as why and where it is needed.
2. The different types of production processes and how they are related.
3. What human and physical resources are needed for production planning.
4. How to determine the capacity and location of production facilities.
5. How to design and lay out production facilities.
6. Materials management by means of purchasing and inventory control.
7. The steps involved in production control.
8. Some of the more useful aids to production control.
9. How to handle maintenance and quality control.

## In This Chapter

What Is Production?
Planning Production
Production Facilities
Design and Layout of Facilities
Materials Management
Production Control

# WHITE CONSOLIDATED INDUSTRIES
*Combining People and Machines*

White Consolidated Industries' specialty is taking over ailing appliance companies, trimming off the fat, and making them profitable. White, an old, low-profile, but aggressive conglomerate, is one of the three largest appliance manufacturers in the United States. Its sales of $2 billion in 1983 were surpassed only by General Electric and Whirlpool, and sales growth has been 230 percent over the last decade.

Founded in 1876 to manufacture and sell the White sewing machine, the company later produced the White steamer, a water-powered automobile. But its real expansion began about twenty years ago. Since then, it has picked up over twenty companies, most of them in deep trouble, and turned them around. Its real achievement has been in buying eight dying appliance divisions from such big firms as Westinghouse, Ford, GM, and American Motors. Each of these divisions had suffered the same perplexing fate. They were financed well enough, their production lines were fully mechanized, and their appliances had widely recognized and highly advertised brand names—Westinghouse, Philco, Gibson, Kelvinator, and Frigidaire. But none of their operations was efficient enough to meet the cutthroat price competition in the appliance trade. So, after "dismal financial returns, and sometimes huge losses," each of the companies sold its production operations to White. Within a year of acquisition, White had nursed the patients back to financial health and transformed them into money makers. As a result, White has become known as a formidable competitor.

White's success comes from a production strategy that's quite simple, even though hard to achieve: increasing production efficiency. Management at White made production and cost control "a corporate religion," to be followed "with messianic fervor." The strategy involved many cost-cutting techniques, rather than capital investment in new machines and equipment. White concentrates on improving production and quality control as well as increasing employee productivity.

Heads roll and pink slips begin to fly within days of a White takeover. For instance, 70 percent of Kelvinator's administrative staff, 40 percent of the workers at three Westinghouse plants, and half the Westinghouse international staff were gone inside of a month. Production is concentrated in the more efficient plants and others are closed. When White bought GM's Frigidaire division, it didn't acquire the plants—just the trademark, inventories, and distribution network. Frigidaires are made in the same plant with appliances sold under the names of Gibson, Kelvinator, White-Westinghouse, and two private brands. This improved plant utilization reduced overhead costs and increased profits.

Whether people, machines, or robots do the job, the dynamic economic development of the U.S. has sprung from the ability to create and produce innovative, marketable goods at low cost. Although robots can't fill teeth or park cars (yet), production techniques are being applied to improve such service activities and decrease their cost. However, people still play an important role in production.

One of management's constant challenges is increasing productivity. A better mousetrap is better only if people need mousetraps and enough can be produced, at realistic cost, to meet market demand and yield a profit for the inventor.

**Productivity,** a measure of the efficiency of production, is the amount of goods (such as mousetraps) or services produced by one worker in a given period of time. Higher productivity can be obtained by improved techniques, better use of resources, and greater efforts by managers and employees. For example, by installing computers, PSA, Inc., a San Diego-based airline, was able to reduce its work force by 900 between 1978 and 1983, even though the number of its daily flights increased. That's basically what this chapter is about.

## WHAT IS PRODUCTION?

**Objective 1**

**What production is, as well as why and where it is needed.**

The term *production,* or *operations,* is often used interchangeably with *manufacturing,* because modern production methods were first developed and applied in manufacturing industries. But even though a service like dry cleaning doesn't produce a tangible object, production figures into the services. If you view production as a process, it becomes clear that even services such as dry cleaning begin with resources—cleaning fluid, machines, presses, and people—and end up with a product—clean clothes. So all business firms are involved in some type of production. **Production,** or **operations,** then, is the use of human, physical, and financial resources to produce products or services.

### Where Production Is Needed

As we've pointed out, production takes place in all kinds of business—as well as nonbusiness—operations. Production in hospitals, for instance, doesn't mean just delivering babies. It also covers the processes of serving meals, performing surgery, taking and reading x-rays, conducting physical therapy, cleaning rooms, and receiving payments. Supermarket production operations include ordering and pricing inventory, stocking the shelves, packaging and displaying meat and produce, and checking out groceries. Governments issue permits and licenses, collect taxes, register voters, provide police and fire protection, and clean and repair streets. Contractors construct, repair, and demolish buildings, build highways, and landscape parks. And banks grant loans, cash or issue checks, and handle deposits and withdrawals.

When you registered for courses at school, you went through what may have been a frustrating sequence of steps. As you've probably guessed by now, that too was a production process. The process probably began when you picked up a registration packet and ended when your tuition and fees were paid. Whether or not the system was hassle-free, production skills were used to design it and put it into practice.

What exactly were the steps involved in your registration?  Was it an efficient and effective system?  What would you do to improve it?  What standards of performance might be used to judge its efficiency and effectiveness?

## The Production Process

Any economic activity creates some type of **utility,** which is the ability of a good or service to satisfy the wants or needs of consumers.  The basic types of utility are form, place, time, and ownership.  Production creates **form utility,** or the change of raw materials into a product or service that satisfies customers' needs.  Marketing creates place, time, and ownership utility.

A more general and useful way of describing the **production process** is that it converts economic inputs into outputs that customers need, want, and are willing to pay for (see Figure 8-1).  For instance, White Consolidated Industries converts inputs such as sheets of metal, wires, motors, paint, plastics, and switches into outputs: appliances for consumers.  In the process, White uses the effort of employees, in plants equipped with machines, equipment, and tools—all paid for with money in the form of cash, checks, or credit.

## How Production Processes Differ

**Objective 2**

**The different types of production processes and how they are related.**

Production processes vary greatly in complexity, production time, the amount of information and planning needed, and the number and type of machines and employees required.  The production of paper takes time and requires a variety of high-producing machines that cost millions of dollars.  Typing a term paper, on the other hand, is a short process using mainly manual operations with relatively inexpensive machines and tools.

▲ **Types of Production**  Production processes also differ according to the way the inputs are processed into outputs.  The two most common types of production processes are the synthetic process and the analytic process.  In the **synthetic process,** two or more basic inputs are mixed or assembled to form the final output or outputs.  Classic examples of the synthetic process are assembling an airplane and an automobile (see Figure 8-2).  Other examples include making watches, books, bread, electronic equipment (such as radios, stereos, TV sets, calculators, and computers), clothing, computer chips, and hamburgers (see FYI on page 203).  As shown in Figure 8-3, this process involves inputs, processing, and outputs.

In the **analytic process,** a raw material is broken down or separated to form a variety of outputs.  Examples of this type of production process are coal being separated into coke, chemicals, and gases; crude petroleum being transformed into gasoline, diesel fuel, lubricating oils, asphalt, and other products; and timber being reduced to lumber, paper, and sawdust (which is used in other building materials).  This process also involves inputs, processing, and outputs, as Figure 8-4 shows.

Both of these processes are often combined into one overall production process.  In other words, both synthetic and analytic processes can be used in

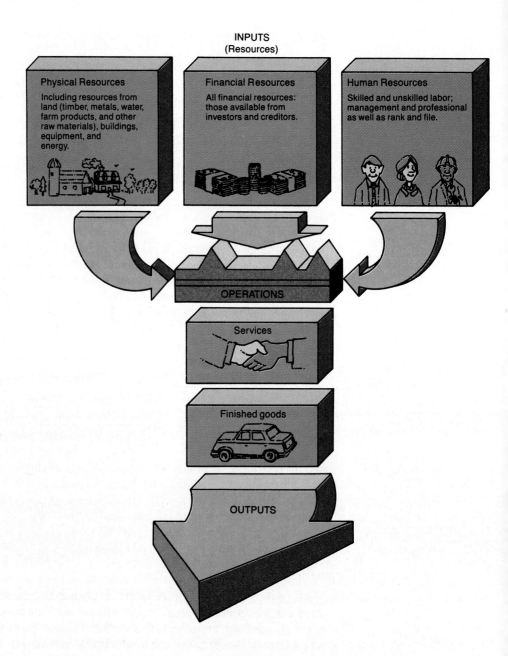

INPUTS
(Resources)

**Physical Resources**
Including resources from land (timber, metals, water, farm products, and other raw materials), buildings, equipment, and energy.

**Financial Resources**
All financial resources: those available from investors and creditors.

**Human Resources**
Skilled and unskilled labor; management and professional as well as rank and file.

OPERATIONS

Services

Finished goods

OUTPUTS

**Figure 8-1** The production process.

the same plant. For instance, after lubricating oil is distilled from crude oil by the analytic process, detergent agents and other components are added by the synthetic process to improve its quality. The same is true of gasoline.

▲ **Timing of Production** Production processes differ in their timing; they may be continuous or intermittent. In a **continuous process,** once production starts, it keeps on for a long time—hours, days, or longer—churning out the same product over and over. Most mass-production industries, such as petroleum refining, paper manufacturing, and chemical production, use the continuous process. Machine shutdowns are costly in terms of wasted time and resources in such industries.

Assembling an airplane is an example of the synthetic process.

The **intermittent process** usually involves short production runs, where the machines are often stopped and started or changed to make a different product or to serve different customers. The operation of most construction projects, radio stations, laundry and cleaning establishments, and auto repair shops is intermittent. For instance, when your car is serviced, the operator pumps the gas—stops; cleans your windows—stops; checks the oil—stops; checks tire pressure—stops; and writes up your charge slip for you to sign. Customer services are almost always the intermittent type of production.

Which types of production processes do you think are used by White Consolidated in producing refrigerators, ranges, washers, and dryers? Why? What process is used by Burger King (see FYI on page 203)? Why?

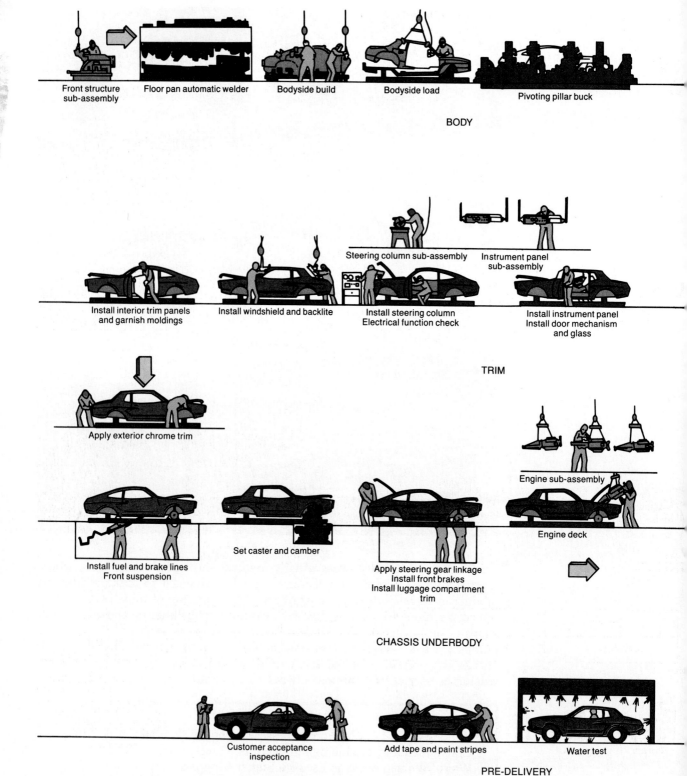

**Figure 8-2**   How a Ford Mustang is assembled. (Reprinted by permission of the Educational Affairs Department, Ford Motor Company.)

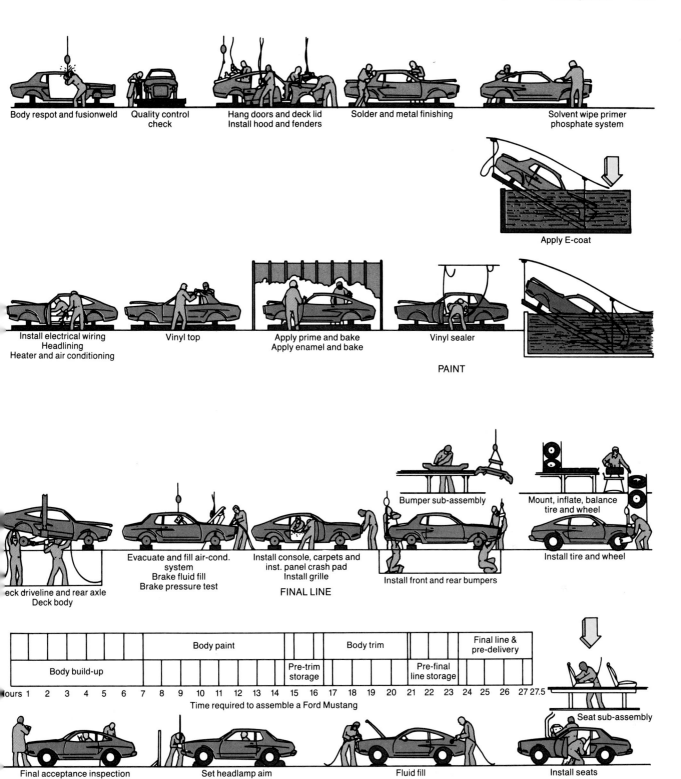

Body respot and fusionweld

Quality control check

Hang doors and deck lid
Install hood and fenders

Solder and metal finishing

Solvent wipe primer phosphate system

Apply E-coat

Install electrical wiring
Headlining
Heater and air conditioning

Vinyl top

Apply prime and bake
Apply enamel and bake

Vinyl sealer

PAINT

...eck driveline and rear axle
Deck body

Evacuate and fill air-cond. system
Brake fluid fill
Brake pressure test

Install console, carpets and inst. panel crash pad
Install grille

FINAL LINE

Bumper sub-assembly

Install front and rear bumpers

Mount, inflate, balance tire and wheel

Install tire and wheel

| | | | | | | | | | Body paint | | | | | | | | Body trim | | | | Final line & pre-delivery | | | |
|---|---|---|---|---|---|---|---|---|---|---|---|---|---|---|---|---|---|---|---|---|---|---|---|---|---|---|---|

Body build-up — Pre-trim storage — Pre-final line storage

Hours 1 2 3 4 5 6 7 8 9 10 11 12 13 14 15 16 17 18 19 20 21 22 23 24 25 26 27 27.5

Time required to assemble a Ford Mustang

Seat sub-assembly

Final acceptance inspection

Set headlamp aim
Set toe-in
Roadability test

Fluid fill

Install seats

FINAL LINE

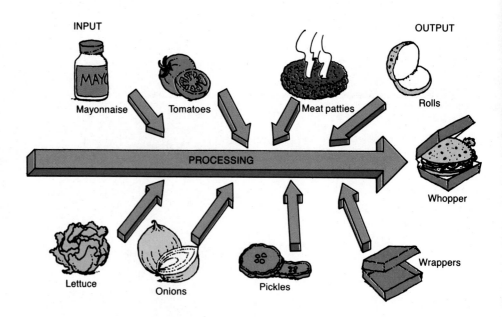

**Figure 8-3** The synthetic production process.

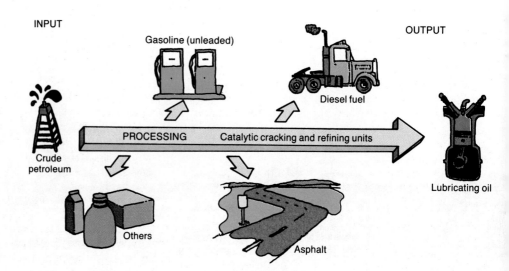

**Figure 8-4** The analytic production process.

## How Production Processes Are Related

Until now, we've been talking about individual production operations as if they were separate processes. But they really aren't. Production starts with such basic ingredients as seed, water, soil, ore, and sunshine and ends with the final delivery of such products as cans of Campbell's soup, an Atari video game, a Kloss Novabeam TV set, a Chrysler Dodge, or Extra-Strength Tylenol, or such services as those of a Ramada Inn, a dentist, a bank, or an auto repair shop. In other words, the whole production process is a **production chain** that includes all activities from the gathering of raw materials to the delivery of the final product or service.

Figure 8-5 illustrates the interdependent nature of production processes. Just to place one can of Del Monte peaches on the grocery shelf requires (1) canning the peaches, which in turn requires (2) producing the basic ingredi-

## FYI

**Fast-Food Operations: Synthetic Production in Action**

Fast-food operations such as Burger King® are designed and operated to supply food quickly and with little customer effort. The process from ordering the food to receiving it has been studied repeatedly and finally divided into two production systems: processing the food and serving it.

The two systems involved in supplying a Whopper® to a Burger King customer include the following activities:

1. *Processing the food.* In the processing system, the ingredients—meat, cheese, buns, and condiments—are stored until needed. Then someone removes the patties, unwraps them, and places them on a conveyor that carries them through the broiler. At the same time, someone else is removing the buns, unwrapping them, and toasting them. Next, mayonnaise is put on the bun and the broiled patty is inserted, along with precut lettuce, tomatoes, onion, and pickles. After the top of the bun is added, the Whopper

is wrapped and stored in a heated bin. By controlling the number of Whoppers in the bin (inventory), Burger King can serve hot food quickly when it is needed. Notice that processing, including cooking and wrapping time, has been separated from the serving time. (Similar systems are used to produce other items, including shakes and French fries.)

2. *Serving the food.* The serving system begins when the customer orders, for example, a Whopper, fries, and a shake. The order is rung up on the cash register and paid for, and the receipt is handed to another clerk. He or she takes the fries and Whopper out of their bins, draws the shake, puts them and the receipt in a bag (or on a tray), and hands it to the customer.

The menu is limited and the facilities are designed to make the operations easier. Note the systems, sequences, and skills involved, as well as the time frames.

ents—cans, cartons, Del Monte labels, sugar, peaches, and so forth. These processes, in turn, require (3) almost innumerable processes that go all the way back to mining the ores for the cans, growing the trees for the boxes and labels, producing the petroleum and gas for label printing, and growing the peaches in the first place. Many other, often invisible, production processes are involved in this and other chains, such as generating and transmitting energy, transportation, finances, and communication.

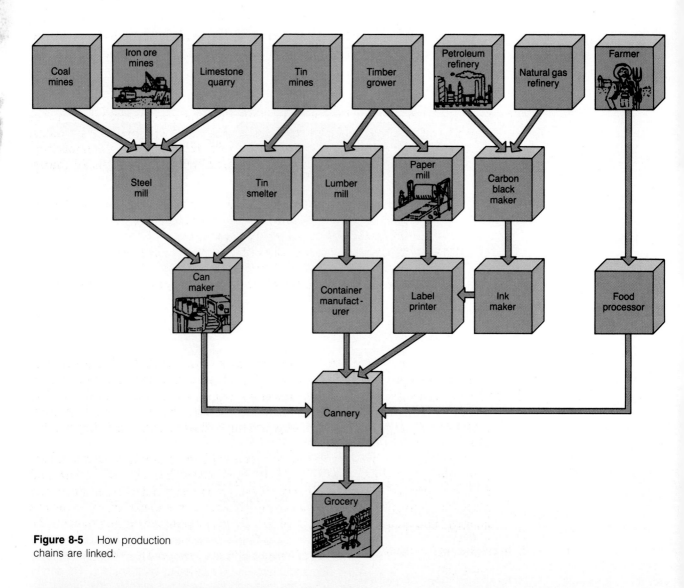

**Figure 8-5** How production chains are linked.

## PLANNING PRODUCTION

Objective 3

What human and physical resources are needed for production planning.

Like any smoothly running machine or economic organization, production doesn't simply start itself running and keep going in perpetual motion. Instead, production requires considerable human and physical resources, as well as the financial resources needed to pay for them—all planned carefully by production managers. But production differs from other economic activities in that it also needs extensive physical facilities. Another difference is the extent to which *either* people *or* machines can be used to do the work. At each stage, managers must do a cost-benefit analysis to determine the desired balance between physical and human resources, with available financial resources, of course, as a limiting factor.

Now that you know what goes into the production process, you should also consider the **production and operations management** process. It can be broken down, like the other management functions, into (1) planning the use

of resources, (2) organizing the use of facilities, materials (inputs), and inventory (outputs), and (3) controlling the efficiency of the whole operation.

## Human Resources

One of the jobs of production managers is planning for the efficient use of capable and well-trained people to run machines, use equipment, and perform work that can't be performed by computerized machines or for which machine production simply isn't economical. Aside from service operations, of course, where people are essential, people are better able to:

1. Perform work that doesn't fit some programmed pattern (see FYI on page 206), such as filling in the gaps in unclear instructions, reacting to breakdowns, and answering grievances.
2. Remember from experience the variations in situations that require modifications of the work being done.
3. Reason, make judgments, and develop entirely new solutions to problems.

## Physical Resources

**Mechanization** is the process of using machines to do work that had previously been done by people or animals. Many manufacturing operations have been mechanized since spinning and weaving machines were introduced over 250 years ago. Now other production activities, such as materials handling, shipping, record keeping, and even engineering and planning, are being mechanized.

Machines are usually used when there's a large amount of standardized, repetitive, routine work to be done. In such cases, human skill, effort, and attention can be economically transferred to the machine. In essence, the more the control of these activities can be shifted to the machine, the more the quantity and quality of production depend on the equipment rather than on the worker.

It can be concluded that machines can replace people when they're required to:

1. Perform repetitive tasks, such as printing newspapers, stamping out cookies, washing clothes, or keeping routine records.
2. Apply great force smoothly and evenly, as in shaping metal, digging trenches, doing heavy construction work, or drilling holes.
3. Count and measure precise physical quantities that might escape the fallible human, as do odometers, weighing scales, or counting machines.
4. Store information in huge quantities for quick, accurate, and consistent retrieval and use, as is done with computer-assisted registration and grade reports or grocery checkouts. For example, in many retail store checkout stations, electronic sensors, connected to computers and cash registers, are being installed to read the bar codes on packages. The checkers and clerks no longer have to key prices into the cash register or update inventory and sales records. Instead, computers do these jobs routinely, rapidly, and accurately, using data stored in their memory banks.

## FYI

### V. Kilena Loveless: Woman Against Machine

Shortly after the new automated subway system opened in Washington, D.C., something happened that reminds us of the need for the human resource. At an otherwise routine stop, the driver got off the train for a minute, and the train pulled out of the station without him. The computer-controlled runaway train passed three stops without opening its doors. Then one of the passengers, V. Kilena Loveless, using her hair barrette, unlocked the operator's booth. She found the "stop" button, brought the train to a halt at the Metro Center station, and stayed at her post while fellow passengers made their escape.

Metro spokespeople claimed that there had been no real crisis. The train was doing what it was supposed to do. The only problem was that there was no human being at the controls to open the doors, which no one had thought to program.

Source: From *Asides*, "Woman Against Machine," Editorial page *The Wall Street Journal*, October 11, 1979, p. 22. Reprinted by permission of *The Wall Street Journal*, © Dow Jones & Company, Inc. 1979. All Rights Reserved.

The increasing use of computers to operate machines is leading to greater automation and changing the sensitive balance between people and machines. **Automation** is the use of a mechanized system with the ability to automatically run and adjust itself to continuous operations as planned and programmed. GE has installed such a system in a seventy-three-year-old plant in Erie, Pennsylvania. Robots, computers, and other automated systems have made it the most cost-efficient locomotive plant in the world. The time required to produce an engine frame has plummeted from sixteen days to sixteen hours.[1]

### The Robot Revolution

At a Panasonic TV plant, the rate of defective products is estimated to be only one-fiftieth of what it was in 1970, before robots took over. At Chrysler's 145-acre Jefferson plant in East Detroit, where it builds the K-cars—the Plymouth Reliant and Dodge Aries—200 welders with masks and welding torches once stood along the assembly line. Now there are no welders to be seen. Instead, robots are working double shifts, spitting sparks, welding the bodies to

Robot welders at Chrysler.

higher standards of quality than ever before. The assembly line's productivity has increased by almost 20 percent since the robots arrived in 1980.

General Electric has found robots far more productive in some work than human workers. In one case, a robot saved enough to pay for itself in ten months. At Ford Motor Company, about fifty small robots are deftly fitting lightbulbs into dashboards and speakers into car radios.

The next phase of the computer revolution may well turn out to be the robot revolution. Robots have been fixtures in comedy and science fiction for a long time, but the first industrial robot wasn't used in the United States until 1961. Industrial robots scarcely resemble the stereotyped humanoid with flashing eyes and a control-panel chest. They're basically just combinations of a computer with very deft and efficient producing machines. What's really new, of course, is the extent to which these electronic wonders are transforming the way people work and the composition of the work force, especially in Japan. There are about 36,000 robots working in Japan and approximately 6,500 in the United States.[2] In early 1982, Raymond Donovan, U.S. Secretary of Labor, predicted that by 1990 half the workers in U.S. factories would be specialists trained to service and repair robots.[3]

It's easy to see why these "steel-collar workers" can be preferable to their human counterparts. They cause fewer personnel problems: they're never absent, and they never ask for more holidays, take vacations, or file grievances. They also give more consistent attention to quality control, are more efficient and effective performers, and are definitely cheaper to keep. Robots, which cost about $30,000 to $150,000 each, usually work two shifts a day. The displaced workers would draw salaries and benefits of about $790,000 a year.[4] However, robots still cannot replace all facets of the human worker. The automated factory is feasible, but when it comes to reason and informed decisions, robots are still in the same league with machines, at least for now.

## PRODUCTION FACILITIES

**Objective 4**

How to determine the capacity and location of production facilities.

There are three decisions that production managers need to make about such physical facilities as plant, machinery, equipment, aisles, storage, and service departments. First, for what production capacity should a company plan? Second, where will the facilities be located? Third, how can the facilities be laid out, or arranged, for greatest effectiveness?

### Plant Capacity

A company's overall **production capacity,** which is the amount of goods or services the facilities can handle during a period of time, is important. It takes time—often years—to add to capacity if it isn't right. If it's too small for the demand, that means loss of sales. But too large a capacity means added cost for idle facilities from which no income is obtained. Finding just the right capacity depends on factors like expected future demand, required investment, and the cost of producing a unit of product. Too much capacity in a restaurant or store has a negative effect on customers, since the place looks empty.

Companies forecast their sales for periods ranging from a few days to twenty or more years into the future. Longer-range forecasts are used to plan the purchase, building, or renting of production facilities at the time when they're most needed. Yet facility changes, many of them forced by competitive pressures, go on almost continuously. By matching the ability to produce with the demand, companies can achieve better results. But this isn't always easy to do. In 1981, Westinghouse invested some $2.5 million for more than fifty robots. After two years, the firm was paying to store more than a dozen unused ones.[5]

Two related subsidiary problems are how large each plant should be and whether it should specialize in producing one product or produce several types of goods. At one time, Johnson & Johnson built its drug supplies plants for 200 or fewer employees. This size was found to be optimum from the standpoint of cost, productivity, employee satisfaction, and nearness to customers. Similarly, Sears, Roebuck and Company has plants specializing in one or a few products. For example, one plant makes cabinets for products such as televisions and sewing machines in one city, another plant in a city forty miles away produces tires, and a third plant eighty miles away makes ladies' underwear.

### Plant Location

Luckily, firms don't have to make decisions about plant location very often. But when a decision is necessary, what are some of the factors involved?

A firm usually has several choices of where to locate its plants. Complicating the location decision is the fact that many communities spend considerable effort lobbying to attract operations that will increase employment and income in their areas.

Among the major factors to be considered in plant location are:

1. *Availability of materials, or the cost of transporting them to the plant.* U.S. Steel located a plant at Sparrows Point, Maryland, because it was the lowest-cost point for shipping iron ore from Venezuela and coal from Pennsylvania.

2. *Availability of personnel with appropriate abilities, experience, productivity, and pay expectations, or training costs to develop personnel.* Nissan Motors built an ultramodern plant at Smyrna, Tennessee, because of employees' favorable attitudes toward work, wages, and unionism.[6]

3. *Types, quantity, cost, and reliability of energy.* Alcoa located an aluminum reduction plant at Chalmette, Louisiana, because of abundant electric power generated from cheap natural gas.

4. *Availability, suitability, costs, and restrictions on use of land and buildings.* Chrysler bought a new 250,000-car assembly plant in Sterling Heights, Michigan, which Volkswagen had built but couldn't use because of inadequate demand for the Rabbit. To cut expenses, Grolier, Inc., a book publisher, moved from New York to Danbury, Connecticut, where rent was cheaper.[7]

5. *Taxes and fees, local zoning and environmental regulations, and attitudes toward business.* Japan's Sanyo Electric opened a TV assembly plant in Tierra del Fuego because of the "very strong incentives" offered by the Argentine government.[8]

6. *Employee attitudes toward the work ethic and unions.* Sharp Corporation of Japan built an ultramodern electronics plant in Memphis, Tennessee, because of the "strong work ethic" found there.[9]

7. *Community relations, such as harmonious living conditions, schools, recreation, crime rate, and quality of life.* The Austin/College Station/Dallas–Fort Worth triangle in Texas is becoming the new mecca for high-tech industries, consultants, and think tanks because of its schools and quality of life.

8. *Nearness to and good interaction with customers.* NCR Corporation and other computer-manufacturing firms—such as Hewlett-Packard, IBM, and Burroughs—are beginning operations in Mexico because the market for computers there is expected to grow at about 25 percent per year after 1984.[10]

The procedures for finding a suitable location usually involve (1) determining the factors to be considered, as well as their relative importance; (2) searching out locations that effectively meet the established requirements; and (3) comparing the locations, using objective and subjective rankings, to determine the best one. This process usually eliminates locations that simply aren't acceptable to a company for one reason or another.

Often, several locations are equally satisfactory from a rational point of view, and the choice or rejection is based on some subjective factor. For example, when asked why he had located his company's facilities where he did, one owner said, "My wife wanted to live in Carmel." Another owner rejected a small town because it didn't have a country club. A third owner chose to return to the small town where she had grown up. These are valid reasons, too, especially for a small business.

## DESIGN AND LAYOUT OF FACILITIES

**Objective 5**

**How to design and lay out production facilities.**

Even if an ideal location is found for facilities, the plant won't work well unless other factors are favorable. So the next chore for the production manager is to resolve some of the potential problems lurking in the design, layout, and operations of production facilities (see FYI on pages 210 and 211). The physical facilities required for production can take the form of a factory, office

# FYI

## Owens Printers: Design for a Headache

"Do I have any problems?" asked Bill Owens, owner and president of Owens Printers. "I've got plenty! Let me explain just a few of our worst ones.

"First, we don't have enough space on the first floor, and there are only stairs going to the second. In any case, we can't move our machines to improve the movement of paper because special reinforced flooring was installed for each machine. It would cost too much to do it again now, or to move to another building.

"Also, it's hard to find enough materials and supplies, especially paper. The type we require is in short supply, so we have to keep a six- to eight-week inventory on hand. Except for special orders, we buy at least four cartons of paper on each order so that transportation costs won't be too high. It's always a problem finding a place to store it.

"Personnel is another critical area. It's almost impossible to find the type of people we need—people who are willing to work as hard as they have to to keep us competitive in this area. There are always some workers absent or late, which makes it hard to schedule work.

"Energy is a constant headache, too. Whenever there are blackouts or even brownouts, we have production problems.

"I guess what I'm saying is that we need more productivity and more volume. Our paper cost has increased from 33 to 38 percent of our cost, labor has risen from 33 to 43 percent, and energy has just about doubled. A more efficient plant layout would really help."

Source: Adapted by permission from Curtis E. Tate, Jr., Leon C. Megginson, Charles R. Scott, Jr., and Lyle R. Trueblood, *Successful Small Business Management,* 3rd ed. (Plano, Tex.: Business Publications, Inc., 1982), pp. 294–300. © 1982 Business Publications, Inc.

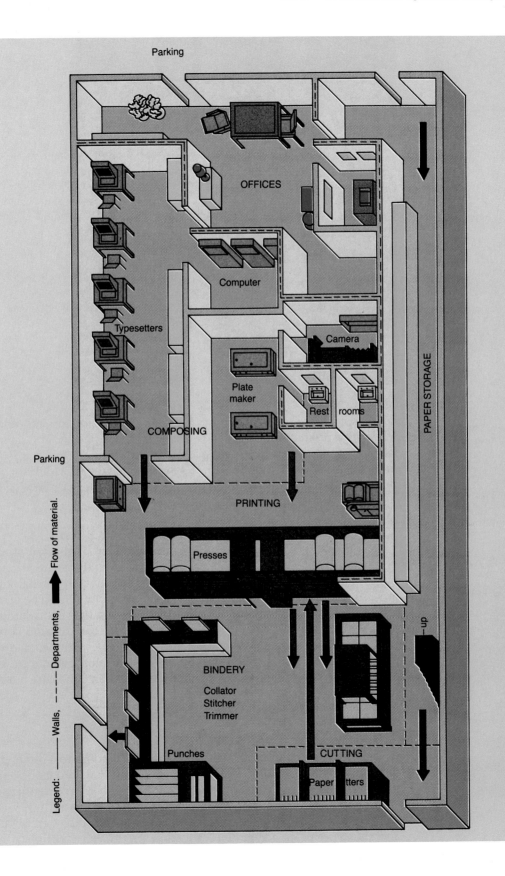

Parking

OFFICES

Computer

Typesetters

Camera

Plate
maker

Rest rooms

COMPOSING

Parking

PAPER STORAGE

PRINTING

Presses

up

BINDERY

Collator
Stitcher
Trimmer

Punches

CUTTING

Paper cutters

Legend: ——— Walls, - - - - Departments, ⬆ Flow of material.

A product layout.

building, eating place, school, hospital, service station, or any other structure where the production of goods or services takes place. The layout of these facilities should be designed so that the planned product can be produced in the most effective and efficient way. **Layout** is the way in which the walls, partitions, machines, tools, equipment, offices, and aisles are arranged.

## Product Layout

There are essentially two types of layout: product layout and process layout. **Product layout** is an arrangement in which work stations are arranged according to the sequence of operations on a given product. It's usually designed to process and move assembled parts to a final assembly line. The drawing above shows a section of a hypothetical chocolate factory that uses a product layout. Notice the conveyor carrying the candy rabbits; the division of work, with each employee doing a different operation; and the working conditions. This is a very efficient production layout, but it's hard for a worker to stand up all day tying bows on rabbits—and what happens when chocolate bunnies are out of season?

## Process Layout

Not all production processes can be planned according to a product layout. A company making small quantities of many different products, such as a job printing shop, needs to use a **process layout,** an arrangement in which machines are grouped together according to the type of work they do. For example, in the layout of Owens Printers, all the printing presses are set up together, and the typesetters are grouped together in another location. This type of layout results in more efficient use of machines but also requires more move-

ment of materials and often results in more inventory on hand—not always a good thing, as we'll see later.

## MATERIALS MANAGEMENT

**Objective 6**

**Materials management by means of purchasing and inventory control.**

Another aspect of effective production is **materials management,** which ensures that the right materials are available when needed at each stage of the production process. This is where purchasing and inventory control come into the production picture.

### Purchasing

Purchasing involves more than just ordering and paying for materials. Like any other production function, it takes planning, communication, and decision making. The steps involved include the following:

1. *Determine what's needed and request its purchase.* After they are evaluated and justified, requests for needed materials come from individual departments. Each request should include a specification and description of the items needed, the quantities to be bought, the price of each unit, and when and where they are to be delivered.

2. *Maintain supplier and transportation information and relations.* The purchasing manager decides which suppliers to use, modes of transportation, and types of packaging (if needed).

3. *Agree on a price.* For most firms, the cost of materials represents a large chunk of the product's selling price. A firm like General Motors spends half of its sales dollar on machines alone. Since most manufacturing firms make only 5 percent net profit on sales (after taxes), a 10 percent increase in materials cost, without any other change, can just about wipe out the company's profit. Needless to say, it's crucial that purchasing managers get a good purchase price.

4. *Place purchase orders.* Purchase orders are sent to suppliers, with copies to the receiving and accounting departments, who must follow up on the orders.

5. *Maintain control.* The purchasing manager should keep an eye on the status of each order to see whether the items are received on time and whether they conform to specifications. If not, the manager should take steps to correct the situation.

6. *Maintain records.* Records of orders and their results provide managers with information for placing future orders.

The Sharp Corporation plant in Memphis has a unique relationship with its seventy suppliers. Its creed, "Practice Sincerity and Creativity," is submitted to vendors along with a statement that Sharp expects "100% quality parts," precisely on schedule. The suppliers then get report cards on their quality, price, promptness of delivery, and other factors.[11]

### Inventory and Its Control

**Inventory** includes all raw materials, supplies, and parts, as well as finished products that aren't currently being moved, used, or sold. All production organizations must have inventories so that operations don't grind to a halt be-

"Who needs computerized production controls? When we run out of parts, we just improvise."

cause of a missing part or unfillable order. But items in inventory that aren't serving a useful purpose become a costly burden.

There's no doubt that inventories are expensive to obtain and maintain, even though the costs don't appear separately in the accounting records. The major costs of keeping inventory on hand result from the facts that (1) it uses up space that could be used for other purposes; (2) insurance and tax costs increase as inventory increases; (3) the items may deteriorate or become obsolete and so depreciate (lose value); (4) items must be moved to and from storage; and (5) money invested in inventory could be earning income elsewhere, through new machines, advertising, or investments.

The costs of not having adequate inventory on hand are (1) lost customer sales (sometimes a permanent loss); (2) idle machines, workers, materials, and trucks; and (3) wasted management time. If a chair manufacturer has a warehouse full of chairs that can't be completed because of a delay in delivery of a special part, people have to be laid off, and the company may have to borrow money to keep going until the part arrives. The use of computer terminals and quality control circles (see next section) by Hewlett-Packard's supervisors and managers reduced inventory by 5 percent—saving nearly $200 million.[12] The use of the **just-in-time (JIT) production system,** a hand-to-mouth method of buying parts and materials in very small quantities just in time for use, with very minimum storage, saves Japanese automakers "hundreds of dollars per car" in storage and carrying costs.[13]

# PRODUCTION CONTROL

First we discussed production as a general process of converting inputs into outputs. Then we saw that human and physical resources had to be planned for and acquired, the facilities laid out for the greatest efficiency, and materials managed for lowest cost and optimum inventory level. Now we come to the point where someone must put all these plans into operation, which requires effective production control. **Production control** is a system for coordinating people, machines, and materials in order to reach objectives. The Profile of Emily Roebling on page 216 illustrates many aspects of production control.

## Steps Involved

**Objective 7**

**The steps involved in production control.**

The usual steps in production control are production planning, routing, scheduling, dispatching, and follow-up.

*Production planning* sets up the production plans and information systems needed to operate the plant. It determines what goods or services will be produced; the personnel, machines, and materials needed to produce them; and a system for obtaining the needed resources at the right time.

**Routing** determines the operations required, the best sequence in which to perform tasks, the machines and tools used, and the paperwork required. A routing system is set up only once for standard products (when there is a model change) but must be done for each job for special products.

*Scheduling* involves the timing of production so that the proper volume is produced and machines and personnel are used efficiently. It takes into account how long each operation takes, in what order operations occur, and at what point in time each operation must be completed in order for other operations to take place. Effective scheduling ultimately ensures that production and delivery schedules are met at a minimum cost. Scheduling becomes more intricate as the complexity of the product being produced increases. For example, a Boeing 727, a small jet as jets go, is composed of over 100,000 different parts, not including the engines. A disastrous chain reaction can result from a delay in production of any one of the well over a million total pieces needed to produce each plane.

**Dispatching** is basically the activating arm of the production process. The dispatcher makes sure that materials, tools, machines, and workers are brought together at the right time and place, and that production proceeds according to the planned schedule. This often involves issuing paperwork such as work orders, routing slips, and memos. Some familiar examples of dispatching are police directing traffic, referees or umpires officiating at sports events, a construction supervisor sending a crew to a work site, a dispatcher sending a freight train on its way, and a manager starting the flow of crude oil through a refinery.

*Follow-up* involves comparing actual output with planned output to see that what was planned has become reality. When production difficulties occur, information must be sent to people who can take corrective action, or else the whole system will fall apart. For example, workers may not be finished with one operation when they are scheduled to begin another. Someone must decide whether to do nothing (a bad option), to work overtime on the first job, to delay the second job, or to take some other action. Follow-up systems are often designed to give early warning of changes in plans that will affect others in the organization. For example, information on the late arrival or

## Profile

### Emily Warren Roebling: Bridge Builder

The Brooklyn Bridge, which recently celebrated its one-hundredth birthday, stands as a symbol of the triumph of the vision and design genius of John and Washington Roebling and the skill of Emily Warren Roebling.

The bridge, conceived and designed for construction by German-born John, was inherited by his son Washington when John died after an accident at the bridge site in 1869. Washington, however, an engineer who had no use for staying at his drawing board, was seriously disabled in the early stages of building the bridge's foundation. In great pain and partially blinded and paralyzed by "caisson disease" (or "the bends," as we now call it), he turned to his wife Emily to oversee the monumental construction project. From his room overlooking the East River, he tutored her on the design, engineering, and construction details of the bridge.

When officials or contractors arrived to discuss bridge matters or negotiate the numerous problems and design changes, it was Mrs. Roebling who received them and talked to them. Countless hours of questioning and being questioned gave all involved the impression that she was in command of the subject, if not the entire project. Her competence and perseverance prevailed over all the criticisms and problems cast her way. For all her power and influence, however, she was willing to accept the role of her husband's agent. Her presence on the job and her skillful handling of public and private meetings earned her the respect of the men who worked on the bridge and the admiration of professionals and politicians alike.

Emily Roebling kept a scrapbook of newspaper articles recording praise and criticism of the bridge, as well as the turbulence of municipal squabbles and scandals surrounding it. Her role as overseer must certainly have been in the eye of the storm.

After the dedication of the bridge, Mrs. Roebling's engineering was limited to supervising construction of a home in Trenton, New Jersey. She traveled extensively, campaigned on behalf of the Woman's Club, and studied law at New York University, where her relentless intellect served to win her awards for legal writing.

Emily Roebling died in 1903. In 1983, she was nominated to the National Women's Hall of Fame. After her induction into the Hall, a national Emily Roebling award was established. It is presented annually to an outstanding American woman.

---

Source: Based on information provided by Citicorp's Public Affairs Department and the National Women's Hall of Fame, Inc.

departure of an airplane flight is passed on to the airline's personnel, such as those in maintenance, catering, and baggage handling, so that their schedules can be adjusted.

## Production Control Aids

As you can see, production can be extremely complex. When there are multiple layers of interacting processes, they simply cannot be controlled through memos or word of mouth. As a result, production managers use graphic tools that allow them to lay out the whole system on paper. A flaw in the system will often show up sooner and more clearly in a Gantt chart or PERT network than it would by trial and error.

▲ **Gantt Charts** **Gantt charts,** developed around 1900 by Henry L. Gantt, graphically measure all production steps performed, the time each is supposed to take, and the time each actually takes. The Gantt chart in Figure 8-6 shows that steps 1 and 5 are progressing according to plan and that step 3 is ahead of schedule. Unfortunately, because step 2 has fallen behind, so has step 4, which depends on step 2 for completion.

▲ **PERT Networks** Useful as they are, Gantt charts proved inadequate for the more complex and dynamic scheduling required to build sophisticated machinery such as atomic submarines, aerospace vehicles, and weapon systems. So PERT was developed. The use of PERT usually results in a minimum of

**Figure 8-6** Gantt chart for completion of a dune buggy.

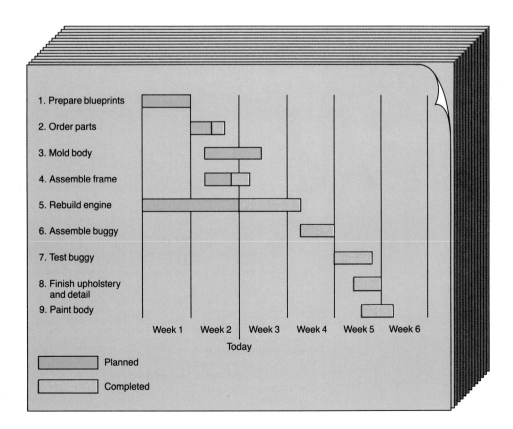

production delays and helps ensure quality production. Essentially, **PERT (Program Evaluation and Review Technique)** is a graphic scheduling and control tool that shows, in linked sequence, all the tasks in a production process, especially the critical path. The **critical path** is the longest sequence of operations or steps in the chart, whose prompt completion is required for the whole project to be done on time. The project can't be done in less than the time needed to complete the critical path.

> Figure 8-7 shows the steps and times needed to produce and ship a textbook somewhat simpler than this one. Which is the critical path—Path A (events 1, 2, 4, 6, 8, 10, 13, 14, 15, and 16) or Path B (events 1, 3, 5, 7, 9, 11, 12, 13, 14, 15, and 16)? Turn to note 14 at the end of the book to see if you answered correctly.

▲ **Computers** Computers are used in almost every aspect of production control. Automakers use them to determine when cars of a certain model, color, and price are to be produced, what resources (especially parts and subassemblies) are needed, and when car assembly should start and finish. A computer routes long-distance phone calls, as well as oil in pipelines and freight in trains and trucks. Airline scheduling, as complex as it is, would be impossible without computers. Computers also dispatch subway systems, as well as high-speed trains in Japan and Europe. Baton Rouge's Exxon refinery has computers hooked to a spectrograph to check on the quality of the product being produced. If it's too rich, the computer adjusts the mixture.

**Figure 8-7** PERT network diagram for a textbook.

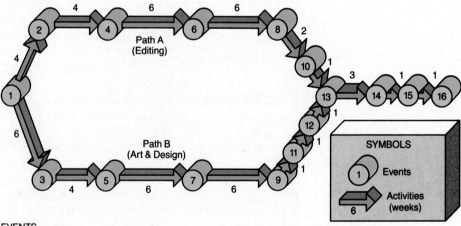

EVENTS
1. Start (receipt of final manuscript)
2. Copy editing complete
3. Interior design of book sketched out
4. Copy editing approved by author
5. Sample design pages received and approved
6. Text typeset
7. Artwork drawn
8. Text proofread and corrected

9. Artwork proofread and corrected
10. Text shipped to printer
11. Artwork shipped to printer
12. Artwork shot by printer
13. Text shot by printer and combined with artwork
14. Text pages and cover printed
15. Pages inserted in book cover
16. End (book's arrival at warehouse)

## Role of Maintenance

Maintenance is still another important part of production control. Your car will probably perform well if you follow the maintenance schedule provided in the owner's manual. Similarly, well-maintained machines and equipment support a high level of productivity in a business. The objective is to prevent unexpected production stoppages. Following a schedule for servicing a machine and making inspections of its critical points reduces breakdowns and permits repairs to be scheduled.

The importance of maintenance was demonstrated in November 1981, when the second flight of the space shuttle Columbia was delayed because two common oil filters became clogged with "gunk."[15]

## Quality Control

**Objective 9**

**How to handle maintenance and quality control.**

**Quality control,** the process designed to ensure that the quality produced is the same as that planned for, is a key part of production control. Most firms would like to produce the product that is best, based on its intended use. The quality actually produced, however, is limited by many factors, such as urgency of customer demand, production capacity, personnel efficiency, type and condition of facilities, and cost.

Production managers usually try to establish the level of quality at the point that balances the customer's needs and the lowest cost of production for the company. The quality level chosen is converted into standard measurements so that machines can be set and run properly. Standards of quality may be set for dimensions, color, strength, content, weight, or other characteristics.

But tradeoffs do take place in the real world. Sometimes the standard used isn't the theoretically ideal one. In order to meet one quality standard, producers may skimp on another. For example, a twelve-ounce box of cereal is supposed to contain at least twelve ounces. However, if it's filled to, say, thirteen ounces, profits will be lower or losses may result. If the contents fall below twelve ounces, on the other hand, customers may complain or government agencies may take legal action. Therefore, machines are set to fill the packages to a point slightly over twelve ounces, which will balance the costs of over- and underweight.

You've seen how production managers use selected standards to set their machines. But it's impossible for firms to produce millions of units each year without some faulty units slipping through the net. The next stage in quality control, then, is to use inspectors to ensure that actual production conforms to the standards. This inspection is usually done on receipt of material from suppliers, at selected points in the production process, and before delivery to customers. It may be a spot check (sampling) or a check of each item. If an unacceptable number of units fail to meet standards, corrective action must be taken. In some places, computers are being used at this stage of production control. For instance, computerized machines at Ford's transmission plant in Batavia, Ohio, measure the dimensions of four parts in minutes rather than the six to eight hours operators needed to measure manually.[16]

The Japanese have developed many effective methods for ensuring quality. One, the quality control circle, recognizes that the quality of a product is determined not only by machines but also by the active participation of the workers involved in its production. A **quality control circle (QCC)** is a group, consisting of the supervisor and workers in a unit, which meets to discuss the quality desired and ways of achieving that level of quality (see Fig. 8-8).

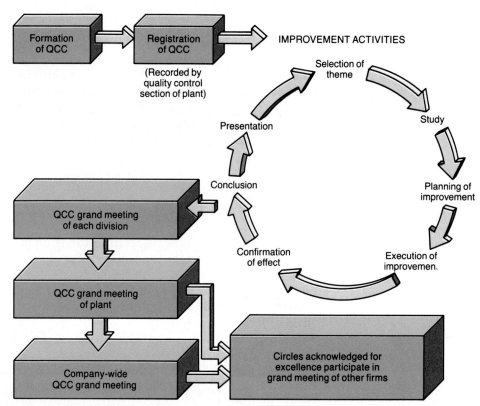

**Figure 8-8** How quality control circles work. (Reprinted from the "Japan: Quality Control and Innovation" Special Advertising Section in the July 20, 1981 issue of *Business Week* by special permission, © 1981 by McGraw-Hill, Inc.)

Quality control circles were used in U.S. plants during World War II. But Japan adopted and further developed them as a way of recovering from the 97 percent devastation of its production system. The Japanese work ethic and national concern for production and quality contributed to their widespread acceptance in Japan. Similar factors have led to their acceptance by many U.S. firms, such as Ford Motor Company. Over 1,000 Employee Involvement Groups (EIGs) have been set up by Ford's managers and the UAW at sixty-five plants around the country.

## ⏺ LEARNING OBJECTIVES REVISITED

1. *What production is, as well as why and where it is needed.*

   Production, or operations, is the use of human, physical, and financial resources to produce products or services. In essence, production is a system for converting inputs into outputs. Such systems are found in all types of organizations, both manufacturing and nonmanufacturing.

2. *The different types of production processes and how they are related.*

   Production processes may be synthetic, in which two or more inputs are mixed or assembled to form one or a very few outputs, or analytic, in which a raw material is broken down, or separated, to form a variety of

outputs. The processes may also be continuous or intermittent.

In any event, the processes are related in a production chain, which includes all the activities from gathering raw materials to delivering the final product or service.

3. *What human and physical resources are needed for production planning.*

Production processes must be designed, work divided, tasks designed, people hired and trained, systems designed and used, and employees motivated for the most effective operations. Whether people or machines are used to perform work depends on the capabilities of each, the nature of the activities to be done, and financial conditions. While mechanization and automation are important to production and the robot revolution is drastically changing the human/machine relationship, people are still the most important resource.

4. *How to determine the capacity and location of production facilities.*

Two major decisions about production facilities are production capacity and location. Both are based on forecasts of future costs and demands. Other factors in location choice are availability of materials, personnel, energy, and land; restrictions and regulations; employee attitudes; surrounding environment; and nearness to customers.

5. *How to design and lay out production facilities.*

There are essentially two types of facility layouts. Product layout arranges work situations according to the sequence of operations on a given product. Process layout groups machines and workers together according to the type of work being done.

6. *Materials management by means of purchasing and inventory control.*

Materials management is needed so that the right materials and supplies are purchased in the right quantity and at the right price, and so that inventory is controlled. Inventory is costly in that it uses space, must be protected and controlled, loses value over time, and ties up money. Yet a lack of adequate inventory is also costly in terms of lost customers and waste of employee and management time.

7. *The steps involved in production control.*

Production control is a system for coordinating people, machines, and materials in order to reach maximum effectiveness. The steps in control are production planning, routing, scheduling, dispatching, and follow-up.

8. *Some of the more useful aids to production control.*

Two useful production control aids are the Gantt chart, which measures the time of actual performance against planned performance, and PERT (Program Evaluation and Review Technique), which determines the critical path for timely project completion. Computers are being used in nearly all phases of production control, from production planning to follow-up.

9. *How to handle maintenance and quality control.*

Other important aspects of production are maintenance and quality control. Quality control is achieved through inspections, spot checks, and sampling, as well as through quality control circles.

## ▲ IMPORTANT TERMS

As an extra review of the chapter, try defining the following terms. If you have trouble with any of them, refer to the page listed.

| | |
|---|---|
| productivity  *196* | product layout  *212* |
| production (operations)  *196* | process layout  *212* |
| utility  *197* | materials management  *213* |
| form utility  *197* | inventory  *213* |
| production process  *197* | just-in-time (JIT) production |
| synthetic process  *197* | system  *214* |
| analytic process  *197* | production control  *215* |
| continuous process  *198* | routing  *215* |
| intermittent process  *199* | dispatching  *215* |
| production chain  *202* | Gantt charts  *217* |
| production and operations | PERT (Program Evaluation and |
| management  *204* | Review Technique)  *218* |
| mechanization  *205* | critical path  *218* |
| automation  *206* | quality control  *219* |
| production capacity  *208* | quality control circle |
| layout  *212* | (QCC)  *219* |

## ▲ REVIEW QUESTIONS

1. What is production?
2. What are the inputs, operating activities, and outputs for (a) a hospital, (b) an airline, (c) a department store, (d) a fast-food establishment, (e) a bank, (f) a print shop, and (g) your school's registration system?
3. What are the main differences between the synthetic production process and the analytic process?
4. What are the differences between a continuous process of production and an intermittent process?
5. Describe a production chain.
6. What is the difference between mechanization and automation?
7. What is the optimum production capacity, and how is it determined?
8. What are the most important factors to consider in locating a firm's production facilities?
9. What is the difference between a product layout and a process layout?
10. What steps are involved in purchasing decisions?
11. Compare the costs of having too much inventory with those of having too little.
12. List and give examples of the steps in production control.

## ▲ DISCUSSION QUESTIONS

1. How does it help a store to have computerized cash registers? Should all stores have them? Why or why not? How do you think workers react when machines take over part of their job?
2. As a manager, how would you determine when to use machines instead of people to do work?

3. Do you think the robot revolution is really a revolution? Is it here to stay? Why or why not?

4. Why would a pocket calculator manufacturer choose to locate or not to locate in your area?

5. What inventory costs can a clothing store avoid (or minimize) with a clearance sale? How might you justify sales of clothing at half price?

6. Prepare a Gantt chart for completion of a term paper.

7. Prepare a PERT network diagram of your school's registration process. Does it have a critical path? Explain.

8. How does increasing the quality of a product affect its costs?

9. Newspapers have reported a variety of complaints about the quality of service from automobile repair shops. If you were managing such a shop, how would you control the quality of your service?

## CASE 8-1  The Crash Program

Bob Redford[17] had recently been appointed district engineer for the Lake District of an independent telephone company in Texas. There were three operating divisions, each with several districts. Bob's boss was Calvin Fall, division engineer of the West Division. The division engineers reported to the company's vice-president in charge of operations.

Shortly after Bob's appointment, the vice-president publicly promised to provide service to the many applicants in a sparsely populated rural area of the Lake District. Little effort had been made through the years to install phones in the area because of the large capital expenditure required; there was no way the service could be profitable. The vice-president promised to provide service in much less time than was normally required for engineering, materials procurement, and construction. The result was a severe peak in the need for engineering personnel. Bob wrote a memo to Calvin Fall requesting more people or overtime pay for his people, but nothing was done.

After five more areas were promised expedited service, Bob told Calvin that he couldn't do the work with his limited staff. Regular maintenance and installation work wasn't being done. Construction work on the new projects couldn't be started until the engineers had completed the detailed designs that Bob needed to purchase materials and issue work orders. Calvin assigned an engineer from another district to do the phase of the engineering that had to be sent to the vice-president for formal approval of the projects, but then that engineer returned to his unit.

When Calvin told Bob that the vice-president had promised that the work on all six projects would be completed, Bob blew his top. He reminded Calvin that his memo requesting more help or overtime, written six months earlier, had never been answered, despite repeated oral requests. Calvin pointed out that company policy prohibited overtime payments for anyone except emergency repair crews. Calvin asked why Bob's engineers, who were professionals, didn't work overtime on their own to help relieve the heavy work load.

**Case Questions**

1. What does this case show about the need to coordinate a firm's sales and operations activities?

2. What does it show about the steps in production control, especially scheduling and sequencing of work?

3. What does it illustrate about the importance of human, physical, and financial resources?

## ▲ CASE 8-2  Scottsville Manufacturing Company

Bill Stevens, operations manager of Scottsville Manufacturing, was known for running an efficient shop. He and Albert Carter, manager of data processing, decided on the basis of a feasibility study to mechanize the materials inventory system. This system was critical to operations because of the large volume of materials used and the importance of having accurate information on the availability, status, and location of all materials for control purposes.

Within a few months, input and output formats, computer programs, and printout schedules had been debugged and the system installed. The printout of the first automated run—placed on Bill's desk at 7:30 A.M., the scheduled time—contained additional information that had been impossible to obtain with previous manual methods. Operating personnel found these neatly printed reports and their arrangement of data very convenient.

Everyone was satisfied with the new mechanized system—until two weeks later when Bill didn't find the materials status report on his desk,

where it had been every morning for the past five years. The night superintendent told him the data processing center had called at 6:30 A.M. to say that the report would be about two hours late. A computer memory component had malfunctioned, causing erroneous information to be generated. This caused much confusion and delay in production. Bill emphasized to Albert Carter the importance of receiving the reports on time, since they were used to schedule the entire day's operations. Albert replied that, while he was sympathetic to Bill's problem, there would sometimes be delays of a few hours or longer. Such problems as program, operator, and magnetic tape read/write errors, failures in hardware or software, and other electronic factors were given as reasons for delay.

Bill was slightly confused. Should they continue with their mechanized system—with its increased accuracy and additional information—and somehow get by when the reports were delayed? Or should they return to the original system and be assured of having access to more limited reports at 7:30 each morning?

**Case Questions**

1. What does the case reveal about the advantages of mechanization?
2. What does it reveal about the disadvantages of mechanization?
3. What does it show about the relative flexibility of humans and machines?
4. What would you do if you were Bill Stevens? How would you justify your decision to your boss?

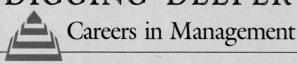

# DIGGING DEEPER
## Careers in Management

Some of the most varied and widespread career patterns in business can be found in management. The many levels of management—first-line supervision, middle management, and top management—and the fact that the basic business functions such as marketing, operations, and finance all require managers creates a variety of opportunities. And the many types of enterprises—restaurants, music stores, radio and television stations, manufacturing plants, insurance agencies, and automobile dealerships, to name just a few—increase the opportunities further. Table II-1 shows where management jobs are.

### What Management Jobs Require

Managers' work is highly complex, since managers must be able to adapt quickly to rapidly changing economic, technological, sociocultural, political-legal, and demographic environments. They must also maintain an appropriate external and internal balance between those having a claim on the firm—employees, customers, suppliers, and the public—and its owners. Managers are, more than anything else, decision makers. They often make decisions in situations in which there is little, and often conflicting, information. Therefore, if you want to succeed as a manager, you must have a high frustration threshold and be able to cope with change and ambiguity. Above all, you must be willing and able to work with and through people.

In spite of these challenges, the competition for management positions is intense. Many people seek the higher status, greater authority, and better salaries associated with these positions. And many people have a strong loyalty and commitment to their organizations and want to contribute to those businesses' growth and development. Although managerial positions are different within and between companies, all managers perform the same basic managerial activities: they communicate with, lead, and motivate employees; allocate scarce resources; and manage conflict and change.

Technical competence and specialization in an area are sometimes quite important to managers. For example, an advertising manager has to have advertising knowledge and skills and a data processing manager needs computer knowledge and skills. In fact, some specialty areas in management have become career options in themselves, such as hotel and restaurant management, hospital administration, airport management, and city management. Yet it isn't the technical expertise of people in these fields that makes them effective managers; it's their understanding of, and ability to use, management skills that lead to success in management.

Career paths in management involve different degrees of authority and responsibility. Supervisors are considered first-line management;

**TABLE II-1. Percentage of employees who are managers, classified by type of industry.**

| Type of Industry | Percentage of All Employees in Industry Who Are Managers | |
|---|---|---|
| | 1976 | 1982 |
| Wholesale and retail trade | 19.2 | 19.3 |
| Public administration | 12.4 | 12.8 |
| Manufacturing | 6.7 | 8.3 |
| Services, except household | 7.3 | 7.9 |
| Finance, real estate, and insurance | 19.8 | 19.6 |
| Construction | 11.9 | 12.9 |
| Transportation & public utilities | 9.3 | 11.0 |
| Mining | 8.3 | 11.7 |
| Agriculture | 0.9 | 1.1 |

SOURCE: Data compiled from U.S. Department of Labor, Bureau of Labor Statistics, *Handbook of Labor Statistics* Bulletin 2175 (Washington, D.C.: Government Printing Office, December 1983).

department managers, including regional and plant managers, are considered middle management; and vice-presidents and chief executives are top management. Technical skills are very important to first-line supervisors because they train their operative employees to perform technical tasks and oversee their performance to ensure that quantity, quality, and cost standards are met. Middle managers need both technical and conceptual skills, and top management, the highest degree of conceptual skills. All managers require considerable human relations skills.

## Some Selected Careers in Management and Administrative Support Positions

Table II-2 shows some selected careers available in management and administrative support. The first salaries for each position were typical of those being offered as this book went to press. The second figures are typical for middle-level positions with above-average abilities in medium-sized and large companies.

**TABLE II-2.  Selected careers in management and administrative support.**

| Job Title | Job Description | Education and Training | Salaries (Beginner Experienced) | Outlook to 1990 |
|---|---|---|---|---|
| Receptionists | Greet customers and other visitors, determine their needs, and refer callers to the person who can help them. May type, file, or operate a switchboard. | High school diploma. Junior or community college. | Average, $9,725 | Number is expected to grow faster than the average for all occupations. |
| Secretaries and stenographers | At the center of communications within the firm; process and transmit information to the staff and to other organizations. | High school diploma. Secretarial training at junior or community college or business school. | Varies | Number is expected to increase faster than the average for all occupations. |
| | *Secretaries* Schedule appointments, give information to callers, organize and maintain files, fill out forms, and take and transcribe dictation. | | Average, $13,365<br><br>Executive secretary to corporate officer, $16,878 | |
| | *Stenographers* Take dictation and transcribe their notes on a typewriter. | | Average, $13,190 | Expected to continue the decline of recent years due to widespread use of dictation machines. |

**TABLE II-2**—*continued*

| Job Title | Job Description | Education and Training | Salaries ( Beginner Experienced ) | Outlook to 1990 |
|---|---|---|---|---|
| Hotel managers and assistants | Responsible for operating their establishments profitably and satisfying hotel guests. Determine room rates and credit policies, direct food service operations and manage the housekeeping, accounting, security, and maintenance departments. | College education is emphasized. Bachelor's degree in hotel and restaurant administration is preferable. Experience is the most important consideration in selecting managers. | $13,500 $20,000–$80,000 | Number is expected to grow faster than the average for all occupations. |
| Personnel and labor relations specialists | Interview, select, and recommend applicants to fill job openings; keep informed of EEO and affirmative action; oversee the implementation of these policies. Handle wage and salary administration, training and career development, and employee benefits. | College degree is required for most beginning positions. Newly hired workers usually enter on-the-job training programs. | $16,500 $50,000–$76,000 in medium-sized and large companies. | Number is expected to grow about as fast as the average for all occupations. Job competition is increasing. Particularly keen competition is anticipated for jobs in labor relations. |
| Health service administrators | Provide effective management for teaching hospitals, clinics, and nursing homes under the supervision of a board of directors. Prepare budgets, establish rates for health services, direct hiring and training of personnel, and coordinate departmental activities. | Master's degree in hospital administration, health administration, or public health is regarded as the standard credential for many positions. | $17,830 $25,000–$40,000 | Number is expected to grow faster than the average for all occupations. |

**TABLE II-2**—*continued*

| Job Title | Job Description | Education and Training | Salaries ( Beginner Experienced ) | Outlook to 1990 |
|---|---|---|---|---|
| Purchasing agents | Buy machinery, raw materials, parts and components, furniture, business machines, vehicles, office supplies; sometimes negotiate for custom-made products. | College degree. Experience in purchasing standard and catalog items and custom-made items. | $17,830 <br><br> $35,000–$53,000 | Employment is expected to increase about as fast as the average for all occupations. |
| Quality assurance managers | Responsible for testing for product deficiencies and detecting and correcting any that exist. Review product design requirements and often participate in selection of materials and supplies. | College degree and experience as inspectors and in performing quality control function. | $17,830 <br><br> $35,000–$60,000 | Employment is expected to increase about as fast as the average for all occupations. |
| Supervisors | Direct the activities of other employees and ensure that equipment and materials are used properly and efficiently. Make work schedules; keep production and employee records. | Growing number of employers are hiring trainees with a college or technical background. Most supervisors rise through the ranks. | $17,832 <br><br> Average, $21,000 | Number is expected to increase about as fast as the average for all occupations. |
| Industrial engineers | Determine the most effective ways for an organization to use people, machines, and materials. Design data processing systems and apply operations research techniques. | College degree is required for most beginning positions. | $24,575 <br><br> $50,000–$63,000 in medium-sized and large companies. | Number is expected to grow faster than the average for all occupations. |

**TABLE II-2**—*continued*

| Job Title | Job Description | Education and Training | Salaries ( Beginner Experienced ) | Outlook to 1990 |
|---|---|---|---|---|
| City managers | Responsible for functions such as tax collection and disbursement, law enforcement, and public works. Budget and prepare for future growth. | Master's degree, preferably in public or business administration. | $26,580<br><br>$33,000–$70,000 | Number is expected to grow about as fast as the average for all occupations. |

SOURCES: U.S. Department of Labor, *Occupational Outlook Handbook*, 1982–1983 (Washington: U.S. Government Printing Office, April 1982) and 1980–1981 (Washington: U.S. Government Printing Office, April 1980); College Placement Council, *CPC Salary Survey, Summer Supplement* (Bethlehem, Pa.: CPC, 1983), pp. 2–5; and Steven D. Ross, "The 12 Top Money-Making Careers of the '80s," *Business Week's Guide to Careers* 1 (Spring 1983):9.

# PART III

## MANAGING HUMAN RESOURCES

The annual report of many companies has a statement that reads something like "People are our most precious asset." This is another way of saying that a firm must have capable, trained, and motivated people if it is to succeed. That's what this part is all about. It explains that the most important resource of any business is its people and that personnel management, as a result, is an important part of managing any business activity.

Many firms have a personnel department with a personnel manager directly responsible for coordinating personnel activities. Yet, whether or not there is a personnel department, *all managers are responsible* for managing human resources.

The personnel management function, which includes planning for, recruiting, training and developing, compensating, evaluating, and maintaining the health and safety of personnel, is discussed in Chapter 9.

In addition, all managers must lead and supervise their employees. This involves communicating with and motivating people. These activities are covered in Chapter 10.

Chapter 11 explains how special groups of personnel—labor unions and employee associations—exert a great influence on all business activities and require a particular management response.

231

# 9

# Managing Personnel

*Management is the development of people and not the direction of things.*

Lawrence Appley

*There is something that is much scarcer, something finer by far, something rarer than ability. It is the ability to recognize ability.*

Elbert Hubbard

**Learning Objectives**

After studying this chapter, you will understand:

1. The meaning of personnel management from the viewpoint of the personnel department and management.
2. How a firm determines future personnel needs and sets up a program for meeting them.
3. The different procedures involved in recruiting, selecting, and orienting new employees.
4. How employees, both nonmanagerial and managerial, are trained and developed.
5. Where employee evaluation fits into the personnel management process.
6. Some of the problems in and methods of compensating employees.
7. The maintenance of employees' health and safety.

**In This Chapter**

What Is Personnel Management?
Planning for Personnel Needs
Recruiting and Selecting Employees
Training and Developing Employees
Evaluating Employees
Compensating Employees
Maintaining Health and Safety

# DELTA AIR LINES, INC.
## A Flying Family

Delta Air Lines began modestly in the 1920s, crop dusting in Louisiana with two World War I "Jennies" (Curtiss JN-4s). By 1929, it had moved up to carrying mail and passengers. Today, Delta has the fewest complaints per passenger boarded of any major airline—no minor accomplishment in a new age of skyjacking and lost luggage.

Behind Delta's astounding record lies a factor that can't be overlooked in any major corporate success: people. Delta has a warm family feeling that makes for doggedly loyal workers and fires the wrath of unions. Delta's personnel policy, for instance, includes open-door access to top management for all employees. The firm promotes from within, its pay and benefits are better than those of most competitors, and it rarely lays off its people. In fact, when other airlines reduced employment during the 1973 oil embargo, chairman and CEO W. T. Beebe warned senior management: "Now the time has come for the stockholders to pay a little penalty for keeping the team together."

Delta management tries to make sure its employees subscribe to the family concept from the beginning by screening job applicants minutely. For example, flight attendants-to-be are skimmed from the top ranks of thousands of applicants, interviewed twice, and then sent to the company psychologist, who tries to evaluate their sense of cooperativeness or teamwork. Top managers have annual meetings with employees, who are encouraged to ask frank questions and make suggestions. Employees are also entrusted with decisions that would normally be restricted to managers alone. A committee of flight attendants chooses their uniforms, and mechanics select their own immediate supervisors.

Of course, Delta could be accused of being a strict, prudish family. Not only did it fire a flight attendant for overexposure in *Playboy,* but, on a more ordinary scale, attendants aren't allowed to wear open-toed shoes while on duty. The firm can be tough, too. It once fired a flight attendant trainee because she griped about having to train between 10 P.M. and midnight on a Saturday night before an 8 A.M. company exam. Her manager explained: "We had visions of her later refusing to go out on flights."

The firm's generous wages and benefits, along with the strong family feeling, have tended to keep the unions out. Without union work rules, Delta has the advantage of being able to switch employees to different jobs as necessary. During a fuel shortage, for example, 700 operating employees were reassigned to jobs handling luggage and taking reservations. Management believed that cross-training helped employees understand how their jobs fitted in with overall company goals.

Says Beebe, "We've got hundreds of college . . . graduates working on the ramp knowing that they will be promoted if their work merits it. But we don't have any 'stars.' We want people who will enjoy and want to be working for the team." But, all the same, Delta's policy of maintaining full employment was starting to hurt in 1982, as over 1,000 of its 36,000 employees were finally seen as "excess" or "underutilized." In spite of its biggest-ever quarterly operating loss of $18 million, it gave employees an unexpected 8 percent pay raise and still refused to lay off. As a show of appreciation, the employees each pledged 2½ percent of their annual salary to buy the company a $30 million Boeing 767 jet.

Like Delta, most companies recognize that people are their most important resource. A firm must have capable, trained, motivated people if it's going to succeed. Researchers at the University of Michigan's Institute of Social Research have asked thousands of top managers to estimate how much it would cost to replace their human organization. The answers are usually something like "over three times our annual payroll" or "about 24 or 25 times our annual earnings."[1] What these responses reveal is that if all the physical and financial resources of a company were taken away, but the people were still there, it would be easier to rebuild the company than if the people vanished en masse.

## WHAT IS PERSONNEL MANAGEMENT?

**Objective 1**

**The meaning of personnel management from the viewpoint of the personnel department and management.**

We've established that the most important resource of any business is its employees. And planning for, recruiting, selecting, developing, evaluating, and rewarding capable employees is an important part of managing any business activity. But what is personnel management, and who does it?

> What do you think would happen if Delta's management were to change its policy and try to make the firm cost-effective by tightening up on performance, wages, and benefits?

You're probably already familiar with the idea of a personnel department. Most medium-sized and large firms have one. The personnel manager is directly responsible for coordinating all the activities involved in finding, hiring, training, and paying employees. But, whether or not there's a personnel department, *all managers are responsible for managing the firm's human resources.* Therefore, someone in every business is responsible for doing **personnel management,** or planning for, recruiting, selecting, training, developing, evaluating, compensating, and protecting the health and safety of employees.

Personnel management is a shared responsibility, based on the line-staff concept. Top management is responsible for developing overall personnel policies. From there, the responsibility for carrying out those policies flows down through operating managers to the first-line supervisors. But these managers can't perform the function alone; they need the help of the personnel department staff.

### Role of Operating Managers

In general, top management sets personnel objectives and policies and does the long-range planning and organizing. Middle-level managers set up and control the operating procedures for carrying out those policies. First-line supervisors are probably at the most important level for achieving effective personnel management. They interpret policies to employees on a day-to-day basis, influence their attitudes, direct their work, and resolve grievances. In turn, they transmit and interpret the employees' needs and interests to higher management.

Part of company report emphasizing human resources.

*"...we have even greater strength than our technology: Bell System people. It is not only their skills but their spirit that makes our business great—and will keep it great."*

Bell System employees pictured are, from left to right: (top row) Pat Isom, AT&T Long Lines-Washington, D.C.; Rau C. Chang, Bell Laboratories-West Long Branch, N.J., and Rochelle Deason, Illinois Bell-Chicago; (bottom row) David J. Calvert, Long Lines-Anaheim, Calif.; Garmayonne D. Tyner, Western Electric Company-Atlanta, Georgia, and Robert Butler, Chesapeake & Potomac Telephone-Washington, D.C.

### Role of the Personnel Department

The personnel manager, who heads the personnel department, provides expert advice, guidance, and assistance to operating managers. In general, the personnel department is responsible for (1) affirmative action programs (AAPs) to ensure equal employment opportunity for all, (2) staffing, (3) training and development, (4) wage and salary administration, and (5) health and safety.

Unfortunately, there tends to be an inherent conflict between the line operating managers and the staff personnel managers. The difficulty, which most firms keep under control, is over who gets credit for successes and blame for failures. Personnel managers say they can't be held responsible for personnel programs unless they have some voice in carrying them out. Yet operating managers say they must have full authority for implementing programs if they're going to be held responsible for their outcome.

## PLANNING FOR PERSONNEL NEEDS

**Objective 2**

How a firm determines future personnel needs and sets up a program for meeting them.

Managers of a business obviously can't wait until they need new employees to plan their personnel needs. Instead, they must work with the personnel department to forecast future needs and decide where they're going to find the right people to fill those needs. **Personnel planning** includes all the activities carried out by both personnel and operating managers in order to provide the right types and numbers of employees to reach a firm's objectives. As FYI on page 237 indicates, personnel management requires a good bit of planning and assessing of the overall business environment.

### Determining Personnel Needs

The process of determining a firm's personnel needs starts with deciding what the firm's objectives and plans are and estimating how many employees will be needed in the future. Then a study of present employees must be made to see who's already able to perform the jobs or can be trained to do so. This is followed by an estimate of how many new people have to be hired.

▲ **Objectives and Plans** The first step in personnel planning is deciding where the business wants to go. What does it plan to do? Expand? Retrench? What new products are going to be introduced? Are new markets going to be opened up? The answers to these and related questions, usually the responsibility of operating managers, will affect the number and types of people to be hired.

> The first objective of Quality Plumbing (FYI, page 237) was to install plumbing, heating, and wiring in commercial buildings and residences. This determined the type and number of people needed. When the partners couldn't obtain the employees needed to reach that objective, how did they adapt to changing conditions?

*FYI*

## The Limited Work Force

In the late 1950s, two friendly competitors formed a partnership—the Quality Plumbing Shop—in a small town southeast of Houston, Texas. It did wiring for commercial buildings and residences. Located in a rapidly developing industrial area, the shop competed for business with several others within a fifty-mile radius. At first, the partners did most of the work themselves and limited their activities to what could be done with two helpers. As business expanded, they hired more craftspeople and other employees, but found it increasingly difficult to find capable employees.

When the Lyndon B. Johnson Space Center was built nearby, many of the town's workers left their jobs for better-paying ones at the center. The result was an acute shortage of skilled workers for the local construction industry.

The partners couldn't hire the competent people they needed to meet their customers' demands. They tried a long-range apprentice training program, but when workers completed the program (which took several years) they often went to work for one of the larger companies instead of staying with Quality.

The partners were forced to reduce the number of jobs they would bid on because of the limited work force. So they started a wholesale plumbing, heating, and electrical supply business on the side. Eventually, there were only three plumbers, three plumber's helpers, two electricians, and two electrician's helpers left. Since most of the craftspeople were nearing retirement age, and since the helpers didn't seem interested in learning the trade, the partners were often unable to bid on construction jobs.

▲ **Job Analysis**  The process used to determine what each job is and what is required to perform it effectively is called **job analysis.** It provides data on required skills, training, effort, qualifications, experience, and responsibilities for various jobs. A **job description,** which lists the job's duties, responsibilities, and working conditions, is prepared from the job analysis. It details the relationships between the particular job, as it's to be done, and the other jobs with which it's associated. When statements of mental, physical, educational, experience, and other qualifications required of a person to successfully perform the job are added, the description is called a **job specification.** These requirements are the basis for selecting new employees for the jobs.

▲ **Personnel Forecasts**  Next, managers must determine the number of employees needed and what skills and abilities they should have. Therefore, the firm's *total* personnel needs must be forecast in terms of desired occupational specialties, job skills, personal characteristics, and number of employees.

Then management must see how many people in the firm can perform those jobs or be trained to do so. This requires that the personnel department prepare an inventory of present employees, matching their skills and capabilities with the overall personnel needs of the business. The difference between overall needs and the number of present personnel capable of doing the work tells how many new people have to be recruited. While the number of people wanted may be known, other factors such as occupational choices, experience, expected retirements, terminations, and transfers must also be considered.

> In FYI on page 237, how did the younger workers' occupational choices and the older workers' expected retirement affect the partners' hiring plans?

## Developing Sources

In general, the more sources used in the search for personnel, the better the chances that people with the desired qualities will be found. Realizing this, effective managers will develop and maintain many sources of supply. Many managers keep up a friendly relationship with selected faculty members at nearby colleges and universities, from whom they get advance notice of capable graduates who are available to fill professional and managerial positions. The personnel department will have sources, too, but they may not be as fruitful as the informed networks that operating managers nurture.

As shown in Figure 9-1, there are really only two sources from which employees can be recruited to fill specific jobs—from within the organization and from the outside. In general, managers prefer to use the internal source whenever possible. It tends to motivate present personnel and is quicker, cheaper, and more effective than scouring unknown outside sources. Some jobs, however, require going outside the firm to find the right people. When a new technological development is introduced, as when a computer is installed, present employees with no experience simply may be unable to do the job. Also, if the internal source is the only one used, there's always the risk of stagnation. Therefore, most employers use a combination of promoting from within and hiring from without.

▲ **Internal Sources** There are three ways to get new employees internally. First, they can be obtained by upgrading someone from the present work force to do the job. **Upgrading** is educating, training, or developing present employees to perform the same job better, as changing circumstances demand. For example, when Mid-South Discount & Closeout Center changed from manual to computerized accounting, management trained the current bookkeeper to use the computer instead of going outside to hire someone else. The bookkeeper not only learned new activities but also grew professionally and earned a higher salary.

Second, jobs can be filled by transferring employees in from other parts of the company. **Transferring** is moving employees from less desirable or less rewarding jobs in the company to others that better satisfy their and the company's needs. Transfers that require relocation to a new geographical area,

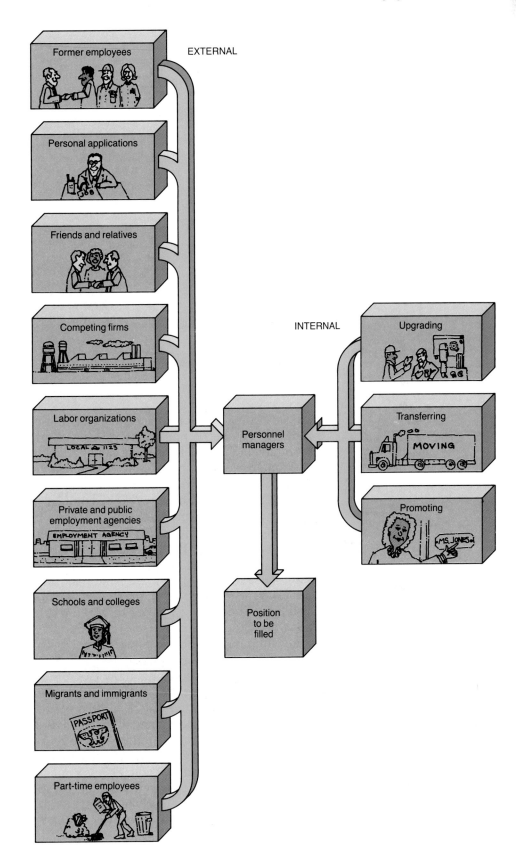

**Figure 9-1** Where to find needed employees.

Some firms utilize workers who only want to work for a limited amount of time.

however, can cause such financial, social, and psychological problems that a transferee may not be immediately effective on the job.

Finally, higher-level positions can be filled by promoting present employees. **Promoting** is moving an employee from a lower-level job to a higher-level one, usually with a higher salary, a new job title, and added duties and responsibilities. Promotion not only takes advantage of skills that have been developed within the company but also serves as a motivator for exceptional performance. Exxon uses primarily internal sources for its higher-level people, as do Caterpillar Tractor and Delta Air Lines.

▲ **External Sources** The specific external source of supply used by a firm depends on the job to be filled, the type of worker needed, and economic conditions. Some sources of employees are (1) former employees, (2) personal applications, (3) friends and relatives, (4) competing firms, (5) labor organizations, (6) private and public employment agencies, (7) schools and colleges, and (8) migrant workers and immigrants.

Many firms are also using many part-time employees, such as students, homemakers reentering the work force, older (often retired) workers, and others who want to work for only a limited period of time. For example, ACS America, a software development firm with sales of $5 million, recently opened a training center for retirees over age fifty-five.[2] Such practices give firms greater staffing flexibility, reduce fixed expenses for employee benefits, and often provide better workers for less money. Also, many companies hire employees from outside concerns that specialize in performing a given service. This method is particularly useful in clerical, custodial, and maintenance operations for which an employee with a given specialty can be hired by the hour or day, as changing work loads dictate.

## RECRUITING AND SELECTING EMPLOYEES

**Objective 3**

The different procedures involved in recruiting, selecting, and orienting new employees.

Once the number and types of new employees to be recruited are known, and the sources from which they're to be recruited have been narrowed down, it's the personnel manager's job to start some type of program of recruitment and selection.

**Recruitment** is reaching out to attract the required number of people with the right abilities to fill available jobs. The recruiter gathers a pool of potential employees from which to select those best qualified to satisfy the firm's needs.

### Affirmative Action Programs

An important part of any program for recruiting and selecting personnel is an effective affirmative action program, which is required by law for firms with fifteen or more employees and for those with government contracts. An affirmative action program requires management not only to provide equal employment opportunity for, but to actively seek out protected groups, such as minorities, women, older employees, the handicapped, and Vietnam veterans. According to legislation such as the Equal Pay Act (1963), Title VII of the Civil Rights Act (1964), and the Equal Employment Opportunity Act (1972), employers must ensure that no group is discriminated against when it comes to employment and advancement.

Affirmative action also assumes that past injustices must be corrected through positive actions to recruit more employees in these categories. Essentially, an **affirmative action program (AAP)** spells out direct and positive actions that a personnel manager will take to search for, recruit, select, train and

An affirmative action program requires management to actively seek out protected groups for employment opportunities.

develop, promote, reward, and maintain individuals who formerly would have been deprived of employment because of race, creed, color, sex, national origin, age, or handicap.

## Methods of Recruiting

The methods used to recruit personnel vary with different companies, in different industries, and in different localities. Some companies passively wait for applicants to come to them. Others go out hunting for potential employees. The usual methods of recruitment include employee referral, advertising, college recruitment, employment agencies, computers, and networking.

▲ **Employee Referral**  **Employee referral** is an employee's suggesting a friend or relative to fill a position that is or soon will be vacant. This is an excellent, inexpensive method of recruiting personnel if it's used properly. Since current employees know the position to be filled and the personal abilities needed to fill it, they may be able to recruit someone better qualified than anyone an outside recruiter could possibly find. However, if the jobs to be filled involve the control and handling of money, or if the company is remiss in its affirmative action, this method should not be used. The basic concept of financial control is that the person who accounts for the money doesn't handle it. If you have friends working together in these situations, this concept is violated.

In light of the overall benefits, some firms that need people give bonuses to employees who attract new employees. A division of Loral Electronics offered a $5,000 bonus to any employee who could find an engineer with a minimum of four years of experience.[3]

▲ **Advertising**  The most common form of recruiting is the use of want ads or display ads in newspapers. Walt Disney got his first job through an ad. And Sears, Roebuck was born when Alvah Roebuck answered an ad placed in the *Chicago Daily News* by Richard Sears. Other forms of advertising include ads in professional journals, on billboards, on radio, and on TV. More than forty major firms use TV to recruit people for hard-to-fill jobs. For example, GTE Lenkurt, Inc., a San Francisco firm, began using TV in 1981 to fill all its engineering and technical job openings.[4]

Although advertising is widely used, most managers would agree that it's a surprisingly poor way to find good managerial, scientific, and professional personnel. Most of these slots are filled by other methods.

▲ **College Recruiting**  College graduates provide the best source of scientific, technical, professional, and managerial personnel. Therefore, many successful firms recruit on college campuses.

▲ **Employment Agencies**  The two main types of employment agencies are private and public. **Private employment agencies** charge a fee to either the employer or the employee for finding an acceptable employee for a given position. If the employee is the one initiating the search for a job, he or she must pay the fee—usually one month's salary. These agencies do some preliminary screening, especially for the higher levels of skilled, clerical, technical, service, and professional occupations. Executive search firms, often called **headhunt-**

**ers,** actively seek managers for given positions in a business. They tend to specialize in a particular occupation, such as marketing managers.

**Public employment agencies** try to match employee qualifications and job needs as part of a public service. The best known is the Job Service, operated by the states in cooperation with the U.S. Labor Department's U.S. Employment Service (USES). These agencies are important sources of skilled and unskilled production and service workers, as well as clerical and technical employees.

▲ **Computers** Just as computers are sometimes used by dating services to match individuals by the characteristics offered and sought, they also can be used to find employees. For example, the U.S. Department of Labor's Job Bank uses a computer to match jobs and people. National Personnel Associates, a group of independent private agencies, has a computer system for pairing professionals with jobs. An agency enters the job specifications for a position into a terminal connected by phone to a central computer which holds applicants' qualifications. In two seconds, the results are announced.[5]

Citibank uses a computerized job-employee matching system, called "Jobmatch."[6] Data about positions are on one program; data about all employees are on another. When there is an opening, employee records are searched to see if anyone in the bank can fill the position. If an employee wants to transfer, his or her record is compared with qualifications needed for various job openings.

▲ **Networking** Operating on the theory that informal ways are sometimes the most effective, a fairly new system called networking is revolutionizing recruitment. Originally associated with women's efforts to advance, **networking** is the transmission of information on job leads and of mutual support via informal business contacts.

### Selecting the Right Person for the Job

Once a group of people have been recruited from the open job market, the next step is **selection,** which is choosing a specific person from among other qualified applicants to fill a vacant position. In theory, selection is simple. The personnel manager decides what the job involves and what abilities an individual needs to perform the job effectively. Then he or she looks at the applicants' records and selects the one whose abilities, experience, and personality most nearly conform to the job requirements. Unfortunately, selection isn't really that simple. While past performance is still the best indicator of future performance, much more is involved. Selection is like an obstacle course. There are certain hurdles and pitfalls a potential employee has to clear before being chosen. An applicant can be disqualified at any stage of the selection procedure. And the decision isn't made by the personnel manager alone.

It's impossible to list all the universal characteristics or abilities to look for in an applicant. They depend on the job. But there are some characteristics that may reveal how well an applicant will perform, including (1) personal background and past performance; (2) aptitudes and interests; (3) attitudes and needs; (4) analytical abilities and technical skills; (5) health, energy, and stamina; and (6) value system. Table 9-1 lists important characteristics, along with sources of information about them. Yet a word of caution is in order. While

**TABLE 9-1. Personal characteristics sought in a prospective employee and sources of information about them.**

| Personal Characteristics Needed to Perform Job Adequately | Sources of Information about Characteristic |
| --- | --- |
| Personal background and past performance | Application blank<br>School records<br>Interviews<br>References |
| Aptitudes and interests | Application blank<br>School records<br>Interviews<br>Psychological tests<br>References<br>Work records |
| Attitudes and needs | Interviews<br>Psychological tests<br>References |
| Analytical abilities | School records<br>Interviews<br>Psychological tests<br>Work references |
| Skills and technical abilities | School records<br>Training records<br>Interviews<br>Work references<br>Performance tests |
| Health, energy, and stamina | Medical examination<br>Interviews<br>Work references |
| Value system | Interviews<br>References |

SOURCE: Reprinted by permission from Leon C. Megginson, *Personnel Management: A Human Resources Approach*, 4th ed. (Homewood, Ill.: Richard D. Irwin, 1981), p. 177. © 1981 by Richard D. Irwin, Inc.

information about a person's personal characteristics can be an important source of valuable knowledge about the applicant, such information must not be used in any way that violates EEOC guidelines.

The selection of employees is a continuous process that can never be thought of as completed, for new people must constantly be selected. The procedure shown in Figure 9-2 and discussed below is as effective a way as any of choosing people.

▲ **Biographical Inventory** An applicant for a copy editor's job in a textbook publishing company has submitted an acceptable résumé and is invited to visit the personnel office. The first thing she has to do is fill out an application blank. This frequently used step in the selection procedure is the first phase in an ongoing search for evidence of acceptable past performance. This evidence

can also be found in an application blank and work, school, and military records as well as the résumé. While the applicant controls what goes into the résumé, the employer determines the information sought in the application blank, such as where the applicant lives, previous employers and supervisors, and prior salary.

▲ **Preliminary Interview** As soon as the paperwork is done, our editorial applicant has a preliminary, screening interview with a personnel department representative and her potential supervisor. The interviewers ask general questions designed to find out if the applicant is unsuitable for the job. Inappropriate experience, lack of serious interest, misunderstandings about the nature of the job, and even personal appearance could disqualify her after a few minutes of questioning. The well-trained interviewer keeps accurate and thorough records at this stage, for future reference in the event of charges of discrimination.

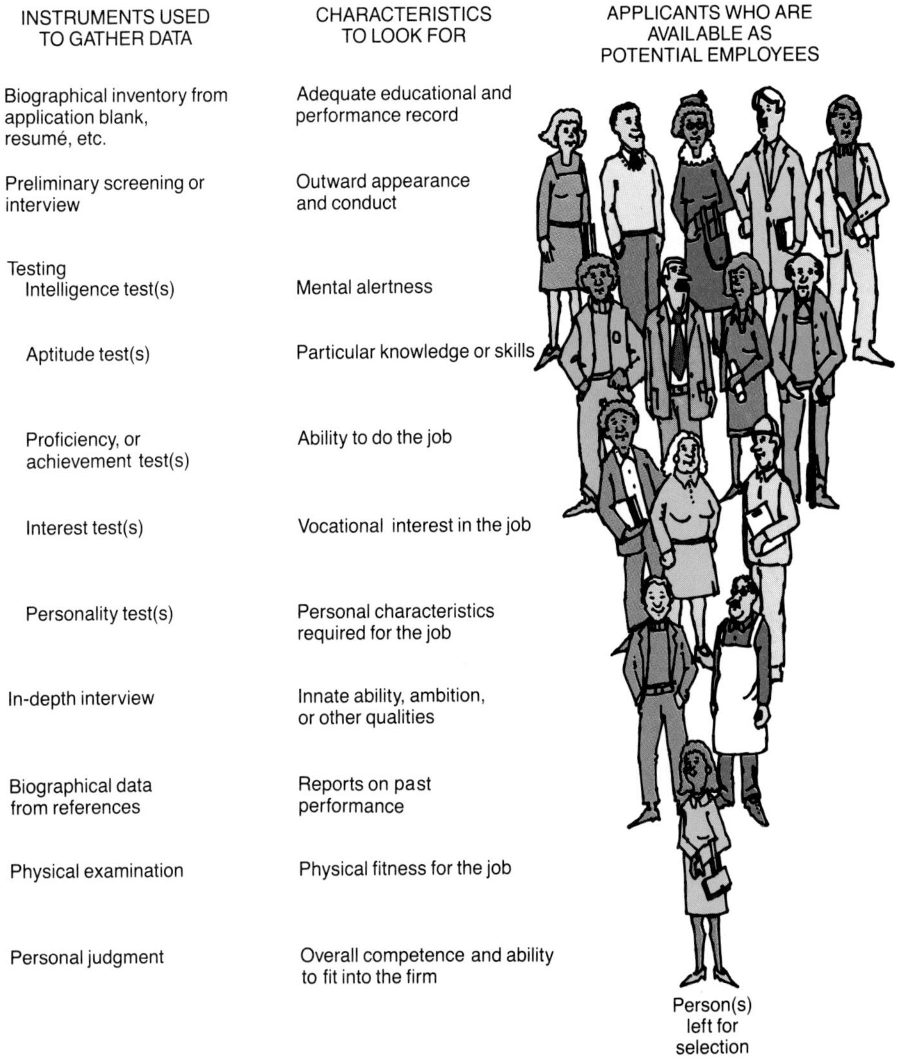

| INSTRUMENTS USED TO GATHER DATA | CHARACTERISTICS TO LOOK FOR |
|---|---|
| Biographical inventory from application blank, resumé, etc. | Adequate educational and performance record |
| Preliminary screening or interview | Outward appearance and conduct |
| Testing Intelligence test(s) | Mental alertness |
| Aptitude test(s) | Particular knowledge or skills |
| Proficiency, or achievement test(s) | Ability to do the job |
| Interest test(s) | Vocational interest in the job |
| Personality test(s) | Personal characteristics required for the job |
| In-depth interview | Innate ability, ambition, or other qualities |
| Biographical data from references | Reports on past performance |
| Physical examination | Physical fitness for the job |
| Personal judgment | Overall competence and ability to fit into the firm |

APPLICANTS WHO ARE AVAILABLE AS POTENTIAL EMPLOYEES

Person(s) left for selection

**Figure 9-2** A suggested procedure for selecting employees. [Adapted by permission from Leon C. Megginson, *Personnel Management: A Human Resources Approach*, 4th ed. (Homewood, Ill.: Richard D. Irwin, 1981), p. 180. © 1981 by Richard D. Irwin, Inc.]

▲ **Testing**  Our applicant is on target for the job so far, but testing is really the only objective basis for judging the quality of her skills.  She's given a sample chapter to take home, copyedit, and mail back to the editorial department supervisor.  With well-developed and well-administered tests, an applicant's ability to perform an important part of the job can be estimated.  But the use of testing is declining because it's difficult both to develop tests that meet affirmative action guidelines and to ensure that *every* applicant takes the same test.  Simple proficiency or achievement tests (such as typing speed tests) are used more frequently.

▲ **In-Depth Interview**  All's going well for our applicant.  She's asked back for a longer, in-depth interview with the supervisor and other key department members—the editor-in-chief and other manuscript editors who can tell her more about the job.  This in-depth interview (or interviews) is quite important in pulling together all the information about the applicant.  Its purpose is to get information about the applicant's attitudes, feelings, and abilities which isn't obtainable elsewhere.  A distinctive feature of this interview is that it's a two-way exchange of information between the potential employee and company interviewers.  In fact, the interviewers may well be trying to sell the applicant on the company at the same time that she's trying to sell them on herself.

▲ **Reference Checks**  The whole editorial department is now in agreement that this candidate looks good for the job.  But one more formality needs to be gone through.  By checking with people our applicant has given as references— three previous bosses and a former professor—management gets subjective information about her past performance.  The one doing the checking must take into account, of course, the possibility of old personality conflicts that may have nothing to do with performance.

▲ **Physical Examination**  Our applicant may be given a physical exam to see whether she has a communicable disease, to decide whether she can physically do the work, and to serve as a defense in case she claims to have been injured on the job.  At one time, the Monsanto Chemical plant in Lynn, Massachusetts, found that 40 percent of the applicants who reached this stage were rejected for "back trouble."  A large energy company found similar results with hearing impairment of applicants who had worked in or frequented discothèques in Los Angeles.  Under U.S. Supreme Court decisions, even handicapped persons can be rejected if they are physically unable to do the particular job.

▲ **Personal Judgment**  Finally, when all else has been done, the personnel manager and those for whom our applicant will work must decide, on the basis of the facts, whether to accept or reject her for employment.  The decision is usually based on the applicant's overall competence and ability to fit into the company.

▲ **Job Offer**  Now that the way has been cleared and a qualified person has been identified, a job offer is made either by the personnel manager or by the editorial supervisor.  Job offers usually spell out the details of starting date, pay, working hours, and vacation time.  There's always a chance, however,

that the applicant will turn down the offer, and then the whole process will have to start over.

▲ **Orientation** After being hired, the new employee is placed on the job and introduced to the company through some form of orientation. This process is important, for a new job is usually difficult and frustrating—even for qualified people. While they may know the job, they simply aren't familiar with the surroundings and the way things are done. For this reason, more employees leave a firm during the first pay period than at any other time in their employment.

The **orientation** process can be a simple introduction of the new employee to co-workers or a lengthy process of filling the employee in on company history, policies, procedures, and benefits. An experimental program at Texas Instruments, consisting of two hours of orientation and six hours of social orientation, resulted in 50 percent less tardiness and absenteeism and two-thirds lower training costs.[7]

## TRAINING AND DEVELOPING EMPLOYEES

**Objective 4**

**How employees, both nonmanagerial and managerial, are trained and developed.**

In general, society is responsible for providing potential employees with a general education, the company for providing job training, and the individual for taking advantage of the learning opportunity. Development can occur formally or informally as the person grows on the job.

### Developing Nonmanagerial Personnel

Beyond simple orientation, there are many methods of training and developing employees. The goal of employee development can be to ensure employees' competence at a given task or job or to help employees qualify for promotion.

▲ **On-the-Job Training** Most employers use some form of **on-the-job training (OJT)**, in which employees perform regular work duties under the supervision and guidance of an experienced worker or instructor. This method provides supervision while the employees are learning the operations involved.

▲ **Vestibule Training** **Vestibule training** is very much like OJT but is done under simulated work conditions, in an area near the production area that's furnished with equipment like that which employees will be using. During training, output isn't a major objective, since the emphasis is on the employees' learning the necessary skills.

▲ **Apprenticeship Training** **Apprenticeship training** is a method of teaching job skills that require an extended period of practice and experience. It's generally used in trades, crafts, and other technical fields. In jobs where skills can be acquired only after a long period of classroom instruction and actual learning experience associated with the job, this training method should be used. The programs are usually jointly developed and supervised by the union and the company, and the union has great say over who enrolls in them.

On-the-job training at Xerox.

▲ **Internship Training** In **internship training,** selected students from a regular academic program work for a company for a limited time to gain employment experience. Internship gives students a better understanding of the relationship between the theory they learn in school and its application in the real world. It also gives them a chance to find out if they like the type of work.

Unfortunately, though, internships don't always work to everyone's benefit. Since they often work on menial tasks, without pay, interns may not be motivated to come to work consistently or to do their best on the job. And managers may feel burdened with an intern's need for direction and lack of experience.

▲ **Programmed Instruction** In **programmed instruction,** material to be learned is presented in a sequential order by means of a TV monitor, film, programmed book, or computer. Learners aren't allowed to proceed beyond a given point until they've demonstrated mastery of the preceding information. In other words, they must learn one part of the training program thoroughly before continuing to the next. In experiments at over 1,500 companies, programmed learning seems to offer improved learning at lower cost.[8] A group of fifty-seven supervisors studying motivation by programmed learning retained twenty-eight factors out of sixty, while the control group retained only fourteen.[9]

▲ **Educational Television** Educational television, which uses either broadcast or closed-circuit television for learning purposes, has the unique advantage of being available to practically unlimited numbers of people, at a drastically reduced cost per person. This method permits managers to do for training and development what industry has done with production, namely, provide mass

development on an assembly-line basis, with quality control, at low cost per person. For example, a group of South Carolina companies used the state's educational TV network to train their middle managers, offering such courses as "Exploring Basic Economics."[10]

## Developing Managerial Personnel

In addition to the usual methods used to develop all employees, there are also some special techniques for development of managerial personnel.

▲ **Coaching** **Coaching** consists of having superiors provide guidance to their subordinates in the course of their regular job performance. The basic idea is for the junior executive to absorb some of the qualities that have made the senior executive successful. Usually, coaching is an informal rather than an officially prescribed procedure. Minorities and women may especially need this type of development to make up for a shortage of role models due to the late entry of minorities and women into management ranks.

▲ **Planned Progression** **Planned progression** is used when the company blueprints the path of promotion that lies ahead of the new manager. Such management progress is frequently charted through successive levels of the operational and functional organizational structure. One form of planned progression is the "assistant to" position, which may be a routine administrative position or one created specifically for training purposes.

▲ **Job Rotation** Through **job rotation,** a young manager learns various operating procedures by temporarily performing many different jobs. Clifton C. Garvin, Jr., chairman of Exxon, was developed this way at the company's Baton Rouge refinery. The short-run inefficiencies are outweighed by the well-rounded development young executives get.

▲ **External Executive Development Program** A well-conceived, well-developed, and well-taught outside executive development program is probably the best way of developing effective managers. Although this method is used for only a relatively few promising managers, its influence is quite significant, for executives trained by this method tend to become the top managers in their organization. This type of program is among the most progressive and dynamic of all the developmental techniques.

## EVALUATING EMPLOYEES

**Objective 5**

Where employee evaluation fits into the personnel management process.

People in business constantly use some form of employee evaluation. For example, employees use it when they discuss how well they and other workers perform. Managers use it—formally or informally—when they praise or criticize employees and when they make salary, promotion, and discharge decisions. Most progressive employers have formal programs for employee growth and development.

## Performance Appraisal

**Performance appraisal** (also called *merit rating, efficiency rating, service rating,* and *employee appraisal*) is the process an employer uses to determine whether an employee is doing the job as intended. Figure 9-3 illustrates an effective appraisal process. You will see that employees have (1) personal qualities that lead to (2) job behaviors that result in (3) work performance. Therefore, a manager needs to do (4) an appraisal of those qualities and behaviors in order to estimate performance as a basis for taking (5) personnel actions. Real performance improvements don't result from the appraisals as much as from follow-up discussions the manager has with employees to explain the evaluation and resulting personnel action.[11] Procter & Gamble product-marketing managers are evaluated on success in increasing unit volume and controlling costs.[12]

## Disciplinary Actions and Terminations

Unfortunately, people in business—and elsewhere—don't always perform as desired. So there's sometimes a need for disciplinary action. Also, because of either undesirable behavior or poor economic conditions, people must occasionally be terminated.

**Discipline** is any action intended to correct wrong behavior and train the individual to perform correctly. The greatest disciplinary problems in business firms are absenteeism and/or tardiness and poor productivity, work habits (including unsafe working practices), and/or attitudes. Absenteeism is the most frequent problem and is apparently increasing. However, safety violations tend to be the most critical problem.

There are three steps in an effective disciplinary program. First, standards of acceptable—and unacceptable—behavior are set up. Second, specific and graduated penalties are established for violating those standards. And third, penalties are imposed fairly and impartially, but only after guilt has been determined by a well-established procedure.

One of the most difficult tasks for a manager is firing an employee for unsatisfactory performance. But if this is required, it should be done decisively and with compassion. Often, this chore is delegated to the personnel department. Another difficult act is terminating people—especially managers and long-time employees—as a way of reducing costs and remaining competitive.

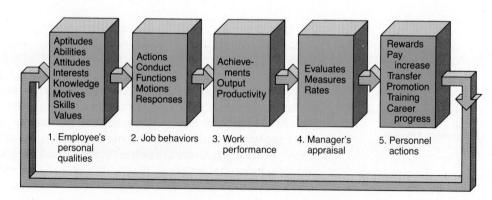

**Figure 9-3** How performance appraisals operate. [Adapted by permission from Leon C. Megginson, *Personnel Management: A Human Resources Approach*, 4th ed. (Homewood, Ill.: Richard D. Irwin, 1981), p. 311. © 1981 by Richard D. Irwin, Inc.]

Enlightened companies are now providing counseling, financial assistance, and help in finding new jobs for terminated employees. This assistance is called **outplacement.** When Goodyear Tire & Rubber Company had to close two plants, idling 1,200 hourly employees, its trained outplacement counselors helped them look for work.[13]

## COMPENSATING EMPLOYEES

**Objective 6**

Some of the problems in and methods of compensating employees.

**Compensation,** or the financial reward provided to employees for past performance and as an incentive to future performance, is one of the most difficult problems for personnel managers. Employees usually consider their income too low, while many employers believe that they are bankrupting themselves to pay undeserved wages. Since the question of pay is probably the most difficult and ticklish personnel issue that management has to deal with, most progressive firms have experts to deal with the problem (see the Profile on page 253).

### Income Differences

Employees usually judge the fairness of their pay by comparing it with that of their fellow employees. Whether they think their income is acceptable will depend on how they see their value relative to that of others with higher or lower incomes. Most employee dissatisfaction is over differences in pay between jobs and individuals. Differences in pay based on occupation, managerial responsibilities, length of service, and geographical location are generally accepted. Differences in pay based on age, race, ethnic group, and sex are now prohibited by law and public policy. Title VII of the Civil Rights Act of 1964 prohibits such discrimination, and the Equal Pay Act of 1963 makes it illegal to pay women less than men for the same general type of work.

However, women's earnings are still lagging behind men's. In fact, women's earnings were still only about 63 percent of men's earnings in 1980, as shown in Figure 9-4. The percentage dropped to 61 in 1981 but rose to 63 in 1983.[14] There are many reasons for this, including the fact that about two out of three new employees are women. They come into companies at the entry level and receive lower rates of pay in those low-level jobs. Also, in spite of all the public policy statements, women are still more heavily concentrated in lower-paid industries and jobs.

### How Management Determines Compensation

A company's compensation policies and practices are determined by the interaction of three factors: what it is *willing* to pay, what it is *able* to pay, and what it is *required* to pay. And have no doubt, if any contention arises, the last of these will probably prevail.

▲ **What the Company Is Willing to Pay** Most managers *want* to pay fair salaries, but they also feel that employees should do "a fair day's work for a fair day's pay." So they encourage employees to increase their output and performance in order to receive higher wages or salaries.

▲ **What the Company Is Able to Pay**  Regardless of all other factors, in the long run, a private firm can only pay salaries based on employee productivity. As indicated earlier, there has to be income before there can be wages. There must also be profits for the owners if wages are to continue to be paid.

▲ **What the Company Is Required to Pay**  In the short run, wages and salaries are based on external pressures from governments, unions, and competitors to pay "prevailing wages." There are several state and federal laws dealing with employee income, in addition to the ones already discussed. The best known is the Fair Labor Standards Act (also called the Wage and Hour Law), as amended. It sets the minimum wage for most employees and the maximum number of hours (forty) they can work per week without receiving overtime premium pay (one-and-a-half times their basic rate of pay). In 1984 the rate was $3.35.

Unions greatly influence wages and salaries, too, whether or not a firm is unionized. Through strike activities, legislative lobbying, and informing the public, unions tend to increase the wages of their own members and, indirectly, those of nonunion employees.

A company's pay practices must conform to wage patterns in its industry and in its community. Competition forces a firm to pay relatively the same wages as others, and trade associations also lead to uniform wages. Certain occupations have relatively the same rate of earnings. Doctors, lawyers, and other professionals, for instance, tend to have similar fee structures within their profession.

## Methods of Compensation

At one time, employees were paid in cash at the end of the day on the basis of the number of hours they had worked. Many lower-level employees are still paid an hourly wage but receive it in the form of a check at the end of the week. This is called **time** or **day wages**. Other, higher-level employees are

**Figure 9-4**  Slight progress for women. (Based on data from U.S. Department of Labor.)

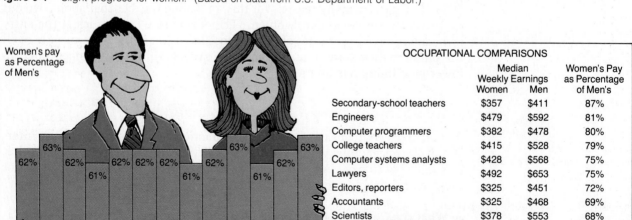

| OCCUPATIONAL COMPARISONS | | |
|---|---|---|
| | Median Weekly Earnings | Women's Pay as Percentage of Men's |
| | Women    Men | |
| Secondary-school teachers | $357    $411 | 87% |
| Engineers | $479    $592 | 81% |
| Computer programmers | $382    $478 | 80% |
| College teachers | $415    $528 | 79% |
| Computer systems analysts | $428    $568 | 75% |
| Lawyers | $492    $653 | 75% |
| Editors, reporters | $325    $451 | 72% |
| Accountants | $325    $468 | 69% |
| Scientists | $378    $553 | 68% |
| Insurance agents, brokers | $284    $419 | 68% |
| Bank officials, financial managers | $336    $574 | 59% |

Women's pay as Percentage of Men's

62% 63% 62% 61% 62% 62% 62% 61% 62% 63% 61% 62% 63%

1971 '72 '73 '74 '75 '76 '77 '78 '79 '80 '81 '82 '83

## *Profile*

## Levy and Partridge: The Texas Troubleshooters

When a growing company starts having performance problems with its personnel, its management often seeks help outside the organization to define and resolve the problem. One such source of help is the husband-wife team of Michael Levy and Mary Partridge, of The Woodlands, Texas. Mike and Mary both own their own consulting firms, but frequently have the opportunity to work together with the same client to do some troubleshooting.

Mary, president of The Woodlands Consulting Group, specializes in personnel management and human resource development systems. With an MBA in industrial management and organization from Florida State University, she taught personnel management at Stetson University; was personnel manager for B. Siegel Company in Detroit; and spent nine years in employee relations at Exxon. Mike, president of Michael Levy & Associates, is a training and organizational development consultant with over a decade of experience in several industries. He was graduated from the University of Houston with a degree in psychology and did graduate work in the field of organization development. His work experience includes positions in the health care field and at Foley's in Houston. Since establishing his own consulting firm in 1979, he's served clients in the oil and gas, retail, health care, and electronics industries, as well as serving as president of the Houston chapter of The American Society for Training and Development.

Together, Mary and Mike are able to provide their cli-

ents with an integrated approach to human resource development. Offering services ranging from the development of personnel policies and systems to executive team development, they are able to be more effective than a consultant working independently. For example, if Mary designs a performance appraisal system for a client, Mike may conduct training in how the system works, as well as how to conduct productive performance discussions with employees. Equally likely, Mike may hear in a seminar that managers are frustrated in their efforts by some inadequacy in the human resource policies or system within the company, and Mary will design a new system to correct it. An added benefit to the client is the vitality that results from this couple's enthusiasm for their respective areas, and the shared values and philosophies that enable them to act as sounding boards or brainstorming partners for each other.

Currently, they share a client in a computer retail chain. Mike's working with the CEO and top management team to clearly define organizational values and objectives and to design a comprehensive management development program. Mary, meanwhile, is designing policies and programs in several areas of human resource management so that the policies of the organization will be in line with the values defined by the management group.

Source: Correspondence and interviews with Mike Levy and Mary Partridge.

paid a **salary,** fixed earnings received by the week, month, or year. About 25 percent of production employees and most sales personnel are paid some form of **incentive wage,** whereby their earnings are directly related to the amount they produce or sell. For example, concessions workers who sell hot dogs at baseball games are paid according to the number of hot dogs they sell. Automobile and real estate salespeople receive a percentage of the sales price as a commission on their sales.

Many firms have a **profit-sharing plan,** under which employees receive a given percentage of the firm's profits as extra income. Profit sharing can be based on the success of the whole company or of an individual unit. United Parcel Service (UPS) has a profit-sharing plan for its hourly employees to which both UPS and the employees contribute. UPS's contribution, plus investment income, in recent years provided a 22.6 percent return on each employee's average monthly balance.[15]

## Employee Benefits

**Employee benefits** are a form of pay over and above regularly paid wages and salaries. Originally called *fringe benefits,* employee benefits now cost about 35 to 40 percent of a firm's basic payroll. Some benefits are required by law. For example, the Social Security Act calls for retirement pay, disability pay, and survivors' benefits, as well as Medicare for medical and hospital payments. Unemployment compensation is also required by the act. All states have workers' compensation laws that provide benefits to workers who contract an industrial illness or sustain an on-the-job injury.

There are many voluntary programs, and they take varied forms. The most popular ones include pay for time not worked (such as paid vacation and holidays), pay for overtime and special activities, retirement pay, health and life insurance, legal services, dental services or insurance, educational benefits, and discounts on purchases of goods and services. All other things being equal, good benefits can swing a job prospect's decision to join a company. Benefits are so important, in fact, that most large firms have an expert assigned to their administration.

Currently, there's a great deal of controversy over whether retirement should be voluntary or mandatory. While many employees retire before age sixty-five, other employees say they shouldn't be required to retire if they don't want to (see the Business Debate on page 255).

## MAINTAINING HEALTH AND SAFETY

**Objective 7**

The maintenance of employees' health and safety.

During the average work day in the United States, one worker is injured every fourteen seconds, and one worker is killed every thirty-seven minutes. Each year, over 14,000 workers are killed in job-related activities, and 2.4 million workers are seriously injured, at a cost of over $12 billion in lost wages, reduced output, and other losses.

While business is doing much to improve this situation, the Occupational Safety and Health Act of 1970 (OSHAct) has speeded up these activities by establishing a regulatory agency, the Occupational Safety and Health Administration (OSHA) to enforce safety standards. OSHA inspectors are concentrating on those industries with the highest accident rates. The law is encourag-

# Business Debate

## Should Retirement Be Mandatory?

According to the Age Discrimination in Employment Act of 1967, employees in a private firm can't be forced to retire before age seventy. Federal employees can't be forced to retire at any time solely because of age. There is *no* permissible mandatory retirement age in California, and legislation has been introduced there to eliminate mandatory retirement entirely. This trend toward removing mandatory retirement because of age is affecting all aspects of human resource management. It especially affects the promotion of younger people, since high-level niches may not be emptied by retirement.

The arguments *in favor of* requiring employees to retire at a given age—usually sixty-five—are that mandatory retirement:

1. Facilitates long-range personnel and career planning, employee training and development, organizational development, and other personnel programs and policies—especially pension planning.
2. Doesn't require management to decide when an employee's performance has become unsatisfactory.
3. Spares older employees the indignity of being forced to quit because of poor performance.
4. Makes room for younger employees to move up in the organization more rapidly.
5. Creates new openings for women and minorities and helps the company meet its affirmative action goals.

The arguments *against* requiring employees to retire at a given age are that:

1. Age isn't an accurate gauge of a person's mental and physical abilities. Therefore the company shouldn't force employees out as long as they receive satisfactory performance ratings.
2. Mandatory retirement is an insidious form of discrimination against aging workers.
3. Mandatory retirement takes away individuals' dignity, sense of worth, and purpose and reduces their ability to provide a livelihood and a higher standard of living in their later years.
4. Management will be more likely to terminate a worker whose performance is unsatisfactory at an earlier age, instead of letting him or her "hang on" until retirement age.
5. The country loses some of its more skilled and capable workers, which reduces the total amount of goods and services produced.

Some issues involved in removing a mandatory retirement age include: Will workers continue to accrue pension benefits beyond age sixty-five? be covered by the medical plan? have life insurance? be eligible for salary increases and vacations? be eligible for promotion or training?

*What do you think?*

ing employers and employees to provide safer and healthier working conditions and to be more responsible for maintaining them. The efforts seem to be paying off. After a decade of experience, the number of injuries and illnesses per 100 full-time workers was down from 10.9 in 1972 to 7.7 in 1982.[16]

## ≜ LEARNING OBJECTIVES REVISITED

1. *The meaning of personnel management from the viewpoint of the personnel department and management.*

   Good workers are required if a firm is to succeed. Both the personnel department and all operating managers are responsible for personnel management. This critical activity includes recruiting, selecting, training, developing, evaluating, compensating, and protecting the health and safety of employees.

2. *How a firm determines future personnel needs and sets up a program for meeting them.*

   In planning for personnel needs, a firm first must consider its objectives and then use forecasts and inventories to decide the number and types of workers wanted. Job analysis is the process used to determine what each job is and what is required to perform it effectively. The job description and job specification then indicate the type of worker qualified to fill the position. Workers can be recruited either from outside the business or from within, by upgrading, transferring, or promoting present employees.

3. *The different procedures involved in recruiting, selecting, and orienting new employees.*

   Once personnel needs are known, management recruits potential employees from as many sources as is feasible. The most common forms of recruiting are employee referral, advertising, college recruitment, employment agencies, computers, and networking. Under affirmative action programs, firms must actively search out minorities, women, veterans, the handicapped, and older employees. The usual procedure for selecting employees involves some combination of preliminary screening and interviewing, testing, in-depth interviewing, reference checking, and giving a physical exam. Selection is completed with a job offer and orientation.

4. *How employees, both nonmanagerial and managerial, are trained and developed.*

   The usual methods of training nonmanagerial employees are on-the-job training, vestibule training, apprenticeship training, internship training, programmed instruction, and educational television. The preferred methods for developing managers include coaching, planned progression, job rotation, and external executive development programs.

5. *Where employee evaluation fits into the personnel management process.*

   Managers use employee evaluations—formal or informal—when supervising employees. Formal performance appraisal is the process used to determine whether an employee is performing the job as intended. If not, disciplinary action, or even termination, may result.

6. *Some of the problems in and methods of compensating employees.*

   A firm should try to set its wage rate high enough to attract capable employees, while still permitting the price of the firm's product to be competitive. Also, the owners must make a profit in order to remain in business. The three forms of pay are time or day wages, salaries, and incentive

wages. Employers may also offer profit-sharing plans. Employee benefits are another important part of a company's compensation program.

7. *The maintenance of employees' health and safety.*

Programs to maintain the health and safety of employees are enforced by the Occupational Safety and Health Administration (OSHA).

## ⬟ IMPORTANT TERMS

As an extra review of the chapter, try defining the following terms. If you have trouble with any of them, refer to the page listed.

personnel management  *234*
personnel planning  *236*
job analysis  *237*
job description  *237*
job specification  *237*
upgrading  *238*
transferring  *238*
promoting  *240*
recruitment  *241*
affirmative action program (AAP)  *241*
employee referral  *242*
private employment agencies  *242*
headhunters  *242*
public employment agencies  *243*
networking  *243*
selection  *243*

orientation  *247*
on-the-job training (OJT)  *247*
vestibule training  *247*
apprenticeship training  *247*
internship training  *248*
programmed instruction  *248*
coaching  *249*
planned progression  *249*
job rotation  *249*
performance appraisal  *250*
discipline  *250*
outplacement  *251*
compensation  *251*
time (day) wages  *252*
salary  *254*
incentive wage  *254*
profit-sharing plan  *254*
employee benefits  *254*

## ⬟ REVIEW QUESTIONS

1. What does *personnel management* mean, and who does it?
2. What does personnel planning involve?
3. What are the most important internal sources of supply of personnel? Explain.
4. What are the most important external sources of supply of personnel?
5. What are some of the methods used to recruit personnel? What are their drawbacks?
6. What are the usual steps in the selection process? How does it end?
7. What are the most popular methods of training nonmanagerial employees?
8. What are the most popular methods of training managerial employees?
9. Why is employee evaluation needed?
10. What three factors combine to determine management's compensation policies and practices? Explain.
11. Describe the basic methods of employee compensation.

# ⏚ DISCUSSION QUESTIONS

1. What are some of the implications of the statement that "all managers are responsible for managing the firm's human resources"? How would a personnel director feel about the statement?

2. How does the recruitment of college athletes differ from the recruitment of employees?

3. There are two applicants for a typist's job—one white, with more skill and experience, and the other a minority-group member whose only qualifications are fair skill and eagerness to learn. Under affirmative action, which person should be hired?

4. Which method or methods of recruitment would you use if you were hiring a managerial assistant? Why?

5. Why are employee training and development so important? Explain.

6. What are some unacceptable income differentials? What is being done to remove them?

## ⏚ CASE 9-1.  Deltech Corporation: The New Assistant-To

Deltech Corporation,[17] a rapidly growing engineering consulting firm, needed additional personnel for certain key executive positions. Because of the technical nature of the business, employees were usually chosen more for their technical qualifications than for their managerial potential. Since technical expertise doesn't necessarily imply managerial expertise, Deltech had a real shortage of qualified managers.

Anne Protheroe, an executive with several years of varied managerial experience but little technical knowledge, was brought in from the outside as assistant to the president. The personnel director had recruited her, with the president's approval. The older department heads felt that someone from inside the organization should have

been promoted to the position and consequently resented the new presidential assistant.

Anne had a hard time obtaining the cooperation of her fellow employees, but she calmly did her job to the best of her abilities. She did what she was asked to do, as long as it was consistent with her professional expertise. She wasn't pushy, but didn't let herself be pushed around without fighting back.

Four years later, Anne was made a vice-president. During her tenure as assistant, she had been able to convince her fellow employees of her managerial abilities and of the need for her services within the business. Her promotion to vice-president was therefore "generally well received."

**Case Questions**

1. What does this problem illustrate about the relationship between the type of organization and the source of personnel?

2. Why was it necessary to go outside the organization for a new manager? What other options were available?

3. What would you have done if you had been the president? Explain.

4. What do you think of the way the presidential assistant handled herself?

## ⏚ CASE 9-2.  Elaine Reeves: Reentry Blues

After over twenty years as a full-time wife and mother, Elaine Reeves[18] had taken her first job outside the home. She was well qualified for the job,

having worked in a Lockheed Aircraft office for several years before marrying. More recently, she had taken an accounting course at a business

school and passed with flying colors. She had been interviewed and hired by the owner of a lumberyard in a small Texas town.

Monday morning, she was greeted by the owner, shown the typewriter, electric accounting machine, and supplies and then left on her own when he went to call on several contractors. She was the only woman in the yard, and the only person in the small office. There were about twenty unskilled and rough-looking workers out in the yard.

Confronted by unfamiliar surroundings and people preoccupied with their own work, which made them seem unfriendly and unhelpful, she was feeling shaken and discouraged and would have liked to turn around and go home.

### Case Questions

1. What type of introduction would you have set up for Elaine?
2. How would you, as the lumberyard owner, approach her about training?
3. Could you expect any resistance to training on her part? Explain your answer.

# 10

# Human Relations

*Treat a man as he is and he will get worse. But treat a man as if he already is what he ought to be and he will become what he ought to be.*

Johann Wolfgang von Goethe

*There are only two stimulants to one's best efforts—the fear of punishment and the hope of reward. When neither is present, one can hardly hope that people will want to be trained or want to do a good job.*

John M. Wilson

*Nature has given to men one tongue, but two ears, that we may hear from others twice as much as we speak.*

Epictetus

## Learning Objectives

1. Individual and group aspects of human relations in business.
2. The motivation process and its role in improving performance.
3. Some popular theories of motivation.
4. The process of communication and its effective use in business.
5. Several means that management can use to improve motivation.

## In This Chapter

What Is Human Relations?
Motivating Employees
Communicating with Employees
How to Improve Motivation

"Hot Rod," a hard-nosed driller (supervisor) on a Slick Oil Company drilling rig in the swamps of Louisiana, treated his crew like dirt. When Hot Rod went on vacation, Jim became the temporary supervisor. He had been a supervisor himself until an accident beyond his control forced him to return to the ranks. Jim had always been considered one of the boys by the other five crew members, who liked and respected him. However, when word got around that Jim would be the relief supervisor, one of the men said, "All drillers are SOB's, and Jim will probably be just the same when he takes over."

At that time, as it happened, the crew was assigned to a new job, using a method that had never been tried in the field. About 20,000 feet of pipe would have to be put in the well in the next twelve hours. All the footage didn't have to go down on Jim's shift, but the driller and crew had set that goal for themselves. The crew had no experience with the technique and no special tools with which to do the job.

Jim's first task was to get the men behind him. Because of their expectations, he knew that this was going to be a major hurdle. Jim called the crew together and said, "This job is new to us, so we'll all have to pull together to get it done. I know we've been goofing off with Hot Rod, but we can't do that now. There's an important job to be done, and I need everyone's cooperation." He asked the crew for suggestions on how they thought the job might be done, and several ideas came out of the brainstorming session. Jim said that they sounded good, and that by using them the crew could probably get the job done. Each man was allowed to choose the job he thought he could do best. And if he tired of one job, he could rotate to another one. Jim told the crew that he would operate at a fast, but safe, speed.

The crew started work on the mammoth job ahead. After many back-breaking hours, they were dead tired and falling behind schedule. Hot Rod would probably have ridiculed, goaded, and cursed them into a faster pace. Jim, however, stopped all work for a few minutes and said, "It's about time we showed the other crews that we're the best. You all know we can outwork any other crew, and so do I. Let's go for it!" Then they really pitched in and worked as hard as they could for the next four hours.

When the shift ended at 5 A.M., they were 150 feet short of their 20,000-foot goal. The day crew had arrived and was ready to take over, but Jim's crew wouldn't leave the derrick floor. They stayed until the job was done. When they finally quit, the men were exhausted but laughing and joking. What's more, they seemed to feel satisfied for the first time in weeks about the job they had done.

In the same way that Jim got the job done by seeking his men's advice, giving them some choice of tasks, and urging them on, good human relations makes a business a much more pleasant and effective place to work. And poor human relations can lead to poor business. Soon after he took over as president of International Harvester in 1982, Donald D. Lennox closed the Fort Wayne truck plant because of the low productivity and morale, which were certainly related.[1]

Simply staffing an organization with the best people is only the first step in an ongoing process of working with people. There are many relationships between managers and others that are classified as human relations. Managers supervise subordinates and guide them to achieve organizational and personal goals. Managers also deal with other managers, owners, the public, government officials, and customers. Therefore, **human relations,** in business, involves getting both managers and others to *want* to strive for organizational goals and objectives. This, in turn, requires motivating and communicating with employees.

**Objective 1**

Individual and group aspects of human relations in business.

## WHAT IS HUMAN RELATIONS?

Over a century ago, human relations in business was very simple. Workers were hired to produce a good or service. They used their own methods and tools and did the work as they pleased. They were paid a given amount per unit (piece rate) for all acceptable production. If their work wasn't acceptable, they were fired. All this was changed by Taylor's **scientific management,** a new method that emphasized the scientific analysis of jobs; selection, training, and motivation of employees to do jobs in the best way; and the separation of management and nonmanagement duties.

### The Scientific Management Movement

Frederick W. Taylor, an engineer, started what came to be known as the scientific management movement at Midvale Steel Company in 1881. This "mental revolution," as he called it, drastically altered the way work was done.[2] Through experiments, Taylor (1) determined the "one best way" to do each job, (2) selected the best people (he called them "first-class men") for each job, (3) trained them to do the work in the prescribed manner, and (4) motivated them with a "differential piece-rate plan." Finally, management duties were separated from nonmanagerial duties for the first time. Planning departments and other management techniques were set up.

Taylor's system was based on human relations in the sense that it selected the best workers for each task. It was based on economics in that it used a highly effective incentive wage system. The human relations approach is still used today, but Taylor's wage system is obsolete; neither unions nor our value system would permit it.

Although Taylor's system was very mechanistic, it did lead to a high material standard of living that lasted until the Great Depression of the 1930s.

The relay room of the Hawthorne plant in 1927.

## The Human Relations Movement

The scientific management movement failed during World War II, largely because of abuse by some inept practitioners. The findings of the Hawthorne studies helped doom it. Carried out from 1924 to 1932 at Western Electric's Hawthorne plant near Chicago, the **Hawthorne studies** were a series of experiments to determine the effect of the environment on employee productivity. From 1924 to 1927, the emphasis of the experiments was on the effects that physical factors—such as layout, heating and cooling, lighting, and methods and dates of paying employees—had on productivity. The results were inconclusive, and this set of studies was abandoned.

x. From 1928 to 1932, the second series of Hawthorne studies focused on sociopsychological factors. The conclusions, published in 1939, emphasized the organization of a business, a plant, or an office as a social system, and the importance of communication and morale.[3] The experiments demonstrated that a sense of recognition may be more motivating than material factors.

The human relations movement became very popular in the 1940s. People were no longer regarded as isolated individuals but as members of social groupings, such as the family and work groups. Work was considered a social, group activity rather than a mere economic endeavor.

The conclusions of both segments of the Hawthorne studies have since been reexamined. For example, the contention that physical factors are not important has been challenged by a study by the Buffalo Organization for Social and Technical Innovation, which concluded that "good office design can boost professionals' and managers' productivity by more than $1,600 a person a year." Control over lighting and privacy were more important to employees than room temperature.[4] Also the concept that morale (job satisfaction) af-

fects production (performance) has been reconsidered in light of foreign competition, automation, and the cost-effective approach to management. One behavioral scientist at the University of Michigan's Survey Research Center has concluded that "productivity and job satisfaction do not necessarily go together."[5] In 1960, Non-Linear Systems, Inc., a private business in Del Mar, California, committed itself to applying human relations concepts (especially those of Abraham Maslow[6]) to a functioning firm. In 1961, profits began "to spiral downward until losses sustained compelled abandonment of the experiment in 1965."[7]

The human resources movement, which developed during the 1960s, has now become popular. The **human resources philosophy** holds that workers should be treated with human dignity, but that their output is an economic resource that must be cost-effective.[8]

### The Japanese Experience

The Japanese have taken the knowledge and experience gained from a massive post–World War II technological transfer (resulting from U.S. investments, enrollment in U.S. colleges and universities, and visiting professorships to Japan) and refined them into an effective management system.[9] The primary elements of the system are (1) company loyalty; (2) commitment to hard work, thrift, and frugality; (3) quality performance, especially in group meetings; (4) suggestion systems; (5) management communication; and (6) union-management cooperation.[10] See the opening case in Chapter 24 for these principles applied to U.S. workers.

All of these features have at one time been (and some still are) applied to U.S. businesses. Although company loyalty may be out of vogue now, especially because of discharge of long-time managers, most workers still take pride in the companies for which they work. The work ethic may be in a decline, but it seems to be still breathing. A National Opinion Research poll found that 72 percent of Americans would still work even if they had enough money to live on for the rest of their lives.[11] Even now, United Parcel Service's managers, supervisors, and hourly workers are proud of their tremendous amounts of initiative, responsibility, hard work, and long hours.[12]

Businesses in the United States have used various quality control systems. Quality control circles, based on the concept of statistical quality control, originated with the trouble-shooting groups of World War II. These were followed by brainstorming and zero defects (Do it right the first time!) programs in the early 1960s.[13] Weatherstripping operations at Ford's Wayne, Michigan, plant are now 99.9 percent perfect.[14] Suggestion systems have been in use at least since World War I.

Communication has been considered one of U.S. management's chief problems for at least two decades.[15] While the Japanese have a reputation for harmonious union-management relations, in the U.S. unions have traditionally been considered the advocate of employees against their common adversary, the employer. This is changing at companies such as AT&T, Chrysler, GM, and Ford. Robert "Red" Little, head of UAW's Livonia, Michigan, local, and Marvin Craig, new manager (1979) of Ford's transmission plant there, wanted to save the plant—and union jobs. They worked up a plan to improve quality and cut costs drastically. The workers bought the idea, including changes in work rules that had been won in thirty years of bargaining, and so

did Ford. The plant became so efficient that it bid lower than a Japanese firm, Toyo Kogyo, for a large transmission contract.[16]

## MOTIVATING EMPLOYEES

Since managers get things done through others, motivating subordinates to perform effectively is an important part of good human relations. **Motivation** is the process by which managers bring out the best in their subordinates by giving them reasons to perform better. The word *motivation* is derived from the word **motive,** which is a drive, impulse, or desire that directs a person to seek to satisfy a need and moves the person toward a goal. In essence, motivation is getting employees to do what you want them to do and to like doing it.

### The Motivation Process

**Objective 2**

**The motivation process and its role in improving performance.**

The motivation process can be viewed as an open system with inputs, processes, and outputs (see Chapter 8 for further details about systems). As shown in Figure 10-1 and Table 10-1, the following steps usually occur when a manager tries to motivate employees:

1. The manager wants to improve performance and productivity.
2. The manager estimates what the employee needs to achieve personal satisfaction.
3. The manager chooses a specific incentive, such as money, a new title, or praise (see the Profile on page 268), that will satisfy the employee's needs and then applies it as a stimulus to induce the employee to respond favorably.

**Figure 10-1** The motivational process as an open system.

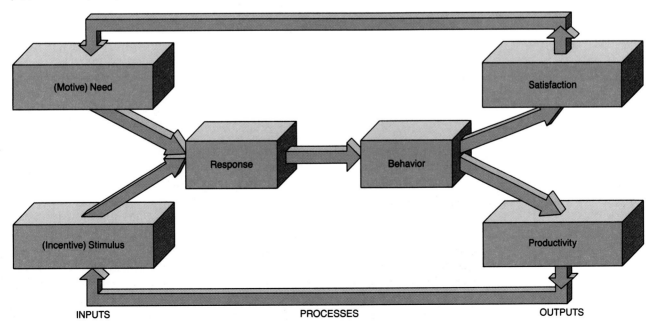

(Motive) Need

Satisfaction

Response

Behavior

(Incentive) Stimulus

Productivity

INPUTS PROCESSES OUTPUTS

**TABLE 10-1.  Practical approach to motivating employees.**

| Manager | | | Subordinates | |
|---|---|---|---|---|
| *Organizational Objectives* | *What Is Needed to Achieve Objectives* | *Incentives That Can Be Used to Motivate Subordinates* | *What Needs Must Be Satisfied for Their Objective to Be Achieved* | *Their Objective* |
| Service and profit | Performance and productivity | Challenging work | Self-fulfillment | Satis-faction |
| | | Merit increases and promotions | | |
| | | | Esteem | |
| | | Praise and recognition | | |
| | | Personal publicity | | |
| | | Responsibility | | |
| | | Job enrichment | | |
| | | Status systems | Social | |
| | | Suggestion system | | |
| | | Communications system | | |
| | | Staff meetings | | |
| | | Training and development | Safety and security | |
| | | Wage incentive plans | | |
| | | Savings plans | | |
| | | Profit sharing | | |
| | | Seniority systems | | |
| | | Insurance | | |
| | | Pensions | | |
| | | Other employee benefits | | |
| | | Money, or sustenance | Physiological | |

SOURCE: Reprinted by permission from Curtis E. Tate, Jr., Leon C. Megginson, Charles R. Scott, Jr., and Lyle R. Trueblood, *The Complete Guide to Your Own Business* (Homewood, Ill.: Dow Jones–Irwin, 1977), p. 78.

4. The employee's resulting behavior will provide him or her with satisfaction and result in performance and productivity, which should satisfy the manager.

This completes one specific motivational cycle, but the process has to be repeated, for employees can't be motivated "once and for all." They need continuing motivation.

### Some Popular Theories of Motivation

**Objective 3**

**Some popular theories of motivation.**

Until the early 1930s, money was thought to be the most important means of motivating employees, so emphasis was put on wages and job security. Then the Hawthorne studies showed that there were other sources of employee motivation. Money is still important as a motivator, however. Its importance is illustrated by the popular quip "Money may not be everything, but it's sure way ahead of whatever's in second place!" Several popular firms still use it as a primary motivator. At UPS, because of the company's profit-sharing plan, no driver makes less than $25,000 a year.[17] At Radio Shack, John F. Pyktel's 1982 salary and profit-sharing bonus totaled $103,900.[18] A Data General sales manager says, "What motivates people? Ego and the money to buy things they and their family want."[19]

Most of the popular motivation theories are built around the idea of **needs,** which are cravings within us that we try to satisfy by our outward behavior. Up to and including our safety-security needs (see Figure 10-2), money seems to be a primary motivating factor; above that level, other factors become more important. The three most popular theories of motivation are Maslow's hierarchy of needs, McGregor's Theory X and Theory Y, and Herzberg's two-factor concept.

▲ **Maslow's Hierarchy of Needs** Psychologist Abraham Maslow introduced the concept of a hierarchy of needs (see Figure 10-2).[20] The **hierarchy of needs** is composed of five levels of needs: physiological, safety and security, social, esteem, and self-actualization.

**Physiological needs** include the need for respiration, elimination, food, drink, sex, and sleep. For example, a man lost in the desert for five days is obviously more interested in these basic needs than in making new friends or being given a new title.

**Figure 10-2** Maslow's hierarchy of needs. (Based on "Hierarchy of Needs" in *Motivation and Personality*, 2nd ed., by Abraham H. Maslow. Copyright © 1970 by Abraham H. Maslow. By permission of Harper & Row, Publishers, Inc.)

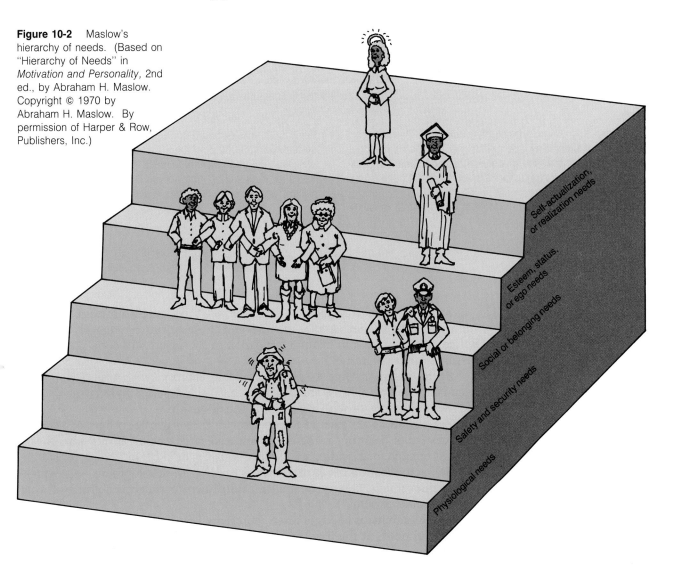

# *Profile*

## Mary Kay: Master Motivator

Mary Kay Ashe, the highly successful founder and chairman of Mary Kay Cosmetics, Inc., attributes her success to the fact that she gives women the ultimate chance to do whatever they are smart enough to do. "I believe you can praise people to success," she says.

She also uses a wide variety of incentives to motivate her 1,500 employees, 200,000 independent beauty consultants, and 5,000 directors. For example, a recent sales whiz was crowned Emerald Director Queen of Unit Sales in 1981 for outstanding unit accomplishment (more than $1 million unit sales). She was also awarded the Queen's sash ribbon, the number one trophy, a bouquet of roses, the

**Safety and security needs** include the need for protection from the environment, as by shelter, regular income, and clothing, or from danger, as by the police. To return to our example, the man in the desert will seek a cave, tree, or some other shelter.

**Social needs** involve association and interaction with others, for love, friendship, belongingness, and acceptance. If the desert wanderer meets people, he will associate with them for companionship.

**Esteem needs** are related to self-respect, the respect of others, job status, the prestige of position, recognition, and ego satisfaction. If our man is safe and has enough food, water, and companionship, he'll begin to look for status.

**Self-actualization needs** motivate us to seek self-development, self-expression, achievement, creativity, and self-fulfillment through becoming all that we're capable of being.

The hierarchy of needs is often represented by a triangle or pyramid with lower-level needs at the base and higher-level needs at the peak. Although in general lower-level (physiological) needs must be met before higher-level needs

Queen's tiara, a gold-and-diamond bar pin displaying her unit accomplishment, a walnut plaque showing her unit production, a 14-karat-gold ring set with 12 diamonds, a Brown Shadow mink stroller with Labrador fox collar and cuffs, a free-form 14-karat-gold ring with a cluster of diamonds, a dream vacation to Costa del Sol, Spain, and a $5,000 shopping spree at world-famous Neiman-Marcus in Dallas, Texas. As icing on the cake, her husband received a 14-karat-gold "husband's ring" set with a diamond. And motivation ran even higher in 1984, when 12 queens were crowned.

Mary Kay's love for people and her determination, talent, and spiritual devotion have helped her attain outstanding success in the world of business. But success didn't come easily. As a seven-year-old, Mary Kay had to keep house and cook for her invalid father and three brothers and sisters while her mother ran a restaurant to support the family. Her mother would tell her, "You can do it," whenever she phoned for help. She says that positive phrase has sustained her throughout her life. A friend who "had everything" also inadvertently inspired Mary Kay. "She made me better than I was," she says.

During 1942 and 1943, as a mother of three, she took premed courses at the University of Houston. Later, she started conducting demonstrations and sales parties in people's homes for Stanley Home Products. At her first company sales meeting, she saw one of the women

crowned Queen of Sales. Afterward, she told the president of the firm, "Next year I'm going to be Queen of Sales." And she was!

Next, she joined World Gift, becoming an area manager within a year and then national training director, but resigned when an efficiency expert said her "power was too great." Only then, in 1963, did she and her son start their own firm with $5,000 of her money, one shelf of cosmetics, and nine people. Now, their annual sales are over $300 million.

Mary Kay uses practical personal touches to motivate people. She personally designs the birthday cards she sends to her consultants—and makes sure they arrive on the person's birthdate. While her son, Richard Rogers, actually runs the company, she is still the vital driving force as chairman. She conducts the annual sales meeting—so large that it's held in the Dallas Convention Center—gives the inspirational speech, and bestows the honors. There's a personal bond between her and her people that is mutually satisfying and is evidence of her belief that success mostly depends on a person's self-confidence.

---

Sources: *News Information* packet from Mary Kay Cosmetics, Inc.; H. Rudnitsky, "Flight of the Bumblebee," *Forbes*, June 22, 1981, pp. 104–6; Paul Rosenfield, "The Beautiful Make-up of Mary Kay," *Saturday Evening Post*, October 1981, pp. 59–63, 106; and Maynard G. Stoddard, "In the Pink," *Saturday Evening Post*, October 1981, p. 108.

become important, a lower-level need doesn't have to be completely satisfied before a higher-level one is sought. Once a particular need has been satisfied, it is no longer an effective motivator.

> Did you notice in the case that opens the chapter that Jim said the crew would operate "at a fast, but safe, speed"? Which employee need was he appealing to with that statement? Explain.

In attempting to fill self-actualization needs, an individual should have a level of aspiration equal to his or her abilities and developmental level. Yet, if one's level of aspiration doesn't increase, one's motivation will be limited. A friend of the great Danish sculptor Albert Thorvaldsen, looking at a piece of sculpture that seemed perfect, said, "Now you must be satisfied with this great

production." The artist answered that this wasn't true "because I must be going downhill when I find my work equal to my aspirations."

▲ **Theory X and Theory Y**  Douglas McGregor, a student of Maslow, divided the assumptions managers make about their subordinates into two philosophies that he called **Theory X and Theory Y.**[21] Theory X is based on satisfying only lower-level needs (physiological and safety) to motivate people in organizations. Theory Y is based on seeking to satisfy higher-level needs (esteem and self-actualization) in trying to reach organizational goals. McGregor's theories include the assumptions shown in Table 10-2.

Managers who follow Theory X assumptions expect employees to hate work and any form of responsibility. They feel employees:

1. Do only the work that is required.
2. Have little interest in improving their jobs.
3. Take as much time off from the job as they can.
4. Are satisfied with merely getting their paychecks.

Managers who follow Theory Y assumptions expect their employees to be striving, self-motivated individuals. They expect employees to:

1. Do more than is required of them and not waste time on the job.
2. Be interested in improving their jobs and their lot in life.
3. Seek self-satisfaction and the respect of others by doing a good job.
4. Seek and accept the rewards of greater responsibility.

A Theory X manager stresses traditional economic incentives. On the other hand, a Theory Y manager tends to be more democratic and stresses the inherently cooperative nature of employees. In other words, because employees seek rewards related to personal achievement, in addition to economic and social ones, they tend to be motivated to participate freely and willingly to reach organizational goals (see the Profile on page 272).

**TABLE 10-2.  Theory X and Theory Y assumptions.**

| Theory X Assumptions | Theory Y Assumptions |
|---|---|
| 1. People are basically lazy, don't like work, and try to avoid it. | 1. People aren't naturally lazy and don't dislike work, for it can be as natural to them as play. |
| 2. It's difficult to motivate people. Managers have to control, manipulate, coerce, and threaten employees to get them to work toward organizational goals. | 2. People are self-motivated to reach company objectives to which they feel committed. |
| 3. People try to avoid responsibility, and prefer to be directed. | 3. People will seek and accept responsibility under favorable conditions. |
| 4. People are irrational, have little ambition, and want security. | 4. People are capable of being innovative and creative in solving organizational problems. |
| | 5. People are bright, but their potential is underutilized; so they strive for self-respect and self-actualization. |

**TABLE 10-3. Comparison of needs, as viewed by Maslow, McGregor, and Herzberg.**

| Maslow's Hierarchy of Needs | McGregor's Theory X and Theory Y | Herzberg's Two-Factor Theory | |
|---|---|---|---|
| Self-actualization needs | THEORY Y | Achievement<br>Work itself<br>Possibility of growth<br>Responsibility | Motivators |
| Esteem needs | | Recognition<br>Advancement | |
| | | Status | Hygiene Factors |
| Social needs | | Interpersonal relations:<br>  Supervisors<br>  Peers<br>  Subordinates<br>  Supervision-technical | |
| Safety and security needs | THEORY X | Company policy and<br>  administration<br>Employee benefits<br>Job security<br>Working conditions | |
| Physiological needs | | Salary<br>Personal life | |

▲ **Herzberg's Two-Factor Theory**   In a study of professional employees, Frederick Herzberg found that there were two sets of motivation factors in each job situation—motivators and hygiene (or maintenance) factors. Logically enough, he called his theory the **two-factor theory.**[22]

**Motivators** are job factors that positively encourage employees to perform effectively. They can include the desire for achievement, responsibility, advancement, growth on the job, and recognition of one's capabilities (satisfaction of esteem and self-actualization needs). Managers must provide these real motivators to achieve the sort of participative attitude that produces outstanding employee performance.

**Hygiene factors** cause dissatisfaction if they're absent, yet don't motivate if they're present. They include such items as proper salary, interpersonal relationships, company policies, job security, working conditions, and quality of supervision. These contribute to job satisfaction by filling the physiological, safety, and social needs. While they're not directly involved in motivating employees, the proper hygiene factors are necessary to satisfy lower-level needs and thereby ensure minimal employee performance.

Table 10-3 compares the needs of employees as expressed in all of these theories. You can see that as our needs approach the higher levels, we become more self-motivated. What the comparison really means for business in the United States is that with machines available to do the tedious and routine work, managers must satisfy employees' higher-order needs so that they'll be truly motivated to do effective decision-making work.

## *Profile*

### The Team Approach to Human Relations

Tom Lasorda's predecessor as manager of the Los Angeles Dodgers was Walt Alston, the "Quiet Man," who managed the team for twenty-three years. Lasorda's personality couldn't be more different from Walt's—he's a bubbly cheerleader of a manager. In contrast to the quiet, re-served Alston, Lasorda is the sort of exuberant manager who hugs his team members for making good plays.

After his team got into the World Series for the third time in 1981, Lasorda's craving for a championship was finally satisfied. Earlier, he'd admitted that it was disap-

## COMMUNICATING WITH EMPLOYEES

**Objective 4**

The process of communication and its effective use in business.

A manager can make good decisions and sound plans, establish an effective organization structure, earn the respect of superiors, peers, and subordinates, work hard at motivating workers—and still be ineffective. All of these activities will be to no avail unless the manager communicates effectively. Communication, of course, involves much more than merely telling a person something. **Communication** occurs when a person or group transmits meaning *and* understanding to another person or group. Don Lennox seems to be succeeding in turning International Harvester around because "He listens well, . . . pushes others to express opinions that contradict his, . . . and once he has the information he is looking for, . . . makes fast decisions, and sticks to them."[23]

### The Communication Process

As shown in Figure 10-3 (page 274), communication is a cycle of events that starts when (1) the sender has an idea, which (2) is translated, or encoded, into

pointing to lose the World Series twice to the New York Yankees, in 1977 and 1978. "But there're twenty-four other clubs that would have loved to be in our place. I told my players I was proud of them winning two pennants in a row against great clubs like the Reds and Phillies and Pirates and Giants. You know if God delays, it doesn't mean God denies. We'll get our turn."

Lasorda was named National League Manager of the Year by the Associated Press when he faced his most difficult challenge in 1981 with an aging team that some baseball buffs believed had passed its peak. But he cajoled the Dodgers into their first world championship since 1965. And he did it in two languages—English and Spanish—in dealing with Fernando Valenzuela, the brilliant rookie left-hander.

When play resumed after the 1981 midsummer baseball strike, Los Angeles was one of four teams assured of a postseason playoff spot. However, the Dodgers appeared to lack incentive in the second half of the season, and they opened the divisional playoffs with two consecutive losses in Houston. Then, only one loss away from elimination, the team came home and won three straight games to knock out the Houston Astros. In the National League Championship Series against Montreal, when the Expos won two of the first three games, the Dodgers were on the brink of extinction again. But Lasorda rallied his team to two straight victories on the road, making it into the World Series again. It appeared unlikely that the Dodgers could bounce back a third time, but they did. After losing the first two games in New York, Los Angeles won three straight at home and then whipped the Yankees in the sixth game at New York. Lasorda said it was the Dodgers' finest moment. In 1983, he was named the National League Manager of the Year for the third time in seven years. He was also rewarded by the Dodgers with an unprecedented three-year contract.

Lasorda is considered the consummate company man. After being part of the Dodgers organization as player, scout, coach, and manager for thirty-four years, he said, "I wouldn't leave the Dodgers unless they cut the cord. There are four things in my life I've never regretted—believing in God, my feeling for my family, being an American, and being with this organization."

Sources: Based on Red Smith, "Of God, Baseball, and Dodger Blue," *The New York Times,* March 14, 1979, p. D21. © 1979 by The New York Times Company. Reprinted by permission. And "LA's Lasorda Named NL's Manager of the Year," *The New York Times,* November 10, 1981, p. C2. © 1981 by The New York Times Company. Reprinted by permission. Also based on "The 700 Club," Christian Broadcast Network, July 19, 1983; correspondence with Tommy LaSorda; and "Lasorda Is Rewarded with Three-Year Contract," *Mobile Register,* October 21, 1983, p. 2E.

symbols, which (3) are transmitted to someone else, who (4) receives them, and (5) decodes them back into an idea—ideally, the same one that started the cycle. Just to be sure, the process must be completed with (6) feedback.

▲ **Thinking** At the thinking stage, the idea is wordless. It's just a thought or feeling that must be translated into such symbols as words, sounds, or gestures before it can be shared with another person or group.

▲ **Encoding** The process by which an idea is transformed into some form of symbol is called encoding or translating. This step is difficult. It's often hard to find exactly the right word to express a thought. How often have you heard someone say, "I'm trying to think of the right word," or "I can't say what I mean," or "I can't put it into words," or "You know what I mean," or simply "You know"?

▲ **Transmitting and Receiving** The symbols are then transmitted to their intended receiver through some medium such as speaking or writing. This

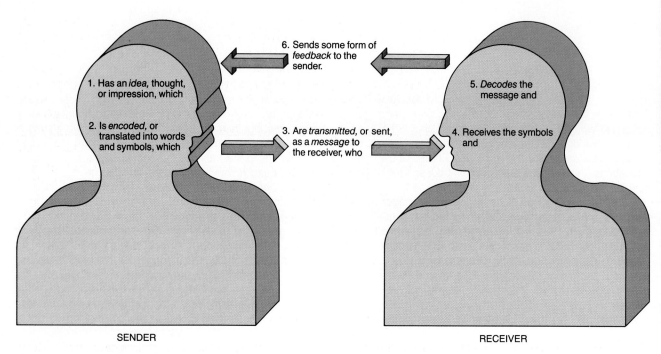

**Figure 10-3** The communication process.

medium will inevitably be subject to some static, noise, filtering, or other environmental interference, so that the messages received often aren't those that were sent. This is a natural tendency that's difficult to overcome.

▲ **Decoding**  Even if the correct symbols are received, the message may be retranslated or decoded into quite different ideas, depending on the receiver's frame of reference. Also, the decoding can be no better than the original encoding. If a message is garbled to begin with, the receiver can't be expected to unscramble it.

▲ **Feedback**  Frequently, communication ceases at this point. Yet, for effective communication, the process must be repeated, in reverse, to make sure that the decoded idea corresponds with the idea as it existed before encoding. This step is called **feedback,** which is a response of some type from the receiver that shows the sender that the idea has been received.

## Methods of Communication

There are many methods of communication, including oral, written, and nonverbal (body language). There is also much informal communication in most organizations, usually in an oral or nonverbal form.

Oral communication is the most direct form of communication and is used by managers for discussions, conferences, and meetings. Other familiar examples are telephone conversations, sales talks, interviews, speeches, and press conferences. In order to be effective, oral communication should be a two-way street, providing the opportunity for feedback.

Written communication is used by managers in performing the basic managerial functions at all levels of the organization. Familiar examples of written communication are memos, letters, reports, and press releases.

Nonverbal communication or **body language** is the transmission of a message without the use of speech or formal language. It permits a message to be conveyed by eyes, eyebrows, facial expression, tone of voice, hand gestures, speech inflection, and other body movements. This type of communication is sometimes quite effective, but it can be confusing, since it can contradict the meaning of other messages. When an employee seems to be responding well to her boss's suggestions, verbally agreeing and promising to try to improve, but her arms are folded and her legs are crossed defensively, body language may be giving a clearer indication of the employee's real feelings.

As you saw in Chapter 7, informal communication, otherwise known as the grapevine, may be quite effective. It tends to (1) provide news quickly, (2) allow employees to let off steam about problems affecting their work, and (3) eventually allow information to work its way to the top, resulting in changes that improve morale.

### Some Practical Guidelines for Communicating

The following practical methods can be used to improve communication:

1. Stress fairness, openness, and straight talk. When Marvin Craig and "Red" Little decided what was needed to save Ford's Livonia plant, they met with the employees in groups of several hundred. After explaining that they had to give up many benefits, Craig said, "Those boys across the pond [Japanese] are beating you in quality and . . . cost. Either we work as a team and do the job or it will be a case of the last guy out, please turn out the lights." The employees stood and applauded.[24]

2. Encourage feedback and response from the receiver. Sandy McDonnell of McDonnell Douglas (see the Profile on page 199) meets with his top team every morning to get feedback on how the company is doing.

3. Listen actively. Listening is more than merely taking in the words so that you can repeat the message. It involves attempting to find and understand the true meaning of the message, from the sender's point of view.
4. Select words carefully, avoiding emotionally loaded terms or accusations, and use the "you" approach. Dr. Sylvia Sorkin, a practicing psychologist, told the participants in a management development program:

> The five most important words you can use are "I am proud of you."
> The four most important are "What do you think?"
> The three most important are "Will you, please?"
> The two most important are "Thank you!"
> The one most important word is "You."

## HOW TO IMPROVE MOTIVATION

**Objective 5**

**Several means that management can use to improve motivation.**

Given that motivation is essential to productivity, what else can one do, besides communicating clearly, to improve it? Some management practices that are designed to improve motivation are management by objectives (MBO), job enrichment, flextime, part-time employment and job sharing, job rotation, merit basis of compensation, profit sharing, and incentive wage plans. Only the first three will be discussed here; the others are covered elsewhere in the book.

### Management by Objectives

Management by objectives (MBO) is a popular management technique whereby managers and subordinates jointly establish specific objectives for subordinates to achieve within a specified time period. Employees are then rewarded on the basis of objectives set and reached.

For an MBO program to be effective, though, the following approach should be followed. Before the beginning of a fiscal year, top management should define the organization's operating strategy, continuing objectives, and performance levels to be achieved. These should be communicated to the heads of subunits and finally to individual managers. At the same time, the managers should be setting up their own specific goals, in cooperation with their subordinates. When the overall objectives of top management are coordinated with the individual managers' and their subordinates' specific goals, the individuals will probably have to modify their goals to fit those of the company, or the company may have to adapt its goals to mesh with those of the individuals. Top management should integrate the goals and objectives and direct how they are to be achieved.

In 1969, a division of Quality Paper Company adopted an overall management by objectives program. One mill manager set a goal of "an overall production increase of 3.7 percent" for 1970. The individual managers of the pulp mill, finishing department, shipping department, power plant, and purchasing

department then set individual targets that their units would have to meet if the overall goal was to be met. The actual overall increase in productivity was 6.2 percent. However, the program was later dropped because existing facilities were inadequate for that production level, and maintenance couldn't repair the equipment quickly enough to keep up the pace.

> Was Jim of Slick Oil Company essentially using MBO? If so, how? Do Mary Kay and her people use MBO? Explain your answer.

### Job Enrichment

**Job enrichment** emphasizes giving employees greater authority and responsibility over their jobs as the best way to motivate them. Under job enrichment, employees are given more say in planning their work and deciding how it's to be done. They're encouraged to learn new and related skills or even to trade jobs with each other. Job enrichment is often used for jobs (1) whose pace is mechanically controlled, (2) that are repetitive and monotonous, and (3) that require minimum skills.

An example of job enrichment can be found at Packard Electric's Austintown, Ohio, plant. A twenty-two-member work team operates a "self-managed" assembly line. The team sets the line's speed, orders materials, checks quality, establishes rules for handling disputes, and does the paperwork. Every day a different employee serves as coordinator and makes the decisions. The workers can rotate jobs on the line, or even leave the line several times a month to handle materials and repairs.[25]

> Can you cite some instances of job enrichment in the case that opens the chapter?

### Flextime

**Flextime,** a concept now being adopted by many businesses, is an arrangement in which workers may schedule their own hours for starting and stopping work, so long as they're present during certain required hours (see Figure 10-4). Notice that all employees must work during the core time from 10 to 2. The rest of their required hours (for a total of eight, usually) can be scheduled within the periods from 7 to 10 and 2 to 5.

Employees often prefer these schedules because of family or personal commitments. They're especially helpful in single-parent and dual-career homes. Managers find in some cases that employees' morale is higher and productivity is improved. On the other hand, some employees become lax about working the full time called for in the work schedule. Flextime may also add to energy costs by extending the work day. Some companies using flextime are Control

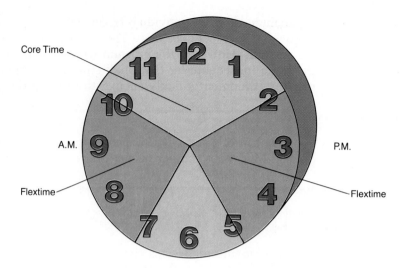

**Figure 10-4** How flextime works.

Data, Smith Kline, John Hancock Life, Blue Cross–Blue Shield of California, and Bank of Boston.

### Techniques Aren't Enough

Regardless of what techniques are used to motivate employees, they won't be effective for very long unless they're backed up by a meaningful philosophy of motivation. The need for such a philosophy was excellently expressed by Clarence Francis when he was chairman of General Foods:

> You can buy a [person's] time; you can buy a [person's] physical presence at a given place; you can even buy a measured number of skilled muscular motions per hour or day. But you cannot buy enthusiasm; you cannot buy initiative; you cannot buy loyalty; you cannot buy devotion of hearts, minds, and souls. You have to earn these things.[26]

Dr. Alfred Haake, lecturer for GM, ended some of his human relations lectures by saying, "'Good human relations is treating people as if it were your last day on earth,' you say. Ah, no! Good human relations is treating people as if it were *their* last day on earth."

### ⬆ LEARNING OBJECTIVES REVISITED

1. *Individual and group aspects of human relations in business.*

   Planning, organizing, and staffing are of little value unless managers establish good human relations. Human relations involves getting employees to want to strive for organizational goals, through motivating and commu-

nicating with them. Human relations concepts have evolved from the scientific management approach of paying incentive wages to first-class workers to the human relations approach, which sees the workplace as a social system in which increasing morale will increase performance, to the human resources approach, which treats workers, individually and in groups, with dignity and respect but evaluates their output by the economic criteria of efficiency and effectiveness.

2. *The motivation process and its role in improving performance.*

Motivation is the process by which managers bring out the best in their subordinates by giving them a reason to perform better. Most popular motivation theories are built around the idea of needs, which are cravings within us that we try to satisfy by our outward behavior.

3. *Some popular theories of motivation.*

The most popular theories of motivation include Maslow's hierarchy of needs, McGregor's Theory X and Theory Y, and Herzberg's two-factor theory.

Maslow's hierarchy is composed of five basic levels of needs: physiological, safety and security, social, esteem, and self-actualization. Lower-level needs must be satisfied before higher-level ones are activated. Once a particular need has been satisfied, it is no longer an effective motivator.

McGregor divided the assumptions managers make about their subordinates into philosophies called Theory X and Theory Y. Theory X assumes that employees seek to satisfy only lower-level needs, while Theory Y assumes that they seek to satisfy higher-level needs as well. Under Theory X, people are considered basically lazy and unmotivated, so that managers have to control, coerce, and threaten them. Under Theory Y, people are assumed to be self-motivated, willing to accept responsibility, innovative and creative, and striving for self-actualization.

Herzberg found that the real motivators are related to achievement, responsibility, advancement, growth on the job, and satisfaction of esteem and self-actualization needs. Maintenance or hygiene factors, such as proper salary, company policies, and working conditions, are related to the fulfillment of lower-level needs and thus do not motivate, although they must be present for workers to be satisfied.

4. *The process of communication and its effective use in business.*

Communication is the process whereby the meaning and understanding of a person or group are transmitted to another person or group. The communication process is a cycle of events that starts with the sender's thought or idea, which is translated or encoded into symbols. These symbols are transmitted to someone else, who receives them and decodes them back into an idea. The receiver then sends feedback to the sender that the message has been received. Transmitting and receiving are subject to some static, noise, or filtering, so that the intended symbols are not always received. Decoding may therefore result in the receiver's having ideas quite different from those intended by the sender. Good communication

is ultimately the result of clear thinking and attentive listening. Informal communication, known as the grapevine, is quite effective.

5. *Several means that management can use to improve motivation.*

   Some of the management practices used to improve motivation are management by objectives (MBO), job enrichment, flextime, part-time employment and job sharing, job rotation, merit wages, profit sharing, and incentive wages. With the MBO technique, managers and subordinates jointly set objectives and then try to reach them. Rewards are based on how well those objectives are achieved. Under job enrichment, employees are given more authority to plan their work and decide how it is to be done. Flextime is an arrangement under which workers are permitted to schedule their own hours for starting and stopping work, within limits set by core time. These and other motivating techniques, however, must be supported by a meaningful philosophy of motivation.

## ⛰ IMPORTANT TERMS

As an extra review of the chapter, try defining the following terms. If you have trouble with any of them, refer to the page listed.

| | |
|---|---|
| human relations  *262* | esteem needs  *268* |
| scientific management  *262* | self-actualization needs  *268* |
| Hawthorne studies  *263* | Theory X and Theory Y  *270* |
| human resources philosophy  *264* | two-factor theory  *271* |
| | motivators  *271* |
| motivation  *265* | hygiene factors  *271* |
| motive  *265* | communication  *272* |
| needs  *267* | feedback  *274* |
| hierarchy of needs  *267* | body language  *275* |
| physiological needs  *267* | job enrichment  *277* |
| safety and security needs  *268* | flextime  *277* |
| social needs  *268* | |

## ⛰ REVIEW QUESTIONS

1. Is good human relations as important as good staffing techniques? Why or why not?
2. Trace the development of the human relations concept through the last century.
3. Describe the motivation process.
4. How have motivation theories changed since Taylor's time?
5. Walk through Maslow's hierarchy of needs. What are its strong and weak points?
6. Compare McGregor's Theory X and Theory Y. What are the strong and weak points of each?
7. Explain Herzberg's two-factor theory. What are its strong and weak points?

8. Describe the communication process. Why is its last step so important?
9. What are the pros and cons of the different communication methods?
10. What employee needs are met by MBO? by job enrichment? by flextime?

## ⬙ DISCUSSION QUESTIONS

1. What are the essential differences among the scientific management, human relations, and human resources approaches as they relate to motivating today's employees?
2. What do you think really motivates someone like Mary Kay? Explain in detail.
3. How can you apply the MBO concept to your schooling?
4. Which theory of motivation do you most believe in? Why? Try forming a theory of your own.
5. Give a few illustrations of informal communications at school or on the job. How effective were they?

## ⬙ CASE 10-1   No Write-Up for Fernando Lopez

Southwest Texas Butane Company (STBC) retailed liquefied petroleum (LP) gas to rural consumers who lived beyond the limits of natural gas pipelines. Fernando Lopez, advertising representative and appliance promoter, was hired by STBC to help Gene Oswell, the merchandise sales manager, increase sales of gas-burning appliances by preparing advertising copy and staging sales promotion campaigns at various retail outlets. He was given the title of director of advertising and sales promotion.

Fernando did an outstanding job, and the store managers liked him and often asked for his services. He enjoyed traveling and didn't complain about being away from home. Apparently, he was quite happy with his job and the company. The managers would often remark, "Fernando is always in such a good mood. He lifts other people's spirits with his pleasant disposition." But after a couple of years of bubbling enthusiasm, he gradually seemed to lose interest in his work. The managers began to complain that "Fernando doesn't have his old zip and enthusiasm anymore. He's not even working up any interest for his promotional activities." Some managers were reluctant to have Fernando do any promotional work for them.

After several complaints reached top management, Annie Sinclair, the personnel manager, called Fernando in. After praising him for his splendid work in the past and expressing faith in his abilities, Sinclair told him about the recent complaints and asked why he thought they were being made. Admitting that he no longer felt the same enthusiasm, Fernando demanded a substantial salary increase. When Sinclair expressed surprise that he'd ask for a raise when his effectiveness was in question, Fernando said he'd been promised a raise in pay after one year if his work was satisfactory. He'd been giving the job all he had for two years, but no raise had come through. Sinclair promised to check with Oswell when he returned from vacation to see if such a promise had been made and what could be done about it. In the meantime, Fernando should try to recapture his old enthusiasm and start doing a better job, or he might be fired instead of getting a raise. Fernando's retort was that if the firm failed to live up to its word, he'd quit rather than wait around to be fired.

Fernando's work seemed to improve for the next month, but he still didn't have his old sparkle. Upon his return, Oswell explained to Fernando that his original promise had been that if sales increased 10 percent the first year, he'd see that Fernando got a substantial raise. However, because of a local recession, sales had climbed little, although they would actually have fallen if it

hadn't been for Fernando's work. He repeated his promise of a raise "if sales increase 10 percent" but added that the first thing necessary was for Fernando to change his attitude. "In your present frame of mind, you can't possibly accomplish much," he concluded.

Fernando then expressed another grievance. About three months earlier, Jim Jones, a manager from another area, had been transferred into Fernando's area. Although his work was inferior to Fernando's, he'd been given a glowing write-up in STBC's newspaper. Why hadn't Fernando been given such a write-up? When he was promised a write-up in a later issue, he was so pleased that he resumed his work with great vigor. Eventually, it was reported that he was again doing a fine job.

After two future issues of the paper came out with no mention of Fernando, he wrote a letter of resignation. The personnel manager asked him to come by the office for further discussion, but he refused.

### Case Questions

1. What motivated Fernando Lopez?
2. Why do you think he resigned the way he did?
3. From the information given, do you think Fernando was more interested in the raise or the article? Why?
4. What would you have done differently if you were Gene Oswell?

## ⚖ CASE 10-2   Communications: Quo Vadis?

The following letter was recently received from a previous student, now an executive with Intel:[27]

I would like to report on an experiment in human relations in which I recently participated in connection with a company training session for third-level managers. The program was designed to enhance management target setting and had to do with communications between superiors and subordinates.

The organization of the experiment was as follows: There were one second-level supervisor, one first-level supervisor, and three "workers" arranged in this manner:

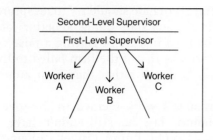

Each participant in the experiment was shielded from the other by a barrier through which notes and slips of paper could be passed. There were two phases to the experiment. In the first phase, each worker was given an envelope containing several slips of paper, each with a symbol (♣, ♥, ♦, etc.). Communication was one way and consisted of written notes from the second-level manager to the first-level manager; from the first-level supervisor to worker A, B, or C. Only the second-level supervisor knew what the objective of the organization (task) was; in this case, it was to exchange the symbols until each member had a matched set.

During the first phase of the experiment, the second-level supervisor wrote notes (letters) to the first-level supervisor, who then wrote notes to A, B, and C.

These notes specified particular actions desired, but did not reveal the objective of the organization. After about 15 minutes of note passing and symbol exchange, the game was stopped.

Then, without further elaboration, the second phase started. The same general arrangement was used except in this case communication was two way; that is, workers A, B, and C could write to the first-level supervisor; the first-level manager could write to the second-level supervisor. The game proceeded again for about 15 minutes.

What were the results of the experiment?

During Phase 1: (a) The workers were confused; (b) the first-level supervisor was confused; and (c) the task was not accomplished.

During Phase 2: (a) The workers were less confused; (b) the first-level supervisor became aware of the objective (task); and (c) the task was accomplished.

**Case Questions**

1. Evaluate the validity of this experiment. Could the results have been forecast from your knowledge of communications? Why or why not?

2. Were the results of this experiment the consequences of the physical arrangement only? Explain.

3. What motivational element was present during the second phase that was missing during the first? How did this presence (and absence) affect the outcome?

4. How would you apply the findings of this experiment to a business organization?

# 11

# Labor Relations

*Unions must change with the times, or risk being run over by them.*

Peter Jennings

*All your strength is in your union,*
*All your danger is in discord;*
*Therefore be at peace henceforward,*
*And as brothers live together.*

Henry Wadsworth Longfellow

## Learning Objectives

After studying this chapter, you will understand:

1. Why unions are so important to U.S. business and what labor relations is.
2. Some of the reasons why people join unions.
3. The development of unions in the United States.
4. The most significant laws affecting labor-management relations.
5. The primary objectives sought by unions for their members.
6. How unions go about achieving their objectives.
7. Current trends in labor relations.

## In This Chapter

Why Are Unions So Important?
Why People Join Unions
How Unions Have Developed
The Legal Basis of Labor Relations
Union Objectives
How Unions Achieve Their Objectives
Current Trends in Labor Relations

## CATERPILLAR TRACTOR STRIKE
*The Cat Purrs Again*

Caterpillar Tractor Company is the world's largest road builder, jungle clearer, earth mover, and mountain reshaper. It makes giant bulldozers, as well as road graders and scrapers, forklifts, backhoes, and diesel engines. They're all painted with Caterpillar's trademark butterscotch yellow (lead-free) paint. The company has twenty-six plants and over 250 dealers who sell to the heavy construction industry worldwide. It's been quite successful and the envy of its competitors. Until 1982, it hadn't had a losing year since 1932—at the depth of the Depression.

By 1982, however, the company had some overriding problems that required it to tighten up on production costs. The recession and foreign competition had cut shipments by around a third, and Caterpillar's financial strength had been declining for two years. Its labor costs for wages and benefits were $19.54 per hour, nearly double its toughest Japanese competitor's. And 14,000 workers had to be laid off. So when the United Auto Workers (UAW), representing Caterpillar's 35,000 workers (including the 14,000 already laid off), went on strike on October 1, the company took a hard stand.

The union was demanding a traditional UAW package containing a 3 percent annual wage increase and cost-of-living adjustments that Caterpillar estimated would raise its wage and benefit costs by 28 percent over three years. The company in turn demanded a contract that would freeze wages for three years, sharply reduce cost-of-living payments, and eliminate up to eleven paid days off per worker over three years. Deadlock!

After a 205-day strike, the longest companywide strike in UAW's history, the workers returned to work on April 25, 1983. Although management won its thirty-seven-month wage freeze and a reduction of 4.5 paid days off, the workers won a profit-sharing plan and wage concessions worth between 18 and 20 percent by 1986. In addition to what it cost Caterpillar and its dealers in lost business, the strike cost workers nearly $20,000 each in wages and benefits. Moreover, the communities where Caterpillar plants operate lost business, tax revenue, and a feeling of goodwill toward the company and its workers.

A wise man had seven sons who were constantly fighting each other, even when they were pitted against outsiders. One day he decided to teach them a lesson. He called them together, gave each one a stick, and said, "Break your stick over your knee." Each one, in turn, easily broke his stick.

Again, he handed each of them a stick. This time he said, "Bind the seven sticks together in a bundle." They did as he asked. "Now try to break the sticks," he said, as he handed the bundle to each of his sons. None of them could break the bundle of sticks.

"Remember," he said, "in union there is strength."

Like the brothers in Aesop's fable "The Bundle of Sticks," an employee has very little bargaining clout when negotiating with management on his or her own. But when employees band together in a union, as Caterpillar's employees did, they're better able to achieve their economic goals. In effect, that's the definition of a **labor union:** an organization of workers banded together to achieve economic goals, especially improved wages, hours, and working conditions.

## WHY ARE UNIONS SO IMPORTANT?

**Objective 1**

**Why unions are so important to U.S. business and what labor relations is.**

Unions are important to managers, employees, the government, and the public, since they affect all aspects of business, one way or another. Unions and their leaders influence a firm's activities, whether it's unionized or not, since supplies, transportation, and maintenance may depend on workers who are unionized. Thus labor relations adds a new wrinkle to managers' human relations task.

The growth of unionism has forced management to change many of its ways of dealing with employees, especially in matters concerning wages, hours, working conditions, and other terms and conditions of employment. Managers of unionized firms face constant challenges from union leaders to consider the rights of workers before developing or applying policies. Managers' freedom of choice has been greatly limited. They can no longer reward one employee on the basis of personal preference or punish another without just cause.

Managers and union members aren't the only ones affected by labor issues. Most of us tend to take for granted such benefits as employee security, better earnings, shorter hours, paid holidays, long vacations, insurance benefits, and improved working conditions. Yet unions have fought for a long time to obtain and preserve these privileges and benefits for all workers.

### What Is Labor Relations?

Many terms are used to refer to the labor relations area of business activity. The terms *labor relations, labor-management relations,* and *industrial relations* are often used interchangeably to refer to the relationships between the managers of an organization and its unionized employees. In brief, **labor relations** is all interactions and relationships between management and its employees where a union is concerned.

Labor-management relations is more than just a power struggle between management and labor over purely economic matters that concern only them. The hurt feelings, bruised egos, disappointments, hopes, and ambitions of managers and labor leaders are also involved (see the Profile on page 288 for an

PROPORTION OF AMERICANS EXPRESSING APPROVAL OF LABOR UNIONS

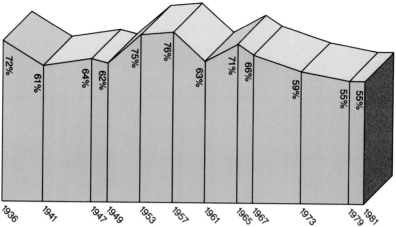

**Figure 11-1** Unions are tending to lose favor with the public. [Based on data from George Gallup, "Union Backing at All-Time Low," *Mobile* (AL) *Register*, September 17, 1981, p. 7-B; and other sources.]

example). Labor-management relationships are affected by—and affect—the total physical, economic, social, technological, legal, political, and cultural environment in which they occur.

## How the Public Views Unions

While unions are still generally accepted by the public, they've lost support recently, even among workers. As Figure 11-1 shows, only 55 percent of the American people favored unions in 1981 (35 percent disapproved), down from 71 percent in 1965 and 76 percent in 1957. Polls also show that one-fifth of families with union members disapproved of unions, and 27 percent of them said that no one should be permitted to strike.[1] Unions rank nineteenth among the country's most powerful institutions in public favor. This is a drastic drop from third in 1977 and fifth in 1974.[2]

There are many reasons why organized labor is now facing its toughest test since the Depression. First, blue-collar industries with card-carrying union members, such as the textile, iron and steel, and auto industries, are being supplanted by card-reading, high-tech ones. Second, people tend to believe that "American labor is simply overprivileged."[3] Third, some workers feel they're actually better off without a union. For example, a worker at the Honda plant in Marysville, Ohio (a heavily unionized state, where the UAW is quite powerful), said that although the union might force a couple of extra dollars out of the firm, it would be bad in the long run. Fourth, management has become more adept at keeping unions out, or minimizing their influence. Fifth, industry is moving from the East and North Central states, where people are favorable to unions, to the West and South, where the environment has been hostile to unions. While 24.5 percent of all U.S. workers were union members in 1980, only 14.1 percent of workers in southern states were.[4]

In other countries, the public's attitude toward unions is mixed. Although Solidarity, Poland's free trade union, was popular with the people—and tolerated by the government—it was curtailed by martial law in December 1981.[5] Unions represent over half of Britain's labor force, but they've lost more than 1.5 million members in the past three years.[6] In Germany and Japan, where unions cooperated with industry to recover from the ravages of World

# *Profile*

## Douglas A. Fraser: Union's Man on the Board

In a staggering break with tradition, the United Auto Workers (UAW) and Chrysler Corporation agreed that Douglas A. Fraser, president of the UAW, would become a member of Chrysler's board of directors—the first American labor leader ever to serve on a company's board. The idea was proposed by the union in 1976 but refused by management. By 1979, however, Chrysler was in such trouble that it accepted Fraser as part of the union's less-costly dispute settlement in May 1980.

Fraser came with his parents from Glasgow, Scotland, to Detroit when he was six years old. After dropping out of high school in his senior year, he lost his first two jobs because of his union organizing activities. His first permanent job was as a metal finisher for Chrysler. After serving in the Army during World War II, Fraser returned to Chrysler, where he again was drawn to union activities. In 1951, he became assistant to the late Walter Reuther, then president of the UAW, largely because of his shrewd bargaining sense. His concern for people and willingness to become involved in plant problems won him enormous respect, even from Chrysler executives. Later, as a vice-president and member of the UAW's executive board, he led the organizing activities of technical, professional, and office employees and workers in skilled trades.

Fraser became president of the UAW in 1977. He's most noted for his negotiating skills, which he used to obtain a comprehensive health care program, unlimited cost-of-living allowances, and favorable pension plans for union members. These skills helped him serve effectively on Chrysler's board, where his primary contribution was to present the workers' point of view.

As a member of Chrysler's board, Fraser emphasized the need for humanizing the assembly line, the four-day work week, assistance to minorities, environmental protection, and comprehensive health insurance. Chrysler officials praised Fraser's performance. Lee Iacocca, Chrysler's chairman, said, "We are lucky to have him. He has fought to keep plants open and save jobs while persuading the firm's employees to give up hundreds of millions of dollars in wages and benefits." Fraser's being on the board smoothed bargaining for concessions from the workers. He could speak with credibility to them because, as a director, he had seen the detailed financial data. He could also speak to management for the workers because he had "walked in their shoes."

Now retired, Doug Fraser, the high school dropout, is teaching courses on the labor movement—and, indirectly, politics—at the University of Michigan and Harvard. His old high school has given him an honorary diploma, and he's received about a dozen honorary university degrees.

Sources: Based on Robert L. Simison, "Chrysler Lauds Strong Performance of UAW's Fraser as Board Member," *The Wall Street Journal*, March 12, 1981, p. 33; and Robert L. Simison, "Douglas Fraser Moves Discussions from Board Rooms to Classrooms," *The Wall Street Journal*, December 1, 1983, p. 31. Adapted by permission of *The Wall Street Journal*, © Dow Jones & Company, Inc. 1981, 1983. Also based on "Fraser Leaves Big Shoes to Fill," *Business Week*, November 15, 1982, pp. 118–23; "A Union Seat on the Board: The Test Isn't Over," *Business Week*, November 22, 1982, p. 30.

War II, they're now becoming more militant as automation and competition reduce employment opportunities.[7]

### Politicians Support Unions

Unions have a great deal of political clout because they're established organizations, just as corporations are. Many state, county, and city officials owe their election to unions, which get out the vote and the contributions for favorite candidates. Even President Jimmy Carter said that he owed his election to unions, especially the National Education Association (NEA), primarily composed of public school teachers.

Historically, a majority of the members of Congress have been favorable to unions. The AFL-CIO endorsed 376 candidates for the U.S. House of Representatives during the 1982 elections. Of these, 238 were elected. Twenty of the 31 candidates backed by the AFL-CIO for the U.S. Senate won. While union leaders' political influence may be waning, at the present time 241 of the 435 House members and 43 of the 100 senators tend to favor union-backed issues.[8]

The AFL-CIO took a big gamble in 1983 by giving its preprimary endorsement to Walter Mondale. By doing so, it gave the candidate access to around $20 million of services and organizational activities, such as phone banks, computerized mailing lists, and so forth. The effort paid off, as he'd essentially won the Democratic nomination for President by mid-May of 1984—two months before the convention.

### Unions Command Large Financial Resources

Unions are powerful also because of the financial resources they can command. Pension funds resulting from union-management agreements total around $300 billion in assets. Pension funds in effect control some corporations. While unions don't have direct control over these funds, they do have indirect influence.

Unions have large sums on deposit in major banks, and union leaders can flex their muscles by threatening to withdraw them. The Amalgamated Clothing and Textile Workers Union used the power of its pension funds to unionize J. P. Stevens & Company. It forced Stevens's board chairman, James D. Finley, to resign as director of Manufacturers Hanover Trust in the face of a threat to withdraw $1 billion from the bank.[9]

## WHY PEOPLE JOIN UNIONS

**Objective 2**

**Some of the reasons why people join unions.**

As powerful as unions may be, there are no simple explanations why workers join or reject them. Pressures are constantly changing, and these pressures influence workers first in one direction and then in another. Union organizers use strong emotional appeals, as well as rational, logical, economic reasons for joining their union.

### Reasons for Joining Unions

In joining unions, workers tend to follow economic motives, including the desire for higher wages, shorter hours, and greater economic security. In addition, employees seek (1) more credible and logical personnel policies, with less

favoritism; (2) the right to have a voice in decisions affecting their welfare; (3) protection from economic hazards beyond their control; and (4) recognition and participation that they couldn't get from management. Workers at certain jobs may be forced to join a union because of a union shop agreement.

### Reasons for Not Joining Unions

Since four out of five employees *don't* belong to a union, there must be some pretty good reasons why they resist joining. Some of the reasons for *not* joining are (1) lack of a compelling reason to unionize; (2) a feeling that the union isn't really needed, as long as benefits can be obtained; (3) worker identification with management; and (4) distrust of and fear of some corrupt union leaders.[10]

To a certain extent, unions are the victims of their own success. They've pushed through state and federal laws giving workers so many benefits that many people take the benefits for granted and think they don't need a union. Also, the majority of workers today have white-collar, managerial, technical, or professional jobs and feel little need for a union.

## HOW UNIONS HAVE DEVELOPED

**Objective 3**

**The development of unions in the United States.**

Until the Industrial Revolution, workers in Europe were mostly independent. Then they became dependent on someone else—especially absentee owners—for their livelihood. This arrangement led to many abuses, as employees were forced to work long hours at hard labor in dingy, windowless, and unventilated factories, in return for low pay and with no job security. Children were also unfairly exploited. Children as young as seven years of age were forced to lift heavy loads and work twelve to fourteen hours a day. When workers were hurt in an accident or became too old or sick to work, they were fired, with no pension.

Working conditions were much better in the early American colonies because of the severe shortage of skilled labor. However, by the latter part of the nineteenth century this had changed. The high birthrate, rapid and uncontrolled immigration, the concentration of wealth and industry in the hands of a few, and political abuses by some employers had led to crowded, oppressive industrial areas. Workers were exploited to such an extent that they tried to fight back.

### Early Union Activities

As we've said, individual employees are weak and powerless when acting by themselves. Although there were labor unions as early as 1776, they tended to be small, isolated, friendly, but ineffective **craft unions**—unions of workers in a specific skill, craft, or trade, such as the union of typesetters.

By the latter part of the nineteenth century, a more concerted effort was needed to improve the workers' plight, so several of the craft unions joined together in 1869 to form the **Knights of Labor,** the first national union. Since its leadership was considered unacceptably radical, even revolutionary, by the general populace, it was only moderately successful. A more conservative national craft union formed in 1881 became the **American Federation of Labor (AFL)** in 1886.

Boys of all ages picked slate from coal in grimy coal chutes.

In 1886, the labor movement became even more unpopular than it had been under the Knights of Labor. During the Haymarket Riot, a bomb killed several Chicago policemen who were trying to break up a union rally. But, because of the enlightened leadership of the AFL's president, cigarmaker Samuel Gompers from London, the union continued to be a national force. Gompers's leadership was based on the economic rather than the social needs of workers. Thus five fundamentals were emphasized: (1) equal pay for the same job; (2) benefits based on seniority; (3) refusal of union members to work on the same job with nonunion workers; (4) collective bargaining and strikes to improve wages, hours, and working conditions; and (5) support of the candidate most favorable to unions rather than identification with any political party.

### Period of Rapid Growth

As a result of backing Woodrow Wilson for president in 1912, unions made many gains. They were exempted from prosecution under the Sherman Antitrust Act by the Clayton Act of 1914, and they were given the Labor Department and many agencies and commissions during World War I. Then workers enjoyed the prosperity of the Roaring Twenties along with everyone else. But when the Depression began in October 1929, workers were again exploited, much as they had been during the Industrial Revolution.

As a result, beginning in 1931, a number of pro-labor laws were passed, including the Davis-Bacon Act (1931), the Norris–La Guardia Act (1932), the National Industrial Recovery Act (1933), the Wagner Act (1935), the Social Security Act (1936), and the Fair Labor Standards Act (1938).

Until that time, the AFL and its affiliates had been organized on a craft basis. Union growth was therefore limited, since there were few craft workers left to unionize. Some union leaders within the AFL decided to organize **industrial unions** composed of all the workers in the same industry, such as the automobile, coal, rubber, and steel industries. The Committee for Industrial Organization (CIO) was formed in 1935. Then John L. Lewis organized the United Mine Workers (UMW), the first union to represent skilled and un-

skilled workers in the same industry. In 1938, after being expelled from the AFL, the CIO changed its name to the **Congress of Industrial Organizations.**

Because of favorable laws—administered by the pro-labor Roosevelt administration—and the increased demand for workers that resulted from World War II, union membership grew from 2.5 million in 1933 to 14 million in 1944—which was nearly 36 percent of the labor force.

### Period of Stabilization

Some unions committed abuses during the war, such as forcing workers to join unions before they could work in war plants, holding no elections or rigged ones, and going on strike when war supplies were badly needed. As a result, the public attitude toward unions changed between 1941 and 1948 (see Figure 11-1), and an anti-labor Congress was elected from 1946 to 1948.

In 1947, the Labor-Management Relations Act (Taft-Hartley Act) was passed—over President Harry Truman's veto—to curb abuses. When Eisenhower took over (1953–1961), he maintained a "hands off" policy toward labor-management relations. The change in the governmental attitude, plus the growth of high-tech industries and white-collar occupations, resulted in a gradual decline in the percentage of the work force that was unionized, as union membership remained stable. To try to combat this trend, the AFL and CIO merged in 1955 into the **AFL-CIO,** with George Meany, head of the Plumbers' Union, as its president and driving force.

About that time, Senate hearings showed that a significant minority of corrupt labor leaders were (1) extorting bribes from companies in return for promises not to strike against them, (2) stealing from employee health and welfare funds, and (3) accepting bribes from management for **sweetheart contracts,** whereby concessions were made to employers at the expense of employees.[11] Again public sentiment turned against unions (see Figure 11-1), and the Labor-Management Reporting and Disclosure Act (Landrum-Griffin Act) was passed in 1959 to prevent this corruption and abuse.

In 1962, President John F. Kennedy issued Executive Order 10988, which permitted government employees to join unions and required federal department heads to encourage such membership. This, plus the fact that professional employee associations, such as the National Education Association, began functioning as labor unions, led to an increase in membership for the next fifteen years or so. Now there are about 20 million union members—or less than 20 percent of the labor force.

## THE LEGAL BASIS OF LABOR RELATIONS

**Objective 4**

**The most significant laws affecting labor-management relations.**

The legal basis of union-management relations is founded on the Norris–La Guardia Act, the National Labor Relations Act, the Labor-Management Relations Act, and the Labor-Management Reporting and Disclosure Act. This complex of laws sets public policy and controls labor relations.

### The Basic Labor Laws

Let's first see the purpose of labor laws. Then we'll see how they operate and are enforced to protect the interests of both labor and management.

▲ **The Norris–La Guardia Act** The earliest piece of federal labor legislation was the Norris–La Guardia Act, passed in 1932. Before its passage, management could get a court order forcing striking workers to either go back to work or face a fine or imprisonment. Not only that, but companies could force employees to sign what were called **yellow-dog contracts,** effectively forbidding them to join a union. If a worker broke the contract, management could use **blacklisting,** which involved listing the names of union troublemakers to keep them from being rehired. The Norris–La Guardia Act took the first step toward making all of these employer weapons unlawful.

▲ **The Wagner Act** The Wagner Act was passed in 1935 to further the growth and recognition of unions as the worker's protector. The act defined specific unfair labor practices that management could no longer commit against the workers and the union. Section 7, the most famous and powerful part of the act, gave employees the right to freely join unions of their choosing and to engage in any and all union activities without fear of punishment.

However, many abuses resulted from the act's failure to mention unfair labor practices to be charged against *unions*. One major issue was whether a union could require all employees to join in order to get, or keep, a job. It was assumed by many managers, as well as employees, that the right to join a union carried with it the right *not* to do so. This assumption was changed during World War II, when union shop and closed shop agreements were accepted by the government. Later, the agency shop was accepted by unions as a second-choice substitute for the union or closed shop.

Under most **union shop** agreements, all employees must join the union within a specified period—usually thirty to ninety days—or be fired. Under a **closed shop** agreement, all prospective employees must be members of the recognized union *before* they can be hired, and all present employees must join to retain their jobs. In an **agency shop,** all employees must pay union dues for the union to serve as their agent even if they choose not to join the union.

---

Do you have trouble seeing the difference between a union shop and a closed shop? In a union shop, management employs the people it chooses, and then they become members of the union. In a closed shop, management must accept the worker(s) sent by the union.

---

▲ **The Taft-Hartley Act** The Taft-Hartley Act of 1947 substantially amended the Wagner Act by making it more even-handed, so that unions as well as management could be charged with unfair labor practices. The law prohibited the closed shop agreement, and Section 14(b) gave states the right to pass laws prohibiting the union shop. By 1981, twenty states had used this section to pass **right-to-work laws** giving employees the right to join or refuse to join a union without being fired. These laws, which take precedence over the federal law, are now found in the states shown in Figure 11-2. Other unfair labor practices outlawed by the Taft-Hartley Act were union refusal to negotiate, striking without sixty days' notice, secondary boycotts (discussed on page 299), and **featherbedding,** or keeping workers on the payroll even when they do no work.

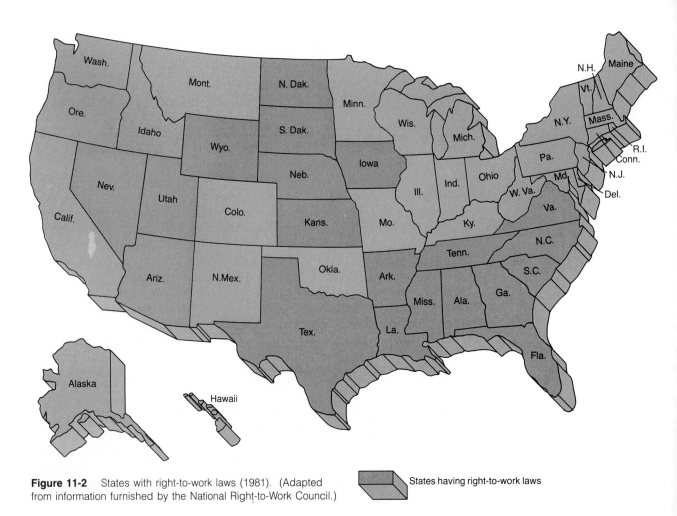

**Figure 11-2** States with right-to-work laws (1981). (Adapted from information furnished by the National Right-to-Work Council.)

States having right-to-work laws

▲ **The Landrum-Griffin Act** As indicated earlier, the Landrum-Griffin Act, which was passed in 1959, aimed to prevent corruption and abuse of employees by some union leaders. It included a bill of rights that protects union members from possible union abuses by requiring regularly scheduled elections of union leaders and placing stricter controls on the use of union funds.

## Rights and Restrictions Under the Law

Employees, management, and unions now have basic rights and restrictions under the labor laws. Employees have essentially five rights under Section 7 of the Wagner Act, as amended. They have the right to:

1. Organize.
2. Form, join, or assist labor organizations of their own choosing.
3. Bargain collectively through their representatives.
4. Engage in concerted activities needed for mutual aid or protection.
5. Refrain from, as well as engage in, such activities, except where there's a valid union shop agreement.

**TABLE 11-1  Unfair labor practices.**

It is an unfair labor practice for *managers* to:

1. Interfere with, restrain, or coerce employees exercising their rights under Section 7 of the Wagner Act.
2. Dominate or interfere with the forming or administering of unions or contribute support to them.
3. Discriminate in hiring or any other terms of employment in such a way as to encourage or discourage membership in a union.
4. Discharge or otherwise discriminate against employees for filing charges or testifying under these laws.
5. Refuse to bargain with the union representative.

It is an unfair practice for a *union* to:

1. Coerce employees into, or restrain them from, engaging freely in union activities.
2. Force management to discriminate against employees in violation of the law.
3. Refuse to bargain in good faith.
4. Require managers to pay money for work not done (featherbedding).
5. Engage in a strike or boycott to force management into illegal acts.
6. Charge excessive initiation fees and dues where there is a union shop.

---

Recall that Douglas Fraser was fired from his first two jobs for union organizing.  Could this happen today—legally?

---

Table 11-1 summarizes some of the things managers can't do under the law, as well as what union leaders can't do.

## How the Law Is Administered

Judicial (judging) powers and administrative (investigating and prosecuting) powers are also prescribed by the law.  The judicial powers of the law are given to a five-person **National Labor Relations Board (NLRB),** first established under the Wagner Act.  The administrative duties are handled by an independent general counsel.  The president appoints these six people, who serve staggered terms, with approval by the Senate.  The board has been quite effective in administering the law since the powers were separated, although it does tend to tilt toward labor when there's a Democratic president and toward management when the president is a Republican.

## UNION OBJECTIVES

**Objective 5**

**The primary objectives sought by unions for their members.**

As shown earlier, the main reason why unions are needed is that individual workers are helpless in the face of the economic and social power of large employer groups.  Workers must also act as groups, not as individuals.  This basic philosophy has been translated into the following principles: strength

through unity, equal pay for the same job, and employment practices based on seniority. If any one of these is threatened, the union will fight back, with predictable management counterattacks. The whole process is illustrated in Figure 11-3.

These principles form the basis for the practical objectives unions have for their members: (1) higher pay, (2) shorter hours of work on a daily, weekly, or annual basis, (3) improved working conditions, both physical and psychological, and (4) improved personal and job security.

## HOW UNIONS ACHIEVE THEIR OBJECTIVES

**Objective 6**

**How unions go about achieving their objectives.**

How do unions achieve these objectives? The usual methods (see Figure 11-3) are:

1. Organization.
2. Recognition as the workers' exclusive bargaining agent.
3. Collective bargaining.
4. Processing grievances and arbitration.
5. Strikes and the threat of strike.
6. Boycotts, union labels, and checkoff of union dues.

### Organization

Obviously, before it can exist, a union must persuade a firm's employees to organize and join the union. This may be done by making them dissatisfied with management because of real or imagined complaints. The union organizer then tries to persuade employees to join the union and to sign a union recognition card. Thirty percent of the employees must sign up before an NLRB election can be held. Litton Industries, the giant high-tech conglomerate, is one of labor's favorite organizing targets. Six unions told a congressional committee that the firm has closed plants before unions could get in, refused to negotiate contracts after workers had voted for a union, and even booted the union out in some cases.[12]

### Recognition

The union then tries to become recognized as the employees' bargaining agent. The bargaining agent acts as the workers' representative in dealings with management over questions of wages, hours, and other terms and conditions of employment. This means that the union has the *sole* right and legal responsibility to represent *all* employees—nonunion members as well as members—in their dealings with management.

Management may voluntarily recognize the union, or it may be forced to accept it because of the union's superior bargaining strength. But the usual way is through a secret-ballot election conducted by the NLRB upon request of the union or the company. If a majority of the eligible employees vote for the union, it's named the employees' exclusive representative in their dealings with management. The number of such elections is now declining, and the unions are winning fewer of them.

**Figure 11-3** How union objectives are met.

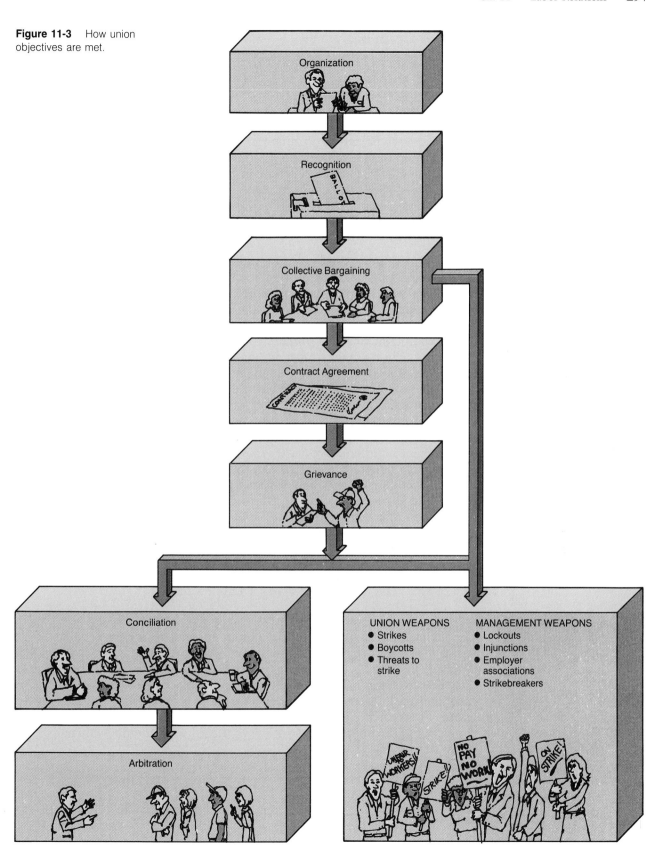

## Collective Bargaining

Once the union is recognized as the employees' bargaining agent, it starts negotiating with management to try to reach an agreement on a contract. In general, **collective bargaining** is the mutual obligation of the employer and employee representatives to meet at reasonable times and places and to confer in good faith over wages, hours, and other terms and conditions of employment. The two parties are required to meet in a reasonable place—usually a hotel or motel—and at reasonable times—usually the firm's normal daily working hours. They must negotiate in good faith, by making valid offers and counteroffers, about any question involving wages, hours, and terms and conditions of employment.

## Grievances and Arbitration

Unions also achieve their goals by interpreting the provisions of the agreement, once it's signed. The contract is a legal document and as such is subject to legal, as well as practical, interpretation. The grievance procedure is an important part of this effort. When an employee feels unfairly treated, the **union steward,** the local union representative, is asked to file a **grievance,** a formal complaint to management about working conditions or terms of employment. The supervisor must answer the grievance by correcting the situation or sending it up the line for higher levels of management to handle.

A grievance is usually settled at the supervisory or middle management level, long before it gets to the executive officers of the company and the union. Frequently, especially during negotiations, the two parties will use **mediation,** in which an outsider meets (jointly or separately) with union and management representatives to try to find an acceptable solution to the problem. If the problem still isn't solved, the dispute must be sent to an outsider for **arbitration,** under which management and the union present their sides of the dispute to a neutral outsider, who weighs the evidence and makes a binding decision that both parties have agreed in advance to accept. For instance, several years ago, a Chicago TV station had a commercial requiring someone to dress up as an animal. The actors' union thought one of its members should have the job, but so did the stage hands' union. The dispute was submitted to an arbitrator, who ruled in favor of the stage hands' union.

## The Strike

The ultimate weapon used by the unions to achieve their objectives is the strike. A **strike** occurs when employees withhold their services from their employer in order to get something, and tell the public why they're doing so by **picketing** (walking back and forth outside the place of employment, usually carrying signs). Most union leaders don't like to use the strike. It's costly, carries a certain stigma for those walking the picket line, and is potentially dangerous to the union because of the possible loss of membership and power if the strike fails.

Notice how much each worker—and the company—lost during the Caterpillar strike.

Strike by Greyhound employees in November 1983.

Although the strike itself is the ultimate device outside of collective bargaining and is the technique of last resort when all other methods of resolving differences have failed, the *threat* of strike is a continuing factor in almost all negotiations. Both union and management tend to act as if one could occur if they don't reach agreement. In 1979, the United Auto Workers had about $280 million (enough for a ten-week strike) in its strike fund, and General Motors had stockpiled an inventory of cars large enough to satisfy its dealers for several weeks. Because both sides were so well prepared, no work stoppages took place in the automobile industry, for the first time in years.

## Other Options

Other, milder weapons that unions can use—both of which have a bit more social acceptability than the strike—are the boycott and union labels. A **boycott** is an attempt by the union to persuade the public not to purchase the employer's product or service. There are two types of boycott: the primary type, which is legal, and the secondary type, which is illegal. Under a **primary boycott,** the union encourages—or even tries to force—its members and others not to buy from the offending employer. A **secondary boycott** is aimed at outside firms dealing with the employer. For example, when the United Farm Workers union struck California's table grape growers several years ago, it asked restaurants, airlines, and other users not to serve grapes and asked the

## *FYI*

### Tips for Managers: Things You Can and Can't Do When a Union Tries to Organize Your Company

*Do*

1. Keep outside organizers off premises.
2. Inform employees from time to time of the benefits they presently enjoy. (Avoid veiled promises or threats.)
3. Inform employees that signing a union authorization card does not mean they must vote for the union if there is an election.
4. Inform employees of the disadvantages of belonging to the union, such as the possibility of strikes, serving in a picket line, dues, fines, assessments, and rule by cliques or one individual.
5. Inform employees that you prefer to deal with them rather than have the union or any other outsider settle grievances.
6. Tell employees what you think about unions and about union policies.
7. Inform employees about any prior experience you have had with unions and whatever you know about the union officials trying to organize them.
8. Inform employees that the law permits you to hire a new employee to replace any employee who goes on strike for economic reasons.
9. Inform employees that no union can obtain more than you as an employer are able to give.
10. Inform employees how their wages and benefits compare with those in unionized or nonunionized concerns where wages are lower and benefits less desirable.
11. Inform employees that the local union probably will be dominated by the international union, and that they, the members, will have little to say in its operations.
12. Inform employees of any untrue or misleading statements made by the organizer. You may give employees corrections of these statements.
13. Inform employees of known racketeering, Communist, or other undesirable elements that may be active in the union.
14. Give opinions on unions and union leaders, even in derogatory terms.
15. Distribute information about unions such as disclosures of congressional committees.
16. Reply to union attacks on company policies or practices.
17. Give legal position on labor-management matters.
18. Advise employees of their legal rights, provided you do not engage in or finance an employee suit or proceeding.
19. Declare a fixed policy in opposition to compulsory union membership contracts.
20. Campaign against a union seeking to represent the employees.
21. Insist that no solicitation of membership or discussion of union affairs be conducted during working time.
22. Administer discipline, layoff, and grievance procedures

public not to buy them. Also, it threatened to boycott the places that did use them.

Many union members will avoid nonunion products, if possible. To encourage this practice, manufacturers use the **union label,** which shows that the

without regard to union membership or nonmembership of the employees involved.

23. Treat both union and nonunion employees alike in making assignments of preferred work or desired overtime.
24. Enforce plant rules impartially, regardless of the employee's membership activity in a union.
25. Tell employees, if they ask, that they are free to join or not to join any organization, so far as their status with the company is concerned.
26. Tell employees that their *personal* and *job* security will be determined by the economic prosperity of the company.

*Don't*

1. Engage in surveillance of employees to determine who is and who is not participating in the union program; attend union meetings or engage in any undercover activities for this purpose.
2. Threaten, intimidate, or punish employees who engage in union activity.
3. Request information from employees about union matters, meetings, etc. Employees may, of their own volition, give such information without prompting. You may listen but not ask questions.
4. Prevent employee union representatives from soliciting memberships during nonworking time.
5. Grant wage increases, special concessions, or promises of any kind to keep the union out.
6. Question a prospective employee about his or her affiliation with a labor organization.
7. Threaten to close up or move the plant, curtail operations, or reduce employee benefits.
8. Engage in any discriminatory practices, such as work assignments, overtime, layoffs, promotions, wage increases, or any other actions that could be regarded as preferential treatment for certain employees.
9. Discriminate against union people when disciplining employees for a specific action and permit nonunion employees to go unpunished for the same action.
10. Transfer workers on the basis of teaming up nonunion employees to separate them from union employees.
11. Deviate in any way from company policies for the primary purpose of eliminating a union employee.
12. Intimate, advise, or indicate, in any way, that unionization will force the company to lay off employees, take away company benefits or privileges enjoyed, or make any other changes that could be regarded as a curtailment of privileges.
13. Make statements to the effect that you will not deal with a union.
14. Give any financial support or other assistance to employees who support or oppose the union.
15. Visit the homes of employees to urge them to oppose or reject the union in its campaign.
16. Be a party to any petition or circular against the union or encourage employees to circulate such a petition.
17. Make any promises of promotions, benefits, wage increases, or any other items that would induce employees to oppose the union.
18. Engage in discussions or arguments that may lead to physical encounters with employees over the union question.
19. Use a third party to threaten or coerce a union member, or attempt to influence any employee's vote through this medium.
20. Question employees on whether or not they have or have not affiliated or signed with the union.
21. Use the word *never* in any predictions or attitudes about unions or their promises or demands.
22. Talk about tomorrow. When you give examples or reasons, you can talk about yesterday or today instead of tomorrow, to avoid making a prediction or conviction which may be interpreted as a threat or promise by the union or the NLRB.

---

Source: Adapted by permission from Curtis E. Tate, Jr., Leon C. Megginson, Charles R. Scott, Jr., and Lyle R. Trueblood, *Successful Small Business Management,* 3rd ed. (Plano, Tex.: Business Publications, Inc., 1982), pp. 224–225. © 1982 Business Publications, Inc.

product is union-made. If you look at the inside pocket of a U.S.-made coat or jacket, you'll probably find a label saying it was made by members of either the International Ladies Garment Workers Union (ILGWU) or the Amalgamated Clothing and Textile Workers Union (ACTWU).

## Management's Response

Management, of course, isn't going to take these actions by unions without fighting back. And it does have several weapons to use, including lockouts, injunctions, employer associations, and strikebreakers.

A **lockout** occurs when management effectively closes its premises to employees and refuses to allow them to continue working. In 1937, Ford Motor Company locked its workers out of its Flint, Michigan, plant, but the workers broke in and refused to leave to let other people work. The union won recognition after a bloody confrontation.

An **injunction** is a court order prohibiting a person or group from carrying out given actions, such as a strike or boycott, that would cause irreparable damage.

Groups of companies will form **employer associations** to negotiate with unions instead of doing so individually. This strengthens the individual firms that must negotiate with one union.

**Strikebreakers,** also called **scabs,** are workers who cross the union picket line to work during a strike. The United Steelworkers struck Phelps Dodge's copper mines in 1983. Management, dead set on breaking the strike, asked workers to cross the picket lines. Within a month, nearly a third of the workers were running the strikers' gauntlet to keep the mines operating at 83 percent of prestrike levels.[13]

Other tactics used by companies are (1) hiring anti-union consultants, (2) filing for bankruptcy to void a union contract, (3) contracting work to outsiders, and (4) shifting work from a struck plant to one of their nonunion plants in other areas. FYI on page 300 tells what management can and can't do when a union tries to organize the firm.

## CURRENT TRENDS IN LABOR RELATIONS

**Objective 7**

**Current trends in labor relations.**

This is an exciting period in labor-management relations. New ideas for cooperation are constantly being developed. Instead of fighting over differences, union leaders and managers are now sitting down together to iron them out. Unions are less militant, partly for economic reasons and partly because of a new breed of leaders who didn't have to fight tooth and nail to get unions recognized. Also, employees are better educated and more capable and have different concerns. For instance, in 1973, Karen Nussbaum, a former clerk-typist at Harvard, founded "9 to 5," an organization of female clerical workers seeking women's rights. It has grown from 10 members to 12,000.[14] Finally, both sides recognize that they must use their energy to fight foreign competitors, not each other.

### New Membership

Unions tend to vary their organizing efforts with changes in the economic, social, and political environments. Because union leaders are now trying to bolster unions' sagging size, power, support, and economic demands, they're

going after what could be termed the "new union mix": younger and better-educated leadership drawn from the new workers entering the labor force. The drive for new members is concentrating on:

1. Employees in the public sector,[15] such as teachers, the police, fire-fighters, and sanitation personnel.
2. Professionals, including teachers, medical personnel, athletes, dentists, and lawyers.
3. People in the service industries, such as communications, finance, insurance, and real estate.
4. Agricultural workers.

In addition to organizing in new industries or professions, unions are trying to reach groups they slighted earlier. These include white-collar workers, women, minorities, and younger employees. In fact, unionism has become more acceptable to middle- and upper-middle-class employees and professionals. For instance, many professional, technical, and managerial personnel at GM are trying to form a union.[16] And the 45,000-member New York State Federation of Physicians and Dentists joined AFL-CIO's American Federation of Teachers in union membership.[17]

The rapid unionization of public employees is causing problems for business as well as for the governments that employ them. While most public employees are prohibited from striking, strikes do occur. And these strikes cause more disruption than those against private employers. Many people are now questioning whether public employees should be allowed to strike, as shown in the Business Debate on page 304. A recent Gallup poll found that 69 percent of respondents thought the police shouldn't be permitted to strike, 70 percent were against strikes by firefighters, 64 percent against postal workers, and 55 percent against sanitation workers.[18] In each case, the public was less tolerant than in earlier surveys, perhaps because of having been hurt by recent strikes.

## New Demands

While unions are still seeking higher wages, shorter hours, and improved benefits and security, they're also seeking to:

1. Eliminate pay differences between comparable jobs.
2. Restore greater pay differences between job classifications, with higher pay for highly skilled jobs.
3. Keep income tied to cost-of-living adjustments (COLAs).
4. Provide better pensions and retirement benefits—especially earlier retirement based on years of service alone, not age plus service.
5. Trade off lifetime guarantees of jobs for union members for the company's right to automate operations or otherwise increase effectiveness.

Conversely, many firms, struggling under economic pressures, are asking unions to make concessions on wages and benefits that employers think are already too high.

# *Business Debate*

## In the Public Interest: Should Public Employees Strike?

The Taft-Hartley Act prohibited government employees from joining unions. The Civil Service Reform Act of 1978 permits federal employees to join unions and engage in collective bargaining but denies them the right to strike. But many federal workers do strike. For example, the Professional Air Traffic Controllers Organization (PATCO) was offered a settlement of bargaining demands in July 1981. After 90 percent of the controllers rejected the offer—at the union president's suggestion—a strike was called for three days later. Four hours after they went on strike, President Reagan reminded the controllers that it was illegal to strike against the government and gave them forty-eight hours to return to work or be fired. The 11,500 who did not return were fired, and PATCO was fined heavily. Unable to pay the fine, PATCO dissolved. Three years later, only a few hundred controllers had returned to work, while others had been hired and trained, and service was back to near normal.

The arguments *for* such employees' being allowed to strike include these:

1. No one should be denied the right to strike if the grievance is strong enough.
2. Since private employees have this right, public employees would become second-class citizens if the right were denied them.
3. Since public workers have the right to collective bargaining, striking is the logical final step in that process.
4. Even public employees must be protected from unfair management actions.
5. Striking is the most dramatic, and sometimes the only, way to publicize abuses.

The arguments *against* public employees' striking include these:

1. Most public employees are bound by their employment oath not to strike.
2. It's against the law for public employees to strike. If they don't set an example by being law-abiding, how can other citizens be expected to be?
3. These employees have some form of civil service protection to obtain and retain benefits for them.
4. There's little to be gained by striking, since wages and benefits are usually set by legislation.
5. The public interest should take precedence over employees' private interests.

*What do you think?*

# ⛰ LEARNING OBJECTIVES REVISITED

1. *Why unions are so important to U.S. business and what labor relations is.*

   Labor unions are among the most powerful groups in the United States. Directly or indirectly, almost all managerial decisions and employee behavior are influenced by unions. Management, instead of acting alone to reward or punish employees, must operate through the union in organized firms. Decisions affecting employees are made collectively at bargaining tables instead of individually by the manager when and where the need arises.

   Labor relations involves all the interactions and relationships between management and its employees where a union is concerned. The growth of unions has changed these relationships—in favor of employees. While the public has generally accepted unions, that acceptance is declining. Part of unions' strength results from their large financial resources and political clout.

2. *Some of the reasons why people join unions.*

   People join unions to seek economic benefits, as well as (1) more credible and rational personnel policies, with less favoritism, (2) the right to have a voice in decisions affecting their welfare, (3) protection from economic hazards beyond their control, and (4) recognition and participation that they might not otherwise get from management. Others refuse to join unions because of (1) lack of a compelling reason, (2) a feeling that unions are not needed, (3) identification with management, and (4) distrust of unions.

3. *The development of unions in the United States.*

   Unions have grown from weak local craft unions in the late eighteenth century to strong national and international unions. These include industrial unions with all skilled and unskilled workers from the same industry in the same union. Real union growth started in the late nineteenth century with the Knights of Labor and the AFL. Later, the CIO was formed, and it then merged with the AFL in 1955.

4. *The most significant laws affecting labor-management relations.*

   The legal basis of present union-management relations is formed by the Norris–La Guardia Act, the Wagner Act, the Taft-Hartley Act, and the Landrum-Griffin Act. The Norris–La Guardia act was the first piece of federal legislation to eliminate employer tactics such as yellow-dog contracts and blacklisting. The Wagner Act gave workers the basic right to organize, join, and participate in union activities, and made it an unfair labor practice for management to interfere with those rights. The Taft-Hartley Act limited unions' activities by prohibiting the closed shop, limiting the union shop, and requiring unions to negotiate if management requested it. The Landrum-Griffin Act established controls for union elections and financial management. These laws are administered by the National Labor Relations Board.

5. *The primary objectives sought by unions for their members.*

   The usual objectives of unions are (1) higher pay, (2) shorter hours of work, (3) improved working conditions, and (4) increased security.

6. *How unions go about achieving their objectives.*

The methods used to achieve these objectives are (1) organizing the workers, (2) becoming recognized as the workers' exclusive bargaining agent, (3) collective bargaining, (4) processing grievances and participating in conciliation, mediation, and arbitration, (5) striking or threatening to strike, and (6) using boycotts and buying by union labels. Management can counter with (1) lockouts, (2) injunctions, (3) employer associations, (4) strikebreakers (scabs), (5) filing for bankruptcy to break a contract, and (6) contracting work out or shifting it to a nonunion plant.

7. *Current trends in labor relations.*

Unions are now trying to fill out their ranks with a new membership mix: young, better-educated workers from the public sector, services, agriculture, and the professions. Their demands are focusing on union security, elimination of pay differences, COLAs, retirement benefits, and lifetime jobs.

## ⬕ IMPORTANT TERMS

As an extra review of the chapter, try defining the following terms. If you have trouble with any of them, refer to the page listed.

labor union  *286*
labor relations  *286*
craft unions  *290*
Knights of Labor  *290*
American Federation of Labor
  (AFL)  *290*
industrial unions  *291*
Congress of Industrial
  Organizations (CIO)  *291*
AFL-CIO  *292*
sweetheart contracts  *292*
yellow-dog contracts  *293*
blacklisting  *293*
union shop  *293*
closed shop  *293*
agency shop  *293*
right-to-work laws  *293*
featherbedding  *293*

National Labor Relations Board
  (NLRB)  *295*
collective bargaining  *298*
union steward  *298*
grievance  *298*
mediation  *298*
arbitration  *298*
strike  *298*
picketing  *298*
boycott  *299*
primary boycott  *299*
secondary boycott  *299*
union label  *300*
lockout  *302*
injunction  *302*
employer associations  *302*
strikebreakers (scabs)  *302*

## ⬕ REVIEW QUESTIONS

1. What have labor unions accomplished for the benefit of nonunion employees?

2. What are some other terms for labor relations?

3. What is the current status of unions in the United States?
4. Why do workers join unions? Why do they reject them?
5. During what period did unions grow the fastest? Why?
6. During what period did union growth stabilize? Why?
7. What laws form the legal basis for labor relations?
8. What are the provisions of Section 7 of the Wagner Act?
9. What are some unfair labor practices that can be charged against management? against unions?
10. How is the Wagner Act administered?
11. What are the primary objectives of unions for their members?
12. What are the traditional means of achieving union objectives?
13. Do labor leaders favor using the strike? Why or why not?
14. What means does management have to respond to union actions?
15. Name two general trends in labor relations.

## ⏏ DISCUSSION QUESTIONS

1. How do you interpret recent union membership trends?
2. Do you believe that union power will increase in the future? Why or why not?
3. Recall the last serious strike you remember, such as the teachers' strikes in 1983. Did it affect you in any way, either directly or indirectly? Even if it didn't affect you, what were the economic, social, political, and cultural effects on the country or community?
4. Would you join a union if you had the option? Why or why not?
5. Are there any really significant differences between the closed shop, the union shop, and the agency shop? Explain.
6. Does public reaction to a strike outweigh its benefits to the union? Why or why not?
7. How are management relationships with employees affected by the presence of a union in an organization?
8. How will the new types of employees affect union-management relations?

## ⏏ CASE 11-1  The Union Organizer (A)

Curtis Kenneth seized what he thought was an outstanding opportunity when he bought Quality Welding Supply Company. Joe Bartlett, from whom Kenneth purchased the small company in Oregon, was in his sixties, ready to retire, and was looking for a young person to buy the business and carry it on. When he took over, Curtis retained the firm's three employees—a young woman who worked as secretary-receptionist and two truck drivers, Frank Boyle and Bill Reinhart.

One morning, a week after he took over, Curtis received a visit from Ben Kelley, the local representative for the Teamsters union. Curtis remembered Ben from their college days, when Kelley had been an outstanding member of the university boxing team and generally known around

campus as something of a tough guy. The two men had been casual acquaintances, but until this meeting their paths had seldom crossed since they left college.

KELLEY: Curt, I'm here to see you about some back wages owed to your two drivers. Although our union signed a contract with this company four months ago, these men have still been getting nonunion wages. We figure you owe each of them close to $400.

KENNETH: Well, Ben, when I bought the business, I didn't assume any liabilities for back salaries owed, and I didn't assume the union contract. If these men are owed anything, they'll have to settle with Mr. Bartlett.

KELLEY: I don't know what kind of arrangements you and Bartlett made, but these men worked here, and I'm going to see that they get paid, even if we have to strike you.

KENNETH: I have no contract with your union, and if these men fail to report for work without good reason, I won't consider it a strike; I'll consider them AWOL and just fire them.

KELLEY: We'll see about that. You'll be hearing from me soon.

After Ben walked out, Curtis felt a little shaken as he called his lawyer. After being reassured that he couldn't be held responsible for the back salaries owed, he felt more relaxed. He knew he could hire two new drivers if the present ones tried to strike, since business was slack and there was considerable unemployment. He'd just have to fire them.

Nothing more was heard from Ben until a week later, when he walked directly into Curtis's office, dropped a union contract on his desk, and said flatly, "Sign it."

Curtis picked it up and scanned it briefly.

KENNETH: I can't do it, Ben. If I had to live up to the letter of this contract, I'd go broke; I won't sign a contract I can't fulfill. This is a small company, and I just can't afford the benefits this contract calls for, desirable though they are. I'm paying close to the union scale now; and as I get my feet on the ground, I'll give the drivers periodic raises—if they deserve them. That's the best I can do.

KELLEY: You'll have to do better, because if you don't, we'll strike.

KENNETH: As I said before, if my drivers fail to show up for work without a good excuse, I'll fire them.

KELLEY: Well, we'll see about that.

Ben picked up the unsigned contract, stuffed it in his pocket, and stalked out.

That afternoon, Frank Boyle, one of the drivers, came in to say he wasn't interested in joining the union, but Bill, the other driver, was hot for it. He said that Bill and Ben were pressuring him into it. He didn't want to buck the group, but he didn't want to lose his job, either.

After two weeks with no word from the union, Curtis decided that if he was going to keep the union out, he'd have to get rid of Bill. Since business was usually slow during the winter months, Curtis laid off Bill Reinhart, telling him that he'd rehire him when things picked up again. In the meantime, Curtis would drive the other truck himself when both were needed.

### Case Questions

1. What response would you have made to the union organizer if you were Curtis?
2. What would you have done after the organizer left (see FYI on pages 300–301 for suggestions)?
3. Could you do today—legally—what Curtis did? Explain.

## 🔺 CASE 11-2   The Union Organizer (B)

After that, things went smoothly for Curtis. Bill got a permanent job elsewhere, and so he didn't have to be rehired. Business grew, and after four years Curtis had thirteen employees, of whom five

were truck drivers. He'd contracted to buy a similar firm nearby, and had ordered three new trucks and was trying to find three new drivers.

Curtis had heard nothing more from the union. Each time he hired a new driver, he inquired about his attitude toward unions and secretly made it a point not to hire those who expressed favorable attitudes toward them. He was firmly convinced that with the featherbedding tactics of union drivers and the "ridiculous demands of the union contract" he couldn't possibly make any profit if his drivers were unionized.

One morning, as Curtis was busy making plans for the new business he'd take over in two weeks, Ben walked in for their first meeting in four years.

KENNETH: Hello, Ben. How've you been?

KELLEY: I've been doing okay, and from the looks of your business, you've been doing okay, too. You've got five trucks going full time, and pretty soon you'll have three more. That'll make eight drivers. The last time I was here, you told me you were too small and couldn't afford to unionize. Now that you're the biggest welding supply company in the city, I think your boys had better be working under contract.

### Case Questions

1. What response would you make this time?
2. What are your legal rights?
3. What's the difference this time?

# DIGGING DEEPER

## Careers in Human Resources Management

The personnel profession has gone through such a revolution during the last decade that its name has changed to conform to its new, wider scope. Today human resources management has many creative, challenging, and well-paying jobs available. Individuals seeking a career in this field may enter it through a personnel department or through an operating department. Depending on their education and experience, new personnel employees can be specialists or generalists. Usually smaller firms look for generalists and give them overlapping responsibilities in all facets of human resources. Larger firms tend to seek specialists in areas such as recruiting and employment; training and development; compensation and benefits; labor relations; and compliance with government regulations, such as equal employment opportunity and health and safety.

### What Human Resources Management Jobs Require

A typical first job for a college graduate with little or no experience would be as a nonmanagerial specialist in government or in a large firm, in employment and placement, say, or in wage and salary administration within the human resources department.

Career paths in human resources management also depend on the firm. Since most large organizations perform all of the personnel functions, they often have units that specialize in various aspects of human resources management. An individual could work in just one unit or in several different units during his or her career. However, employees in the health, safety, and security units tend to specialize throughout their careers.

In large organizations, the path to a position such as vice-president for resources management, or corporate personnel director, is taken by moving up through the ranks of the human resources department, as shown in Figure III-1. Often the personnel director has served as manager of all the personnel functions in a plant or regional office of the firm. An individual may (1) be a specialist either in the firm's headquarters or at a plant or regional office, then (2) perform as manager of a specialized unit, (3) become a generalist manager of all personnel functions in a plant or office, (4) return to headquarters as an assistant director or vice-president in charge of one or several functions, and finally (5) move to the directorship or vice-presidency of human resources management.

The top position is usually designated as *personnel director* or *vice-president of human resources*. Holders of this position (1) confer with managers of other departments to determine their future personnel needs, (2) define training and development needs, (3) develop and implement performance appraisal programs, (4) suggest guidelines for promotion and firing, and (5) serve in many other capacities.

### Employment and Placement

Employment and placement is an area involving numerous positions with a variety of duties. The *employment manager*, or *employment supervisor*, has overall responsibility for the selection of qualified employees with growth potential. Working in this unit are (1) *interviewers*, who evaluate applicants on the basis of personal interviews; (2) *test administrators*, who administer and score tests designed to measure applicants' competence to do selected jobs; and often (3) *college recruiters*, who conduct on-campus interviews to identify prospects for employment. After applicants are hired, an *employee orientation specialist* provides them with information needed for smooth integration into the firm.

These professionals work with the employment manager to develop sources of potential employees to fill current and future human resources needs, counsel employees concerning placement, and administer promotion and transfer systems.

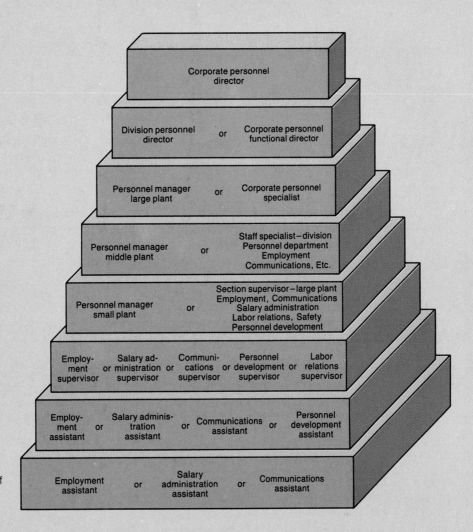

**Figure III-1** Some sample career paths in personnel or human resources departments. (Adapted from "Selecting and Developing Personnel Professionals," by Howard N. Mitchell, copyright July 1970. Reprinted with the permission of *Personnel Journal*, Costa Mesa, Calif.; all rights reserved.)

## Training and Development

Training and development and career management are also important career areas. Under a *training director*, a staff of training and career specialists (1) develops and conducts programs to meet specific training needs; (2) administers on-the-job training programs; (3) maintains records of employee participation in training, such as apprenticeship and management development; (4) coordinates employee appraisal programs; and (5) communicates information about promotion opportunities to help interested employees expedite their personal growth and career development.

## Wage and Salary Administration

Wage and salary administration also provides many opportunities. The *wage and salary ad-* *ministrator* establishes policies and practices that ensure employees equitable compensation. The *job analyst* analyzes job duties and writes job descriptions or specifications. Jobs are evaluated by a *wage and salary specialist* to determine their proper pay ranges. Compensation surveys are conducted to determine how competitive the firm's pay range is with similar jobs in other firms in the industry or area.

## Benefits, Safety, and Services

Benefits, safety, and services are growing personnel areas, usually under the supervision of a *benefits coordinator* and a *safety director*. Working under the benefits coordinator is a *benefits planning analyst,* who helps design and administer medical, disability, retirement, and pension plans.

The *safety director*, with the assistance of *plant safety specialists*, works with management to (1) develop and administer safety programs, (2) conduct safety inspections, (3) maintain accident records, and (4) submit required governmental health and safety reports. *Nurses and physicians* may also be assigned to this unit.

### Labor Relations

Labor relations is usually headed by a *labor relations director*. He or she and a staff of *labor relations representatives* interact with union officials and employee members. Duties such as negotiating labor contracts with union representatives, interpreting labor contracts to supervisors, resolving employee grievances, and collecting and analyzing information related to labor contracts are performed by them.

### EEO and AA

Equal employment opportunity and affirmative action activities are under an *equal employment opportunity coordinator*, who coordinates management efforts to comply with equal opportunity

**TABLE III-1  Selected careers in human resources management.**

| Job Title | Job Description | Education and Training | Salaries ( Beginner Experienced ) | Outlook to 1990 |
|---|---|---|---|---|
| Labor relations representatives | Help company officials prepare for collective bargaining, participate in contract negotiations, and handle labor relations matters that arise daily. | A college degree is required for most beginning positions. A law degree is an asset. | $17,000 $21,000–$33,600 Labor relations directors, $27,700–$50,000 | The number of positions is expected to grow about as fast as the average. Particularly keen job competition is anticipated in this area. |
| Personnel specialists Recruiters EEO or affirmative action coordinators Job analysts Wage and salary specialists Training directors Benefits coordinators | Assist management in making effective use of employees' skills and help employees to find satisfaction in their jobs. Interview, select, and recommend applicants to fill job openings. Administer affirmative action and EEO programs. Write job descriptions. Handle wage and salary administration, training and career development, and employee benefits. | A college degree is required for most beginning positions in this field. Newly hired employees usually enter on-the-job training programs, where they classify jobs, interview applicants, or administer employee benefits. | $17,000 $21,000–$33,600 Average for personnel directors, $27,700–$50,000 | The number of specialists is expected to grow about as fast as the average for all occupations. |

SOURCES: U.S. Department of Labor, *Occupational Outlook Handbook*, 1982–1983 (Washington: U.S. Government Printing Office, April 1982) and 1980–1981 (Washington: U.S. Government Printing Office, April 1980); College Placement Council, *CPC Salary Survey, Summer Supplement* (Bethlehem, Pa.: CPC, 1983), pp. 2–5; and Steven D. Ross, "The Top 12 Money-Making Careers of the '80s," *Business Week's Guide to Careers* 1 (Spring 1983): 9.

laws and regulations. Aided by specialists, the coordinator performs such duties as (1) writing the organization's affirmative action plan, (2) assisting managers to develop affirmative action programs, (3) advising management of legal requirements, (4) investigating employee complaints and charges of discrimination, (5) maintaining liaison with minority and women's organizations, and (6) representing the company in government investigations.

## Selected Careers in Human Resources Management

Table III-1 includes some selected positions college graduates can enter. In addition to the salaries shown, the American Society for Personnel Administrators (ASPA) has found that large firms pay their human resources managers as much as $105,000 a year. The average for small firms was $44,000.[1]

# PART **IV**

## MARKETING

You've studied many types of businesses in this book. Yet they all had some activities in common—such as determining the need for their product, deciding what quality of service to provide, doing word-of-mouth advertising, determining the price to be charged, deciding the kind of customers wanted, and choosing the methods to be used in attracting them. You may not have recognized it at the time, but those and other related activities are part of the marketing process. Marketing is one of the basic functions of any organization, business or otherwise. All organizations market some type of product or service for use by their customers, clients, or members. The material in this part will help you to understand marketing and its use.

The marketing process, and how it's based on satisfying customer needs, is covered in Chapter 12. It emphasizes such topics as the role of marketing, the marketing concept, marketing strategies, and the marketing environment.

Chapter 13 deals with marketing decisions about what products to sell and what prices to charge for them. The discussion covers such topics as new-product development, product life cycle, identification of products, the role and importance of pricing, pricing policies, and how prices are determined.

Developing promotional strategies is covered in Chapter 14. Topics such as advertising, personal selling, sales promotion, and publicity are discussed.

In Chapter 15, you will learn about the dynamic nature of distribution. The marketing channels and the physical distribution of products are described.

315

# 12

# The Marketing Process: Satisfying Customer Needs

*No one returns with good will to the place which has done him a mischief.*

Phaedrus

*Marketing is the whole business seen from the viewpoint of its final result, that is, from the customer's point of view.*

Peter Drucker

## Learning Objectives

After studying the material in this chapter, you will understand:

1. What marketing is and its role in a business enterprise.
2. How the marketing concept has evolved.
3. What a market is and the different types of markets.
4. Different market characteristics.
5. How target markets are used.
6. What marketing research is and what it reveals about consumer behavior.
7. How marketing strategy is built on the marketing mix.
8. The environments that affect marketing decisions.

## In This Chapter

What Is Marketing?
The Role of Marketing
The Marketing Concept
What Is a Market?
Target Markets
Marketing Research
Marketing Strategy and Marketing Mix
Marketing Environments

## BABY FOOD OR DESSERT?
*Gerber Makes Teens Its Business*

Hit by the declining birthrate in the late 1970s, Gerber Products Company sought ways to expand its market by getting teenagers (ages fifteen to twenty-two) to try its baby foods. But it learned that the name "baby food" can be a real turnoff.

Late in 1979, Gerber anonymously conducted a "Secret Snack Sweepstakes," with ads in several magazines, including *Glamour* and *Seventeen.* When about 30,000 readers received a free jar of Gerber's Dutch Apple Dessert and a coupon to get another jar free, half of them went back to the store for more. Encouraged, Gerber decided to try some named-brand ads in teen magazines. The ads featured a youthful model saying to a friend, "The secret's out. Gerber isn't just for babies!" and offered a free sample. Most young people didn't bite, but many did write to say, in effect, "You're crazy if you think I'm going to eat baby food."

Still, Gerber intends to keep after the teen market. Gerber has about 70 percent of the baby food market, which is expected to keep growing now that the birthrate is rising again. Eventually, that will mean a large growth potential in the teen market.

According to J. Walter Thompson Company, the ad agency developing other teenage marketing tests for Gerber, "The difficult part is to play down the name as much as possible while guaranteeing Gerber quality and yet avoiding the stigma of eating baby food."

317

The United States has developed an efficient system of mass production. But fields and factories pumping out products are useless unless ways are devised to get the products to the consumers who want them. Production, important as it may be, isn't an end in itself. Rather, consumption—the satisfaction of wants—is the ultimate goal of business, from which a satisfactory profit can be derived. Now, Gerber could simply have continued to produce baby food, aimed at its original market: babies. But a change in the social environment forced the company to reconsider its target market and expand it to include different kinds of consumers. And that focus on understanding, finding, and reaching the consumer is what marketing is all about.

## WHAT IS MARKETING?

**Objective 1**

What marketing is and its role in a business enterprise.

**Marketing** is the determination of customers' needs and wants, the development of goods and services to satisfy those needs and wants, and then the delivery of those goods and services to the customer. Marketing activities really begin with understanding the consumer. Then come conceiving, designing, developing, and producing new products or services to fill present or expected unfilled consumer needs. The next step is providing (or gathering) the products or performing the services where and when the customer needs them. The final stage is the transfer of the products from the seller to the buyer and the movement of the goods or services to where the customer will obtain them.

You'll notice that we've included services in our definition. Just as a product must be aimed at the right market, a service must be marketed effectively, too. A computer dating service, for instance, wouldn't find much of a market in a family-oriented suburban community. Its customers would be concentrated in a metropolitan area.

## THE ROLE OF MARKETING

The word *marketing* is sometimes used interchangeably with the word *distribution.* But the marketing function involves more than the physical transportation of goods to where they're needed. As we've said, it includes determining what consumers need or want and seeking to satisfy these needs by providing the right products or services.

### Marketing Functions

The marketing process involves several specialized functions, each of which contributes to the whole system for getting goods and services from the producer to the consumer. As shown in Figure 12-1, these functions are usually classified—moving backward from the consumer to the store—as (1) **exchange,** which is buying and selling, (2) **physical distribution,** which is storing and transporting goods, and (3) **facilitation,** which is financing, risk taking, standardizing and grading, and researching. Most companies perform all of these functions. The success or failure of firms selling similar goods or ser-

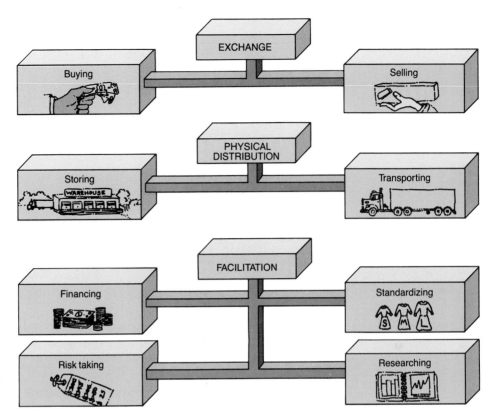

**Figure 12-1**  Marketing functions classified into three groups. [Adapted by permission from Walter W. Perlick and Raymond W. Lesikar, *Introduction to Business: A Societal Approach,* 3rd ed. (Dallas, Tex.: Business Publications, Inc., 1979), p. 208. © 1979 Business Publications, Inc.]

vices often depends on the effectiveness with which they carry out each function.

### Allocates Abundant Supplies

Marketing can be relatively unimportant in some of the world's marketplaces. Sellers of rice in underdeveloped parts of the world don't need to advertise or promote their product. Customers stand in line waiting to buy it as soon as it's available. But a company that sells rice in the United States must not only advertise its product but also persuade the customer to buy it in preference to other foods that are equally nutritious, tasty, and available. The customer who wants rice therefore finds a whole grocery shelf full of choices—raw rice, enriched rice, quick rice, "wild" rice, rice with macaroni and seasonings, and rice in boilable bags—all at different prices.

What makes the difference between the two situations is the fact of abundance in the United States. Wherever there's abundance, marketing techniques are needed to convince consumers to buy the specific goods and services they most need or want.

### Provides Utility

Marketing activities are means of creating utility, which is the ability of a product or service to satisfy the needs or wants of consumers. There are at least four kinds of utility, as shown in Figure 12-2: utilities of form, place, time, and ownership. As was shown in Chapter 8, production is concerned

**Figure 12-2** Four kinds of utility.

with the creation of form utility, or converting raw materials into finished products. Marketing provides place, time, and ownership utility, as will be shown in this and the next three chapters.

**Place utility** results from providing the product or service to customers at a convenient location. Transportation and channels of distribution help create place utility.

**Time utility** is created by having the product or service available when consumers want to buy it. The storage of a product creates time utility.

**Ownership utility** is created through arranging for the transfer of title to the goods from seller to buyer. Advertising and promotion help create ownership utility by providing useful information to the consumer.

The importance of marketing is far from universally accepted, as shown in the Business Debate on page 322. Yet, whether or not marketing really benefits the U.S. economy, its importance can be considered from the viewpoint of (1) society, which uses the marketing system to provide the goods and services people need and want, and (2) the business firm, which depends on the marketing department to sell its products.

## THE MARKETING CONCEPT

Objective 2

How the marketing concept has evolved.

Since the mid-1940s, the concept of marketing has changed greatly in the United States. Before the Depression, it was assumed that anything produced that was of reasonable quality and price could be sold without any problem. The Depression proved this belief—the **production concept**—to be a myth. After World War II, our productive capacity had been geared up so high to run the war that there was much excess capacity. There was also over $160 billion

of savings waiting to be spent for goods and services that had been unavailable for years. And the G.I. Bill made it possible for over 11 million ex–service personnel to borrow money at a low interest rate to buy homes and businesses.

These factors of supply and demand combined to force a drastic marketing change. After the war, more companies adopted the **marketing concept,** the belief that a business must attempt to determine and satisfy the desires and needs of customers in order to reach the ultimate goal of making a profit.

## How the Marketing Concept Works

According to the marketing concept, the needs, wishes, and desires of customers are management's primary concern. In fact, an organization's mission should focus on the broad class of customer needs it's seeking to satisfy, not on the product or service it wants to offer. If the mission is properly focused, a firm's management is customer-oriented; if improperly focused, its management is product-oriented.

Railroads, for instance, made the fatal mistake of letting other forms of transportation, especially buses and trucks, take customers away from them because they saw themselves as being in the railroad business rather than in the transportation business. The reason they defined their mission incorrectly was that they were railroad-oriented instead of transportation-oriented. In other words, they were product-oriented instead of customer-oriented.[1]

Following the marketing concept and being customer-oriented should enable management to deal with constantly changing demands. As customer demand changes, products and services must also change. Management should attempt to serve the changing market by whatever means are required and feasible for the organization. Present products may be altered, new products may be developed, or new business arenas may be entered. In 1974, while gasoline prices (and oil company profits) were skyrocketing because of OPEC's restriction of petroleum exports, Mobil Oil Corporation bought MARCOR in order to obtain Montgomery Ward. Mobil was severely criticized for making tremendous profits from gas buyers and using them to buy a department store instead of reinvesting in oil exploration. Yet the action was perfectly logical from Mobil's point of view. The automobile-servicing market had changed, and Mobil had to change with it. Self-service filling stations were replacing full-service garages. People were having their cars serviced in shopping centers, particularly at department store auto service centers.

Was Gerber Products following the marketing concept? Explain.

Under the marketing concept, managers determine what their customers' needs are and how to satisfy those needs. In the process, they should gain that ever-desired goal: a competitive edge. A **competitive edge** isn't just something that's desirable from the customer's viewpoint, but also a quality that sets a firm apart from, and gives it an advantage over, its competitors. The owner of a small ladies' clothing store in a rural community had a profitable business. Most of her customers lived in a city fifty miles away. Her competitive edge was that she knew her customers by name, understood their needs, bought

## *Business Debate*

### Is Marketing Good for the U.S. Economy?

Marketing's advocates say that marketing plays an important role in the U.S. economy and greatly improves our material well-being. Yet there are just as many critics who claim that the benefits hardly justify the cost involved.

The usual arguments that marketing *does benefit* the economy are:

1. The marketing function adds value to material goods by creating time, place, and ownership utility. Physical resources would be of limited value if they weren't gathered together, processed, moved to where they're needed, and made available to consumers at a price they're willing—and able—to pay.
2. The activities required to gather the many products from multiple sources and distribute them to a multitude of customers in many different places can be performed better and more effectively by the marketing system.
3. Marketing is responsible (through advertising and promotion) for creating demand and persuading people to buy products they might not otherwise know about. This not only adds to total consumption but also creates employment and income.
4. Marketing is responsible for creating new products and services that otherwise wouldn't be available.

The arguments that marketing *doesn't benefit* the economy are:

1. Too much money is spent on marketing. While marketing makes a valid contribution, its costs are too high because of the many activities involved. These costs should be reduced.
2. Marketing allocates scarce resources improperly, since a disproportionate amount of resources is used to market goods and services rather than to produce them. Also, because of the obsolescence built in by producers, perfectly usable products are often unnecessarily discarded.
3. Through advertising and sales promotion, marketing encourages people to think of their own material welfare instead of what's best for society. An example is the past emphasis on high-powered engines for cars instead of on energy-saving ones.
4. The marketing system is inefficient. Far too much repetition occurs in the buying and selling function, which takes place at each step in the marketing process.

*What do you think?*

with them—as individuals—in mind, and phoned each customer to inform her of special purchases.[2] In order to compete with discount drug chains, small, independent drugstores will check prescriptions to make sure that they don't conflict with other medication the customer is taking. Many also maintain computerized records of all drug purchases for tax purposes.

As AT&T entered the highly competitive business communications field, it aggressively adopted the marketing concept used by IBM for years. IBM's

service personnel always wear a jacket, although they may remove it before working. Now AT&T is asking its service personnel, called system technicians, to dress up when they call on business firms—a shirt and tie for men and a business suit for women. They carry their tools in attaché cases provided by the company, rather than on belts strapped around their waists. The technicians also are using marketing techniques, such as answering questions about AT&T services and products.[3]

## Not All Companies Use the Marketing Concept

Of course, not all companies practice the marketing concept. Many companies seem less concerned with the customers' needs than with their own wishes. A classic example is Henry Ford, who wanted to provide customers with a low-priced, dependable car through mass production. When customers asked for more variety, at least in body color, he's reported to have said, "They can have any color they want as long as it's black." If Ford Motor Company had never changed that strategy, it wouldn't be here today.

Sometimes management may misinterpret the market, or customers may say one thing and buy another, or the firm's interests and customers' interests may conflict. Since business owners tend to be profit-oriented, marketing managers may face a conflict between profit and consumer satisfaction. U.S. automakers faced that conflict in the 1970s. While the public was seeking fuel-efficient cars, the manufacturers continued to make large luxury models because of their larger profit margin. GM failed to provide small, fuel-efficient cars when the public demanded them and then had to spend over $40 billion just trying to stay competitive.[4]

Moreover, marketing is so complex that it's impossible to please all customers. For example, a low-priced product may satisfy certain buyers, but customers seeking high quality or prestige may be unhappy with it.

## WHAT IS A MARKET?

**Objective 3**

**What a market is and the different types of markets.**

The term *market* can be used in any number of ways. For example, we say that a person is in the market for an automobile or a stereo, which is on the market. Or a person may invest in the stock market. In some parts of the country, one goes to the market for groceries. In general, though, a **market** is people (including governments and institutions) who have the necessary authority, purchasing power, and willingness to buy a good or service. For instance, fifteen-year-olds may have the wherewithal and willingness to buy alcohol, but not the authority. Many people may have the authority and funds to buy elephants, but aren't willing to. In neither of these cases is the group a real market.

### Types of Market

There is no such thing as one national market. Instead, there are hundreds of unique small markets. For a firm to prepare an effective marketing strategy, it must first pinpoint its markets. These are usually classified as consumer markets, industrial markets, and international markets.

There are usually many products and brands appealing to the consumer market.

▲ **Consumer Markets** **Consumer markets** consist of individuals or households that purchase goods and services for their own use. For example, every time you buy groceries, toiletries, furniture, tools, clothing, sports equipment, music systems, and books, as well as dry cleaning and term-paper typing, you're part of these consumer markets.

▲ **Industrial Markets** **Industrial markets** consist of firms that buy goods for resale and firms or institutions that buy goods and services to use in performing their operations. There are many different industrial markets that buy goods to sell at a profit or to use in performing their operations. These goods include raw materials, fabricated materials, equipment, tools, office supplies—even company airplanes.

Some items, such as typewriters, microcomputers, and security systems, may be classified as either consumer or industrial goods. The proper classification depends on the purchaser and the reason for buying the good. If you bought a typewriter for your own use, it would be considered a consumer good. On the other hand, if the typewriter was purchased for use by a secretary at your school, it would be classified as an industrial good.

> Suppose you decide to use your typewriter to type papers for fellow students, for a fee. Which kind of market would you represent when you bought typing paper and ribbons?

▲ **International Markets** In a free enterprise economy, when demand for goods is less than productive capacity for the present and immediate future, people become more aware of the significance of **international markets:** buyers of goods and services from other countries.

In the United States, more foreign-made goods are now being purchased in the consumer market than ever before. Consider the growing sales of such foreign-made goods as automobiles, television sets, stereos, radios, calculators, watches, cameras, apparel, and shoes. Goods from other countries are also abundant in the industrial market.

The available natural resources and the status of economic development in a particular country or geographic region determine the dimension of the market for international products. As one European economist put it, "The highly developed economies are your best customers. For it is these people who have resources to purchase your goods and services."

## Market Characteristics

**Objective 4**

**Different market characteristics.**

To be most effective, marketing managers need to understand completely the characteristics of the markets they are trying to serve. **Market characteristics** include population, age, income, and regional patterns that affect market strategies.

▲ **Population Patterns**  The underlying market factor determining consumer demand is the number and type of people with the purchasing power to buy a given product or service. This factor is important to the business owner-manager who asks the question "Are there enough potential customers to justify my going into business here?" These patterns are also important to managers of national retailing chains. The population trend for the country and the specific location would affect where a new store could be located or an old one closed, as shown in Figure 12-3 (page 326). Notice that the population is shifting away from the Northeast and to the South and West.

Other important population characteristics are household formations and education. The proportion of married couples is declining, while the proportions of single people, single-parent families, and unmarried couples are increasing. Also, fewer children are expected, although the "baby bust" of the 1960s and 1970s may be ending. The population has become more educated, as over two-thirds of those twenty-five years and older have completed high school and nearly a fifth have finished college.

▲ **Age Groups**  The average age of Americans is now rising and is expected to continue to rise in the foreseeable future. The average age rose from twenty-six in 1966 to thirty-one in 1983. Figure 12-4 (page 327) shows a bulge in the population for people from eighteen to thirty-seven: the baby boom generation. At the same time, the percentage of children and middle-aged is declining, while the sixty-five-and-over group is increasing rapidly.

Each age group has different consumption patterns, and marketing managers tend to design their marketing strategies accordingly. For example, young children need baby food, toys, and clothing. School-aged children purchase clothing, sports equipment, records and tapes, school supplies, cosmetics, and used cars. The young-adult and middle-aged groups purchase homes, second cars, new furniture, stereo systems, recreational equipment, and sports cars. And, although television commercials may make it appear that golden-agers are interested only in laxatives and high-fiber cereals, parents whose children have left home find themselves free to enjoy travel (including ocean cruises) and other luxuries they may formerly have denied themselves. They may be able to buy retirement homes in New England or the Sun Belt and engage in recreational activities. They're also good customers for goods and services for their children and grandchildren.

In an effort to cater to adults, Hershey Chocolate has become Hershey Foods Corporation, a diversified, decentralized company that includes Friendly

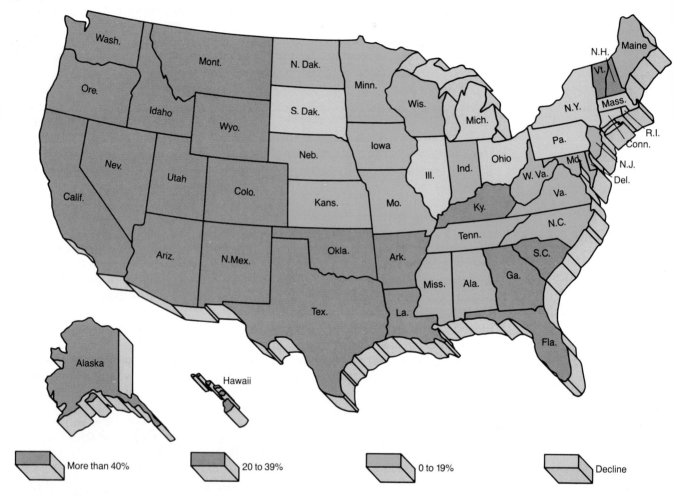

**Figure 12-3** Population change, 1980 to 2000. (Data from U.S. Department of Commerce.)

Restaurants, San Giorgio and Skinner Pasta, and Cory Coffee Service. It has further retargeted its marketing program toward adults by introducing new boxed candy and candy pieces in addition to the usual bars.[5] Its status product, the Golden Almond Bar, in an elegant gold wrapper, is really a fat Hershey bar with an extra helping of almonds.

Epcot Center is evidence of a change in corporate strategy at Walt Disney Productions to cope with the altered age composition of the population. Long dependent on young children and families for the success of its theme parks and movies, Disney is now trying to broaden its appeal to teenagers and adults. Epcot Center, located on a 260-acre tract near Orlando, Florida, has two distinct realms that appeal to adults. They are Future World, whose corporately sponsored pavilions celebrate the limitless potential of science, industry, and technology in creating a better tomorrow, and World Showcase, which displays the architecture and culture of nine countries. To escape the negative effects of the U.S. baby bust, the company is also beginning an expansion overseas, where the population and age patterns are more in its favor.[6]

▲ **Income Levels** The most important source of consumer purchasing power is personal income. The total personal income of Americans has increased more than twelve times from 1940 to the present. Even with an adjustment for inflation, this is still a dramatic increase in income. However, the savings rate has declined.

During the same period, the percentage of families earning over $10,000 increased almost fivefold and the percentage earning less than $3,000 decreased fivefold. Considering these data, you can imagine where the marketing programs of companies are now being directed—namely, toward middle-income consumers.

As shown in Figure 12-5 (page 328), income varies considerably by region and state. As you'll see, this sort of distribution will also affect a firm's marketing plans.

▲ **Regional Differences** Not only do total and per capita incomes vary by region, but so do buying habits and purchasing patterns. Many progressive companies use research firms to find out what kinds of people they could reach with their products and sales pitches and what kinds of people currently buy their goods—even down to their eating habits, religious beliefs, and voting patterns (see FYI on page 329).

Detroit is tailoring cars to specific regions to exploit regional differences in taste. Drivers in the Northeast, where freeways are crowded, are highly concerned about safety, while in less crowded states, such as Wyoming and Nebraska, people want to be sure that parts and service will be available. Drivers

**Figure 12-4** The baby boom generation comes of age. (Based on data from the U.S. Bureau of the Census.)

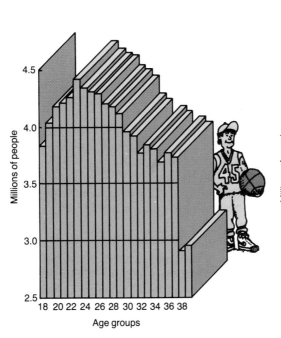

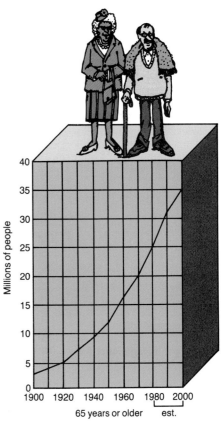

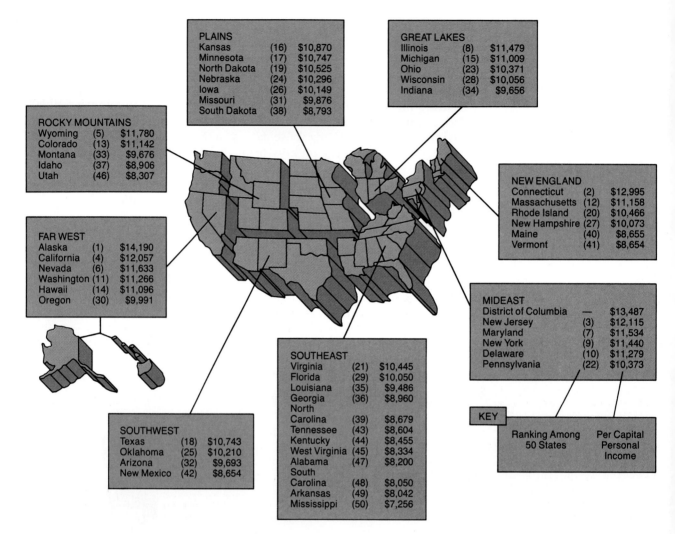

**PLAINS**

| | | |
|---|---|---|
| Kansas | (16) | $10,870 |
| Minnesota | (17) | $10,747 |
| North Dakota | (19) | $10,525 |
| Nebraska | (24) | $10,296 |
| Iowa | (26) | $10,149 |
| Missouri | (31) | $9,876 |
| South Dakota | (38) | $8,793 |

**GREAT LAKES**

| | | |
|---|---|---|
| Illinois | (8) | $11,479 |
| Michigan | (15) | $11,009 |
| Ohio | (23) | $10,371 |
| Wisconsin | (28) | $10,056 |
| Indiana | (34) | $9,656 |

**ROCKY MOUNTAINS**

| | | |
|---|---|---|
| Wyoming | (5) | $11,780 |
| Colorado | (13) | $11,142 |
| Montana | (33) | $9,676 |
| Idaho | (37) | $8,906 |
| Utah | (46) | $8,307 |

**NEW ENGLAND**

| | | |
|---|---|---|
| Connecticut | (2) | $12,995 |
| Massachusetts | (12) | $11,158 |
| Rhode Island | (20) | $10,466 |
| New Hampshire | (27) | $10,073 |
| Maine | (40) | $8,655 |
| Vermont | (41) | $8,654 |

**FAR WEST**

| | | |
|---|---|---|
| Alaska | (1) | $14,190 |
| California | (4) | $12,057 |
| Nevada | (6) | $11,633 |
| Washington | (11) | $11,266 |
| Hawaii | (14) | $11,096 |
| Oregon | (30) | $9,991 |

**MIDEAST**

| | | |
|---|---|---|
| District of Columbia | — | $13,487 |
| New Jersey | (3) | $12,115 |
| Maryland | (7) | $11,534 |
| New York | (9) | $11,440 |
| Delaware | (10) | $11,279 |
| Pennsylvania | (22) | $10,373 |

**SOUTHEAST**

| | | |
|---|---|---|
| Virginia | (21) | $10,445 |
| Florida | (29) | $10,050 |
| Louisiana | (35) | $9,486 |
| Georgia | (36) | $8,960 |
| North Carolina | (39) | $8,679 |
| Tennessee | (43) | $8,604 |
| Kentucky | (44) | $8,455 |
| West Virginia | (45) | $8,334 |
| Alabama | (47) | $8,200 |
| South Carolina | (48) | $8,050 |
| Arkansas | (49) | $8,042 |
| Mississippi | (50) | $7,256 |

**SOUTHWEST**

| | | |
|---|---|---|
| Texas | (18) | $10,743 |
| Oklahoma | (25) | $10,210 |
| Arizona | (32) | $9,693 |
| New Mexico | (42) | $8,654 |

**KEY**

| Ranking Among 50 States | Per Capital Personal Income |
|---|---|

**Figure 12-5** Regional income patterns. (Adapted from *Mobile Press-Register*, May 30, 1982, p. 3-F. Reprinted by permission. © 1982 by NEA, Inc.)

in Texas tend to stress horsepower and acceleration, while California drivers emphasize dependability and passenger comfort. Buick produces a hopped-up car called the Regal Grand National for Southerners. In California, the same car is sold in a high-fashion, two-tone version called the Somerset Regal.[7]

## TARGET MARKETS

**Objective 5**

**How target markets are used.**

As you can see from the above discussion, no business can satisfy all customers. Most marketing managers therefore try to attract the part of the market that matches their product or service. This is called its **target market**—the specific group of customers, as defined by factors like age, education, occupation, economic status, and location, toward which a firm directs its marketing efforts. A firm can have several target markets at the same time.

## FYI

# Where You Live Affects the Kind of Goods You Buy

Mediamark Research, Inc., a New York market research firm, analyzes the buying behavior of Americans by geographic regions. For example, Chrysler Corporation automobiles sell extremely well in Cleveland, compared with other makes, because the buyers seek quality and dependability. Yet the same cars do poorly in San Francisco, where people seek powerful cars to climb the hills. Philadelphia is an excellent market for American Motors cars, possibly because of the patriotic associations—and low fuel costs. On the other hand, Los Angeles is a poor one because of the desire for speed.

Mediamark produced city-by-city findings for 1,000 product categories on the basis of buying strength in the ten cities where the major broadcast networks own and operate television stations. Those cities are New York, Los Angeles, Chicago, Philadelphia, San Francisco, Boston, Detroit, Washington, Cleveland, and St. Louis.

To simplify comparisons, Mediamark indexed local percentages in each case against a national average of 100. In the Chrysler example, Cleveland rated 179 and San Francisco 42. The American Motors figure was 191 for Philadelphia and 50 for Los Angeles. Other comparisons by make were Cadillac: Washington, 171, and Boston, 53; Oldsmobile: Chicago, 153, and Washington, 56; Toyota: Los Angeles, 222, and Cleveland, 41; and Datsun: San Francisco, 217, and Detroit, 25.

Source: Based on Eugene Carlson, "Where You Live Often Affects the Kinds of Goods You Buy," *The Wall Street Journal*, September 14, 1982, p. 29. Adapted by permission of *The Wall Street Journal*, © Dow Jones & Company, Inc. 1982. All Rights Reserved.

In the 1970s, as discount and specialty stores eroded their traditional middle-class clientele, Sears, Roebuck and Company had to scramble to find its market niche. First, it promoted itself as an upscale, fashion-oriented department store for more affluent customers. When that failed, Sears experimented with budget shops and embarked on a disastrous price-slashing binge. It then shifted back to stocking more middle-of-the-road staple goods and designer products.[8] It also sells insurance, real estate, securities, and computers, in addition to servicing automobiles.

Many firms attempt **market segmentation,** or dividing the total market into groups with similar characteristics. While at GM, John De Lorean regularly listened to rock-music radio stations to hear what was being discussed. By keeping up with shifting trends among young and affluent car buyers—his market segment—he was able to pinpoint a market for smaller, sportier, and more efficient cars and helped quadruple Pontiac sales.

Regional differences in advertising are shown by these contrasting ads for the same car.

# The hottest Buick this side of a banked oval.

Shown above is the 1984 Buick Regal Grand National Coupe, caught in a very uncharacteristic pose...at rest. Cooling its more than slightly sinister, wedge-shaped body until it's called on to show its rear deck spoiler to the pack far behind.

When it does, this very special Regal will be exercising some mighty impressive muscle.

To begin with, a sequential-port fuel-injected and turbocharged 3.8 litre V-6 engine that puts some 200 powerful horses at your disposal via a four-speed automatic transmission with overdrive.

You'll make good use of them, too. Thanks to other standard Grand National fare such as a 3.42 performance

axle ratio, fast-ratio power steering, and a special Gran Touring suspension that gets the most out of P215/65R15 steel-belted radials set on black-accented aluminum road wheels.

Little chrome and a lot of power in basic black attire. That's what the Buick Regal Grand National Coupe is all about. We know you'll approve.

Firms also try **product differentiation,** or distinguishing their goods or services from those of other companies. For instance, some companies are now producing goods for the "super baby" trade. These gourmet babies, whose upwardly mobile parents, usually both employed, want the best possible start for them, are being showered with expensive clothing and toys. The *Ultimate Baby Catalog* offers a set of Steuben Glass crystal baby blocks for $275,000 and Chippendale chairs for $990.[9] That's product differentiation! It's also **market positioning,** or placement of a product in the market so as to convey a desired image and make the product attractive.

The product or service that meets the needs and wants of a specifically defined group of people is preferable to a product or service that is a compromise to suit widely different tastes. Often a firm attempts to identify a market segment that's not well served by other companies. Although each Camel

**Limited appeal.**

The 1984 Buick Regal Somerset is clearly not for everyone. In fact, we never intended it to be. That's why we planned this Regal as a limited edition for a select few...right from the very beginning.

You see, we realized that for every dozen or so new Regal owners there's at least one more who wants his or her next car to be exceptionally distinctive... even for a Regal.

We think we've achieved this level of uniqueness with our latest edition of the Somerset. This Regal's aerodynamic elegance is further enhanced by special Designers' Accent paint in light and dark brown.

The standard steel-belted, radial-ply whitewall tires are set on Designer wheels with light brown accents.

Tasteful Somerset ornamentation highlights the hood, front fenders, and rear roof panel areas.

It all adds up to an exterior treatment that will really catch eyes and turn heads. Even those of other Regal owners.

As good as all that looks and sounds, there's even more. So turn the page and step inside our '84 Somerset.

cigarette has more unfiltered tar than an entire pack of some brands, and although Camels aren't extra-long or filter-tipped or even heavily advertised, they're the seventh-largest-selling brand in the United States. Camels are smoked regularly by almost 1.5 million people, primarily middle-aged or elderly men living in the rural areas of the South, Midwest, and East who tend to live dangerously.[10]

More often, though, a firm will try to capture part of someone else's market, if it's big enough. By producing a more desirable product, a company will try to penetrate a given market, even if it's already well served. For instance, Brother Industries, Ltd., a Japanese manufacturer, drives hard to achieve its objectives. It earned its reputation before World War II by selling a copy of Singer's classic sewing machine outside the United States. Then it captured a sizable share of the portable typewriter market. Now Brother is after a solid

chunk of the booming office-automation market. Its target is the office type-writer market, dominated for over twenty years by IBM's Selectric models.[11]

> For what products or producers are you a target market? How is advertising for these products directed at you?

## MARKETING RESEARCH

**Objective 6**

**What marketing research is and what it reveals about consumer behavior.**

The way marketers find out about their target's market characteristics is through **marketing research,** the systematic gathering, recording, and analysis of data about problems related to the marketing of goods and services. Some of the more important areas of marketing research are:

1. Estimating sales potential for the industry and the company.
2. Selecting the most appropriate channels of distribution for the company's products.
3. Identifying customers for the firm's products or services and determining their needs.
4. Evaluating the company's advertising efficiency.

Marketing research is usually used to develop marketing strategies that help business perform the marketing function better. Failure to use market research effectively to develop a marketing strategy can be disastrous, as shown by the Edsel (see FYI, page 333).

### Sources of Information

Effective marketing managers have both formal and informal sources of information about consumer needs and about products to satisfy those needs. Some informal sources are social and sports clubs, lunches with suppliers and competitors, and trade newspapers and magazines. Examples of formal sources of information are test markets (see the Profile on page 334), computer systems that provide daily analysis of sales trends in the company and its industry, pilot projects, user testing, and market research firms.

Many producers are now using their employees to try out new products. It's more convenient, less expensive, and quicker than testing with outside consumers. Possible disadvantages are lack of objectivity and employees' desire to please management. Dr Pepper, for example, has for years relied solely on its employees to taste soft drinks. It found that workers care about improving the product.[12] Polaroid uses this method to prevent leakage of trade secrets. On the other hand, employees of Puritan fashions didn't even tell the company when new Puritan clothes shrank and the color bled on them.

Some more reliable, standard sources of data are government publications, trade association reports, Chamber of Commerce studies, university research publications, trade journals, newspapers, company records, and data obtained from dealers, sales representatives, customers, and competitors.

# *FYI*

## The Edsel: Marketing Mistake

In 1957, a Ford Motor Company marketing manager declared that the Edsel car would become an important part of automotive history. Ironically, the Edsel has become part of history, even part of the English language, but the name conjures up images of failure and self-inflicted wounds.

Ford executives set out to design the perfect car, with the latest features in design and engineering. Money was no object. Probably more research and development went into the Edsel than into any other car. Three years of intensive research and development and $250 million went into building, advertising, and promoting the new car, but it was an instant flop. Factors contributing to its failure were a recession, overpricing, controversial styling, poor quality, and insincere dealers, who told Ford how wonderful it was and told customers something else. The name, which was chosen by executives for sentimental reasons—Edsel was the deceased son of Henry Ford, the founder, and the father of Henry, the chairman in 1957—was later found to have inhibited sales. Yet the name was retained even after market research showed that it should be changed.

The basic reason for failure, however, was the curiously unscientific approach of Ford's management. For instance, the car was designed in group sessions, with too many fingers leaving their marks on its identity. Also, it was ordered into production without research to determine whether or not there was a need for it. Then, to compound the error, it was pushed through production so rapidly that there were more than the usual number of flaws and defects. And once produced, the Edsel was undermined by Ford executives, who almost immediately wrote it off after a disappointing introduction to the market. Perhaps no product could have survived with all these handicaps, and certainly not one called Edsel. After spending a total of over $350 million on research, development, and tooling, and after losing $50 million on sales, Ford finally took the Edsel off the market. It's now a collectors' item.

Sources: David Abodaher, *Iacocca* (New York: Macmillan, 1982), pp. 99–100, 112, 117; "The Edsel Affair," *Sales and Marketing Management* 125 (December 8, 1980):92; and others.

## Consumer Behavior

Consumers favor those businesses that give them what they want in products, prices, promotion, and convenience. However, consumer wants are always changing. As a result, it's no wonder that consumers—the basis for the marketing concept—are constantly being studied by marketing managers. In

## *Profile*

### Fred's Place: Exclusive Test Market

Fred Cianciolo owns and operates Cianciolo & Co., or Fred's Place, three blocks from Proctor & Gamble's (P&G) headquarters building. The twenty-five-by-seventy-foot establishment is the only grocery store left in downtown Cincinnati. It's an old-fashioned neighborhood grocery store, with a fruit stand and a green awning out front. The customers are down-to-earth types who live nearby.

P&G has been using Fred's Place as a test market for almost twenty years. Nearly every product that P&G is testing is stacked on shelves in a rear corner of the store. P&G offers the products to Fred's, as well as to several other stores in the Cincinnati area, as a convenience to its employees, who often like to try out the firm's new products. Fred orders the new products just as he does other products.

Based on customer purchases and reactions, Fred is able to tell P&G consumer products sales reps—as well as competitors—what a new product's chances of success are. For example, he predicted that Pringle's potato chips wouldn't be much of a success, since they were too different from the chips people were used to. Yet he says that Duncan Hines yellow cake mix for microwave ovens is a real winner.

Source: Based on Paul Ingrassia, "P&G's Rivals Often Show Up at Fred's Place," *The Wall Street Journal*, November 1, 1982, pp. 27 and 35. Adapted by permission of *The Wall Street Journal*, © Dow Jones & Company, Inc. 1982. All Rights Reserved.

short, the *who, what, when, where, how,* and *why* of consumer behavior have to be determined before marketing plans can be made.

▲ **Who Is the Buyer?** An important step in market research is to find out who uses, buys, or makes the decision to buy a given product or service. The person who decides what to buy may be neither the user nor the purchaser. In the marketing process, therefore, most marketing tactics deal directly with the decision maker and buyer rather than the user. For example, babies and children are users but not buyers or decision makers. As a result, many Fisher-Price toy ads are aimed at demonstrating to parents the educational quality or safety of toys, and Mattel ads stress durability and wholesome play value.

> Who chose this book for you to use?  You?  Your teacher?  A faculty committee?

▲ **What Is Needed?**  What is the need that must be satisfied by the product? Many new products have failed because their makers didn't know about or weren't able to satisfy those needs.  One study, for instance, found that travelers are more dissatisfied with the bath soap at hotels than with any other single item.  Complaints included the small size of the bars and their failure to lather.[13]

▲ **When Is It Needed?**  Determining when the buyer wants the product is important.  As you are probably aware, items purchased mainly for Christmas, such as toys, Christmas trees, tree lights, and seasonal cards and foods, have a marketing program different from that for products sold uniformly throughout the year.

▲ **Where Is It Bought?**  In determining the *where* of consumer buying habits, one must see where the buying decision is made, as well as where the actual purchase occurs.  For instance, about 30 percent of decisions to buy groceries are made at home and about 70 percent in the store.  The place where the buyer goes for the product is also vital to marketing plans.  Does the buyer want to buy it in a retail outlet, at home, over the phone, or by mail order?

▲ **How Is It Bought?**  Does the purchaser want to buy the product singly, in six-packs, in cases, or in bulk?  Is the product to be delivered or picked up by the buyer?  Is it to be paid for with credit or cash?  How frequently is the product purchased?

▲ **Why Is It Bought?**  Sound marketing policies are based on a knowledge of customers' buying motives, or why they buy a particular product.  Is it price? Status?  Is the product being used in ways other than its originally intended use?  If so, these could be promoted.  The motives of the final purchaser are important, but so are those of the wholesalers and retailers who will handle the item.

Buying motives may be divided into rational and emotional.  Rational buying motives usually are concerned with such factors as price, cost of use, durability, ease of servicing, and reliability.  Some examples of emotional buying motives are security, curiosity, ego, comfort, and pride.  Fear is one of the strongest and most influential of all buying motives in the United States.  It underlies the sale of insurance, drugs, burglar and fire alarms, and even deodorant.

> What are the motives that cause people to buy high-priced cars, loaded with extras, instead of cheaper, stripped-down models for basic transportation?

## MARKETING STRATEGY AND MARKETING MIX

Once a target market has been pinpointed and a thorough marketing research effort has been made, it's the job of marketing managers to work out **marketing strategy:** the overall plan for developing the marketing process to reach a firm's objectives. Usually, marketing strategies revolve around product, pricing, and promotional strategy, as well as distribution plans.

**Product planning** (to be covered in Chapter 13) includes decisions about package design, branding, trademarks, copyrights, warranties, and new product development. The product is appraised on how well it satisfies the consumers' needs and desires. The diet movement led G. D. Searle & Company to introduce aspartame (Nutrasweet), the new diet sweetener, and the emphasis on health foods resulted in No Salt, a salt substitute. The older population's craving for chocolate and deemphasis on hard candies caused Life Savers to close one of its plants and Perugina, the Italian firm famous for its milk chocolate with cream of hazelnut, to introduce collections of chocolate for Christmas, Valentine's Day, and Easter.

**Pricing strategy** (to be covered in Chapter 13) deals with the methods of setting profitable and justified prices. If a product is priced too high, as the TI 99/4A apparently was when it was introduced at $1,195 in 1980, customers won't buy it. But if the price is too low, like the price tag of under $100 on the TI 99 in 1983, losses will occur. However, as new products begin to be sold in larger quantities, the price can be lowered. For instance, the Atari 400 went from $630 in 1980 to $79 in 1983; the Commodore VIC-20 from $299 in 1981 to $89 in 1983; and the Timex 1000 from $99 in 1982 to $49 in 1983.[14]

**Promotional strategy** (to be covered in Chapter 14) involves personal selling, advertising, and sales promotion tools and techniques. Are you going to use celebrities? It may or may not work. Bill Cosby rates high in Jell-O Pudding commercials but low in Ford ads. Nancy Walker's commercials for Bounty paper towels rated higher than Madge the Manicurist ads for Palmolive Liquid. Should you use humor or be serious? Two of the highest-rated ads, for Dr. Scholl's foot powder and American Tourister luggage, use humor successfully.[15] Or do you use the "hard sell," as the Seven-Up Company did with its "no caffeine, no sugar, and no artificial flavor or color" ads during 1983? The hotel industry is baffled as to how to appeal to women, who account for about 30 percent of all business travelers.[16]

**Distribution strategy** (to be covered in Chapter 15) involves the physical distribution of goods and the selection of marketing channels, or the steps a product follows from producer to final consumer. This decision can be crucial to a company. For instance, Levi Strauss & Company started selling its jeans through mass merchandisers such as J. C. Penney and Sears in 1982. But sales through regular department store chains declined, for the move damaged Levi's fashion credibility.[17] Book sales escalated when books were introduced into shopping centers by national chains such as B. Dalton and Waldenbooks, and into airport newsstands and supermarkets. Over two-thirds of all gasoline is sold through self-service stations, and Southland (7-Eleven stores) is the second-largest U.S. distributor of gasoline. A store named Banana Computer sells non-Apple brands. And where would you go to buy an industrial robot? In Tokyo, you could go to Seibu's department store.

The **four P's** of marketing are product, price, promotion, and placement. Marketing managers try to find the proper—and most profitable—marketing

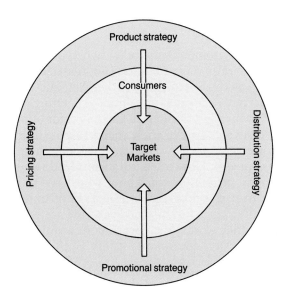

**Figure 12-6** The marketing mix.

mix of these strategies. The **marketing mix** is the combination and blending of the four P's into an overall strategy designed to satisfy chosen consumers.

The diagram of the marketing mix (see Figure 12-6) provides a roadmap for our remaining discussions of marketing. As you can see, the mix operates to satisfy consumer needs by developing the right product, pricing, promotional, and distribution strategies. Small changes in any segment of the mix can have a dramatic impact on the overall strategy. For instance, Coca-Cola sales went through the roof when A. B. Candler gave two Chattanooga lawyers the right (for one dollar) to bottle and distribute his beverage in virtually the entire United States.[18]

## MARKETING ENVIRONMENTS

**Objective 8**

**The environments that affect marketing decisions.**

Marketing strategies must also take into account the environments in which the firm operates, including the competitive, legal, economic, and social environments. While these environmental factors are largely beyond the control of management, the firm's manager must constantly evaluate them when making marketing decisions. Part I provided a background on these environments, so only a few marketing-related factors are presented here.

### The Competitive Environment

There are many examples of firms that have succeeded or failed because of the way they adapted or failed to adapt to the competitive environment. For example, the American Motors Company's compact car, the Rambler, succeeded during the recession of the early 1960s but fell from popularity in the late 1960s and early 1970s because of competition from the larger, more comfortable cars produced by Ford, GM, and Chrysler. The larger cars, in turn, lost out to smaller, more fuel-efficient foreign imports such as Volkswagen, Toyota, and Datsun.

Competition exists not only among companies in the same industry but also among substitute products. An example of the latter would be the competition of steel, aluminum, and glass as building materials.

### The Legal Environment

The legal environment includes two types of laws and regulations that are particularly important to marketing managers: those that maintain competition, such as the Sherman Antitrust Act, and those that regulate specific marketing activities, such as the Pure Food, Drug, and Cosmetic Act and the Consumer Product Safety Act (see Chapter 2 for others). Most firms now conform to these laws as part of their social responsibility.

However, legal factors often shackle managers who try to follow the marketing concept. How often, for example, do you use the seatbelt in your car? How many people do you know who have modified their cars with broom handles to use regular gasoline instead of unleaded? Yet both seatbelts and narrow filler pipes for unleaded gasoline are mandated by government regulation. In other words, the government requires automobile manufacturers to provide emission control and safety equipment that customers don't always want or even use.

### The Economic Environment

Three aspects of the economic environment that are especially important to managers are the business cycle, inflation, and the energy crisis. The business cycle determines the demand for goods and services. Inflation largely determines the types of goods sold, for, when income remains constant and the cost of necessities rises, less is left for other goods and services. The energy crisis has led to increases in the cost of many goods and services.

### The Social Environment

The social environment is also important to business, especially the changing social responsibilities of business (see Chapter 2). Companies are now paying more attention to such issues as pollution control, the presence and image of blacks and women in TV commercials, and consumer safety.

The role of consumer advocates, exemplified by Ralph Nader, can be decisive. A case in point is that of the Corvair automobile produced by General Motors in the 1960s. In Ralph Nader's opinion, the Corvair was flawed. He maintained that internal proving grounds tests by GM in the early 1960s showed that company engineers were very worried about the car's instability on the highway. Millions of dollars have been spent in legal expenses and out-of-court settlements in compensation for those killed in Corvairs.[19]

---

Business firms were the original users of burglar and fire alarms. Who now make up the primary market? How has the legal/social environment affected this change?

---

## ⌂ LEARNING OBJECTIVES REVISITED

1. *What marketing is and its role in a business enterprise.*

   Marketing is the determination of customers' needs and wants, development of goods and services to satisfy those needs, and delivery of the goods and services to the consumer. The usual marketing functions are ex-

change, which includes buying and selling; physical distribution, which includes storing and transporting; and facilitation, through financing, risk taking, standardizing and grading, and researching.

Marketing, which provides place, time, and ownership utility, enables consumers to have a higher standard of living, employment, and income. Without it, other business activities would be in vain.

2. *How the marketing concept has evolved.*

   Until the 1930s, the production concept, or concentration on producing and selling, predominated in U.S. business. When using the marketing concept, on the other hand, a company tries to determine and meet the needs of its customers in order to reach its long-run goal of profit. Firms try to gain a competitive edge, which is a quality that is desirable from the customer's viewpoint and that sets the firm apart from, and gives it an advantage over, its competitors.

3. *What a market is and the different types of markets.*

   A market consists of people (including institutions and governments) with the willingness to buy a good or service, the necessary purchasing power, and the authority to make purchase decisions. Markets can be classified as consumer, industrial, and international markets.

4. *Different market characteristics.*

   The market characteristics for a given business can be defined in terms of differing population patterns, age groups, income levels, and regional differences.

5. *How target markets are used.*

   A target market is the specific group of customers, defined by market characteristics, toward which a firm directs its marketing efforts.

6. *What marketing research is and what it reveals about consumer behavior.*

   Marketing research is the systematic gathering, recording, and analysis of data about problems related to the marketing of goods and services. Marketing managers use both informal and formal sources of marketing research information.

   Market planning begins with a careful study of consumers. The major areas for study include questions of who buys what goods and services and when, where, how, and why they buy them.

7. *How marketing strategy is built on the marketing mix.*

   Marketing strategy is the overall plan for developing the marketing process to meet a firm's objectives. Usually, marketing strategies revolve around the marketing mix of product, pricing, promotional, and distribution plans. Product planning includes decisions about package design, branding, trademarks, copyrights, warranties, and new product development. Pricing strategies deal with the methods of setting profitable and justified prices. Promotional strategies involve personal selling, advertising, and sales promotion. Distribution strategies involve the physical distribution of goods and the selection of marketing channels.

8. *The environments that affect marketing decisions.*

   Managers make decisions within interacting environments. The competi-

tive, legal, economic, and social environments vitally influence marketing strategies.

## ▲ IMPORTANT TERMS

As an extra review of the chapter, try defining the following terms. If you have trouble with any of them, refer to the page listed.

marketing  *318*
exchange  *318*
physical distribution  *318*
facilitation  *318*
place utility  *320*
time utility  *320*
ownership utility  *320*
production concept  *320*
marketing concept  *321*
competitive edge  *321*
market  *323*
consumer markets  *324*
industrial markets  *324*
international markets  *324*

market characteristics  *325*
target market  *328*
market segmentation  *329*
production differentiation  *330*
market positioning  *330*
marketing research  *332*
marketing strategy  *336*
product planning  *336*
pricing strategy  *336*
promotional strategy  *336*
distribution strategy  *336*
four P's  *336*
marketing mix  *337*

## ▲ REVIEW QUESTIONS

1. How would you define marketing from the viewpoint of a firm's management?
2. Distinguish marketing from production and distribution.
3. What are three kinds of utility that marketing provides? Explain each.
4. How does the marketing concept differ from the production concept?
5. What are the differences among consumer, industrial, and international markets?
6. Describe the four different market characteristics.
7. What are the primary purposes of marketing research in a firm?
8. How is marketing research information gathered?
9. How is marketing strategy based on the marketing mix?
10. What are the four P's?
11. What are four interacting environments in which marketing managers make decisions? How do they affect those decisions?

## ▲ DISCUSSION QUESTIONS

1. Is marketing good for the U.S. economy? Explain.
2. Do you expect that the marketing concept will be as relevant in the late 1980s and 1990s as it has been? Why or why not?
3. Describe the possible overlaps of consumer, industrial, and international markets.
4. How may market characteristics such as population patterns, age groups, income levels, and location differences affect your employment and/or your buying habits in the next decade?
5. Some firms, such as Sears, have appealed to different target markets in the

last two decades. Do you anticipate stability in firms' selection of target markets in the next decade, or do you anticipate continued change in firms' target markets?

6. What is your prediction concerning the strength of the consumerism movement in the 1980s? Cite a few illustrations of the expected impact of this movement on marketing strategies.

## CASE 12-1   Tom Rush: The Case of the Aging Audience[20]

When, in the mid-1970s, folksinger Tom Rush found his popularity slipping, he set about analyzing the problem. He had been one of the sixties' most popular college-circuit performers, with hits like "Urge for Going" and "Circle Game." But in the seventies, when groups like the Bee Gees were selling millions of albums, his albums peaked at only about 100,000 copies.

It seemed that his music just didn't sell as well anymore. In 1981, though, a University of New Hampshire marketing student asked for permission to research Rush's audience for his master's thesis. The conclusion? Rush should target his merchandising at the older, baby boom audience—not at the younger, rock audience. He should play locations seen by the older, professional baby boomers as "special and nice."

Since then, Tom Rush has sold out a concert at Boston's prestigious Symphony Hall, had a PBS special, and produced an album himself, which he's marketing through such solid magazines as *New Yorker* and *Yankee*. Says Rush, "I'm having the best time of my life, and the curve is headed up."

### Case Questions

1. How long can Tom Rush expect to continue using his new marketing strategy?
2. How might a "baby boom" marketing strategy change in the next twenty years?
3. What other products or services might find their marketing efforts affected by the baby boom phenomenon?

## CASE 12-2   The Aging Consumers[21]

In 1900, 13.2 percent of the U.S. population was fifty years of age or older; that figure increased to 22.5 percent by 1950 (nearly thirty-four million people), and 26.0 percent in 1980 (over sixty million). It is expected to be 27.6 percent by the year 2000 (seventy-two million).

In addition to these growth percentages, around 53 percent of all discretionary income is in the hands of those over forty years of age; 28 percent is in the hands of consumers fifty-five and over—twice that of households headed by persons thirty-four and under, the age group most often courted by the retail industry.

According to Montgomery Ward's executive vice-president of marketing, persons fifty-five and over (1) are the best credit risks, (2) outspend other consumers on a per capita basis, (3) have a lower delinquency rate, and (4) have the lowest bankruptcy rate.

The year 1983 was a turning point. For the first time ever, there were more Americans over sixty-five than there were teenagers. Moreover, some of the most popular women today, such as Jane Fonda, Linda Evans, Linda Gray, Stephanie Powers, and Joan Collins, are "fashionable forties and fifties."

Older persons now form a large, highly diverse, well-heeled, and eager market. Yet marketers have acted as though people at fifty just drop off a cliff and die—and thus cease being consumers.

### Case Questions

1. What should the preceding information mean to marketers?
2. How would you go about trying to capture the older market?
3. What kind of products would you design for them?

# 13

# Product and Price

*If a man has good corn, or wood, or boards, or pigs to sell, or can make better chairs or knives, crucibles or church organs, than anybody else, you will find a broad hard-beaten road to his house, though it be in the woods.*

Ralph Waldo Emerson

*What we obtain too cheap, we esteem too lightly; 'tis dearness only that gives everything its value.*

Thomas Paine

## Learning Objectives

After studying the material in this chapter, you will understand:

1. The classification of products as durable or nondurable goods and consumer or industrial goods.
2. How new products are developed.
3. The stages in a product's life cycle.
4. Product identification by brands, trademarks, and labels.
5. The role played by product packaging.
6. How pricing objectives relate to a company's product decisions and marketing objectives.
7. How prices are determined.
8. Various pricing policies used by business firms.

## In This Chapter

Classifying Products
New-Product Development
The Product Life Cycle
Identification of Products
Packaging
The Role and Importance of Pricing
Pricing Objectives
Determining Prices
Pricing Policies

# HEAD'S "SNOWSHOE"
## *The New-Product Racquet*

Since 1976, Pam Shriver, who was ranked 24th in the world in tennis, has gone to 5th and won the Wimbledon Doubles Championship. Gene Mayer leapt from 148th to 6th, Kathy Renaldi jumped from 181st to 14th, and Vincent Van Patten moved up from 385th to 31st. What they all had in common wasn't a revolutionary new training regime, but a switch to the Prince tennis racquet. Even though better performance and the use of the new, oversized racquet may be merely coincidental, it looks as if the Prince may not just dominate the market by 1993, when its patent runs out, but virtually own it.

Called "the snowshoe" when it was introduced in 1976, the Prince was seen as an amusing novelty. But now it's grabbed the lion's share of the high-priced racquet market. Its market share—8.5 percent in 1979 and 31 percent in 1981—makes a quantum leap every year and should be over 50 percent of racquet sales by 1985, according to an independent market analyst.

This amazing success is due largely to the technical and marketing genius of its inventor, Howard Head. Head became familiar with the uses of aluminum when he was an aircraft engineer during World War II. In the early 1950s, he designed a pair of aluminum skis to improve his own performance. They proved to be so popular that he founded his own company to produce them. Before selling the company to AMF in 1969, he'd started selling conventional-sized aluminum tennis racquets under the Head label.

Head's next step was to buy the Prince Manufacturing Company, a small firm that made machines to shoot tennis balls to a player practicing alone. Realizing that tennis authorities had never set limits on the size of racquets, even though almost everyone used the standard 70-square-inch racquet, Head developed his 110-square-incher. In order to obtain his patent, which covers racquets ranging from 85 to 130 square inches, he had to prove that the Prince had unique playing characteristics. Although the same weight and length as conventional racquets, his is wider and more oval and has strings that are spaced farther apart at the edges and closer together at the center to form a "sweet spot" that is three and a half times larger. It has less wobble, less twist (which reduces the risk of tennis elbow), more power, and greater control.

Luck helped Head's genius, for the International Tennis Federation, which could have banned oversized racquets, authorized the Prince and gave it a virtual monopoly on the oversized oval racquet market. This permitted Head to charge a higher price for his "amusing novelty."

When a company has an idea for a new product, whether it's Head's Prince racquet or Pepperidge Farm's Vegetables in Pastry, many decisions have to be made. How will the product be classified? How will its sales grow compared with competitors'? How will it be labeled and packaged? And, last but not least, how will it be priced? The first two P's of the marketing mix—product and price—represent the startup decisions in the marketing of any product, whether good or service. You can see from the orange area in Figure 13-1 how these two interlocked decision areas fit into the whole marketing mix.

## CLASSIFYING PRODUCTS

**Objective 1**

**The classification of products as durable or nondurable goods and consumer or industrial goods.**

You've already learned that for any company to be profitable and survive it must provide goods or services that satisfy its customers. If products are to be marketed appropriately, an often-unstated classification must be made. This classification will determine many strategies for handling a product. From the physical point of view, a product may be *tangible*, like your clothing, or *intangible*, like life insurance policies or shares of stock. The tangible items are usually called products or goods, while the intangible ones are called services. Tangible products, in turn, can be classified as durable or nondurable goods.

### Durable Goods

**Durable goods** have physical qualities and uses that permit them to last a relatively long time, even while being used. They're designed to be used up over an extended period of time and are made of materials that will take considerable wear and tear. For example, you probably own such durable goods as a car, tape deck, cassette player, TV set, or stereo that should remain usable for several years—or at least until the warranty runs out. Houses are built to last thirty to fifty years or more. Refrigerators and mattresses both have a life

**Figure 13-1** Product and price in the marketing mix.

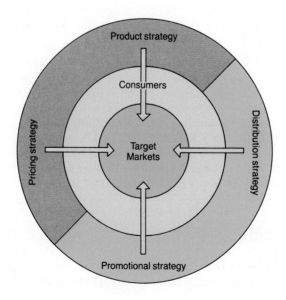

expectancy of about twenty years, and quality jewelry, silverware, china, and furniture are frequently handed down from one generation to the next.

The fact that a product is durable influences its whole marketing strategy. Obviously, goods like these are packaged differently, sold more personally and aggressively, and priced higher than a tube of toothpaste or a bottle of shampoo.

## Nondurable Goods

**Nondurable goods,** on the other hand, have physical qualities and uses that cause them to be used quickly or only a few times. In other words, they're made to be used up. Food, flowers, oil, gasoline, cosmetics and toiletries, batteries, paper, pencils, magazines, newspapers, and paper plates are examples.

## Consumer Goods

Durable goods can be further classified as either consumer goods or industrial goods, each of which requires a different set of marketing strategies. **Consumer goods** are used by the consumer or household that buys them and come in a ready-to-use form that calls for no further industrial or commercial processing. On the basis of how much effort a consumer takes to obtain them, consumer goods can be further subdivided into (1) convenience goods, (2) shopping goods, and (3) specialty goods.

**Convenience goods** are sold to the consumer whose shopping time is limited and who buys them often, routinely, quickly, and in any outlet that carries them. Examples are candy bars, cigarettes, milk, bread, and detergent. The first two of these are often **impulse goods,** bought on sight to satisfy a need that is strongly felt at the moment.

**Shopping goods** aren't bought very often, are bought only after the consumer has compared their features with those of competing brands, and are found in only a few stores in one area. These goods usually have a higher unit price than convenience goods, and an individual salesperson, rather than a cashier, may be needed to sell them. Examples of shopping goods are automobiles, furniture, men's suits, ladies' wear, shoes, and major appliances.

**Specialty goods** like prestige automobiles, photographic equipment, fine jewelry, and high-fashion clothing and furniture are bought by consumers after a special shopping effort. They're bought infrequently and are generally available only in exclusive outlets. They're usually high-priced, but price isn't the main consideration of a customer buying them. A customer is often willing to go out of the way to find a certain brand.

Specialty goods prove the point that goods are often considered not just for their physical qualities but also for the economic utility, ego enhancement, status, and satisfaction they carry with them. For example, when people buy a new car, they may want it not just for basic transportation but also for recognition, status, or prestige.

You've probably figured out that this classification of consumer goods is far from rigid. It may differ according to a buyer's intent or wishes. As consumers' incomes and buying habits change, or as prices drop, goods shift from one classification to another. Usually they shift downward, from the specialty to the shopping, or from the shopping to the convenience goods category. Television sets became shopping goods years ago. When microwave ovens

Convenience goods are sold to a consumer who buys them often and routinely.

Shopping goods are usually bought less frequently and after comparison with competing brands.

first came on the market, they were regarded by many as an expensive new toy—a specialty good—for the rich. Now they're considered indispensable shopping goods by working couples and single people who buy them to save cooking time.

### Industrial Goods

Instead of being bought by the ultimate consumer, **industrial goods** are used by businesses to produce other goods or to provide services to customers. These goods are usually bought by institutions such as manufacturers, utilities, government agencies, contractors, wholesalers, retailers, hospitals, and schools that use them in producing their own products or services. Buyers of these goods usually provide prospective suppliers with a description of the product or service and request that bids or price quotations be submitted. The buying decision is usually based on technical performance, cost, or expected monetary gain.

There are many types of industrial goods, but the most common ones are (a) *raw materials,* such as the special silicas produced by Degussa for skin-care products and cosmetics; (b) *component parts,* such as Monroe's ride control

Specialty goods are bought infrequently and are generally available only in exclusive outlets.

products and Walker's exhaust system parts; (c) *installations,* such as International Paper's new Mansfield, Louisiana, containerboard mill; (d) *transportation systems,* such as Fairchild's corporate jet; (e) *tools,* such as Nordson's coating robots; (f) *equipment,* such as Raytheon's radar system; (g) *materials,* such as Crown Zellerbach's coated papers used in publishing; and (h) *supplies,* such as 3M's Post-it Note products.

## NEW-PRODUCT DEVELOPMENT

The development of new products to satisfy changing trends is vital to the marketing program of any company that is trying to retain old customers while also attracting new ones. A recent study showed that companies get an average of 15 percent of their total sales from products introduced within the past five years.[1] The success of a new product depends first and foremost on analyzing the market to see whether a new-product idea fills the needs of the market at that time. Then the marketing mix is developed, and a prototype of the product is test-marketed. Only then does the product begin its life cycle

## *Profile*

### George E. Johnson

George E. Johnson, grandson of a Mississippi sharecropper, is what *Time* magazine has called an example of "black capitalism at its bootstrap best." His fast-growing and very popular Johnson Products Company (JPC), which in 1969 became the first black publicly owned company when it was listed on the American Stock Exchange, has garnered a lion's share of the black hair-care market. Johnson's family owns more than two-thirds of the firm's common stock.

Born in Mississippi but reared in Chicago, Johnson quit high school in the eleventh grade to work for a black-owned cosmetics company as a salesman and production chem-

with the introduction stage. This is the approach that was used by Johnson Products Company to introduce a new hair-grooming product for blacks (see the Profile above).

Only a decade ago, the strategy was still (1) see a need, (2) design and produce a product that best fit the company's resources and needs, and then (3) try to sell it to the customers. This is basically the same strategy used by the young Gillette company in 1895 (see FYI on pages 350 and 351). Probably more research went into the Edsel than into any other automobile, but customers just didn't want it. So Ford lost over $400 million on it before taking it off the market. Similarly, Texas Instruments (TI) used its technological expertise, developed in the aerospace program, to design a digital watch that could be easily and cheaply produced and sold for around $20. Yet its pricing was so inept that, although it soon dominated the market, the watch was dropped in 1980 when its low price (at the time around $10) produced huge losses.

The Japanese had great success using the marketing concept: (1) monitor customer needs, (2) assess how the company can satisfy those needs with avail-

ist. In 1954, Johnson, then twenty-seven, was convinced that he had an improved chemical hair straightener that could be commercially successful. Needing $500 to start his own firm, he visited a commercial loan company in Chicago to borrow half of it. A loan officer decided that lending money to a black high school dropout was too risky and turned Johnson down.

Battered but not beaten, he walked three blocks to a branch of the same loan company and received the $250 after explaining that the money was for a vacation. And Johnson began marketing his hair straightener. At that time, hair straighteners and skin lighteners were quite popular with blacks. But with the Civil Rights movement of the 1960s came "black pride," with its emphasis on the Afro hairstyle and the natural look. Hair straighteners were passé.

Though slow to detect this trend, Johnson in 1968 introduced his Afro-Sheen line of hair sprays and conditioners for taming the hairdos. By 1973, sales had quadrupled and net income had more than tripled. Part of the reason for that massive growth was Johnson's identification with the "black is beautiful" concept. He also developed cosmetics specifically for black women, because their skin tends to be oilier than white skin and their makeup requires a different base. Thus, Johnson exploited weaknesses in the product lines of competitors who tried to sell their existing lines to blacks.

In 1975, the Federal Trade Commission (FTC) required the firm to warn consumers that some of its hair-care products contained lye, which could burn the scalp and cause eye damage. Johnson claims that FTC officials assured him that like products of competitors would also have a printed warning, but for almost two years they didn't. Consequently, by 1977 sales had dropped to $32.3 million, from the 1975 total of $37.6 million. Earnings during this period fell from $1.40 to $0.35 a share.

In 1980, JPC introduced Precise, a revolutionary product that straightens and conditions hair simultaneously. JPC now has a line of about 110 hair-care items, including sprays, conditioners, shampoos and 100 cosmetic items. Its leading product is Gentle Treatment No-Lye Conditioning Creme Relaxer.

JPC distributes its products through high-volume drug, variety, and discount stores and supermarkets. While its largest markets are in New York, Chicago, and Los Angeles, the lucrative African market is perhaps the firm's most promising prospect for the future. Accordingly, JPC has built a $2 million manufacturing plant in Lago, Nigeria, in a joint venture with that country's government, and the company is currently investigating other business opportunities in Africa.

Source: Correspondence with Johnson Products Company. Used by permission of Johnson Products Company, Inc.

able resources, and then (3) react to those needs by efficiently producing and marketing the desired product. With this approach, one out of seven new-product ideas is a winner—much better odds than fifty-seven to one just a decade ago.[2]

In spite of the casualties, new food and drug products keep pouring into the market. In 1982, there were around 1,500 such new entries, as compared to about 800 in 1973. Yet *Dun's Business Month* predicts that in the future there will be fewer and fewer of these new products.[3] The reasons are a decline in population growth and oversegmentation of the market. It's become increasingly difficult for a new product to succeed, since most consumer needs have been identified and met in the grocery and drug lines. Finally, new products are all too often only slight variations of existing ones that may add little to sales while increasing costs. For instance, PepsiCo now has five different cola drinks—Pepsi, Diet Pepsi, Pepsi Free (its decaffeinated drink), Pepsi Light, and Sugar Free Pepsi Free. Coca-Cola appears to have kept Tab in addition to Diet Coke, and is now advertising caffeine-free versions of each, in addition to decaffeinated Coke.

## THE PRODUCT LIFE CYCLE

**Objective 3**

**The stages in a product's life cycle.**

Products, like people, go through a life cycle. They are born, grow, and mature. But only sometimes do they die, for, unlike people, products can be reintroduced in a new form and start all over again. The **product life cycle** is the series of increases and decreases in sales and profits that all products go through from their first appearance until their eventual disappearance. The stages, as shown in Figure 13-2, are introduction, growth, maturity, and decline. The life cycle of a product is important to managers because different competitive strategies are required for products at different stages.

During a product's introduction stage, it's new to the world, and a great deal of effort goes into the birth announcements involved in making its name, package, and features known. Because of the expense of promotion and the time it takes people to become aware of a new product, profits are low and sales climb slowly at introduction.

As a product moves into the growth stage, both sales and profits rise rapidly. Since word is spreading about the product, startup expenses are past, and the competition hasn't caught on yet, profits often peak at this stage.

more, and with every additional customer you get, you are building a permanent foundation of profit." And Gillette found the right disposable product. Until the invention of Gillette's safety razor, shaving could be done only with a straight razor—a piece of steel that had to be stropped regularly and honed by a professional knife sharpener. Small wonder that beards and mustaches were so popular! Those who could afford it used the services of a barber, but for many the professional shave was more a luxury than a routine.

Gillette described the idea for his invention in words that had the ring of a mystical experience, rather than a new-product plan:

> It was in the summer of 1895, when like a child that has been looked and longed for, the razor was born as though its embryonic form had matured in thought and only awaited its appropriate time of birth. On one particular morning, when I started to shave, I found my razor dull beyond the point of successful stropping and it needed honing. As I stood there with the dull razor in my hand, my eyes resting on it as lightly as a bird settling down on its nest, the Gillette razor was born. . . . All this [the design] came more in pictures than in thought as though the razor were already a finished thing and held before my eyes. I stood there in a trance of joy at what I saw.

But Gillette's ecstasy evaporated as he tried to construct a practical model. Since he didn't know how to hone

the steel to a sufficiently sharp edge, Gillette kept looking for the special man who would have the right technical knowledge. Persistence paid off.

On New Year's Day 1900, Gillette, who by then lived in Boston, happened to discuss his idea of a razor with a disposable blade with Edward Stewart, a soft-drink bottler. Stewart introduced Gillette to financier Jacob Heilborn, who, in turn, found William E. Nickerson, that special man who could make the razor and blade. Nickerson, an MIT-trained engineer, spent a month mulling over the hardening and sharpening processes. Within six months, he gleefully concluded that it was his "confident opinion that not only can a successful razor be made on the principles of the Gillette patent, but that if the blades are made by proper methods a result in advance of anything known can be reached."

On September 28, 1901, the new company was incorporated under the name of American Safety Razor, later changed to the Gillette Safety Razor Company.

---

Source: Prepared for this book by Heidi Vernon Wortzel, Northeastern University. Information from *The Gillette Blade,* February 1918, pp. 6–10; January 1919, p. 11; and September 1926, pp. 7, 9. *The Gillette Blade* was published monthly as a house organ of the Gillette Safety Razor Company from 1917 to 1922. For a year it was published in alternate months, and it became a quarterly publication in 1924. It ceased to exist when the company merged with the Autostrop Company in 1929.

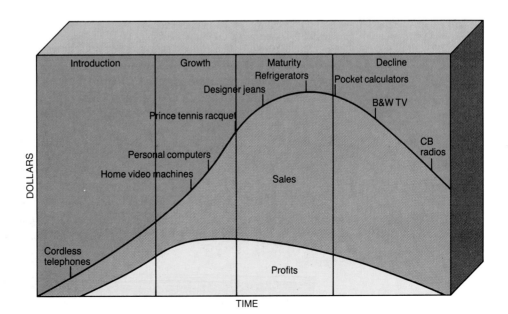

**Figure 13-2** The product life cycle.

Product life cycle, stage 4?

"Of course our problem is productivity. What else could it be?"

⤬ As a product reaches maturity, competitors are gaining on it in the marketplace. At this point, a company may have to lower prices and target promotion at competitors in order to stay competitive. Toward the end of this stage, sales begin to decline, while profits have already started a downhill slide.

Decline, as the word implies, is a continuing dropoff in sales and profits. Newer, better replacement products are hitting the market, further price cuts dig into profits, and consumers lose interest in the product. At this point, a company may try to resurrect the product with improved features, simultaneously start a different product at the introduction stage, or—more likely—discontinue the product.

The length of the life cycle varies with the product. A fad like Cabbage Patch Kids may peak early, often around the Christmas season, and drop off within months (see FYI on pages 354 and 355). Other fads may last several years. For example, Radio Shack stores sold an average of forty CB (citizens' band) radios per month in the late 1970s but now sells less than a dozen a month.

On the other hand, a basic product that serves a real need may show constant growth for years. TV dinners, frozen foods, instant coffee, herb teas, and cassette players are examples of innovative products that have survived. It seems unlikely that videodiscs and videotape cassettes will disappear from the market, although, like microwave ovens, they were slow getting started.

## IDENTIFICATION OF PRODUCTS

**Objective 4**

**Product identification by brands, trademarks, and labels.**

When a business develops a product, it wants customers to be able to pick that product out of a group of competitors. Such product identification is usually achieved by using a brand, trademark, or label.

### Brands

A **brand** is a name, term, design, sign, symbol, or combination of these used to

identify a company's products and to distinguish them from competitors' products. Sunkist, Dodge, Coke, Pepsi, Levi's, Calvin Klein, and Pierre Cardin are brand names. The Texaco red star, McDonald's golden arches, Kellogg's Tony the Tiger, and Goodyear's blimp are brand symbols. One reason brands are so important is that they help develop and enhance a product's image. When a particular brand is familiar to you, its appearance has the same effect on you as advertising would.

Another branding policy also exists in business. When a wholesaler or retailer sells and sponsors its own brand, it's called a **private** or **house brand.** Sears, with its private brands such as Allstate, Craftsman, and Kenmore, or Montgomery Ward, with its Riverside brand, may be familiar to you. You may also buy less expensive store brands (such as A&P's Ann Page). Private brands permit such chains to control their marketing effort more closely and to avoid direct product competition with other distributors.

Some retailers are now selling lower-cost **generic products,** slightly lower-quality goods that have no brand name or symbol and only limited black-and-white labeling. Interestingly, consumers seem to move away from generics, in spite of their lower cost, preferring the consistent quality offered by a brand name.

### Trademarks

Brand names and symbols can be registered with the U.S. Patent and Trademark Office as trademarks. A **trademark** is a brand that has been given legal protection so that only its owner has the right to use it. Many firms, therefore, use a trademark or logo, as well as a brand name, to identify their products.

To keep brands and trademarks effective, an owner must register and renew them as required by law. The trademark owner has the right to insist

Back to basics.

# *FYI*

## Cabbage Patch Kids™: Fad or Fancy?

There was a greater than normal element of lunacy about the Christmas selling season of 1983. After two lean recession years, Americans were spending money at a furious pace—literally cleaning out merchandise inventories of popular toys, games, home computers, and other electronic gadgets. The most popular item, however, was distinctly low-tech. It was a simple doll that had no batteries or mechanical features, didn't wet its pants, couldn't even say "Mama," and was marketed under the name of Cabbage Patch Kids™.

on capitalization of the brand name and the use of such symbols as ® and ™. This is especially important in the case of names often used generically, such as Coke, Xerox, Kleenex, and Scotch tape. To prevent such brand names from becoming the name of all makes of the product, the trademark owner must insist that they not be used for other brands of cola drink, copier, facial tissue, or cellophane tape. In 1970, General Brands began advertising Sanka as "Sanka brand" to keep it from becoming the generic term for decaffeinated coffee.

Did you know, for instance, that Ping-Pong and Fiberglas are registered trademarks? In fact, such common words as *aspirin, cellophane, shredded wheat,* and *thermos* were once trademarks. Now they can be used by any company, although Thermos is still a brand name, and Aladdin Industries, Inc. cautiously calls its thermos a "thermo bottle." Johnny Carson, host of NBC's *Tonight Show,* is welcomed with the phrase "Here's Johnny!" The phrase has become so closely identified with him that he's licensed its use by a restaurant and for a line of clothing. When a Troy, Michigan, firm began marketing a portable toilet under the brand name Here's Johnny, Carson sued, charging

A more unlikely hit product would be hard to imagine. The dolls were mass produced, retailed for a modest $25 each, and weren't even pretty—some people called them more than a little ugly. Further, they weren't even produced in the usual manner. Standing the Industrial Revolution on its head, Coleco Industries programmed its computers to make each doll slightly different from all others.

Yet these dolls quickly became not only one of the most successful consumer products in U.S. history, but also a social phenomenon that was earnestly debated by psychologists, sociologists, newspaper writers, and TV commentators. To be the parent of a female child and not to at least try to buy her a Cabbage Patch doll was soon seen as subjecting one's child to a mild form of sensory deprivation. In the face of this unbelievable surge in demand, the legal supply of dolls was quickly exhausted, and a black market sprang to life where the Kids changed hands at exorbitant prices, as high as $1,500.

Several factors lay behind the dolls' unique success. The most important of these was the fact that Cabbage Patch Kids aren't purchased—they are "adopted." The original developer of the idea, Xavier Roberts, set up Babyland General Hospital in Columbus, Georgia, in 1977, where his kids were "born" and then put up for "adoption." Naturally, since no two real infants are identical, no two of these handmade dolls were, either. Roberts's dolls were an immediate success, and six years later Coleco acquired the rights to mass-produce them—and also agreed to keep each one unique.

The entry of Coleco into the Cabbage Patch biography is the stuff of which marketing legends are made. By retaining the adoption procedure and by avoiding standardized manufacture, Coleco was able to create the illusion of "mass-produced individuality." And its advertising was brilliant. Aimed at parents, it instilled the idea that a Cabbage Patch Kid should become a member of the family—that it should be loved and cherished in a way that no mere toy would be. Since the dolls are indeed "cuddly," parents bought the sales pitch.

Unusual social events don't go unreported by the media for long. Once the hunt for the scarce dolls took on a note of frenzy, it became news. And the economics of scarcity mated with the popular fascination with human interest stories to form a potent marketing mix. Cabbage Patch Kids and Santa were in for a memorable Christmas.

Of course, it remains to be seen whether Cabbage Patch dolls will become the Barbie dolls of the 1980s or prove to have been just another Christmas flash in the pan. Coleco and independent entrepreneurs are trying to generate an aura of permanence by launching Cabbage Patch newsletters and "Stork" announcement services.

Source: Prepared for this book by William L. Megginson, Florida State University, from various media sources.

trademark infringement and invasion of privacy and publicity rights. He sought to prevent the use of the phrase as a corporate or product name. His claim was upheld by the Sixth U.S. Circuit Court of Appeals.[4]

### Labels

The purpose of a label on a product or package is to identify the brand and to assist the consumer in making a buying decision. There are many types of labels, but only two—grade labels and universal product code labels—will be discussed here.

A **grade label** specifies the quality level of a good by using words, letters, or numbers. For example, the U.S. Department of Agriculture (USDA) has established five grades for beef: prime, choice, good, standard, and commercial. Eggs are graded by both size and quality, such as Grade A Large.

The **universal product code (UPC)** label (see Figure 13-3) is a bar code used by supermarkets and other stores that have computerized checkout stations with optical sensors. The sensors read these labels as they pass over. This is

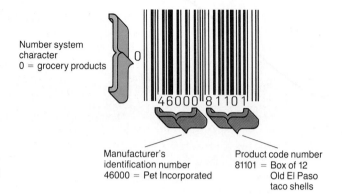

Number system
character
0 = grocery products

Manufacturer's
identification number
46000 = Pet Incorporated

Product code number
81101 = Box of 12
Old El Paso
taco shells

**Figure 13-3** Sample universal product code (UPC) label.

called scanning, and is a fairly new marketing technique that is probably the hottest innovation in retailing today. Well over three-fourths of all supermarket items now have UPC labels. Scanning is changing many marketing concepts and routines, as inventory control, out-of-stock recording, reordering, and checkout activities are taken over by the computer. Some checkout computers even "read" the price of each item aloud.

## PACKAGING

**Objective 5**

**The role played by product packaging.**

**Packaging,** the external presentation of a product, is an essential part of marketing. An appealing package, of the right size, shape, and appearance, will increase sales of even the best product, not to mention a mediocre one; an unappealing package will restrict sales. For instance, one study found that, when faced with more attractive packages, one-third of consumers who bought because of advertising switched products.[5] Packaging can also create an entirely new product from an old one: apple juice and other fruit drinks in foil pouches and cardboard boxes are no different from similar drinks in glass bottles, but the container is a novelty.

Packaging serves many purposes. It may make the product more attractive, thus encouraging purchases. Sales of women's and men's cosmetics, for instance, increase when the shape, color, and design appeal to the buyer. Men's products may come in packages with angular shapes, natural colors, and wooden or rugged textures. Women's products feature rounded shapes, pastel shades, and soft textures.

Packaging also provides convenience. The sale of Campbell's soups and juices increased when the single-serving size was introduced. Disposable aluminum cans, especially when joined by plastic rings into a six-pack, improved sales of soft drinks and juices. More frozen foods are now being packaged in cardboard rather than aluminum for the convenience of microwave oven users.

The product's use may be improved through better packaging. Facial tissues are interleaved so that another tissue pops up when one is removed; aluminum drink cans have pull tabs or foil closures to permit opening without an opener; and other drinks are packaged in bottles with screw-off caps, in foil pouches to be pierced with a straw, or even in cardboard boxes requiring no

refrigeration. Packaging also can prevent damage to the product. One of the key features of the ill-fated Pringle's potato chips was a package that prevented crushing. However, it seems that taste was more important to consumers.

A package may increase safety, too. The danger of breakage in bathrooms and swimming pools was minimized when glass containers were replaced with plastic ones. Many drugs and potentially dangerous household chemicals now have childproof caps to prevent accidental poisoning. Protection is still another function of packaging: after the Tylenol scare (Chapter 2) drug companies began to package in tamperproof containers.

## THE ROLE AND IMPORTANCE OF PRICING

**Objective 6**

**How pricing objectives relate to a company's product decisions and marketing objectives.**

Once a company has developed, branded, packaged, and introduced a product, what should it charge for the product? The price can't be much higher than the market will bear, yet it must be high enough to allow the producer to recoup the costs of production and promotion and to earn a profit. As you saw in Chapter 1, supply and demand interact to establish prices, but in most companies, the question of the right price to charge is more complex than that. Managers can control the supply available, but they can't control demand. Not only should prices *be* fair, but customers should *perceive* the firm's price as fair, or else they won't buy.

## PRICING OBJECTIVES

**Pricing objectives** are the long-term goals a firm hopes to achieve through its pricing policies and procedures. In turn, pricing policies and procedures must help to achieve the pricing, marketing, and overall company objectives. For example, management may state the company's overall objectives as "To become the dominant company in the domestic market for our products." The *marketing* objective then might be "To achieve maximum sales penetration in all sales regions." The overall *pricing* objective might be "To achieve sales maximization." Other, more specific pricing objectives might be "To obtain a 20 percent return on investment before taxes," "To increase current market share," "To be the price leader in our industry," "To meet competition," or "To maximize cash flow."

Pricing objectives aren't always economic; they may set status and prestige goals for the firm's products. For example, the firm making Mercedes-Benz automobiles has declared that its objective is to sell a high-quality, prestige automobile. Therefore, it restricts production volume in order to produce the required quality product. Owners of these cars not only recognize their prestige and status value but also believe that they receive considerable practical value for the high price they pay. One owner of a Mercedes driven over 150,000 miles proudly announced that the car was "just getting broken in" at a point when other cars would long since have "hit the junkheap."

Still, the usual pricing objectives of a firm include (1) generating revenue and profit, (2) balancing supply and demand, and (3) allocating scarce resources.

### Generating Revenue and Profit

The price charged by a firm for its product or service is very important in determining both its revenue and its profit. The situation is complicated, though, because the volume sold depends on the price charged. Furthermore, costs are often affected by volume and hence by prices.

In general,

$$\text{Profit} = \text{Revenue} - \text{Expenses}$$

But total revenue results from the selling price and the quantity sold:

$$\text{Total Revenue} = \text{Price} \times \text{Quantity Sold}$$

Therefore, profits can be increased by raising price, increasing the volume sold, or some combination of both.

One difficulty with price is that its rules sometimes work in reverse. In some special situations, the volume sold may increase as the price increases. For example, a retailer found some high-quality linen tablecloths that gave her a substantial profit when priced at $10 each. However, customers, perhaps suspicious of what seemed to be too much of a bargain, didn't buy them. So she stored the tablecloths for a month and then returned them to the shelves at $40 each—which may have seemed a more reasonable price—and soon sold out.

Pricing tended to be neglected by manufacturers of consumer goods during the prosperous 1970s. But, with the 1981–1982 recession, many consumer-goods firms made price cuts in order to increase sales. This action had been almost unheard of among packaged-goods marketers. Their prior sales practice had been "cents-off" coupons, bigger advertising budgets, sweepstakes, refunds, temporary price discounts, or minor product changes resulting in claims that brands were "new and improved." Not any more. "We're paying a lot more attention to price now," said the marketing director for one firm. "It's a tool that's been neglected." For example, leading consumer-products marketers, such as Procter & Gamble, Kellogg, Coca-Cola, Scott Paper, Mobil, Union Carbide, and Lever Brothers, have all cut their prices on certain brands.[6]

### Balancing Supply and Demand

As shown in Chapter 1, prices serve to bring about a proper balance between the demand for a product and the company's ability to produce it. But, when there's high unemployment and falling family incomes, price cuts become more important as a means of increasing the demand for growing supplies of goods and services. This is especially true of necessities like food, an area where no-frills products and stores are growing.

Nonexistent in 1977, no-frills operations had captured about 5 percent of the $200 billion grocery market by the early 1980s.[7] They did this by selling generic (nonbrand) products or large volumes of a limited selection of national products and by reducing services—eliminating elaborate shelf displays, bagging and carryout, check cashing and credit card use, and, in some cases, individual pricing of items. Following their lead, other large chains, such as Grand Union, have reduced the variety offered and are concentrating on volume sales. Optical scanners permit elimination of individual item pricing as consumer acceptance of the practice grows.

Price also determines who a firm's customers will be. Some firms, such as prestigious jewelry and clothing stores, deliberately use high prices to attract a certain clientele. For example, Levi Strauss Canada, Inc. is issuing a limited edition of Levi 555s at a higher price than its regular 555s. It's producing only 30,000 to 50,000 of them, and each one will have a small copper plate on the rear pocket with a five-digit serial number. The buyers will receive a certificate documenting their ownership.[8]

Conversely, a low price may result in an undesirable clientele. The owner of a tavern in a college town dropped the price of a pitcher of beer to one dollar. The reduction attracted not students, as expected, but street people.

Price affects the amount of promotion a firm can afford. Higher prices make more money available for promotion.

---

Which of these pricing policies do you think would sell more Bayer aspirin? (1) Reducing the product's price by 50 percent and cutting the budget for promotional efforts by an equivalent amount, or (2) maintaining the current price and continuing the present high level of promotion.

---

The second policy is the one preferred by Bayer's management.

### Allocating Scarce Resources

In a free-enterprise system, price allocates scarce resources. Resources are attracted to industries and firms where relatively high prices and profits are found. Price encourages the production of goods society wants and discourages those it doesn't want. For example, if society wants more petroleum and petroleum-based products, it must be willing to pay dearly for them—at least in the short run. In early 1981, President Reagan lifted federal controls on the price of gasoline and let it find its natural level. After rising about $0.10 a gallon, prices stabilized. After adequate supplies became available, prices declined so that by late 1983 they were about $0.25 to $0.35 below the regulated price.

## DETERMINING PRICES

**Objective 7**
**How prices are determined.**

The five most frequently used approaches to determining prices are (1) supply and demand pricing, (2) markup pricing, (3) breakeven point analysis, (4) the market approach, and (5) price leadership.

### Supply and Demand Pricing

In Chapter 1, you learned that price is set by supply and demand. Therefore, the **equilibrium price** is that price at which the amount of a product demanded just equals the available supply of that product.

Managers rarely use this theory for determining price, for many reasons. First, individual firms have little control over prices because of the actions of others. Second, most firms seek only a satisfactory profit, not the maximum profit. Third, the real world is too complex for managers to apply the theory in actual practice.

### Markup Pricing

In markup pricing one takes the cost figure for an item and adds a fixed percentage markup to it to find the selling price. Therefore, the **markup** is the difference between the cost of an item and its selling price. It must cover the cost of selling the item plus a profit for the risks taken.

Most retailers use this approach. They take the invoice cost of a product and add a markup percentage to it to find the price. The **markup percentage** is found by dividing the amount of the markup by what it cost to buy the product. The formula for this percentage is:

$$\text{Markup percentage} = \frac{\text{Amount added to } cost \text{ (markup)}}{\text{Cost of production}}$$

Thus, if an item costs the retailer $4.00 and sells for $5.00, its markup is $1.00/$4.00, or 25 percent.

Figure 13-4 shows how automobile dealers compute their sticker (sales) prices using the markup approach. They add their desired markup percentage (22 percent) to the cost of the automobile from corporate headquarters ($6,296) and get a markup of $1,385, which is added to the cost to get the sticker price of $7,681.

### Breakeven Point Analysis

Breakeven point analysis involves computing the **breakeven point,** which is the level of sales, at a given price, that will cover the total fixed and variable

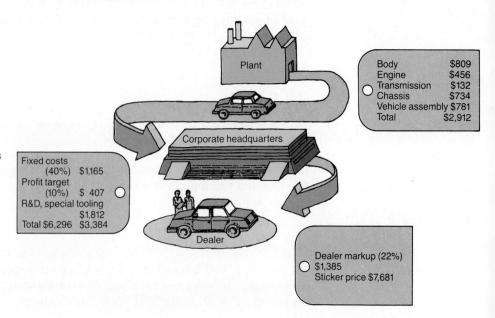

**Figure 13-4** How a small car's price grows from the assembly line to the showroom.

**TABLE 13-1  Breakeven point (BEP) analysis for a hypothetical product.**

| | A<br>Volume | B<br>Fixed Cost | C<br>Variable<br>Cost<br>(A × $5) | D<br>Total Cost<br>(B + C) | E<br>Total<br>Revenue<br>(A × $15) |
|---|---|---|---|---|---|
| | 1,000 | $40,000 | $ 5,000 | $45,000 | $15,000 |
| | 2,000 | 40,000 | 10,000 | 50,000 | 30,000 |
| | 3,000 | 40,000 | 15,000 | 55,000 | 45,000 |
| BEP | 4,000 | 40,000 | 20,000 | 60,000 | 60,000 |
| | 5,000 | 40,000 | 25,000 | 65,000 | 75,000 |
| | 6,000 | 40,000 | 30,000 | 70,000 | 90,000 |

costs. **Fixed costs** are those that remain the same regardless of the amount of production, such as property taxes. **Variable costs** are those that increase directly as production increases, such as materials or parts. The breakeven point is the minimum sales volume the seller needs to keep from suffering a loss. Sales above that point will provide a profit, and sales below that point will result in a loss. Table 13-1 shows how the breakeven point (BEP) was determined in this hypothetical case, where the total fixed costs of producing a product are $40,000, the variable costs equal $5 per unit, and the sales price is $15 per unit.

### The Market Approach

While the above and other rational approaches can be used to set prices, they rarely are. Instead, many other social, psychological, cultural, and political factors, as well as whim or chance, influence pricing. Under this type of pricing, called the **market approach,** a company sets its prices in terms of the current market prices for similar products or services. Some frequently purchased convenience goods, such as candy bars and soft drinks, have a low unit price that is set by market conditions. These prices are frequently related to "what the market will bear"; that is, the price charged is as high a price as customers are willing—and able—to pay. When there is no regulation by government, trade unions, or trade associations, other types of firms also use this approach.

Prices may also result from **price leadership,** which exists when all the firms in an industry follow the pricing practices of one dominant company. When the market leader increases or decreases prices, the followers immediately react in the same way. For many years, U.S. Steel was the leader in the iron and steel industry, but foreign competition has lessened its influence.

## PRICING POLICIES

**Objective 8**

**Various pricing policies used by business firms.**

The purpose of pricing policies is to have consistent and uniform pricing decisions throughout a company. Some of the most popular pricing policies are (1) high, competitive, or low pricing, (2) skimming or penetration pricing for new products, (3) odd pricing, (4) price lining, and (5) discount policies.

### High, Competitive, or Low Prices?

Depending on its target markets, a firm may select a high-price, a competitive-price, or a low-price policy. If it's attempting to appeal to the prestige market with a high-quality product, it will charge a high price. Tiffany & Company, Saks Fifth Avenue, and Neiman-Marcus are examples of retailers who have a high-price policy. National retailers such as Sears, J. C. Penney, and Montgomery Ward usually try to appeal to customers with lower-middle, middle, and upper-middle incomes and price their products competitively. On the other hand, discount department stores like K mart and Zayre appeal to the mass market by charging low prices for their products.

### Skimming or Penetration Pricing?

The pricing of new products is difficult and risky, and it's difficult to change prices during the introduction stage of the product life cycle. Consequently, many new products or packages are test-marketed in restricted areas that are representative of national or regional markets.

The two alternative strategies that may be used in pricing these products are (1) a skimming pricing policy and (2) a penetration pricing policy.

Under a **skimming pricing** policy, a new product is priced relatively high in comparison to substitute products in order to allow the company to make quick, high profits—that is, to skim off the top of the market. Then the price is gradually lowered in the face of competition. Du Pont followed a skimming policy in pricing its synthetic materials such as Dacron and Qiana relatively high in the beginning.[9]

Under a **penetration pricing** policy, a new product is priced low in comparison to substitute products in order to allow the company to achieve broad market acceptance and gain a large market share. In using the penetration policy, management hopes that brand acceptance will allow for increasing prices later. Health and beauty aids, such as hair conditioners, soaps, and toothpastes, are familiar examples of products to which this policy is applied. They are frequently available in small trial sizes, and sometimes free samples are mailed or distributed to homes.

A variation on penetration pricing is **extinction pricing,** which is used to wipe out competition. It involves pricing the new product far below cost in order to eliminate independent or weak competitors. Once these are disposed of, the firm raises its prices to normal levels.

### Odd Pricing

In **odd pricing,** sellers set the price at some odd amount, such as $3.97, $49.98, or $99.99. Some retailers believe that a price like $3.97 is more appealing because it makes the prospective customer think of three dollars and some cents instead of a price only slightly under four dollars. Gasoline is still priced this way, even though dropping the tenths of a cent would have eliminated the need to retool pumps and the confusion of half-gallon pricing when prices first went over a dollar a gallon.

### Price Lining

In **price lining,** sellers set the prices of their goods around a few specific pricing points instead of pricing each item individually. Thus a store may have a line

# Business Debate

## Should There Be Discounts for Cash Payment?

A large share of spending by consumers is paid for with credit cards instead of currency and checks. When you make a purchase with a credit card, the company issuing the card pays the seller 94 to 95 percent of the total charge and bills you for the full amount of the purchase. Some people feel that this is unfair to those who pay cash, since they wind up paying the cost of credit for those who use credit cards. Therefore, they argue, customers who pay cash should pay a lower price than those who use credit cards.

The arguments *for* this practice are that:

1. Most cash buyers are deceived in that they're unaware that they're really paying more than credit-card buyers for purchases.
2. Cash customers subsidize the convenience that credit-card customers enjoy because, while credit customers end up paying the same amount, they're able to use their money longer than the cash customer and can even earn interest on that money.

3. When customers pay cash, the seller gets immediate possession and use of the money, instead of having to wait to be paid by the credit-card company.

The arguments *against* this system are that:

1. The U.S. economy is based on buying on credit, so it's appropriate that people be discouraged from paying with cash.
2. People pay cash because for them it's the best way to manage their finances. For instance, buyers who only use cash probably won't be as impulsive with their shopping as a credit card user who doesn't have to hand over the hard cash.
3. Having more people pay with cash would be a disadvantage to retailers, since having a large amount of cash on hand encourages robberies. Also, it's more trouble to process and store cash at the end of the day than to process and store credit-card receipts.

*What do you think?*

---

of similar suits for $60, others for $80, and still others for $100. Similarly, a department store may have a sale of kitchen gadgets, all priced at 88¢, or a grocery store may sell produce by the piece instead of by weight. Those who follow price lining believe that it simplifies customer buying decisions by giving them a limited number of prices to choose from. It is also easier for clerks and cashiers who have to deal with a great variety of items.

When customers have to choose among many different models of an appliance, they can easily become confused. When there are only three distinct models, and their prices are easily accounted for by the pronounced difference in features (as is the case with Sears' Good, Better, and Best lines), customers can compare them and make a decision more easily.

## Discounts

A **discount** is a reduction in price offered by a seller to a buyer. The types of discount frequently used are (1) trade, (2) quantity, (3) cash, (4) seasonal, and (5) loss leader.

A **trade discount** is offered by a producer to an intermediary, as compensation for selling, transporting, and processing goods.

A **quantity discount** is given to buyers who order large quantities of goods. Generally, the seller's storage, shipping, and billing costs per unit are decreased by the larger sales order.

A **cash discount** is offered by the seller to encourage customers who pay their bills early or use cash instead of credit cards (see the Business Debate on page 363).

A **seasonal discount** is sometimes given on seasonal products if they're bought out of season. The major reason for such discounts is to spread out sales into those months when business is slow. Products frequently sold at seasonal discounts are cards, gift wrappings, and decorations after Christmas; winter clothing in February; and swimsuits in August.

Some retailers use **loss leaders,** where the price of the product is set very low—even below cost—to attract customers into the store. They hope the customers will then buy other, more profitable items. Supermarkets use this practice in their weekly ads. An unethical variation of this method is the **bait-and-switch** technique, where an item is advertised at a low price and then the customer thus lured to the store is pressured into buying a different, more expensive item. You may be familiar with the practice of firms that advertise photographic portraits at a very attractive price, such as 88¢ for an 8 × 10. This is a good deal if you can confine yourself to just that one picture, but you'll have to have very strong sales resistance to withstand the pressure to buy other sizes and poses at much higher prices—very difficult if they're pictures of your own child.

## ⏶ LEARNING OBJECTIVES REVISITED

1. *The classification of products as durable or nondurable goods and consumer or industrial goods.*

   Durable goods have traits and uses that permit them to last a relatively long time, while nondurables have traits that result in their being used only once or a very few times. Durable goods can also be classified as either consumer or industrial goods. Consumer goods are used by the consumer who buys them and require no further industrial or commercial processing. They are subdivided into convenience goods, shopping goods, and specialty goods. Industrial goods are used by businesses to produce other goods or to provide services.

2. *How new products are developed.*

   The development of new products is vital in the marketing programs of many companies. Since only one in seven new products is successful, a market analysis of the probable demand for a new product is essential for success. The Japanese have very effectively used the new marketing approach, which involves monitoring customer needs, assessing how the company can satisfy those needs with available resources, and then producing and marketing the desired products efficiently.

3. *The stages in a product's life cycle.*

The product life cycle is a sequence of introduction, growth, maturity, and decline in sales and profits. All products go through this cycle—from their initial appearance to their disappearance. Different marketing strategies are required for products at different life cycle stages.

4. *Product identification by brands, trademarks, and labels.*

A brand is a name or symbol used to identify the products of a manufacturer and to distinguish them from competitors' products. Brands are important because they help develop and enhance a product's image. A trademark is a legally protected brand name or symbol. The purpose of a label is to identify the brand and to assist consumers in making a buying decision.

5. *The role played by product packaging.*

Packaging involves giving a product a size, shape, and appearance that will please customers and increase sales. Packaging provides attractiveness, convenience, safety, protection, and sometimes the illusion of a new product.

6. *How pricing objectives relate to a company's product decisions and marketing objectives.*

The price of a product or service must be high enough to cover costs but no higher than the market will bear. The usual pricing objectives are generating revenue and profit, balancing supply and demand, and allocating scarce resources.

7. *How prices are determined.*

Some approaches that are used in pricing decisions are using supply and demand to find the equilibrium price, applying a markup to an item's cost, computing the breakeven point, and following the market approach, which relates prices to current market prices for similar goods or services.

8. *Various pricing policies used by business firms.*

Some of the pricing policies that are used are high, competitive, or low pricing; skimming or penetration pricing for new products; odd pricing; price lining; and discount policies.

## ⬛ IMPORTANT TERMS

As an extra review of the chapter, try defining the following terms. If you have trouble with any of them, refer to the page listed.

## REVIEW QUESTIONS

1. What is the difference between tangible and intangible goods?
2. What is the difference between consumer and industrial goods?
3. Name four different types of consumer goods.
4. Describe each stage of the product life cycle and its effects on sales and profits.
5. List three reasons why brands and trademarks are so important.
6. What roles does packaging play in marketing a product?
7. How do pricing objectives fit into the firm's hierarchy of objectives?
8. How would you distinguish (a) markup and market approaches to determining prices?  (b) skimming and penetration pricing?
9. List the most important approaches used in determining prices.
10. What are some examples of (a) odd pricing?  (b) price lining?  (c) seasonal discounts?

## DISCUSSION QUESTIONS

1. Is it correct to label intangible goods as *goods*?  Why or why not?
2. Is a typewriter in a stationery store a consumer good or an industrial good?  Explain.
3. Classify each of the following as a convenience, shopping, or specialty good.  If your answer is more than one classification, explain why.
   a. Haagen-Dasz ice cream.
   b. A $24.95 pocket calculator.
   c. Designer jeans.
   d. A disposable toothbrush.
   e. The Prince tennis racquet.
   f. Godiva chocolates.
   g. A home videocassette player.
   h. An Apple IIe microcomputer.
4. Do you think the product life cycle will continue to be relevant to marketing, or will it become antiquated?  Defend your answer.
5. What is the difference between a brand and a trademark?
6. Will branded products continue to be important, or will generic products replace them?
7. Will the universal product code label be used to a greater or lesser extent? Explain your answer.

8. How would you package Gerber products differently to appeal more to teenagers?

9. Is the law of supply and demand dead as far as pricing is concerned? Explain.

10. How do prices act to allocate scarce resources?

11. Do you think most retailers use one of the rational approaches to setting prices, or do they use the "what the market will bear" approach?

12. Should cash customers receive a special discount? Why or why not?

## ⏚ CASE 13-1    Component TV: New Twist for a Mature Product

A "new product" was unveiled at the Consumer Electronics Show in Chicago in 1982—component TV. And Sears had a component TV with videocassette recorder in its *1982 Christmas Book*.

TV set makers are breaking the standard receiver into separate parts to be purchased and used individually, like the now-common component stereo systems with their separate tuner, amplifier, turntable, tape deck, and speakers. Adding a separate TV monitor and a control device to a TV set will permit family members to watch a regular program and use a computer, watch a recorded tape or disc, or play video games whenever they want. Other advantages are a sharper, clearer picture and improved sound from better speakers. The systems won't be cheap, though. A good monitor and tuner control will cost more than a comparable TV set.

There are several marketing problems involved with this new product. One thing to consider is how to price each of the components: should there be a separate price for each component or a "package" price for the entire group of components? Another question is whether to make the components in basic colors or with the same furniture-like finish as regular TV cabinets. If colors are used, should one color be used for all the components, or should matched colors be used? If colors are used, will retailers have to carry enough colors of each component to harmonize with their various customers' decors? Finally, should the manufacturers start from scratch to produce all-new components, or should they build incremental components to be added to existing sets?

### Case Question

1. How would you answer these questions if you were the marketing manager of a producer, such as RCA, Zenith, or Magnavox?

## ⏚ CASE 13-2    The Selling of *Annie*

The Broadway musical hit *Annie* was made into a big-screen movie by Columbia Pictures, at a cost of $50 million. It was released in mid-June 1982 and opened in movie houses throughout the country.

Before its release, Columbia had used almost every conceivable promotional technique to publicize the picture. TV commercials, a one-hour documentary on public TV stations, special screenings for listeners of more than 100 rock stations, an *Annie*-related college tour, and licensing of around 250 *Annie* items were used to "sell" the movie. Yet crowds stayed away from the theaters in droves, and the film was a financial failure. It grossed only $32 million. The critics almost unanimously panned it, saying that the movie was a poor copy of the stage play. At the time the movie came out, several live road shows of the play were touring the nation and it was still playing on Broadway.

### Case Questions

1. Why do you think the movie was a failure?
2. What role did supply and demand play?
3. Can sales promotion overcome a poor product? Explain.

# 14

# Promoting, Advertising, and Selling

*He who whispers down a well*
*About the goods he has to sell*
*Will never reap the golden dollars*
*Like him who shows them round and hollers.*

Quoted by the Prince of Wales (later Duke of Windsor)

*One saying I have always tried to remember in*
*retailing is "You can't do business from an empty*
*wagon." Another I have added is "If you ever stop*
*telling, then you'll stop selling."*

Jeane D. Byrd, toy retailer

**Learning Objectives**

After studying the material in this chapter, you will understand:

1. The objectives of promotion and the importance of choosing the right promotion mix.
2. The differences between product and institutional advertising.
3. The advantages and disadvantages of different advertising media.
4. Public attitudes toward advertising.
5. The types and process of personal selling.
6. Some different kinds of sales promotion.
7. How publicity differs from other forms of promotion.

**In This Chapter**

Developing a Promotional Strategy
Advertising
Personal Selling
Sales Promotion
Publicity

# 7UP
*No Caffeine, Artificial Flavor, or Artificial Color*

"No Caffeine, No Artificial Color, No Artificial Flavor. No wonder 7UP has a clean, refreshing, unspoiled taste," claimed the double-page ads in national magazines and commercials on TV. With this advertising campaign, the Seven-Up Company, a subsidiary of Philip Morris, Inc., started another raging controversy among its competitors in the soft-drink industry. The campaign was based on research that found that the public was concerned about ingredients in foods and beverages. The ads show that other drinks have artificial colors and flavors that might be harmful to customers' health. They imply that people should drink 7UP because it is less harmful to them. The company hopes the ad campaign will result in a profit—for the first time since 1979.

This ad campaign followed by less than one year a similar no-caffeine campaign in 1982 that turned caffeine-free soda into a national craze. The 1982 campaign not only raised the Seven-Up Company's sales of 7UP and Diet 7UP but also increased its market share by 0.4 percent to 6.5 percent in 1983, breaking a six-year market share slide. Also, its giant competitors, PepsiCo and Coca-Cola, as well as Dr Pepper, introduced decaffeinated brands shortly after 7UP's no-caffeine campaign. They'll have a hard time imitating the "no artificial color" claim, though, for their cola products contain caramel coloring.

Seven-Up advertising executives claim the new ads—which saturated television from May 25 through July 4, 1983—are primarily designed only to make consumers aware of brand differences, for they even include Like, which is Seven-Up's recently introduced artificially flavored and colored, but caffeine-free, cola drink. Then it's up to informed consumers to make their own decision. Included in the campaign are direct-mail solicitations to health officials and local school authorities.

The magazine and newspaper ads invite consumers to write to the company for coupons worth one dollar off on their next purchase of 7UP or Diet 7UP, along with "more information on ingredients in all soft drinks." The TV ads featured Geoffrey Holder, the mellow-voiced actor who appeared for several years in 7UP's "uncola" and no-caffeine ads.

Needless to say, competitors cried foul, as they had with the no-caffeine ads. Dr Pepper suggested that the ads were untrue, as 7UP did have two artificial ingredients—citric acid and sodium citrate. Coke called the ads "false, misleading and detrimental to the soft-drink industry." It also wrote its bottlers that it would soon begin a marketing program for Sprite, its lemon-lime competitor to 7UP, that would "communicate positively and aggressively" about the product. Canada Dry wrote the three major television networks to protest the ads, which it said were "deceptive to the consumer." Seven-Up officials call the complaints "sour grapes."

369

When an ad campaign like 7UP's makes such a success of a product, promotion—the third P in the marketing mix—is responsible. Once a producer has decided what product to sell, what price to charge for it, and through which channels to distribute it, potential customers must be told that it's available. This final activity is probably the most important and familiar part of marketing, since a product's chances of success depend on customers' knowing about it. **Promotion,** then, is the process of informing, persuading, and influencing customers in their decisions about purchasing products or services.

## DEVELOPING A PROMOTIONAL STRATEGY

**Objective 1**

The objectives of promotion and the importance of choosing the right promotion mix.

In developing a promotional strategy for a product or service, managers usually decide on the purposes of promoting it, select the methods to be used in promoting it, and choose exactly what promotion mix of those methods will be used. Figure 14-1 shows the relationship of the promotional strategy to the consumer and the target market, both of which were discussed in previous chapters.

The general objective of promotion is to reinforce existing consumer behavior or to change it. Either way, the goal can be met by stimulating the demand for goods or services. Specifically, promotion involves providing useful information, increasing sales, and stabilizing sales.

There are many ways of promoting goods or services. The ones most frequently used are advertising, personal selling, sales promotion, and publicity. Managers must determine the **promotion mix,** or the best combination of these promotional methods, since it isn't wise to use any single method by itself. Important decisions must be made about the extent to which the company is going to emphasize advertising, use personal selling, rely on sales promotion, or try to get free publicity. All these decisions are based on the nature of the product, the target market, and available funds.

For example, producers of consumer goods who are trying to sell to a mass market will probably try to stimulate consumer demand through advertising

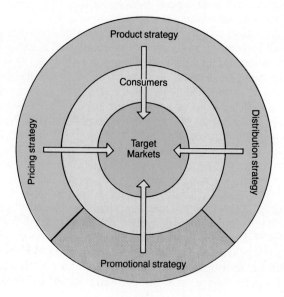

**Figure 14-1** How promotion fits into the marketing mix.

and sales promotion, if they have sufficient funds. This was the mix used by Johnson & Johnson (J&J) when it introduced Tylenol as a consumer product, especially after competition entered the field in 1975. On the other hand, a producer of industrial goods being sold to a specialized market will very likely use more personal selling and sales promotion. This was the mix used by J&J when Tylenol was a prescription drug. Its salespeople called on physicians to give them literature and free samples.

In some situations, and under unusual circumstances, several or all promotion methods will be used. After the Tylenol poisoning disaster, J&J used an all-out blitz of advertising, personal selling (calling on physicians and pharmacists), sales promotion (coupons in newspapers), and publicity (news conferences and TV appearances) to introduce the newly packaged Tylenol.

## ADVERTISING

**Advertising,** which is any paid form of nonpersonal sales or promotion, usually directed toward a large number of possible customers, is big business in the United States. For example, annual advertising expenditures in most years average about 1 percent of sales, and for some products the figure is even higher.

Companies are willing to put so much into advertising budgets because it usually pays off in sales. In early 1981, RCA gave a glittering closed-circuit television presentation to some 5,000 dealers meeting in seventy-four locations around the country. As the guests were being wined and dined, RCA announced its SelectaVision Videodisc, which was being launched with a $22 million advertising and promotion campaign.[1] Unfortunately, in this case the product's sales figures hardly paid for its debut, and its production was halted in early 1984.

**Objective 2**

**The differences between product and institutional advertising.**

There are many types of advertising, but in general they can be categorized as product and institutional advertising. **Product advertising** is the nonpersonal selling of specific products or services. **Institutional advertising** is used to develop goodwill for a company, industry, or other organization.

### Product Advertising

Product advertising, which describes the product's good qualities and price, varies from one situation to another. In general, it tries (1) to stimulate an interest in and desire for certain goods, especially new products, or (2) to influence consumers to buy a particular brand. The advertiser may use mass advertising to appeal to a broad cross-section of the population or direct the ad to special groups of people, such as college students, homeowners, or mothers of infants. In general, the nature of the product or service determines the way it's advertised—if at all. A good example of products that aren't advertised to the mass market is school and stationery supplies. The makers of pencils, notebook paper, and the like rely on personal selling to persuade store owners or managers and distributors to carry only their line.

Product advertising is so popular today that we have come to associate the characters in ads with their product. Morris the cat, much mourned at his death, is still synonymous with Nine Lives cat food, Mr. Whipple with Charmin toilet tissue, Kellogg's Tony the Tiger with Frosted Flakes, Mrs. Olsen with Folger's coffee, and Brooke Shields with Calvin Klein jeans.

Product advertising.

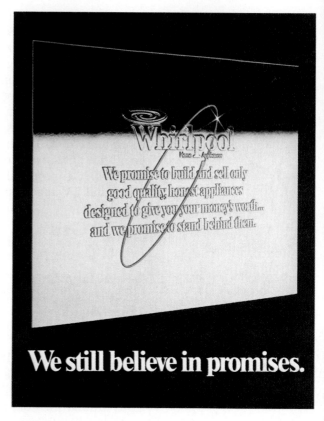

Institutional advertising.

Some ads promote specific features of the product ("Rolaids spells relief"). Others merely claim that the product is "new and improved" (detergents and cleaning agents). Still others try to develop a certain atmosphere around the product or to associate it with desirable traits. Some claim benefits that are totally unrelated to the product in order to expand the market. (For example, Listerine's claim that it helped cure colds and sore throats had to be dropped.) What all of them have in common is influencing your buying decisions.

## Product Life Cycle and Advertising

As products go through their life cycle (see Chapter 13), their advertising varies, too. **Informational advertising,** which tells what the product is or does, is used in the *introduction* stage. This is the type of advertising Kodak used in making its disc camera familiar to sellers and buyers.

**Persuasive advertising,** which tries to improve the product's competitive edge, is used during the *growth* and *early maturity* stages. At that point, the customer has to be coaxed away from the competition more aggressively, through offers of free extras or through direct attacks on other brands.

Comparative advertising—a form of persuasive advertising—can be brought in at this point. In **comparative advertising,** two or more products—mentioned by name—are compared in terms of quality. Only 14 percent of the commercials on ABC television were of this type in 1979, but in 1981, 23

percent were.[2] This form of advertising is now causing a furor in advertising circles—and the courts. Before, ads referred to rivals with a whitewashed "Brand X" or "other leading brands" or ignored them completely, because TV networks and industry regulatory codes prohibited naming competitors. Now, the manufacturers of the products being criticized are challenging the offending ads by filing complaints with the radio or television network that played them or in the courts. In 1980, ABC received 131 challenges to these ads and upheld 30 percent of them.

Notice how 7UP's competitors challenged its ads in the opening case. In still another famous case, Burger King ads claimed that Burger King's Whopper, which is broiled, was found to taste better than McDonald's and Wendy's fried burgers. What's more, the Whopper was supposed to be bigger. Both McDonald's and Wendy's sued, unsuccessfully, to stop the ads.[3] And Burger King's sales increased 16 percent the next year, as compared to only 5 percent for McDonald's and the industry.[4]

**Reminder advertising,** which attempts to keep the product's name before the public, is used to rejuvenate the product during later stages of its life cycle, as for the old Bell System and Whitman's Sampler. Hershey Foods' chocolate products were so well entrenched through personal selling and other promotional strategies that advertising wasn't used until Hershey began to lose business to other chocolate firms that did advertise extensively. Of course, not all products follow this pattern. As shown in Table 14-1, Coca-Cola kicked off one of the most expensive ad campaigns in history to change the theme of its hundred-year-old product.

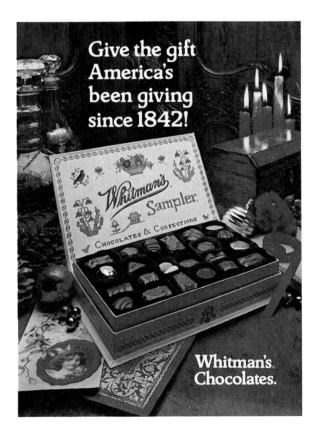

Reminder advertising.

## TABLE 14-1 Some of Coca-Cola's ad themes through the years.

| | |
|---|---|
| 1886 | Drink Coca-Cola |
| 1905 | Coca-Cola revives and sustains |
| 1906 | The Great National Temperance Beverage |
| 1922 | Thirst knows no season |
| 1925 | Six million a day |
| 1927 | Around the corner from everywhere |
| 1929 | The pause that refreshes |
| 1938 | The best friend thirst ever had |
| 1948 | Where there's Coke there's hospitality |
| 1949 | Along the highway to anywhere |
| 1952 | What you want is a Coke |
| 1956 | Makes good things taste better |
| 1957 | Sign of good taste |
| 1958 | The cold, crisp taste of Coke |
| 1963 | Things go better with Coke |
| 1970 | It's the real thing |
| 1971 | I'd like to buy the world a Coke |
| 1975 | Look up, America |
| 1976 | Coke adds life |
| 1979 | Have a Coke and a smile |
| 1982 | Coke is it |

SOURCE: From John Huey, "Lots of Hoopla About Three Little Words as Coca-Cola Kicks Off New Ad Campaign," *The Wall Street Journal*, February 5, 1982, p. 29. Adapted by permission of *The Wall Street Journal*, © Dow Jones & Company, Inc. 1982. All Rights Reserved.

### Institutional Advertising

Institutional advertising is used to create a favorable impression or goodwill for a business or industry in general. It may be used to better identify the company or to improve its image. For example, when a survey showed that 60 percent of respondents confused ITT with AT&T, ITT launched a $10 million per year ad campaign to change its image.[5] In turn, when AT&T was forced to shed its twenty-two operating companies, it wanted to retain the Bell name for its marketing subsidiary, American Bell. But, after it had spent $30 million on splashy TV and print ads to publicize the new American Bell name and symbol, the presiding judge ruled that the Bell name was to be reserved for the local and regional companies. AT&T then spent another $30 million to erase the Bell name from buildings, business cards, trucks, and signs and replace it with the globe-shaped AT&T logo.

Institutional advertising is also used to counteract negative publicity or consumer reaction. The energy crisis of the 1970s resulted in unfavorable publicity for oil companies. Most of them began to use institutional advertising to stress the benefits they provided. Mobil bought full-page ads to emphasize its environmental protection efforts. Texaco even went so far as to point out that many of its owners were widows and orphans. (See FYI on p. 375 for Shell's strategy.) Similarly, so many consumers have been cutting down on caffeine that the National Coffee Association has presented upbeat television spots featuring celebrities claiming that coffee "lets you calm down and picks you up."

*FYI*

## Come to Shell for Answers

An excellent example of institutional advertising is the "Come to Shell for answers" advertising program, with its Shell Answer Books. The objectives of this program are to:

1. Enhance Shell's reputation for responsible behavior.
2. Contribute to the credibility of its representatives and public statements.
3. Support the reputation for excellence of Shell products, services, and people.
4. Favorably differentiate Shell from the other major oil companies.

Shell's strategy was to demonstrate its social responsibility by providing useful consumer information in its areas of expertise. Its most obvious area of expertise was gasoline and automobiles, though some of the Answer Books have expanded Shell's image as an energy company by discussing energy efficiency in homes.

Shell Answer Books have appeared as inserts in most of the popular magazines. Television commercials are constructed around the tips contained in the books. Booklets are also distributed through Shell dealers and have been used as a permanent part of the driver education curricula in five states. By 1983, over thirty different booklets were being distributed.

Shell's management has been gratified by the results of the program. In early 1980, Shell had the highest consumer awareness of any oil company, and people believed that Shell did more than other oil companies to help its customers.

Source: The description of the "Come to Shell for Answers" program was developed from materials provided by the Corporate Advertising division of the Public Relations Department of Shell Oil Company.

## Advertising Media

**Objective 3**

The advantages and disadvantages of different advertising media.

In 1982, around $61 billion was spent on advertising in the United States, and in 1983, the figure was estimated to be $75 billion. Figure 14-2 shows how some of the 1982 money was divided among the **advertising media,** which are the different means, devices, or vehicles through which advertisers reach their audience. A brief evaluation of each of these media is presented below, with more details in Table 14-2.

▲ **Newspapers** In the United States newspapers are the medium that receives by far the largest number of advertising dollars. Both local and regional daily newspaper advertising is very important, as newspapers provide wide coverage at a reasonable cost. Also, changes in text and format can be made quickly and

Creating a favorable impression.

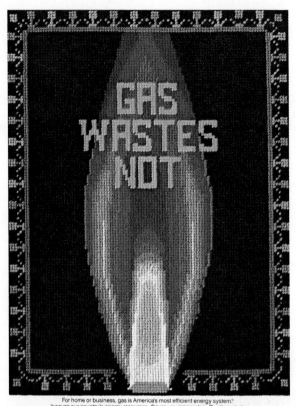

easily. *USA Today*, the first truly national newspaper, sprang to life in living color on September 15, 1982. It's been well received (1.1 million daily circulation and 750 national advertisers), and its ad sales, which have been disappointing, are expected to improve soon.[6] Weekly newspapers are also growing in popularity as an advertising medium, especially for small businesses. One daily paper, the *Chicago Daily News*, was forced out of business by the intense competition of the weeklies in its area.

▲ **Television** Although television advertising is one of the newest forms of advertising, it's also the fastest-growing one. Television is the most pervasive

**Figure 14-2** Percentage of advertising expenditures in the United States, classified by media used. (Based on data from *Statistical Abstract of The United States, 1982–1983* (Washington, D.C.: U.S. Government Printing Office, December 1982), p. 566.

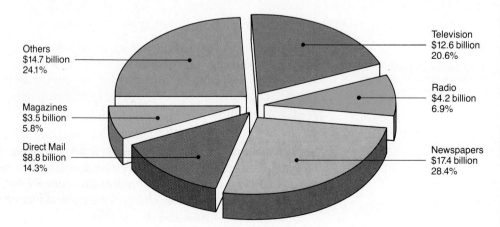

Others
$14.7 billion
24.1%

Magazines
$3.5 billion
5.8%

Direct Mail
$8.8 billion
14.3%

Television
$12.6 billion
20.6%

Radio
$4.2 billion
6.9%

Newspapers
$17.4 billion
28.4%

**TABLE 14-2  Profile of major advertising media, 1982.**

| Medium | Volume in $Billions | Percentage of Total Volume | Advantages | Disadvantages |
|---|---|---|---|---|
| Newspapers | $17.4 | 28.4 | Wide coverage. Short time lag from when ad is ordered to when it runs. Changes can be made quickly. | Short life; hasty reading. Lack creative, "eye-grabbing" appeal. Poor color reproduction. Ads compete with news, sports, comics, and other features. |
| Television | 12.6 | 20.6 | Ads available in almost all homes. Appeals to two senses— sight and sound. Flexibility permits advertising in different areas simultaneously | Cost. Time required to prepare and change ads. Ads presented so fleetingly that they may not be noticed or recalled unless very dramatic. |
| Magazines | 3.5 | 5.8 | Can have specialized market. Remain in home or office for some time. Can have attractive art, layout, and color reproduction. | Relatively inflexible. Material must be planned months in advance and often published weeks in advance. Cost. |
| Direct mail | 8.8 | 14.3 | Rapid preparation and delivery. Easy to change. Can saturate a specific area. Ads can be kept and referred to later. | Difficulty of keeping mailing list current. Can be costly unless trying for mass market. Consumer resistance to junk mail. |
| Radio | 4.2 | 6.9 | Low cost. More accessible than other media. Quite flexible, as ads can be changed quickly and easily. Specialized programs create homogeneous audiences for advertisers. | Only one sense—hearing— is involved. Messages so fleeting that they can't be examined carefully. People tend to use radio only for background noise and don't hear commercials. |
| Others | 14.7 | 24.1 | | |

medium in our society today, since almost all families have at least one TV set that is watched around seven hours a day.

As shown in Table 14-2, cost is the main disadvantage to the advertiser. The price of a commercial depends on a show's rating, which is the estimate of the percentage of TV households watching it. For instance, a thirty-second commercial on a top-rated show like the Super Bowl or the final episode of $M^*A^*S^*H$ would cost $400,000 or $450,000.[7] The average fee for such a spot for the 1984 Olympics was $125,000.

## *FYI*

### The Best of TV Advertising

In 1982, for the second straight year, the most popular TV advertising campaign was for Miller Lite beer. But when it came to being remembered by potential customers, no well-liked brand did better than Oscar Mayer. In a telephone survey, Video Storyboard Tests, Inc., a New York ad-testing company, asked 22,000 adult viewers to name the "most outstanding" TV commercial they'd seen during the year. The results are shown in the table below.

The firm then asked regular users of a given product—such as soft drinks—to mention a TV commercial for that product during the previous week. The number of mentions was divided by that product's budget to find out how cost-efficient (that is, the cost per 1,000 retained impressions) the ad was. That figure is shown in the right column in the table.

Some authorities are beginning to question the effectiveness of advertising on TV. In fact, there's evidence that the number of sets turned on doesn't accurately measure the effectiveness of TV ads. For instance, two studies found that around 40 percent of commercials are wasted because people either miss or forget the advertiser's name.[8] And the most popular ads aren't the most efficient (see FYI above).

Three out of five commercials feature name talent (see the Profile on page 380). Movie and TV stars, sports and music personalities—even painters, astronauts, former politicians, opera singers, and Nobel Prize–winning authors and scientists—now sell products or services on TV. Some stars even subdivide their talents. Cheryl Tiegs has sold the right to exploit her lips, eyes, and face to the Noxell cosmetics group for $1.5 million for five years. Bristol-Myers already owned the right to advertise her hair.[9] And Sears has marketed a clothing line bearing her signature and featuring her photograph in its catalog and advertising.

| 1982 Rank | 1981 Rank | Brand (Agency) | 1982 TV Spending (Millions) | 1982 Cost Efficiency |
|---|---|---|---|---|
| 1 | 1 | Miller Lite (Backer & Spielvogel) | $44.4 | $29.86 |
| 2 | 2 | Coca-Cola (McCann-Erickson) | 38.6 | 8.96 |
| 3 | 16 | Federal Express (Ally & Gargano) | 19.9 | 22.01 |
| 4 | 5 | McDonald's (Leo Burnett) | 59.9 | 11.50 |
| 5 | 3 | Pepsi-Cola (BBDO) | 42.0 | 10.35 |
| 6 | * | Burger King (J. Walter Thompson) | 35.4 | 9.08 |
| 7 | * | Budweiser Light (Needham, Harper & Steers) | 31.2 | 41.67 |
| 8 | 4 | Dr Pepper (Young & Rubicam) | 13.3 | 7.83 |
| 9 | * | Atari Video Games (Doyle Dane Bernbach) | 46.9 | NA |
| 10 | 6 | Bell System (N.W. Ayer) | 66.7 | 18.33 |
| 11 | 7 | Polaroid (Doyle Dane Bernbach) | 31.8 | 13.89 |
| 12 | 10 | Oscar Mayer (J. Walter Thompson) | 11.7 | 6.37 |
| 13 | * | Shasta (Needham, Harper & Steers) | 5.3 | 11.33 |
| 14 | * | Velveeta (J. Walter Thompson) | 13.8 | NA |
| 15 | 14 | Tab (McCann-Erickson) | 18.0 | 19.33 |
| 16 | 11 | Life Cereal (BBDO) | 7.2 | 13.40 |
| 17 | 9 | Seven-Up (N.W. Ayer) | 24.5 | 10.00 |
| 18 | 8 | French's Mustard (J. Walter Thompson) | 3.4 | 10.16 |
| 19 | * | Toyota (Dancer Fitzgerald Sample) | 66.0 | 29.44 |
| 20 | 12 | Kibbles 'n Bits (J. Walter Thompson) | 5.5 | 16.56 |
| 21 | * | Levi's (Foote, Cone & Belding) | 12.1 | 6.81 |
| 22 | 25 | Kodak (J. Walter Thompson) | 69.1 | 22.22 |
| 23 | 21 | Ford (J. Walter Thompson) | 107.7 | 32.56 |
| 24 | * | MCI Communications (Ally & Gargano) | 21.1 | 11.77 |
| 25 | * | Wonder Bread (Ted Bates) | 9.4 | NA |

How many of the following have you recognized in commercials? Can you remember what they were selling?

| | | |
|---|---|---|
| Lee Iacocca | James Garner | Billy Martin |
| Pete Rose | Ricardo Montalban | Roger Staubach |
| O. J. Simpson | Joe DiMaggio | John McEnroe |
| Lauren Bacall | Mariette Hartley | Bill Cosby |
| Karl Malden | Bubba Smith | Michael Jackson |

The Federal Trade Commission recommends that celebrities sign a written testimonial for the products they plug, and, except in obvious cases (Joe Namath doesn't really have to wear pantyhose), they must actually use the products.[10]

# Profile

## Victor K. Kiam II: "I Bought the Company"

Although you've never seen him in a movie or on a TV program, Victor Kiam is a TV star both here and in Japan. You've almost certainly seen his TV commercial for Remington Products, Inc.'s electric razor. He intones: "I was a dedicated blade shaver until my wife bought me this Remington micro screen shaver. . . . I was so impressed, I bought the company." For Japan, he even struggled through commercials in Japanese. He's now so well known and easily recognized that he can't relax unshaven on weekends.

Mr. Kiam, born in 1927, formerly sold bras and girdles for International Playtex, packed goods for Lever Brothers, and sold watches and jewelry for Wells Benrus Corporation.

Whether he really bought Remington because of his wife's generosity is unknown, but he did pick the firm up from Sperry Corporation in 1979 for a mere $25 million, most of which was provided by Sperry and banks. Since then, Remington's annual sales have increased from $49 million to about $100 million. Its market share has increased from 19 percent to over 33 percent, and its 1982 pretax profits are estimated to have been at least $75 million. (It lost $30 million in the four years before Kiam purchased it.)

How did the new owner turn the company around? It was "larded with middle managers," and so Kiam fired seventy of them during his first two weeks—for an annual saving of $2 million. Then he cut the price of existing shavers, introduced new and cheaper models, removed frills such as chromium trim and fancy cases, added new retail outlets like Sears, and started the new ad campaign with himself as the star—backed by a $17 million budget in thirty countries. The results were phenomenal.

Some problems developed for Mr. Kiam and his firm in mid-1981, when the North American Philips Corporation (NAPC), makers of the Norelco rotary head shaver, sued Remington for trademark infringement. The suit, which claimed that Remington's use of the term *triple head* in its ads infringed on Norelco's "Triple Header" trademark, was settled out of court. Then, in early 1982, Kiam found out that NAPC had bought the Schick shaver trademark and was going to market a cheaper razor to compete with Remington. Remington filed a $300 million antitrust suit against NAPC and Schick, for the Norelco shaver already had 55 percent of the market.

Kiam has revised his marketing strategy to protect his share of the U.S. market. He's increased domestic advertising by $3 million for 1982, reduced overseas advertising, cut down on research and development, and concentrated on the electric shaver business.

---

Source: Based on Bill Abrams, "Remington's Kiam Seeks to Protect Gains in Face of Potential Challenge by Schick," *The Wall Street Journal*, August 20, 1982, p. 37. Adapted by permission of *The Wall Street Journal*, © Dow Jones & Company, Inc. 1982. All Rights Reserved. Also based on "Remington's New Antitrust Jab," *Business Week*, April 5, 1982, p. 58.

▲ **Magazines** General-interest magazines have declined in importance as an advertising medium because of the greater popularity of television and the demise of once-popular magazines like *Look*. *Reader's Digest* is one of the few left, but it claims 50 million readers every month.[11]

Many successful magazines cater to special target markets, such as working women (*New Woman, Savvy,* and *Working Woman*) or retirees (*Modern Maturity*). Furthermore, they have subscription lists classified by characteristics important to advertisers, and some, like *U.S. News & World Report* and *Good Housekeeping,* publish regional editions with several pages for local ads. Trade magazines and business papers are an effective medium for companies selling to industrial markets.

▲ **Direct Mail Direct mail,** which includes catalogs, letters, folders, pamphlets, handbills, and postcards, is the most selective of all advertising media. Computerization has made mailing lists for various target markets more readily available. This method is relatively expensive because of the costs of mailing lists and the steep increase in third class postage rates. Still, many advertisers find that the cost in terms of increased sales is well worth it. Mail-order catalogs have proliferated to the point where *Consumer Reports* rated forty of them in 1983.[12]

The Soviets sell subscriptions to *Soviet Life,* an English-language monthly magazine, to American consumers by direct mail. In 1982, only about 45,000 of the 62,000 copies allowed under a cultural exchange agreement were being sold. So about 250,000 American households received subscription solicitations, including the following enticement: "If, like most Americans, your exposure to the Soviet Union is basically confined to borscht, babushkas, and the Bolshoi, you have some exciting discoveries ahead." The mailing list also contained a sweepstakes offer and a colorful brochure listing story topics.[13]

▲ **Radio** With an average of five radios in every household in the United States, car radios, and the unavoidable portables, radio remains a valuable, if noisy, advertising medium. Many businesses that aim at specific target markets use particular radio stations that have the appropriate audience characteristics, or profiles. One station in New York broadcasts to forty-five different ethnic minorities.[14] The effectiveness of radio advertising is believed to be greater during the daylight hours since many people are watching television at night. Radio advertising costs much less than the other major forms of advertising.

> Who are the advertisers on your favorite radio program or station? Do they fit a pattern? What target market are they aiming at?

▲ **Other Media** Some other forms of advertising are outdoor, personal distribution, transportation, and personal advertising. **Outdoor advertising** includes billboards, neon and other lighted signs, and advertising space on trash cans and benches. **Personal distribution ads** include handbills, shopping newspapers, and other advertisements distributed by hand. Examples of **transportation advertising** are posters and placards on buses, taxis, railway cars, subways,

Outdoor advertising aimed at minority neighborhoods.

and even alongside ski lifts. Many companies, especially those performing services, rely heavily on the personal, word-of-mouth advertising provided by satisfied customers.

How effective is each medium? It all depends on what the advertiser wants from it. Figure 14-3 shows how one survey rated the most popular media on twenty-eight variables.

## Advertising Agencies

After reviewing these advertising media and their potential, you can see that it would be difficult for management to do all advertising activities by itself. It would be hard to select the most effective media and to prepare appropriate advertising materials to reach desired target markets. Advertising agencies are there to furnish assistance in these areas. Agencies also assist their clients in package design, sales research and training, merchandising displays, preparation of house newsletters, and publicity.

J. Walter Thompson (JWT) is one of the world's largest and most integrated advertising agencies. Many agencies split up advertising activities among specialized groups. But JWT insists on performing full service—research, creative art, media buying, marketing the ads, and public relations—for its clients. It emphasizes creating a sound marketing strategy, meeting high standards in copy and art, and having a thorough knowledge of the client's marketing problems.[15]

## Attitudes Toward Advertising

**Objective 4**

**Public attitudes toward advertising.**

The attitude of the public toward advertising ranges from lavish praise to intense criticism. Advertising is praised for providing information that performs the worthwhile economic function of relating demand to mass production and distribution. It's criticized for (1) being unpleasant, intrusive, and repetitive, (2) increasing the cost of products and services, (3) creating artificial demand instead of filling greater social needs, and (4) presenting untruths or half-truths.

Better Business Bureaus try to protect consumers by registering complaints about undesirable advertising practices (as well as other undesirable business practices) of offending firms. They rely heavily on persuasion to correct abuses, as they have no legal standing. The Federal Trade Commission has been active in enforcing federal and state legislation that mandates truth in

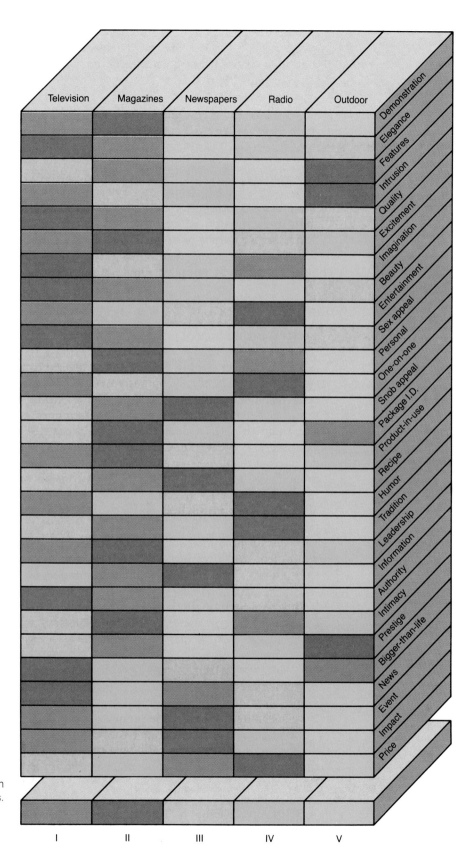

**Figure 14-3** Which media do it best. (Reprinted by permission of Needham, Harper and Steers. Richard C. Anderson, Executive Vice President, Needham, Harper & Steers/USA; Inc.)

advertising. And the media themselves engage in policing activities to protect consumers, as shown in the discussion of comparative advertising. Ultimately, consumers have recourse to the federal courts when false advertising is sent through the mails.

## PERSONAL SELLING

**Objective 5**

**The types and process of personal selling.**

**Personal selling,** the oldest form of promotion, is a sales presentation made directly to a potential customer by a salesperson. It has the greatest flexibility of all forms of promotion because salespeople can adapt their messages, on the spot, to each potential customer. Advertising can create attention and build desire for a product or service, but nothing replaces salespeople for actually completing the sale. And since most companies depend heavily on repeat business for their sales, personal selling must be performed effectively.

### Types of Selling

The two main kinds of personal selling are retail selling and business selling.

▲ **Retail Selling** **Retail selling** takes place primarily in department or specialty stores. The salespeople involved are often merely order takers, particularly when self-service is the rule. Many stores are now abandoning any attempt at personal selling because of customers' growing price-consciousness. The main thing that does the selling in cases like this is the price tag. For example, J. P. Stevens & Company has developed an electronic merchandising device that displays over 2,000 types of textile items, writes up the customer's order, and suggests additional items. It consists of a desk-sized console placed in front of a large TV screen. The customer pushes a button to start the device, after which it's automatic. But a clerk is still needed to bring the items out of inventory.[16]

Certain products, such as automobiles, expensive photographic or stereo equipment, video games, and high-fashion clothing, require expert personal sales efforts. And services, such as insurance, are most often sold personally.

▲ **Business Selling** Both consumer and industrial goods may be involved in **business selling,** personal selling to businesses and institutions rather than to individuals. Two special types of business selling are technical and missionary selling.

**Technical selling** is usually done by attempting to persuade the potential customer's technical staff of the superiority of a company's products. For example, high-technology companies such as Digital Equipment Corporation have specialists who provide technical and operating assistance to customers.

**Missionary selling** is done to develop goodwill and demand for a new product. An example is sales calls by a drug company's detail person, who leaves samples with doctors and pharmacists and informs them about new prescription drugs.

▲ **Selling by Telephone** Telephone selling or solicitation has grown rapidly in recent years, mainly because of wide-area telephone service (WATS) lines, whose cost has declined and will doubtless continue to do so now that compe-

tition has entered the field of long distance service. In addition, innovations in automatic dialing have now made it possible to dial systematically through all possible number combinations and play a recording (and record a response) each time a connection is made, thus eliminating the cost of human telephone solicitors. However, consumers, long weary of junk mail (direct mail advertising), have raised such strenuous objections to the prospect of junk telephone calls that legislation against them has been proposed.

## The Sales Process

There are some well-defined steps in the selling process, and salespeople know them by heart. They are prospecting, approach, presentation, answering objections, close, and follow-up.

▲ **Prospecting** **Prospecting** involves identifying and qualifying potential customers. Salespeople have a number of sources for prospects, such as present or former customers, friends, neighbors, other salespeople, and nonsales employees in the company. For example, realtors, banks, and insurance firms use lists of newly hired employees in the community, such as new university professors, to develop prospects. Of course, not everyone is in a position to buy, so prospects must also be qualified. When selling a family a new car, for instance, the salesperson tries to determine who the decision maker is and whether she or he is in a financial position to buy a car at that time.

▲ **Approach** In the **approach,** the salesperson tries to get the prospect's attention and interest, often by setting a definite appointment to talk further. The approach used by insurance salespeople is to offer to inventory and evaluate the prospect's current insurance coverage.

This step is important because it gives the prospect an initial impression of the salesperson that will affect his or her future attitude. Too hard a sell or an abrasive approach will turn some customers off. Even clothing makes a difference: For example, clerks behind perfume counters usually wear "dressy" clothes and jewelry.

▲ **Presentation** A critical step in the selling process is the **presentation,** where the salesperson informs the prospect of how the product or service fills his or her wants or needs. The salesperson describes the product or service, emphasizes its advantages, and gives examples of customer satisfaction. Demonstrations are often done at this point, to show how a product is used—especially for products that take some practice and have to be operated properly for best results. Vacuum cleaners, sewing machines, and complex kitchen gadgets are examples. A modified example is the automobile salesperson who hands the customer the keys and says, "Take it for a spin."

▲ **Answering Objections** Prospects' objections usually have to do with product features, cost, need for the product, timing of the purchase, or the reputation of the company. A salesperson should expect objections and consider them a positive sign, since they may show that the prospect is seriously considering the product.

▲ **Close** Another critical point in selling is the **close,** or asking the prospect for an order. A close can be handled by assuming or implying that the sale has

been completed, as when the salesperson asks, "Do you want it delivered, or would you like to carry it yourself?" The direct approach would be to ask, "Are you interested in buying this stereo?" Proposing alternative purchases is a last resort: "This luxury model may be too steep for your budget at this time, but you *could* afford our standard model."

The salesperson may sometimes use a **trial close** before closing, to determine whether the prospect is really interested in buying the item. For example, an effective salesperson may show the customer two differently priced stereo systems and ask, "Which one do you prefer?" to lead the customer into a decision.

▲ **Follow-up**   **Follow-up** consists of postsale activities, such as completing the order processing quickly, reassuring the customer about a purchase he or she may be having second thoughts about, and checking with the customer to see that the product or service was satisfactory. Companies want repeat customers, and effective follow-up helps them to get and keep them. The good car salesperson may call the new owner after a few days to ask how he or she likes the car, whether it needs any servicing, and so on.

## SALES PROMOTION

**Objective 6**

**Some different kinds of sales promotion.**

**Sales promotion** includes specialized activities—other than personal selling, advertising, and publicity—designed to help transfer ownership and move goods from the manufacturer to the customer more effectively. There are many types of sales promotion, but the most popular are displays, specialty advertising, trade shows, coupons and trading stamps, and sales contests.

### Displays

**Displays,** or **point-of-purchase (POP) advertising,** are designed to reflect a store's image, feature products, or promote a service. The most frequently used types are interior displays and window displays.

Interior displays include all forms of displays inside a store. Colorful, attractive goods may be set up on a countertop or center island for customers' examination. Related merchandise, such as clothing, shoes, and accessories, may be shown on mannequins. In order to enhance the display of their merchandise, manufacturers and distributors often provide retailers with special racks (like the L'eggs display and TicTac racks), banners, and other materials—even personnel to assist in installing displays.

Window displays are intended to entice potential customers into the store as they pass by. They tend to reflect the store's image and the quality of the merchandise and may emphasize featured merchandise. A noteworthy piece of promotion is Neiman-Marcus's annual event known as "Fortnight," held in October of each year. The purpose of Fortnight is to present the best of a selected country's merchandise and culture. Items reflecting the fashions, foods, furnishings, customs, and cultural life of the country being featured are available for sale. Schools, universities, museums, libraries, and theaters participate by presenting programs and exhibits related to the cultural life of the country, often with native artisans and entertainers. The result is enormous

Creative Systems Group robot.

interest in the country, an increase in travel, a boost in sales, and a stimulus to international goodwill.

### Specialty Advertising

Familiar examples of **specialty advertising** are inexpensive pens, calendars, keyrings, frisbees, and the like that are imprinted with an advertiser's name or logo. One form of specialty advertising involves inducing customers to pay for the privilege of becoming walking advertisements. T-shirts, beach towels, beach bags, ice chests, tires, caps, and other items imprinted with an advertising slogan or facsimile of products like Coppertone tanning lotion or Nike sports shoes are offered to customers at a bargain price.

Creative Systems Group, Inc., of Atlanta, has developed a series of promotional robots resembling R2D2, the charismatic, beeping character of *Star Wars* fame. The little fellows run on a car battery, have two-way wireless radios, and chat spontaneously with clientele at trade shows, grand openings, supermarkets, hospitals, and sporting events.[17]

### Trade Shows

Wholesalers and retailers attend trade shows and conventions where manufacturers exhibit their product lines. Familiar examples are mobile home, business equipment, small business, and recreational vehicle shows.

### Coupons and Trading Stamps

**Coupons** are advertising inserts or package enclosures used to reduce the price of an established product and to promote new or different products. Many advertisers believe that coupons increase sales, and certainly coupon use is on the rise in these economically depressed times. Manufacturers distributed 110 billion coupons in 1982, and consumers used them to save almost $1 billion. Strangely enough, better-off families use coupons more than poorer ones; surveys show that most coupon users were college graduates with an annual household income of $25,000 to $34,999.[18] Coupons are popular with advertisers because they inform customers as well as entice them to respond to the price discounts involved in their redemption. Coupons also motivate retailers to stock up on the product. After the Tylenol poisoning disaster, Johnson & Johnson placed 40 million coupons worth $2.50 (about the price of a bottle of 100 Tylenol capsules or pills, and far more than the average coupon value of $0.20) in three different newspaper ads to promote the new, safer Tylenol package.[19]

**Trading stamps,** which retailers give as a bonus based on the amount of purchase, may be redeemed by a customer for additional merchandise. Sometimes retailers use them to build customer loyalty. Their use is now declining, as many stores are offering double redemption value on coupons instead of stamps.

### Sales Contests

Sales contests are used by many companies to encourage competition among their salespeople and to increase sales volume. The salesperson's spouse can be a powerful motivator. Some years ago, a manufacturer of heavy earth-moving equipment was having difficulty motivating its salespeople. They got such a high commission on each unit they sold that they could make a good living working only six months of the year. So a sales contest was held, and the firm took the winners and their spouses to Paris on an all-expense-paid vacation, where they stayed at the best hotels and took in the best restaurants and nightclubs. After they returned home, motivation was no longer a problem.

## PUBLICITY

**Objective 7**

How publicity differs from other forms of promotion.

**Publicity** is any nonpaid information concerning an organization and its products or personnel that appears in any published or oral medium. Familiar examples of publicity are news releases about the development of new products or processes. The business sections of newspapers consist primarily of writeups about actions of local companies with interesting products or services and about hirings, promotions, and personnel activities in those companies. And many features in homemaking pages are thinly disguised plugs for a particular product that's featured in the recipes or craft hints.

Publicity can also take a number of other forms, for it includes anything that directly or indirectly increases sales of the firm's product or service. For example, Hershey Foods Corporation received invaluable free publicity when

the hero of *E.T., the Extra-Terrestrial* ate its candy, Reese's Pieces. In *Rocky III*, Sylvester Stallone trained on Wheaties, long advertised as "the Breakfast of Champions,"[20] while Burt Reynolds is a walking billboard in *Stroker Ace*. Of course, few manufacturers pay directly to have their products and trademarks seen in the movies. Instead, they pay intermediaries who cultivate friendships with producers, property managers, and others, who then use the product. Lots of merchandise is also given to actors, directors, and crews in the name of "product sampling."

Another aspect of publicity—both good and bad—is the appearance of company executives on TV news and talk shows. Since many business executives aren't very effective public speakers, these appearances can result in a negative impression of the company. For this reason, companies are now seeking advice from TV experts. For example, Standard Oil of California spends about $60,000 each year for media consultants to help its officials come across better on TV. Its economists, for instance, are taught how to make their responses briefer and more quotable.[21]

## ⏚ LEARNING OBJECTIVES REVISITED

1. *The objectives of promotion and the importance of choosing the right promotion mix.*

   The objectives of promotion are to provide information, to increase sales, or to stabilize sales. The promotion mix is a combination of advertising, personal selling, sales promotion, and publicity. Managers need to determine the best mix, based on the nature of the product, the target market, and available funds.

2. *The differences between product and institutional advertising.*

   Product advertising is the nonpersonal selling of specific products and services. A product's life cycle affects its advertising. Informational ads are used during the introduction stage. Persuasive and comparative ads are more suited to the growth and early maturity stages. Then, during the late maturity and decline stages, reminder advertising is best.

   Institutional advertising is used to develop goodwill for a company, industry, or other organization rather than to try to sell specific goods or services.

3. *The advantages and disadvantages of different advertising media.*

   The usual advertising media are newspapers, television, magazines, direct mail, and radio. Newspaper advertising is quite flexible but has a short life and lacks "eye-grabbing" appeal. Television advertising provides mass coverage with great impact but is fleeting in its presentation and quite expensive. Magazine advertising is attractive and effective in reaching

specialized markets but is relatively inflexible, since material must be prepared far in advance. Direct mail, in the form of letters, folders, pamphlets, handbills, and postcards, is the most selective of all advertising media. Major advantages of radio advertising are its greater accessibility to the consumer and its specialized programming, which provides a homogeneous audience. But its message is fleeting and may not be heard. Miscellaneous forms of advertising are outdoor, personal distribution, transportation, and personal word-of-mouth advertising.

4. *Public attitudes toward advertising.*

   Public attitudes toward advertising range from praise to criticism. Advertising is praised for providing information and encouraging mass distribution; it is criticized for creating artificial demand and increasing the costs of products and services.

5. *The types and process of personal selling.*

   Personal selling is a sales presentation made directly to a potential customer by a salesperson. It has the greatest flexibility of all promotional methods because salespeople can adjust their messages even while talking to a potential customer. Two main kinds of personal selling are retail and business selling. The steps in the sales process are prospecting, approach, presentation, answering objections, close, and follow-up.

6. *Some different kinds of sales promotion.*

   Sales promotion includes specialized activities—other than personal selling, advertising, and publicity—that are intended to help bring about transfers in ownership and move goods from the manufacturer to the customer more effectively. Examples are displays (point-of-purchase advertising), specialty advertising, trade show exhibits, coupons and trading stamps, and sales contests.

7. *How publicity differs from other forms of promotion.*

   Publicity is any nonpaid information concerning an organization and its products or its employees that appears in any published or oral medium.

## ⏚ IMPORTANT TERMS

As an extra review of the chapter, try defining the following terms. If you have trouble with any of them, refer to the page listed.

# REVIEW QUESTIONS

1. What are the objectives of promoting products or services?
2. Why does a promotion mix vary?
3. Distinguish between the following, and give examples.
   a. Product advertising and institutional advertising
   b. Informational, persuasive, and reminder advertising
   c. Retail selling and business selling
   d. Interior displays and window displays
4. Why and how does advertising vary with each stage of a product's life cycle?
5. What are some of the advantages and disadvantages of newspapers as an advertising medium?
6. What are some of the advantages and disadvantages of television as an advertising medium?
7. What are some of the advantages and disadvantages of magazines as an advertising medium?
8. What are some of the advantages and disadvantages of direct mail as an advertising medium?
9. What are some of the advantages and disadvantages of radio as an advertising medium?
10. Give three examples of sales promotion.
11. Describe and give examples of each of the steps in the sales process.

# DISCUSSION QUESTIONS

1. How would you characterize the attitude of the public toward advertising? Is it justified? Why or why not?
2. What products have you bought that were never advertised? Why weren't they?
3. What is your reaction to comparative advertising? Is it justified? Does it hurt or help a product?
4. Are some products advertised only in magazines? in newspapers? on television? Why?
5. Do you favor selling by telephone? Explain.
6. Is publicity a valid type of promotion? Explain.
7. What can be done to make promotion of goods and services more effective?
8. What sort of promotion mix would you devise for earth-moving equipment? a new brand of instant popcorn to compete with Jolly Time? the IBM PCjr microcomputer? Defend your answer.

## ⬙ CASE 14-1   The Masked President[22]

Several years ago, Roger Strauss, campaigning with a paper sack over his head, was chosen president of the University of Georgia Student Government Association.

"I just can't believe it," exclaimed the twenty-year-old junior from Atlanta. "We ran the campaign as a joke. My platform was that we had to upgrade the student government from a farce to a joke. I took the idea from the *Gong Show*—you know, the unknown comic. We thought the un-

known candidate who would go around cracking bad jokes might be an idea that might catch on here. I always wanted to be a stand-up comic who stole everybody's jokes. We really didn't expect to get this far."

Strauss's platform included pledges to have dining halls redecorated by Saks Fifth Avenue and to add five bagpipe players to the university marching band.

### Case Questions

1. What do you think of this unique way of promoting oneself for a student political office?
2. What suggestions does it provide for marketing managers?

## ⬙ CASE 14-2   The Condominium Blitz[23]

It was a classic example of how a well-planned ad campaign can give a product high visibility. For almost two years, the sixteen-floor Ocean Point condominium development sat in Virginia Beach, Virginia, with only two units sold.

Fred Davis, the flamboyant twenty-eight-year-old maverick of a Tulsa advertising agency, dressed the condo in a new name, Dolphin Run; painted over the water stains; hung new awnings; did a little landscaping; remodeled one floor, the lobby, and elevators; and raised the prices. A bash—complete with hors d'oeuvres, three bands, fireworks seen from the roof, and helicopter and cruise

ship rides—gave the ad executive a chance to show off his product to prospective buyers. The invitations were worded to make the guests feel special. Yet, when they arrived, their acquisitiveness was pricked by the presence of 2,000 people, all of them competing for the 108 condos. "We wanted them to forget the empty buildings, . . . the water stains, . . . and that it was across the street from the 'red light district,'" Davis said.

Evidently they forgot, for forty-seven of the units sold that night, thirty-seven the next day. Within six weeks, the development was sold out.

### Case Questions

1. What made this an effective promotional effort?
2. Do you agree with the way it was done? Explain.
3. What would you have done differently?

## ⬙ CASE 14-3   The Graying of a Sales Force[24]

More and more companies are now hiring older people as salespeople. Many firms seek retirees to fill high-technology and computer sales jobs. One of Texas Refinery Corporation's top sales representatives is Robert Stacey, seventy-four years old, who was named "rookie of the year," with $45,000 in commissions. He was a pharmacist before his

first retirement. Twenty salespeople over seventy joined this firm in 1981.

The main reason for this trend is that companies have realized that older people are among the top salespeople. "A graying or balding head is an asset. It seems that the grayer the hair, the more they'll take your recommendations." Older cus-

tomers particularly like to interact with older salespeople.

The trend pleases the older salespeople too. Some retirees dislike retirement and believe that "people who retire tend to kick off." And the new tax law also makes work more attractive to older folks. A person over age sixty-five can now earn up to about $6,000 in outside income without losing Social Security benefits.

### Case Questions

1. Do you think this trend is only a result of the recession of 1982–1983, or is it a permanent trend? Explain your answer.
2. What possible disadvantages do you see to using the older salesperson?

# 15

# Channels and Distribution

*When is a refrigerator not a refrigerator?*
*When it is in Pittsburgh at the time it is desired in*
*Houston.*

J. L. Heskett,
N. A. Glaskowsky,
R. M. Ivie

*If you have it, it came by truck.*

Trucking industry slogan

## Learning Objectives

After studying the material in this chapter, you will understand:

1. What channels of distribution are and how intermediaries operate within them.
2. The major types of distribution channels for consumer and industrial goods.
3. The criteria used in selecting channels of distribution, including intensity of market coverage.
4. The types of wholesalers and their functions.
5. The types of retailers and their functions.
6. How warehousing, order processing, and transportation function as part of physical distribution.

## In This Chapter

What Are Channels of Distribution?
Wholesalers
Retailers
Physical Distribution

# IS SEARS STILL A RETAILER?

Sears, Roebuck and Company began in 1886 when Richard W. Sears, a railroad station agent, acquired some watches and started peddling them to farmers in the area. He made enough profit to buy more watches, sell them by writing letters to people in a wider area, quit his railroad job, and start the Richard W. Sears Watch Company in Chicago. Later, he and Alvah C. Roebuck organized Sears, Roebuck and Company as a mail-order business, first in Minneapolis and later in Chicago. The firm continued to expand its product line, adding retail stores but remaining primarily a mail-order operation through World War I.

Later Sears executives Julius Rosenwald and General Robert Wood made decisions that kept Sears at the forefront of retail marketing. In the 1920s, with the introduction of the automobile and postwar mobility, a migration took place from the farms to the cities. Sensing that this shift would vitally affect Sears, Rosenwald in turn changed the firm's emphasis from mail-order business to urban merchandising. Later, the firm anticipated the mall era, opening up stores outside the cities where there was plenty of parking space.

In the late 1940s, anticipating the effects of World War II's G.I. Bill on U.S. business, General Wood started a modernization and expansion program that put Sears well out in front of Montgomery Ward and other competitors for over two decades. Wood also got Sears into auto service and rental, insurance, gardening, and home decorating.

By the end of 1981, Sears had become prominent in real estate and securities investing through acquisition of Dean Witter Reynolds, the fifth-largest securities brokerage firm in the United States, and Coldwell Banker & Company, the nation's largest independent real estate broker. Since then, Sears has also moved into sales of personal computers, calculators, copiers, word processors, and telephones.

Sears held its own in the earnings war, managing to stay ahead of K mart, J. C. Penney, and Montgomery Ward. But over the years, it had developed the dowdy image of a utilitarian store where one went to buy work clothing and washing machines. People didn't "shop" there the way they did at Bloomingdale's. This led management to question the idea of the "all things for all people" type of retailing that Richard Sears had begun. New management was brought in to close unprofitable stores and consolidate offices. Zeroing in on a target market with more shopping money, Sears went after signature collections like its Cheryl Tiegs line, at the same time adding big-name national brands like Levi Strauss.

But bringing out designer lines and introducing national brands isn't enough if the customer can't find them and doesn't perceive the change in the store's atmosphere. So Sears also began to reorganize its stores along "store within a store" lines. In addition to their 800 product lines, the new Sears stores will now have special areas in which other items and services, such as telephones, computers, insurance, stocks, and real estate, will be sold.

Rigorous planning, good communication, cost controls, and a new merchandising strategy have put Sears in motion. Although some of these techniques are new, Sears still follows the same basic retailing principles that Richard Sears established nearly 100 years ago. In the future? Sears executives envision ventures in mortgage origination, communications, and, possibly, automatic teller machines in stores.

Even if a firm has the perfect product, it can't count on the world to beat a path to its door. Without a good distribution system to get products to customers, sales are going to be poor or nonexistent. An effective distribution system gets the goods or services that customers want into their hands at the right time and place and still falls within the seller's cost constraints. Three of the four types of economic utility—time, place, and ownership—are thus provided by an effective distribution system. And, as shown in Figure 15-1, the last of the four P's of marketing—placement—is achieved by performance of the distribution function.

## WHAT ARE CHANNELS OF DISTRIBUTION?

**Objective 1**

**What channels of distribution are and how intermediaries operate within them.**

**Channels of distribution** are the different paths that goods pass through in moving from the producer to the consumer. The decisions about which channels to use are important ones; some products and services are best sold one way, others another way, as we'll soon see.

During their early days, movie producers had their own theaters, where they showed only their own films. Now they sell the right to show their movies to thousands of independently owned theaters around the country on a royalty basis. Ice, milk, and vegetables used to be sold from wagons and trucks—like the Kraft cheese wagon—moving directly from the producer to the consumer. Given the current size of the consumer goods market and the ability to distribute goods widely, a door-to-door cheese wagon wouldn't be a marketing manager's choice today.

### The Role of Intermediaries

The individual steps in channels of distribution are the groups of businesspeople or firms that help to pass goods along on their way to consumers. **Intermediaries** are these units or institutions in the channel of distribution that either take title to goods (that is, buy and sell in their own names) or negotiate a sale as an agent or broker for the producer. They may take physical possession of, or title to, the goods, as wholesalers and retailers generally do, or they may simply obtain an order for goods to be shipped by the supplier directly to the customer.

In general, intermediaries perform the following marketing functions for those they serve: (1) buying and selling; (2) storing, transporting, and distributing goods; (3) setting and maintaining grades and standards; and (4) in many cases, financing the purchase of the goods or services. The main reason for using intermediaries is to move products from the producer to the consumer more efficiently. Although you might think that having such intermediaries would add to the cost of a good, that isn't necessarily so. Efficiency can be improved and cost reduced by cutting down the number of individual transactions and by relating the amount demanded to the amount supplied. Intermediaries also help to bring buyers and sellers together and to speed the flow through the channels of distribution. If Levi Strauss & Company tried to sell its jeans directly to consumers, it could sell a few thousand pairs each year. But by selling through retailers, it can sell millions.

**Figure 15-1** How distribution strategy fits into the marketing mix.

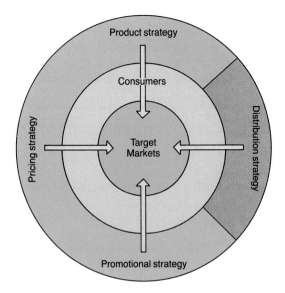

▲ **Reducing Number of Transactions** Intermediaries greatly reduce the number of transactions required between production and ultimate consumption of goods and services. For example, suppose that there were twenty-five students, each enrolled in four classes, and that each instructor required the students to buy two textbooks, each from a different publisher. If a bookstore didn't exist as intermediary, 200 transactions (twenty-five students multiplied by four classes multiplied by two publishers each) would be necessary for all the students to obtain the required books. The presence of a bookstore cuts the number of transactions to no more than 33 (twenty-five students buying from the bookstore and the bookstore buying from, at most, eight publishers).

▲ **Relating Demand to Supply** It isn't economical for suppliers to produce in very small quantities or for consumers to buy goods or services in enormous amounts. Therefore, intermediaries buy in relatively large quantities and break them down into smaller, more purchasable amounts for consumers. If you bought cassettes or records directly from the producer, you'd have to buy in larger quantities or pay higher prices because of the cost of distributing them to you.

▲ **Locating Buyers** Intermediaries locate buyers for producers' goods. This saves the producers from having to search for customers and customers from having to try to find suppliers. Where would you go to find a producer of notebook paper if there were no bookstore?

Objective 2

The major types of distribution channels for consumer and industrial goods.

## Types of Distribution Channels

In Chapter 3, we distinguished between consumer goods and industrial goods. As you might expect, since the markets are different for these two types of goods, so too are the distribution channels.

Have you noticed throughout this part of the text, especially in the examples, how the line of distinction between the classes of goods is blurring?  Is a home computer an industrial good or a consumer good?

▲ **For Consumer Goods**  The usual distribution channels for consumer goods, as shown in Figure 15-2, are:

1. Producer → consumer.
2. Producer → retailer → consumer.
3. Producer → wholesaler → retailer → consumer.
4. Producer → agent or broker → wholesaler → retailer → consumer.

The most direct channel for distributing consumer goods is the first, from the *producer directly to the consumer.*  If you send away for something you see advertised in a magazine, you're using this channel.  Most small service businesses, such as dry cleaners and window washers, use this channel.  This channel gives the producer great control over the condition and price of the goods, along with a larger share of the profit.  However, it does limit the number of customers and may be more costly, unless there is quite large-scale distribution.  This channel is the one used by manufacturers who establish their own

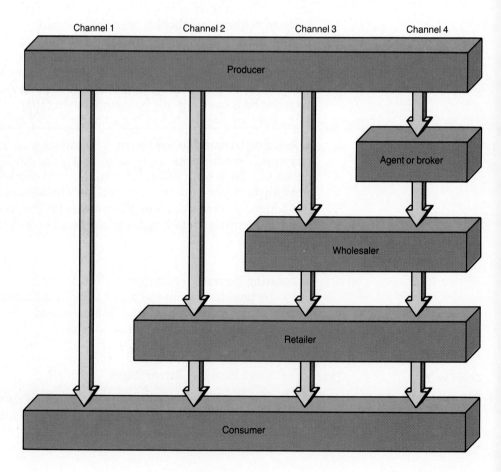

**Figure 15-2**  Channels for distributing consumer goods.

retail stores for their goods, such as Kuppenheimer men's wear, Red Cross shoes, B. F. Goodrich tires, and Radio Shack computers.

Sometimes, of course, there's a sales intermediary in the channel acting as the spokesperson of the producer. Many personal and home-use items, such as

Manufacturers who establish their own retail stores are using the most direct channel for distributing consumer goods.

# KUPPENHEIMER SUITS COST US LESS TO SELL. AND YOU LESS TO BUY.

**OUR FACTORY**   **OUR STORE**   **OUR CUSTOMER**

At Kuppenheimer, we make our own high quality suits, sportcoats and slacks. Then we sell them direct to our customers in our own Kuppenheimer Factory Stores. We don't pay one penny extra for anybody's markups. And neither do you.

KUPPENHEIMER

Amway and Avon products, are sold door to door, for example, rather than in stores. To overcome negative reactions to solicitors, some manufacturers of cookware, dresses, and costume jewelry prefer to have their representatives arrange for home parties at which their products may be displayed and sold. Tupperware is probably the best-known of the products sold this way.

Department stores are examples of participants in the second channel, from the *producer to the retailer to the customer*. For example, Hershey Foods sells its candy directly to large retailers, who then sell it to consumers. This channel provides wider coverage and potentially greater sales, but the producer begins to lose a little control over price and distribution.

The route from *producer to wholesaler to retailer to consumer*, the third channel, is still the most-used channel for goods that are sold by independent retailers, such as pharmacies and grocery and hardware stores. It's more reasonable, for instance, for a wholesaler to purchase large quantities of nuts and bolts and then resell them in usable quantities to hardware stores. In fact, producers of agricultural and petroleum products often use two or more wholesalers to divide, sort, and distribute bulky quantities. This channel is probably the most economical one for the producer, for less selling, credit, and bookkeeping are required.

In some instances, the fourth channel, from *producer to agent or broker to wholesaler to retailer to customer*, is used. This route tends to be used for specialized products of which there are only a few producers. The **agent** or **broker** is a representative who doesn't take title to or possession of the products but only brings the buyer and seller together. For instance, if the farmers waited to find buyers when strawberries began to mature around Hammond, Louisiana, the berries might spoil. Instead, the strawberries are loaded into cooled railroad cars and shipped to Chicago. While the berries are in transit, brokers find wholesalers who want them. Then the berries are diverted to the buyer.

A company producing consumer goods might adopt two or more of these channels. For example, it could sell directly to chains and large independent stores, while at the same time using wholesalers to sell to small independent retailers. However, these multiple distribution channels sometimes create conflicts. To use Hershey Foods as an example again, it sells candy to wholesalers for resale to retailers, while also selling candy directly to chains and large retail stores.

▲ **For Industrial Goods** The most common channels of distribution for industrial goods, as shown in Figure 15-3, are:

1. Producer → industrial user.
2. Producer → wholesaler or industrial distributor → industrial user.
3. Producer → agent → wholesaler or industrial distributor → industrial user.

As you can see, retailers aren't usually used in distribution of industrial goods. The first channel, from the *producer directly to industrial user*, is the approach most frequently used for distributing industrial goods, except for small items of equipment and supplies. For example, Caterpillar Tractor sells heavy earth-moving equipment directly to road contractors, and McDonnell Douglas sells planes directly to airlines or governments.

The second channel, *producer to wholesaler or industrial distributor to industrial user*, is used for some accessories, equipment, and supplies that are

**Figure 15-3** Channels for distributing industrial goods.

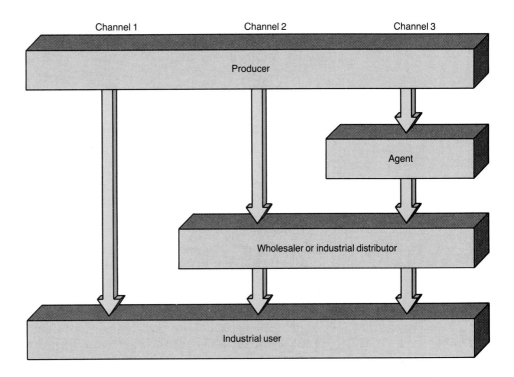

produced in large quantities but used in relatively small amounts. Building materials such as lumber, roofing materials, central heating units, toilet fixtures, and paints are sold this way.

Imported petroleum is an example of a product that follows the third channel, *producer to agent to wholesaler or industrial distributor to industrial user.* Unsold crude oil is shipped in tankers from the North Sea wells to the United States. While it's in transit, an agent finds a distributor to buy the oil. The distributor then finds a refinery that needs the oil and diverts the tanker to the nearest port.

## Selecting a Channel of Distribution

**Objective 3**

**The criteria used in selecting channels of distribution, including intensity of market coverage.**

The choice of a channel of distribution depends on the market the producer is trying to satisfy. As indicated above, if the product is bought by several different types of customers or is used by both consumers and industrial users, more than one channel may be used. In fact, it's possible for one producer to use all the channels.

The need to change or select a distribution channel can arise from the introduction of a new product; changes in target customers' buying habits; inefficiencies in existing channels; changes in the marketing mix, such as a new price strategy; expansion into new territories; or changes in intermediary functions. The key steps in the channel selection process are to:

1. Identify the target market.
2. Determine customers' buying habits for the type of product.
3. Locate potential customers geographically.
4. Determine and evaluate alternative channels.
5. Select the most effective channel.
6. Use the channel and then evaluate its performance.

You may recall that Johnson Products Company (see the Profile on page 348) distributes its products through high-volume drug, variety, and discount stores and supermarkets. This represents a change from the company's original marketing strategy. When its products didn't sell well, the firm abandoned sales through department stores and shifted to another channel.

## Market Coverage

The type of product sold and the image sought by its producers will determine not only the channels selected but also the intensity of market coverage. Market coverage can be intensive, selective, or exclusive, depending on the number of outlets used to distribute the product, as shown in Figure 15-4.

▲ **Intensive Coverage** Since producers of basic consumer products try to achieve complete coverage of the market, they use **intensive distribution.** Little effort goes into choosing which intermediaries to use, and as many channels as needed are used. For instance, Hershey candy is sold to large retailers and to wholesalers who sell it to retailers. The products are sold in as many outlets as possible, with every promotional effort being used to get as many consumers as possible to buy them. Convenience goods, such as candy, soft drinks, gum, basic foods, tobacco products, essential clothing, newspapers, and magazines, are usually distributed intensively.

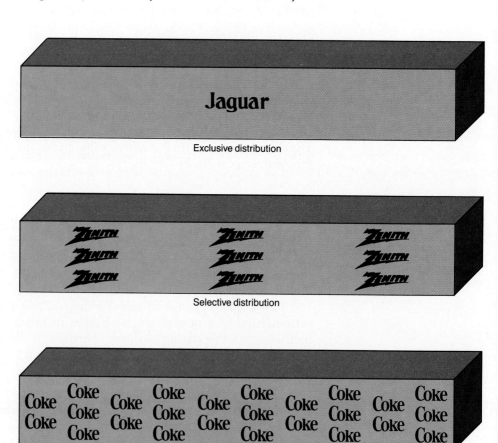

Exclusive distribution

Selective distribution

Intensive distribution

**Figure 15-4** Exclusive, selective, and intensive distribution.

▲ **Selective Coverage** In **selective distribution,** the producer screens dealers and outlets in order to select a limited number of better outlets for the particular type of product. Since the number of retailers is limited, customers must be willing to travel and shop for the desired product, which is usually a shopping good. Examples are television sets, stereo systems, kitchen and other household appliances, name-brand suits and dresses, lower-priced automobiles, and some cosmetics and personal care items.

▲ **Exclusive Coverage** In **exclusive distribution,** a single dealer, like Neiman-Marcus, is given the exclusive right to sell the item in a specified area. This type of market coverage is used by manufacturers of expensive items and specialty goods with high status and ego appeal. Examples of such products are prestige cars, such as Jaguars, Cadillacs, and Chryslers; exclusive clothing lines, such as Pierre Cardin and Gucci; and expensive cosmetics like Germaine Monteil. Also, exclusive showings of first-run movies such as *Return of the Jedi* take place only at selected theaters, sometimes "by invitation only."

## WHOLESALERS

**Objective 4**

**The types of wholesalers and their functions.**

**Wholesalers** are people or firms that buy finished products from manufacturers and other producers and sell them to retailers, other wholesalers, industrial users, and government agencies. They rarely sell directly to the ultimate consumer. Wholesalers provide invaluable services to both manufacturers and retailers. For example, for manufacturers and other producers, they provide a sales force; store goods; divide large, unwieldy shipments into smaller, more salable amounts; offer credit; and provide market information. For retailers, wholesalers serve as purchasing agents, storage centers, assemblers of goods from various manufacturers, prompt deliverers, sources of credit, and marketing information specialists.

There are many differences among wholesalers. Some of the differences involve (1) whether or not they take ownership of the goods they sell; (2) whether they carry general merchandise, a general line of goods, or specialty products; (3) whether they perform a broad range or a limited number of services; and (4) whether or not they're owned by a given manufacturer.

Most wholesalers are **merchant wholesalers,** who take possession of the goods they buy from producers and sell to small or moderate-sized retailers, industrial users, or other large-scale buyers. They receive and store the goods and later ship them to buyers. For instance, a grocery wholesaler buys goods such as sugar, flour, and canned goods in large quantities, stores them until they're sold, then ships them to the buyer, usually on credit.

Some wholesalers carry only one or two lines of goods. For example, ARA of Mobile carries only air conditioning and heater parts. Some wholesalers are specialty sellers who offer only part of a line to target customers. For instance, Duncan's Wholesale Floral sells only custom orders of dried, silk, and polyethylene flowers. As mentioned previously, most industrial distributors typically sell only to industrial users.

**Manufacturers' sales offices and branches** are wholesalers owned and managed by large manufacturers. Since the late 1960s, they've experienced the most rapid growth of all wholesalers. For example, The B. F. Goodrich Company sells its tires through its own sales offices.

**Manufacturers' agents and brokers** are representatives of only one manufacturer or of manufacturers of several complementary lines. They follow the terms set by those manufacturers. Unlike merchant wholesalers, agents and brokers don't take title to goods, rarely handle them, and act mainly to bring buyer and seller together. They perform fewer services than other wholesalers, work on a commission basis, and generally have good knowledge of the product and of the preferences of users within their territories. Consolidated Investments, Inc. is a broker for sugar, rice, and petroleum products.

## RETAILERS

**Objective 5**

**The types of retailers and their functions.**

**Retailers** are firms or people who obtain goods from wholesalers, brokers, and agents, and sell them to the ultimate consumer for personal, nonbusiness use. Most retail stores are owner-managed. Many of them are "mom and pop" stores that exist because retailing is an easy business to get into: the capital requirements may be only a few thousand dollars, and there are relatively few legal or other requirements for becoming a retailer. On the other hand, retailing can be highly competitive. The failure rate for small retailers is quite high.

### Types of Retailing Operations

Even though most retailers are quite small, the industry is dominated by a few giant organizations, the ten largest of which are listed in Table 15-1. Notice the predominance of food and clothing stores, the basics required by consumers. F. W. Woolworth, number six in 1981, and the Great Atlantic & Pacific Tea Company (A&P), number ten, were replaced in 1982 by Household International and Winn-Dixie. As you'll see from the following definitions of different retail types, it's quite difficult to distinguish between retailers, and the types can overlap.

▲ **Department Stores** A **department store** consists of several different departments located together under one roof to achieve economies in buying, service,

**TABLE 15-1 The ten largest retailers (1982 sales).**

| Company | Sales (In Thousands of Dollars) | Number of Employees |
|---|---|---|
| 1. Sears, Roebuck and Company | $30,019,800 | 403,600 |
| 2. Safeway Stores | 17,632,821 | 156,478 |
| 3. K mart | 16,772,166 | 240,000 |
| 4. Kroger | 11,901,892 | 131,962 |
| 5. J. C. Penney | 11,413,806 | 173,000 |
| 6. Lucky Stores | 7,972,973 | 64,000 |
| 7. Household International | 7,767,500 | 84,000 |
| 8. Federated Department Stores | 7,698,944 | 124,600 |
| 9. American Stores | 7,507,772 | 62,449 |
| 10. Winn-Dixie Stores | 6,764,472 | 64,500 |

SOURCE: Reprinted by permission from "The Fifty Largest Retailers," *Fortune*, June 13, 1983, p. 168. ©1983 Time, Inc. All rights reserved.

promotion, and control. Each department is usually managed by a buyer, who chooses and buys the merchandise, promotes and sells it, and may even select and manage the department's personnel. Higher management coordinates the activities of all the departments and establishes the store's image. This image is set by top management through the type of merchandise carried, the dress and manners of sales personnel, and the store's advertising. Floor space and positioning of items are based on profitability. For instance, perfumes, cosmetics, and jewelry are located in heavy traffic areas, as they are quite profitable.

Some well-known department stores are Rich's in Atlanta, I. Magnin in San Francisco, Bullock's in Los Angeles and Northern California, Filene's in Boston, and Bloomingdale's in New York—all owned by Federated Department Stores, the largest of the department store chains; Lord & Taylor in New York (and elsewhere) and Goldwater's in Arizona, owned by Associated Dry Goods; Marshall Field of Chicago; Neiman-Marcus, based in Dallas; and Macy's in New York, which owns Davison's in Atlanta. Notice how conglomerates dominate the department store field; there are few large independent stores.

▲ **Mass-Merchandising Shopping Chains** **Mass-merchandising shopping chains** like Montgomery Ward, Penney's and Sears are basically similar to department stores (see the Profile on page 406) but quite different in some ways. For instance, they're huge organizations, as shown in Table 15-1, in terms of sales volume, number of stores, use of store brands, and promotion. They're also vertically integrated, owning all or part of many manufacturers that provide their merchandise. They almost always purchase directly from manufacturers. Most of their buying is centralized, but local managers are granted limited purchasing authority.

▲ **Specialty Stores** As their name implies, **specialty stores** handle only one type of merchandise, such as children's clothing, men's clothing, electronic equipment, fabrics, or sporting goods. These stores often carry a greater assortment of merchandise in their specialty than department stores carry. They also attempt to provide more effective customer service. Bill Rodgers Running Centers are a good example, as is Banana Computer Showroom in Silver Spring, Maryland, which sells non–Apple brand computers.

▲ **Discount Stores** **Discount stores** stress high volume and low prices. They often carry a complete line of national-brand merchandise, such as GE and RCA appliances, and generally price the items well below the suggested retail price. These stores tend to stress convenience of location, parking, and hours, as well as ease of purchase (with a centralized check-out). National chains, such as K mart, National Automotive Superstores, and Woolco, used to dominate the discount industry, but now Woolco is gone. (See Case 15-1 at the end of this chapter. Also see FYI on page 408 for an up-and-coming competitor.)

Another type of discount store that is becoming a big factor in the industry is the **off-price store,** which sells high-quality, usually high-priced name brands at 30 to 80 percent off the stated price. By negotiating with suppliers who are in trouble, the owner gets good prices on large quantities of such items as Ralph Lauren shirts, Jaeger sweaters, Albert Nipon dresses, and Izod/Lacoste clothes, which he or she then sells at less than the wholesale price. Some examples of

# *Profile*

## J. C. Penney: The "Golden Rule" Retailer

James Cash Penney once said that the things that lead to success in life are confidence in people, hard work, honesty, preparation, and applying the golden rule.

The seventh of twelve children, J. C. Penney was born in 1875 on a farm in Missouri. His father, a farmer and old-school Baptist minister, preached on Sunday without pay at the Log Creek Baptist Church near Hamilton, Missouri. He taught his son the value of behaving ethically and treating people as he'd want them to treat him. These precepts, embodied in the Golden Rule, guided Penney from his first business experience at age eight. He bought some pigs with $2.50 he'd saved from running errands. When the pigs bothered the neighbors, his father made him sell them prematurely at a much lower price than he would have gotten later for fully developed pigs.

Penney failed in his first business position, as owner of a butcher shop in Longmont, Colorado, because he wouldn't bribe a chef with a bottle of whiskey each week in order to keep the business of a local hotel. Undaunted, he went to work with The Golden Rule Mercantile Co. chain in Longmont. Then, in 1902, he opened The Golden Rule, a dry goods and clothing store, in Kemmerer, Wyoming, in partnership with his former employer. There, he introduced a marketing strategy new for the area—cash sales only, low prices, low markup, low overhead, volume sales, and satisfaction guaranteed on all goods sold. His unique ideas

also applied to employees, whom he considered and referred to as "associates." Managers were paid low salaries but shared in decision making, and were made partners, with a one-third interest in the stores.

Through hard work, sacrifice, and prudent management, The Golden Rule chain prospered, becoming one of the nation's largest retailers after it was incorporated in 1913 as the J. C. Penney Company. Penney served as president of the company from 1913 until 1917, when Earl Sams became president and Penney became chairman of the board. During the stock market crash of 1929, Penney lost much of his stock. He had put it up as collateral for loans to carry on several of his philanthropies and was unable to redeem it on short notice. Despite his loss of stock in the company, Penney served as chairman until 1946, when Sams became chairman and Penney became honorary chairman. When Sams died in 1950, Penney was reelected chairman, a position in which he served until 1958, when he retired. He remained a director until his death at age ninety-five in 1971.

Penney's now ranks fifth among U.S. retailing chains and continues to be highly respected for its quality merchandise and value.

---

Source: Correspondence with J. C. Penney Co.

these outlets are Marshalls in Chicago; Rick Pallack of Sherman Oaks, California; Zayre's Hit or Miss stores in Massachusetts; K mart's Designer Depot; Burlington Coat Factory Warehouse outlets in the New Jersey area; and Zayre's T. J. Maxx in the South.

▲ **Factory Outlets** **Factory outlets** are a form of direct retailing in which the producer sells its products directly from the factory to consumers, usually at a substantial discount. In layout these outlets usually look more like a warehouse than a retail store, with the merchandise displayed in large quantities, closely grouped together. Travelers in North Carolina are pleased with the bargains they find at the state's many textile mill and furniture factory outlets. Another variation of this type of retail operation is the **catalog showroom.** These stores are able to sell merchandise more cheaply because display, sales, and service costs are lower.

▲ **Supermarkets** **Supermarkets** are large-scale self-service food stores laid out by department, such as meats, produce, baked goods, frozen foods, and canned goods. They now frequently have a delicatessen and bakery to cater to shoppers' demand for carry-out food. The more successful supermarkets, such as Kroger, give up to 60 percent of their space to nonfood items, such as drugs, flowers, cosmetics, clothing, and even small TV sets.[1] The line between supermarkets and discount stores is beginning to blur, since Giant Foods' Super Giants and J. C. Penney's Treasure Island discount stores both have grocery sections.

A variation on the theme, **convenience stores** are small supermarkets, like 7-Eleven and Store 24, that offer late-hour shopping seven days a week in exchange for higher prices and limited selection.

▲ **Direct Retailers** The **direct retailer** sells directly to the customer, by telephone, catalog, television, radio, newspaper, magazine, and mail-order advertising, or through personal visits. Mail-order sales have increased between 10

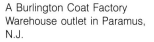

A Burlington Coat Factory Warehouse outlet in Paramus, N.J.

# FYI

**Wal-Mart Stores: Future King of Discounters?**

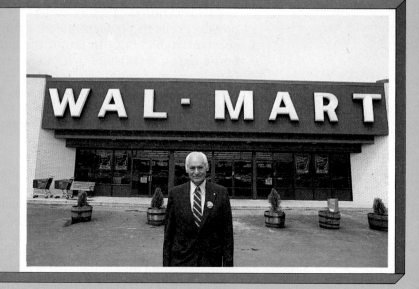

How would you like to vault from being the fifteenth-largest shopkeeper in the nation in 1980 to being ninth in 1983? That's what Wal-Mart Stores did. Sam Walton, chairman, leads cheers of "Wal-Mart, we're number one" at Saturday morning meetings with buyers and managers. With the chain growing at the rate of nearly two new stores each week, and with sales increasing at the rate of 32 percent annually, Walton expects to challenge K mart as the king of discounters by 1987.

Based in the small (population 8,756), sleepy mountain town of Bentonville, Arkansas, Wal-Mart now operates in fifteen southern and midwestern states. It was founded in 1962 by Sam, a former J. C. Penney employee and World War II veteran, and his brother Bud, now a senior vice-president. Many of J. C. Penney's precepts are followed, such as strict observance of the Golden Rule. At the

7:30 A.M. Saturday meetings, new merchandise samples are shown, and Mister Sam motivates those attending with inspirational talks and company cheers.

Wal-Mart's strategy is to offer big discounts on quality merchandise, individually tailored to the small towns where its stores are located. Also, its employees, called "associates," share in Wal-Mart's profits and receive bonuses for suggesting new merchandise ideas and for reducing shoplifting. This strategy has made Wal-Mart the nation's fastest-growing major retailer, with sales increasing almost three times as fast as the discount store industry average.

---

Sources: "Small-Town Hit," *Time*, May 23, 1983, p. 43; Milton Moskowitz, Michael Katz, and Robert Levering, eds., *Everybody's Business: An Almanac* (New York: Harper & Row, 1980), p. 328; *USA TODAY*, March 16, 1984, p. 2B; and others.

and 15 percent a year since 1977, while in-store sales rose only 2 to 3 percent. While Sears is the nation's largest mail- and phone-order catalog seller, around 5 billion copies of 4,000 different catalogs are sent out each year. Direct mail marketing offers customers the convenience of being able to order merchandise without leaving home, along with liberal policies for returning unwanted items. Newspaper and magazine advertisements that ask consumers to call or to send a coupon are another popular form of direct marketing. A third form is door-to-door retailing, as used by Avon, Fuller Brush, and *World Book* encyclo-

pedias. The largest direct marketers in 1983 were Sears Merchandising Group, J.C. Penney's, Montgomery Ward's, Colonial Penn Group, and Spiegel's.[2]

▲ **Vending Machines** Tremendous growth has occurred in vending machine sales. This is understandable when you consider how often consumers buy items like cigarettes, coffee, candy, gum, books, newspapers, soft drinks, stamps, and subway farecards—even air travel insurance and credit cards— from machines. They're appropriate when there's a need for certain products but the demand isn't great enough to justify a full-time salesperson.

## Trends in Retailing

Retailing is in a state of continual change. The **wheel of retailing** is a concept used to describe this perennial state of flux. New retail enterprises enter the market as low-cost, low-price operations. In time, the enterprise moves to a better location, offers higher-quality merchandise, supplies more services, and raises prices. This "trading up" creates a gap in the lower segment of the market, which is then filled by new low-priced enterprises.

Another current trend in retailing is, of course, failure. Retailing, except in larger firms, is a high-risk business. In late 1982, small retailers were struggling when consumers were either unemployed or saving frantically in anticipation of being unemployed. Small retailers were among the hardest-hit victims of the recession, facing profit squeezes and even the loss of their stores. Dun & Bradstreet Corporation said that 8,937 retail stores went out of business between January and November 1982, a 40 percent increase over 1981. This figure was the highest in at least twenty years.

Small retailers don't have the wherewithal to finance slow-moving inventory, and they frequently can't afford to slash prices enough to move their

Mail-order sales and phone-order catalog sales are examples of direct marketing.

stock. As a result, there are many instances of family-owned businesses struggling just above the survival line.[3]

## PHYSICAL DISTRIBUTION

**Objective 6**

How warehousing, order processing, and transportation function as part of physical distribution.

**Physical distribution** consists of all business activities that are concerned with storing and transporting finished inventories or raw materials so that they arrive at the proper place, at the right time, in the desired condition. Physical distribution managers are responsible for getting finished products to the consumer or user effectively and efficiently. Recently, physical distribution management has taken on major importance as managers have become more aware of its cost-saving potential. Physical distribution is part of **logistics,** which is the process of managing the storage of goods and physical movement from producers to users. The usual logistical functions are warehousing, order processing, and transportation.

### Warehousing

Warehouses are places where goods are stored, usually in large quantities, while waiting to be sold or used. Most producers and wholesalers, as well as the larger retailers, have their own warehouses. But there are also **public warehouses,** independently owned facilities that often specialize in handling certain products, such as furniture or refrigerated products. Public warehouses are especially useful when a business wants to place inventory close to key

customers for quick delivery, avoid investment in new facilities, increase flexibility when entering a new market, or temporarily store products to meet seasonal demands.

**Distribution centers** are warehouses of a special type. They serve a regional market, consolidate large shipments from different production points, process and regroup products into customized orders, and maintain a full line of products for customer distribution. The computer is the key to the success of these centers.

### Order Processing

An effective and efficient order-processing system is the next necessity after goods have been warehoused for easy access. Order processing begins the moment a customer places an order. A salesperson sends the order to the office, usually on a standardized order form. The order is then filled and the goods are sent to the customer. Proper order processing is vital to reduce or eliminate customer dissatisfaction due to slow shipment and incorrectly or partially filled orders.

### Transportation Modes

The total transportation bill for the United States is around 22 percent of its gross national product. About 85 percent of that is for moving freight rather than people, which shows how important the transportation of materials and products really is. Materials and products are moved hundreds of times and many miles before the end product reaches consumers. More complex routing, tighter schedules, and the need for quicker and more efficient delivery have forced managers to study the feasibility of using different **transportation modes,** which are the methods used to take people and products from place to place.

A company has many choices of modes or methods of moving goods to and from its plants and/or warehouses. Each of these has advantages and disadvantages, so managers often find it difficult to determine which is best. Even within each method, the various carriers differ in the quality of service they offer, as well as in the rates they charge. So shippers must choose not only among modes but also among different carriers within the same mode.

Selection of the mode of transportation depends on the bulk or perishability of the items to be moved; the distances involved; the availability, dependability, and capacity of each mode; and the costs involved (see Figure 15-5). Specific items to be considered when comparing modes are:

1. *The time within which goods must be delivered.* Some perishable goods, such as flowers, need fast delivery, while some bulky, low-cost items need low-cost transportation and can have longer delivery times.

> Which of the modes shown in Figure 15-5 is least effective in terms of speed? Why do you think that's so?

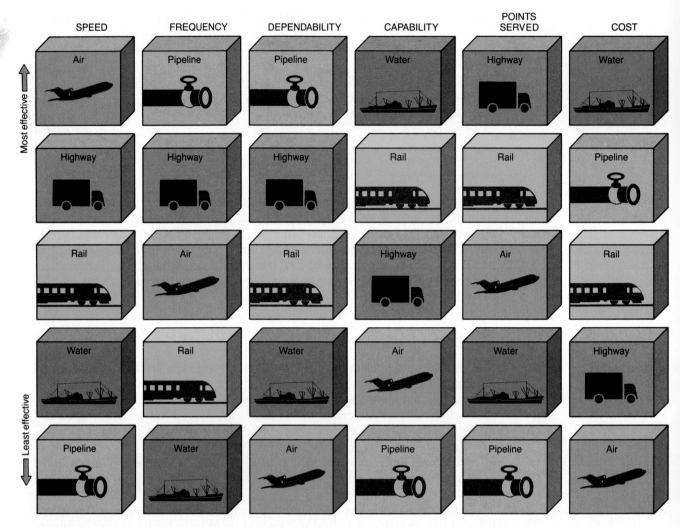

**Figure 15-5** Comparison of the basic modes of transportation. [Adapted from J. L. Heskett, Robert M. Ivie, and Nicholas A. Glaskowsky, Jr., *Business Logistics:* Management of Physical Supply and Distribution (New York: Ronald Press, 1964), p. 71. Copyright © 1964 by Ronald Press. Used by permission of John Wiley & Sons, Inc.]

2. *The service available between the source and the demand location.* If a mode of transportation isn't available to move goods between two desired locations, obviously it can't be used. The choice of plant and warehouse locations often depends on available transportation service and its cost between those points.

> Which modes are most and least effective from the standpoint of points served? frequency of service? Why?

3. *How dependable the service is.* If planned schedules aren't met, operations are disrupted and larger inventories must be carried.

Which modes are most and least dependable? Why?

4. *The carrier's capability of performing desired services.* Transportation managers must match the carrier's ability to carry many types and sizes of payloads with their needs. For example, barges can carry large quantities of material in one trip up the river, while airplanes can't do this except in rare cases.

5. *The cost of the transportation service.* Each mode of transportation has its own cost characteristics. These costs are affected by the size of the load, cost per ton-mile of the transporting unit, handling needed, and government regulation and subsidies.

Most firms use more than one mode of transportation. There are so many different materials, parts, and products and so many terminal locations that frequent study of transportation alternatives is required. Also, changes in methods, government regulations, and competitive situations require specialized attention in large companies. The more popular modes of transportation, though, are railroads, highways, waterways, pipelines, and airlines. Figure 15-6 shows the relative use of each mode. Notice that the use of waterways, pipelines, and railroads has increased, while the use of airlines and highways has declined, perhaps because of their high cost.

▲ **Railroads** Railroads are still the most important freight carrier in terms of intercity ton-miles carried. They are low-cost movers of large tonnages over long distances. Also, they can provide door-to-door service when loading and unloading points are located on rail sidings. Railroads provide nationwide service, as cars can be interchanged between lines. In fact, long moves usually involve two or more rail lines. Trains can run at relatively high speeds and are less affected by congested traffic or bad weather conditions. Therefore, one can usually expect quick and reliable delivery. However, delays due to old and obsolete equipment and time for switching cars lessen this advantage.

▲ **Highways** Trucks serve more points and companies than any other transportation mode. Many firms offer actual door-to-door service, speedy delivery, and relatively economical rates. Since trucking involves fewer transfers from one mode to another, and since the ride is generally smoother, trucking is appropriate for finished goods and fragile products. Large intercity tractor-trailer rigs compete with railroads for short-distance hauling—up to about 500 miles. The national network of highways makes the choice of routes more flexible for trucks than for other modes of transportation. However, weather conditions, traffic congestion, government regulations, and the high cost of fuel are problems for truckers.

▲ **Waterways** At one time, the major way of moving large quantities of goods was by boat. Now, water transport is used mainly to move large shipments of goods that aren't needed very quickly. This mode is limited to situations in which there are available and suitable waterways going from the source to the destination. While boat transportation is slow and adversely affected by icing, it's the lowest-cost means of shipping on a ton-mile basis.

**Figure 15-6** Volume of domestic freight carried by each transportation mode. (Adapted from *Statistical Abstract of the United States,* 1980, p. 639, and 1982, p. 607.)

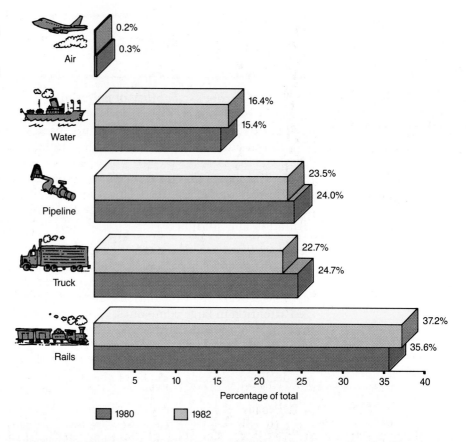

Air freight offers the advantage door-to door, fast delivery of parcels.

▲ **Pipelines**   There's a network of pipelines in the United States that can handle specialized materials such as oil, natural gas, and chemicals. Research is now being done on moving coal in a liquid suspension called *slurry*. While pipelines are restricted in their location and very expensive to build, they provide a continuous flow and at low cost. Thus they're a dependable and economical choice where they're available.

▲ **Airlines**   When speed is a factor, as in the delivery of flowers, business correspondence, and critical spare parts, airplanes are used. Speed is by far their main advantage. On the other hand, shipping by air is limited by aircraft carrying capacity and the location of landing fields. Improvements in helicopters, which can land almost anywhere, are increasing their potential for short hauls and light loads. And there's the space shuttle for future transportation.

Federal Express, which virtually created the overnight package delivery industry, will now pick up a letter from the sender's office, deliver it by 10:20 A.M. the next day to any of thousands of communities, send proof of delivery, and trace it if it goes astray—all for $11. Emery Air Freight Corporation has instituted fast international freight service, with door-to-door delivery of parcels of any size, weight, or value.

▲ **Other Modes of Transportation**   Many changes have led to improved service to customers. Small containers in which to ship goods have been used for a long time to provide easy handling. Now, large containers are filled, locked, and placed on trailers, rail cars, ships, or cargo planes. This method has reduced handling, pilferage, and breakage costs.

**Piggybacking,** or loading specially designed truck trailers onto flat railroad cars, is very common. Other developments are **fishybacking,** in which rail or

Large containers are often filled and placed onto trailers, rail cars, ships, or cargo planes.

truck carriers are loaded onto water carriers, and **birdybacking,** in which truck trailers are loaded onto airplanes. Special containers that can be transferred from one type of carrier to another enable railroads, trucking companies, airlines, and shipping lines to link services. Other specialized types of equipment to meet the needs of particular goods are jumbo tank cars for liquid and gaseous materials; supertankers for oil; open-sided boxcars for lumber and building materials; and enclosed automobile transport cars that protect cars from damage in transit. These designs minimize handling, increase capacities, speed up movement, and reduce damage and theft. CSX Corporation has an integrated system using several modes of transportation. For example, its trains carry trailers, which can then be pulled by truck rigs to the receiver or loaded on ships, barges, or planes for further shipment.

## ⬙ LEARNING OBJECTIVES REVISITED

1. *What channels of distribution are and how intermediaries operate within them.*

   Channels of distribution are the paths that goods take as they move from the producer to the consumer. Intermediaries are those units or institutions in the channel of distribution that either take title to or negotiate the sale of goods and services. The principal role of any channel of distribution is to move products efficiently. Channels bring buyers and sellers together and perform other functions such as reducing the number of transactions, relating the amount demanded to the amount supplied, locating buyers, and improving flows in the distribution of goods.

2. *The major types of distribution channels for consumer and industrial goods.*

   Distribution channels differ for consumer and industrial goods. The usual route for consumer goods is from producer to wholesaler to retailer to consumer. This route can be shortened—or lengthened, by the addition of an agent or broker. The channels of distribution for industrial goods are from producer to industrial user and from producer to wholesaler or industrial distributor to user—with agents or brokers also sometimes being used.

3. *The criteria used in selecting channels of distribution, including intensity of market coverage.*

   The key steps in the channel selection process are to (1) identify the target market; (2) determine customers' buying habits for the type of product; (3) locate potential customers geographically; (4) determine and evaluate channel alternatives; (5) select the best channel; and (6) use the channel and evaluate its performance. Products also differ in intensity of market coverage. They may be placed in many outlets (intensive distribution), with a limited number of retailers (selective distribution), or with one dealer (exclusive distribution).

4. *The types of wholesalers and their functions.*

   Wholesalers are people or firms that sell to retailers, other wholesalers, industrial users, and government agencies, but rarely directly to the consumer. The usual types of wholesalers are merchant wholesalers, manu-

facturers' sales offices and branches, and manufacturers' agents and brokers. Unlike merchant wholesalers, agents and brokers do not take title to the products, rarely handle them, and act mainly to bring the buyer and seller together.

5. *The types of retailers and their functions.*

Retailers are firms or people who sell to the ultimate consumer. The more important types of retailers are department stores, mass-merchandising shopping chains, specialty stores, discount stores, factory outlets, catalog showrooms, supermarkets, convenience stores, direct retailers, and vending machines.

6. *How warehousing, order processing, and transportation function as part of physical distribution.*

Physical distribution includes all business activities that are concerned with transporting finished inventories or raw materials so that they arrive at the right place and time, in the desired condition. It is part of logistics, which is the process of managing the storage of goods and physical movement from producers to users. The usual logistical functions are warehousing, order processing, and transportation. The most frequently used modes of transporting freight are railroads, highways, waterways, pipelines, and airlines.

## ▲ IMPORTANT TERMS

As an extra review of the chapter, try defining the following terms. If you have trouble with any of them, refer to the page listed.

channels of distribution  *396*
intermediaries  *396*
agent (broker)  *400*
intensive distribution  *402*
selective distribution  *403*
exclusive distribution  *403*
wholesalers  *403*
merchant wholesalers  *403*
manufacturers' sales offices and
   branches  *403*
manufacturers' agents and
   brokers  *404*
retailers  *404*
department store  *404*
mass-merchandising shopping
   chains  *405*
specialty stores  *405*

discount stores  *405*
off-price store  *405*
factory outlets  *407*
catalog showroom  *407*
supermarkets  *407*
convenience stores  *407*
direct retailer  *407*
wheel of retailing  *409*
physical distribution  *410*
logistics  *410*
public warehouses  *410*
distribution centers  *411*
transportation modes  *411*
piggybacking  *415*
fishybacking  *415*
birdybacking  *416*

## ▲ REVIEW QUESTIONS

1. How does distribution function as part of the marketing mix?
2. What are the roles and functions of intermediaries?
3. What are the different channels of distribution for consumer goods? What are their advantages and disadvantages?

4. What are the different channels of distribution for industrial goods? What are their advantages and disadvantages?
5. What are the key steps in the channel selection process?
6. Describe the three different kinds of market coverage for manufactured products and the types of goods they apply to.
7. What functions do wholesalers perform?
8. Describe three different types of wholesalers.
9. How does a retailer differ from a wholesaler?
10. Describe the following retail operations: (a) department stores, (b) mass-merchandising shopping chains, (c) specialty stores, (d) discount stores, and (e) direct retailers.
11. What does physical distribution involve?
12. What are the logistical functions?
13. What are the advantages and disadvantages of the most frequently used modes of transportation?

## DISCUSSION QUESTIONS

1. Will there continue to be differences in the channels of distribution used for consumer and for industrial goods in the future? Why or why not?
2. Why doesn't the use of intermediaries increase the cost of goods?
3. What would be the best channel for forklift trucks? office typewriters? wallpaper and paint? home computer cables? Explain your answers.
4. What intensity of market coverage would you choose for Jantzen swimwear? the IBM Personal Computer? *Time* magazine? *Tennis* magazine? the Toyota Celica? Avon cosmetics?
5. Will there continue to be an important role for wholesalers as intermediaries? Why or why not?
6. Will independent department stores be able to survive as retailers in competition with mass-merchandising shopping chains and discount stores? Why or why not?
7. What changes do you see occurring in retailing?
8. What mode or modes of transportation would be best for Frito-Lay's potato chips? Saab automobiles? certified mail? fresh milk? Why?

## CASE 15-1 The Death of Woolco[4]

In November 1982, Woolworth announced that it was closing its largest division, the 336-unit Woolco discount operation. The discounter was losing money, and there were no signs that losses were declining. In its last full year of operation, Woolco had sales of $2 billion.

In 1962, Woolworth was much larger than Kresge, a rival variety-store chain. But then Kresge started opening K mart discount stores and phasing out its variety stores. Woolworth reluctantly followed Kresge's example by opening a few Woolco stores, while still expanding its variety-store operations. Woolworth officials tried to run the discount operations the same way they operated the variety stores. Their buyers bought the same merchandise for both chains, especially artificial flowers and cheap ceramic figurines, which were best sellers in the variety stores, and didn't stock the appliances and other household items that sold well in K mart stores.

Emotional ties to variety-store merchandising prevented Woolco officials from learning the discount business or trying to make it work.

Case Questions

1. What could Woolworth's managers have done differently to save Woolco?
2. What would you suggest that Woolworth's managers do now to improve their variety-store operations?

## ⚖ CASE 15-2  Penney's Streamlines Its Line[5]

When J. C. Penney opened his first dry goods store in 1902, he stocked it with just what his value-conscious customers wanted: gingham dresses for women and denim overalls and suspenders for men. By the 1970s, the Penney chain had grown to more than 2,000 stores selling everything from auto service and appliances to woolens. But profits shrank as merchandise lines expanded. So, in early 1983, Penney's announced that it was dropping its household appliance and hardware lines and service activities and closing its 434 automotive service centers. These back-to-basics moves had been made by many other department stores several years earlier to improve profits. Penney's found, for instance, that appliance sales failed to bear their "fair share" of overhead costs. Women's apparel lines and some other high-markup home furnishings grossed more than three times more profit per foot of floor space than appliances.

Penney's is now spending over $1 billion to revamp and update over 450 of its stores. The entire chain will begin to concentrate on clothing and other "soft" goods. It'll emphasize men's, women's, and children's apparel and home furnishings. It will deemphasize or eliminate less profitable lines such as fabrics, hardware, and lawn and garden supplies.

Case Questions

1. To what extent is Penney's reverting to the basic marketing strategy upon which the earlier stores were founded (see the Profile on page 406)?
2. To what extent do you think these moves will make Penney's more competitive?

# DIGGING DEEPER
## Careers in Marketing

There are many employment opportunities in the marketing and distribution system. In fact, over half the labor force in service occupations is working in one phase or another of marketing. According to one survey, demand for sales and marketing executives reached a five-year high in late 1983. Demand was greatest in the Southeast and Midwest, but also up in the Southwest, West, and Northwest.[1]

### What Marketing Jobs Require

Marketing is a very broad field, involved with a product or service from the time it is created until after it is sold, including service and maintenance. Therefore, generalizations about marketing careers are difficult to make because marketing organizations range from small neighborhood or community retailers to giant multinational firms, as well as giant transportation systems. But many career opportunities do exist in selling, advertising, sales promotion, public relations, product management, marketing research, retailing, wholesaling, physical distribution, and marketing management.

### Selling

Selling offers a wide range of career opportunities because it has more employees than any other single marketing occupation. In some sales jobs, workers are their own boss and determine their own schedules, and their earnings depend entirely on their performance. But most other jobs are routine, with structured work schedules and regular pay. Education and training vary for sales work. For jobs selling standardized goods or services, only high school graduates are required, and more experienced clerks train them. But those whose selling is more complex need more education and training.

Most college graduates with marketing majors enter retailing at a higher level than salesclerk. Initially, they tend to be *trainees* in execu-

tive development programs that lead to positions as *managers* and *buyers*, with opportunities to advance to *merchandising managers* and to top management.

A wide variety of sales jobs are associated with manufacturers, intermediaries, and marketing services, for sales may be directed at producers, wholesalers, retailers, service organizations, or ultimate consumers. But all *salespeople* need product knowledge and customer knowledge to present products effectively and to persuade potential customers that the product they are selling will meet customers' needs better than any other.

### Advertising

Careers in advertising not only are considered glamorous but also are highly competitive. Advertising jobs exist in the advertising departments of producers and intermediaries, in advertising agencies, and with media firms that provide advertising space, time, and supplies for business and industry. It's common for advertising people to change jobs frequently in their advancement. However, some giant advertising agencies do provide attractive advancement opportunities.

A firm's advertising program is directed by the *advertising manager*, who determines how advertising expenditures are allocated, the type of ads and media to use, and the advertising agency to be employed.

*Research directors* and their assistants survey customers' buying habits and motives and test sample ads to find the theme or medium that sells the product or service best. *Copy writers* use research results to write the text or scripts for ads and commercials. They also work closely with *artists* and *layout workers*.

*Production managers* arrange to have ads printed for publication, filmed for television, or recorded for radio. *Media directors* negotiate contracts for advertising space or air time and select the best medium and time to reach prospective customers at the lowest cost.

The job of *account executives* is described in Table IV-1.

## Sales Promotion

Sales promotion involves all activities, including personal selling, required to promote sales, beyond media advertising. *Sales promotion specialists* may work directly for firms or for sales promotion houses to "dress up" products to attract consumers' attention.

## Public Relations

The *director of public relations* and his or her staff develop action programs to build and maintain a positive image of the firm and communicate the attitudes and concerns of employees, customers, stockholders, and government agencies to the firm's management. They provide information about the organization to news media and other channels of communication and arrange speaking engagements and write speeches for the firm's management. They write press releases and articles for publication, including the firm's own publications. Much face-to-face communication with personnel, legal, and marketing staffs within the firm is also part of the public relations job.

## Product Management

Many firms who handle various products or brands employ *product* or *brand managers*, who are responsible for all activities related to that product or brand.

## Marketing Research

The position of *marketing research analyst* is described in Table IV-1.

## Retailing

Most salespeople work in retail outlets. The *department manager* is responsible for inventory maintenance, coordinating the work of buyers and salespeople, and maintaining the overall efficiency of the department's operation.

A *buyer*, as shown in Table IV-1, has the "glamour" job in retailing; all the merchandise sold in a store is there because of some buyer's decisions.

*Merchandise managers* plan and coordinate buying and selling activities for large and medium-sized retail stores. Their responsibilities are to decide how much merchandise to stock, assign buyers to purchase certain goods, divide the budget among buyers, and review buying decisions. College graduates are often assigned to executive development programs that lead to such positions.

## Wholesaling

Many jobs in wholesaling are similar to those in retailing. The principal difference is that the customers are producers, industrial users, and retailers rather than consumers. The position of *wholesale trade salespeople* is described in Table IV-1.

## Physical Distribution

The functions of transportation and warehousing offer many career opportunities. Logistics, practiced by producers, intermediaries, common carriers, and warehouses, is a good growth area.

## Marketing Management

In addition to the marketing management positions described above, three others are emphasized: *sales managers* or *district sales managers*, *product* or *brand managers*, and the *marketing manager*. The marketing manager, or marketing vice-president, is in charge of the marketing function, say, for a manufacturing firm. The product or brand manager position provides excellent training and experience for this position.

Table IV-1 shows some selected positions available in the many marketing areas.

**TABLE IV-1  Selected careers in marketing.**

| Job Title | Job Description | Education and Training | Salaries ( Beginner / Experienced ) | Outlook to 1990 |
|---|---|---|---|---|
| Retail trade salespeople | In jobs selling standardized products, try to interest customers in merchandise by describing its construction, demonstrating its use, and showing various models and colors. Prepare sales slips, receive cash, and give change and receipts. | High school diploma. Associate degree often preferred. For some jobs, special knowledge or skills may be needed. | $7,000<br><br>$8,300–$14,200 | Employment is expected to grow about as fast as the average for all occupations. |
| Buyers | Job of retail buyer is associated with high fashion and also with all merchandise sold in a retail store. Select goods that satisfy customers and sell at a profit. Often specialize in one or a related line of goods. | College degree preferred. Many stores have six- to eight-month training programs for buyer trainees. | $16,930<br><br>$19,000–$28,000<br><br>In addition, cash bonuses, profit sharing, and stock option incentives. | Employment is expected to grow about as fast as the average for all occupations. |
| Automobile salespeople | Assist customers or potential customers in choosing a car that will meet their needs as well as their personal tastes. Are expected to negotiate, especially if cars are overstocked. | High school diploma. Associate degree preferred. | $10,000–$12,000<br><br>Average, $18,000 | Employment is expected to grow faster than the average for all occupations. |
| Advertising agency account executive | In charge of advertising for one or more of the agency's clients. Determine the nature of the advertising to be produced, coordinate all activities involved in producing the advertising, and maintain good relations between the agency and the client. | Minimum requirement is usually a bachelor's degree with a liberal arts, journalism, art, or business major. | $16,930–$18,000<br><br>$25,000–$40,000<br><br>Much higher for senior executives and highly talented individuals. | Employment is expected to grow about as fast as the average for all occupations. |
| Marketing research analysts | Analyze the buying public and its wants and needs. Plan, design, implement, and analyze the results of surveys. Often are concerned with finding out customers' preferences and buying habits. | Bachelor's degree is sufficient for trainees. However, graduate education is necessary for many specialized positions. Trainees usually start as research assistants or junior analysts. | $16,930<br><br>For directors of marketing research, $27,000–$50,000 | Employment is expected to grow about as fast as the average for all occupations. |

**TABLE IV-1**—*continued*

| Job Title | Job Description | Education and Training | Salaries ( Beginner Experienced ) | Outlook to 1990 |
|---|---|---|---|---|
| Manufacturers' salespeople | Sell mainly to factories, banks, wholesalers, retailers, hospitals, schools, libraries, and other institutions. Visit prospective buyers to inform them about products, analyze the buyers' needs, suggest how products can meet these needs, and take orders. | College degree is increasingly desirable. For nontechnical products, degrees in liberal arts or business; for technical products, degrees in science or engineering. | $14,880<br><br>$26,200–$33,500 | Employment is expected to grow about as fast as the average for all occupations. |
| Wholesale trade salespeople | Help move goods from the factory to the consumer. Visit buyers for retail, industrial, and commercial firms and institutions. | For nontechnical goods, familiarity with manufacturers and their brands and sales ability are important. More complex products require a more technical background. | $18,500<br><br>$23,000–$49,500 | Employment is expected to grow about as fast as the average for all occupations. |
| Travel agents | Have information and know how to make the best travel arrangements to match their clients' budgets and other requirements. Consult a variety of sources for information about departure and arrival times, fares, and hotel ratings and accommodations. | College education is often preferred. | $9,500<br><br>$18,000 | Employment is expected to grow much faster than the average for all occupations. Travel industry is sensitive to economic conditions. |
| Public relations personnel | Help organizations build and maintain a positive public reputation. May handle press, community, or consumer relations, as well as interest-group representation and fund raising. Must understand the attitudes and concerns of these publics and communicate this information to management to help formulate policy. | College education combined with public relations experience is excellent preparation. Most beginners have a college degree in journalism, communications, or public relations. | $17,800<br><br>Directors of public relations, $38,000 | Employment is expected to increase about as fast as the average for all occupations. Demand may slacken as employers delay expansion or reduce their staff during business slowdowns. |

SOURCES: U.S. Department of Labor, *Occupational Outlook Handbook*, 1982–1983 (Washington: U.S. Government Printing Office, April 1982) and 1980–1981 (Washington: U.S. Government Printing Office, April 1980); College Placement Council, *CPC Salary Survey, Summer Supplement* (Bethlehem, Pa.: CPC, 1983), pp. 2–5; and Steven D. Ross, "The Top 12 Money-Making Careers of the '80s," *Business Week's Guide to Careers* 1 (Spring 1983): 9.

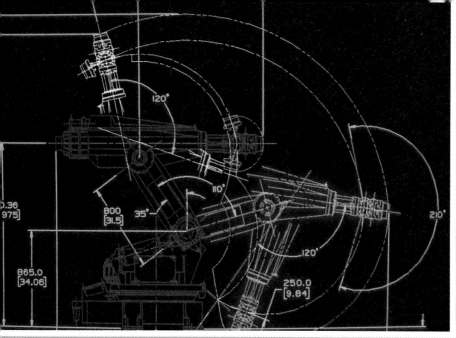

# PART V

## TOOLS OF BUSINESS

Managers need mental and physical tools to help them run a business. In order to effectively manage and organize the business, manage human resources, produce goods and services, and handle financial details, they must have an efficient information system available. This information system is now provided by, and based upon, the computer and an accounting system. Of course, there are other skills, tools, techniques, and systems involved, but these are the critical ones.

Chapter 16 explores in depth what a computer is, how it was developed, the parts of a computer system, how it operates, and how it's used in business.

Accounting procedures, the most important financial statements, and suggestions for interpreting the statements are discussed in Chapter 17.

425

# 16

# Computers and Data Processing

*It is unworthy of excellent men to lose hours, like slaves, in the labour of calculation.*

Baron Gottfried W. von Leibnitz

*We're in the throes of another mighty technological revolution, and the people who are alive today are the first ones to be a part of that revolution.*

Carl Sagan

## Learning Objectives

After studying the material in this chapter, you will understand:

1. The different types of computers and what they can do.
2. The development of the computer from its beginnings to the present.
3. The roles of the hardware and software components of a computer system.
4. How a computer operates, using computer languages, memory, and different methods of processing data.
5. How the computer is used in business.

## In This Chapter

# INTERNATIONAL BUSINESS MACHINES
*A Giant Reawakens*

When people think of computers, they tend to think of IBM. But what few people realize is that for several years after the computer's introduction in the late 1940s, IBM resisted developing computers of its own. Today's computer giant was convinced that they were unprofitable. And since it controlled 97 percent of the punched card tabulating business—and owned the equipment, which was only leased to users—it had a huge stake in maintaining that status quo.

IBM was founded in the early 1900s by Thomas J. Watson, Sr., an Ohio farm boy turned salesman. It was first known as the Computer-Tabulating-Recording Company (CTR), whose main product was an electrical punched card computing system developed for use in the 1890 census. Watson revitalized the tired company, transforming its sales force into dedicated supersalespeople. Pep talks from Watson and songs from the firm's songbook, *Ever Onward,* began each day; dark suits, white starched shirts, and conservative striped ties became regulation attire. And after the name change to IBM in 1924, the now-famous "THINK" signs were posted around company offices, even popping up in closets and washrooms. The strategy of enthusiasm worked to the point that IBM totally dominated the market for time clocks and punched card tabulators in the 1920s and 1930s.

When Watson's son, Tom, Jr. (see photo), took over the company in the 1950s, IBM had grown into one of the nation's largest corporations. But then came the computer. IBM had spent $500,000 to help underwrite the building of the Mark I, a more sophisticated computing device based on electromechanical technology, in the 1930s. But when it was completed in 1944, IBM donated it to Harvard. The reason for such cavalier generosity was that the senior Watson, still chairman of the board at that time, wasn't interested in the big machines. He felt that eight to ten of these newfangled "electrical brains" would fill the needs of engineers and scientists, and that businesses wouldn't have much use for them. His son felt differently but could do little about it.

But when IBM finally made its late and cautious entry into the field, IBM was able to compete as effectively as Tom, Jr., had hoped. IBM's domination of the office machinery field meant that it could make use of an established reputation, sales force, and support services. By the end of 1956, IBM computers were outselling other computers by almost two to one. From that point on, IBM was fully committed to computer production.

IBM reached near-monopoly in sales of mainframe computers in the 1960s and 1970s, but IBM again let competitors get ahead—for a while—in a new area: microcomputers. Until 1981, IBM failed to market a computer for small business and home use, again feeling that the market was too small to be profitable. However, after watching companies like Apple Computer put their machines into thousands of small businesses, IBM introduced its Personal Computer (PC) in 1981 and began to sell it aggressively through retail outlets as diverse as Sears, Computerland, and its own retail product centers.

By late 1983, IBM had surpassed Apple in the $2,500 to $5,000 market. Then it entered the low-priced end of the microcomputer market with the PCjr, designed to sell for under $700. The sleeping giant had reawakened!

427

IBM is certainly no longer dragging its heels in the midst of the computer revolution. And, like business itself, computers now affect nearly everything we do. When we buy anything with a credit card, computers process and store the information, which goes into our computerized credit history. Our income checks are computer-calculated and printed, and our bank deposits are handled by a computer. When you registered at school, a computer was probably used somewhere in the process.

Computers are even changing our language in much the same way that the automobile did. With that new invention, not only did we need to know new terms like *carburetor*, *piston*, and *odometer*; we also had to give new names to old objects: *window* became *windshield*. There were also new commands—*downshift*, *accelerate*—and brand names—Ford, Chrysler, Pontiac, and Rambler—to remember.

Today, the public is in about the same fix. While new computers are readily available, we still don't fully understand their purpose and uses because of unfamiliar terminology. Just as with cars, we have to learn the new vocabulary. There are new objects, like *disk drives, microprocessors*, and *card readers*. New commands include RUN, BREAK, GOTO, and CLEAR. There are even new names for old objects: the simple TV screen becomes a *CRT*, and the user's guide, *documentation*. But, as foreign as the terms and concepts sound today, within a decade they'll be as widely accepted and used as *front-wheel drive* is today.

Webster defines the term *computer* itself as "one who computes; an automatic electronic machine for performing calculations." Indeed, until around 1950, the first definition was the rule. In this chapter, we'll discuss the second meaning—an electronic information processor, a piece of equipment that's become as indispensable to business as paperclips.

## WHAT IS A COMPUTER?

**Objective 1**

**The different types of computers and what they can do.**

For our purposes, we'll define a **computer** as an electronic device that can perform computations, or process data, without the intervention of a human. This device is a remarkable invention, producing reliable, complex analyses in the blink of an eye. For instance, Dartmouth College's John Kemeny, one of the authors of the computer language BASIC, has observed that while it took dozens of experts a full year to do the calculations needed for the Los Alamos atomic tests, today a single student could do them all in one afternoon at a computer terminal.

Although it's extremely fast, the computer, like manual computing systems (basically, paper, pencil, and brains), is still limited to three basic operations. A computer can:

1. Do arithmetic operations—add, subtract, multiply, and divide.
2. Perform logical operations, such as sorting or comparing two items to see if they're equal.
3. Input and output data. The computer accepts information for storage and later presents this information for use when it's needed.

These three operations may not seem like much, but they're performed with extraordinary speed and accuracy. It's this speedy accuracy that gives computers their enormous power.

The Cray-1 computer.

The information a computer uses, called *data*, consists of facts, concepts, and instructions in a form the computer can use. These data, whether the numbers in a mathematical equation or the words in a report, are manipulated, or processed, by the computer to give a desired result. **Data processing,** then, means routine use of a computer to manipulate data and other types of information. Businesses, of course, use the data processing capabilities of computers to make their activities more effective and efficient.

Computer systems are grouped into three types. The type that usually springs to mind is the mainframe computer—a roomful of whirring tape drives, blinking lights, and memory banks flanked by printers. A **mainframe** is a full-scale computer with large memory storage and complex capabilities. The Cray-1 computer (list price, $5 to $15 million) is one of the world's largest, fastest, and most powerful mainframe computers.[1] Such mainframe systems are used mainly by large firms and complex government and research organizations.

A smaller computer system is much handier for most small firms. Such a **minicomputer** may be able to store enormous amounts of data and perform calculations in billionths of a second, just like a mainframe. Yet the actual hardware involved fits into the corner of a room.

The third, and newest, type of computer system, the **microcomputer,** consists of a single unit housing all memory, processing circuits, and wiring, as well as some input-output devices. The microcomputer's great advantage is its near-portability. In fact, the Osborne 1—pioneer in the field—and the Kaypro, Compaq, and Gavilan are truly portable.

As you can see from Figure 16-1, the mainframe's share of the market is declining, while those of the other two types are rapidly increasing. By 1986, sales of personal computers should exceed those of both mainframes and minicomputers. There are now over 200 companies making personal computers.[2] It has been estimated that by 1986 there may be only a dozen left because of the competitive pressures.[3] As FYI on page 432 shows, the shakeout has already started.

**Figure 16-1** The mainframe's share of the computer market is shrinking. (From "Moving Away from Mainframes," *Business Week*, February 15, 1982, p. 78. Reproduced with permission of *Business Week* and Steven Max Singer Designs. © 1982, McGraw-Hill, Inc.)

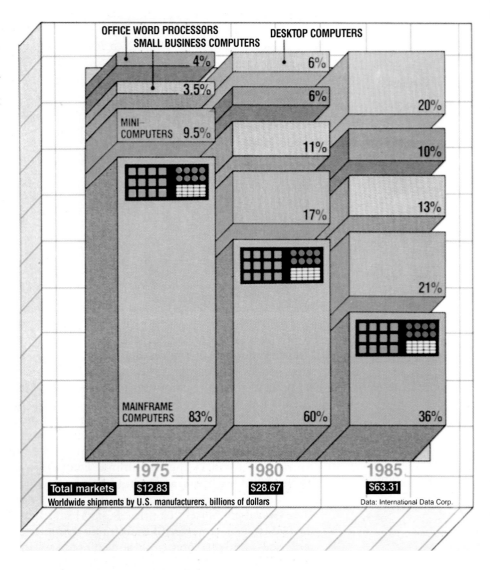

Do you think this is an isolated case, or do you expect other computer companies to fail? Why?

## THE DEVELOPMENT OF THE COMPUTER

**Objective 2**

The development of the computer from its beginnings to the present.

For something that has so radically affected our lives, the computer really hasn't been around for very long. The farthest back we can look for the computer's forerunners is 1642, when French mathematician Blaise Pascal invented an automatic device that added and subtracted with the turning of little wheels. And Charles Babbage, an English mathematician, at one point became

so irritated with errors that he found in mathematical tables that he spent the next forty years developing the Analytical Engine to calculate mathematical functions. Perfected in 1832, it embodied all the concepts of a modern computer but was hardly practical. It required parts so precise that the craftspeople of the period couldn't machine them, so it was never built.

### The First Computer

The first true, operating electronic computer was designed and built in the late 1930s by Dr. John V. Atanasoff, a mathematics professor at Iowa State University, and his assistant, Clifford Berry.[4] The machine, dubbed the Atanasoff-Berry Computer, or simply "ABC," provided the necessary technical groundwork for the advances that took place in the late 1940s. The ABC was used at Iowa State University to perform mathematical operations for the school's master's and doctoral candidates.

### The First Generation: Vacuum Tubes

With the outbreak of World War II and its endless demand for precisely calculated artillery trajectories, the concepts developed by Atanasoff and Berry took on new importance. The Army saw the advantage of having a machine that could rapidly perform calculations that then took people fifteen minutes or more each. Dr. John Mauchly and J. Presper Eckert took on the challenge and in 1943 received government funding to work on a "differential analyzer."

▲ **ENIAC** After three years and nearly $500,000, the machine was completed and christened ENIAC (Electronic Numerical Integrator and Calculator). ENIAC performed the then-amazing feat of multiplying two numbers in about

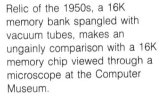

Relic of the 1950s, a 16K memory bank spangled with vacuum tubes, makes an ungainly comparison with a 16K memory chip viewed through a microscope at the Computer Museum.

# *FYI*

## Osborne Failure: The Shakeout Begins

Author-publisher Adam Osborne was always a gadfly for the computer industry. He minced no words about what companies should do to improve quality: match equipment to users' needs and lower prices. When personal computers started to catch on in the mid-1970s, Osborne began to make a name for himself by speaking, writing, and even publishing in the field. His own publishing company put out about forty books, including nearly a dozen written by Osborne himself. One of his books, *Introduction to Micro-computers*, sold over 300,000 copies from 1975 to 1982.

Born in Thailand, the son of a British professor, Osborne came in 1961 to the United States, where he earned a Ph.D. in chemical engineering. He had absolutely no training in business, electronics, or computer science, so when he sold his printing company to McGraw-Hill in 1979 to build his own personal computer, most industry experts raised skeptical eyebrows.

It took the unfazed Osborne only four months to build a

three-thousandths of a second, an accomplishment easily bettered by any of today's calculators. The computer had 19,000 vacuum tubes, 1,500 relays, and hundreds of thousands of resistors, capacitors, and inductors. It was estimated that a vacuum tube failed, on the average, once every fifteen minutes. Whenever a new procedure was to be run, the whole machine had to be rewired. The vacuum tubes were so bulky and produced so much heat that the computer weighed thirty tons, took up 1,500 square feet of floor space, and had to be specially cooled. But ENIAC was still light-years ahead of existing calculating machines and ushered in the computer age.

▲ **UNIVAC** Other computers were designed and built using ENIAC's technical concepts. For lack of a better information storage device, vacuum tubes continued to be used. Mauchly and Eckert founded their own company and

prototype from cheap, easily obtainable parts. It took only a little over an hour, and forty screws, to put together an Osborne 1. The unit, first shipped in July 1981, was a complete, twenty-four-pound system in a portable plastic case that could fit under an airplane seat. It had a 5-inch display screen on a console that looked like "the instrument panel on a DC-3." Osborne's little dynamo could operate on a portable battery pack, had a detachable keyboard and 64K of memory, and cost only $1,795, including five software packages worth up to $1,500 if purchased separately. It was so portable that it was used in courtrooms for lawyers' briefs, in Afghanistan to file news reports, and in the wilds of Kenya for zoological research.

By February 1983, Osborne Computer Corporation was selling about 10,000 units a month, for annual revenues of over $100 million. But Adam Osborne, while marketing-savvy and brash, lacked the management experience or engineering expertise to run a large company in this competitive field. So Robert Jaunich II was brought in from Consolidated Foods as CEO, and Osborne devoted his time to developing the new Osborne Executive model. But Jaunich, too, had difficulty adjusting to the industry's fast pace and was aloof and ineffective.

The company planned to sell stock to the public in the spring to get badly needed funds, but poor 1982 earnings delayed the issue. By then, it was too late. When the new model was announced—before it was ready for delivery—orders for Osborne I dried up, along with corporate cash flow. Many dealers had already cut back on orders because of poor customer service.

By early September, Osborne had resigned from the company he'd founded. Then, at a hastily called meeting on Friday morning, September 9, 1983, the management announced that 80 percent of the firm's staff—400 employees—would be furloughed indefinitely. They were given a check and two hours to clear out their desks and vacate headquarters. Later, the company filed for Chapter 11 bankruptcy in an effort to regroup its resources. Its investors lost $20 million.

While Osborne may have been down, he wasn't out. Within six months, he'd invested $150,000 of his own capital and up to $1 million of investors' commitments to found Paperback Software International, Inc. Working out of the guest house of his estate overlooking San Francisco Bay, he's trying to act as the central marketer, distributor, and packager for twenty-five or thirty small software companies that are unable to do these functions on their own.

Sources: Based on Richard Shaffer, "Riding the Success of Hot Product, Osborne Computer Is Going Public," *The Wall Street Journal,* January 19, 1983, pp. 22–26. Reprinted by permission of *The Wall Street Journal,* © Dow Jones & Company, Inc. 1983. All Rights Reserved. Also based on "Osborne: From Brags to Riches," *Business Week,* February 22, 1982, pp. 86, 90; Frederic Golden, "Other Maestros of the Micro," *Time,* January 3, 1983, pp. 28–29; Michael Rogers, "A Pioneer Loses His Way," *Newsweek,* September 19, 1983, p. 69; "A Pioneer Goes Bankrupt," *Time,* September 26, 1983, p. 52; correspondence with Osborne Computer Corporation; "Carry Along, Punch In, Read Out," *Time,* June 21, 1982, pp. 65ff.; "Adam Osborne Is Back in Computers—With Software," *Business Week,* April 2, 1984, p. 37; and various others.

developed UNIVAC, the first business application for computer technology. They later sold the company to Sperry Rand, which marketed UNIVAC. Until the development of UNIVAC, computers were used only by electronic engineers and mathematicians. But UNIVAC was designed for business applications; it was the first computer capable of processing words as well as numbers. The first UNIVAC was delivered to the U.S. Bureau of the Census for use in the 1950 census. Its first business installation was at General Electric's innovative plant at Appliance Park, Kentucky, in January 1954. UNIVAC was used by Walter Cronkite and CBS (with some misgivings) to predict the outcome of the 1952 presidential election. Although CBS didn't have much faith in UNIVAC's predictions at first, the predictions proved to be perfectly accurate. For the first time, the public had a massive demonstration of computer power, and UNIVAC won national credibility for computers.

The UNIVAC I being used by CBS and Walter Cronkite to predict the outcome of the 1952 presidential election.

### The Second Generation: Transistors

By the mid-1950s, there were still fewer than 250 computer systems in the United States. One reason for that was the unreliability of vacuum tubes, which were bulky, generated tremendous heat, and were annoyingly slow. But in 1947, three Bell Laboratories scientists developed the **transistor,** an electronic device for transferring an electrical current across a resistor (they received a Nobel Prize for this invention).[5] However, no one knew what to do with it, so the manufacturing rights were sold to Sony Corporation for $25,000. A transistor was first put in a computer in 1954. Development of this small, durable, energy-efficient, and cheap device led to the second generation of computers. Computers became less expensive, and companies that previously couldn't afford them flocked to buy computer systems. By 1964, there were 18,200 computers in the country.

### The Third Generation: Integrated Circuits

Transistors reduced the size and cost of machines, but they had their limitations, too. IBM led the way to the third generation of computers in 1964 with the use of integrated circuitry in the System/360 mainframe. Instead of consisting of several separate parts, or components, the control unit was stored on one small **integrated circuit,** or **chip,** a miniaturized electronic component made of silicon. Computer reliability increased dramatically; these chips, which weren't much bigger than a contact lens, failed only once in 33 million hours of operation—a far cry from once every fifteen minutes for vacuum tubes. Also, the 64K chips could store 65,536 bits of information,[6] and a 256K chip had the capacity of 262,000 transistors.[7]

### The Fourth Generation: Micro Chips

Computer technology took another leap forward with the development of the **microprocessor** by a young engineering graduate, Ted Hoff. In 1971, Hoff, working for Intel Corporation, conceived the idea of putting not just the control unit but the entire processor, or brain, of the computer on a single silicon chip. When this computer on a chip was combined with other chips for storage of information, a complete computer system could be put on a circuit board less than one foot square.

The microcomputer age had really begun. It became possible to have a computer in a small console rather than an entire room, paving the way for the development of the personal computer. These microprocessor chips could also be put into cars to control gas consumption, into microwave ovens for temperature and time control, or into typewriters for instant word processing capability. And not only size, but also cost, was shrinking. Today all the circuitry for a computer can be put on a chip that costs less than $25 to produce.

The race to produce the fifth generation is already on between Japanese and U.S. companies. These companies are researching artificial intelligence and trying to build supercomputers a thousand times faster than today's, performing 100 billion operations per second.[8] No one quite knows what effect these "geniuses" will have on us as individuals and organizations.

## PARTS OF A COMPUTER SYSTEM: HARDWARE AND SOFTWARE

Objective 3

The roles of the hardware and software components of a computer system.

When faced with a problem or decision, we humans gather as much information as possible about the situation, develop alternative solutions, and finally choose the most appropriate alternative. We *input*, or gather, information; *process* the information and arrive at a decision; and *output* the results, based on the best information, thinking, or logic available.

A 64K silicon computer chip with over 65,000 bits of data can fit easily on a paper clip.

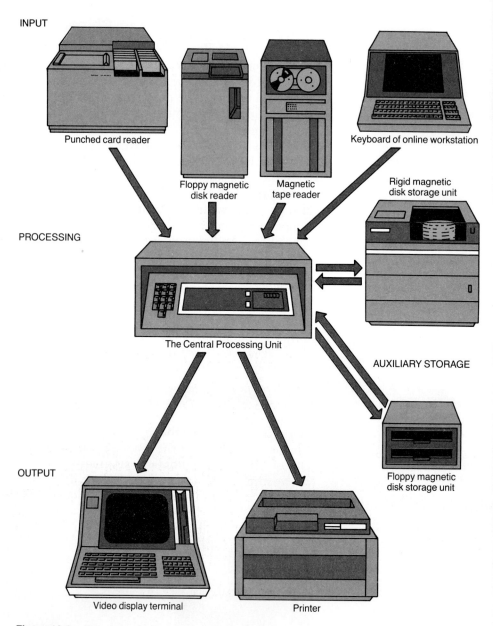

INPUT

Punched card reader

Floppy magnetic disk reader

Magnetic tape reader

Keyboard of online workstation

Rigid magnetic disk storage unit

PROCESSING

The Central Processing Unit

AUXILIARY STORAGE

Floppy magnetic disk storage unit

OUTPUT

Video display terminal

Printer

**Figure 16-2**  The parts of a computer system.

Just as in the human decision-making process, a computer system goes through a three-step cycle, as shown in Figure 16-2.[9]  Information, or data, is put into the computer in one of several ways, to be discussed later.  The computer's central processing unit sorts and manipulates those data under the control of a set of instructions, or program, it has received.  Once the data have been processed, the results are sent out, by means of output devices, as printed words or characters on a video screen.  The process may become quite complex, as we'll see, but all applications involve input, processing, and output of data.

A **computer system** is a collection of all the devices a computer needs to

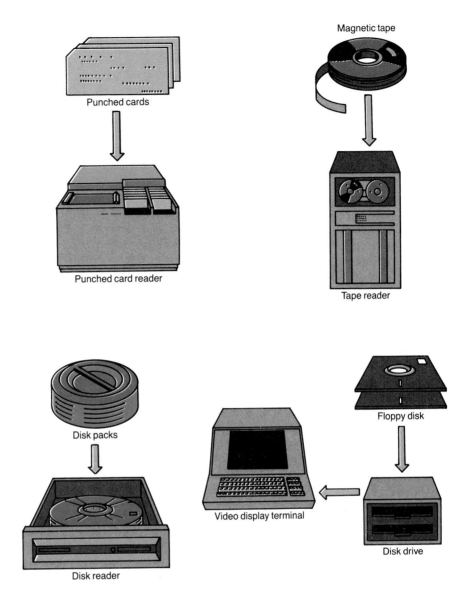

**Figure 16-3** Computer input devices.

input, process, output, and store data. For a microcomputer, they may all fit into a single console. For a mainframe computer, they may be many machines in a large, air-conditioned room. The physical components themselves are called the **hardware;** the instructions (programs and languages used with them) are the **software.**

## Input Devices

Before processing can happen, of course, the information has to be presented to the computer in a form it can digest. Data are inputted in a number of ways: through punched card readers, magnetic tape readers, or computer terminal keyboards (see Figure 16-3).

> Do you know of other ways of inputting data into a computer?  If so, what are they?

▲ **Punched Cards**  One of the earliest ways to input data was through the use of **punched cards,** which have holes punched in them to correspond to characters.  The system was adapted from the card system that Tom Watson's company developed to process the 1890 census.

Each card contains twelve rows of eighty columns that may represent up to eighty letters, numbers, symbols, or spaces.  The operator enters the information on a card using a typewriterlike machine called a **keypunch,** which punches the holes in the cards.  The cards are then put into a card reader, which converts the punched holes into electric impulses that the computer can understand.

▲ **Magnetic Tape and Disks**  Punched cards are bulky to handle and store, and reading them into the computer can seem to take forever.  In the 1960s, a substitute was developed to speed up the input process.  Data are recorded on **magnetic tape,** which can then be entered, or read, into the computer by a magnetic tape reader.  The tape used is a thin mylar strip coated with iron oxide (rust) particles, which can be specially magnetized to accept 800 to 1600 characters per inch.  The tape reels are easier to store than cards, and data can be entered more quickly into the computer.

Despite its advantages, tape has one drawback.  Information must be stored and retrieved in sequence.  Information stored on the end of a tape reel can be retrieved only by first passing through the entire reel, as you would a stereo cassette.  This disadvantage has been eliminated by the development of the magnetic disk and its smaller cousin, the **diskette.**  The **magnetic disk** is a magnetized metal or mylar platter, much like a grooveless phonograph record.  Data can be retrieved from any given part of it, much as any song can be played by putting a needle down at any location on a record.  Information stored on disks is read into the computer by a **disk drive,** a device which keeps the disk spinning, like a phonograph record, under a stationary read/write head.  The advantage of using disks is that data can be retrieved directly, at random, without reading through an entire disk first—a much faster process.

▲ **Computer Terminals**  In many cases, when information must be available in seconds, direct access to the computer processor is provided by a **computer terminal.**  The keyboard of a terminal—very much like a typewriter keyboard—can enter data directly into computer memory.  A reply comes almost instantaneously.  The terminal is the primary input medium for small computer systems and home computers and is used in combination with other devices in most larger systems.

## The Processor

The heart of the computer is the processor, where the data inputted into the system are actually used and analyzed.  Although it's very important, the processor itself can be one of the smallest components of the system.  In microcomputers, it consists of a single microprocessor chip.

The processor is made up of two parts: the central processing unit and **main computer storage.** The main computer storage is where data are kept after they are read into the system through an input device. The instructions, or program, that the processor uses are also stored here. The **central processing unit (CPU)** is the controller for the system. It contains the logic and arithmetic circuitry that allows the computer to perform its basic functions.

### Output Devices

Once data have been processed, the results must be made available to users by means of an output device.[10]

▲ **Printers** The most widely used output device is the **printer,** which can range from a small desktop unit cranking out twenty-five characters per second to a huge high-speed printer churning out 20,000 lines per minute. An office needing only one or two short reports a day may use a desktop unit, while a large utility company printing millions of computerized bills each month would need a high-speed model.

▲ **The CRT** Data also can be outputted from the computer on a video screen, called a **cathode ray tube (CRT).** When information is needed immediately, a computer terminal with keyboard and CRT is used. The screen image can also be reproduced by the printer or another recording device.

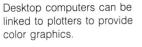

Desktop computers can be linked to plotters to provide color graphics.

> Can you envision other types of output devices?  If so, what are they?

### Auxiliary Storage

The space available in main computer storage is limited.  Previously used data must be put elsewhere or destroyed when new information is entered.  But these data can be stored for future use on many of the same types of media used to input data.  Information can be recorded on reels of magnetic tape, which can be stored and then pulled out for use when the information is needed again.  Magnetic disks, however, are rapidly replacing tape as the auxiliary storage medium of choice.

Large-scale computer systems typically use a **disk pack** consisting of hard disks stacked in bundles of eleven.  Each surface, except the top and bottom ones, is coated with magnetic oxide and can accept information.  The latest disk packs can store up to 200 million characters.  These packs are placed in disk drives, which spin the packs at speeds of 3,600 revolutions per minute.  A read/write head, or access arm like a phonograph's tone arm, swings between the disks to store or retrieve data.

Smaller quantities of data can be stored on diskettes called **floppy disks,** which are often used with microcomputers.  These are thin, flexible (hence their name) mylar disks that can contain up to 1.5 million characters.  A floppy disk drive is needed to store and read the data on these disks.

### Instructions Please: The Software

The system we've described so far is made up of individual components—hardware.  The hardware, however, can't do a thing without very specific instructions.  The set of instructions given to a computer is called a **program.** The program is extremely important, for just one small error—an instruction out of sequence, a punctuation mark omitted or misplaced, or a misspelled word—can completely confuse the machine.  In fact, it was the omission of one punctuation mark from hundreds of pages of a computer program that caused the failure of a space shot in the 1960s.[11]

Computers need instructions simply to understand commands.  The set of instructions that controls the inner workings of the computer is called the **systems software** and is built into the computer by its manufacturer.  The user can simply forget it exists.  The systems software translates typed commands into electronic impulses and sends them to the precise location where they are needed for processing.  The systems software is the traffic cop of the system.

In order for the computer to generate useful information, another type of program is needed: **applications software.**  This is a series of commands written by the user, or purchased from another programmer or a software company, which gives the system specific instructions for a given job.  Applications programs may keep track of bank account balances, monitor heating and air-conditioning systems, record inventory levels, calculate income tax returns, compose letters, check spelling, or help set up family budgets.

Computer hardware technology has advanced more rapidly in recent years than software technology.  Practical applications programs are needed to make

computer hardware useful, and each new computer design requires new software. The programming bottleneck has resulted in a tremendous demand for computer programmers to design and write programs. One of the disadvantages of IBM's late entry into the microcomputer field, for instance, was the shortage of software available for its Personal Computer as compared, say, with the Apple. Its strategy in dealing with a potential marketing disaster was to open its doors to user-developed software.

The software industry is fiercely competitive, with much of the development being done—and companies being formed—by young users, especially students. One of the most successful, VisiCorp, was started in a walk-up apartment in 1978 by Daniel Fylstra, a graduate student at Harvard Business School. With $500, he started publishing software to make personal computers more useful for professional and business people. In 1981, his sales of products like VisiCalc, a computer financial spreadsheet program, reached nearly $25 million.[12]

## HOW DOES IT COMPUTE?

### Computer Languages

**Objective 4**

**How a computer operates, using computer languages, memory, and different methods of processing data.**

Since computers' electronic circuits operate in either an *on* or an *off* state, computers only understand instructions written in **machine language,** a binary code in which all letters and numbers are represented in terms of only two different digits. Communicating with the computer's processor using binary code is a tedious, time-consuming task. But the only way to transfer meaning to and from the earliest computers was through machine language.

## *Profile*

### Captain Grace Hopper: The Grand Old Lady of Software

"I told the admiral, I plan to die on active duty so he'll have to pay for my funeral. That's the Scot in me," said the ever-so-opinionated Captain Grace Murray Hopper, or the "Grand Old Lady of Software," as she's been dubbed. She says it's her "youth" that keeps her going. Nearly eighty, she's the oldest Navy person on active duty. These com-ments are typical of this vivacious and dynamic expert on computers and computer software.

Dr. Hopper is a pioneer, both in the field of computer science and as one of the first persons to be promoted to captain by a special act of Congress. No one on the Reserves' retired list had ever received such a promotion.

In an effort to simplify the instruction process for human operators, some experiments were carried out in the early 1950s by Dr. Grace Hopper (see the Profile above) and others. The results were higher-level programming languages that transmit information to the computer with more comprehensible words and notations instead of numbers. The earliest widely used programming language was **FORTRAN** (FORmula TRANslation), a number-crunching language developed for use by scientists and engineers.

As computers began to be used in business, weaknesses were encountered in FORTRAN and other engineering languages. And many computer models had individual languages which could be used on no other machine. In the late 1950s, a committee sponsored by the Defense Department developed a programming language that simplified programming and could be used on computers made by different manufacturers. **COBOL** (COmmon Business-Oriented Language), which approximated normal business English, rapidly became one of the most widely used programming languages in the world.

Microcomputers today use a simpler language, **BASIC** (Beginners' All-Purpose Symbolic Instruction Code). The commands are in easy-to-understand

Her extensive educational background includes a degree in mathematics from Vassar (1928) and a master's degree (1930) and a Ph.D. (1934) in math and physics from Yale. Then she taught math while waiting for a more challenging opportunity. It came in 1943 when she left her position as an assistant professor of math at Barnard College to enlist as a WAVE in the Naval Reserves. Since then, she's been awarded a dozen honorary doctorates and the prestigious "Man of the Year" honor from the Data Processing Management Association.

In 1944, Dr. Hopper began working with Dr. A. Howard Aiken at the Navy's Bureau of Ordnance Computation at Harvard University—and the rest is history. Dr. Hopper, together with the Navy team, developed the Mark I, Mark II, and Mark III computers. After leaving the Navy, she joined the Eckert-Mauchly Computer Corporation (later Sperry Rand) and aided in the development of UNIVAC-I, the first large-scale mainframe digital computer, which became operative at the Census Bureau in 1951. With the advent of more efficient computers, she formed the first complete list of computer commands, such as ADD, EXECUTE, and STOP. Her most important contribution was helping to develop the language COBOL, which revolutionized the way businesses could use computers.

Captain Hopper isn't impressed with the women's movement, though. She thinks too many women are preoccupied with the idea and says, "If you want to do something, go ahead and do it—you don't have to wait for permission." For Grace, a gutsy attitude and willingness to take risks (not necessarily her "youth") have led to success. When she has an idea, she follows through with it, then asks permission to do it. "The big rewards go to the people who take big risks," she says.

Perhaps the other key to Captain Hopper's success has been her ability to adapt to change. She loves lecturing to, and working with, young people because they aren't afraid of new ideas. She believes that continuous learning is the essential element one needs in order to adapt because "when you stop learning, you die." With this attitude, it's understandable that Captain Hopper pokes fun at those who resist change. For example, she tells the story of how the term *debug*, meaning to straighten out a computer program, began. When something went wrong with the Mark I about forty years ago, she and the others found a moth stuck to one of the parts. They removed the moth and wrote in the records, "The Mark I was debugged today."

She's convinced that the computer revolution is in the beginning stages; she calls it the "Model T" stage. And those who know Captain Grace Hopper would say she's probably right.

Sources: An interview with Brightman Brock, "This Navy Captain Knows Her Stuff," *Mobile Register*, October 13, 1983, p. 11-A; "Navy Captain Has a Message for Her Public," *Mobile Register*, June 1, 1983, p. 7-A; and "Older than UNIVAC," *Forbes*, August 30, 1982, p. 141.

English, and the language is so logical that it can be learned quickly. Most small business systems use BASIC because of its clarity and simplicity.

Since computers speak and understand different languages, and even different versions of the same language, one of the pressing needs today is for a way to make them more compatible. For instance, if you bought an IBM PC, you couldn't use Apple software on it because the machines use different systems software as well as different versions of BASIC. To combat this problem, Quadram Corporation has developed the Quadlink, a card that fits inside an IBM PC and runs programs written for the Apple IIe—in effect, the card makes the PC think like an Apple.[13]

### Memory and Its Measurement

A computer's memory is measured in units called **bytes.** If the main computer memory can store 16,000 characters, or bytes, it is said to have 16 kilobytes of memory, or simply 16K. You can get an idea of how much information a kilobyte contains by imagining a letter-size page with normal margins and

double-spaced typing. There are approximately 2K bytes of information on that page. Small microprocessors, or personal computers, usually start with 64K memory storage, but some of them can now be expanded beyond 256K.

### Running a Program

Let's follow the processing cycle through to see how the computer operates. Say that a bank has a computer program set up to prepare its monthly checking account statements (see Figure 16-4). The records for all its accounts are recorded on magnetic disks, with deposits and withdrawals coded differently. On the day that the monthly statements are prepared, the computer operator puts these disks into a disk drive, which reads the information into main computer storage. A detailed program outlining how the statements are to be prepared is also put into the computer's main computer storage.

Within the CPU, all activity is controlled by the program. The information for the first account file, including the balance, is moved by the program from memory into the CPU, where calculations are done. First, the processor uses its logic function to see whether a transaction is a check or a deposit. Then its arithmetic function subtracts the check amount from or adds a deposit to the previous balance. Next, the computer uses its logic function again. It asks, "Are there any more transactions?" If so, it goes through the "check or deposit?" routine again. If there are no other transactions, the program tells the computer to print out the result and go on to the next account—until all the accounts are finished.

While the processor tackles the next account, the control system sends the first account to the printer and puts the new account balance onto magnetic disk or tape for storage. The printer then prints out the statement.

### Methods of Processing Data

The computer can process data in groups, called batches, or it can respond to individual commands to provide desired information instantly.

▲ **Batch Processing** The checking account program just described illustrates the oldest method of data processing—grouping records, in this case checking account records, into batches for the computer to process together, or **batch processing.** Batch processing works well for applications such as payroll, monthly sales reports, or mailing lists. All the information can be read in, processed, and printed out together. Before recent technological advancements, batch processing was the only method available.

▲ **On-Line Processing** Preparing monthly checking account statements may lend itself to batch processing, but what if you want to know what your checking account balance is *now*? Unless the bank has just processed all its records, it would be difficult to use the computer to determine your balance. Therefore, modern computer systems have the ability to process data immediately upon receiving an inquiry.

**On-line processing** allows the user to communicate directly with the processing unit of the computer to obtain or retrieve information. This capacity lets travel agents make airline and hotel reservations instantly and permits the sale of tickets to cultural and sporting events at any number of remote locations, through outlets like Ticketron's.

**Figure 16-4** Simplified flowchart describing how a computer program reads and calculates the balance for a set of bank checking accounts.

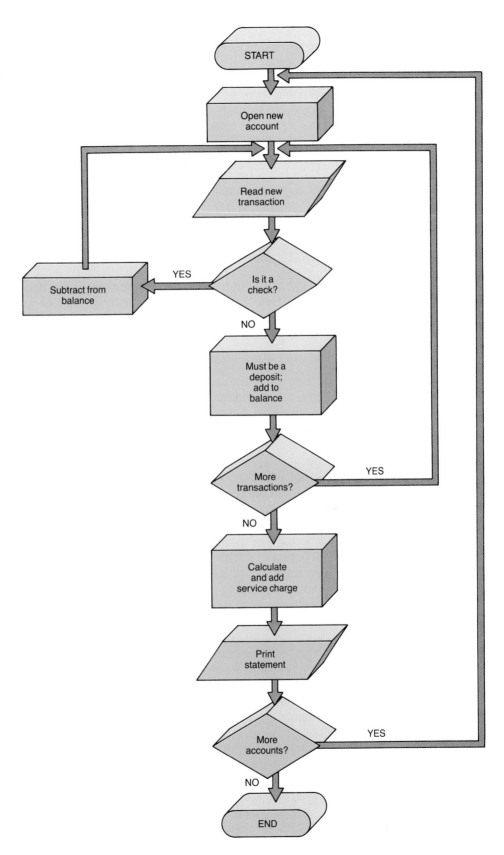

The keys to on-line processing are the computer terminal and random access memory. Data must be stored on random access media such as disks so the computer can retrieve information quickly. The computer terminal, with keyboard and video screen, enables anyone to have access to the computer. When a typed inquiry is sent to the processor, a reply is displayed on the video screen in seconds. If you've used a bank's twenty-four-hour automated teller, you've experienced a simplified form of on-line processing.

On-line processing requires careful planning, as the operators using the system may know very little about computer terminology and operation. User-friendly computer programs, which lead the user through each step with prompting questions and responses, have been developed to ease this dialog.

## USING THE COMPUTER IN BUSINESS

**Objective 5**

**How the computer is used in business.**

It's impossible to describe all the uses of the computer in business. Instead, we'll show how it processes business data in general and explain its most frequent applications.

### Computer Applications

Computers are useful to small firms as well as to large corporations. These firms may find that a computer can provide benefits far exceeding its cost. For example, accounting for most firms can be handled more quickly and efficiently by a computer. Accounting programs let the operator input data, such as a customer's cash or credit payment, and then the computer automatically updates all the records affected by that payment. The customer's account balance is reduced, the firm's cash account is updated, and the accounts receivable balance in the general ledger is reduced, all in one entry.

One of the most widespread uses of computer technology in both small and large businesses is **word processing.** By coupling the small computer with a letter-quality printer, one can type, edit, check spelling in, and correct over 100 pages of type on the video display before sending it to the printer. A perfectly typed letter or report then emerges. Once the letter is in the computer's memory, the user can easily send the same letter to many different persons, changing the address and salutation. With mailing-list programs like MailMerge, these changes are automatic.

Computers can also help businesses keep track of inventory and signal when supplies are running low. Other computers may handle a doctor's patient records, help a real estate agency locate available houses, or handle an investor's financial planning.

Spreadsheet programs like the VisiCalc program mentioned earlier enable businesspeople to plan "what if" scenarios. For example, what would the company's profit be if it increased the price of its product by $1.00, if costs were reduced by 5 percent, or if output were increased by 3 percent? These calculations would take hours if done manually but can be done in seconds on a computer. With such programs, planners have access to more complete and timely data for decision-making.

Computers are beginning to be an important feature of hotel rooms. Travelhost network has its Quazon computer terminals hooked up to the

phone and TV set in 100 of Chicago's Midland Hotel's 300 rooms. Over 120 other hotels, including Hiltons, Holiday Inns, Marriotts, and Sheratons, are installing the system in over eighty cities. With this system, guests can check airline schedules and make reservations, catch late sports scores, play games, check the latest news and stock reports, and receive messages transmitted from their offices.[14]

Larger businesses have developed ingenious uses for computer systems. The automatic teller machines (ATMs) and electronic funds transfer (EFT) used by banks (see Chapter 18) are some examples of the computer's use in banking and finance. The U.S. government routinely uses computers to send Social Security and retirement payments directly to recipients' banks. Some businesses are using computers to send electronic mail between branches and to other firms.

Large retailers have adopted computer-based sales registers to aid sales personnel. Many use hand-held tag readers that enter sales information into the register automatically. Some newer systems can use the data entered to update inventory and automatically print out purchase orders when new merchandise is needed. Large supermarkets use laser scanners to read the universal product codes printed on almost all grocery items (see Chapter 13). The sales tape records for purchasers what was actually bought, and the data entered in the computer system help management analyze which products are selling well. Some of the latest systems are even saying "Thank you for shopping with us."

---

What are some other computer business applications you've experienced? What are some other possible applications?

---

## Data Bases and MIS

Computer systems that use the concept of data bases are called **management information systems (MIS),** or data base management systems (DBMS). This type of computer data system maintains a comprehensive master file of all data relating to each subject.

To understand data base systems you must know what type of system they replace. Conventional systems work on the concept of individual files—for example, a storage file for inventory, a storage file for customer accounts, a separate mailing address file, and a file for customer purchase orders. When a customer's address changes, three files have to be updated; when an order is received, three files have to be changed.

With proper programming, a computerized master file can be created to store all this information together, including customer addresses, account balances, and order information. Retrieving the desired information, whether for the accounting department or for the shipping department, becomes a simple, one-step process. The master data base can be designed to store any type of information the company uses routinely.

Despite the complexity involved in setting up management information systems, their use has become widespread. With their increasing use, however, have come problems of data security and protection of individuals' pri-

vacy. As the film *War Games* made clear, access to the data base must be restricted to ensure data security. Internal security can be strengthened by use of passwords or identification numbers keyed to different security levels. In response to the concern for individual privacy, Congress passed the Privacy Act of 1974, restricting the right of federal agencies to establish data banks and giving individual citizens the right of access to stored information about themselves upon request.

## ⬛ LEARNING OBJECTIVES REVISITED

1. *The different types of computers and what they can do.*

   The computer is an electronic device that can perform computations, or process data, without the intervention of a human. It can do arithmetic operations, perform logical operations, and input and output data. Data processing means using a computer routinely to process data and other types of information.

   Computers vary from (1) mainframe computers, which are giant machines with banks of processors and output devices, to (2) minicomputers, which can store and process large amounts of data but are small enough to fit in the corner of a room, to (3) microcomputers, consisting of a single unit housing all the memory, processing circuits, and some input/output devices.

2. *The development of the computer from its beginnings to the present.*

   Probably the first automatic data processing device was built in 1642 by Blaise Pascal. Then Charles Babbage perfected his Analytical Engine in 1832. But the first generation of operating computers was developed in the United States in the late 1930s. Real progress toward programmable operating computers was made during the 1940s and early 1950s with ENIAC and UNIVAC. They used vacuum tubes; were slow, bulky, and massive; and had only limited applications.

   The second generation began in the mid-1950s and was based on the transistor. A rapid growth in the development and use of computers resulted in reduced prices and new applications.

   The third generation was based on the use of integrated circuits, or chips. Computer reliability increased dramatically, as did memory storage capabilities.

   The real explosion in computer development, programs, use, and reduced cost occurred during the fourth, and current, generation. Based on the microprocessor chip, the personal and business microcomputer began to open up new applications and led to new types of users.

3. *The roles of the hardware and software components of a computer system.*

   The computer, like humans, inputs (gathers) information, processes it, and outputs the results. The computer does this with a combination of hardware, or operating mechanisms, and software, or instructions.

   Hardware consists of (1) input devices, including punched cards, magnetic tape or disks, and computer terminals; (2) the processor, including the central processing unit and main computer storage; and (3) output devices, including printers and computer terminals. In addition, auxiliary

storage is provided by magnetic tape and disks, disk packs, and floppy disks.

Software includes programs for instructing the computer. Built-in systems software constitutes a program that controls the inner workings of the machine. Applications programs are the user's commands for the device to perform specific functions.

4. *How a computer operates, using computer languages, memory, and different methods of processing data.*

All computer commands must be translated into some machine language, which is based on a binary code. Higher-level languages like FORTRAN, COBOL, and BASIC more closely resemble English.

Memory is measured in units called bytes. Memory capacity is one way of classifying the power of a computer.

Computers can process data in groups, through batch processing, or they can respond immediately, through on-line processing.

5. *How the computer is used in business.*

Some of the more popular business applications of the computer are in accounting activities, payroll, word processing, inventory control, automatic banking, supermarket checkout, and management information systems, or data base management.

## ⛛ IMPORTANT TERMS

As an extra review of the chapter, try defining the following terms. If you have trouble with any of them, refer to the page listed.

## ⛛ REVIEW QUESTIONS

1. What are a computer's strengths and weaknesses?
2. Explain the differences among mainframe computers, minicomputers, and microcomputers. How would each best be used?

3. What happened in each of the computer's four generations?

4. How does the basic cycle followed by the computer parallel human data processing?

5. Classify each of the following as hardware or software:
   a. A deck of punched cards
   b. A disk drive
   c. The CPU
   d. 16K of memory
   e. A disk pack

6. Describe some basic input devices.

7. What are the parts of the processor?

8. What are some output devices? Describe each.

9. Why is auxiliary storage needed?

10. How would you distinguish between systems software and applications software?

11. How would you distinguish among machine language, FORTRAN, COBOL, and BASIC?

12. What is the difference between batch processing and on-line processing of business data? What are some applications of each?

## ⏚ DISCUSSION QUESTIONS

1. Aside from those mentioned in the text, what are some new terms—or new meanings for old terms—created by the computer?

2. What do you see as some of the next major breakthroughs in computer technology?

3. (a) What organizations maintain a data file on you? (b) What would happen if they lost your file? (c) What are some possible problems involved in the security of data files?

4. What are some applications of the computer not mentioned in the chapter?

5. Which kinds of work should be assigned to a computer and which to people? Why?

6. Try preparing a flowchart of a process you're familiar with.

## ⏚ CASE 16-1  Edge 1000: New Baseball Management System?

In 1981, the Oakland Athletics professional baseball team bought an Edge 1000 computer system to help its broadcast team keep track of such mundane things as runs batted in and batting averages. Later it was programmed to analyze how well—or poorly—certain batters performed against opposing pitchers, and vice versa. Billy Martin, the A's flamboyant manager, kept his own statistics and strategies in his head and would have nothing to do with the new toy.

On the other hand, Tony La Russa, the Chicago White Sox's manager, was quite willing to pioneer baseball's use of a computerized managerial system. (It may be only coincidental that, in 1983, with the 1000, the White Sox won the American League pennant for the first time in over twenty-five years, but they did!) After La Russa's success with using the system to analyze play-by-play accounts of each game and provide detailed performance evaluations of players in the American League, the A's began using it. Later, in 1983, Billy Martin and George Steinbrenner bought a system for the New York Yankees.

The managers use the ballpark terminal,

which is hooked up by telephone to a mainframe in Philadelphia, to assist in planning game tactics, scouting the opposition, contract negotiations, and even arbitration with disgruntled players, by storing reams of performance data. The White Sox even used its data to move its home plate eight feet forward in an effort to produce more home-team homers. Oakland has used it to juggle its batting order.

### Case Questions

1. Do you think this baseball computer system will be an effective management technique? Why?
2. How would you feel if you were a player and the managers made a decision affecting you based on the computer's printout?
3. Do you think it will replace managers? Why?

## ⬚ CASE 16-2 United Technologies: Computers for Managers

United Technologies (UT) is a high-tech company producing goods such as air conditioners, elevators, and helicopters. Yet the giant firm only became part of the computer revolution around 1978—by introducing its secretaries to word processors. Then some of its younger, more adventurous engineers and financial experts began sneaking their own personal computers (PCs) into company headquarters. So UT began to buy its higher-paid executives PCs and programs and offered them a three-day intensive training course on how to use the equipment.

About 1,100 executives were scheduled to take the course. There was considerable resistance from those managers who thought their time could be better spent "working with people" than "feeding data into a machine." Then UT's chairman, Harry Gray, issued a videotaped message saying he thought the program was "a good idea."

After 300 or so executives had finished the course, less than 20 percent of them were using their PCs on the job, and over 60 percent never used them. The others used the computers occasionally. Incidentally, Chairman Gray hadn't taken the course.

The primary value of this effort was to prepare top managers for multifunction work stations uniting the telephone, the computer, and voice-activated dictating machines. The work stations could be hooked up to each other so the managers could exchange messages and share data.

### Case Questions

1. Are you surprised that so few executives used the computers after training in their use? Why or why not?
2. Why do you think the chairman didn't take the course? Did this influence the attitude of the other executives? Why or why not?
3. What could be done to encourage the use of the PCs?

# 17

# Accounting for the Firm's Resources

*Double-entry bookkeeping discloses to us the cosmos of the economic world.*

Werner Sombart (1902)

*[Accounting] is a tool and, like most tools, cannot be of much direct help to those who are unable or unwilling to use it or who misuse it.*

Financial Accounting Standards Board

## Learning Objectives

After studying the material in this chapter, you will understand:

1. The role of accounting and accountants in recording and presenting a firm's financial information.
2. How the accounting equation and the double-entry system are used to classify business transactions.
3. The purpose of the balance sheet and its information on assets, liabilities, and owners' equity.
4. The purpose of the income statement and its information on revenues, expenses, and profits.
5. The purpose of the statement of changes in financial position.
6. How financial statements can be interpreted.

## In This Chapter

What Is Accounting?
Accounting Procedures
The Financial Statements
Interpreting Financial Statements

## TANDY CORPORATION
*Profit Margin or Market Share?*

In the fall of 1983, John V. Roach, chairman of Tandy Corporation, had a real problem: profits were expanding, but Tandy's share of the personal computer market was shrinking. The company's 1983 profits were over $278 million, up 24 percent from 1982's and up over 400 percent from 1978's earnings, yet its personal computer market share had declined from 40.5 percent in 1979 to 8.6 percent in 1983.

There were several consequences of this problem. First, Tandy's very high margins of profit, usually close to 60 percent of sales, couldn't stay that high if the prices of its personal and small business computers were cut to meet those of competitors, who were slashing prices. Second, the upheaval in the computer field had scared investors, so that Tandy's stock had declined $20, to $39. This decline had caused its employees—who earn part of their income from a highly favorable profit-sharing plan—to lose half a billion dollars, at least on paper. Motivation was suffering, and there was pressure to reduce staff, especially employees who didn't contribute directly to sales income. Finally, there was pressure on Roach to cut back on low-profit activities, such as product service and support to customers.

Tandy started in 1899 as a small family-owned leather goods store but by 1963 was a national leathercraft and hobby chain. Then Charles Tandy, the owner, bought Radio Shack, a nine-store electronics firm. In 1975 Tandy Corporation spun off its hobby, crafts, and other operations to concentrate exclusively on the electronics field. First it rode the CB radio wave (Charles Tandy's own "handle" was "Mr. Lucky") until it receded. Then Radio Shack helped start the home computer fad with its TRS-80; its stores were the first ones where a customer could stroll in and walk out with a computer. Later, it offered the TRS-80 Model II, which has a much larger memory than the original machine and is twice as fast. When Charles Tandy died in 1978, Radio Shack had more outlets (over 7,000) than any other firm in the world.

With around 9,000 outlets, over 32,000 employees, annual sales close to $900 million, and its share of the computer market declining, Radio Shack entered the lucrative telephone business—with the hope that this move would revive profits, morale, and stock prices.

An important feature of Tandy's accounting system which may help that revival is a monthly income (profit-and-loss) statement for each store. On penalty of discharge, each manager of a company-owned store must file a daily sales report so that the statement can be prepared and circulated by the tenth of each month.

Accountants have an image that belies their importance to a firm like Tandy. Far from being dull Bob Cratchit types, slaving in a maze of corporate cubicles, accountants are responsible for a company's financial lifeblood. The report of an accountant can determine employees' earnings. For example, John F. Pyktel, manager of a Dallas Radio Shack, earned $103,900 in salary and bonuses in 1982. You can bet he looks forward to seeing the monthly income statements. The accountant's statements can also turn investors on or off about a firm. Former accountants fill the ranks of corporate executives. And corporate planning and strategy would be impossible without an accountant's records on where the firm has been, is now, and will go financially.

From the beginning of this book, we've stressed the role of profits in a successful business. Naturally, managers want to know how much profit they've made, but *how* can they find out whether they're making a profit—or have suffered a loss? To do this, they need some method of keeping score, which accounting provides. It uses standardized principles and methods so that anyone studying the firm's financial statements can understand how they were prepared and what they mean. This is crucial in cases of acquisition, merger, or mere investment in the firm.

## WHAT IS ACCOUNTING?

**Objective 1**

The role of accounting and accountants in recording and presenting a firm's financial information.

**Accounting,** sometimes called the language of business, is a system of principles and techniques used to record, classify, summarize, and interpret financial information. Only by evaluating accurate records of present and past performance can managers plan realistically for the future.

The score-keeping function of accounting, called financial accounting, uses standardized procedures and rules for presenting financial information, demonstrated throughout this chapter. **Financial accounting,** then, is used to develop financial information needed by outsiders, such as government agencies, financial institutions, investors and creditors, and suppliers, as well as by insiders, such as the owners and managers (see Figure 17-1). Therefore, the information must be readily understandable and must conform to generally accepted rules and procedures.

Information regarding the firm's financial structure and profits is required by various government agencies such as the Securities and Exchange Commission, the Federal Trade Commission, and federal, state, and local taxing authorities. Data about the company's cash flow and credit history are of interest to financial institutions, investors, and suppliers. Financial institutions need this information as the basis for buying or selling the company's securities. And the owners themselves want to know how much profit has been made with their invested funds and whether the firm is financially healthy. Therefore, formal financial statements must be submitted regularly to these and other groups.

The bulk of the financial information gathered by a firm, however, doesn't leave the firm. It's retained for use by the company's managers. A less formal field of accounting, **managerial accounting,** provides management with financial information to be used in decision making. Because the information is used only by insiders, a less structured, more flexible system may be developed. Managerial accounting involves budgeting, cost analysis, tax planning,

**Figure 17-1** The role of financial accounting in the flow of financial information.

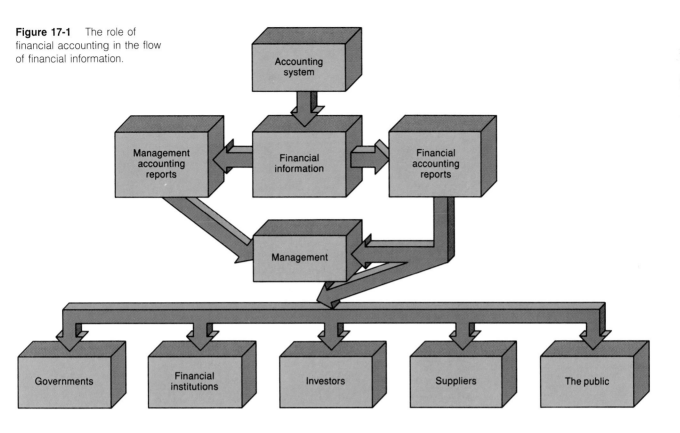

and other activities that help managers plan and control operations. Introduction of a managerial accounting system for comparing operating results with forecasts helped Sherwin Williams, the nation's largest paint firm, to increase profits by 38 percent.[1]

### The Accountant's Role

Much of a business's accounting is routine **bookkeeping,** or the clerical side of accounting, which is simply recording the data of financial transactions. But before routine bookkeeping can be done, someone has to answer such questions as: What is to be recorded? How will the data be used? Who will do the recording? How often will financial reports be prepared? What are the reporting needs of the business? The answers to these questions are used to develop the accounting system.

The person who designs and oversees that system is the accountant. Large firms employ their own accountants to handle the business's records and prepare financial statements. Some firms hire specialists in cost accounting, budgeting, financial forecasting, or other specialized areas. Smaller firms may employ a bookkeeper to handle routine procedures and hire a public accounting firm to advise them on accounting systems. There are nearly 30,000 of these firms nationwide. The ones at the top, otherwise known as the Big Eight, are Arthur Andersen; Arthur Young; Coopers & Lybrand; Deloitte, Haskins & Sells; Ernst & Whinney; Peat, Marwick, Mitchell; Price Waterhouse; and Touche Ross.

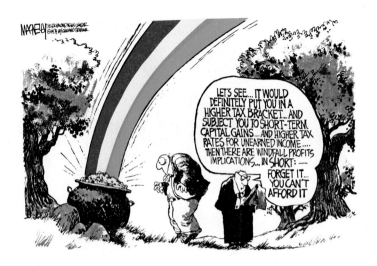

### The CPA

**Public accountants** are independent of a firm, offering their services to the general public in much the same way other professionals, such as consultants, lawyers, and physicians, do. A public accountant who has completed a full accounting education and passed a uniform exam prepared by the American Institute of Certified Public Accountants (AICPA) earns the title of **certified public accountant (CPA).** Only about one out of five accountants has achieved this status. Although CPAs are employed in all areas of accounting, over half of them work in public accounting. A certified public accountant who meets the state's requirement can advise clients on a wide range of financial matters, help with tax planning, prepare tax returns, and assist firms in developing accounting systems to suit their needs (see the Profile on page 458).

The main function of a CPA, however, is auditing. **Auditing** involves reviewing a firm's accounting system, gathering information about its operations, examining its accounting records, and giving a professional opinion as to the reliability and fairness of the financial statements. Figure 17-2 shows the report of an independent accounting firm verifying the fairness of the financial reports included in Sears, Roebuck's annual report. Because CPAs are independent of the companies they audit, their report is supposed to assure creditors, suppliers, government agencies, and stockholders that the financial reports present a fair picture of a company's financial position and results of operations. As FYI on page 461 shows, however, this isn't always the case.

CPA firms will often advise businesses on ways of improving their operations. Because CPAs deal with all of the business's financial records, they can sometimes spot problems in their client's financial system and offer suggestions for correcting them. Since individual CPAs directly affect their firm's profits, image, and client relations, they're often made partners. For example, Price Waterhouse, the fifth-largest public accounting firm in the United States, has 629 partners.

Why do you think Ernst & Whinney's auditors failed to help United American Bank?

The faces of accounting.

## ACCOUNTING PROCEDURES

**Objective 2**

**How the accounting equation and the double-entry system are used to classify business transactions.**

Almost everyone dislikes keeping detailed records. Yet, for a business, accounting records are vital (1) to determine how much the firm is worth, (2) to see how well it has been doing, and (3) to help managers make decisions. At the root of all accounting records are some very elementary rules, founded on the accounting equation and double-entry bookkeeping. These rules have been in use for thousands of years, and becoming familiar with them will give you a basic understanding of accounting that you can use in your own daily business transactions.

**Figure 17-2** Report of an independent accounting firm. (Reprinted by permission from Sears, Roebuck and Co., Sears Tower, Chicago, Ill. 60684.)

To the Shareholders and Board of Directors of Sears, Roebuck and Co.:

We have examined the Consolidated Statements of Financial Position of Sears, Roebuck and Co. as of December 31, 1982 and 1981 and the related Consolidated Statements of Income, Shareholders' Equity and Changes in Financial Position for each of the three years in the period ended December 31, 1982. Our examinations were made in accordance with generally accepted auditing standards and, accordingly, included such tests of the accounting records and such other auditing procedures as we considered necessary in the circumstances.

In our opinion, the financial statements referred to above present fairly the financial position of Sears, Roebuck and Co. as of December 31, 1982 and 1981, and the results of its operations and the changes in its financial position for each of the three years in the period ended December 31, 1982, in conformity with generally accepted accounting principles applied on a consistent basis.

*Touche Ross & Co.*

Chicago, Illinois
March 22, 1983

# *Profile*

## Sidney Kess: Guru of Taxation

He could be a candidate for an American Express ad—people may not recognize Sidney Kess, but his name is well known in the accounting world. A certified public accountant and tax lawyer, Kess is a tax partner in the international public accounting firm Main Hurdman/KMG and an adjunct professor at New York Law School. For the past eighteen years, Kess has been making the rounds from one end of the United States to the other, conducting tax seminars on behalf of the American Institute of Certified Public Accountants. His audiences consist primarily of accountants from small and medium-sized firms, who readily attest to the Kess expertise. Paying a tax-deductible entrance fee of $250, about 30,000 accountants attend the Kess seminars annually.

At these seminars, Kess uses his traveling library—six suitcases filled with reference materials and his personal computer terminal—to provide his audience with a rundown of tax proposals which Congress failed to act on before it adjourned. This information allows accountants' clients to act on these tax incentives while they still can. Besides giving planning tips (like which cruises can be written off if combined with conventions), Kess spends a great deal of time reviewing principles in recent Internal Revenue Service rulings and U.S. Tax Court cases.

Although the seminars themselves move at a quick clip with no interruptions or questions, Kess is quite approachable. He announces the times that he will be available before or after sessions to resolve questions, and he even takes telephone calls until 11:00 P.M. He freely socializes with those in attendance and makes good use of the time to direct interested parties to various publications for additional information.

Perhaps the real success of the Kess approach lies in its simplicity. Kess himself says his basic strength is his ability to take the complex and bring it down to earth, to put the technical in a real-world setting. He begins with basic definitions and builds up to new developments. The information he gives must be quite valuable, as many of those in attendance have been returning year after year for an up-to-date briefing.

Sources: Beth Brophy, "Accountant Who Has the Answers," *USA Today,* Dec. 20, 1983, pp. 1-B, 2-B; and Deborah Rankin, "Taxes Complicated by Changes in Laws," Your Taxes, Part I, *New York Times,* February 2, 1981, p. D-1.

## The Accounting Equation

Have you ever calculated how much you're worth financially? If not, give it a try. You may be surprised at how much you have, even if you're always running short of cash.

Figure 17-3 shows a list of things you may own and some debts you may owe. Enter your estimates of the dollar value of the items shown. Then add up the columns and subtract the total amount you owe from the total amount you own. The difference is your net financial worth. It's an estimate of your financial worth at this time. These figures will probably change quickly, so it's important to make estimates of this sort often.

A business is also interested in what it's worth at a given time, usually at the end of the fiscal year. But since managers are responsible for how they use other people's funds, they can't be as casual as you are in estimating net value. They must keep exact records of all items in order to show how the money is used. Also, the terms they use are different from those you used.

Like all the items you own, including cash and prepaid items (items such as insurance and rent that are paid before being used), anything of value owned by a business is called an **asset.** Anything owed is called a **liability,** which is an obligation to pay money to someone for something. The difference between what is owned and what is owed is called **owners' equity,** or a firm's worth after all debts have been taken into account. These three categories—assets, liabilities, and owners' equity—are the terms in the **accounting equation,** shown in Figure 17-4. You can see that no matter how you put it, whether

$$\underbrace{\text{Assets} - \text{Liabilities}}_{\$490{,}000} = \text{Owners' Equity}$$
$$\$500{,}000 - \$10{,}000 = \$490{,}000$$

or

$$\text{Liabilities} + \text{Owners' Equity} = \text{Assets}$$
$$\underbrace{\$10{,}000 + \$490{,}000}_{\$500{,}000} = \$500{,}000$$

both sides of the equation are the same. The relationship among the parts of the equation is still in balance.

## The Double-Entry System

In 1494, an observant Italian monk, Fra Luca Pacioli, developed the system of double-entry bookkeeping based on this unchanging balance in the accounting equation. The **double-entry system** assumes that there are two sides, two effects to every business transaction. Whether a transaction is a product sold, a check written, or a building bought, it must be recorded in two places to keep the accounting equation in balance.

**Figure 17-3** Calculating your financial worth.

Date _____

**How Much I Own** | **Value**

Cash in pocket .......................................... $_____
Money in bank .......................................... _____
Money owed to me ..................................... _____
Prepaid items
   Insurance _____
   Tuition and fees _____
   Room and board _____
   Utility deposits _____
     Total prepaid items .......................... _____

Books, paper, pencils, etc. .......................... _____
Clothes, shoes, etc. .................................. _____
Automobile or other vehicle (appraised value) ........ _____
Furnishings, including music systems ................. _____
Other items I own

   _____ _____
   _____ _____
   _____ _____

   Total other items I own ........................... _____
     TOTAL AMOUNT THAT I OWN      $_____

**How Much I Owe to Others** | **Value**

For tuition or books ................................. $_____
On credit cards ...................................... _____
On utility bills ..................................... _____
On installment payments .............................. _____
On loans ............................................. _____
Other debts

   _____ _____
   _____ _____
   _____ _____

   Total other debts ................................. _____
     TOTAL AMOUNT THAT I OWE      $_____
MY NET FINANCIAL WORTH
(Total Amount Owned − Total Amount Owed)      $_____

After each transaction, the financial elements are classified and recorded into one of accounting's storage units: the **accounts.** For example, when a firm purchases material for cash, the cost of the material is added to an Inventory account, and the cash is deducted from the Cash account. Every transaction you make also involves two changes. For example, when you purchase a

# FYI

## United American Bank: The Audit That Failed

On February 14, 1983, Tennessee's commissioner of banks declared the United American Bank of Knoxville (UAB) insolvent because of "large and unusual . . . losses" on loans made by Jake F. Butcher, its CEO (see photo). The next morning, UAB opened under the hastily applied logo of its new owner, First Tennessee Bank of Knoxville. Between $50 and $60 million of UAB's nearly $478 million of loans had to be written off at once as uncollectible, and the value of the rest of the loans was reduced $1.5 million. This was the fourth largest failure among commercial banks in U.S. history.

As early as November 1981, the Federal Deposit Insurance Corporation (FDIC) had become concerned that UAB was trying to conceal its increasingly bad loans by transferring them to other banks that Butcher had an interest in. The FDIC and the office of the Comptroller of the Currency (which supervises such banks) started comprehensive audits of UAB's books. In December 1982, the FDIC issued three orders for UAB to stop "hazardous lending and lax collection practices."

One of the biggest mysteries about the collapse was how UAB's outside auditor, Ernst & Whinney (E&W), one of the Big Eight accounting firms, missed what was going on.

Just three weeks before the FDIC declared the bank insolvent, E&W gave its financial report "unqualified approval." E&W's people had made no contact with FDIC examiners who were in the bank at the same time.

The UAB case naturally has bank-auditing experts worried about what it might do to auditing's image. What went wrong? First, independent auditors and bank regulators look for different things. Auditors look at whether the reserve for loan losses is adequate, while regulators try to see whether the loans are collectible. Some accounting authorities say E&W may have relied too heavily on the judgment of the bank's own inside auditors because of the pressures of time and economy.

---

Sources: Based on Gregory Stricharchuk and Damon Darlin, "Ernst & Whinney's Audit of Bank That Failed Puzzles Investigators," *The Wall Street Journal,* March 4, 1983, p. 18. Reprinted by permission of *The Wall Street Journal,* © Dow Jones & Company, Inc. 1983. All Rights Reserved. Also based on "An Overnight Bank Rescue in Knoxville," *Business Week,* February 28, 1983, pp. 29–31; Tom Nicholson, "Butcher's Bank on the Block," *Newsweek,* February 28, 1983, p. 58; and "Tapped Out: A Knoxville Bank Goes Under," *Time,* February 28, 1983.

**Figure 17-4**  The accounting equation.

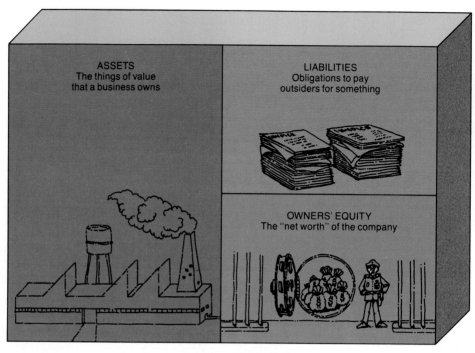

ASSETS
The things of value
that a business owns

LIABILITIES
Obligations to pay
outsiders for something

OWNERS' EQUITY
The "net worth" of the company

Assets = liabilities + owners' equity
Assets − liabilities = owners' equity

book for cash, you reduce your cash balance and increase your assets (book). If you buy the book on credit, you increase your assets (book) and your liabilities (debts). Many combinations of changes can occur, such as the loss in value of a textbook after you've used it. (It declines in value even more when it's no longer used at your school.) Our point is that each transaction involves at least two changes. Double-entry bookkeeping records these transactions in at least two accounts, which must then be equal.

Assume for a moment the unlikely situation that your financial status is as follows:

$$\text{Assets} \quad = \text{Liabilities} + \text{Owners' Equity}$$
$$\$10,000 \ (\text{cash}) = \quad 0 \quad + \quad \$10,000 \ (\text{cash})$$

You perform the following transactions:

1. You borrow $30,000 from friends, which you must pay back later.
2. You buy a supply of 1,000 printed T-shirts for $1,500, or $1.50 apiece.
3. You sell 100 T-shirts at $2.50 apiece to other students, collecting $250, or earning a profit of $100 ($250 − $150).
4. You pay your tuition bill of $1,000.

These transactions would be reflected in double-entry form as shown in the accounting equation in Figure 17-5. Notice that the sides of the equation always remain in balance.

### Accounting as a System

As you can see from Figure 17-6, the accounting process involves the basic input/process/output systems approach of the computer, studied in the last chapter. In fact, most large firms today use computers to handle their account-

**Figure 17-5** The double-entry system in action.

| | | ASSETS | | = | LIABILITIES | + | OWNERS' EQUITY |
|---|---|---|---|---|---|---|---|
| | Cash | Prepaid Tuition | Inventory | = | Loan | | |
| | + 10,000 | | | = | | + | 10,000 |
| (1) | + 30,000 | | | = | +30,000 | + | |
| Bal. | + 40,000 | | | = | +30,000 | + | 10,000 |
| (2) | − 1,500 | | +1,500 | = | | + | |
| Bal. | + 38,500 | | +1,500 | = | +30,000 | + | 10,000 |
| (3) | + 250 | | − 150 | = | | + | 100 |
| Bal. | + 38,750 | | +1,350 | = | +30,000 | + | 10,100 |
| (4) | − 1,000 | +1,000 | | = | | + | |
| Bal. | + 37,750 | +1,000 | +1,350 | = | +30,000 | + | 10,100 |
| | | $40,100 | | | | $40,100 | |

ing system. A computerized system gives accuracy, speed, dependability, and otherwise unavailable data to the firm's record-keeping and frees employees for more subjective planning and decision making. Computerized accounting systems will never replace people, however. There must be someone to enter the data into the computer system, to tell the computer what to do, and to interpret the results.

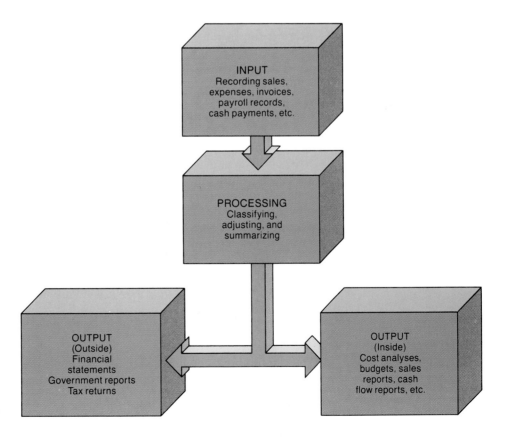

**Figure 17-6** Accounting as a system.

▲ **Recording Transactions (Input)**  The procedure starts with detailed records of company activities such as sales, purchases, and employee payroll.  The data are entered in journals (or books of original entry) that are used to record each transaction.  In a computerized system, the data are entered on computer terminals, which take the information to the main computer processing unit for classification and storage.  Each transaction changes the values that appear in one or both of the financial statements.

▲ **Processing**  At the end of a given period, the data for transactions made during the period are used to obtain the figures for the financial statements.  The computer processes the data into the forms needed for internal and external use.

▲ **Output**  Financial statements are then prepared from the processed data.  These statements summarize what the firm has accomplished during the accounting period—usually a year.  These statements are normally printed for distribution.  But Abbott Laboratories, realizing that people prefer watching television to reading, produces a videotaped version of its annual report for its employees.

## THE FINANCIAL STATEMENTS

We've previously classified accounts into assets, liabilities, and owners' equity.  Each of these categories represents many other accounts, such as cash or inventory.  For simplicity's sake, though, we'll divide the accounts into the same three groups accountants use in presenting information: those that appear on the balance sheet, those that appear on the income statement, and those that show changes in financial position.

The **balance sheet** shows a firm's financial status *at one moment in time*. The balance sheet can be compared to a snapshot, showing a frozen instant. The **income statement** reflects results of operations, or the *change in status between two points in time*, corresponding roughly to a movie, following the action over a month, quarter, or year.  If you look at a firm's balance sheet for the past year and for the present year, you get a picture of where it was and where it is now, at the same fiscal point in time.  By looking at the income statement, showing income and expenses over the year, you can fill in the gaps and see how the firm got where it is now.  A third financial statement is now required, the **statement of changes in financial position.**  While the balance sheet concentrates on things owned and owed, and the income statement on results of operations (or profit or loss), this third statement focuses on the *flow of funds (either cash or working capital) into and out of a business.*  The statement of changes in financial position helps explain a company's cash flow, for example, showing where the company got its cash and how it was used.

### The Balance Sheet

You can tell how a business stands at a given time by examining the data in the statement of its financial position or the balance sheet.  It is based on the principle that what a business owns (its assets) and the claims that people have on those assets must balance out.  Like the accounting equation, the balance

**Objective 3**

The purpose of the balance sheet and its information on assets, liabilities, and owners' equity.

sheet shows the recorded amounts of the assets of a firm as equal to its liabilities, plus the owners' equity (net worth). Thus, for everything owned, there is someone, either an outside creditor or an owner of the firm, who has a claim on it.

Figure 17-7 shows Whizbang Manufacturing Company's balance sheet for two years. Note how much it's like your statement of financial worth (Figure 17-3), even though the terms used are different and the sizes of the values differ. Notice also that the total assets ($5,076,800) equal total liabilities ($2,084,800) plus owners' equity ($2,992,000).

**Figure 17-7**  Sample balance sheet.

**WHIZBANG MANUFACTURING COMPANY**
Balance Sheet
December 31, 19X4 and 19X5

| | December 31, 19X5 | | December 31, 19X4 | |
|---|---|---|---|---|
| **ASSETS** | | | | |
| **Current Assets** | | | | |
| Cash | | $ 51,200 | | $ 67,900 |
| Marketable Securities | | 214,800 | | 233,100 |
| Accounts Receivable | | 725,000 | | 712,000 |
| Inventories | | 758,500 | | 780,000 |
| Prepaid Expenses | | 50,700 | | 51,200 |
| Total Current Assets | | $1,800,200 | | $1,844,200 |
| **Property, Plant, and Equipment** | | | | |
| Land | | 1,404,600 | | 1,215,700 |
| Buildings and Equipment | $2,080,000 | | $2,080,000 | |
| Less Accumulated Depreciation | − 208,000 | | − 104,000 | |
| Total Property, Plant, and Equipment | | 1,872,000 | | 1,976,000 |
| | | 3,276,600 | | 3,191,700 |
| Total Assets | | $5,076,800 | | $5,035,900 |
| **LIABILITIES AND OWNERS' EQUITY** | | | | |
| **Current Liabilities** | | | | |
| Accounts Payable | $ 319,900 | | $ 356,900 | |
| Notes Payable | 188,300 | | 189,900 | |
| Accrued Expenses | 535,400 | | 489,100 | |
| Total Current Liabilities | | $1,043,600 | | $1,035,900 |
| **Long-Term Liabilities** | | | | |
| Mortgage on Building and Equipment | $1,041,200 | | $1,059,600 | |
| Total Long-Term Liabilities | | 1,041,200 | | 1,059,600 |
| Total Liabilities | | $2,084,800 | | $2,095,500 |
| **Owners' Equity** | | | | |
| Common Stock | | $ 576,000 | | $ 576,000 |
| Retained Earnings | | 2,416,000 | | 2,364,400 |
| Total Owners' Equity | | 2,992,000 | | 2,940,400 |
| TOTAL LIABILITIES AND OWNERS' EQUITY | | $5,076,800 | | $5,035,900 |

▲ **Assets** As you know, assets are the tangible and intangible things of value that a company owns. They're usually classified as either current or long-term assets.

**Current assets** are those that are used or sold in less than a year. Since they change form rapidly and can be converted to cash easily and quickly, they're often referred to as **liquid assets.** Current assets usually come in the form of cash, marketable securities, accounts receivable, inventories, and prepaid expenses.

1. *Cash* consists of funds on hand or in the bank that are readily available for use and free from any restrictions.
2. *Marketable securities* are short-term investments of funds that can be quickly converted to cash.
3. *Accounts receivable* are the delayed payments by a customer for items purchased from the firm on credit.
4. *Inventories* are stocks of items that are to be sold or used in production or operations.
5. *Prepaid expenses* are assets resulting from paying in advance for items such as insurance, taxes, and future services.

**Fixed assets,** or **property, plant, and equipment,** are relatively permanent investments that the company intends to keep for longer periods of time to produce income. These longer-lived, higher-cost investments include items such as land, buildings, machinery, and equipment. The costs of fixed assets, except land, are depreciated or allocated over their estimated useful lives. They are included on the balance sheet at the actual cost to the company less the amount of depreciation accumulated to date. It's often possible to improve profits by reducing these assets. For instance, Quaker Oats Company took a $60 million loss in 1983 by selling three poorly performing businesses in order to improve its later profits.[2]

▲ **Liabilities** Whenever a company buys something on credit, it creates a debt, or liability. Simply stated, a liability is an obligation to pay money to someone for something of value received from that person. These obligations may be for a short period of time, in which case they are called *current liabilities*, or for a longer period, in which case they are called *long-term liabilities*.

**Current liabilities,** as you can guess, are debts that are normally repaid within one year. The usual ones are accounts payable, notes payable, and accrued expenses.

1. *Accounts payable* represent debts to suppliers, resulting from purchases of supplies.
2. *Notes payable* are short-term loans, usually from a bank, which are scheduled to be repaid in less than a year and are a source of funds from creditors.
3. *Accrued expenses* are debts, such as wages and taxes, that have been incurred but not yet paid.

Financial managers don't normally finance long-term assets with short-term liabilities—at least not if they can help it! Instead, they use long-term borrowing to finance fixed assets and other basic investments. These **long-term liabilities** are contracts to repay the loan in the future and to pay a regular

interest charge on the money used. Mortgage loans and bonds are the usual types of long-term liability. (These will be discussed in detail in Chapter 19.)

▲ **Owners' Equity** Profit-seeking businesses are owned by individuals, or groups, who have invested money in the firm. This ownership interest, called owners' equity, is the value of the assets, less any liabilities. The owners' equity is sometimes called a capital account. Equity in a corporation is called stockholders' equity; in a partnership it is called partners' equity. As stated earlier, the sum of the firm's liabilities plus owners' equity equals the amount of the firm's assets.

## The Income Statement

**Objective 4**

**The purpose of the income statement and its information on revenues, expenses, and profits.**

You're probably very interested in the changes in your finances that occur as you pay tuition, buy food, go to a movie, buy gasoline, or receive income. These transactions change your financial condition. Business firms use accounting to collect and record similar data in a statement of income, which shows the results of operations over a given period of time. As shown in Figure 17-8, the income statement shows the profit (or loss) that's left after expenses are subtracted from revenues received.

Figure 17-9 is a form that you can use to analyze your own "operations." Did you gain or lose during the period? You can also do this analysis on a longer time period—such as a quarter, a semester, or a year.

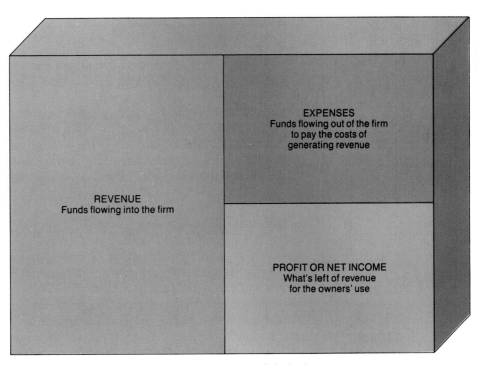

**EXPENSES**
Funds flowing out of the firm to pay the costs of generating revenue

**REVENUE**
Funds flowing into the firm

**PROFIT OR NET INCOME**
What's left of revenue for the owners' use

revenue − expenses = profit (or loss)

**Figure 17-8** The income statement equation.

**Figure 17-9** Your personal income statement.

For the month of _____

|  | Value |
|---|---|
| **My Revenues** | |
| From parents | $_____ |
| From wages | _____ |
| From scholarships or grants | _____ |
| From other sources | |
| _____  _____ | |
| _____  _____ | |
| Total income from other sources | _____ |
| MY TOTAL REVENUES | $_____ |
| **My Expenses** | |
| Room and board | $_____ |
| Tuition and fees | _____ |
| Transportation | _____ |
| Recreation | _____ |
| Books, paper, and supplies | _____ |
| Clothes, shoes, and grooming | _____ |
| Other expenses | _____ |
| _____  _____ | |
| _____  _____ | |
| Total other expenses | _____ |
| MY TOTAL EXPENSES | $_____ |
| NET GAIN (LOSS) IN MY REVENUE | $_____ |

Now look at the statement for a large company in Figure 17-10. Note that both your statement and that of the firm start with income, or revenues.

▲ **Revenues**  **Revenues,** or income from sales of either products or services, are the lifeblood of a business, for without income a business will die. Sales revenue in the form of cash or credit is received from selling the business's goods and services. A business may be interested in obtaining other revenue, such as from short-term investments, but it concentrates its efforts on sales revenue.

▲ **Expenses**  **Expenses** are the cost of doing business. Products and services must be bought and used to generate sales. The main expense items are cost of sales, selling and administrative expenses, and taxes.

As goods are made and services performed, resources are consumed. Materials and parts are made into products. The costs of the labor used to make the product, electricity, supervision, repair and maintenance, and raw materials are grouped together to establish the "cost" of producing the product, or *cost of sales.*

*Selling expenses* are the costs of promoting, selling, and distributing the product or service. *Administrative expenses* are those items that can't be

identified elsewhere, such as the president's salary and the cost of clerical work in the general office.

▲ **Profits** The **income before tax** is found by summarizing expenses and deducting them from income. The result is the amount used to calculate corporate income taxes. Income taxes must then be deducted before the firm has any profit for its owners. **Net income** is the amount remaining after deducting all costs and expenses from revenues. If revenues exceed expenses, a profit is earned. This profit can be used by the firm to pay dividends to stockholders, or it can be retained in the business, but a combination of the two is usually done. If it is retained, it shows up on the balance sheet as an increase in retained earnings.

Notice in Figure 17-10 that Whizbang Manufacturing made $390,000 net income in 19X5. Of that amount, $338,400 was distributed as dividends to stockholders. The remaining $51,600 was added to 19X4's retained earnings of $2,364,400 (see Figure 17-7), increasing the retained earnings account to $2,416,000 in the year 19X5.

## Statement of Changes in Financial Position

**Objective 5**

**The purpose of the statement of changes in financial position.**

As its name implies, the statement of changes in financial position, often called the *funds statement,* summarizes the changes that have occurred in the company's financial position during the accounting period. It aids one in understanding the firm's financial position by supplying answers to questions such as: How many dollars of funds flowed into the business from operations? How were these funds used? What were the proceeds of a bond issue used for? What was the source of funds to finance the new plant? Why were there fewer current assets and more current liabilities at the end of the period than at the beginning?

The statement helps answer these questions by showing where a business got funds and how it used them. Funds may be defined as cash or as working capital (current assets minus current liabilities). Regardless of the definition of

| WHIZBANG MANUFACTURING COMPANY | | |
|---|---|---|
| Income Statement | | |
| For the Years Ending December 31, 19X4 and 19X5 | | |
| | **19X5** | **19X4** |
| SALES REVENUE | $7,800,000 | $6,240,000 |
| COSTS AND EXPENSES | | |
| Production expenses | 5,720,000 | 4,410,000 |
| Selling and administrative expenses | 1,174,000 | 1,075,000 |
| Depreciation on building and equipment | 104,000 | 104,000 |
| Other expenses | 52,000 | 51,000 |
| Total costs and expenses | $7,050,000 | $5,640,000 |
| INCOME BEFORE TAX | 750,000 | 600,000 |
| Less income taxes (@48%) | 360,000 | 288,000 |
| NET INCOME | $390,000 | $312,000 |

**Figure 17-10** Sample income statement.

**Figure 17-11** Sample statement of changes in financial position. [Reprinted from William W. Pyle, John Arch White, and Kermit D. Larson, *Fundamental Accounting Principles,* 8th ed. (Homewood, Ill.: Richard D. Irwin, 1978), p. 605. © 1978 by Richard D. Irwin, Inc.]

**Delta Company**

Statement of Changes in Financial Position

For Year Ended December 31, 1979

| | | | |
|---|---|---:|---:|
| Sources of working capital: | | | |
|   Current operations: | | | |
|     Net income for 1979* | | $12,200 | |
|     Add expenses not requiring outlays of working capital in the current period: | | | |
|       Depreciation of buildings and equipment | | 4,500 | |
|       Working capital provided by operations | | $16,700 | |
|   Other sources: | | | |
|     Sale of common stock | | 12,500 | |
|       Total new working capital | | | $29,200 |
| Uses of working capital: | | | |
|   Purchase of office equipment | | $ 500 | |
|   Purchase of store equipment | | 6,000 | |
|   Addition to building | | 15,000 | |
|   Reduction of mortgage debt | | 2,500 | |
|   Declaration of dividends | | 3,100 | |
|     Total uses of working capital | | | 27,100 |
| Net Increase in Working Capital | | | $ 2,100 |

*Delta Company reported no extraordinary items during 1979.

funds, the statement is designed to emphasize the increases or decreases in the fund that took place during the year. Hence transactions that increase the fund are called *sources* of funds, and those that decrease working capital are called *uses* of funds. Figure 17-11 is an example of one of these statements based on working capital.

# INTERPRETING FINANCIAL STATEMENTS

**Objective 6**

**How financial statements can be interpreted.**

To find out the true meaning of a financial statement, you must analyze it. The statement's individual items are relatively meaningless. It's only when relationships and changes between items and groups of items are interpreted that significant aspects of the business become clear. We could go into detail as to how to interpret these statements, but CBS-TV *Morning News*'s business commentator, Jane Bryant Quinn, has done it better than we can. See FYI on pages 471–473 for her excellent—but simple—explanation.

It's important to first try to determine the validity of the data in the statements through independent audits, as they may be illusions rather than reality (see the Business Debate on page 474). There are many ways of doing "creative accounting" that distort accounting results. For example, a senior vice-president of the JWT Group, Inc. (parent of the J. Walter Thompson advertising agency) programmed $24.5 million of "fictitious" revenues into its computer. The write-off of these revenues reduced net income by 60 percent.[3] And Datapoint Corporation, a one-time favorite of Wall Street, rushed out shipments of computers at the end of each accounting period to inflate revenues and accounts receivable.[4]

# FYI

## How to Read an Annual Report
*by Jane Bryant Quinn*

To some business people I know, curling up with a good annual report is almost more exciting than getting lost in John Le Carré's latest spy thriller.

But to you it might be another story: "Who needs that?" I can hear you ask. *You* do—if you're going to gamble any of your future *working* for a company, *investing* in it, or *selling* to it.

### Why Should You Bother?

Say you've got a job interview at Galactic Industries. Well, what does the company do? Does its future look good? Or will the next recession leave your part of the business on the beach?

Or say you're thinking of investing your own hard-earned money in its stock. Sales are up. But are its profits getting better or worse?

Or say you're going to supply it with a lot of parts. Should you extend Galactic plenty of credit or keep it on a short leash?

### How to Get One

You'll find answers in its annual report. Where do you find *that*? Your library should have the annual reports of nearby companies plus leading national ones. It also has listings of companies' financial officers and their addresses so you can write for annual reports.

So now Galactic Industries' latest annual report is sitting in front of you ready to be cracked. How do you crack it?

Where do we start? *Not* at the front. At the *back!* We don't want to be surprised at the end of *this* story.

### Start at the Back

First, turn back to the report of the *certified public accountant*. This third-party auditor will tell you right off the bat if Galactic's report conforms with "generally accepted accounting principles."

Watch out for the words "subject to." They mean the financial report is clean *only* if you take the company's word about a particular piece of business, and the accountant isn't sure you should. Doubts like this are usually settled behind closed doors. When a "subject to" makes it into the annual report, it could mean trouble.

What else should you know before you check the numbers?

Stay in the back of the book and go to the *footnotes*. Yep! The whole profits story is sometimes in the footnotes.

Are earnings down? If it's only because of a change in accounting, maybe that's good! The company owes less tax and has more money in its pocket. Are earnings up? Maybe that's bad. They may be up because of a special windfall that won't happen again next year. The footnotes know.

### For What Happened and Why

Now turn to the *letter from the chairman*. Usually addressed "to our stockholders," it's up front, and *should* be in more ways than one. The chairman's tone reflects the personality, the well-being of his company.

In his letter he should tell you how his company fared this year. But more important, he should tell you *why*. Keep an eye out for sentences that start with "Except for . . ." and "Despite the . . ." They're clues to problems.

## Insights into the Future

On the positive side, a chairman's letter should give you insights into the company's future and its *stance* on economic or political trends that may affect it.

While you're up front, look for what's new in each line of business. Is management getting the company in good shape to weather the tough and competitive 1980's?

Now—and no sooner—should you dig into the numbers!

One source is the *balance sheet*. It is a snapshot of how the company stands at a single point in time. On the left are *assets*—everything the company owns. Things that can quickly be turned into cash are *current assets*. On the right are *liabilities*—everything the company owes. *Current liabilities* are the debts due in one year, which are paid out of current assets.

The difference between current assets and current liabilities is *net working capital,* a key figure to watch from one annual (and quarterly) report to another. If working capital shrinks, it could mean trouble. One possibility: the company may not be able to keep dividends growing rapidly.

## Look for Growth Here

*Stockholders' equity* is the difference between total assets and liabilities. It is the presumed dollar value of what stockholders own. You want it to grow.

Another important number to watch is *long-term debt*. High and rising debt, relative to equity, may be no problem for a growing business. But it shows weakness in a company that's leveling out. (More on that later.)

The second basic source of numbers is the *income statement*. It shows how much money Galactic made or lost over the year.

Most people look at one figure first. It's in the income statement at the bottom: *net earnings per share*. Watch out. It can fool you. Galactic's management could boost earnings by selling off a plant. Or by cutting the budget for research and advertising. (See the footnotes!) So don't be smug about net earnings until you've found out how they happened—and how they might happen next year.

## Check Net Sales First

The number you *should* look at first in the income statement is *net sales*. Ask yourself: Are sales going *up at a faster rate* than the last time around? When sales increases start to slow, the company may be in trouble. Also ask: Have sales gone up faster than inflation? If not, the company's *real* sales may be behind. And ask yourself once more: Have sales gone down because the company is selling off a losing business? If so, profits may be soaring.

(I never promised you that figuring out an annual report was going to be easy!)

# ⧋ LEARNING OBJECTIVES REVISITED

1. *The role of accounting and accountants in recording and presenting a firm's financial information.*

Accounting information is needed by managers, owners, government agencies, financial analysts, creditors, and many others in order to make intelligent decisions. Accounting is the system of principles and techniques used to record, classify, summarize, and interpret this financial information.

Bookkeeping involves the routine aspects of accounting, such as recording data about financial transactions. Accounting includes answering the important questions, such as what data and records are needed, how they will be kept and reported, and what the significance of the figures is. The accountant designs and oversees the accounting system, including the input, processing, and output of financial information. Most firms also use the services of an outside Certified Public Accountant (CPA), a specialist who has completed formal training and passed a professional exam.

### Get Out Your Calculator

Another important thing to study today is the company's debt. Get out your pocket calculator, and turn to the balance sheet. Divide long-term liabilities by stockholders' equity. That's the *debt-to-equity ratio.*

A high ratio means that the company borrows a lot of money to spark its growth. That's okay—*if* sales grow, too, and *if* there's enough cash on hand to meet the payments. A company doing well on borrowed money can earn big profits for its stockholders. But if sales fall, watch out. The whole enterprise may slowly sink. Some companies can handle high ratios, others can't.

### You Have to Compare

That brings up the most important thing of all: *One* annual report, *one* chairman's letter, *one* ratio won't tell you much. You have to compare. Is the company's debt-to-equity ratio better or worse than it used to be? Better or worse than the industry norms? Better or worse, after this recession, than it was after the last recession? In company-watching, *comparisons are all.* They tell you if management is staying on top of things.

Financial analysts work out many other ratios to tell them how the company is doing. You can learn more about them from books on the subject. Ask your librarian.

But one thing you will *never* learn from an annual report is how much to pay for a company's stock. Galactic may be running well. But if investors expected it to run better, the stock might fall. Or, Galactic could be slumping badly. But if investors see a better day tomorrow, the stock could rise.

### Two Important Suggestions

Those are some basics for weighing a company's health from its annual report. But if you want to know *all* you can about a company, you need to do a little more homework. First, see what the business press has been saying about it over recent years. Again, ask your librarian.

Finally, you should keep up with what's going on in business, economics and politics here and around the world. All can—and will–affect you and the companies you're interested in.

Each year, companies give you more and more information in their annual reports. Profiting from that information is up to you. I hope you profit from *mine.*

Source: Reprinted by permission of International Paper Company, 77 West 45th Street, New York, New York 10036.

2. *How the accounting equation and the double-entry system are used to classify business transactions.*

   The accounting equation, Assets = Liabilities + Owners' Equity, establishes the principle of balance in all accounting records. The double-entry system requires that each transaction be recorded in two places, to maintain this balance.

3. *The purpose of the balance sheet and its information on assets, liabilities, and owners' equity.*

   The balance sheet shows—for a moment in time—a firm's financial position. It is based on the concept that the two sides of the accounting equation must balance—that is, be equal. The usual accounts included in a balance sheet are current assets; fixed assets (or property, plant, and equipment); current liabilities; long-term liabilities (or debt); and owners' equity.

4. *The purpose of the income statement and its information on revenues, expenses, and profits.*

# *Business Debate*

## Does Corporate Financial Reporting Represent Reality or Illusion?

Does corporate financial reporting—that is, income statements and balance sheets—represent genuine operating performance or the illusion of performance?

Those who believe that financial statements *represent genuine operating performance* include some managers, investors, and creditors. They present the following arguments to support their position.

1. The accounting equation (Assets − Liabilities = Owners' Equity, or Assets = Liabilities + Owners' Equity) underlies the balance sheet, and figures don't lie. Total assets on the left side and total liabilities and owners' equity on the right side must balance.
2. There are many areas of accounting in which generally accepted accounting principles (GAAP) exist for reporting identical business situations.
3. Management is responsible for measuring and reporting on performance, and its judgments should lead to the use of the most appropriate accounting principle in a particular situation. It's in management's best interest to communicate its objectives, policies, and the factors involved in decision making.
4. The Financial Accounting Standards Board (FASB) develops and issues rules on accounting practice.
5. Flexibility in using accounting principles is needed because of the existing variations in basic business policies and management attitudes toward risks. If generally accepted accounting principles become too inflexible, business practice may be unduly restricted.

Those who believe that *corporate financial reporting represents illusion* present the following arguments.

1. Managers aren't fulfilling their public reporting responsibilities objectively, as pressures from stockholders to achieve increased annual earnings per share are so great that they are tempted to puff up the corporation's earnings through accounting policy decisions.
2. There are difficulties involved in making meaningful comparisons of the financial reports of different firms, for managers can choose between several equally authoritative accounting treatments to report various items. Thus profits vary greatly, depending on the alternative chosen.
3. Some managers have taken advantage of accounting alternatives to report profits in the way that best serves their own purposes rather than those of the owners, investors, and the public. This practice has made it more difficult for business as a whole to fulfill its public responsibility in corporate financial reporting.
4. Managerial accounting provides management with useful financial information for operating its firm. Therefore, some managers have decided not to use the same accounting principles for *managerial* and *financial* accounting purposes, on the grounds that some external reporting practices can't be used internally because they might introduce an undesirable behavioral bias in decisions of unit managers.
5. *Tax* accounting may conflict with *financial* accounting, since their objectives are different. Because taxes are based on profits, reported profits should be as low as possible to minimize taxes. But financial accounting is pressured to make the firm—and its managers—look good. So there's pressure to have differences in the accounts.

Does corporate financial reporting represent reality or illusion? *What do you think?*

The income statement indicates—over a prescribed period of time—the results of a company's operations by reflecting changes in status between two points in time. It's based on the equation Revenues – Expenses = Profit (or Loss).

5. *The purpose of the statement of changes in financial position.*

This statement summarizes the changes that have occurred in the company's financial position during the accounting period. Its main function is showing where a firm got its funds and how it used them.

6. *How financial statements can be interpreted.*

In interpretation of financial statements, the individual items in the statements are relatively meaningless. The relationships and changes between items and groups of items are the significant factors to look for.

## ⏶ IMPORTANT TERMS

As an extra review of the chapter, try defining the following terms. If you have trouble with any of them, refer to the page listed.

accounting  *454*
financial accounting  *454*
managerial accounting  *454*
bookkeeping  *455*
public accountants  *456*
certified public accountant
 (CPA)  *456*
auditing  *456*
asset  *459*
liability  *459*
owners' equity  *459*
accounting equation  *459*
double-entry system  *459*
accounts  *460*

balance sheet  *464*
income statement  *464*
statement of changes in
 financial position  *464*
current assets  *466*
liquid assets  *466*
fixed assets (property, plant, and
 equipment)  *466*
current liabilities  *466*
long-term liabilities  *466*
revenues  *468*
expenses  *468*
income before tax  *469*
net income  *469*

## ⏶ REVIEW QUESTIONS

1. What is the difference between bookkeeping and accounting?
2. Categorize the following as financial accounting or managerial accounting:
   a. Preparation of income statements.
   b. Working out a department budget.
   c. Filling out a tax form.
3. Why are CPAs special?
4. What is the role of auditing?
5. Describe the relationship between the accounting equation and the double-entry system.
6. Classify each of the following as an asset, a liability, or owners' equity:
   a. Cash in the bank.
   b. A loan on your car.
   c. Tuition paid in advance.
   d. A 10-speed bike.

7. What is meant by the statement that the accounting process involves a basic input/process/output system?
8. Define the following accounts:
   a. Cash
   b. Accounts Receivable
   c. Marketable Securities
   d. Accounts Payable
   e. Selling Expenses
   f. Administrative Expenses
9. What is the primary purpose of the statement of changes in financial position?
10. What is involved in interpreting financial statements?

## ▲ DISCUSSION QUESTIONS

1. If CPAs make mistakes like they did at the UAB, why do firms continue to use them and pay them large fees?
2. How would you distinguish between the balance sheet and the income statement with respect to (a) purpose, (b) timing, and (c) accounts?
3. How do you think computers will affect, or change, accounting? Do you see any pitfalls?
4. What are some of the changes the computer will make in accounting records and statements?
5. Does corporate financial reporting represent reality or illusion? Explain.

## ▲ CASE 17-1  The Affluent Graduates

Joan, a finance major, and Tim, a chemistry major, married three years ago, just after they graduated from college. She went to work in the credit department of a large department store, while he became a chemist in a local chemical plant. At night, he worked on an MBA degree at a local university.

Recently, he became chief chemist for a small refinery in another city, and she became a management trainee in a bank. He continued his schooling but had to drive fifty miles to and from school two nights a week. When they moved, they had the chance to buy, for $250,000, some land that they could subdivide and sell for a substantial profit. Their first reaction was "There's no way we can swing it! We don't have the money." The lawyer who was handling the sale, however, urged them to analyze their financial situation to see if they could obtain the funds.

They studied their income, debts, and belongings and were surprised to discover how well off they were. First, their combined income was now over $38,000—and going up. Then, when they added up their equity in two cars, two lots, a thrift fund, paid-up insurance, books, art, music systems, clothes, furniture, and other belongings, they found they were "worth" over $40,000.

They were able to dispose of some of their assets and borrow the balance to buy the property.

**Case Questions**

1. What is your reaction to the way they evaluated their financial position?
2. Would you have handled it any differently? How?
3. How does their approach conform to that used by a business?
4. How does it differ?

## ⚖ CASE 17-2 Closing the Hospital's Emergency Room

In 1970, the University of South Alabama Medical Center (USAMC) contracted with the Mobile County Hospital Board (MCHB) to provide care for the county's indigent patients "to the extent that a three-mill ad valorem tax fund permitted."

By the end of 1982, USAMC, one of the nation's finest teaching and research institutions, had an annual budget of $43 million and was receiving only about 2 percent of that from the county for indigent care. Yet it handled about 90 percent of the indigent care in the county, and 35 percent of its patients were indigent. In 1982, indigent care cost the hospital $19.9 million, of which only $2.3 million was covered by county funds. The net cost of indigent care was $8 to $11 million.[5] USAMC's bad debts increased from $9.1 million in 1979 to $19.9 million in 1982, and it was losing around $25,000 a day on indigent care in 1983.[6] Yet, by state law, no government agency can operate at a deficit.

Previously part of the deficit had been transferred to paying patients, but this was no longer possible because insurance companies and government agencies had tightened up restrictions on payments. Personnel and other expenses had already been reduced as far as possible. Compounding the problem was the wide difference of opinion as to what the financial situation *really* was. An audit by a national auditing firm showed a "profit" of around $1.6 million.[7] But, according to the hospital administrator, the audit did not show a $1.7 million expense for "funded depreciation," which caused a $138,939 deficit, the second in two years. The auditors answered that "generally accepted accounting principles for colleges and universities" do not recognize depreciated expenses. Yet most hospitals use money from operations and depreciation for expansion.

During the first three months of fiscal 1983, the number of nonpaying patients rose to 41 percent, up from about 35 percent a year earlier. The administration decided to close the emergency room from Friday at 7 P.M. to Monday at 7 A.M., as that was when many indigents entered the hospital. After several weeks of legal battling, the Alabama Supreme Court permitted the closing as a cost-saving measure to permit the hospital to continue operating. The city and county governing authorities are paying for another audit of USAMC's books.

### Case Questions

1. What accounting issues are involved in this problem?
2. Why do you think there was so much difference of opinion as to USAMC's true financial condition?
3. What do you think of the practice of transferring indigent costs to paying patients?
4. Should the hospital be forced to remain open even if it has $19.9 million of bad debts and is losing $25,000 a day?
5. How would you resolve the difficulty if you were the president of the University of South Alabama?

# DIGGING DEEPER

## Careers in Data Processing and Accounting

Computer systems have enabled companies to process great amounts of data quickly and in many forms. Businesses are now able to serve customers more effectively, maintain better records, have better employee relations, and provide management with vital information for effective decision making. Career opportunities are excellent for those who want to enter this field. Since 1979, computer specialists have been singled out by personnel recruiting firms as the most sought-after employees in the country. Demand for them far exceeds the supply, and salaries are rising so rapidly that published figures quickly become outdated. Every issue of *Computerworld*, a weekly newspaper for the computing industry, contains page after page of help wanted ads.

Accountants provide financial information about a business to those who need it. Major users of this information are (1) the firm's managers; (2) current or potential investors in the company; (3) government tax agencies, such as the Internal Revenue Service; and (4) government regulatory agencies. The financial information provided to the users deals with company activities and its current position and situation resulting from those activities.

### What Data Processing Jobs Require

*Information systems managers* should have both technical knowledge and managerial skills, with managerial skills relatively more important. These managers must clearly understand the firm's business, its mission and objectives, and its data base needs. They must be able not only to direct and motivate their employees effectively but also to command the respect of other executives. They should have college degrees and practical experience.

*Data base administrators* establish a data dictionary, coordinate the data collection and storage needs of users, act as file design and data base consultants to other managers, and design the data-base user system in order to prevent un-

authorized use. They should have college degrees and practical experience.

*Software/systems engineers and analysts* are described in Table V-1. There tends to be a geographical concentration of these positions in the Midwest and Northeast. Two-thirds of systems analysts are employed in these two regions. These jobs are currently increasing at over 15 percent per year nationwide, but 60 percent of new jobs in the Midwest are computer-related.[1]

*Programmers*, also described in Table V-1, may be classified as applications programmers or systems programmers. The former take the systems specifications of analysts and transform them into programs of instructions for computers. The latter select, modify, and maintain operating system software and participate in decisions involving hardware and software additions or deletions.

*Telecommunications personnel* design the data communications networks. They interact with systems programmers to select communication processors used in the networks. They analyze network traffic and prepare data communication software. Their technical skills should be strong, but formal education is relatively unnecessary compared with expertise, knowledge, and motivation.

*Computer operations personnel* are described in Table V-1.

### What Accounting Jobs Require

A national examination for Certified Managerial Accountant (CMA), prepared and graded by the Institute of Management Accounting, has been developed, and an internal auditor can take a similar examination to earn a Certified Internal Auditor (CIA) designation. Certified Public Accountant (CPA) firms hire thousands of college graduates with accounting majors each year. Career options consist of remaining with the firm in which they were initially employed, joining other CPA firms, taking employment with busi-

**TABLE V-1  Selected careers in data processing and accounting.**

| Job Title | Job Description | Education and Training | Salaries (Beginner / Experienced) | Outlook to 1990 |
|---|---|---|---|---|
| Computer operations personnel<br><br>Keypunch operators<br><br>Console operators | Specialized workers in data systems who enter data and instructions, operate the computer, and retrieve the results. | Community or junior college training, especially in data processing | $10,400<br><br>$15,600–$19,600 | Employment of console and peripheral equipment operators is expected to rise much faster than the average for all occupations. |
| Printer and card-tape converter operators | Keypunch operators prepare input by punching patterns of holes in computer cards. | | | Employment of keypunch operators should continue to decline. |
| Tape librarians | Console operators monitor and control the computer, decide what equipment should be used by examining special instructions prepared by programmers. | | | |
| Software/systems engineers and analysts | Plan efficient methods of processing data and handling the results. Discuss the data processing problem with managers. Devise a new system. Prepare charts and diagrams that describe operations. Translate systems requirements into capabilities for computer hardware. Prepare specifications for programmers. | College graduates are generally sought. Background in accounting, business management, and economics desired for business applications. Background in physical sciences, mathematics, or engineering desired in scientific systems. | $17,150<br><br>$20,300–$25,500 | Employment is expected to grow much faster than the average for all occupations. |
| Programmers | Write detailed instructions that list in a logical order the steps the computer must follow to organize data or solve a problem. Usually work from descriptions prepared by systems analysts. | Most programmers are college graduates, especially for scientific or engineering applications. | $17,800<br><br>$25,400 | Employment is expected to grow faster than the average for all occupations. |

SOURCES: U.S. Department of Labor, *Occupational Outlook Handbook*, 1982–1983 (Washington: U.S. Government Printing Office, April 1982) and 1980–1981 (Washington: U.S. Government Printing Office, April 1980); College Placement Council, *CPC Salary Survey, Summer Supplement* (Bethlehem, Pa.: C P Council, 1983), pp. 2–5; and Steven D. Ross, "The 12 Top Money-Making Careers of the '80s," *Business Week's Guide to Careers* 1 (Spring 1983):9.

**TABLE V-I**— *continued*

| Job Title | Job Description | Education and Training | Salaries (Beginner / Experienced) | Outlook to 1990 |
|---|---|---|---|---|
| Bookkeepers and accounting clerks | Maintain systematic, up-to-date records of accounts and business transactions in journals, ledgers, and other accounting forms. Prepare periodic financial statements. Use calculators, check-writing, and bookkeeping machines. | High-school graduates who have taken bookkeeping and business arithmetic, completed courses at a community or junior college or business college | $9,600<br><br>$11,400–$16,900 | Employment is expected to grow about as fast as the average for all occupations. Increased use of advanced computing systems will reduce need. |
| Accountants | Provide financial information about an organization to the firm's managers, current or potential investors, government tax and regulatory agencies. Design and supervise accounting systems. Computers and other modern information-processing equipment are used extensively. Often specialize in one area. | B.S. in business administration with major in accounting | $18,800<br><br>$40,000–$68,000 | Employment is expected to grow faster than the average for all occupations. |
| Economists | Study the way a society uses scarce resources—land, labor, new materials, and machinery—to provide goods and services. Determine costs/benefits of making, distributing, and using resources. Focus on energy cost, inflation, business cycles, unemployment, or tax policy. Concerned with practical applications of economic policy. | Bachelor's degree with a major in economics. Graduate training is increasingly required. | $19,100<br><br>Medium base salary for business economists, $38,000<br><br>Top salary range for corporate economists, $50,000–$61,000 | Employment is expected to grow faster than the average for all occupations. |

**TABLE V-I**—*continued*

| Job Title | Job Description | Education and Training | Salaries (Beginner/Experienced) | Outlook to 1990 |
|---|---|---|---|---|
| Statisticians | Devise, carry out, and interpret the numerical results of surveys and experiments. May use statistical techniques to predict population growth or economic conditions or to develop quality control tests for manufactured products. | Bachelor's degree with a major in statistics or mathematics. Courses in computer use and techniques are highly recommended. Opportunities are best for those with advanced degrees. | $20,800 $29,300 | Opportunities are expected to be favorable. |

ness or nonprofit organizations, or establishing their own practices.

In addition to CPA firms and private businesses, many professional accountants are employed by federal, state, and local governments and nonprofit organizations. About 25 percent of practicing accountants are employed by public accounting firms, about 60 percent by profit and nonprofit organizations, and the remainder by governments and colleges and universities.

Accounting is one of the best entry-level jobs, as accounting experience provides a fine background for other management positions. Many members of top management in large firms started in accounting.

Accountants often specialize in one area during their careers. These areas include *general accounting, controlling, auditing, tax accounting, systems and procedures accounting, cost accounting, budgetary accounting,* and *public accounting.* The demand for tax consultants and cost analysts was increasing at the rate of over 12 percent in 1983–1984, and for controllers, over 15 percent.[2] One career path for accountants is shown in Figure V-1.

*Economists* (see Table V-1 for details) are hired by some private firms, but most are in government and nonprofit organizations in major cities throughout the country.

*Statisticians* (see Table V-1 for details) are primarily employed in metropolitan areas such as New York City, Washington, D.C., and Los Angeles, and are concentrated in finance, insurance, and manufacturing firms.

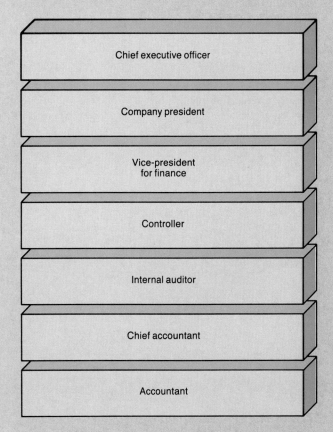

**Figure V-1**    One career path for accountants.

PART **VI**

# FINANCE

Businesses are as dependent on a flow of cash as you are. However, they have many more sources of funds, different uses of money, and obligations to more people than you do. Business managers are given the trusteeship of money by the owners, who expect the managers to use the funds to make a company successful, while protecting its assets. This trusteeship involves two separate functions: (1) obtaining and using money to make a profit and protect and increase assets and (2) keeping track of money and reporting the progress of the company.

There are many kinds of money, which is a scarce resource that must be wisely used. A description of the various types appears in Chapter 18, along with an explanation of the whole U.S. financial system, especially the Federal Reserve System.

The role of financial management within a firm, uses of funds, and short- and long-term sources of funds are discussed in Chapter 19.

Chapter 20 covers securities and securities markets in more depth, as well as discussing personal investments.

The management of risk, especially the use of insurance for that purpose, is dealt with in Chapter 21.

# 18

# The American Financial System

*If you have money, it doth not stay,*
*But this way and that it wastes [away].*

François Villon

*Business! It's quite simple. It's other people's*
*money.*

Alexandre Dumas

**Learning Objectives**

After studying the material in this chapter, you will understand:

1. What money and a monetary system are.
2. The financial institutions that serve individuals and businesses.
3. The purpose and organization of the Federal Reserve System.
4. The functions performed by the Federal Reserve System.
5. The tools available to the Federal Reserve System to create and control the money supply.
6. Some of the newer developments in the U.S. financial system.

**In This Chapter**

What Is Money?
Financial Institutions
The Federal Reserve System
Creating and Controlling the Money Supply
New Developments

## CITICORP
### *Leader of Banking's Big Ten*

New York's First National Bank, better known as Citibank, or Citicorp, isn't a conventional stuffy, dignified, cautious bank. Instead, it's adventurous, aggressive, and daring. It has neither the stately aura of the Bank of America nor the high visibility of the Chase Manhattan. What it does have is a no-nonsense chief executive, Walter Wriston, whose team of young managers has led Citicorp nearly to the top of the banking world. Citicorp holds about one out of every twenty dollars of deposits in all U.S. banks. And its assets of over $130 billion make it the leader of America's ten largest banks.

Citicorp is based in New York but operates nationwide and around the world. Its 840 banking offices in ninety-two foreign countries make it by far the largest U.S. bank overseas. In fact, about three-quarters of its deposits are overseas, and it derives more than two-thirds of its profits from international activities. In addition, there are 270 branch banks in the New York City area and 31 in upstate New York.

Citicorp has sunk over $225 million into new consumer technology. It has installed about 500 automated teller machines on the streets of New York City. The new tellers, which can take deposits, issue cash, and transfer funds from a savings account to checking, already handle about a third of the bank's consumer business at half the cost of human tellers. Says bank chairman Wriston: "People love them. The machines are polite, bilingual in English and Spanish, and are available twenty-four hours a day, without coffee breaks."

In another futuristic move, a trial group of Citibank customers gave up their checkbooks in 1981 in favor of small computer terminals installed by the bank in their homes. These desk-top devices enable customers to pay their bills or rent, stop payment on a previously paid bill, take out a loan, open a new savings account, or check on the balance of an existing one, all electronically, without leaving their homes.

In spite of its huge size and worldwide reputation, Citibank has never been particularly well known in the United States outside New York City. Many people in the United States first heard of it in the late 1970s when Citibank decided to go after the nation's credit card business in a big way. It blanketed the nation with 26 million offers of Visa and Master-Charge cards—in the process angering many other banks that also issue the cards. But a lot of people took advantage of the offer. By 1980, nearly 6 million Americans held bank cards issued by Citibank, and some 80 percent of them lived outside New York State.

You may not hold an account at Citibank or, in fact, at any bank with services quite like Citibank's. But you probably cash checks at an automatic teller machine, perhaps pay bills by phone, and definitely spend money. We've been talking about money since the beginning of this book, whenever profits, revenues, or expenses have been mentioned. In this chapter, you'll come to understand what money really is, how the U.S. banking system works, and how the Federal Reserve System (FRS) directs it all. And you'll discover that money and finance—essential to the U.S. business world—aren't that difficult to understand.

## WHAT IS MONEY

**Objective 1**

**What money and a monetary system are.**

Money makes modern economic and business systems possible. It's necessary not only for a private business to start, grow, and survive, but also for entire economic systems to exist. Without it, we'd still be trading bushels of corn for medical services, and herds of cows for clothing and shelter.

### The Development of a Monetary System

In our study of accounting, we saw how businesspeople account for the money that flows through their companies. But now we'll take a deeper look at what money really is—and does. At its most basic level, money is what we give up in exchange for things of value. In the United States, we give up dollars; in Belgium and France, people give up francs; in Portugal, escudos; in Germany, marks. Thus we regard printed and minted dollars, francs, escudos, and marks as money. But the whole concept of money encompasses more than simply printed currencies. It really revolves around the basic principle of exchange.

Centuries ago, the development of a system of money allowed society to progress from simple person-to-person trade to widespread commerce. In the first human societies, the only form of trade was **barter,** or trading things for other things. If a farmer with extra grain wanted a pottery bowl, he had to arrange a trade with the potter—his grain for the potter's bowl. Of course, this system had its limitations. It only worked if the potter wanted the farmer's grain and the farmer needed a bowl. To make things more convenient, people devised a system of accepting common items as tokens of value. With the acceptance of these tokens as a unit of exchange throughout society, people progressed from a barter system to a **monetary system.**

In primitive cultures, a number of different things have been used as money, including shells, gold, cattle, and tobacco. In ancient Abyssinia, slabs of rock salt ten inches long by two inches thick were the coins of the realm[1]— but hardly convenient as pocket change. All these items, or tokens, have one thing in common: they were all accepted as a medium of exchange for goods or services.

### Types of Money

We can thus expand our definition of **money** to include anything generally accepted as (1) a medium of exchange, (2) a store of value, and (3) a measure of value. Anything that performs these three functions is money. A dollar bill is

used as a medium of exchange when we use it as "legal tender for all debts, public and private." You can keep it in your pocket for years and still trade it later for merchandise; therefore, it's a store of value. Finally, since we can refer to a car as a "$35,000 luxury car," we also use dollars as a measurement standard to determine an item's value.

In our financial system, money includes coins and bills, but it's many other things as well. For example, checking accounts must be included in our definition of money, since checks are accepted as a means of payment. In fact, coins and currency make up only about a fourth of the total U.S. money supply. Checking accounts and other forms of money make up the remaining 75 percent, the largest and most important portion. One widely used term for money is **M-1**, which includes all coins and currency, as well as all checking accounts.

## FINANCIAL INSTITUTIONS

**Objective 2**

The financial institutions that serve individuals and businesses.

**Financial institutions** are businesses that distribute or deal in money and financial affairs. The number and types of these institutions are quite varied and complex. Traditional distinctions are becoming fuzzy, and new institutions designed to meet new financial needs are springing up almost daily. For clarity's sake, we'll discuss only the most familiar institutions.

### Commercial Banks

As shown in FYI on page 488, commercial banks, the oldest of our financial institutions, began centuries ago. Today, they're the heart of the U.S. financial system, the type of bank you're most familiar with. It's through these state and nationally chartered banks that most of our financial activities are channeled. In effect, they're the department stores of finance.

A **commercial bank** is a privately owned, profit-seeking corporation organized to serve individuals' and businesses' financial needs. Banks serve individuals by offering such services as checking accounts, savings accounts, and consumer loans. The commercial bank is also the most important financial institution for businesses, which use many of the same services that individuals do, including checking accounts.

A bank's most important service to a business is usually its lending activities. The commercial bank is the most important source of short-term loans for businesses, whether they're one-person proprietorships or billion-dollar corporations. Banks lend organizations money to finance inventory or to meet seasonal cash needs. Sometimes these loans are made on the condition that the corporation pledge some item of value as security. This type of loan is called a **secured loan.** If the borrower defaults, or fails to pay the money back, the bank may take possession of the pledged item.

It's no surprise that businesses carefully protect their credit ratings and their relationships with commercial banks. The most credit-worthy businesses are able to borrow solely on the basis of their good reputation. Such unsecured loans are less expensive for the borrower and give the business more flexibility. These very credit-worthy firms are given the **prime rate,** which is the lowest commercial interest rate available at a particular time and place.

# FYI

## Goldsmith Banking

Modern banking had its origins in ancient England. In those days, people wanting to safeguard their coins or gold had two choices—hide it under the mattress or turn it over to someone else for safekeeping. The logical people to turn to for storage were the local goldsmiths, since they had the strongest vaults.

The goldsmiths accepted the gold for storage, giving the owner a receipt stating that the gold could be redeemed at a later date. When a payment was due, the owner went to the goldsmith, redeemed part of the gold, and gave it to the payee. After all that, the payee was very likely to turn around and give the gold back to the goldsmith for safekeeping.

Gradually, instead of taking the time and effort to physically exchange the gold, businesspeople began to exchange the goldsmiths' receipts as payment. Therefore, the gold never left the goldsmiths' vaults. It wasn't long before enterprising goldsmiths saw the potential for profit in this arrangement. As long as the gold remained in the vaults, the owners wouldn't miss it if it were loaned to someone else—for a fee. The odds were overwhelmingly against all the depositors' wanting their gold at the same time—and few people would ever demand their very own gold coins back.

The circulation of goldsmiths' receipts was the beginning of paper currency and of commercial banking. And the enterprising goldsmith who first lent somebody else's gold for a fee was the first to make a bank loan for interest.

Source: Eugene S. Klise, *Money and Banking*, 5th ed. (Cincinnati: South-Western, 1972), pp. 132–34; and "Silversmiths' and Goldsmiths' Work," *Encyclopaedia Britannica*, 1949, vol. 20, pp. 688–91.

The accounts that commercial banks offer their customers are of two types: demand deposits and time deposits. **Demand deposits** are simply checking accounts. They're called *demand* deposits because the money in them is available to depositors immediately, without prior notice—"on demand." For this instant availability, depositors forfeit the chance to receive interest. We'll see later how important demand deposits are in the control of our money supply.

**Time deposits** are savings accounts and certificates of deposit. Technically, time deposits require depositors to leave their money with the bank for a stated period of time. In actual practice, though, some time deposits, such as passbook savings accounts, are available on demand, although there may be an interest penalty for immediate withdrawal. In return for allowing their money to be tied up during the stated time period, depositors are paid interest by the banks.

In addition to the most widely used type of savings account, the passbook account, most banks offer a bewildering variety of savings certificates, called **certificates of deposit.** Savers may elect to put their money into thirty-day, six-month, or two-and-one-half-year certificates. These savings instruments tie up depositors' money for longer periods of time, but they also pay higher interest. As a result, many corporations buy large-denomination bank certificates of deposit, considering them a low-risk place to temporarily store their surplus cash.

Most banks are full-service banks, offering the above accounts plus safe deposit boxes, trust services, consumer loans, traveler's checks, electronic funds transfer, bank credit cards, and financial advice. These services are constantly expanding and becoming more sophisticated.

## Savings and Loan Associations

**Savings and loan associations (S&Ls)** were created specifically to finance the housing industry. Depositors placed their money in S&L savings accounts, and the association used these funds to lend money to home builders and buyers. Because S&Ls weren't originally allowed to accept demand deposits, they were allowed to pay a slightly higher rate of interest than commercial banks to attract depositors.

The modern savings and loan association has changed radically from that traditional concept, however. Now S&Ls offer a type of demand deposit, called a **negotiable order of withdrawal (NOW) account,** which is essentially a checking account that pays interest but requires a minimum balance in the account. Most S&Ls are also expanding into consumer loans other than home mortgages. In fact, beginning in 1982, customers could consolidate their savings, checking, and investment accounts in S&Ls, getting convenient, one-step financial shopping.

## Savings Banks

**Savings banks** serve small savers by accepting time deposits and paying interest. Like S&Ls, they invest their depositors' money in real estate and government securities. Savings banks are most common in the northeastern section of the nation. These banks pioneered in developing NOW accounts during the late 1970s.

## Credit Unions

Groups of people with a common interest, place of employment, or occupation can form **credit unions.** Members can have money deducted from their paychecks or make individual deposits into a credit union savings account. The credit union then uses the funds from these accounts to make low-interest loans to members. Because all borrowers and depositors are linked by a common interest, the risk in lending is reduced. Credit unions are able to pay slightly higher interest on savings accounts and charge slightly lower interest on loans than other institutions. Most can now offer a form of NOW account called a share draft account.

## FYI

### The Fall of the Franklin National Bank

In 1974, the Franklin National Bank of Long Island was apparently doing pretty well. It was the twentieth-largest bank in the country, and it had $5 billion in assets in over 100 branches. But below the surface, Franklin was in deep trouble. It had encountered financial reverses and had made risky loans to bring in business that other banks had declined. It had also taken a gamble on interest rates, betting that they would fall. Instead, they rose rapidly. By April of 1974, the bank was losing $3 million a month on bad loans, bad debts, and bad foreign exchange transactions. When the rumor of failure reached the public in the summer of 1974, customers withdrew over $1.7 billion, or 53 percent of the bank's deposits.

When the end came, it came quickly. On a pleasant October day, the FDIC secretly took bids for a takeover of the bank. At 3 P.M. that day, when the bank closed, it was declared insolvent. Two hours later, the winning bidder was announced. The next morning, all branches opened as usual—but a sign in the window of each read "European-American Bank and Trust Company," the name of the winning bidder. The Franklin was no more. At that time, it was the biggest bank failure in U.S. history. While no depositors lost money—they just found themselves customers of a new bank—the stockholders' investments were wiped out.

Sources: Adapted from *Everybody's Business: An Almanac,* edited by Milton Moskowitz, Michael Katz, and Robert Levering, p. 487. © 1980 by Harper & Row, Publishers, Inc. Reprinted by permission of Harper & Row, Publishers, Inc.

### Investment Banks

Investment banks don't accept deposits from the general public. In fact, you may never come in contact with one unless you buy securities or become a corporate financial officer. When a corporation wants to sell a new issue of stock or bonds, it arranges to have an investment bank handle the transaction. The **investment bank,** also called an underwriter, buys the corporation's entire issue of securities and then sells them to individuals or institutions such as pension funds. Its profit is the difference between the price it receives when it sells the securities and the price it paid for them.

### Factoring Companies

Businesses that sell on credit have a large portion of their assets tied up in accounts receivable—the accounts of persons or businesses that have bought

goods or services on credit—which will be collected within a short period of time. A business that needs cash immediately may choose to sell its accounts receivable to a **factoring company,** or **factor,** which pays the business the amount of the accounts receivable after deducting a percentage as its fee. Customers then pay their accounts to the factoring company. Factoring companies are an important source of funds to businesses. The business firm doesn't have to tie up its funds in accounts receivable, and factoring often reduces the firm's collection costs.

## Insurance Companies

Insurance companies collect premiums from individuals in return for providing insurance protection. As a result, these companies amass large pools of funds, some of which are loaned to businesses. A firm that borrows from an insurance company avoids the expense of issuing stock or bonds through investment banks.

## Trust Companies

A **trust company** is a financial institution that handles the protection of a company's bond holders' interests. It safeguards property by allowing individuals to set up trusts at large commercial banks to administer their estates. Large corporations also use trust companies to safeguard the funds entrusted to them by investors.

A corporation selling bonds appoints a **trustee,** usually a trust company, to protect the bond holders' interests. The trustee makes certain that the corporation abides by all the requirements of its agreement with investors. The trustee issues dividend and interest checks and keeps up with the names and addresses of stockholders and bond holders.

Commercial banks in many states also provide trust services. These banks usually have the term *trust* in their title, as in First National Bank and Trust Company.

## Commercial Paper Houses

Large corporations may also borrow money by issuing **commercial paper,** which is essentially a very short-term unsecured IOU from the corporation. This paper is to be repaid within 270 days. Only the largest and most financially secure corporations can issue commercial paper. Commercial paper houses purchase commercial paper from corporations and resell it to investors, much as an investment bank does with stock and bond issues. Because the minimum denomination is very high, usually $100,000, commercial paper is sold mainly to institutions such as pension and mutual funds.

## Deposit Insurance

A sad chapter in the history of banking occurred in the 1930s. At the height of the Depression, individual banks failed in record numbers. In 1932 alone, a total of 1,456 banks ceased operation. Depositors in most of these institutions lost all their savings.[2]

As a result of this experience, Congress passed **deposit insurance** legislation guaranteeing the deposits of customers at banks and S&Ls. The Federal

Deposit Insurance Corporation (FDIC), created in 1933, now guarantees customer deposits of up to $100,000 in any member bank. Nationally chartered banks are required to join the FDIC, and state-chartered banks may do so if they meet the requirements. In 1981, over 98 percent of all commercial banks and about 80 percent of all bank deposits in the United States were insured by the FDIC.[3]

If a financial institution that is a member of the FDIC goes bankrupt, the FDIC will step in and try to arrange for another institution to take over customers' accounts. The majority of bank failures are handled this way. Only rarely is it necessary for the FDIC itself to step in and pay depositors out of its own reserves, but it will do so if necessary. The full commitment of the federal government is behind these accounts. No depositor has ever lost a penny in an insured checking or savings account (see FYI on page 490).

## THE FEDERAL RESERVE SYSTEM

**Objective 3**

**The purpose and organization of the Federal Reserve System.**

In any privately owned, profit-seeking business, there's always the possibility not only of profit but also of loss. There's also the potential for business failure, bankruptcy, or unethical business practice. The commercial bank, in its early stages, was no exception.

Until 1913, private banks were able to issue their own notes, or paper money, which functioned as a medium of exchange. When a bank failed, its notes became worthless, throwing the area's money supply into chaos. Then in 1913, the **Federal Reserve System (FRS),** commonly called "the Fed," was established by Congress to serve as a central bank for the nation, with the implied objective of controlling the money supply. It created a national money supply by issuing its own Federal Reserve notes, which took the place of the earlier individually issued bank notes. Federal Reserve notes circulating today range in value from $1 to $100,000, although no denomination larger than $100 has been printed since 1969.

> Look at a piece of U.S. currency, such as a $1, $5, $10, or $20 bill. Notice that it reads "Federal Reserve Note," indicating that it was printed and circulated by the Federal Reserve System.

This currency is backed by the "full faith and credit" of the U.S. government. It has value as long as people have faith in the U.S. government and trust it to be able to redeem the money. A dollar bill in itself is worth no more than the paper it's printed on. Its real value depends on how much people think it can buy.

### The Organization of the Fed

Although the Federal Reserve System was established by Congress, the U.S. government doesn't own it. When it was created, its stock was sold to member banks, which were private commercial banks. This puts the Fed in the unique position of being privately owned, yet operated by government officials in the public interest.

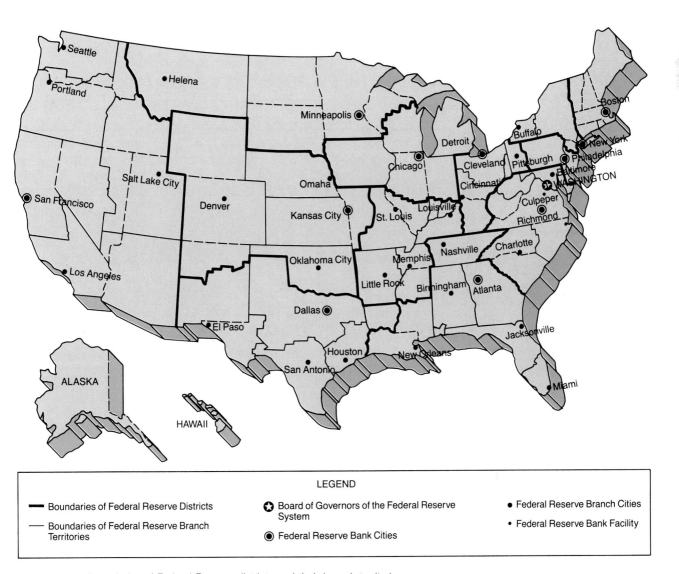

**LEGEND**

| | | |
|---|---|---|
| ▬ Boundaries of Federal Reserve Districts | ✪ Board of Governors of the Federal Reserve System | • Federal Reserve Branch Cities |
| — Boundaries of Federal Reserve Branch Territories | ◉ Federal Reserve Bank Cities | • Federal Reserve Bank Facility |

**Figure 18-1**  Boundaries of Federal Reserve districts and their branch territories.

▲ **Federal Reserve Districts**   There are twelve Federal Reserve districts scattered across the country, as shown in Figure 18-1.  Each of these districts has its own president, board of directors, and district bank, and each district bank has several branch banks.  Individual commercial banks in these areas own stock in the district FRS bank and elect some of its directors.  Other directors are appointed by the Board of Governors, the Fed's seven-member main governing body.  Of the nine directors of each FRS district bank, three may be bankers, three must be businesspeople, and three must represent the general public.

▲ **The Board of Governors**   As we've said, the FRS has a Board of Governors, headquartered in Washington, D.C., one of whose members serves as chairperson (see the Profile on page 494).  The President of the United States appoints the Board of Governors, with the consent of the U.S. Senate.  All members are appointed for fourteen years, with staggered terms, effectively taking the operation of the Fed out of the control of any single president or Congress.

## Profile

### Paul A. Volcker: Inflation Fighter

This good gray banker isn't without humor. Invited to a Halloween party in 1970, six-foot, seven-inch Paul Volcker painted his balding head with green body paint, donned a pair of emerald tights, and arrived as the Jolly Green Giant. Even at work, the chairman of the Fed appears equally un-bankerly. He's seldom without a twenty-cent, gold-seal stogie clamped between his teeth. Ashes invariably litter the lapels of his rumpled suits, some of them clearly past their prime. Says his wife Barbara: "He's got one suit that he thinks looks like silk, but it's just shiny."

But Paul Volcker is a maverick only in appearance and style. His reputation as a staunch defender of the dollar is cast iron, and international and U.S. bankers were equally enthusiastic when he was appointed Fed chairman in 1979. Faced with a 13 percent inflation rate, the Carter Administration was forced to appoint a solid, conservative inflation fighter, and Volcker's credentials were far more impressive than anyone else's.

Son of a New Jersey city manager, Volcker received a B.A. degree summa cum laude from Princeton and a mas-

The relationship between the Board of Governors and the twelve Federal Reserve banks isn't unlike that between the federal government and the various state governments. Like the federal government, the Board usually concentrates on matters of national importance. Like the states, the district banks tend to specialize in matters within their districts.[4] The Board of Governors sets the general direction for the member banks.

▲ **Member Banks** While there are over 14,000 commercial banks in the United States, only about 5,500 are member banks belonging to the Federal Reserve System. These banks, however, control about 70 percent of the nation's total bank deposits.

National banks, which are chartered by the federal government and have the term *national* in their title, must join. State-chartered banks may join if

ter's degree in political economy from Harvard. After a few months of studying for a doctorate at the London School of Economics, Volcker quit, saying, "My lasting memory of the place is the repeated need to put shillings into a heater in a small, cold flat at night."

Shucking the academic world for the real thing, Volcker signed on as an economist with the New York branch of the Fed. After five years, he jumped into private enterprise at the Chase Manhattan Bank. Five more years and he became chief financial analyst at the U.S. Treasury in Washington, D.C., a remarkable achievement at age thirty-four.

The dazzling promotions continued. Volcker rose to Deputy Undersecretary for Monetary Affairs, took time out for four years to be a Chase vice-president, and then served Richard Nixon in the Treasury Department, defending the dollar against attacks from abroad. The experience strengthened his view that the Fed had to take strong action to fight inflation and thus defend the dollar overseas. For a year, Volcker was a senior fellow at Princeton, but in 1975 he returned to the New York Fed as its president.

In July 1979, Volcker stood near the peak of a brilliant career, commanding a salary of $110,000 as president of the Federal Reserve Board of New York. Upon accepting President Carter's appointment as chairman of the Fed, Volcker moved to a small one-bedroom apartment in Washington, took a 45 percent pay cut, and began his campaign to strengthen the dollar and reduce inflation. On weekends, he visited his wife in New York. She has arthritis but worked as a bookkeeper and took in a boarder to help pay the bills.

In his position as chairman, Volcker fought hard and successfully to limit the growth of the money supply, thus depriving inflation of its monetary fuel. When he took office in 1979, the inflation rate stood at an eye-popping 13.3 percent. In 1983, it had been reduced to less than 5 percent.

Historically, Fed chairmen have remained relatively unnoticed among Washington's glamour-seeking politicians. But Volcker's position as the nation's chief inflation fighter made him uncomfortably prominent. His office mail was filled with two-by-fours and keys sent by contractors and auto workers protesting houses that can't be built and cars that can't be sold. Frequent television appearances and his outsize frame made it impossible for him to walk down the street without being noticed.

Why did he sacrifice his personal finances (his assets totaled only $56,000 in 1981, and his salary was only $60,000 in 1983 when he was reappointed by President Reagan) to help save this nation's economy? According to a friend, he saw inflation as society's greatest hardship, especially to the poor and elderly, and was willing to make a personal sacrifice for the general good of the people.

---

Sources: Based on Kenneth H. Bacon, "Challenges for Fed: Volcker, Reappointed, Is Facing Severe Tests at Home and Abroad," *The Wall Street Journal*, June 20, 1983, pp. 1, 18. Reprinted by permission of *The Wall Street Journal*, © Dow Jones & Company, Inc. 1983. All Rights Reserved. Also based on "Behind the 20¢ Cigar," *Time*, March 8, 1982, pp. 80–81; "The Dollar Chooses a Chairman," *Business Week*, August 6, 1979, pp. 20–21; A. F. Ehrbar, "A Real Inflation Fighter Takes Charge at the Fed," *Fortune*, September 10, 1979, pp. 62–64; "When Fed's Chief Counts His Money," *U.S. News & World Report*, June 21, 1982, p. 6; "The Fed's Plan for Economic Recovery," *Business Week*, December 13, 1982, pp. 90–97; and "No. 2 in Washington," *Time*, February 28, 1983, p. 44.

they meet all the Fed's requirements. The major advantage of being a member is the right to borrow funds at a discount through the Federal Reserve System.

## Functions of the Fed

**Objective 4**

The functions performed by the Federal Reserve System.

The Federal Reserve System performs six basic functions for the nation: (1) it acts as a bank for financial institutions; (2) it serves as the government's bank; (3) it supervises member banks; (4) it protects consumers in credit transactions; (5) it facilitates the movement of money; and (6) it controls the nation's money supply.

▲ **Acting as a Bank for Financial Institutions** Financial institutions need a bank for many of the same reasons consumers do—to borrow money, make

deposits, cash checks, and so on. The Fed provides these services. In 1982, it processed over fifteen billion checks. Most banks must keep reserves against their demand deposits. These reserves may be deposited in a Fed bank account. Banks can draw on these accounts to do business but are subject to penalties if the balance falls too low, somewhat like an individual's checking account with a minimum balance requirement.

Sometimes banks need extra money, too. When this happens, banks go to the Fed to borrow funds. They're actually exchanging some of their assets, government securities, for cash. The Fed pays the bank the face value of the security, less a discount as a fee for the loan.

▲ **Serving as the Government's Bank**  The federal government earns, spends, and owes more than any other organization in the world. The Fed does two types of jobs for the government: it keeps its checking accounts and handles its borrowing. When individuals pay their taxes, the money is deposited in the nearest Federal Reserve bank. As the government spends money—to build submarines, pay salaries, or buy computers—it writes checks on its Federal Reserve account.

When the government has to borrow, it has the Fed arrange a loan between individuals or institutions and the federal government. A U.S. savings bond is such a loan. The Fed prints these IOUs, or securities, and sells them, handling most of the government's financial paperwork.

▲ **Supervising Member Banks**  The Federal Reserve writes the rules under which member banks must operate. To make certain that these rules are obeyed, it employs a staff of bank examiners, who visit those members that are not national banks. These examiners spend anywhere from a week to several months going over the bank's financial records to make certain that everything is in order and that these banks are maintaining a safe, risk-free environment for consumers' deposits.

▲ **Protecting Consumers' Credit Transactions**  After Congress passed the Truth in Lending Act in 1968, the Fed was given the responsibility of drawing up detailed regulations and putting them into effect. Since then, it has issued consumer protection regulations such as those giving married women the right to establish credit histories in their own name and prohibiting discrimination in credit based on race, color, sex, marital status, religion, or national origin. It also requires lenders to state in specific terms such essentials as annual percentage rates and finance charges.

▲ **Facilitating the Movement of Money**  The Fed keeps a huge supply of printed or minted currency and coins in its vaults. This cash comes from the U.S. Treasury, where it is printed or minted. When a bank needs more coins or paper money to meet customer needs, it notifies the Fed, which ships the money by armored car.

Yet three-fourths of our money supply isn't in cash but in **checks,** which are unconditional promises directing a bank to pay out certain sums of money under specified conditions. These are usually—but not always—small pieces of paper used in commercial transactions in exactly the same way currency is used (see FYI on page 497). A commercial bank receives thousands of them each day, deposited by consumers. It gives depositors credit for the amounts of

# FYI

## A Check Is a _____?

For almost 3,000 years, checks have permitted us to do business without handling currency. Almost all checks are written on special checkbook paper, but they needn't be. So don't worry if you run out of your beautifully printed personalized checks one day. Through the years, perfectly valid checks have been written on some curious surfaces: on handkerchiefs, cigarette paper, calling cards, fragile valentines, and newspapers.

One written on the shell of a hard-boiled egg was cashed without trouble by the Canadian Bank of Commerce. A Midwest lumberman made out so many checks on his own brand of shingle that his bank had to construct a special filing cabinet for them. And a contractor in Memphis once settled his weekly payroll by drawing on the banks with slabs of wood.

One story tells of a sailor in San Diego who was plagued with requests from home for money. He engraved a check on a piece of battleship plate with a blowtorch and sent it home, confident the annoying requests would stop. At the end of the month, though, the steel check came back with the rest of his canceled checks, with a proper endorsement—also made with a blowtorch.

Somewhat similar is the bizarre tale of a solid-steel check the size of a small headstone that was carried into the Cleveland Trust Company by two men in 1932. The teller handed over $7,500, then called bank guards, who carted the oversized check outside and canceled it with submachinegun bullets. The check is now in the world-famous Chase Manhattan Bank Museum of Moneys of the World.

Source: Adapted from Irwin Ross, "Please Cash My Shingle," *Sky*, June 1980, p. 76. This article has been reprinted through the courtesy of Halsey Publishing Co., publishers of *Sky* magazine.

the checks and then sends the checks to the institutions on which they were drawn, asking for payment.

The Fed helps banks collect on the checks they receive. In effect, it says, "Send us all your checks, and we'll sort them and present them for payment. Then we'll pay you." This saves the bank the trouble and expense of sorting the checks and mailing them individually. It also cuts the time it takes for checks to clear. If the checks handled by the Fed each day were taped end-to-end, they'd reach from New York to Alaska.

The Federal Reserve System also wires money. If a business in Washington needed to transfer $10,000 to Seattle to close a business deal, it would call a commercial bank, which would in turn call the nearest FRS bank. The Fed would then electronically wire the money to the FRS bank in San Francisco, which would send the money to Seattle, where it could be picked up.

▲ **Controlling the Money Supply**  The last, and probably the most important, function of the Fed is controlling the supply of money in circulation. This is the primary purpose of the Fed, the reason it was created. Essentially, this function involves creating money and then controlling its supply and movement.

## CREATING AND CONTROLLING THE MONEY SUPPLY

**Objective 5**

**The tools available to the Federal Reserve System to create and control the money supply.**

Before the Fed was established, individual banks could issue their own notes, or paper money. The volume of money increased or declined as a result of business conditions. With the development of a central bank, the responsibility for controlling the money supply was transferred to the Fed.

The amount of money in circulation vitally affects our economy. When too little money is available, interest rates—the price of money—increase. Business can't afford to borrow at high prices, and the nation's economic health is affected. Too much money tends to result in inflation. Therefore, the Fed tries to walk a tightrope between too small and too large a supply.

### How the Fed Creates Money

The Fed doesn't, by itself, create money. Rather, commercial banks create money, in cooperation with the Fed.

▲ **The Fractional Reserve System**  Each commercial bank can accept customers' checking account deposits. The bank doesn't simply put that money in its vault, but instead uses it to make loans to businesses or individuals. Thus it uses the deposited money to make a profit.

If the bank lent the entire amount of its demand deposits, it would have no money on hand should a customer want to withdraw his or her entire account. To protect customers, the Fed requires that banks keep a certain portion, or fraction, of each demand deposit "on reserve" to meet withdrawal demands.[5] (A smaller reserve is required on time deposits.) This is why our banking system is referred to as a **fractional reserve system,** using a changing percentage or **reserve requirement.**

▲ **How Deposits Expand**  Suppose that the Fed sets 10 percent, or one-tenth, as the fraction that banks must hold in reserve. If a customer deposits $100 cash in a checking account in Bank A, the bank must keep one-tenth, or $10, as a reserve. The remainder, $90, may be loaned out, and so forth (see Table 18-1 for the further progress of our initial $100). The process continues until, at some point, the remainder available for further loans is $0. Notice that, although no new coins or currency have been put into circulation, a total of $900 has been loaned out. The initial $100 has simply been respent and expanded throughout the commercial bank system. A total of $900 in *new* money has been "created" by the process of deposit expansion ($1,000 − $100 = $900). If each bank in our example decided to lend less than the maximum, the process wouldn't create the maximum $900 of new money.

▲ **How Changing Reserve Requirements Affect the Process**  The commercial banks above were required to hold 10 percent, or one-tenth, of their deposits as a reserve. If, however, the reserve requirement were increased to 20 percent,

### TABLE 18-1 How deposits expand under the fractional reserve system.

If $100 is deposited in the commercial banking system with a reserve requirement of 10 percent, that original $100 can be loaned until a maximum of $900 in new money is created.*

|  | New Deposit | Required Reserve | Maximum Available for New Loans |
|---|---|---|---|
| Bank A | $100.00 | $10.00 | $90.00 |
| Bank B | 90.00 | 9.00 | 81.00 |
| Bank C | 81.00 | 8.10 | 72.90 |
| Bank D | 72.90 | 7.29 | 65.61 |
| Bank E | 65.61 | 6.56 | 59.05 |
| Totals for the first five banks | $409.51 | $40.95 | $368.56 |
| Total for the entire banking system | $1,000.00 | $100.00 | $900.00 |

*For simplicity's sake, assume that the proceeds of each new loan are deposited in a different bank.

each bank would have to withhold 20 percent of each deposit as a reserve, and the total amount of money that could be "created" would thus be reduced from $900 to $400 (see Table 18-2).

## How the Fed Controls the Money Supply

The Fed's assigned task of controlling the money supply isn't simple. Because individual banks themselves determine how much they will lend, the Fed can't directly control the volume of money in circulation. Instead, it must use indirect tools to force banks to adjust the amount of money created. Table 18-3 shows these tools and how they can be used to help increase or decrease the money supply.

▲ **The Reserve Requirement** One tool the Fed can use is a change in the reserve requirement. In the above example, when the amount commercial

### TABLE 18-2 How increasing the reserve requirement reduces the amount of "new money created."

If $100 is deposited in the commercial banking system with a reserve requirement of 20 percent, that original $100 can be loaned until a maximum of $400 in new money is created.

|  | New Deposit | Required Reserve | Maximum Available for New Loans |
|---|---|---|---|
| Bank A | $100.00 | $20.00 | $80.00 |
| Bank B | 80.00 | 16.00 | 64.00 |
| Bank C | 64.00 | 12.80 | 51.20 |
| Bank D | 51.20 | 10.24 | 40.96 |
| Bank E | 40.96 | 8.19 | 32.77 |
| Totals for the first five banks | $336.16 | $67.23 | $268.93 |
| Totals for the entire banking system | $500.00 | $100.00 | $400.00 |

**TABLE 18-3  Tools the Federal Reserve System can use to control the money supply.**

| If the Fed wants to → <br> It can use: | Increase the Money Supply | Decrease the Money Supply |
|---|---|---|
| THE RESERVE REQUIREMENT | Decrease the reserve requirement, allowing banks to lend more money. | Increase the reserve requirement, preventing banks from lending as much money. |
| THE DISCOUNT RATE | Reduce the discount rate, encouraging banks to borrow more from the FRS, so that they will have more money to lend. | Increase the discount rate, discouraging banks from borrowing from the FRS, so that they will have less money to lend. |
| OPEN MARKET OPERATIONS | Buy government securities on the open market, putting money into circulation. | Sell government securities on the open market, taking money out of circulation. |
| THE MARGIN REQUIREMENT | Reduce the margin requirement, allowing investors to buy stocks with a smaller cash down payment, so that they will borrow more. | Increase the margin requirement so that investors must put up more cash in order to buy stocks. |

banks had to hold as reserve was increased from 10 to 20 percent, the amount of total possible loans declined from $900 to $400.

The Fed is quite reluctant to use this tool. It's like killing a fly with a shotgun. Changing the reserve requirement only 10 percentage points, from 10 percent to 20 percent, cuts the amount of potential new money by over half, severely disrupting banking transactions and the entire economy. Therefore, the reserve requirement is very rarely changed.

▲ **The Discount Rate**  One of the functions performed by the Fed is to lend money to member banks. The price of such loans is the amount of interest the Fed charges on the securities it buys from the banks, known as the **discount rate.** The discount rate is changed fairly frequently as the Fed attempts to expand or reduce the money supply. It, too, however, affects the entire banking system and isn't appropriate when only a small correction is needed.

▲ **Open Market Operations**  The seven-member Board of Governors and five representatives of the district Federal Reserve banks form the Federal Open Market Committee (FOMC). This body determines whether or not the Fed, by buying or selling securities on the open market, should increase or reduce the money supply. As we'll see in Chapter 20, securities, such as stocks, bonds, and government debt issues, can be bought or sold secondhand on several organized exchanges. The Fed uses these exchanges to buy or sell government securities in order to directly increase or decrease the money supply.

If the FOMC decided to make credit easier to obtain by increasing the money supply, it would direct the Fed to go to the open market and buy up government securities, as shown in Figure 18-2. Securities dealers and banks would exchange their government securities for money. The Fed would receive the paper securities and the dealers would receive cash, which they would deposit in banks, thus increasing the supply of money in circulation.

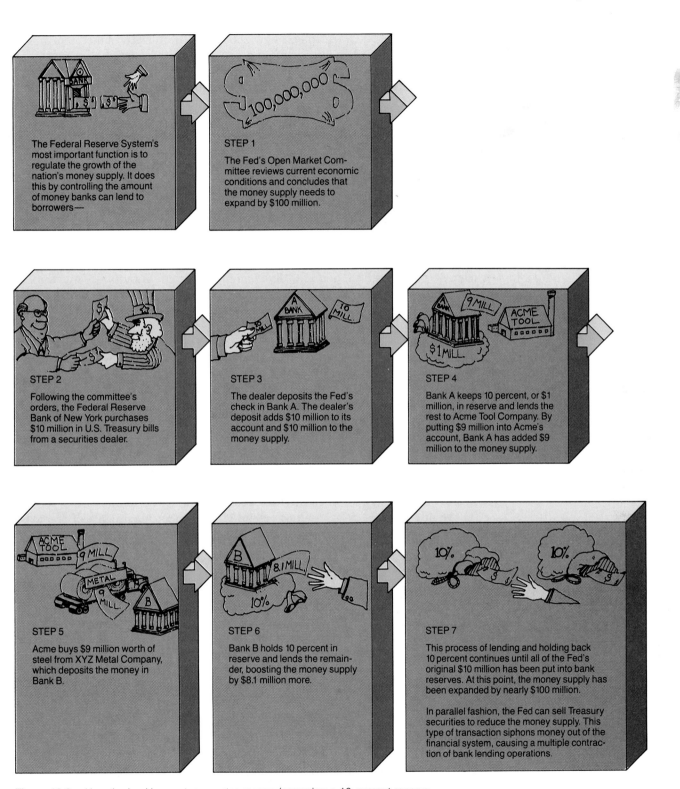

The Federal Reserve System's most important function is to regulate the growth of the nation's money supply. It does this by controlling the amount of money banks can lend to borrowers—

**STEP 1**

The Fed's Open Market Committee reviews current economic conditions and concludes that the money supply needs to expand by $100 million.

**STEP 2**

Following the committee's orders, the Federal Reserve Bank of New York purchases $10 million in U.S. Treasury bills from a securities dealer.

**STEP 3**

The dealer deposits the Fed's check in Bank A. The dealer's deposit adds $10 million to its account and $10 million to the money supply.

**STEP 4**

Bank A keeps 10 percent, or $1 million, in reserve and lends the rest to Acme Tool Company. By putting $9 million into Acme's account, Bank A has added $9 million to the money supply.

**STEP 5**

Acme buys $9 million worth of steel from XYZ Metal Company, which deposits the money in Bank B.

**STEP 6**

Bank B holds 10 percent in reserve and lends the remainder, boosting the money supply by $8.1 million more.

**STEP 7**

This process of lending and holding back 10 percent continues until all of the Fed's original $10 million has been put into bank reserves. At this point, the money supply has been expanded by nearly $100 million.

In parallel fashion, the Fed can sell Treasury securities to reduce the money supply. This type of transaction siphons money out of the financial system, causing a multiple contraction of bank lending operations.

**Figure 18-2** How the banking system creates money (assuming a 10 percent reserve requirement, or $1 million reserve on $10 million deposits). (Adapted from "How the Banking System Creates Money," *U.S.News & World Report,* April 26, 1982, pp. 48–49. Reprinted from *U.S.News and World Report;* Copyright 1982, U.S.News & World Report, Inc.)

If the FOMC decided to sell new securities in order to make credit more difficult to obtain, it would direct the Fed to sell its securities for investors' cash. The investors would receive the securities, and the Fed would receive the cash, thereby taking money out of circulation and reducing the money supply.

These **open market operations** of buying and selling securities are the most important tool the Fed uses to control the money supply. Small changes in the money supply can be made quickly, without effects on the entire commercial banking system.

▲ **Margin Requirement** A fourth tool the Fed uses infrequently is a very selective one, the control of the **margin requirement** on the purchase of securities. When investors buy stocks, they usually don't have to put up the entire amount in cash. Instead, a portion can be borrowed from the stockbroker "on margin." This margin, or percentage that must be put up as cash, has varied from 10 to almost 100 percent. By changing the margin requirement, the Fed can increase or decrease the amount of money flowing into the stock market. In this way, speculation can be controlled or investment encouraged.

In 1929, investors were allowed to buy stock on margins of only 10 percent, so that they had to pay only 10 percent of the purchase price in cash. Small investors flocked to the market, attracted by the glamour and easy credit terms. In October of that year, the stock market took a nose-dive. On October 29, 1929, the stock market crashed—stock prices dropped by 13 percent in one day and many of those same small investors were wiped out. By 1932, investors had lost more than $74 billion, and many banks had run out of money and closed.[6]

Despite all the tools available to control the money supply, it's extremely difficult for the Fed to "fine-tune" the economy. There are many reasons for this inability to effectively control the money supply. In spite of the best efforts of Chairman Volcker and the other governors, the main reasons remain (1) the difficulty of defining money and (2) the sheer magnitude of the task.

## NEW DEVELOPMENTS

**Objective 6**

**Some of the newer developments in the U.S. financial system.**

New developments are occurring on the U.S. financial scene, especially in banking. Most of them result from a political development—deregulation—and a technological innovation—electronic funds transfer. These, in turn, have led to a third development—financial supermarkets.

### Deregulation

Until 1980, financial institutions were bound by a complex set of government regulations limiting the services they could offer. The Fed's Regulation Q limited the rate of interest banks and S&Ls could pay on savings accounts. S&Ls were allowed to pay ¼ percent more interest than commercial banks could pay on comparable accounts. The Fed also prohibited these institutions from paying interest on checking accounts.

No more! In 1980, a total revision of banking regulation was put into motion. Both banks and S&Ls now offer interest-bearing checking accounts, the NOW accounts. The maximum interest ceiling on savings deposits will be

totally phased out by 1986, allowing banks to pay whatever interest the market will bear.

Financial institutions have also been freed to offer new types of investments, such as certificates of deposit tied to the interest paid on U.S. Treasury bills. These are often called money market certificates. Some banks are experimenting with accounts that automatically transfer depositors' excess money into a higher-yielding investment fund.

The traditional barrier prohibiting banks from operating across state lines is under assault, and interstate banking has become available. While Congress is hesitating to formally approve interstate banking, several states—believing that Congress *will* do so—have paved the way for it. Massachusetts, Connecticut, and Rhode Island have enacted legislation authorizing interstate acquisition among banks in the three states.[7] And multibank holding companies are permitted in forty states. BankAmerica, the holding company that owns the Bank of America, is acquiring Seafirst, the parent of Seattle–First National Bank. Already, BankAmerica and Citicorp have offices in all but ten states.[8]

### Electronic Funds Transfer

Tied into this rapid change in the structure of banking is the rapid development and acceptance of electronic banking. By blending computer technology with banking ingenuity, financial institutions have created **electronic funds transfer (EFT),** whereby money is transferred from individual to bank, bank to individual, bank to bank, and city to city instantly, through a computerized electronic system. The federal government uses EFT extensively to credit Social Security payments to individual recipients' bank accounts without writing and mailing checks.

Large commercial banks and S&Ls have installed electronic transfer devices, called **automatic teller machines (ATMs),** outside their buildings and even in shopping centers and on university campuses. You can get cash, make loan payments, or transfer money from one account to another on weekends, during holidays, or at any time of the day or night, instead of being limited to traditional banking hours.

The key to EFT is the customer's plastic access card, called a **debit card.** Although the debit card looks much like a credit card, it functions very differently. A credit card lets you charge products and services and pay later. A debit card, in conjunction with an automatic machine, makes transfers directly to and from a customer's checking account. Of course, as with other forms of plastic cards and even paper checks, there's always the danger of misuse and abuse.

Some large retailers, such as grocery stores, have installed EFT devices at their checkout stations. Shoppers may use their debit cards to instantly transfer the amount of their purchase from their checking account to the store's account. The long-awaited checkless society hasn't arrived yet, and may never arrive, but financial institutions are becoming more creative in their use of EFT to attract customers.

EFT has made it possible for banks to bypass the inconvenience created by a federal law making it illegal for commercial banks to accept deposits outside their home states. Groups of banks have set up automatic teller machine networks whereby their customers can use their debit cards to withdraw cash, transfer funds from one account to another, and check balances on ATMs in other states. The customer pays a fee (of forty cents to a dollar) for each trans-

action outside the state. In 1982, Bank of America, Chase Manhattan Bank, and Continental Illinois National Bank and Trust Company joined twenty-three other banks to establish a *national* ATM network. More than 3,000 other banks were expected to join the network by 1984.

### Financial Supermarkets

In earlier periods, banking was easier to define. No one thought of making financial transactions anywhere but at a bank. Stocks and bonds were purchased through stockbrokers, and insurance was purchased through an insurance company. But with deregulation, a new generation of financial supermarkets, handling all types of financial transactions, has upset traditional definitions. Prudential recently merged with the Wall Street brokerage firm of Bache. American Express, the traveler's check company, merged with Shearson Loeb Rhoades, Inc. These combinations have created radically new financial opportunities. The world's largest brokerage firm, Merrill Lynch, can now sell life insurance to its customers, buy or sell their homes, and lend them money, in addition to providing the traditional services involved in stock and bond transactions.[9] Nowhere is this trend seen more dramatically than in the transformation of Sears, Roebuck from a top retailer to the company behind the Sears Financial Network (see Case 18-2 at the end of the chapter).

The shape and operations of the U.S. banking system are changing daily. For example, American National Bank and Trust Company of Chicago tripled the minimum balance required for free checking from $500 to $1,500 in 1981. The bank was delighted when nearly 20 percent of its checking and savings accounts were closed by irate customers. It was then in a position to offer a greater array of new services to its preferred customers—those with a household income of $100,000 or more.[10]

In the future, our concepts of banking and finance will continue to change, making old definitions obsolete.

## ⬛ LEARNING OBJECTIVES REVISITED

1. *What money and a monetary system are.*

   Money is anything that is generally accepted as a medium of exchange, a store of value, and a measure of value. A monetary system is such a medium of exchange used throughout a society. In the United States, money, narrowly defined as M-1, includes coins and currency, as well as such things as demand deposits, NOW accounts, and automatic transfer accounts.

2. *The financial institutions that serve individuals and businesses.*

   The most popular financial institutions are commercial banks, savings and loan associations, savings banks, credit unions, investment banks, factoring companies, insurance companies, trust companies, and commercial paper houses.

   Commercial banks are privately owned, profit-seeking corporations organized to serve most individual and business financial needs. Their usual accounts are demand deposits, or checking accounts, and time deposits, or savings accounts. Full-service banks perform a multitude of services for their clients.

   Savings and loan associations (S&Ls) were created to serve the housing industry but now perform most of the same services as banks. Savings

banks serve small savers by paying interest on time deposits. Credit unions are formed by groups with a common interest, place of employment, or occupation. They use members' funds to make loans to members, usually at a rate of interest lower than that of other financial institutions.

The financial institutions primarily serving businesses are investment banks, factoring companies, insurance companies, trust companies, and commercial paper houses.

Because of bank failures during the 1930s, most customer deposits are now insured by federal agencies such as the FDIC.

3. *The purpose and organization of the Federal Reserve System.*

The Federal Reserve System (FRS), or the Fed, was established by Congress to serve as a central national bank, controlling the money supply. It is governed by a chairperson and six other governors and has twelve Federal Reserve districts, each with a district bank and several branch banks.

4. *The functions performed by the Federal Reserve System.*

The Fed acts as a bank for other financial institutions, serves as the government's bank, supervises member banks, protects consumers in credit transactions, facilitates the movement of money, and controls the nation's money supply.

5. *The tools available to the Federal Reserve System to create and control the money supply.*

Money is created by commercial banks under the fractional reserve system. When a sum of money is deposited with banks, they can lend out all of that money above the legal reserve requirement. Thus the original sum can be expanded many times, the exact number depending on the reserve requirement. With a 10 percent requirement, a $100 deposit can be expanded to $1,000, creating $900 of new money.

The tools available to the Fed to control the money supply, in addition to the reserve requirement, are the discount rate, which is the percentage the Fed charges member banks for securities it buys from them; open market operations, which involve buying and selling securities in the securities markets; and the margin requirement, which is the percentage of the total value of a stock that a purchaser must pay in cash. It is difficult for the Fed to effectively control the money supply because of the sheer magnitude of the task and the difficulty of defining what money really is.

6. *Some of the newer developments in the U.S. financial system.*

Some new developments in the U.S. financial system are deregulation, electronic funds transfer (EFT), and the emergence of financial supermarkets. A particularly interesting development is the combination of individual banks' automatic teller machines (ATMs) into regional and national ATM networks. This is the beginning of interstate banking, which will favor the larger banks.

## ⏚ IMPORTANT TERMS

As an extra review of the chapter, try defining the following terms. If you have trouble with any of them, refer to the page listed.

barter  *486*                          money  *486*
monetary system  *486*                 M-1  *487*

## ⬓ REVIEW QUESTIONS

1. How did our monetary system develop?
2. What are the characteristics of money?  Why is each important?
3. Distinguish among the types of money.
4. What are the financial institutions that serve individuals?  Explain each.
5. What's the main difference between demand deposits and time deposits?
6. Why is a secured loan desirable from the lending institution's point of view?
7. What are the financial institutions that serve businesses?  Explain each.
8. What is the FDIC?
9. Why was the Federal Reserve System established?
10. How is the Federal Reserve System organized and governed?
11. What are the functions of the Fed?
12. Describe each of the tools available to the Fed to control the money supply.
13. How is money created by the banking system?
14. Why is it so difficult for the Fed to control the money supply?

## ⬓ DISCUSSION QUESTIONS

1. What's happening to the differences among the types of financial institutions?  Are these changes desirable or undesirable?  Explain.
2. Do you think that the present limit of insurance on deposits ($100,000) is sufficient?  Why or why not?
3. Do you favor the long terms and staggered appointments for governors of the Fed?  Why or why not?
4. How does writing a check on a coconut differ from using a barter system?
5. What do you think of the fractional reserve system?  Can you think of a better method of creating money?
6. Do you think the Fed is too reluctant to use the reserve requirement and the discount rate to control the money supply?
7. What do you think of the newer developments in the U.S. financial system?  How will they affect consumers?  Explain.

# ≜ CASE 18-1   The First Women's Bank[11]

First Women's Bank is small and insignificant compared to its competitors. Yet it has carved out a market for itself—and is serving that market quite well. The reason? It offers what giants like Citibank and Chase Manhattan can't—personalized service.

First Women's offers financial advice and small loans to people and businesses that can't find anyone who even knows their names at big banks. According to Judy H. Mello, president since 1980, the bank can't offer "mass-market, people-intensive banking," but "We know our customers. If you overdraw your checking account, if you're a good customer, there's no way I'll bounce your check."

Promising to meet the financial service needs of women, First Women's Bank has evoked applause from every woman who ever felt she'd been denied credit because she was unmarried, divorced, widowed, or just plain female. After a shaky start resulting from offering more services than its size warranted and not being selective enough in lending money to women to start new businesses, the bank is now doing quite well. Assets and profits are steadily increasing.

Yet even First Women's can't overlook costs and profits. So it's weeding out small, unprofitable accounts. Many of the bank's 7,000 checking and savings accounts were opened as a gesture of support when it was the first all-women's bank, founded in 1975 by feminists under a federal program to aid women's banks. In 1981, letters were sent to these inactive accounts thanking them for their earlier support but saying that token accounts were no longer needed.

### Case Questions

1. Is there really a need for a bank such as First Women's? Explain.
2. Can a bank of this nature succeed without concern for costs and profits? Explain.
3. Would you like to invest in First Women's Bank? Why or why not?

# ≜ CASE 18-2   The Sears Financial Network[12]

The retail side of Sears' business is still important, providing the company with $209 million profit in 1980. However, Sears' financial subsidiaries provided the corporation with over $522.5 million profit during the same year.

The Sears Financial Network owns Dean Witter Reynolds, Inc., one of the largest brokerage firms; Coldwell Banker, the nation's largest real estate firm; and Allstate Savings & Loan (in California); as well as its long-time insurance subsidiary, Allstate Insurance. Sears is apparently living up to its old slogan, "Sears has everything."

Sears is already experimenting with a financial department in its retail stores. Its future potential is mind-boggling, for over 48 million households in the United States, an astonishing 57 percent of the total, have a Sears credit card. If Sears decides to put electronic funds transfer (EFT) machines in its stores, it could use this base of cardholders to develop a debit card system, allowing customers to instantly pay for purchases as well as tying these customers in with the other Sears financial services.

Sears is pushing its financial services to "Middle America," primarily married householders between the ages of twenty-five and forty-four, with an average income of $30,000. But it's encountering some trouble in selling its financial services. For instance, a mailing to 19 million of its cardholders in early 1983 generated only 1,000 new IRAs.

### Case Questions

1. Do you think Sears should put EFT machines in its stores? Why or why not?
2. To what extent does the financial network add to, or detract from, Sears' "regular" retailing? Is it a problem?
3. What other possibilities do you see for Sears to become even more involved in the U.S. financial system? Explain.

# 19

# Managing Financial Resources

*The world is his, who has money to go over it.*

Ralph Waldo Emerson

*The use of money is all the advantage there is in having it.*

Benjamin Franklin

## Learning Objectives

After studying the material in this chapter, you will understand:

1. The role of financial management in a business.
2. How funds flow through a business and how they are used.
3. The primary short-term sources of funds, both within and outside of a business.
4. Sources, advantages, and disadvantages of debt financing.
5. Sources, advantages, and disadvantages of equity financing.

## In This Chapter

What Is Financial Management?
How Funds Flow Through a Business
Uses of Funds
Short-Term Sources of Funds
Long-Term Sources of Funds

# BACK TO BASICS AT EXXON

In 1982, a hundred years after its founding by John D. Rockefeller, Exxon, the largest industrial corporation in the United States, had financial problems that forced it to abandon its grandiose plans for diversifying into advanced technology and to return to the basics of the energy industry. In an effort to boost profits and conserve cash, Exxon reduced its staff by 15 percent and cut back on advertising—especially institutional advertising. It even required managers to abandon first class for business class on overseas flights and eliminated the coffee and pastries that had been served at all-morning meetings of its investment advisory committee.

In 1981, Exxon had been first in sales ($108.1 billion), assets ($62.9 billion), net income ($5.7 billion), and stockholders' equity ($28.5 billion). Yet in 1982, its profits had shrunk to half of 1981's, and its stock had fallen 40 percent since 1980. More importantly, Exxon's $6 to $7 billion efforts to expand its base for future earnings had been disappointing, to say the least. Its $606 million effort to get into mining and minerals lost $250 million; $435 million spent to develop uranium and nuclear fuels lost $273 million; $1.2 billion spent on an energy-saving firm earned only $31 million; and nearly $2 billion was forfeited in an effort to create an information processing and office systems business. But Exxon's most publicized retreat was its May 1982 withdrawal from the $6 billion Colony Shale Oil Project it had launched in Colorado in 1980, when oil prices were shooting toward $40 a barrel. It had spent close to $1 billion on the project.

What happened? An unfortunate combination of several external and internal factors hit the giant firm at once. Externally, crude oil prices fell to around $33 a barrel instead of rising to $50 as the oil industry had expected. A worldwide recession lowered demand for—and prices of—metals, and the nuclear energy movement essentially halted. Internally, miscalculations about entering non-oil industries probably resulted from the inbred nature of the firm's management. Wall Street analysts wondered if these lifelong oilmen were versatile enough to succeed in high-technology areas. Anyway, Exxon is turning its attention back to "established business lines of demonstrated profitability."

On a scale such as Exxon's, financial management takes on mammoth proportions. Regardless of size, though, businesses must make sure that they have funds available not only to pay daily bills but also to finance the major expansions like the Colony project. You've seen how a company keeps track of its money with accounting, and how financial institutions keep the whole economy's money rolling. A company's financial manager makes use of in-depth knowledge of the financial situation of both the company and the economy as a whole to plan and control how the company obtains and uses its money. But closer to home, let's first look at how *you* operate as a financial manager.

## WHAT IS FINANCIAL MANAGEMENT?

**Objective 1**

**The role of financial management in a business.**

Ever notice how easy it is to spend money and how hard it is to keep a cash balance to meet the next need that comes along? Did you ever run short and have to put off an important purchase or borrow some money? It almost goes without saying that the need for funds is a common problem for people as well as for businesses. All people and businesses have practically unlimited wants and needs that call for money. Yet individuals and businesses—regardless of size—have limited funds to spend on those needs. As a result, **financial management,** the business function involved in effectively raising and using funds, is required.

### Managing Your Own Finances

Basically, your situation is like that of any business. Since you know your own "business," that seems a logical starting point for seeing what financial management is all about. If you're a typical student, you're probably straining your resources. Your financial situation may look like that shown in Figure 19-1. The demands on your resources may be greater than the resources available to meet those demands. While our figure isn't detailed enough to give the total view of your money income and outgo, it should give a general idea of your basic financial situation. Let's see what else is involved.

Figure 19-2 (page 512) shows how your planned or budgeted expenses for the school year (the red bars, appropriately enough), along with the money available to pay them (green bars), may look. Notice how the monthly outgo varies because of lump sum payments for clothes, tuition, books, and supplies, and other infrequent or irregular payments you have to make in some months, like for gifts in December and for income tax in April. You can also see that your money doesn't come in at the same time or in the same amounts as the payments must be made. For example, the high level of money available for tuition, books, and supplies in September and January might be from savings and scholarships, while the money coming in each month may be only from your earnings or a grant. Individuals as well as businesses need a positive **cash flow,** which is the amount of money coming in from all sources and the amount going out for all purposes.

It's probably obvious to you that, over a period of time, the funds available must average out to an amount equal to or greater than the expenses. That's what makes you solvent—or a business profitable.

**RESOURCES AVAILABLE**

Money
   Savings
   Scholarships
   Wages/salary
   Loans
   Investments
   Federal tuition grants
Assets
   Clothes
   Sports equipment
   Cosmetics
   Car
   Food
   Home—if owned
   Household furnishings
     and equipment

**DEMANDS ON YOUR RESOURCES**

   Tuition
   Books
   Supplies
   Transportation
   Rent
   Utilities
   Food
   Clothes
   Recreation
   Taxes

**Figure 19-1** Your financial resources and the demands made on them.

## Planning and Control

You must plan and control your finances just as a business does. To do this, you need to:

1. *Determine your overall needs,* and estimate when you must satisfy those needs. For example, tuition, books, and supplies must be paid for in September and January; travel and gifts come in December; taxes are paid in April; and living expenses must be met daily, weekly, and monthly.

2. *Convert those needs into the amount of money needed.* In our example, $1,000 is needed for tuition, books, and supplies in September and January; $300 for new clothes in September; $300 for gifts and travel in December; $100 for taxes in April; and $400 for living expenses each month.

3. *Determine what sources of funds you have.* For example, you may have a part-time job that meets your usual living expenses; a grant or scholarship to cover tuition; a savings account that can be used for clothes, books, and supplies. And you can borrow for Christmas and your taxes. For other purposes and for emergencies, you'll also have to borrow.

4. *Find out the amount of funds coming from each source,* as well as when the money should arrive. For example, in September, you may have $600 of savings left over from your summer work. You also may have a grant or scholarship of $800 available during both September and January, and you earn $400 each month. This gives you a total of $1,800 ($600 + $800 + $400) to pay your September expenses of $1,700, so you're in good shape.

5. *Match available funds with expenses on a month-by-month basis.* If the results are satisfactory, continue what you are doing; if not, revise earlier steps. For example, you can use the extra $100 left over in September to pay part of your Christmas expenses. You'll have to borrow the other $200, as well as $200 for books and supplies in January. Then, in April, you'll need to borrow another $100 for taxes.

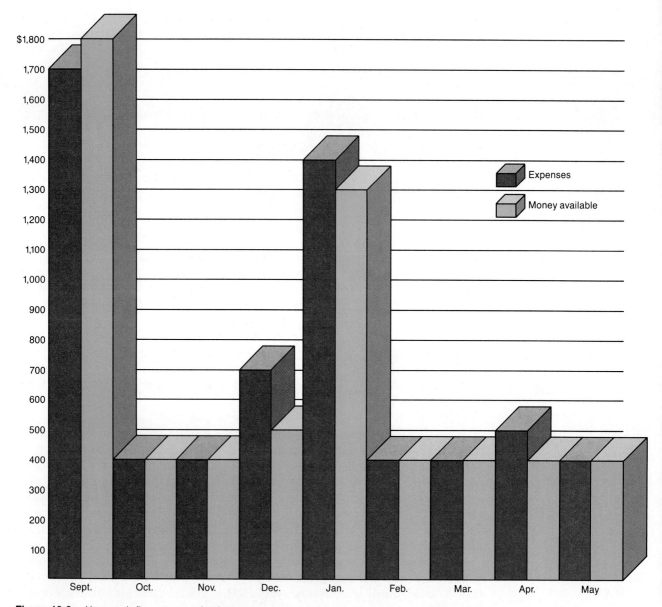

**Figure 19-2** Your cash flow over a school year.

6. *Arrange to obtain the needed funds.* You might ask a bank to lend you $200 in December and January and $100 in April, to be paid back from summer employment.

7. *Establish an effective system for recording financial transactions.* As shown in Chapter 17, you should prepare a form for recording daily expenses—and then faithfully enter the information.

8. *Establish a system of financial feedback and control.* Total up your actual expenses at regular intervals and compare them with your budgeted amounts in order to see if changes in your financial program are needed.

Most successful firms use these same basic steps in planning and controlling their finances. This basic plan-spend-record-control cycle is required by

businesses, governments, and nonprofit organizations. In February 1983, the State of California had to temporarily issue registered warrants, a legalized form of IOU, to vendors and recipients of income tax refunds because of a shortage of cash. The practice stopped when $200 million in cash from a loan became available.[1]

Think of the different types of organizations you come into contact with, such as schools, churches, governments, small businesses, large firms, service organizations, and concert groups. All of these try to develop various sources of funds such as investments, bake sales, taxes, donations, and dues. These organizations know that funds are limited, so they have organized programs to obtain the needed funds. Then they decide how to allocate those scarce resources. Finally, they must control the use of those funds.

### The Financial Manager's Role

Identifying the areas where funds are to be used is one of the duties of the firm's financial manager. Of course, the financial manager's basic job is to help the firm achieve its overall objectives of earning a satisfactory profit while keeping enough money on hand to meet ongoing financial obligations. These, then, become the goals of the financial manager, too.

In addition to identifying uses for the firm's funds, the financial officer also must perform the equally important task of finding sources of these funds. For each use of funds, the financial officer must determine an appropriate source of funds, balancing the firm's profitability with the need to have enough money to meet its obligations.

"My goodness, man, you don't need a loan granted, you need three wishes granted."

However, the role of financial executives is rapidly changing. They're now being asked to aid in strategic planning, mergers, acquisitions, operations, and even putting together and promoting comprehensive profit improvement plans. In fact, they're beginning to be viewed as financial miracle workers who often rise to the top of the corporate ladder. For example, the chief financial officer of the relatively small Sargent-Welch Scientific Company helped its personnel department revise the employee benefit package to include dental insurance coverage without increasing costs. He also invested some idle funds in much higher yielding securities so that a larger profit was made.[2]

## HOW FUNDS FLOW THROUGH A BUSINESS

**Objective 2**

How funds flow through a business and how they are used.

Now let's look at the flow of funds through a hypothetical organization. Basically, this flow involves:

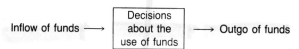

Figure 19-3 shows how funds usually flow through the financial system of a real business. Notice at the left how some funds come from outside sources such as banks, insurance companies, and the owners. The managers then decide how to use those funds. The way funds are used to pay for the goods and services needed to produce and sell the firm's product or service is shown on the right. You can see at the bottom and to the left of the figure that when the goods and services are produced and sold, this provides another source of funds.

Some movements in the figure are of cash, while others are of credit. The various flows are planned so that the desired amount of money is obtained, the best source of funds is used, and a profit is made—all with the right timing.

## USES OF FUNDS

The flow of funds can be best understood by looking at exactly how and when those funds are used in a business. Basically, money goes into purchasing assets, paying operating expenses, and producing income.

### Purchasing Assets

Some very small firms try to operate on a cash basis: no credit given, no money borrowed. But the size of these companies is limited—and their life may be jeopardized—by the amount of cash available at any given time. Other firms extend their resources through the use of credit. An automobile agency, for instance, may have its building constructed and then finance it through an insurance company; its tools and equipment may be bought on credit from the manufacturers; and its cars may be financed by a credit subsidiary of the manufacturer, such as General Motors Acceptance Corporation. Thus the agency owner has some of his or her own money invested but has a lot more of other

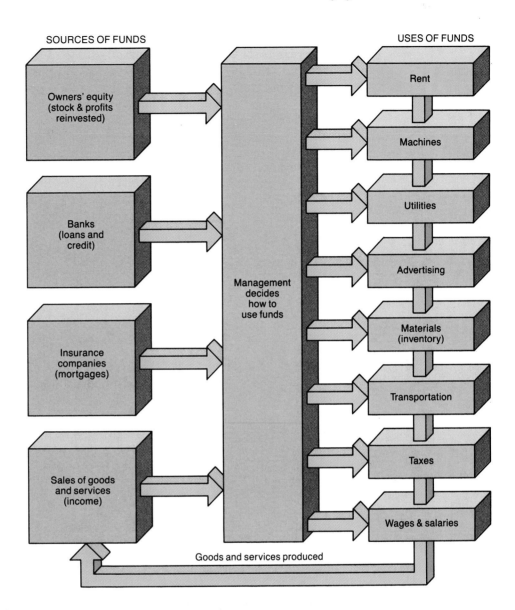

SOURCES OF FUNDS

Owners' equity (stock & profits reinvested)

Banks (loans and credit)

Insurance companies (mortgages)

Sales of goods and services (income)

Management decides how to use funds

USES OF FUNDS

Rent

Machines

Utilities

Advertising

Materials (inventory)

Transportation

Taxes

Wages & salaries

Goods and services produced

**Figure 19-3** Movement of funds through a business.

people's. The monthly payments are manageable, so the agency owner enjoys the privilege of using the facilities without having to pay for them all at once.

You can see that businesses use money to buy assets like land; buildings and furnishings; and tools, machines, and equipment. These assets are often purchased with mortgage loans secured by the building or equipment itself. In other words, the bank, savings and loan, or insurance company really owns the property until the mortgage has been paid in full. The financed assets are used by the firm to generate revenue, which, in turn, is used to pay off the loan. Under a cash plan, the purchase of a machine would have to be delayed until enough cash was available. The use of debt, or credit, however, increases both the assets and the income of the purchaser. This use of borrowed money to make more money is called **leverage.**

The decision to purchase fixed assets, which pay for themselves only over a period of several years, is sometimes quite difficult because of external factors. Notice that Exxon had to cancel the Colony Shale Oil Project because of the falling price of crude oil. Exxon had to make another difficult decision in 1983. The firm had already committed $1.65 billion to build two units of a four-unit power station in Hong Kong, to be completed in 1987. Construction of the remaining two units was scheduled to start, in order to be completed in 1990, at a cost of $850 million. But Britain's lease on the Hong Kong territory from mainland China is due to expire in 1997, and no one knows whether it will be extended, or whether profits can be taken out after that date. The loans Exxon arranged for the construction aren't due to be repaid until 2002.[3]

> What would you have decided if you were Exxon's financial manager? (See Chapter 22 for Exxon's actual decision.)

## Paying Operating Expenses

As shown earlier, you need funds to pay your everyday expenses. Businesses use funds to pay operating expenses such as the cost of materials and supplies needed to produce goods and services for sale. A manufacturer of wooden desks, for instance, must buy lumber, hardware, nails, glue, varnish, and so forth. Funds are also needed to pay such current expenses as employee wages, rent or mortgage payments, insurance premiums, and utility bills.

If one could be sure that cash would be available exactly when expenses had to be paid, no cash reserve would be necessary. But this rarely happens. Instead, a reserve supply of cash on hand is needed to take care of the differences. Notice, too, that cash flow needs to be rapid. The cost of leaving productive assets idle is reduced by efficient cash flow, but a business must maintain some reserves to avoid the cost of being without the products wanted by customers. Having readily available cash to meet expenses as they come due is called **liquidity.**

Cash reserves are necessary in any dynamic business system. But this poses a problem for management. Idle cash earns no profit and declines in value because of inflation. It's therefore more effective to have a low cash reserve, which leads to a greater profit. Yet the reserve must be large enough for the firm to avoid bank charges and the image of being a poor credit risk. Firms granting credit to their customers must have a cash reserve to finance those sales, as shown in FYI on page 517.

## Producing Income

Instead of simply lying idle, cash can be used to produce income. It can be put into financial institutions such as banks, savings and loan associations, and credit unions to draw interest. Sometimes a company, finding itself with excess funds, will buy securities listed on one of the exchanges and let them earn income until the company needs funds. Then it will sell the securities to get the needed funds. These securities are called **near money.**

# *FYI*

## Chrysler Pays Back

Chrysler Corporation "consumes about $250 million in cash per week" to finance its operations. But it's been difficult for the firm to obtain funds since 1978, when, for various reasons, it was essentially bankrupt. Losses were tremendous, sales plummeted, and financial circles refused to provide credit.

Thanks to a new chairman, Lee Iacocca, the management at Chrysler worked a financial miracle, with the help of many individuals and institutions. The turnaround, called the largest financial transaction in U.S. history, involved 452 banks, several cities and states, three foreign countries, about 1,500 dealers and suppliers, the United Auto Workers union (UAW) and five other unions, and the Congress and the executive branch of the U.S. government.

In 1979, the government guaranteed $1.5 billion in loans from private sources, although only $1.2 billion was actually borrowed. The loans were to be repaid by 1990. Also, the unionized production employees gave up nearly $1 billion in wages and benefits, and half of the firm's managers and white-collar employees were terminated or laid off. In the last three quarters of 1982, Chrysler made its first profit since 1977. However, it had to sell its profitable defense (tank) division to General Dynamics for $239 million to maintain the flow of funds it needed to remain operational.

By 1982, Chrysler had paid off $1.3 billion of bank debt and had $1.1 billion in cash reserves. But it still needed cash to finance credit sales. The first new credit since 1979 came in the form of a $500 million loan to Chrysler Financial Corporation. That credit permitted the firm to finance an additional 100,000 vehicles and improve its chances of further recovery.

In June 1983, Chrysler unexpectedly repaid $400 million of the $1.2 billion federally guaranteed loans. Then, declaring the firm's financial independence from the U.S. Treasury, Chairman Iacocca repaid the remaining $800 million—seven years before it was due. Chrysler did this to save an estimated $392 million in interest payments and to free itself from several restrictions imposed by the government's loan board. Now it can pay dividends to stockholders, give bonuses to executives, and resume normal borrowing arrangements with banks, because of its improved credit rating.

Iacocca poked fun at his—and Chrysler's—critics by paraphrasing fellow TV star John Houseman's ad: "We at Chrysler borrow money the old-fashioned way: we pay it back."

---

Sources: "The Banks Like Chrysler's Line," *Business Week,* August 2, 1982, p. 18; Lally Weymouth, "Has Chrysler Been Saved?" *Parade,* September 12, 1982, p. 7; Sally Jacobsen, "Iacocca Ready to Repay Loans," *Mobile Register,* July 14, 1983, p. 3-B; and Tom Nicholson, "Back to Cruising Speed," *Newsweek,* July 25, 1983, p. 63.

# SHORT-TERM SOURCES OF FUNDS

**Objective 3**

The primary short-term sources of funds, both within and outside of a business.

As shown throughout this chapter, most firms, like most individuals, don't have perfectly level financial needs. Instead, they may spend more money early in the year to buy raw materials and less later in the year, as finished products are sold and revenues come in. Such seasonal needs are financed by short-term sources of funds. **Short-term sources of funds** must be paid off within one year. As a result, they're used for short-term needs like salaries, and for emergencies.

As you can see in Figure 19-4, a hypothetical firm's expenses are higher from May to July than they are from August to October. The revenue the firm earns is quite low in the earlier period, however, and increases during the latter period. Since revenues are less than expenses, the firm needs to find a short-term source of funds for the months of May, June, and July. By August, the firm is bringing in enough revenue to begin paying off its suppliers of short-term funds, and by October, the debt can be paid off completely.

Congress Sportswear Company, a Boston manufacturer of winter coats and jackets since 1926, provides a perfect example of the need for short-term credit to finance seasonal operations. In February of each year, it starts producing garments for the next winter. Congress has a $1.5 million credit line at a local bank from which it borrows funds to pay 130 factory employees and to buy 700,000 to 800,000 yards of fabric and other items used in production. Usually, the garments are shipped in August and September, and payment is received thirty days later. But during the 1981–1983 recession, the garments were shipped in October and November, and payment was received forty-five to sixty days later. "You can't operate this business without borrowing," said its owner.[4]

Short-term funds can be obtained either from sources within the firm or from outside sources such as trade credit, loans, factoring, or commercial paper.

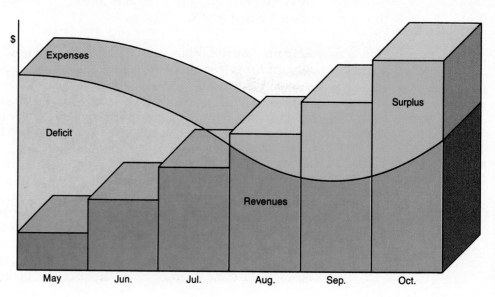

**Figure 19-4** Revenue and expenses for seasonal operations of a hypothetical firm.

## Internal Sources

The cheapest, safest, and most obvious source of funds for a business is the money it already has. Businesses have money tied up in machinery, inventory, accounts receivable, and personnel. By simply using these assets more effectively, the firm can free some of its original investment. For example, speeding up collection of accounts receivable brings in cash more quickly and reduces the amount of funds tied up in credit accounts. Shortening the time it takes to convert resources into finished products, and thus speeding up sales, will also generate funds more quickly. And these funds can be used profitably elsewhere in the firm.

Late in 1979, for instance, LTV Corporation's management, having decided that high interest rates would be a long-term problem, started generating funds internally. The chief financial officer received daily cash generation reports that emphasized efforts to raise cash by selling off marginal lines, cutting inventories, and speeding up collection of accounts receivable. The firm's short-term debt declined from $242 to $51 million in one year.[5]

## Outside Sources

Businesses today have many outside sources from which to obtain short-term funding. These sources include trade credit, loans, factoring, and commercial paper.

▲ **Trade Credit** One of the most commonly used, and least expensive, sources of short-term funds for business is **trade credit,** or credit extended by the firm's suppliers of goods and services. About 85 to 90 percent of all U.S. business transactions involve some form of trade credit. When a business orders goods or services, it doesn't normally pay cash for them. Instead, the supplier provides them, along with an invoice requesting payment within a specific time period, say thirty days. During that time, the purchaser is able to use the goods or services without paying for them. If the transaction were on a cash basis, it would be necessary for the purchaser to borrow the funds from a financial institution and pay one month's interest, or tie up its own scarce funds for that period.

▲ **Loans** Small businesses can sometimes tap private sources of funds in the form of loans from friends, family, or local lending institutions. Such loans generally require less paperwork and can be made on an informal basis. Commercial banks are probably the second most important source of short-term funds, after trade credit. Banks lend money to their business customers in one of two ways—by direct loans or by setting up lines of credit.

Like a personal loan, a commercial loan from a bank may be either secured or unsecured. An unsecured loan is simply an unconditional promise to repay with no collateral, or security, backing it. The borrower signs a note promising to repay the loan on a certain date, plus a certain percentage for interest. Unsecured loans aren't usually made for large amounts or for longer than one year. The firm must have an excellent credit rating to qualify for an unsecured loan, since the bank has nothing of tangible value to protect its interests. The interest rate that commercial banks charge on unsecured loans to their best business customers is the prime rate, discussed in the previous chapter. Other

business loans are made at higher rates usually quoted as "one point above prime" or "two points above prime," which means that the interest rate on the loan will be one or two percentage points higher than the lowest, or prime, rate.

A secured loan is usually required for larger amounts or for newer, less well known companies. As we mentioned in Chapter 18, a secured loan requires the borrower to pledge something of value to back the loan should it not be repaid. Some secured loans are backed by a firm's inventory. Still others are secured by accounts receivable or by a specific piece of equipment. The bank can sell any of these items to recover the value of the loan should the borrower default.

Of course, businesses don't run back to the bank and arrange a separate loan every time they need funds. Usually they arrange a **line of credit,** which is the amount they can borrow without making a new request. With a $100,000 line of credit, for example, a company can borrow up to $100,000 any time it chooses simply by notifying the bank. The bank will probably require the business to keep some of its funds on deposit at the bank or impose other restrictions. A line of credit provides a business with flexibility in financial planning.

▲ **Factoring**  Business firms that sell on credit have an important asset on their books, accounts receivable, which should be converted into cash quickly. Most credit customers pay off their accounts within a month or two, but in the meantime unpaid receivables tie up the firm's funds. When an unexpected need for cash arises, a company might sell its accounts receivable to the financial broker we talked about in Chapter 18: a factoring company, or factor. The factor immediately pays the firm cash, usually 50 to 80 percent of the value of the accounts receivable. Then, when customers make payments on their accounts, the money goes directly to the factor, and the loan is gradually paid off. Often the firm's customers aren't even aware that this has happened, since they never come in contact with the factor. Still other companies sell *all* their accounts receivable to factors, thereby eliminating the need for, and expense of, their own credit departments. In cases like these, customers are instructed to make payments directly to the factor.

▲ **Commercial Paper**  Financially strong firms may use commercial paper as a source of credit. Commercial paper simply consists of unsecured promissory notes, in denominations from as low as $25,000 to as high as $1,000,000, that mature in 270 days or less. Since commercial paper is unsecured, only the most credit-worthy firms can use it. Commercial paper gives the issuer access to short-term funds at interest rates lower than those charged by banks and gives buyers a method of profitably investing temporarily idle cash for short periods.

## LONG-TERM SOURCES OF FUNDS

What's a business to do if it needs funds to construct a new assembly line or to do extensive research and development? These activities require financing for longer periods of time. Similarly, a new product developed by the company's research and development department may not begin to bring in revenues for

several years, so short-term financing wouldn't work. **Long-term sources of funds,** to be paid off over periods longer than a year, are needed.

The business may choose to finance its long-term needs with **debt financing** (borrowing), **equity financing** (allowing others to acquire part interests in the firm), or a combination of the two (see FYI on page 523). Still a third option is to use the present owners' equity by retaining the earnings of the corporation instead of paying dividends to stockholders.

## Debt Financing

**Objective 4**

Sources, advantages, and disadvantages of debt financing.

A firm may choose to finance long-term operations by borrowing from outside sources. Such debt financing, which involves a promise by the company to repay the loan with interest, may be in the form of a mortgage, a long-term loan, or a bond issue. Even Du Pont had to borrow millions of dollars when it acquired Conoco, Inc., and mighty IBM borrowed over a billion dollars in 1981 and 1982.[6]

▲ **Mortgage Loans** A **mortgage loan** is a type of secured loan against which the borrower has pledged some fixed asset, such as real estate, as a guarantee that the loan and interest will be repaid when due. Mortgages are usually used to finance new buildings and to buy needed tools, machines, equipment, furniture, and fixtures. For example, Ford Motor Land Development Corporation borrowed $200 million to build and run Phase I of the Renaissance Center, the office-hotel-retail center completed in Detroit in 1977.[7]

---

Do you own a house or an automobile? If so, how was it paid for: with cash or credit? If with credit, did you have to sign a mortgage? If not, what process was used to obtain the funds to pay for it?

---

Insurance companies, by their very nature, accumulate large amounts of idle funds that must be invested to generate income to pay off claims. They lend billions of dollars to companies each year in the form of mortgage loans. Aetna Life & Casualty Company, Travelers Corporation, John Hancock Mutual Life Insurance Company, and Equitable Life Assurance Society paid for $180 million of the Renaissance Center, and Ford Motor Credit Company paid for the other $20 million.[8]

Banks, insurance companies, and other institutions will also make unsecured long-term loans to well-established, credit-worthy companies on the basis of a note signed by their responsible officials.

▲ **Bond Issues** A commercial loan may be for a smaller amount than the business wants, or for a shorter time period than it may wish. If a business does need larger sums or needs the funds for longer than a year, it may divide the loan into smaller packages and borrow from more than one source. It can do this by means of **bonds,** which are basically corporate IOUs obligating the corporation to pay the amount of the bond at a specified time in the future.

There are two basic types of corporate bonds: debenture bonds and mortgage bonds. **Debenture bonds** are unsecured except by the creditworthiness of

Specimen debenture bond.

the issuing corporation. **Mortgage bonds** are secured by a pledge of specific assets of the corporation. Mortgage bonds tend to be more secure than debentures, but not always. For example, from 1977 to 1982, a GM debenture bond was probably safer than a Chrysler mortgage bond.

Actively traded through stockbrokers, bonds have a face value, such as $1,000, $5,000, or even $50,000, which is the principal that must eventually be repaid. In addition, investors are entitled to receive interest once or twice a year for the use of their funds. This interest, being a legal obligation, must be paid whether or not the corporation makes a profit. If the bond holders aren't paid the stated interest on time, the company can be forced into bankruptcy. Should the corporation go out of business, bond holders have first claim on its assets.

LTV Corporation (mentioned previously) used both loans and bonds for long-term financing. It borrowed $111 million on a 10½ percent mortgage note and sold $65 million worth of 11 to 14 percent bonds.[9]

▲ **Advantages of Debt Financing** For the corporation, securing funds by means of mortgages, long-term loans, and bonds has two advantages over issuing other types of securities:

1. *Holders of the corporation's mortgage, notes, and bonds are creditors, not owners.* They have no voting rights and can't participate in the operations of the corporation. By using these types of debt, the corporation gives itself more management control over budgeting and financial planning, as it's dealing with fixed, known expenses.

2. *The interest paid by a corporation to these creditors is tax deductible.* It can be subtracted from the company's earnings before income taxes are calculated. This reduces the amount of corporate income tax that must be paid, making mortgages, notes, and bonds a relatively cheap form of financing. In good years, the fixed interest rate paid limits the amount of profit that must be given to creditors, so the corporation's owners can keep a larger portion.

## *FYI*

### How Scott Paper Paid for Expansion

Scott Paper Company recently began a five-year, $1.6 billion program to buy new machinery, upgrade some aging plants, and expand capacity. About half of the funds are coming from within and half from outside the company.

First, Scott sold $102 million of new common stock to Brascan, Ltd., a Toronto-based holding company. Then it sold $100 million worth of motors, compressors, and spare parts to a group of British banks and leased them back, with a low interest rate to Scott and a tax break for the banks. A similar arrangement in the United States raised $92 mil-

lion. A seven-year line of credit with a U.S. bank and a ten-year one with foreign banks raised another $400 million.

Finally, Scott has 3.3 million acres of timberland it can either develop in a joint venture with some other company or sell outright.

Source: Based on "Scott's Crafty Capital Spending Push," *Business Week*, March 8, 1982, pp. 91–92.

▲ **Disadvantages of Debt Financing** Using debt financing also has several drawbacks that must be considered:

1. *Unlike ownership securities, these obligations must eventually be repaid.* This commits the company to a huge repayment at some point in the future.

2. *Bond interest payments are a fixed legal obligation.* In bad years, interest payments can't be reduced or postponed. If the company can't pay its interest obligations, its bond holders can reclaim the assets backing the bonds.

3. *Bond agreements often contain restrictive provisions* that may limit a corporation's flexibility in handling its future finances.

### Equity Financing

**Objective 5**

Sources, advantages, and disadvantages of equity financing.

Another financing option is for a company to allow outsiders to invest in the firm. If the business is a proprietorship, it can become a partnership. Or, if it's already a partnership, the firm can bring in more partners. A partnership, or even a corporation, can form a tax-sheltered limited partnership with outsiders, as shown in Chapter 3. For example, Metro-Goldwyn-Mayer Film Company (MGM) offered the investing public a chance to help finance half the cost

of all its films until 1986. It offered 10,000 limited partnership interests of $5,000 each. Each buyer was required to buy at least two of them.[10]

Also, a company can sell shares of its stock to raise money. For example, Ford Motor Company raised $658 million when it first sold shares to the public in 1956; Merrill Lynch raised $112 million in 1971; and Apple Computer raised $101 million in 1980.[11] When a corporation issues stock, it is obtaining permanent ownership financing, a form of equity financing. The stockholders need never be repaid, as bond holders must be, for stockholders are owners, not creditors. Equity financing may be obtained through issuing of either common stock or preferred stock.

At times, when a corporation is in financial trouble, an outsider may buy enough of its stock to gain control (see the Profile on page 525). Also, it may obtain funds by selling part of its assets. When Occidental Petroleum Corporation (Oxy) acquired Cities Service Company in 1982, it found itself with $8.8 billion of debt and preferred stock. It then raised close to $3 billion by selling part of its assets (including selling Cities Service's refining and marketing operations to Southland Corporation to ensure the availability of gas for its 7-Eleven stores).[12]

▲ **Common Stock** In Chapter 3, we discussed the characteristics of a corporation and listed the rights enjoyed by its owners. Ownership is evidenced by shares of common stock. Owners' rights include the right to elect corporation directors, vote on major issues, attend stockholders' meetings, inspect the corporation's books, and receive a share of the corporate profits, if any. These rights mean that the corporation must consider common stockholders' preferences when making major business decisions. Corporate officers may find themselves without jobs should their actions not come up to stockholders' expectations.

Corporations usually prepare a report on their operations for stockholders. This annual report includes a letter from the chairperson of the board or

Specimen certificate for a share of common stock.

## Profile

### William E. Simon: Financial Wizard

Bill Simon is a busy man—busy making money. His quick moves, fast talk, and dedication to work have made him a very wealthy man. In just two years, Simon, a free-enterprise enthusiast of the first order, has used his economic knowledge, financial expertise, connections, reputation, and good name to make a fortune in a series of business deals in which he and his partner, Raymond G. Chambers, bought and rehabilitated seventeen companies.

Simon served as U.S. Secretary of the Treasury from 1974 to 1977. Before that, he was Deputy Secretary of the Treasury from 1973 to 1974 and was chairman of the Economic Policy Board, the Federal Energy Office, and the East-West Foreign Trade Board. After leaving government service in 1977, he became a senior advisor to the consulting firm of Booz, Allen & Hamilton and a senior consultant to Blyth Eastman Dillon and Company, Inc.

Simon concedes that his number one job is that of opening doors, and he's the first to admit that his connections are invaluable. Top business executives don't turn down lunch invitations from a former treasury secretary, head of the U.S. Olympic Committee, and candidate for commissioner of professional baseball. Simon knows that his name is worth millions.

Bill Simon knows he is a strong, aggressive player who constantly uses the system to get ahead. Milton Friedman, Nobel Prize–winner in economics, calls Simon "a brilliant and passionate man." Just as Simon knows where his strong points are, he also knows his weaknesses. Thus, when he's considering buying a new company, he leaves the bargaining to his partner, Chambers. He also refrains from becoming very involved in managing the acquired companies. Instead, he either leaves the current managers in place or finds new ones and lets them run the show.

As a result, Simon has become a personal conglomerate. Together with Chambers, he founded Wesray Corporation, now one of the largest private firms in America. Sales are close to $2 billion and still growing, as the company continues to buy out and rejuvenate ailing companies. For example, Wesray purchased Gibson Greeting Cards from an unhappy RCA. Simon then sold about a third of the shares to the public for $27 a share. The result? Simon's shares in Gibson are worth $70 million.

Sources: "Bill Simon's New Treasury," *Newsweek*, August 8, 1983, pp. 62–63; "Dealing in Secondhand Companies," *Forbes*, February 28, 1983, pp. 66–67; William E. Simon, *A Time for Truth* (New York: Reader's Digest Press, McGraw-Hill, 1978); and an interview with William Simon by the senior author.

chief executive officer explaining what the corporation did during the year. It also contains the corporation's financial reports—its income statement, balance sheet, and a description of the sources and uses of funds. This report fulfills the corporation's obligation to allow stockholders to inspect its books and provides an opportunity for communication with the owners.

LTV Corporation also used equity financing to raise long-term funds. It sold $4 million worth of common stock in 1981—its first offering in fourteen years. This issue, together with other equity financing, raised $171 million.[13]

▲ **Preferred Stock**  Another type of stock frequently issued by corporations is preferred stock, or ownership shares that entitle their holders to special treatment. Preferred stockholders receive their annual dividend before common stockholders are paid and are promised that, should the corporation earn a profit, they will receive a fixed annual payment. In good years or bad, the corporation promises to pay that dividend. Only if it finds its earnings aren't large enough to pay preferred dividends may it omit the dividend. When this happens, however, no common stock dividends may be paid to the owners until the preferred stockholders have received their payment. Usually the missed dividend becomes a liability of the corporation in future years until it is repaid. For example, when Chrysler was in trouble, many creditors, especially banks, accepted preferred stock in the company rather than lose everything. In 1983, they were owed $100 million in accrued dividends on that stock.[14]

If a company is in such bad straits as to be liquidated, preferred stockholders also come before common stockholders in the distribution of assets. In exchange for this special treatment, preferred stockholders give up certain rights. They aren't allowed to vote on corporate decisions or to elect directors. In a sense, then, preferred stockholders are treated more like bond holders than owners. They receive a fixed annual return and are unable to influence the management of the corporation. Unlike bond holders' interest payments, however, their annual dividend isn't a legal obligation of the corporation.

▲ **Advantages of Equity Financing**  Equity financing has certain advantages for the corporation:

1. *Because stockholders are permanent owners of the business, their investment never has to be repaid.*

2. *Annual dividends aren't a fixed legal obligation.* Common stock dividends are issued at the discretion of the board of directors. Preferred stock dividends are fixed, but if they are not paid, stockholders have no legal right to claim them.

3. *Issuing stock gives the corporation a healthier balance sheet.* Because stock is ownership, no debt is added. The corporation is in a better position to borrow money in the future.

▲ **Disadvantages of Equity Financing**  The disadvantages of equity financing, however, can be significant:

1. *Common stockholders can vote on corporate affairs.* This limits the flexibility of management decision making.

2. *Stockholders expect to be compensated for their investment in some way.* Although annual dividends aren't a legal obligation, investors do expect a reasonable return on their investment at some point. They're buying stock to

## FYI

## Sources and Uses of Funds at Gillette

When the Gillette Safety Razor Company was incorporated under the name of American Safety Razor in 1901 (see FYI on page 350), little did King Camp Gillette know what financial management worries he would shoulder. Gillette was made president, while Jacob Heilborn, the financier, was given the job of treasurer. Neither of them, nor Edward Stewart, the third member of the board, received any compensation. In fact, engineer William Nickerson was the only salaried member of the firm, and even he agreed to work half-time for $40 a week.

The founders hit their first roadblock trying to get start-up capital, even though they had a unique new product—the disposable-blade razor—in stock. Almost at the last minute, they were bailed out by Heilborn's brother-in-law, a prominent Boston stockbroker, who bought some shares himself and sold the rest to friends.

By summer 1902, the owners had spent the entire $5,000 of original capital and were nearly $12,000 in debt. "In fact," Gillette reported, "we were busted and apparently done for." Several sample razors made by Nickerson and his two assistants had been distributed to potential investors, but no one seemed interested. Gillette, determined to get the company going at almost any cost, even *gave* some of his stock to outsiders.

A sense of gloom settled over the board. Gillette noted that "no one had any suggestions that seemed likely to relieve the situation in time to avoid a receiver, so we broke up with clouds settling down on the business—the end had apparently come." Still in the doldrums, Gillette went to lunch at his favorite restaurant, where he happened to meet John Joyce. Joyce, who had invested in one of Gillette's earlier unsuccessful inventions, had been given a sample razor and over a thousand shares of the still-worthless stock. When Gillette told Joyce that his razor company was near failure even before the first razor hit the market, Joyce offered to make a substantial investment in the firm. Seeing an opportunity to recoup the $20,000 that Gillette still owed him and to get in on the ground floor of a potentially successful enterprise, Joyce offered to finance the company with constant small infusions of cash in exchange for bonds and a substantial portion of stock.

The first commercial shipment of five-dollar razor sets was completed on New Year's Day 1904. Within a few months sets were being shipped by the thousands, and soon they were being sent around the world.

Source: Prepared for this book by Heidi Vernon Wortzel, Northeastern University. Information from *The Gillette Blade*, February 1918, pp. 6–10; January 1919, p. 11; and September 1926, pp. 7, 9.

participate in the future growth of the company. If dividends aren't paid, or if the value of the stock doesn't increase, shareholders will show their displeasure, either by their voting at a stockholders' meeting or by selling their shares.

3. *Equity financing is a very expensive type of financing.* Bond interest is deductible from corporate income before taxes are paid. Corporate dividends aren't. They are paid out of the income left after taxes. Thus a corporation that pays close to 50 percent in income tax would have to earn twice as much to pay stockholder dividends as it would to pay bond holder interest.

## Retaining Earnings

A third option for the corporation is to keep its annual profits and reinvest them in the business as "seed money." In retaining earnings, the corporation reduces or eliminates its annual payment, or dividend, to stockholders. Many new, small, fast-growing companies have to keep their profits as their primary source of financing. For example, Apple Computer and Apollo Computer paid out no dividends at all during their first few years. Instead, earnings were retained to expand the business. However, retaining earnings may increase taxes as well as the company's book value—thus inviting a takeover by outsiders.

Each corporation has its own corporate philosophy and faces unique investment circumstances. In making the debt, equity, or profit reinvestment decision, management must balance the advantages and disadvantages of all these options.

## The Debt Versus Equity Decision

A corporation looking for long-term financing has to weigh the advantages and disadvantages of both debt and equity, as shown in Table 19-1. If it uses equity, new owners—stockholders—will be added, and each of them will have a voice in governing the company. Stockholders also expect a reasonable return on their investment in the form of increasing market value of their stock or extensive dividends.

Debt financing, on the other hand, doesn't dilute management control. But the company is legally bound to pay bond holders interest each year, and at the end of the loan period, each bond holder must be repaid in full. In addition, excessive debt financing can leave a firm in financial difficulty if its profits aren't adequate.

**TABLE 19-1  Advantages and disadvantages of debt and equity financing.**

|  | Advantages | Disadvantages |
| --- | --- | --- |
| Debt financing | Interest is tax deductible. | Bonds must be repaid. |
|  | Investors have no voting rights. | Interest is a legal obligation. |
|  | Relatively inexpensive. | May contain restrictive provisions. |
| Equity financing | Investment never has to be repaid. | Stockholders share management control. |
|  | Annual dividends aren't mandatory. | Investors expect a healthy return on their investment in the form of dividends or increase in market value. |
|  | Gives the corporation a healthier balance sheet. |  |
|  |  | Dividends aren't tax deductible. |

Most companies, especially new, struggling ones, use both types of financing. During its early years, Ford Motor Company used both, as did the young Gillette Company (see FYI on page 527).

## ⏚ LEARNING OBJECTIVES REVISITED

1. *The role of financial management in a business.*

   Financial management is the business function involved in effectively raising and using funds. The need for funds is a common problem for people as well as for businesses. Also, the process of planning and controlling the flow of funds is similar for all people and organizations. The process involves (1) determining overall needs, (2) converting those needs into the amount of money needed, (3) determining sources of funds, (4) finding out the amount of funds coming from each source, (5) matching available funds with expenses on a month-by-month basis, (6) arranging to obtain needed funds, (7) establishing an effective system for recording financial transactions, and (8) establishing a system of feedback and control.

   The job of the financial manager is to keep enough money on hand for the firm to meet ongoing financial obligations and earn a satisfactory profit.

2. *How funds flow through a business and how they are used.*

   The flow of funds through a firm involves the inflow of funds, decisions about their use, and the outgo of funds. Cash reserves are needed because the inflow of funds seldom coincides with their expenditure. Funds are used to purchase assets, pay operating expenses, and produce income. Since idle funds earn no income, businesses usually lend excess funds to some financial institution in order to earn interest.

3. *The primary short-term sources of funds, both within and outside of a business.*

   Short-term funds are usually used to pay operating expenses; short-term loans are payable within one year. The primary internal source of these funds is money already invested in the company, which is freed through speeding up collection of accounts receivable, reducing inventory, and shortening the time needed to convert resources into finished products, thus speeding up sales. The primary external sources include trade credit, secured and unsecured loans from individuals and banks, factoring of accounts receivable, and commercial paper.

4. *Sources, advantages, and disadvantages of debt financing.*

   A firm may need long-term funds to buy or construct new buildings; acquire new machines, tools, equipment, furniture, or fixtures; or do extensive research and development. Essentially, long-term funds are obtained by means of debt financing or equity financing.

   Debt financing can be obtained from mortgage or other long-term loans and from bond issues. Advantages of this type of financing are that interest is tax deductible, investors have no voice in management, and it is a relatively inexpensive method of financing. Disadvantages are that it is a legal obligation that must be repaid, and the debt agreement may contain restrictive provisions.

5. *Sources, advantages, and disadvantages of equity financing.*

Equity financing includes taking in new partners, issuing common or preferred stock, and retaining earnings in the firm. Advantages of equity financing are that the investment need never be repaid, annual dividends are not mandatory, and it gives the corporation a healthier balance sheet. On the other hand, stockholders share management control and expect some kind of return on their investment, in the form of either dividends or an increase in market value. Moreover, dividends are not tax deductible, which makes this an expensive form of financing.

## IMPORTANT TERMS

As an extra review of the chapter, try defining the following terms. If you have trouble with any of them, refer to the page listed.

| | |
|---|---|
| financial management 510 | line of credit 520 |
| cash flow 510 | long-term sources of funds 521 |
| leverage 515 | debt financing 521 |
| liquidity 516 | equity financing 521 |
| near money 516 | mortgage loan 521 |
| short-term sources of funds 518 | bonds 521 |
| | debenture bonds 521 |
| trade credit 519 | mortgage bonds 522 |

## REVIEW QUESTIONS

1. Describe the plan-spend-record-control cycle for planning and controlling finances.
2. Why is the financial manager so important?
3. Basically, how do funds flow through an organization?
4. For what uses are funds needed by a business?
5. How is a mortgage used by a business?
6. How is leverage used by a business?
7. What are cash reserves, and why are they needed by a business?
8. Why is liquidity important?
9. What are the primary sources of short-term funds? Why is each used?
10. What are some differences between debt and equity financing?
11. What is the difference between a bond issue and a mortgage loan? between bonds and stock?
12. What are some differences between common and preferred stock?
13. What are the pros and cons of debt and equity financing?

## DISCUSSION QUESTIONS

1. Do you agree that financing a business is similar to managing your own financial affairs? Why or why not?
2. Which source of short-term funds—internal or external—do you think is more desirable for a small business without unusual financial problems? Why?
3. From the point of view of a business, which is more desirable—a secured or an unsecured loan? Why?

4. Why would a line of credit be important to a prosperous business?
5. If you were the owner of a prosperous small business, would you use equity or debt financing? Why?

## ⛰ CASE 19-1  G. D. Searle: To Sell or Not To Sell?

In mid-1983, the management of G. D. Searle & Company had to make a tough decision: whether or not to sell its profitable 1,100-unit Pearle Vision Centers.

Between 1977 and 1982, Searle—under the leadership of Donald Rumsfeld—had turned losses into a $120 million profit on sales of over $1 billion. It had test-marketed aspartame, its highly successful sweetener; its spending on research into new drugs had more than doubled; the number of Pearle Vision Centers had tripled; and the number of new products it introduced each year had increased nearly 1,000 percent. But during the first quarter of 1983, earnings had plunged nearly 40 percent, largely because of a drop in sales of prescription drugs—the company's basic business.

Searle needed money badly for research and development of new drugs. Too many of its drugs had outlived their patents, permitting competition from generic products. Also, management was concentrating on short-term profits by selling drugs developed by other companies instead of concentrating on high-reward—but high-risk—research into new drugs.

One possibility for obtaining funds was to sell Pearle Vision for about $300 million. After all, Pearle wasn't exactly compatible with Searle's basic business. What made the decision difficult was that, in 1982, Pearle's earnings had grown 48 percent, to $35 million, while Searle's overall earnings had grown only 7 percent, to $140 million, on sales of $1.04 billion, a 10 percent increase. (During the previous five years, sales had grown nearly 15 percent per year.) Searle had slashed its advertising budget and cut its ethical drug sales force by almost 25 percent.

While aspartame was popular, Searle had to invest $155 million in 1982 to expand its capacity to produce it. Also, aspartame was overpriced compared to other artificial sweeteners.

### Case Questions

1. Would you sell Pearle? Why or why not?
2. What would you try to do about increasing Searle's profitability?
3. What do you think aspartame (sold as Equal and NutraSweet) will do to Searle's profitability? Explain.

## ⛰ CASE 19-2  Montgomery Ward: The Credit Grantor

Montgomery Ward and Company, the merchandising subsidiary of Mobil Corporation, has always used commercial bank loans extensively to finance its sales. In the past it encouraged customers to open accounts with easy-payment terms and then borrowed the money to finance the accounts receivable. At one time, nearly 60 percent of all Ward sales were on credit, and the firm did well. Then interest rates skyrocketed to over 20 percent, and many state usury laws prevented the firm from charging its credit customers that much. Consequently, by 1981, Ward was losing an estimated $100 million annually just financing its $4 billion of receivables. Those losses helped contribute to the company's $415 million losses in just three years.

Since interest rates have declined to around 12 to 13 percent, Ward's is again breaking even—or making a little profit—on its credit sales.

### Case Questions

1. What should Ward's have done when interest rates went to over 20 percent? Explain your answer.
2. Should Ward's now try to reduce the percentage of its sales being made on credit? Why?

# 20

# Securities

*The secret of making money in the stock market is simple: buy low, and sell high.*

J. P. Morgan

*Money is the seed of money, and the first guinea is sometimes more difficult to acquire than the second million.*

Jean Jacques Rousseau

## Learning Objectives

After studying the material in this chapter, you will understand:

1. What securities are.
2. The different types of securities that are available, including equity and debt issues and government securities, and the reasons for investing in each.
3. How primary and secondary securities markets operate and are regulated.
4. Why people buy securities.
5. How to read published data about securities.

## In This Chapter

What Are Securities?
Securities Markets
Personal Investing
Reading Published Data About Securities

# A TALE OF TWO WEDNESDAYS

*Wednesday, October 10, 1979*

During the week of October 8, 1979, the stocks on the New York Stock Exchange (NYSE) dropped a total of 58.62 points, for the second-worst one-week decline in history. On Tuesday, the ninth, the Dow Jones Industrial Average (DJIA), an index of stock market activity, suffered its worst reverse in six years. It dropped a staggering 26.45 points, partly because the Federal Reserve had announced its decision to raise the discount rate. These activities set the stage for a selling binge the following day. As *Time* magazine described it:

> Even before the opening bell rang, the . . . specialists . . . who work on the floor of the New York Stock Exchange sensed that Wednesday would not be an ordinary day. . . . At brokers' booths and trading stations, everybody was fretting about what worried investors would do next. . . .
>
> Only minutes after trading opened, brokers were deluged with orders to sell. By the time trading had been under way for an hour, everyone realized that the rush was on. . . . At brokerage houses around the city, investors were trying to cut their losses. . . .
>
> By early afternoon, the market was down 20 points and the tape . . . was running nearly half an hour behind the trading. As it did so, the tension increased. . . . At a trading station, a specialist berated a clerk who had just placed a slice of pizza on a pile of papers. "Dammit!" he shouted. "The bottom's falling out of the market, and you're stuffing your face with mozzarella!" . . .
>
> As the tape fell a full 60 minutes behind trading, everyone understood that history was being made. Finally, as . . . the gong signaled an end to . . . trading, those on the floor celebrated, in a time-honored Wall Street tradition. Scooping up armfuls of the paper that lay ankle-deep on the trading floor, they tossed it into the air with a cheer that reflected as much exhaustion as exhilaration.
>
> Their attitude was understandable. Though most had anticipated a big day, few had expected that the volume would approach 82 million shares.

*Wednesday, August 18, 1982*

Wednesday, August 18, 1982 was the day the traders didn't even go to lunch—they stayed right on the exchange floor, creating the biggest trading day in financial history. It was the day the number of shares traded hit 132.9 million, the largest number sold in one day up to that time.

In the visitors' gallery, spectators watched as the floor swarmed with moving people and flying slips of notepaper. In the opposite gallery, television crews set up their cameras to record the setting of the record, the closing bell, and the commotion. They weren't disappointed. With the digital clocks on the wall reading 3:59:49, the clanging that marks the end to the day's trading began, sparking cheers and yelling from the floor. "They were hamming it up for the press," said Josephine Lombardi, who works in the NYSE News Bureau. "They're all hams on the floor. . . . Nobody went to lunch today," Lombardi noted.

It's hard to be bored with finance once you get to know the dynamic, exciting, and constantly shifting nature of the securities markets. The numbers alone are mind-boggling. Over 12 billion shares of stock were sold during 1982, and over 160 million shares changed hands on the NYSE on January 5, 1984, setting another record for the number of shares traded in a day. In fact, more shares were sold in that one day than were traded during the entire year of 1942. And the effects on the economy are profound. Vast amounts of wealth are being gained, lost, or exchanged in securities trading every year. It's estimated that every American benefited by over $1,500 during the three-month rally in late 1982, since the 40 percent increase in stock values increased the value of pension funds and insurance investments by that amount.[1]

In the previous chapter, we saw stocks and bonds through the eyes of a firm's financial manager, whose interest is in making the best use of available sources of funds. In this chapter, we'll look at stocks and bonds both on the floor of securities markets like the New York Stock Exchange and where they ultimately pay off—in the hands of the wise investor.

## WHAT ARE SECURITIES?

**Objective 1**

**What securities are.**

Although we called them by different names, we showed in Chapter 19 that **securities** are essentially pieces of paper issued by corporations and governments, representing an obligation by the issuing corporation to provide a stated, or expected, return on the funds invested in them. These pieces of paper are traded in **securities markets,** exchanges that provide investors with a convenient means of buying and selling their securities. These markets may be organized exchanges like the NYSE, individual investment banks or groups of such banks that issue new securities, or nationwide securities dealers linked electronically by computer networks.

Just as there are two forms of financing (see Chapter 19), there are essentially two types of securities: equity issues and debt issues. Only corporations can issue equity securities, but both governments and corporations can issue debt securities (see Figure 20-1). As we've discussed, equity issues represent shares of ownership, while debt issues represent promises to repay an investment in the future.

### Equity Issues

**Objective 2**

**The different types of securities that are available, including equity and debt issues and government securities, and the reasons for investing in each.**

Shares of stock are units of ownership in a corporation. Although stock may take the form of common or preferred stock, most corporations issue only common stock.

▲ **Common Stock** If you inspect the piece of paper that is a share of stock, some interesting details come to light. For instance, common stock may be issued on a par or no-par basis. **Par value** is simply the dollar amount printed on the face of each stock certificate. Since this figure has little real value, except for calculating state incorporation taxes, most corporations now either issue **no-par stock** (stock with no given value) or give their stock an arbitrary value of, say, $1 per share.

Holders of common stock have two potential sources of return on their investment: from cash dividends and from increases in the market value of

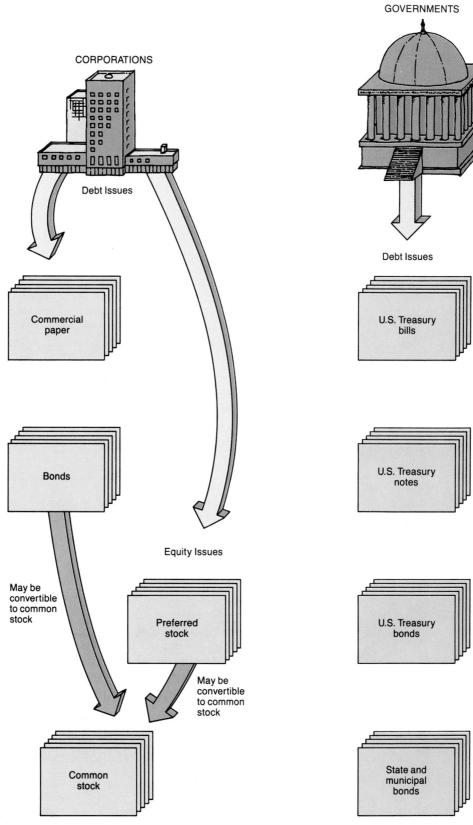

**Figure 20-1** Types of securities issued by corporations and governments.

each share. Cash dividend is the amount of money stockholders receive per share when a distribution is declared by the corporation's board of directors—usually four times a year. **Market value** is the current price at which each share of stock is being bought and sold.

Your portion of ownership in a corporation is determined by the number of shares you own, divided by the total number of shares. Since a drop in the size of that portion would jeopardize your rights, most companies give their common stockholders the **preemptive right** to buy a proportionate amount of any new stock issue, to protect their percentage of ownership. IBM stockholders recently voted to give up this right in order to make their stock more attractive to potential investors.

From the investor's point of view, all stocks, especially common stocks, are riskier than debt investments. The corporation may not make a profit or be able to pay you dividends, and you always run the risk of losing your entire investment should the company go bankrupt. There's also a market risk, which is that the price of your stock will increase (to your benefit) or decrease (to your disadvantage). Stocks that fluctuate wildly in market value are the riskiest but also may have the highest returns.

▲ **Preferred Stock** In addition to common stock, some corporations issue preferred stock, which gives its holders preference over common stockholders in the payment of dividends and distribution of assets if the company is dissolved.

This type of stock is usually issued to attract buyers who want a regular, but sure, income and are willing to accept a lower rate of return to get it. Preferred stock is safer than common stock, for it has a fixed dividend rate and its market value doesn't change as rapidly or as greatly. But its yield is lower, and its owners don't share in the operations of the company.

### Debt Issues

The two types of corporate debt issues are commercial paper and bonds. From the investor's point of view, they're extremely solid, offering a predictable, fixed return, but no share in the company's growth.

▲ **Commercial Paper** Commercial paper is a corporate IOU sold to raise money for short-term needs (see Chapters 18 and 19 for further details). In recent years, commercial paper has been one of the most profitable investments around. The risk involved is very low, as only the most respected, credit-worthy corporations may use commercial paper , and its short maturity (up to 270 days) gives it high liquidity. Its primary disadvantage for small investors is the large minimum investment—often $100,000. General Motors, for instance, frequently uses large quantities of thirty-, sixty-, and ninety-day paper to finance its short-term needs.

▲ **Bonds** Bonds are also corporate IOUs, issued to raise long-term funds (see Chapter 19 for details). They have high face values ($1,000 to $50,000) and long maturities (five to forty years) and may be secured (mortgage) or unsecured (debenture). With unsecured bonds, the corporation is saying, in effect, "I promise to use all my resources to pay you back. I'm pledging my credit rating."

Some corporations issue **convertible bonds,** which give investors the option of trading their fixed-rate bonds for a certain number of shares of common stock. The advantage for investors is that they can choose to share in the corporation's growth if it begins to prosper, or they can keep their fixed-annual-interest bond if business conditions deteriorate. The advantage for the corporation is that, if the investor converts to stocks, a portion of its debt is converted to equity, or ownership, which never has to be repaid.

Corporations make the investor certain promises in exchange for their loan. The corporation makes these promises to its investors in a contract called an indenture. The **bond indenture** gives the details of the loan—annual interest to be paid, repayment date and procedure, and a description of the security that the corporation puts behind the loan. Bond indentures may also contain restrictions on the issuing corporation, such as a requirement that it limit future borrowing or maintain a certain debt-to-equity ratio in its financial structure.

Because bond holders could be doing other things with their money while the company has it, the bond issuer promises to pay bond holders interest, either annually or semiannually, on their investment. If the interest is not paid on time, or if the principal is not repaid at maturity, bond holders have legal rights to seek repayment. Thus payment of interest and repayment of principal are legally binding.

These promises make bonds a relatively safe investment. Like all good things, though, safety comes with a price—namely, low yield. Therefore, the more safety provisions a company offers to investors, the less interest it will have to offer. A secured bond, issued by an old, established corporation with a superior credit rating, would provide an investor with maximum safety and minimum risk. But the interest rate on such a high-quality bond would be comparatively low. A riskier bond would have to pay higher interest in order to compensate the investor for taking the additional risk. So a debenture bond with no restrictive provisions, issued by a newly established firm, would have to carry a much higher interest rate.

## Government Securities

Securities also may be issued by either the federal government or a state or local government unit. As we've mentioned, these securities are debt issues only. Since all "the people" own a government, no single individual can own a part of it. Ideally, governments would be financed entirely by taxes and would operate under a perfectly balanced budget. But this is usually impossible, since the inflow of taxes rarely matches, in volume or timing, the outflow for programs and benefits. So governments, too, must borrow money by issuing various securities to pay their bills.

▲ **U.S. Savings Bonds**  The U.S. debt security most familiar to you is probably a U.S. **savings bond.** These bonds are of low face value. For example, a person buying a $50 Series EE savings bond is lending the government $50, less interest. These bonds, backed by the full faith and credit of the U.S. government, are the most widely held securities in history.[2]

▲ **U.S. Treasury Bills**  Although savings bonds are more familiar, U.S. **Treasury bills (T bills)** are the securities most often used to finance the government's

short-term debt. They have a minimum face value of $10,000, mature in 30 to 270 days, and pay no interest. Instead, they're sold in weekly auctions at a discount, which means that a $10,000 T bill may be bought for, say, $9,000, or $9,100—as determined by bidders. Since they're virtually risk-free and can be quickly and readily sold with little fluctuation in value, they tend to be an attractive investment, except for the high face value.

▲ **U.S. Treasury Notes and Bonds**  To finance long-term needs, the government issues **Treasury notes** for up to ten years and **Treasury bonds** for up to twenty-five years. The minimum investment in these securities is usually $5,000, and they pay a fixed amount of interest once or twice a year. For investors willing to tie up their money for that long, these notes and bonds provide a balance between low risk—since they're backed by the government—and adequate income. For example, the investment officer for Du Pont's $6 billion pension fund sold all of its $1.3 billion worth of corporate bonds in 1979 and put the proceeds into U.S. Treasury and Government National Mortgage Association (GNMA) bonds to ensure the pension fund's safety.[3]

▲ **State and Municipal Notes and Bonds**  Since state and local governments can't issue stock as corporations can, they raise money by taxing or by borrowing money, usually by issuing bonds. These governments generally issue notes or bonds when there's a specific project to be financed, such as construction of a bridge or a hospital. The face value is usually $5,000, although the actual amount will vary with the project being financed. These securities have one advantage over those of the federal government and corporations: their interest is exempt from federal income taxes. For this reason, investors in higher tax brackets find them especially attractive.

From the investor's viewpoint, there are significant differences between types of municipal bonds. **Revenue bonds** are securities issued to finance a specific project. If the project generates revenue, annual interest is paid; if no money is earned, no interest is paid. **General obligation bonds,** on the other hand, are issued to finance general operations and are fully backed by the issuing government. The government promises to use its full power to assess and collect taxes behind the bond issue. Annual interest will be paid out of the government's tax collections, if necessary.

Both types of bonds have the same advantages as corporate bonds—fixed annual return and safety of the principal. Their interest rates can be considerably lower, however, because their interest payments are exempt from federal taxes. Still, one serious problem with these securities is their lack of liquidity. The secondary market for municipals isn't well established, and an investor may find it difficult to convert them quickly into cash.

## SECURITIES MARKETS

**Objective 3**

How primary and secondary securities markets operate and are regulated.

Now that you have some idea of the types of securities that are available, where do you find them? Where are they bought and sold? The answer is that there are essentially two types of securities markets: primary markets, which issue new securities, and secondary markets, where previously issued securities are bought and sold.

## Primary Markets

A corporation generally doesn't try to sell a new issue of stock or bonds itself. Rather, it negotiates with an investment bank, or underwriter, to sell the securities for it. If the issue is extremely large, the underwriter may bring in other investment banks to form an underwriting syndicate. The underwriter buys the securities from the corporation, then resells them to individual investors through the secondary markets. The underwriter's profit is the difference between the price it paid for the securities and the price it can obtain for them from investors.

## Secondary Markets

Once the corporation sells its securities, it receives no further money for them, even if they're resold at a higher price. Purchasers who wish to convert their securities into cash must find another investor to buy them. Going to the issuing corporation is useless; it doesn't usually buy back its own stock and may not even be interested in redeeming its bonds before maturity. As a result, nine organized security exchanges have developed to make the buying and selling of securities of about 2,800 corporations easier.[4] These exchanges consist of the individual investors, brokers, and intermediaries who deal in the purchase and sale of secondary securities. Exchanges are simply auctions where investors get together to bid for stocks and bonds. While exchanges have become more formalized over time, the hurly-burly auction atmosphere still remains.

▲ **The New York Stock Exchange**  The largest organized security exchange is almost as old as the country itself. The New York Stock Exchange (NYSE) was established in 1792 when a group of merchants and traders decided to meet daily at regular hours, under a buttonwood tree on Wall Street, to exchange (buy and sell) securities. Later, the NYSE moved indoors to its present location on the corner of Wall and Broad streets. Now there are fourteen electronically sophisticated trading posts where specific stocks are traded. A separate bond exchange is housed in a nearby building.

Each trading day, over 2,000 issues of stock of about 1,500 of the strongest corporations are exchanged on the trading floor of the "Big Board," as the exchange is called.[5] The stock of corporations that meet the exchange's strict qualifications are "listed." Only listed corporation securities are traded. Each individual stock issue is traded at one of the fourteen trading posts, but only the 1,366 members—various stock brokerage firms like Merrill Lynch (see FYI on page 542) and some larger individual investors—may trade. A **seat,** or membership, must be bought and approved, for as much as $625,000 (in 1929) or as little as $17,000 (in 1942). In 1983, the price ranged from $310,000 to $425,000, but only twenty-five seats were sold.

▲ **American Stock Exchange and Regional Exchanges**  Over 800 stock issues of about 600 other reputable companies that aren't traded on the NYSE are listed on the American Stock Exchange (AMEX), also located in New York.[6] The basic procedures on the AMEX are the same as for the NYSE, although listing requirements aren't as strict. In 1976, for instance, An Wang moved Wang Laboratories' stock from the NYSE to the AMEX, which permitted him to create a separate limited-voting class of stock. The Wang family controls more than 40 percent of the voting stock and wants to keep it that way.

The trading floor of the NYSE as it appeared when the present building opened in 1903.

Some of the fourteen trading posts on the trading floor of the NYSE now.

Close to 4,000 issues are traded at the country's seven regional exchanges, such as the Mid-West Stock Exchange, the Pacific Coast Stock Exchange, and the Philadelphia-Baltimore-Washington Exchange.[7] Stocks traded are usually those of smaller companies with only regional appeal.

▲ **The Over-the-Counter Market** Originally, stocks actually were sold "over the counter" between two individuals. A more extensive system has since evolved, of course, but it has its limitations. While there are over 14 million corporations, only about 3,000 stock issues are listed on the organized exchanges. Therefore, the majority of stock issues aren't traded on any exchange. Either they're closely held and not actively traded, or they're traded in small volumes, infrequently, between individuals in a true bid auction. The stocks of 12,000 such small to medium-sized firms are sold in the **over-the-counter (OTC) market** by a network of securities dealers.

There is no central market for OTC trading, and there are no listing requirements. But 3,700 dealers from around the country are linked by an automated quotation system that displays the most recent asking price and bid for about 4,000 stocks of 3,600 companies.[8] The National Association of Security Dealers developed the computerized communication system **NASDAQ** (National Association of Securities Dealers Automated Quotations System) in the early 1970s to tie the OTC market together in one vast electronic stock mar-

ket. Now it's the second-largest market, ahead of AMEX, and so well thought of that some 600 companies that qualify for the Big Board prefer to remain in it. Some of the better-known companies in the NASDAQ System, which has as many as 1.58 million shares changing hands in one day, are Tandem Computers, Apple Computer, Apollo Computer, Intel Corporation, Turner Broadcasting System, and MCI Communications.[9]

### Regulating the Markets

The securities markets are regulated to some degree by the federal and state governments. Prices and quality aren't established, nor are investors' profits guaranteed. Rather, the law provides protection against blatant abuses and fraud and assures investors that an orderly exchange system will be maintained. Most states have passed **blue-sky laws,** designed to protect the public from unscrupulous securities dealers who would sell securities with promises as empty as the blue sky. In general, these laws require that issuing corporations back up their securities with something more than thin air and that stockbrokers be licensed.

The Securities Act, passed in 1933, was designed to insure full disclosure of information about new securities issues, and to try to prevent another stock market crash. The following year the Securities and Exchange Commission was created to control the trading of securities on exchanges. In general, the SEC is a watchdog, protecting investors against fraud in the sale of securities, illegal sales practices, market manipulation, and other violations of their trust by brokers.

Before any company offers its securities for sale to the general public, it must file a registration statement with the SEC. The registration statement must include information about the firm, its management and operations, and the type of security being issued, as well as copies of financial statements certified by independent public accountants. One portion of this statement is the **prospectus,** which must be offered to each potential investor.

Despite the many protections provided by federal and state laws, however, it's important for investors to realize that they have the ultimate responsibility for their own protection. The SEC can't protect an investor against an unwise investment; only the investor can make the final decision.

## PERSONAL INVESTING

**Objective 4**

**Why people buy securities.**

So far, we've talked about types of securities and their general advantages to investors. But you, as an individual, are probably getting more interested in exactly where to start with securities as a personal investment. The majority of you now own, or will eventually own, some type of security, either directly or indirectly as a member of a pension fund or life insurance company. How do you manage that investment wisely?

### Why Buy Securities?

There are many places for you to invest your funds, as we've shown. But regardless of where people put their money, they have two primary motives for buying securities: speculation and investment.

## *FYI*

### Merrill Lynch: Bullish on Expansion

Merrill Lynch, Pierce, Fenner & Smith, Inc. is the world's largest and most "bullish" stock brokerage house, with 12 percent of all stock trading volume. It's larger than its three closest competitors—Dean Witter Reynolds, E. F. Hutton, and Shearson Loeb Rhoades—combined, and its share of the market is almost three times as great as its nearest competitor's.

There are many reasons for Merrill Lynch's success, including its aggressive courting of new clients, its emphasis on selling securities to everyone—not just the wealthy elite—and its many innovations in serving as many of a person's financial needs as possible. It's trying to become a complete financial services company by expanding into almost all financial areas. Throughout its eighty-one-year

▲ **Speculation** People interested in purchasing stocks and bonds may hope to get rich quick; in other words, they are speculating. They buy cheap or underpriced stock, hoping it will go up rapidly so it can then be sold at a large profit. For example, if you buy stock at $0.50 a share, and it goes up a dollar to $1.50, you've made 200 percent profit. But if your $10 stock goes up a dollar, you've made only 10 percent.

Stock prices are a combination of rational factors, such as the company's annual earnings and reputation, and irrational factors, such as rumors and national events. For example, Apple Computer stock fell $8.25 in one day in October 1983 on news that September quarterly earnings would be "sharply lower." The stock, which was issued for $22 in 1980, was selling at $63 in June 1983, but dropped to $23 in October. Steven Jobs, Apple's co-founder, saw the value of his shares drop from $435 million in June to $159 million in October.[10]

history, Merrill Lynch has tried to bring Wall Street to Main Street. Now, about 75 percent of all Americans live within 25 miles of one of Merrill Lynch's nearly 500 offices.

From this position of strength, Merrill Lynch has helped change the ways that Americans save, invest, and spend their money. Not content to be the top trader in securities, the company is now challenging such venerable Main Street businesses as banks, insurance agencies, and real estate firms.

Merrill Lynch's efforts to attract new clients were increased in the early 1940s by its founder, Charles E. Merrill. While other brokers often relied on social and family ties and recruited their customers at elite social gatherings, Merrill introduced mass merchandising to the stock market. He wooed Middle America by abolishing service charges, slashing markups on many stock trades, and running lively advertising campaigns in national newspapers and magazines. The aggressive firm grabbed a lead over its stuffy competitors and has never looked back.

During the stagnation of the 1970s, Chairman Donald Regan realized that diversification was the only way to grow. He established a strategy that led the firm to become the financial supermarket that it now is. Its Cash Management Account (CMA®) is a single account that permits clients (with $20,000 or more) to write checks, write their own loans, make purchases on a special card, and withdraw cash almost anywhere in the world—in addition to having their investments managed. Merrill Lynch was also an in-novator in tax shelters; it and E. F. Hutton are the two biggest retailers of tax shelters. During Regan's decade as chairman, Merrill Lynch's revenues surged nearly 350 percent. (In January 1981, Regan resigned to become Ronald Reagan's Secretary of the Treasury.)

Not all of Merrill Lynch's projects succeed, however. In 1977, it unveiled plans for a computerized stock market. This nationwide computer network, linking brokers to all stock exchanges, would match up buyers and sellers wherever the price was best, without necessarily going through the NYSE. Experiments with the system were so impressive that it was considered to pose "the most serious threat yet to the old-style trading system." But in practice, the volume on this automated exchange was so skimpy—100,000 to 300,000 shares a day, compared with 100 million for the Big Board—that Merrill Lynch withdrew from it in mid-1983.

---

Sources: Based on the following articles in *The Wall Street Journal:* Tim Carrington, "Merrill Lynch to Stop Making Markets in Listed Stocks, Calls Test Cumbersome," March 22, 1983, p. 10; and Tim Carrington, "Merrill Lynch Ends Computer Trading Role," July 3, 1983, p. 2. Reprinted by permission of *The Wall Street Journal,* © Dow Jones & Company, Inc., 1983. All Rights Reserved. Also based on Milton Moskowitz, Michael Katz, and Robert Levering, eds., *Everybody's Business: An Almanac* (New York: Harper & Row, 1980), p. 485; Jean A. Briggs, "Should You Tax Shelter?" *Forbes,* April 26, 1982, pp. 107ff.; Richard L. Stern, "Could This Be the Black Box?" *Forbes,* February 15, 1982, p. 46; and "A Step Backwards for a National Stock Market," *Business Week,* August 8, 1983, pp. 27, 30.

---

The value of your investment may change from day to day in response to market conditions. In a **bull market,** all stock prices tend to move up together. In a **bear market,** all stock prices tend to move down. For that reason, an investor who's optimistic about prices rising is called "bullish," while a more cautious investor is "bearish."

The wide fluctuations in the return on stocks show why they're used for speculative purposes. Speculators are sometimes able to achieve fantastic returns, but they can also sustain great losses. For example, someone who had the foresight to invest $1,000 in McDonald's Corporation stock in 1967 would have had an investment worth over $33,000 by 1973—an astounding 3,200 percent increase. However, if that same investor had bought $1,000 of McDonald's stock in 1973, by mid-1979 it would have been worth only $519. Similarly, investors who bought $1,000 worth of Chrysler Corporation's stock in 1976 would have seen their investment shrink to only $370 by 1979. That's

"It should be some evening. I've seated everyone Bull-Bear, Bull-Bear."

a yearly return of minus 27 percent. Yet $1,000 paid for Chrysler stock in early 1982 (at $3.375 a share) would have been worth $5,260 (at $17.75 a share) by the end of that year, for a gain of 426 percent.[11]

▲ **Investment** Those interested in committing funds to securities for the long run are looking for income, growth (they hope), and safety. Long-term investments in common stocks have tended to keep pace with inflation more than other investments. The return on government and corporate bonds tends to vary less than that on stocks, making them a safe investment. While bonds weren't a profitable investment in the late 1970s, they have been attractive since 1980, because interest rates have declined.

1. *Income.* Your investment should earn you money. No one intentionally puts money into an investment that will lose money, except as an income tax write-off. You expect to be compensated for taking a risk and tying up your funds. This compensation can be by one of two methods. Investments such as corporate bonds and savings accounts pay investors annual interest. Most corporate stocks also pay an annual profit to investors in the form of dividends. This annual income—interest or dividends—is one part of your investment's total return. The *yield* an investor is receiving is determined by dividing this income by the market value of the security and expressing the result as a percentage.

2. *Growth.* In addition to providing annual income, your investment may also increase in value. A common stock purchased last year for $35 may be selling for $40 now. Over the past year, that stock has increased in value by $5. If that stock also paid dividends during the year of $2, it provided a total annual return of $7 ($2 in annual income plus the $5 increase in market value). An increase in market value is called a **capital gain.** A decrease of $5 in the stock price would be a $5 **capital loss.** Some investments, such as passbook savings accounts, don't increase in market value at all. The total

return on these funds is simply the fixed annual interest received. An investment in rare coins, on the other hand, pays no annual income to its owner. Any return on that investment would be in the form of an increase in market value, a capital gain. Between those extremes are other forms of investment that both pay annual income and increase or decrease in value; these vary as to safety. Equity securities, such as preferred and common stock, and debt securities, such as corporate bonds, usually provide both types of return. The total return on investment would be a combination of annual income and capital gains or losses.

3. *Safety.* In general, people who buy securities as an investment also seek safety. Safety is determined by the type of security (see Table 20-1), the type of organization issuing the securities, the nation's economic condition, and the care and attention of the investor.

---

Do you own any securities? If so, why did you acquire them? Why do you keep them?

---

## Choosing Your Investments

A potential investor faces the same basic decision a corporation faces—debt or equity securities. From the investor's standpoint, however, the pros and cons of the two options are different.

▲ **Debt Investments** Debt investments provide a fixed annual return, since you're functioning as a lender to a corporation or government. Debt investments all have the same characteristics—a fixed annual income and repayment of the principal at the time the security matures. In return for this safety, investors forgo the opportunity to share in the corporation's growth. As creditors, they have no ownership interest.

▲ **Equity Investments** Equity investments include buying common or preferred stocks, becoming a partner in a business firm, collecting coins or stamps, buying antiques or works of art, investing in gold, and speculating in

**TABLE 20-1 How securities vary as to income, growth, and safety.**

| Type of Security | Possibilities for | | Safety |
| | Income | Growth | |
|---|---|---|---|
| U.S. Treasury bills | Fixed at time of purchase | Practically none | Outstanding |
| U.S. Treasury bonds | Very regular | Very little | Excellent |
| Corporate bonds | Very regular | Very little | Very good |
| Preferred stock | Very regular | Very little, unless they are convertible into common | Good |
| Common stock | Varies widely and often quickly | Greatest possibility for growth—or decline | Poorest |

**commodities**—raw materials such as corn, cattle, soybeans, or wheat. All of these options make you an owner, with ownership rights. The return you receive from your investment depends on the success of that investment. Should the project prove extremely successful, your return will be spectacular, as your loss may be if the project fails. You aren't guaranteed income or the return of your investment, and there is no maturity date. You're trading safety for the potential of unlimited return when you make such an investment.

In order to reduce the risk incurred in buying stocks, a good strategy is not to put all your eggs in one basket. Invest in more than one company and industry. For example, a **diversified portfolio** may include stocks from a grocery store chain, a defense contractor, an electronics company, and a public utility. The electronics company and the defense contractor stocks have the potential for rapid growth, whereas the grocery store should have moderate profits—even in a recession. The utility stock, an income stock, will provide steady annual income.

**Mutual funds,** from mutual investment companies, provide one way to obtain the benefits of diversification without a huge investment. These companies pool money from many investors and then invest the funds in a wide range of stocks and bonds. Each investor thus owns a fraction of several companies. The advantage of mutual funds, in addition to diversification, is that your investment is professionally managed.

Another diversification alternative is **money market funds,** whereby investors pool their money and the fund invests in short-term securities, such as commercial paper and T bills. The small investor can thus share in the high return available on such investments.

Choosing investments, then, involves balancing the risk you can tolerate with the return you want, as shown in Figure 20-2. As a rule, the higher the rate of return, the riskier the investment. For maximum safety, leave your money in a U.S. Treasury bond or an S&L savings account. You should also choose an investment that suits your investment goals. If you want your money in a year or so, a short-term investment such as T bills or commercial paper (or a money market fund) may be best. If you have excess funds that you can commit for ten to fifteen years, want high returns, and can tolerate a bit of risk, common stocks may be your best alternative.

## READING PUBLISHED DATA ABOUT SECURITIES

**Objective 5**

**How to read published data about securities.**

With over 2,000 stocks traded on the NYSE, it would be difficult for you to get a good reading of the state of the stock market without some composite index, or score sheet, to summarize the market's performance. Luckily, you don't have to guess blindly—over the years, several stock indexes have been developed to help you follow stock price trends.

### Stock Averages

When people say, "The market is up today," they're probably referring to the **Dow Jones Industrial Average (DJIA),** the most closely watched composite index of overall market performance. The DJIA was begun in 1884 by Charles Dow, who chose eleven important stocks, added their prices together, and then divided the total by eleven. The resulting figure could be compared from day to day to see if stock prices generally were rising or falling. In 1928, the index

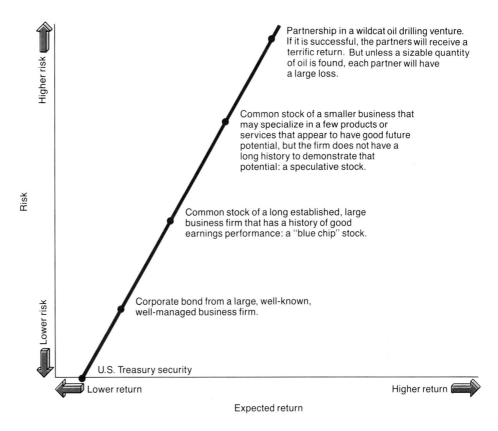

**Figure 20-2** General pattern of risk-return tradeoff. For most investments, the higher the rate of return (horizontal axis), the higher the risk (vertical axis). [Adapted from Larry R. Lang and Thomas H. Gillespie, *Strategy for Personal Finance* (New York: McGraw-Hill, 1981), p. 638. © 1981 McGraw-Hill, Inc.]

Partnership in a wildcat oil drilling venture. If it is successful, the partners will receive a terrific return. But unless a sizable quantity of oil is found, each partner will have a large loss.

Common stock of a smaller business that may specialize in a few products or services that appear to have good future potential, but the firm does not have a long history to demonstrate that potential: a speculative stock.

Common stock of a long established, large business firm that has a history of good earnings performance: a "blue chip" stock.

Corporate bond from a large, well-known, well-managed business firm.

U.S. Treasury security

was expanded to include the stocks of thirty industrial companies. The companies included have changed as corporate conditions have changed. For example, Chrysler was dropped in 1979 when it came near bankruptcy, and IBM was added. In 1982, the first financial company, American Express, made it into the DJIA, replacing Manville Corporation, which had declared bankruptcy. Two companies, General Electric and American Brands (formerly American Tobacco), have been included in the average throughout its history.

Standard & Poor's Corporation also tracks stock prices with its **Standard & Poor's 500 Composite Index.** This index uses a broader group of 500 stocks, made up of 400 industrial stocks, 20 transportation stocks, 40 utilities, and 40 financial stocks. The Standard & Poor's index and the Dow Jones index tend to move in the same direction.

## Trends in the Indexes

The DJIA and other averages have tended to rise and fall in cycles, roughly every four years. Stock prices rise rapidly as investment conditions improve, after which they peak out and then rapidly decline. The most rapid decline was the notorious stock market crash of 1929 (see Fig. 20-3 and the Business Debate on pages 548 and 549). The long-term trend, however, has been generally upward, with market lows and peaks being progressively higher with each cycle.

Economists watch the published indexes as closely as investors, for basic changes in common stock prices tend to precede basic changes in the nation's business climate by about five to nine months. Thus, a rising stock market, or bull market, would tend to indicate that the nation's economy was starting to

# Business Debate

## Could the Great Crash of 1929 Happen Again?

The memory of the stock market crash of 1929, which was followed by a decade of depression, haunts those who invest in securities. Could such an event be repeated today? Authorities are divided on the subject.

Those who believe that *it could happen again* are quick to point out that the sequence of events leading up to—and following—a collapse during the 1980s would likely be much different from that which accompanied the Great Crash of 1929. The primary causes of the 1929 crash—and the subsequent depression—were (1) excessive speculation in common stocks, much of it on small margin; (2) an unbalanced private economy, where personal income had failed to keep pace with the massive growth in industrial productive capacity; (3) a skewed distribution of wealth, where 1 percent of the population owned over half of the nation's financial and real assets; and (4) the straitjacket of classical economic theory, which stifled any federal efforts to fight the depression.

The sparks that might ignite an economic collapse today would be primarily foreign in origin. By far the most dangerous international economic problem is the Third World debt load, which will soon exceed one trillion dollars. Much of this debt is relatively short-term (three to five years' maturity), and a large portion of it is owed to U.S. commercial banks. If one or more large debtor nations were to default, this could precipitate a wave of defaults against which U.S. banks would be powerless to intervene.

A widespread international debt crisis would quickly drive many of this nation's largest banks to the brink of collapse. Faced with such a prospect, government officials would almost surely devise a massive financial rescue package that at the very least would cause interest rates to rise substantially. At worst, the sight of the strongest financial institutions in the U.S. on the edge of bankruptcy, and

recover from recession. A falling stock market, or bear market, could indicate that a recession was in the near future. Conversely, national events can change the trend of the market. On October 6, 1979, the Federal Reserve Board announced a historic change in monetary policy, which had the effect of making money harder to borrow. Within a week, the DJIA dropped fifty-nine points, about a 6 percent change.

## Understanding Financial Quotations

Notice in one of the opening quotations that J. P. Morgan said the way to make money in the stock market is to buy "low" and sell "high." What do you think he meant by that statement? We'll now see.

the prospect of a highly inflationary financial rescue package, would shatter the public's confidence in the entire banking system—which is ultimately the only real source of U.S. financial stability.

There are several other international economic problems that could easily degenerate into major crises. Twice during the last decade, the world has suffered through serious recessions in the wake of oil supply interruptions and price increases; a third oil shock could well prove catastrophic. Another source of weakness in the current international financial system is the size and volatility of capital flows among the major western nations. These, coupled with highly erratic exchange rate fluctuations, could easily turn a manageable financial problem into a deepening panic.

Other authorities believe that *it couldn't happen again.* They argue that the safeguards that exist today effectively ensure against another Great Crash. Businesspeople, economists, and public policy makers have had half a century in which to make the U.S. economy less susceptible to depressionary tendencies.

Perhaps the most important safeguards that have been erected are those that deal with securities trading and the nation's banking system. Capital markets are now highly regulated, and blue-sky laws ensure that the financial reports of U.S. corporations are timely, relevant, and accurate. Furthermore, the Federal Reserve Board exercises close control of the country's banking system and effectively controls the nation's money supply. The Fed has repeatedly shown that it is able to adjust to rapidly changing economic conditions and to contain potentially dangerous financial problems.

The U.S. economy is also much more balanced today than it was fifty years ago. This strength and diversity are a result of the growth of both old and new industries—particularly service industries, which are relatively insensitive to business cycles. In addition, the federal government now plays a critical—perhaps dominant—role in the nation's economy and is therefore in a position to decisively influence the course of business activity.

Another bulwark of economic stability is the fact that Americans are now far wealthier than they were during the 1920s, and the national income is more evenly distributed. Largely because of this, financial markets have become much larger, more competitive, and more efficient—and wider investment opportunities have encouraged much greater diversification of financial investment.

Finally, international economic and financial cooperation has become deeply ingrained in the political thought of all the major industrialized countries. Since World War II, the benefits of unrestricted world trade have become so self-evident that few governments have been willing to impose serious protectionist trade policies. And the international financial markets and institutions that developed in the postwar era have repeatedly demonstrated their capability to cope with financial crises and to help countries that are experiencing difficulties. If confronted with a 1929-style panic, it seems likely that these markets and institutions would be able to effectively contain, and then overcome, the crisis.

*What do you think?*

Source: Written for this book by William L. Megginson, Florida State University.

▲ **Reading the NYSE Quotations** The financial section of your daily newspaper or the *Wall Street Journal* can yield a tremendous amount of information about a stock. Consider the following NYSE stock quotation for November 9, 1983, for General Motors, taken from the November 10, 1983, *Wall Street Journal* (see also Figure 20-4):

| 52 Weeks | | | | Yld | P-E | Sales | | | | Net |
|---|---|---|---|---|---|---|---|---|---|---|
| High | Low | Stock | Div. | % | Ratio | 100s | High | Low | Close | Chg. |
| 80 | 53⅝ | GMot | 4 | 5.3 | 9 | 12884 | 76⅛ | 74¼ | 76⅛ | +1¾ |

The first two figures give the stock's fifty-two-week high and low prices. During the past year, GM's stock sold for as much as $80.00 and as little as $53.625. The wider the range, the more unstable, or volatile, the stock price probably is.

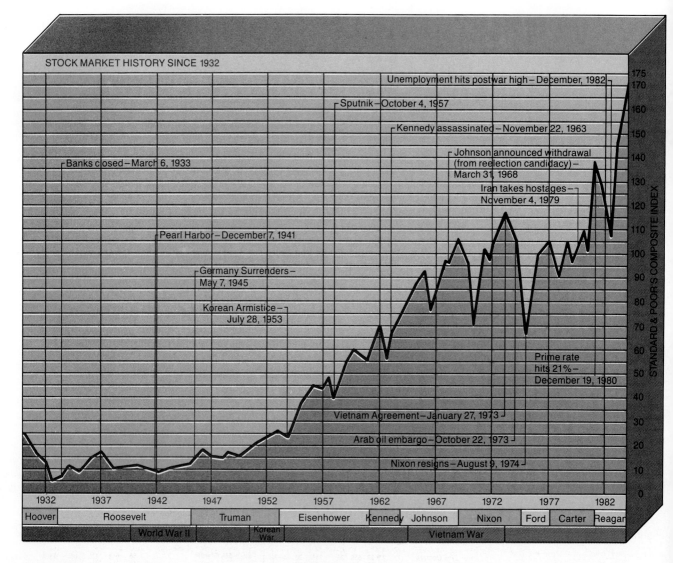

**Figure 20-3** Stock market history as charted by financial indexes. (Adapted by permission from Standard & Poor's Corporation, Trendline Division, 1980.)

The name of the corporation is given next, followed by the most recent dividend paid on that corporation's stock. The last dividend GM paid was $4.00 annually per share. If the letters "pf" appear before the dividend, the stock is a preferred stock.

The next two figures, yield percentage and P-E ratio, are ratios of interest to an investor. We'll come back to these later.

Sales volume is given next, before daily prices. Notice that the figure given is "sales [in] 100s," or hundreds of shares. On November 9, 1,288,400 shares of GM were bought and sold. A high volume may indicate that something significant happened regarding the company, such as a new earnings report or a news story about the company's product. Stocks that haven't traded 100 shares aren't listed that day.

The last four figures show the stock's price during the trading day. First is the highest price paid for the stock. Next is the day's lowest trading price.

# NYSE-Composite Transactions

## *Wednesday, November 9, 1983*

**Quotations include trades on the Midwest, Pacific, Philadelphia, Boston and Cincinnati stock exchanges and reported by the National Association of Securities Dealers and Instinet**

| 52 Weeks High | 52 Weeks Low | Stock | Div. | Yld % | P-E Ratio | Sales 100s | High | low | Close | Net Chg. |
|---|---|---|---|---|---|---|---|---|---|---|
| 36⅞ | 22⅛ | Coopr | 1.52 | 4.6 | 34 | 563 | 33⅝ | 33¼ | 33⅜ | ..... |
| 38½ | 29½ | Coopl | pf2.90 | 8.0 | .. | 11 | 36½ | 36¼ | 36¼ | ..... |
| 49 | 21¾ | CoopLb | s.40 | 1.5 | 20 | 2471 | 27⅜ | 25¼ | 26½ | −1 |
| 22¾ | 12⅜ | CoprTr | s.36 | 2.2 | 7 | 185 | 16½ | 16⅛ | 16⅜ | + ⅛ |
| 19⅞ | 14¾ | Copwld | .58 | 3.5 | .. | 75 | 16⅝ | 16⅛ | 16⅝ | + ⅛ |
| 25⅝ | 23½ | Cpwld | pf2.48 | 11. | .. | 64 | 23½ | 23½ | 23½ | ..... |
| 25¾ | 14½ | Cordura | .68 | 3.6 | 14 | 403 | 18¾ | 17⅞ | 18¾ | +1⅛ |
| 17⅝ | 11⅜ | Coreln | .48 | 3.4 | 19 | 11 | 14⅜ | 13⅞ | 14¼ | + ⅝ |
| 90¼ | 55⅝ | CornG | 2.32 | 3.3 | 13 | 200 | 71 | 69⅞ | 71 | +1¼ |
| 32⅜ | 20⅞ | CorBlk | 1.80 | 7.5 | 11 | 11 | 23⅞ | 23¾ | 23⅞ | − ⅛ |
| 22 | 14 | Cowles | .40 | 2.0 | 19 | 5 | 20½ | 20⅜ | 20⅜ | ..... |
| 55¼ | 39½ | CoxCm | .30 | .7 | 18 | 1244 | 45½ | 44½ | 44½ | − ¾ |
| 9¾ | 6½ | Craig | | .. | .. | 17 | 6⅞ | 6¾ | 6⅞ | + ⅛ |
| 36 | 22⅝ | Crane | 1.60b | 5.8 | .. | 30 | 27½ | 26½ | 27½ | + ⅞ |
| 54⅞ | 35⅝ | CrayRs | | .. | 38 | 893 | 51 | 48¾ | 50⅞ | +1¾ |
| 35 | 27 | CrockN | 2.40 | 8.5 | 9 | 83 | 28¼ | 28 | 28¼ | + ¼ |
| 25½ | 21¼ | CrckN | pf2.18 | 9.9 | .. | 12 | 22½ | 22⅛ | 22⅛ | − ¼ |
| 28⅞ | 14⅞ | CrmpKn | 1.12 | 5.6 | 10 | 43 | 20 | 19¾ | 19⅞ | − ⅛ |
| 38¾ | 27½ | CrwnCk | | .. | 12 | 68 | 38 | 37⅝ | 37⅞ | + ¼ |
| 34¼ | 25 | CrwZel | 1 | 2.9 | .. | 398 | 34¼ | 33⅜ | 34 | + ⅜ |
| 49½ | 41 | CrZel | pf4.63 | 9.7 | .. | 38 | 48 | 47½ | 47¾ | − ¼ |
| 57½ | 49½ | CrZel | pfC4.50 | 7.9 | .. | 5 | 57 | 56¾ | 57 | + ½ |
| 52⅞ | 32⅜ | Culbro | 1 | 2.1 | 12 | 6 | 48⅜ | 48 | 48⅜ | + ⅜ |
| 50½ | 22⅜ | Culinet | s | .. | 41 | 828 | 36¼ | 34¼ | 36¼ | +2¼ |
| 73⅛ | 41½ | CumEn | 2 | 2.7 | .. | 448 | u75¼ | 72¾ | 74¾ | +2¼ |
| 9⅞ | 8¾ | CurrInc | 1.10 | 12. | .. | 7 | 9¼ | 9¼ | 9¼ | + ⅛ |
| 57¼ | 39⅝ | CurtW | 1.20 | 2.7 | 12 | 39 | 45¼ | 45 | 45 | −1 |
| 34¾ | 17½ | Cyclops | 1.10 | 3.6 | .. | 15 | 31 | 30⅝ | 30⅝ | − ⅛ |
| | | **– D–D–D –** | | | | | | | | |
| 4¾ | 2¼ | DMG | | .. | .. | 215 | 4¼ | 4⅛ | 4⅛ | − ⅛ |
| 39⅞ | 9½ | Damon | .20 | 1.2 | 84 | 589 | 16⅞ | 15⅜ | 16⅞ | ..... |
| 50 | 29 | DanaCp | 1.60 | 3.6 | 23 | 1633 | 44 | 43 | 44 | +1 |
| 32 | 19¼ | Dana | wi | .. | .. | 1100 | 30 | 30 | 30 | + ¾ |
| 14⅞ | 9¼ | Daniel | .18b | 1.8 | 11 | 81 | 9⅞ | 9⅝ | 9¾ | − ⅛ |
| 77¼ | 63 | DartKr | 3.84 | 5.8 | 8 | 792 | 66 | 65¾ | 65¾ | − ¾ |
| 82¾ | 35⅛ | DataGn | | .. | 38 | 781 | 74½ | 72½ | 74 | +1¼ |
| 27⅜ | 17 | Datpnt | | .. | 63 | 1854 | 25 | 23½ | 25 | +1⅜ |
| 15 | 8⅝ | Dayco | .16 | 1.1 | 39 | 95 | 14⅞ | 14⅝ | 14¾ | ..... |
| 80 | 48 | Dayc | pf4.25 | 5.4 | .. | z10 | 78½ | 78½ | 78½ | −1½ |
| 41 | 25 | DaytH | s .66 | 1.8 | 16 | 1749 | 37¼ | 36 | 37¼ | +1 |
| 19⅛ | 12½ | DaytPL | 2 | 14. | 5 | 6089 | 13⅞ | 13⅜ | 13⅞ | + ⅞ |
| 62 | 52 | DPL | pf 7.48 | 14. | .. | z90 | 52½ | 52½ | 52½ | −1 |
| 64 | 56 | DPL | pf 7.70 | 14. | .. | z400 | 56½ | d55 | 55½ | − ½ |
| 62 | 51¼ | DPL | pf 7.37 | 14. | .. | z110 | 52 | 51¾ | 51¾ | ..... |
| 103¼ | 91 | DPL | pf12.50 | 14. | .. | z650 | 91¾ | 91¾ | 91¾ | + ¾ |
| 39¾ | 19⅛ | DeanF | s .60 | 1.7 | 16 | 26 | 34¾ | 34⅜ | 34¾ | + ⅛ |
| 42⅜ | 27¼ | Deere | 1 | 2.7 | .. | 596 | 37½ | 37⅛ | 37⅜ | + ⅛ |
| 19⅝ | 14⅜ | DelmP | 1.64 | 9.2 | 7 | 546 | 18⅜ | 17¾ | 17⅞ | − ½ |
| 51 | 29 | DeltaAr | .60 | 1.6 | .. | 1174 | 38¾ | 38¼ | 38½ | − ⅛ |
| 15⅛ | 7¼ | Deltona | | .. | .. | 232 | 9⅝ | 9⅜ | 9⅜ | − ¼ |
| 47¾ | 33⅜ | DlxChk | 1.36 | 3.6 | 12 | 532 | 39⅛ | 38¼ | 38¼ | − ⅜ |
| 39 | 22⅛ | DenMfg | 1.60 | 4.6 | 13 | 12 | 34⅝ | 34⅜ | 34⅝ | + ⅜ |
| 36⅞ | 27⅛ | Dennys | .72 | 2.0 | 13 | 658 | 36 | 34¾ | 36 | + ¾ |
| 37¼ | 23½ | DeSoto | 1.24 | 4.2 | 10 | 32 | 29¼ | 28⅝ | 29¼ | + ⅝ |
| 16 | 12⅝ | DetEd | 1.68 | 11. | 7 | 2060 | 15¾ | 15½ | 15⅝ | + ⅛ |
| 86 | 67¾ | DetE | pf5.50 | 6.5 | .. | 1 | 84¼ | 84¼ | 84¼ | − ¾ |
| 74 | 66 | DetE | pf9.32 | 13. | .. | z320 | 70 | 69 | 70 | +1 |
| 62¼ | 53½ | DetE | pf7.68 | 13. | .. | z60 | 57¾ | 57¾ | 57¾ | +1¾ |
| 60 | 52½ | DetE | pf7.45 | 14. | .. | z30 | 54¾ | 54¾ | 54¾ | −1 |
| 61 | 51½ | DetE | pf7.36 | 13. | .. | z1150 | 54⅞ | 54¼ | 54⅞ | − ⅜ |
| 23¾ | 20 | DE | pfF 2.75 | 12. | .. | 41 | 23⅝ | 23⅝ | 23⅝ | + ¼ |
| 25½ | 24 | DE | prR3.24 | 13. | .. | 5 | 24¼ | 24⅛ | 24⅛ | − ⅛ |
| 25⅞ | 22½ | DE | pfQ 3.13 | 13. | .. | 22 | 23½ | 22⅞ | 23½ | + ¼ |
| 24 | 19½ | DE | pfB 2.75 | 13. | .. | 8 | 22½ | 22 | 22 | − ⅜ |
| 27½ | 23⅞ | DE | pfO 3.40 | 13. | .. | 25 | 25⅝ | 25¼ | 25½ | − ⅛ |
| 28 | 21⅝ | DE | pfM3.42 | 14. | .. | 50 | 25⅝ | 25¼ | 25¼ | − ⅛ |
| 32¼ | 27⅞ | DE | prL 4 | 13. | .. | 13 | 30⅛ | 29¾ | 29¾ | − ⅛ |
| 33 | 28¾ | DE | pfK 4.12 | 13. | .. | 13 | 30¾ | 30½ | 30¾ | − ⅛ |
| 19 | 16 | DetE | pr2.28 | 13. | .. | 13 | 17⅞ | 17⅝ | 17⅝ | ..... |
| 29⅛ | 16¾ | Dexter | s .72 | 3.3 | 12 | 239 | 21¾ | 21½ | 21½ | − ⅛ |
| 15⅞ | 10⅜ | DiGior | .64 | 5.0 | 13 | 70 | 12¾ | 12½ | 12¾ | ..... |
| 26⅝ | 20¼ | DiamS | 1.76 | 7.3 | 15 | 5149 | 24¼ | 23⅞ | 24 | − ¼ |
| 41⅛ | 35⅛ | DiaSh | pf 4 | 9.9 | .. | 24 | 40⅜ | 40¼ | 40⅜ | ..... |
| 102 | 65¼ | Diebld | 1 | 1.2 | 17 | 124 | 83¼ | 81 | 83¼ | +1⅞ |
| 132⅛ | 64 | Digital | | .. | 16 | 2964 | 69½ | 68¾ | 69¼ | + ½ |
| 84¾ | 55⅞ | Disney | 1.20 | 2.0 | 21 | 2369 | 60½ | 57⅝ | 58¾ | −1⅝ |
| 36½ | 20½ | DEI | 2.40 | 7.2 | 7 | 21 | 33⅜ | 33⅛ | 33⅛ | ..... |
| 6⅞ | 2¼ | Divrsln | | .. | .. | 37 | 4½ | 4⅜ | 4½ | + ⅛ |
| 17⅛ | 11¾ | DrPepp | .84 | 5.1 | 43 | 1806 | 16⅜ | 15⅝ | 16⅜ | + ⅝ |
| 22¼ | 9 | Dome | g .12 | .. | .. | 857 | 12¾ | 12¼ | 12¾ | + ½ |
| 23¾ | 19½ | DomRs | 2.40 | 10. | 8 | 3416 | 23¼ | 23 | 23¼ | + ⅛ |
| 24 | 16⅛ | Donald | .66 | 3.2 | .. | 12 | 20⅜ | 20⅜ | 20⅜ | − ¼ |
| 24⅞ | 15¼ | DonLJ | .24 | 1.5 | 10 | 110 | 16¼ | 16 | 16¼ | + ¼ |
| 39¼ | 13½ | GCA | s | .. | .. | 2237 | 34⅜ | 32 | 34⅛ | +2⅛ |
| 64 | 37¼ | GEICO | .72 | 1.2 | 12 | 1002 | 58 | 56½ | 58 | + ½ |
| 14½ | 8⅛ | GEO | .18j | .. | .. | 786 | 8⅝ | 8¼ | 8⅜ | ..... |
| 7⅝ | 2¾ | GF Cp | s | .. | .. | 91 | u 7¾ | 7⅜ | 7¾ | + ⅜ |
| 48⅜ | 35¾ | GTE | 3 | 6.4 | 9 | 3078 | 46⅞ | 46⅛ | 46⅝ | − ⅛ |
| 23⅜ | 20⅜ | GTE | pf 2.48 | 11. | .. | 4 | 22¼ | 22⅛ | 22¼ | ..... |
| 22¼ | 8¼ | GalHou | .05j | .. | .. | 13 | 9 | 8¾ | 9 | + ¼ |
| 72 | 51⅜ | Gannett | 1.92 | 3.3 | 17 | 488 | 59¼ | 57¾ | 58½ | − ½ |
| 45¼ | 16 | GapSt | s .40 | 1.6 | 10 | 72 | 24¾ | 24½ | 24¾ | + ⅜ |
| 26⅛ | 11½ | Gearht | .40 | 1.9 | 77 | 387 | 21¼ | 20¾ | 20¾ | − ½ |
| 27⅛ | 16¼ | Gelco | .56 | 2.9 | .. | 184 | 19 | 18¾ | 19 | ..... |
| 63¼ | 45 | GemCa | | .. | 121 | 6 | 61⅞ | 61¾ | 61⅞ | + ¼ |
| 17 | 14¾ | GemIn | 3.20a | 21. | .. | 2 | 15¼ | 15⅛ | 15⅛ | ..... |
| 22¼ | 16 | GAInv | 1.51e | 7.2 | .. | 43 | 21 | 20⅝ | 21 | ..... |
| 31⅞ | 18½ | GnBcsh | 1 | 3.3 | 7 | 73 | 31⅜ | 30¾ | 30¾ | − ⅞ |
| 45½ | 25¾ | GCinm | .64 | 1.5 | 9 | 91 | 42¼ | 41¾ | 42 | ..... |
| 29⅝ | 13⅞ | GnData | | .. | 49 | 91 | 24½ | 24⅜ | 24½ | + ⅛ |
| 57 | 29 | GnDyn | 1 | 1.8 | 13 | 1590 | 55¾ | 55 | 55¾ | + ⅝ |
| 57¾ | 43⅛ | GenEl | s1.90 | 3.5 | 13 | 4243 | 54⅜ | 52¾ | 54¼ | +1⅜ |
| 53½ | 36⅝ | GnFds | 2.40 | 4.7 | 9 | 961 | 50⅞ | 50¼ | 50⅝ | − ⅜ |
| 22⅝ | 15⅞ | GGth | .60a | 2.9 | 24 | 41 | 20⅞ | 20½ | 20⅞ | + ⅜ |
| 5⅜ | 1½ | GGth | wt | .. | .. | 119 | 4½ | 4 | 4⅜ | + ½ |
| 23⅞ | 21¾ | GGth | pf1.90 | 8.3 | .. | 2 | 22⅞ | 22⅞ | 22⅞ | + ¼ |
| 22 | 11⅛ | GHost | s .44 | 2.1 | 12 | 118 | 20¾ | 20½ | 20¾ | + ⅜ |
| 29¾ | 14⅜ | GnHous | .20 | 1.3 | 9 | 211 | 16⅜ | 15⅞ | 16 | − ⅜ |
| 66⅞ | 29⅛ | GnInst | .50 | 1.6 | 14 | 4711 | 32¼ | 31 | 31¾ | + ¾ |
| 57¾ | 44¼ | GnMills | 2.04 | 3.8 | 10 | 839 | 53½ | 52¼ | 53½ | +1¾ |
| 80 | 53⅝ | GMot | 4 | 5.3 | 9 | 12884 | 76⅛ | 74¼ | 76⅛ | +1¾ |
| 40 | 33½ | GMot | pf3.75 | 11. | .. | 245 | 36 | 35⅛ | 35⅛ | − ½ |
| 52⅛ | 44 | GMot | pf 5 | 10. | .. | 25 | 48⅝ | 48¼ | 48⅜ | − ¼ |
| 29⅝ | 11⅞ | GNC | s .16 | 1.1 | 16 | 118 | 14¾ | 14 | 14 | − ⅝ |
| 9¾ | 5⅞ | GPU | | .. | 10 | 1294 | 7⅜ | 7¼ | 7¼ | − ¼ |
| 73 | 52 | GenRe | 1.28 | 2.1 | 13 | 1247 | 62½ | 62 | 62 | ..... |
| 7⅛ | 3 | GnRefr | | .. | .. | 28 | 5⅜ | 5¼ | 5⅜ | + ¼ |
| 50 | 40½ | GnSignl | 1.68 | 3.6 | 16 | 303 | 47¼ | 46⅞ | 47¼ | ..... |
| 11⅝ | 10 | GTFI | pf1.25 | 11. | .. | z320 | 11 | 11 | 11 | ..... |
| 74⅝ | 64 | GTFI | pf8.16 | 12. | .. | z2000 | 67½ | 67½ | 67½ | + ½ |
| 38 | 24¾ | GTire | 1.50b | 4.2 | 36 | 45 | 35½ | 35¼ | 35½ | + ⅛ |
| 10⅜ | 4⅛ | Gensco | | .. | .. | 224 | 8⅜ | 8⅛ | 8⅛ | − ¼ |
| 46⅜ | 17⅝ | GnRad | s .08 | .2 | 41 | 377 | 33¾ | 31⅜ | 33½ | +1¾ |
| 31½ | 15⅛ | Genst | g .60 | .. | .. | 563 | 22⅝ | 22½ | 22⅝ | + ⅛ |
| 48⅜ | 38½ | GenuPt | 1.38 | 3.2 | 15 | 645 | 43 | 42½ | 43 | − ¼ |
| 31⅞ | 21⅜ | GaPac | .60 | 2.5 | .. | 1586 | 24⅜ | 23⅝ | 24¼ | + ⅝ |
| 37 | 29½ | GaPc | pf2.24 | 6.6 | .. | 10 | 34⅛ | 34⅛ | 34⅛ | − ⅛ |
| 29½ | 25⅜ | GaPw | pf3.44 | 13. | .. | 27 | 27¼ | 26⅞ | 26⅞ | − ⅜ |
| 31¾ | 25⅜ | GaPw | pf3.76 | 13. | .. | 4 | 29¼ | 29 | 29 | ..... |
| 22¼ | 18½ | GaPw | pf2.56 | 13. | .. | 4 | 19⅞ | 19⅞ | 19⅞ | − ⅜ |
| 25¼ | 23⅛ | GaPw | pf2.75 | 11. | .. | 1 | 24⅜ | 24⅜ | 24⅜ | + ⅛ |
| 67⅞ | 57½ | GaPw | pf7.80 | 13. | .. | z200 | 60 | 60 | 60 | −1¼ |
| 42¾ | 21⅞ | GerbPd | 1.48 | 3.7 | 12 | 473 | 40 | 39¼ | 40 | + ¾ |
| 29¼ | 7¼ | GerbS | s .12 | .5 | 37 | 2002 | 23¼ | 21¾ | 22¾ | +1 |
| 73¼ | 44¼ | Getty | 2.60e | 3.6 | 14 | 2460 | 73 | 69¼ | 73 | +3¾ |
| 9½ | 5⅜ | GiantP | | .. | .. | 56 | 6⅞ | 6½ | 6¾ | − ⅛ |
| 16 | 7⅛ | GibrFn | | .. | 6 | 140 | 11½ | 11¼ | 11¼ | ..... |
| 23 | 15¾ | GiffHill | .52 | 3.2 | 149 | 51 | 16¾ | 16⅜ | 16⅜ | − ¼ |
| 51½ | 40⅞ | Gillette | 2.44 | 5.1 | 10 | 453 | 48⅜ | 47⅛ | 48⅛ | + ⅞ |
| 17⅞ | 8½ | GleasW | | .. | .. | 49 | 13⅝ | 13¼ | 13⅝ | + ⅛ |
| 13 | 7⅜ | GloblM | .24 | 2.7 | 4 | 523 | 8⅞ | 8¾ | 8⅞ | ..... |
| 19⅜ | 5½ | GldNg | s | .. | 13 | 2341 | 13¼ | 12½ | 13¼ | + ¼ |
| 8 | 4¾ | GldN | wt | .. | .. | 566 | 5 | 4¾ | 5 | ..... |
| 30½ | 11½ | GldWF | .06e | .3 | 6 | 592 | 20¾ | 20 | 20¾ | ..... |
| 43⅞ | 29⅜ | Gdrich | 1.56 | 5.2 | .. | 401 | 29⅞ | 29½ | 29⅞ | + ¼ |
| 36⅞ | 27 | Goodyr | 1.40 | 4.5 | 12 | x4032 | 31⅛ | 30¾ | 31 | + ⅛ |
| 30 | 16¾ | GordnJ | .56 | 2.1 | 11 | 45 | 26¾ | 26 | 26¾ | + ¾ |
| 43¾ | 25¾ | Gould | 1.72 | 5.9 | 17 | 1056 | 29¼ | 28⅝ | 29⅛ | + ⅝ |
| 50⅜ | 35¾ | Grace | 2.80 | 6.2 | 14 | 151 | 45⅛ | 44⅝ | 45 | + ⅛ |
| 63¼ | 46¾ | Graingr | 1.20 | 2.0 | 18 | 45 | 59¼ | 59 | 59¼ | − ⅛ |
| 17¼ | 8¾ | Granitv | | .. | .. | 3 | 17 | 16⅞ | 16⅞ | ..... |
| 14¼ | 7⅜ | GtAtPc | | .. | 16 | 136 | 11¼ | 11⅛ | 11⅛ | ..... |
| 40⅜ | 22½ | GtLkln | .80a | 2.4 | 9 | 5 | 33¼ | 33¼ | 33¼ | ..... |
| 26⅝ | 15¾ | GNIrn | 1.50e | 7.4 | 17 | 5 | 20⅜ | 20⅜ | 20⅜ | ..... |
| 54 | 34¼ | GtNoNk | 2.10 | 4.1 | 12 | 256 | 51¼ | 50⅞ | 50⅞ | − ⅛ |
| 31½ | 18⅝ | GtWFin | .88 | 4.0 | 17 | 373 | 22 | 21⅝ | 22 | + ¼ |
| 19⅛ | 8¾ | GWHsp | | .. | 19 | 129 | 10⅝ | 10⅛ | 10¼ | − ⅛ |
| 15⅛ | 12½ | GMP | 1.64 | 11. | 6 | 9 | 14⅞ | 14⅝ | 14⅝ | − ⅛ |
| 28 | 17⅛ | Greyh | 1.20 | 5.3 | 10 | 4118 | 22⅝ | 21⅝ | 22½ | + ⅞ |
| 47 | 37 | Greyh | pf4.75 | 11. | .. | z100 | 43 | 43 | 43 | ..... |
| 8⅜ | 2 | Groler | n | .. | 5 | 484 | 4⅝ | 4⅜ | 4⅝ | + ¼ |
| 17½ | 9¾ | GrowG | .40 | 2.2 | 19 | 526 | u18¼ | 17½ | 18 | + ½ |
| 5⅞ | 2¼ | GthRty | | .. | .. | 41 | 3⅝ | 3⅝ | 3⅝ | ..... |
| 11½ | 4¼ | GrubEl | | .. | 21 | 73 | 7¾ | 7½ | 7½ | − ¼ |
| 33⅝ | 21 | Grum | s .90 | 3.3 | 8 | 85 | 27½ | 27⅛ | 27½ | + ⅛ |
| 25¼ | 21 | Grum | pf2.80 | 12. | .. | 30 | 24¼ | 24⅛ | 24¼ | ..... |

**Figure 20-4** Sample NYSE stock quotations. (Adapted from *The Wall Street Journal,* November 10, 1983. Reprinted by permission of *The Wall Street Journal,* Dow Jones & Company, Inc. 1983. All Rights Reserved.)

**Closing** is the price paid in the last trade of the day. Our example's closing price was $76.125, or $1.75 more than yesterday's closing price. Notice that stock prices are given in eighths of a dollar: ⅛ is $0.125, ¼ is $0.25, ⅜ is $0.375, and so on. Net change is the amount the closing price differed from that of the day before.

Now return to the two ratios in the middle of the quotation, "Yld %" and "P-E Ratio." These ratios show the relationship between two financial figures. The yield percentage is the dividend yield, or the percentage return you'd earn from dividends if you bought GM's stock today. Think of it as a comparison figure similar to interest on a bond. It's calculated by dividing the current dividend by the stock's closing price ($4.00 ÷ $76.125 = 0.0525, or 5.3%).

A stock's **P-E ratio** is also a comparison figure, but one that compares the stock's closing price to the company's earnings. It's calculated by dividing the stock's closing price by the amount of profit the company earned for each share of stock, called **earnings per share (EPS).** The value for a stock's EPS can be found in the company's annual report or one of several financial publications, such as *Standard & Poor's Stock Guide.* The P-E ratio is calculated as follows: $76.125 (closing price) ÷ $8.50 (EPS) = 9. Investors are willing to pay $76.125, or nine times earnings, for a stock that earns only $8.50 for each share. The P-E ratio provides a method of gauging investor preferences. If investors are willing to accept a high P-E ratio, say 20 or 25, they must feel the stock has the potential for extraordinary growth. Stocks that investors expect to grow rapidly often carry high P-E ratios.

▲ **Reading Corporate Bond Quotations** Understanding corporate bond quotations requires more background. First, you must realize that the data are given in financial jargon and may not mean what they appear to mean. Look at the following quotation for Chrysler (see also Figure 20-5):

| Bonds | Cur Yld | Vol | High | Low | Close | Net Chg |
|-------|---------|-----|------|-----|-------|---------|
| Chrysl 8⅞95 | 12. | 21 | 75¼ | 74⅞ | 75¼ | +¼ |

The corporation's name is the first line item. Notice that some companies are listed several times. This is because they have more than one bond issue outstanding. General Motors Acceptance Corporation (GMAC), for example, has thirty-seven separate bond issues quoted.

Each of the issues has a different maturity date and interest rate, which are given next. Chrysler's bond is listed as 8⅞95, meaning that it pays an annual interest rate of 8⅞ percent and will mature in the year 1995. These two factors are the major influences on the bond's price. Generally, the higher the interest rate, the more attractive the bond is. Also, the shorter the maturity, the less risk involved.

---

Notice in Figure 20-5 that maturity dates vary from 1984 to 2019. If you were going to tie your money up that long, what kind of interest rate would you want as compensation for the uncertainties?

---

The next figure, current yield, is the bond's annual interest divided by its current price. This figure is given as a percentage. Generally, a higher figure indicates a higher-quality bond.

# New York Exchange Bonds

*Wednesday, November 9, 1983*

**Total Volume $25,750,000**

| | Domestic Wed. | Domestic Tue. | All Issues Wed. | All Issues Tue. |
|---|---|---|---|---|
| Issues traded | 956 | 908 | 965 | 916 |
| Advances | 388 | 284 | 392 | 286 |
| Declines | 344 | 398 | 347 | 401 |
| Unchanged | 224 | 226 | 226 | 229 |
| New highs | 10 | 7 | 10 | 7 |
| New lows | 23 | 23 | 23 | 23 |

**SALES SINCE JANUARY 1**

| 1983 | 1982 | 1981 |
|---|---|---|
| $6,615,655,000 | $5,936,034,000 | $4,680,754,000 |

## Dow Jones Bond Averages

| 1981 High | 1981 Low | 1982 High | 1982 Low | 1983 High | 1983 Low | | Wednesday 1983 | Chg. | 1982 | Chg. | 1981 | Chg. |
|---|---|---|---|---|---|---|---|---|---|---|---|---|
| 65.78 | 54.99 | 71.52 | 55.67 | 77.84 | 69.85 | 20 Bonds | 70.79 | +.05 | 71.06 | +.15 | 59.31 | +.47 |
| 66.18 | 53.61 | 72.71 | 53.80 | 78.88 | 67.42 | 10 Utilities | 68.58 | +.06 | 72.37 | +.57 | 60.22 | +.89 |
| 66.15 | 56.32 | 71.23 | 57.36 | 77.13 | 71.51 | 10 Industrial | 73.00 | +.04 | 69.75 | −.27 | 58.40 | +.04 |

**CORPORATION BONDS**
**Volume $25,460,000**

| Bonds | Cur Yld | Vol | High | Low | Close | Net Chg. |
|---|---|---|---|---|---|---|
| APL 10¾97 | 14. | 1 | 77 | 77 | 77 | ..... |
| ARA 4⅝s96 | cv | 29 | 61 | 60⅞ | 61 | ..... |
| AVX 13½00 | 14. | 1 | 97 | 97 | 97 | −4 |
| Advst 9s08 | cv | 92 | 96 | 94 | 94 | −2⅛ |
| AetnLf 8⅛07 | 12. | 31 | 70½ | 70½ | 70½ | +1⅜ |
| AlaP 9s2000 | 13. | 20 | 72 | 72 | 72 | −½ |
| AlaP 8¼s03 | 13. | 20 | 66 | 66 | 66 | −⅜ |
| AlaP 10⅞05 | 13. | 1 | 84 | 84 | 84 | −⅜ |
| AlaP 8¾07 | 13. | 30 | 69 | 68 | 68¾ | +¾ |
| AlaP 9¼07 | 13. | 15 | 72¼ | 72 | 72¼ | ..... |
| AlaP 15¼10 | 14. | 23 | 109⅞ | 108 | 108 | +¾ |
| AlaP 17⅜11 | 15. | 1 | 115⅝ | 115⅝ | 115⅝ | −⅛ |
| AlaP 18¼89 | 16. | 144 | 112¾ | 112 | 112¾ | −¼ |
| AlskH 16¼94 | 15. | 15 | 110¼ | 110¼ | 110¼ | +¼ |
| AlskH 17¾91 | 15. | 2 | 115 | 115 | 115 | ..... |
| AlskH 18⅜01 | 16. | 28 | 114¾ | 114 | 114¾ | +1¾ |
| AlskH 15s92 | 14. | 11 | 105 | 105 | 105 | +¼ |
| Alexn 5½96 | cv | 45 | 70 | 68¼ | 70 | +1¾ |
| Allgl 10¾99 | 14. | 1 | 77 | 77 | 77 | −¾ |
| Allgl 9s89 | 12. | 10 | 78¼ | 78¼ | 78¼ | −1⅞ |
| AlldC 9s2000 | 12. | 6 | 73⅞ | 73⅞ | 73⅞ | −2⅝ |
| AlldC zr92 | .. | 22 | 35⅛ | 35 | 35 | −⅛ |
| AlldC zr96s | .. | 25 | 26⅞ | 26⅜ | 26⅞ | +½ |
| AlldC zr98s | .. | 25 | 20⅛ | 20 | 20⅛ | +⅛ |
| AlldC zr2000s | .. | 150 | 16⅝ | 16¼ | 16¼ | −½ |
| AlldC 6s88 | 8.0 | 4 | 75⅛ | 75⅛ | 75⅛ | −1 |
| AlldC 6s90 | 8.7 | 3 | 69⅛ | 69⅛ | 69⅛ | −⅞ |
| AlsCha 12s90 | 13. | 5 | 90 | 90 | 90 | −⅜ |
| Alcoa 6s92 | 8.9 | 1 | 67½ | 67½ | 67½ | +¼ |
| Alcoa 9s95 | 11. | 30 | 81⅞ | 81⅞ | 81⅞ | +1⅞ |
| AluCa 9½95 | 12. | 5 | 82 | 82 | 82 | +⅞ |
| AMAX 8s86 | 8.6 | 3 | 93 | 93 | 93 | ..... |
| AMAX 9⅜00 | 13. | 10 | 70 | 70 | 70 | −4 |
| Amax 14¼90 | 14. | 16 | 102½ | 102 | 102 | +¼ |
| AForP 5s30 | 13. | 10 | 39 | 38 | 38 | −1 |
| AAirl 10⅞88 | 11. | 51 | 98 | 97⅝ | 98 | +½ |
| AAirl 10s89 | 10. | 1 | 96⅝ | 96⅝ | 96⅝ | +½ |
| ABrnd 8⅛85 | 8.4 | 25 | 96⅜ | 96⅜ | 96⅜ | −⅛ |
| ABrnd 11⅛89 | 11. | 5 | 97 | 97 | 97 | −¼ |
| ACan 6s97 | 11. | 1 | 55¾ | 55¾ | 55¾ | +1½ |
| ACan 13¼93 | 13. | 46 | 102⅛ | 102 | 102⅛ | −⅜ |
| ACeM 6¾91 | cv | 8 | 87¾ | 87¾ | 87¾ | +1¾ |
| AExC 8½s86 | 8.9 | 15 | 95 | 95 | 95 | −¾ |
| AExC 11¾12 | 13. | 9 | 91½ | 91½ | 91½ | −1½ |
| AmGn 11s07 | cv | 12 | 131½ | 130½ | 131½ | +1½ |
| AmGn 11s08 | cv | 229 | 131½ | 129½ | 131½ | +1½ |
| AHoist 5½93 | cv | 15 | 79 | 79 | 79 | +3½ |
| AmMed 8¼08 | .. | 10 | 85½ | 85½ | 85½ | +1 |
| AmMot 6s88 | cv | 17 | 99 | 98⅛ | 99 | −½ |
| ASmel 4⅝s88 | 6.1 | 21 | 76 | 75 | 76 | +1 |
| AmStr 9⅞90 | 11. | 1 | 92¾ | 92¾ | 92¾ | −⅛ |
| ASug 5.3s93 | 8.7 | 3 | 61 | 61 | 61 | ..... |
| ASu 5.3s93r | 8.7 | 2 | 61 | 61 | 61 | ..... |
| ATT 3¼s84 | 3.4 | 30 | 95⅝ | 95 9-32 | 95 9-32 | −5-32 |
| ATT 4⅜s85 | 4.7 | 30 | 93⅛ | 92¾ | 93⅛ | +⅝ |
| ATT 2⅝s86 | 3.1 | 1 | 85½ | 85½ | 85½ | +¾ |
| ATT 2⅞s87 | 3.6 | 30 | 79¼ | 79¼ | 79¼ | −¾ |
| ATT 3⅞s90 | 5.7 | 28 | 68¼ | 67⅞ | 68 | +½ |
| ATT 8¾00 | 12. | 294 | 76¼ | 75¾ | 75¾ | ..... |
| ATT 7s01 | 11. | 180 | 63 | 62⅞ | 62⅞ | ..... |
| ATT 7⅛s03 | 11. | 59 | 62⅞ | 62⅝ | 62⅞ | +½ |
| ATT 8.80s05 | 12. | 269 | 74½ | 73¾ | 74¼ | −¼ |
| ATT 8⅝s07 | 12. | 67 | 73 | 72½ | 72⅞ | +½ |
| ATT 10⅜90 | 11. | 17 | 93½ | 93⅛ | 93½ | +⅛ |
| ATT 13¼91 | 13. | 98 | 105¼ | 104⅞ | 104⅞ | ..... |
| Amfac 5¼94 | cv | 4 | 78 | 76¼ | 76¼ | ..... |
| AMP 8⅝s85 | 8.9 | 5 | 96⅞ | 96⅞ | 96⅞ | +⅛ |
| Ampx 5½94 | cv | 5 | 85½ | 85½ | 85½ | −1½ |
| Ancp 13⅞02 | cv | 172 | 78½ | 77⅛ | 77¾ | −1 |
| Anxtr 8¼03 | cv | 6 | 100 | 100 | 100 | ..... |
| AppP 10½84 | 11. | 10 | 99½ | 99½ | 99½ | +2½ |
| AppP 11s87 | 11. | 5 | 99¼ | 99¼ | 99¼ | +1¾ |
| Arco 8s84 | 8.0 | 15 | 99½ | 99½ | 99½ | +1-32 |
| ArizP 12⅛09 | 13. | 22 | 93 | 92¾ | 92¾ | −⅝ |
| Armr 5s84 | 5.0 | 10 | 99½ | 99½ | 99½ | ..... |
| AshO 11.1s04 | 13. | 14 | 83½ | 83½ | 83½ | −⅛ |
| AsCp 9¼90 | 10. | 5 | 91¼ | 91¼ | 91¼ | ..... |
| AsCp 12⅜89 | 12. | 50 | 101¼ | 101¼ | 101¼ | +1 |
| AsInv 4⅝85 | 5.1 | 10 | 91¼ | 91¼ | 91¼ | −¼ |
| Atchsn 4s95 | 7.9 | 3 | 50½ | 50½ | 50½ | ..... |
| Athlne 11s93 | 13. | 4 | 81⅝ | 81⅝ | 81⅝ | ..... |
| ARich 5⅝97 | 9.0 | 3 | 62⅜ | 62⅜ | 62⅜ | −1 |
| ARich 7.7s00 | 11. | 15 | 67¼ | 67¼ | 67¼ | −1¾ |
| ARch d7s91 | 9.4 | 15 | 74¼ | 74¼ | 74¼ | +¼ |
| ARch 12½12 | 13. | 10 | 99½ | 99½ | 99½ | +⅛ |
| AvcoC 5½93 | cv | 11 | 73 | 73 | 73 | ..... |
| AvcoC 7½93 | 11. | 1 | 68 | 68 | 68 | ..... |
| AvcoF 9⅛98 | 12. | 5 | 77⅝ | 77⅝ | 77⅝ | −⅜ |
| Avnet 8s13 | cv | 16 | 102¾ | 102 | 102¾ | +¾ |
| Bache 14s00 | 13. | 30 | 104 | 102⅝ | 104 | −½ |
| BakInt 7.55s87 | 8.6 | 30 | 87⅝ | 87¼ | 87⅝ | +⅜ |
| BldwU 10s09 | 23. | 150 | 46 | 44 | 44 | −2 |
| Bally 6s98 | cv | 55 | 82½ | 82 | 82 | −¼ |
| Bally 10s06 | cv | 42 | 93 | 92¾ | 92¾ | ..... |
| B O 4¼95 | 7.7 | 4 | 55 | 55 | 55 | ..... |
| B O 4½10A | cv | 18 | 185 | 184⅞ | 185 | −4 |
| BalGE 8⅜06 | 12. | 5 | 68 | 68 | 68 | −½ |
| BalGE 16¾91 | 14. | 17 | 116½ | 116 | 116 | +1 |
| BangP 11½98 | 14. | 25 | 85 | 85 | 85 | +1⅜ |
| Bevrly 7⅝03 | cv | 27 | 82½ | 81½ | 82 | −½ |
| Boeing 8⅞06 | cv | 45 | 116 | 115½ | 116 | +2 |
| BorW 7⅞s91 | 10. | 15 | 78½ | 78 | 78 | −1 |
| BosE 9¼07 | 13. | 5 | 72¼ | 72¼ | 72¼ | −¾ |
| BrkUn 8¾99 | 12. | 3 | 71½ | 71½ | 71½ | −1 |
| BrkUn 17⅜91 | 15. | 2 | 116 | 116 | 116 | +½ |
| BwnSh 9¼05 | cv | 5 | 74 | 74 | 74 | ..... |
| Bulova 6s90 | cv | 4 | 71 | 71 | 71 | ..... |
| BurNo 8½96 | 11. | 18 | 74⅞ | 74⅞ | 74⅞ | −1⅛ |
| BurNo 8.6s99 | 12. | 2 | 74⅛ | 74⅛ | 74⅛ | −⅝ |
| Butte 10¼97 | 15. | 41 | 69 | 68½ | 68½ | −⅛ |
| CCI 13⅞00 | 15. | 9 | 90 | 90 | 90 | −4⅜ |
| CIGNA 8s07 | cv | 11 | 95½ | 95½ | 95½ | ..... |
| CIT 8¾08 | 12. | 15 | 70¼ | 70¼ | 70¼ | +1¼ |
| CIT 15½87 | 14. | 11 | 111¼ | 111¼ | 111¼ | ..... |
| Caesr 12½90 | 13. | 3 | 94⅞ | 94¾ | 94⅞ | +¼ |
| Caesr 11¼97 | 13. | 6 | 84¼ | 84½ | 84½ | ..... |
| Caesr 12½00 | 14. | 5 | 89 | 89 | 89 | ..... |
| CPc4s perp | 11. | 11 | 36½ | 36½ | 36½ | +½ |
| Carr 8⅛s96 | 11. | 25 | 73½ | 73½ | 73½ | −1 |
| CartH 9¼96 | 13. | 8 | 74 | 74 | 74 | ..... |
| CastlC 5⅜94 | cv | 57 | 96½ | 96½ | 96½ | −3½ |
| CatTr 5½00 | cv | 13 | 91 | 91 | 91 | −1¾ |
| CatTr 14⅜88 | 14. | 5 | 107½ | 107½ | 107½ | +½ |
| Celanse 4s90 | cv | 2 | 85 | 85 | 85 | ..... |
| Celanse 9¾06 | cv | 20 | 113½ | 113½ | 113½ | −½ |
| Centel 8.1s96 | 11. | 4 | 71⅞ | 71⅞ | 71⅞ | −⅞ |
| CtrlTel 8s96 | 11. | 15 | 71½ | 71½ | 71½ | +1 |
| Cessna 8s08 | cv | 40 | 94 | 93½ | 94 | ..... |
| CATS zr91 | .. | 6 | 42 | 42 | 42 | +⅛ |
| CATS zr92 | .. | 100 | 39 | 38 | 38 | −1⅞ |
| CATS zr95 | .. | 30 | 32⅞ | 32⅞ | 32⅞ | −1⅞ |
| CATS zr96 | .. | 33 | 28 | 27⅝ | 28 | ..... |
| CATS zr97 | .. | 1 | 23⅜ | 23⅜ | 23⅜ | ..... |
| CATS zr98 | .. | 1 | 23 | 23 | 23 | −1⅛ |
| CATS zr99 | .. | 20 | 22⅛ | 22⅛ | 22⅛ | −2⅝ |
| CATS zr01 | .. | 21 | 18¾ | 18¾ | 18¾ | ..... |
| CATS zr02 | .. | 3 | 16⅜ | 16⅜ | 16⅜ | +¼ |
| ChrtCo 10⅝98 | 16. | 76 | 69 | 68 | 68 | −1 |
| ChrtCo d14¾02 | 16. | 10 | 92⅜ | 91¼ | 91½ | +1 |
| ChsBk 8¾86 | 9.3 | 33 | 94 | 93⅝ | 94 | +¼ |
| ChsCp 6½96 | cv | 14 | 80 | 78½ | 80 | +1⅜ |
| ChsCp 9.2s99t | 9.3 | 5 | 99⅜ | 99⅜ | 99⅜ | +⅛ |
| ChsCp 9.35s09t | 10. | 22 | 90⅜ | 90¼ | 90⅜ | ..... |
| Chelse 5¼93 | cv | 10 | 72⅛ | 72⅛ | 72⅛ | +⅛ |
| ChNY 8.4s99 | 12. | 6 | 69⅝ | 69⅝ | 69⅝ | −⅛ |
| ChNY 9¾04t | 10. | 10 | 95½ | 95½ | 95½ | −¼ |
| ChO 3½96Dr | 3.8 | 5 | 91 | 91 | 91 | ..... |
| CPoM 7¼12 | 12. | 15 | 59⅜ | 59⅜ | 59⅜ | +⅛ |
| CPoV 9½19 | 12. | 15 | 76⅛ | 76⅛ | 76⅛ | −1 |
| CPoW 13s17 | 13. | 5 | 99 | 99 | 99 | ..... |
| CPWV 7¼13 | 12. | 2 | 58¼ | 58¼ | 58¼ | ..... |
| ChesbP 10⅝90 | 11. | 1 | 94 | 94 | 94 | −¼ |
| ChCft 13s99 | 14. | 8 | 94 | 92⅝ | 92⅝ | −1⅜ |
| ChCft 15s99t | 14. | 6 | 105⅝ | 105½ | 105½ | −⅛ |
| Chrysl 8⅞95 | 12. | 21 | 75¼ | 74⅞ | 75¼ | +¼ |
| Chryslr 8s98 | 12. | 5 | 64⅞ | 64⅝ | 64⅞ | −¼ |
| ChryF 7⅜86 | 8.4 | 60 | 88¼ | 87⅝ | 87⅝ | −⅜ |
| ChryF 9s86 | 10. | 10 | 90⅛ | 90⅛ | 90⅛ | ..... |
| ChryF 8⅞84 | 9.0 | 10 | 98⅜ | 98⅜ | 98⅜ | +11-32 |
| ChryF 9⅜87 | 10. | 61 | 91½ | 91 | 91 | −½ |
| CinGE 4⅛87 | 5.5 | 14 | 75 | 74⅝ | 74⅝ | −⅝ |
| Citicp 9¼89t | 9.3 | 3 | 99½ | 99⅜ | 99⅜ | −⅛ |
| Citicp 5¾00 | cv | 1 | 82½ | 82½ | 82½ | −1 |
| Citicp 8.45s07 | 13. | 40 | 67⅛ | 67⅛ | 67⅛ | +¼ |
| Citicp 11.1s98t | 12. | 34 | 95⅝ | 95⅝ | 95⅝ | +⅛ |
| Citicp 9.8s04t | 10. | 20 | 94½ | 94½ | 94½ | ..... |
| ColSO 7⅝85 | 8.2 | 6 | 93 | 93 | 93 | −¼ |
| Cmdis 8s03 | cv | 194 | 81 | 79½ | 80 | +2 |
| CmlCr 8⅞86 | 9.4 | 10 | 94⅝ | 94⅝ | 94⅝ | ..... |
| CmlCr 8.35s86 | 9.1 | 13 | 92¼ | 91⅞ | 92¼ | +⅝ |
| CmwE 8s03 | 12. | 27 | 65⅞ | 65⅝ | 65⅝ | +⅜ |
| CmwE 8⅛07D | 13. | 6 | 64⅞ | 64⅞ | 64⅞ | +⅜ |
| CmwE 8¼07 | 13. | 31 | 64⅞ | 64¾ | 64¾ | ..... |
| CmwE 9⅛08 | 13. | 20 | 70¾ | 70¾ | 70¾ | ..... |
| CmwE 9¼84 | 9.3 | 7 | 99 3-16 | 99 3-16 | 99 3-16 | +1-16 |
| CmwE 12½86 | 12. | 10 | 101¾ | 101½ | 101¾ | +¾ |
| CmwE 11⅛10 | 13. | 18 | 83½ | 83½ | 83½ | +⅜ |
| CmwE 16¼89 | 15. | 20 | 112 | 112 | 112 | +⅜ |
| CmwE 17⅞88 | 15. | 18 | 118½ | 118¼ | 118¼ | −¾ |
| CmwE 13s12 | 13. | 35 | 96⅝ | 96½ | 96½ | ..... |
| CmpSci 6s94 | cv | 14 | 82½ | 82½ | 82½ | ..... |
| Conoco 13¼11 | 13. | 10 | 103¾ | 103¾ | 103¾ | +1½ |
| ConEd 3⅜85 | 3.8 | 2 | 88 | 88 | 88 | +⅜ |
| ConEd 4¼86 | 5.1 | 1 | 83⅞ | 83⅞ | 83⅞ | −⅝ |
| ConEd 4s88 | 5.3 | 74 | 75¼ | 75 | 75 | +¼ |
| ConEd 5s90 | 7.4 | 5 | 69½ | 67½ | 67½ | −2 |
| ConEd 4⅜92V | 7.4 | 20 | 59½ | 59½ | 59½ | −¾ |
| ConEd 9⅜00 | 12. | 7 | 77½ | 77½ | 77½ | +⅜ |
| ConEd 7¾03 | 12. | 10 | 65⅛ | 65⅛ | 65⅛ | −⅛ |
| ConEd 8.4s03 | 12. | 5 | 68⅝ | 68⅝ | 68⅝ | ..... |
| ConEd 9⅛04 | 12. | 26 | 74½ | 74 | 74 | ..... |
| CnNG 7¾94 | 11. | 10 | 72¾ | 72¾ | 72¾ | +⅝ |
| CnNG 8¼94 | 11. | 5 | 77 | 77 | 77 | ..... |
| CnNG 9s95 | 11. | 3 | 80⅝ | 80⅝ | 80⅝ | +¾ |
| CnNG 7⅞95 | 11. | 5 | 71⅝ | 71⅝ | 71⅝ | −¾ |
| CnNG 9¼95 | 11. | 15 | 81⅝ | 81⅝ | 81⅝ | ..... |
| CnNGS 8⅜96 | 11. | 11 | 79½ | 79½ | 79½ | +3⅜ |
| CnPw 4⅛88 | 6.5 | 35 | 69¼ | 69¼ | 69¼ | −⅜ |
| CnPw 6⅞98 | 12. | 2 | 55⅞ | 55⅞ | 55⅞ | +⅛ |
| CnPw 6⅝98 | 12. | 5 | 53¾ | 53¾ | 53¾ | −1¼ |
| CnPw 7⅝99 | 13. | 24 | 59⅞ | 58 | 58 | −¼ |
| CnPw 8⅝00 | 13. | 5 | 65 | 65 | 65 | +½ |
| CnPw 8⅛01 | 13. | 52 | 60½ | 60 | 60½ | −½ |
| CnPw 11⅝94 | 13. | 20 | 89¾ | 89¾ | 89¾ | ..... |
| CnPw 11½00 | 13. | 25 | 86⅛ | 85½ | 86⅛ | +⅝ |
| CnPw 9s06 | 14. | 10 | 64⅞ | 64⅞ | 64⅞ | ..... |
| CnPw 8⅞07 | 13. | 2 | 66 | 66 | 66 | +⅜ |
| CnPw 8⅝07 | 14. | 1 | 63 | 63 | 63 | ..... |
| Ct IC 8½85 | 8.9 | 5 | 95¼ | 95¼ | 95¼ | −¾ |
| CtlOil 7½99 | 11. | 1 | 67¼ | 67¼ | 67¼ | −¾ |
| CtlOil 9⅛s99 | 12. | 3 | 77⅛ | 77⅛ | 77⅛ | −1⅛ |
| CornG 7¾98 | 11. | 5 | 68⅝ | 68⅝ | 68⅝ | +1⅝ |
| Crane 7s94 | 12. | 5 | 60⅝ | 60⅝ | 60⅝ | −⅛ |
| CrdF 8s92 | 10. | 5 | 79⅜ | 79⅜ | 79⅜ | −1⅜ |
| CrdF 9s86 | 9.8 | 10 | 92 | 92 | 92 | ..... |
| CrocN 8.6s02 | 12. | 75 | 70⅛ | 70⅛ | 70⅛ | +½ |
| CrwnZ 8⅞00 | 12. | 2 | 71⅛ | 71⅛ | 71⅛ | −2⅛ |
| Culb 11½05 | 14. | 1 | 83 | 83 | 83 | −2 |
| Dana d5⅞06 | cv | 30 | 72¾ | 72½ | 72½ | ..... |
| Datpnt 8⅞06 | cv | 12 | 72¼ | 72 | 72¼ | −¾ |
| Dayc 6s94 | cv | 4 | 77 | 77 | 77 | −1½ |
| Dayc 6¼96 | cv | 8 | 97 | 96 | 96 | −1 |
| DaytP 8⅛01 | 13. | 48 | 63¼ | 62⅝ | 62⅝ | −⅝ |
| DaytP 12⅛09 | 14. | 1 | 87½ | 87½ | 87½ | ..... |
| DaytP 16¾12 | 15. | 3 | 114 | 114 | 114 | +3⅞ |
| Deere 7.9s87 | 8.8 | 25 | 89¾ | 89¾ | 89¾ | +⅛ |
| Deere 8.45s | 12. | 5 | 72 | 72 | 72 | −¾ |
| Deere 11⅞89 | 12. | 15 | 98 | 98 | 98 | ..... |
| Deere 9s08 | cv | 13 | 111¾ | 111¼ | 111¾ | ..... |
| Denny 9½07 | cv | 1 | 112 | 112 | 112 | −2½ |
| DetEd 9s99 | 13. | 5 | 71⅝ | 71⅝ | 71⅝ | +⅛ |
| DetEd 9.15s00 | 13. | 18 | 72 | 71¼ | 71¼ | −⅛ |
| EatnCr 8½84 | 8.6 | 20 | 98 11-16 | 98 11-16 | 98 11-16 | +3-16 |
| Ens 10s01 | cv | 19 | 101¾ | 101⅛ | 101¾ | −⅛ |
| Enstar 12¾99 | 14. | 10 | 92½ | 92½ | 92½ | ..... |
| Entex 8⅞01 | 13. | 15 | 71⅞ | 69½ | 69½ | −½ |
| EqutG 9½06 | cv | 34 | 125 | 123¼ | 125 | +2½ |
| Exxon 6s97 | 9.7 | 64 | 62⅜ | 61½ | 61⅝ | −½ |
| Exxon 6½98 | 10. | 40 | 64⅝ | 64¼ | 64¼ | −¼ |
| ExonFn 10½89 | 11. | 5 | 97½ | 97½ | 97½ | ..... |
| ExxP 9s04 | 12. | 7 | 77 | 77 | 77 | +⅝ |
| ExxP 8¼01 | 11. | 1 | 72 | 72 | 72 | −¼ |
| Farah 5s94 | cv | 25 | 85¾ | 85⅝ | 85⅝ | ..... |
| Feddr 5s96 | cv | 5 | 42 | 42 | 42 | +1¼ |
| Finan 10¼90 | 11. | 6 | 90⅛ | 90⅛ | 90⅛ | ..... |
| FinCpA 6s88 | 8.0 | 28 | 75⅛ | 74⅞ | 74⅞ | −¼ |
| FinCpA 11⅞98 | 14. | 20 | 85⅛ | 85 | 85 | −1 |
| FinCp d11½02 | cv | 4 | 141½ | 141½ | 141½ | −1½ |
| FtPenn 5s93 | cv | 30 | 55⅛ | 55 | 55 | −⅛ |
| FleetF 10½07 | 8.3 | 1 | 127 | 127 | 127 | −⅞ |
| Ford 9¼94 | 12. | 52 | 79¾ | 79 | 79 | +½ |
| Ford 14¾85 | 14. | 23 | 104¾ | 104¼ | 104½ | −⅛ |
| FrdC 8⅞90A | 11. | 25 | 84½ | 83⅝ | 84½ | +½ |
| FrdC 8½91 | 10. | 50 | 81 | 80½ | 81 | +2 |
| FrdC 7½91 | 10. | 40 | 75 | 75 | 75 | +1 |
| FrdC 4½96 | cv | 57 | 105½ | 104 | 105½ | +2¾ |
| FrdC 4⅞98 | cv | 36 | 118 | 117½ | 118 | +2½ |
| FrdC 8.7s99 | 12. | 7 | 70¼ | 70¼ | 70¼ | −1¾ |
| FrdC 7⅞93 | 11. | 55 | 74⅛ | 73⅜ | 74⅛ | +1⅛ |
| FrdC 10½94 | 12. | 15 | 88½ | 88 | 88 | ..... |
| FrdC 8.85s85 | 9.2 | 16 | 96⅛ | 95⅝ | 96⅛ | +¼ |
| FrdC 9¾01 | 13. | 4 | 78 | 78 | 78 | +¾ |
| FrdC 8⅝86 | 9.3 | 5 | 93 | 93 | 93 | +¼ |
| FrdC 9⅛01 | 13. | 7 | 73 | 73 | 73 | ..... |
| FrdC 8.1s84 | 8.3 | 7 | 97⅜ | 97⅜ | 97⅜ | ..... |
| FrdC 8¼88 | 9.8 | 5 | 84 | 84 | 84 | +⅜ |
| FrdC 7.85s88 | 9.2 | 45 | 85⅝ | 85½ | 85⅝ | +⅜ |
| FrdC 8⅛88 | 9.7 | 175 | 87½ | 87⅜ | 87½ | +1 |
| FrdC 9s84 | 9.0 | 10 | 99 9-16 | 99 9-16 | 99 9-16 | −1-16 |
| FrdC 8⅞90 | 11. | 52 | 82¾ | 82¼ | 82¾ | +½ |
| FrdC 9⅛85 | 9.6 | 83 | 98½ | 97½ | 98½ | +½ |
| FrdC 9.55s89 | 11. | 18 | 88⅝ | 88⅜ | 88⅝ | +⅞ |
| Fruf 5½94 | cv | 30 | 96 | 96 | 96 | ..... |
| FrufF 7.6s84 | 7.7 | 4 | 98½ | 98½ | 98½ | ..... |
| Fuqua 7s88 | 7.9 | 3 | 88½ | 88½ | 88½ | ..... |
| Fuqua 9½98 | 13. | 3 | 73⅜ | 72¾ | 72¾ | −⅝ |
| GTE 10½07 | cv | 75 | 115½ | 115¼ | 115⅜ | −⅛ |
| Gelco 14⅝99 | 14. | 28 | 101 | 100¼ | 101 | +¾ |
| GnATr 5¾99 | cv | 11 | 66¾ | 66¾ | 66¾ | −¾ |
| GCinem 10s08 | 9.2 | 130 | 108½ | 108½ | 108½ | +1½ |
| GnEl 7½96 | 10. | 34 | 73¼ | 72⅝ | 73¼ | ..... |
| GnEl 8½04 | 11. | 30 | 75⅞ | 75 | 75 | +⅝ |
| GElCr 8¼86 | 8.7 | 27 | 94⅜ | 93⅞ | 94⅜ | +⅝ |
| GElCr 7⅝88 | 8.7 | 16 | 87½ | 87½ | 87½ | −¼ |
| GElCr 9⅛84 | 9.2 | 15 | 99 19-32 | 99 19-32 | 99 19-32 | +1-32 |
| GElCr 9⅜87 | 10. | 63 | 95¼ | 95 | 95 | −½ |
| GElCr 11½90 | 12. | 74 | 99½ | 99¼ | 99½ | +¼ |
| GElCr 11¾05 | 12. | 10 | 98 | 98 | 98 | +1⅝ |
| GHost 7s94 | 11. | 3 | 65⅞ | 65⅞ | 65⅞ | ..... |
| GMills 8⅞95 | 11. | 5 | 78¾ | 78¾ | 78¾ | −1½ |
| GMills zr88s | .. | 4 | 62⅜ | 62¼ | 62¼ | −⅛ |
| GMA 4½85 | 5.0 | 35 | 89½ | 89½ | 89½ | +⅛ |
| GMA 4⅞87 | 6.2 | 44 | 79½ | 79⅛ | 79⅛ | −⅞ |
| GMA 6¼88 | 7.8 | 36 | 81 | 80⅛ | 80½ | ..... |
| GMA 8s93 | 10. | 2 | 76¾ | 76¾ | 76¾ | +¼ |
| GMA 7¾94 | 11. | 40 | 73 | 73 | 73 | +¾ |
| GMA 7⅛92 | 9.8 | 7 | 73 | 73 | 73 | +1 |
| GMA 7.85s98 | 11. | 30 | 69⅝ | 69⅝ | 69⅝ | +⅞ |
| GMA 8⅞99 | 12. | 14 | 75 | 75 | 75 | ..... |
| GMA 8⅝s85 | 9.0 | 10 | 95½ | 95½ | 95½ | +⅛ |
| GMA 8¾s00 | 12. | 5 | 73⅛ | 73⅛ | 73⅛ | −⅛ |
| GMA 8⅛96 | 11. | 5 | 73¼ | 73¼ | 73¼ | +½ |
| GMA 7.35s87 | 8.3 | 10 | 88¼ | 88¼ | 88¼ | −¼ |
| GMA 8s02 | 12. | 29 | 67 | 67 | 67 | ..... |
| GMA 7.3s85 | 7.8 | 20 | 94⅛ | 93¾ | 93¾ | −1⅛ |
| GMA 8⅛06 | 12. | 2 | 67⅜ | 67⅜ | 67⅜ | −1⅜ |
| GMA 8.2s88 | 9.3 | 40 | 88¾ | 88 | 88⅝ | +⅝ |
| GMA 8⅝88 | 9.7 | 5 | 88¾ | 88¾ | 88¾ | ..... |
| GMA 8⅞85 | 9.2 | 18 | 97 | 96¼ | 96⅜ | −⅛ |
| GMA 9s84 | 9.1 | 17 | 99 17-32 | 99 5-16 | 99 5-16 | −3-16 |
| GMA 9⅝89 | 11. | 25 | 90¾ | 90¾ | 90¾ | +¼ |
| GMA 9¾03 | 12. | 85 | 80½ | 79⅛ | 80½ | −⅜ |
| GMA 9⅛89 | 10. | 20 | 89 | 89 | 89 | +½ |
| GMA 11.9s87 | 12. | 10 | 101⅜ | 101⅜ | 101⅜ | ..... |
| GMA 11⅝90 | 12. | 143 | 98⅝ | 98⅛ | 98⅜ | −⅛ |
| GMA 12s05 | 13. | 31 | 95⅛ | 94¼ | 95⅛ | +½ |
| GMA 10⅞87 | 11. | 14 | 99 | 99 | 99 | +⅛ |
| GMA 11¾00 | 13. | 27 | 93⅝ | 93⅝ | 93⅝ | +¼ |
| GMA 11.55s90t | 11. | 20 | 103 | 103 | 103 | +⅜ |
| GMA d6s11 | 12. | 44 | 51⅝ | 51⅜ | 51⅝ | +⅝ |
| GMA 14⅝89 | 14. | 10 | 107½ | 107½ | 107½ | −⅜ |
| GMA 10.10s92t | 10. | 10 | 100 | 99⅞ | 100 | +⅛ |
| GMA 14.40s85 | 14. | 5 | 104⅞ | 104⅞ | 104⅞ | ..... |
| GMA 12⅝85 | 12. | 5 | 102⅝ | 102 | 102 | −⅝ |
| GMA 12s86 | 12. | 5 | 102⅛ | 101½ | 101½ | ..... |
| GMA 11¾89 | 12. | 108 | 99½ | 99½ | 99½ | +⅛ |
| GMA zr12 | .. | 25 | 69⅛ | 69 | 69 | −½ |
| GMA zr15 | .. | 19 | 59½ | 59 | 59½ | −⅝ |
| GM 8.05s85 | 8.3 | 15 | 96½ | 96½ | 96½ | ..... |
| GM 8⅝s05 | 12. | 15 | 73½ | 73 | 73 | −½ |

**Figure 20-5** Sample bond quotations. (Adapted from *The Wall Street Journal*, November 10, 1983. Reprinted by permission of *The Wall Street Journal*, Dow Jones & Company, Inc. 1983. All Rights Reserved.)

Volume is given somewhat differently for bonds than it is for stocks. Bond volume is the dollar amount of trading in *thousands of dollars*. Trading in Chrysler's bond on this day amounted to $21,000.

The final figures show daily price, as stock quotations do. There is one major difference, however, that complicates bond listings. Price is in percentages, not dollars. Chrysler's bond closing price of 75¼ means that it sold for 75.25 percent of its face value, or $752.50 for a $1,000 bond.

Some bonds sell for more than their face value. Look at the Bache bond in the first column, selling for 104 at the close. This bond is selling at a **premium,** or more than its face value. By looking at the bond's interest rate, you can see why: it's 14 percent, much higher than most other bonds, making Bache's bond a more attractive investment than, say, Chrysler's, which pays only 8⅞ percent per year.

## ⌂ LEARNING OBJECTIVES REVISITED

1. *What securities are.*

   Securities are essentially pieces of paper issued by corporations and governments, representing obligations by the issuing organization to provide a stated, or expected, return on the funds invested in them.

2. *The different types of securities that are available, including equity and debt issues and government securities, and the reasons for investing in each.*

   Equity issues represent shares of ownership, so only corporations can issue them. Governments can't issue them because governments belong to all the people, and no individuals can own them. Shares of common and preferred stock are units of ownership of corporations. People buy common stock for income and financial growth, but also so they can be owners of, and exercise indirect control of, a business. People buy preferred stocks for income and because they are safer, as dividends must be paid on them before any can be paid to holders of common stock.

   Corporate debt issues include (1) commercial paper, a corporate IOU used to raise money for short-term needs, which is relatively safe and has a short maturity and high liquidity; and (2) bonds, IOUs used to raise long-term funds. Bonds may be secured with pledges of specific assets or only the full faith and credit of the corporation. They pay annual or semiannual interest and are relatively safe but have long maturities, so the investor's money is tied up for long periods.

   Government securities are issued by federal, state, and municipal governments. The U.S. government issues U.S. savings bonds, U.S. Treasury bills, and U.S. Treasury notes and bonds. They're all safe, since they have the full faith and credit of the government behind them. T bills have short maturities and good yields. The notes and bonds have long maturities and good yields. State and municipal notes and bonds vary as to their safety, depending on their purpose and maturity and the quality of officials involved. Revenue bonds are issued to finance specific projects, while general obligation bonds are for general operations.

3. *How primary and secondary securities markets operate and are regulated.*

Primary markets underwrite a security issue by buying securities from a corporation and then reselling them to individual investors through secondary markets. Secondary markets are organized security exchanges with brokers and intermediaries who buy and sell previously issued securities to interested investors. There are nine of these markets. The largest and oldest is the New York Stock Exchange (NYSE), called the "Big Board." The American Stock Exchange (AMEX) is another respected market, with less stringent listing requirements than the NYSE. The over-the-counter (OTC) market, the second-largest exchange, has an automated quotation system, NASDAQ, which links 3,700 dealers around the country.

The Securities and Exchange Commission (SEC) regulates the securities business for the nation. But it only tries to prevent fraud, illegal sales practices, and violations of investors' trust; it can't protect the individual investor from poor judgment in buying decisions.

4. *Why people buy securities.*

People buy securities for either (1) speculation, hoping to get rich quick by buying cheap stock and seeing its price skyrocket, or (2) investment, hoping for long-run income and growth—with safety.

5. *How to read published data about securities.*

The primary sources of data about stocks are the Dow Jones Industrial Average (DJIA) and the Standard & Poor's 500 Composite Index. When these indexes rise, there's a bull market, which indicates a rising economy; when they fall, there's a bear market, which indicates a poor economy.

## IMPORTANT TERMS

As an extra review of the chapter, try defining the following terms. If you have trouble with any of them, please refer to the page listed.

## ◬ REVIEW QUESTIONS

1. Explain the essential differences between equity and debt issues.
2. What are the differences between common and preferred stock?
3. Distinguish between the par value of a share of stock and its market value.
4. What is the role of a bond indenture?
5. Distinguish among the following U.S. government securities: T bill, U.S. Treasury note, and U.S. Treasury bond.
6. What distinguishes a secondary market from a primary market?
7. Differentiate the NYSE, AMEX, and the OTC market.
8. What are the essential differences between investing and speculating?
9. Why are stock averages used?
10. Translate the following NYSE quotation from the *Wall Street Journal:*

    81¾   50¾   CBS   2.80   3.7   13   426   75¾   75   75   −⅝

## ◬ DISCUSSION QUESTIONS

1. How do you explain the real difference between the events of the two Wednesdays—October 10, 1979, and August 18, 1982? What caused things to happen so differently?
2. What types of companies would issue commercial paper? Why? Why would purchasers buy it?
3. Assume that a relatively well managed city issued a twenty-year revenue bond to build an auditorium as well as a twenty-year general obligation bond. If the yield were essentially the same for both, which would you prefer to buy? Why?
4. Why did a company as prosperous and well organized as Wang Laboratories, Inc. take its securities off the NYSE and list them on the AMEX? Why do you think it issued convertible debenture bonds rather than mortgage bonds?
5. Do you think there will be another stock market crash similar to that of 1929 in your working life? Explain your answer.

## ◬ CASE 20-1   People Express: The Gamblers' Special[12]

In 1981, People Express Airlines, Inc. was launched as the answer to the deregulation of airlines. Its ambitious mission is to compete head-to-head with the big, established airlines, and beat them. Its strategy is to charge low fares and operate at very low costs, with no frills, using general-purpose employees who can sell tickets, clean planes, handle baggage, and serve as flight attendants. Even its pilots handle clerical chores in addition to jockeying the planes from one airport to another, and its executives pour coffee for passengers.

When People Express inaugurated flights from its base in Newark, New Jersey, to Atlantic City, New Jersey, in the summer of 1983, it was nicknamed "the gamblers' special." Many people think its stock should be similarly named. Even with a depressed stock market in May 1983, its stock was selling at 40½, or twenty to thirty-five times its anticipated 1983 earnings. Yet, in 1982, it netted only $1 million on revenues of close to $140 million, or $0.17 per share. And it earned only $2.1 million, or $0.35 per share, in the first quarter of 1983.

With twenty-one used planes serving sixteen cities in the Northeast and Florida, with cheap transatlantic flights now in operation, with a load

factor averaging 80 percent, which is essentially full utilization of its capacity, and with three dozen other used planes being purchased from distressed airlines such as Braniff and Continental, People Express should prosper. But its primary drawing card is its low fares, and these can be raised only a very little without losing customers to the well-established, full-service lines. Therefore, People Express's future may be in expanding its service to more destinations.

### Case Questions

1. Would you have invested in People Express stock in the summer of 1983? Why?
2. How do you explain the very high price-earnings ratio?
3. What do you think is the future for People Express?

## CASE 20-2   The New Stockholders[13]

In December 1983, the NYSE released the results of a survey of new owners of stock purchased on the exchange. It showed that the typical new stockholder was a thirty-four-year-old woman with a stock portfolio worth about $2,200. From 1981 to 1983, over half (57 percent) of all new stock purchasers were women. Also, over 10 million more Americans owned stock in 1983 than had in 1981, and three-fourths of them had never owned stock before. From July 1982 (a month before the bull market began) to June 1983, nearly five million new customers bought shares of stock.

By December 1983, 18 percent of all Americans owned some stock, as opposed to 14 percent in 1981 and 12 percent in 1975.

### Case Questions

1. How do you explain this surge in new stockholders?
2. Could the influx be a cause—or an effect—of the booming economy from the fall of 1982 to the winter of 1983–1984? Explain.
3. Were you one of the new stockholders? If so, why?

# 21

# Risk Management and Insurance

*Everything is sweetened by risk.*
Alexander Smith

*And down in fathoms many went the*
  *captain and the crew;*
*Down went the owners—greedy men whom*
  *hope of gain allured;*
*Oh, dry the starting tear, for they*
  *were heavily insured.*
William S. Gilbert, "Etiquette," in *The "Bab" Ballads*

## Learning Objectives

After studying the material in this chapter, you will understand:

1. What risk and risk management entail.
2. The three fundamental principles of insurance.
3. The different types of private and government insurers.
4. The different kinds of property and liability insurance affecting business.
5. How health insurance provides medical coverage and income maintenance.
6. The different types of life insurance policies that are available.

## In This Chapter

Risk and Its Management
Insurance Fundamentals
Types of Insurance Companies
Types of Insurance

# LLOYD'S OF LONDON

Lloyd's of London isn't an insurance company, but an association of about 250 brokers, who present clients' requests to over 415 privately owned underwriting syndicates. These groups are in turn each composed of 20 to over 1,000 wealthy investors, most of whom aren't professional insurers, who put up $140,000 each. These syndicates and over 23,000 individuals share in Lloyd's' profits and losses.

Lloyd's operates all over the world and is particularly well known for insuring unusual risks, including space satellites. For example, Elizabeth Taylor and Richard Burton aren't known for their responsibility in meeting performance schedules. So when they teamed up to do the play *Private Lives* on Broadway, Lloyd's was the main insurer underwriting their appearance, to the tune of $3.5 million. Lloyd's has also insured the lives of celebrities such as Bing Crosby, Bob Hope, and Frank Sinatra, as well as parts of others' anatomies. It insured Marlene Dietrich's and Betty Grable's legs, tennis star Bjorn Borg's arm, Frank Sinatra's voice, and Jimmy Durante's nose. Elizabeth Taylor's violet eyes were insured for $1 million against damage from heavy makeup during the filming of "Ash Wednesday," for a premium of $2,000 a day.

Historically, Lloyd's has been very profitable. But lately it has suffered some severe losses, many as a result of poor judgment. For example, it lost about $340 million on some $2.4 billion of insurance policies issued against loss from cancellation of computer leases. It assumed that the equipment would retain around 40 percent of its value until the end of the leases—an assumption that turned out to be totally unrealistic in this rapidly expanding field. It also had to pay NBC $40 million when the United States boycotted the 1980 Olympics. In 1981, it had to pay team owners $50 million when major league baseball players went on strike. In late 1982, with its 300-year-old reputation for reliability at stake, Lloyd's faced a nasty scandal that shook the insurance world on both sides of the Atlantic. The scandal involved a former underwriter known as "Goldfinger," who was later acquitted in court. But Lloyd's flexibility, integrity, and business acumen permitted it to bounce back— it's still quite profitable.

Luckily, not every business is hit with misfortunes like Lloyd's $40 million loss from the U.S. boycott of the Olympics or $340 million loss from cancellation of computer leases. But part of the financial security of every company depends on preparing for unexpected disaster to strike. What would a publisher do if several truckloads of its books were buried in volcanic ash? What if a computer company's directors were eliminated en masse in a plane crash? These are some questions answered by the main subject of this chapter: risk and its management.

## RISK AND ITS MANAGEMENT

**Objective 1**

**What risk and risk management entail.**

A business constantly faces potential loss of property or personnel through fire, explosion, windstorm, flood, theft, lawsuits, and death or disability of its key personnel. For example, a physical peril like fire may destroy the property outright, causing direct loss. Or the loss may be indirect: income may be reduced because business is interrupted while a burnt-out plant is being rebuilt. Goods may be stolen, damaged, destroyed, or spoiled in transit, for which the common carrier isn't liable. Improper storage facilities may cause unexpected spoilage. Forgery of warehouse receipts may result in product loss. Banks may either call in or refuse to renew loans. Customers may become insolvent and be unable to pay accounts receivable. And sometimes whole business areas are characterized as high-risk because of weather conditions, crime, fire hazards, or political unrest. Given this rogues' gallery of lurking perils, what's a business to do?

**Risk management** is the process of conserving a firm's earning power and assets by minimizing the financial shocks of such accidental losses. It lets a firm regain its financial balance and operating effectiveness after suffering an unexpected loss. This is done by paying a short-term fixed loss (the premium paid for the insurance) in order to minimize long-term loss from risks.

### Kinds of Risk

There are different kinds of risk, of course. A **pure risk** is uncertainty as to whether there will occur some unpredictable event that can only result in loss or, at best, breaking even. This is insurable risk. For example, when the Hyatt Regency hotel in Kansas City was being built, to speed up construction a design change was made in the skywalks spanning the lobby. Later, stress and vibration caused the walks to collapse, killing 114 persons and injuring 216, resulting in $3 billion in lawsuits.[1]

On the other hand, a **speculative risk** is uncertainty as to whether a voluntarily undertaken activity will result in a gain or a loss. Production risks such as building a plant that turns out to have the wrong capacity or keeping an inventory level that turns out to be too high or too low are speculative risks.

Speculative risk is the name of the game in business. For example, tennis players scoffed when Howard Head risked introducing the outsized Prince racquet in 1976, but now it's a leader in the field. Texas Instruments risked lowering the price of its TI 99/4A to increase sales, but financial losses were so

great that it dropped its line of low-priced computers entirely. Levi Strauss risked selling its jeans through mass merchandisers such as Sears and Penney's, only to have department store chains turn to Lee jeans. A classic example of a speculative risk is the one taken by the Great Wallendas (see FYI on page 562).

As you can see from the previous business examples, some business risks are simply uninsurable. And, as you know, the greatest risk facing any business firm—the ever-present possibility that it will be unprofitable—is uninsurable. Other uninsurable risks are associated with the development of new products, changes in customers' preferences, price fluctuations, and changes in laws.

## Coping with Risk

The main ways for a business to cope with either kind of risk are (1) risk avoidance, (2) risk prevention or loss control, (3) risk assumption, and (4) risk transfer.

*Risk avoidance* is refusing to undertake—or abandoning—a venture in which the risk seems to be too costly. For instance, Lockheed Corporation stopped producing the L-1011 jet after fifteen years of troubled operations and $2.5 billion in losses. Citibank experimented with having depositors of less than $5,000 either pay a fee to see a teller or use an automatic teller machine. When customers rebelled, the project was dropped as too risky.[2]

*Risk prevention*, or loss control, consists of using any of various methods to reduce the probability that a given event will occur. The primary control technique is prevention, including safety and protective procedures. Cancer, for example, strikes around 120,000 people in the work force each year and causes more than $10 billion in lost earnings. Groups like the American Cancer Society are trying to reduce this loss by helping to prevent cancer through improved protective measures.

Most large firms try to control losses by providing first aid offices, driver training, and work safety rules, not to mention security guards used to prevent pilferage, shoplifting, and outright theft.

*Risk assumption* is a procedure whereby financial losses caused by chance events are met through the firm's own financial resources without recourse to professional risk takers. Through **self-insurance,** a firm sets aside a certain amount of its own funds to meet losses that are uncertain in size and frequency, yet large enough to result in financial embarrassment or even insolvency. Generally, more than one method of handling risks is used at the same time. For example, a firm may use self-insurance for all automobile damage, since the amount of potential loss is relatively small and is known (it is the total value of all its cars). Yet the firm would probably use commercial insurance against all liability claims arising from operating the cars negligently, for, in that case, the potential losses are unknown and may be prohibitively great.

*Risk transfer* means shifting the risk to persons or organizations outside the firm who agree to shoulder the risks of others. The best known form of risk transfer is **insurance,** which is the process by which an insurance company agrees, for a fee (a premium), to pay an individual or organization an agreed-upon sum of money for a given loss.

## *FYI*

### The Great Wallendas

Helen Wallenda began urging Karl, her husband, to retire from the high wire in 1970 when he was sixty-five years old. He'd reply: "Look, honey, let me do it as long as the good Lord lets me. He's up there with me." She'd respond: "How will you know when He tells you to stop?" "When He leaves me, I'll know," Karl said. Before stepping out on the wire, the greatest high-wire performer in circus history always put a piece of hard candy into his mouth to prevent nausea and said silently, "God, please . . . ."

Karl was born in 1905 into a German family that had been acrobats and trapeze artists for three generations. At six, he performed in the family show; at eleven, he was

## INSURANCE FUNDAMENTALS

**Objective 2**

**The three fundamental principles of insurance.**

Insurance companies are in business to assume other people's risks, but there are certain principles they must follow in doing so if they are to remain in business themselves. It would be easy to imagine an insurance company refusing to insure Karl Wallenda. That's because insurance is based on certain rules—namely, insurable interest, insurable risk, and the law of large numbers.

### Insurable Interest

According to the principle of **insurable interest,** no one can be insured unless he or she stands to suffer financially or emotionally when a loss occurs. The main reason for this requirement is to permit measurement of the extent of the loss. For example, ownership conveys an insurable interest in property, since its loss by fire, theft, or disaster would mean a loss of assets. Therefore, the

doing stunts in beer halls.

In the early 1920s, Karl met Louis Weitzmann, who taught him to "walk the wire." Karl appeared in an act with Louis in which Karl did a handstand on Louis's shoulders at the center of the wire. This innovative stunt was booked throughout central Europe. Later, Karl formed his own troupe, the Great Wallendas, with his brother Herman and Helen Kris. In 1927, they performed in Havana without a net under the forty-foot-high wire. John Ringling saw the performance and offered Karl a contract with "The Greatest Show on Earth."

The act that established the Wallendas as truly special was the seven-person pyramid, consisting of Karl and Herman, Helen Kris and her younger sister, and three others. Helen married Karl in 1935 and retired from the circus in 1959.

In 1962, tragedy struck the act when one of the performers let a pole slip and was killed when he toppled thirty-five feet to the arena floor. Of the other performers, Karl's son-in-law was killed; an adopted son suffered a spinal injury that paralyzed him for life; Karl was hospitalized with a pelvic injury, a double hernia, and bruised ribs; and Herman sustained a gash. The following morning, Karl, running a high fever and hurting all over, asked to be discharged from the hospital. "I feel like a dead man on the ground," he told Helen. "The wire is my life."

In middle age, Karl became increasingly popular as a "skywalker," walking across cables between buildings and across sports stadiums. At age sixty-five, he did a 1,000-foot walk at a height of over 700 feet above Tallulah Gorge in Georgia. About 30,000 spectators were present to see the sensational twenty-minute walk.

In March 1978, Karl and three protégés, including his seventeen-year-old granddaughter, Rietta, went to Puerto Rico to join the Pan-American circus. Karl was asked to do a skywalk as a promotional stunt. The walk was particularly hazardous because the wire would be strung 100 feet above the street where gusts of wind from the sea couldn't be measured. Helen tried to dissuade Karl from doing it, but he insisted. About midway across the wire, the wind ballooned his shirt and whipped his trousers. Karl attempted to take a sitting position, but his feet slipped from the wire, and he plummeted to the street. After fifty-seven years on the high wire, the greatest of the Great Wallendas was dead at age seventy-three, and with him went the most tangled legend of romance and tragedy the circus had known. The three protégés did the matinee that day to carry out Karl's tradition that the show must go on.

Sources: Based on Joseph P. Blank, "The Wire Is My Life," *Reader's Digest*, July 1979, pp. 89–94; "The Wallendas Still on the Wire, Rick and Rietta," *Newsweek*, August 27, 1979, p. 9; and others.

owner or mortgage holder may insure property to the extent of his or her investment in it. Also, business partners can insure each other's lives because the death of one partner may cause the firm to fail and the remaining partners to lose financially.

### Insurable Risk

As we mentioned before, not every risk is insurable. There are generally four conditions that qualify something as an **insurable risk:**

1. The potential losses must be reasonably predictable, in accordance with the law of large numbers (described next). A catastrophic loss, as from nuclear war or riot, can't be insured against because it's so devastating and unpredictable.
2. The risk should be spread over a broad geographic area. It would be unwise, for instance, to insure just San Francisco businesses against earthquake losses, for a single earthquake might be catastrophic for

the insurer. As a result, earthquake coverage applies throughout California, as does sinkhole coverage in Florida.

3. The insurer should be able to determine when a loss has occurred and what its extent is.
4. The loss must be accidental, or beyond the insured's control. If the owner of a business burns down one of his or her own plants, the insurance company certainly won't pay for the loss.

### The Law of Large Numbers

The **law of large numbers** works to the advantage of both insurer and insured, reducing the risk for the former and the cost for the latter. Basically the same as the law of averages, it states that as the number of individuals covered increases, the chance of something unpleasant unexpectedly happening to any one of them decreases. Insurance companies use mortality tables like Table 21-1 to predict the likelihood of deaths, fires, automobile accidents, and so on in the overall population. From these predictions, they know what premiums are needed to cover probable losses.

For example, if an uninsured $60,000 house burns, the owner loses $60,000. But if each homeowner in a population of 5,000 houses worth around $60,000 has paid $600 a year into an insurance pool, the loss to the person whose house burns is only $600, the same as the cost to everyone else (see Figure 21-1). And the cost to the insurance company is nil, since it's been collecting $3,000,000 a year in premiums—enough to cover the cost of fifty houses, or 1 percent of the insured population, which is probably more than can be expected to burn down.

## TYPES OF INSURANCE COMPANIES

Both private insurers and government agencies sell insurance.

### Private Insurers

**Objective 3**

**The different types of private and government insurers.**

Private insurers are primarily (1) **stock companies,** which are corporations owned by stockholders and operated for their profit; or (2) **mutual companies,** which are corporations owned by policyholders (the insured), for whom no profit is intended apart from premiums or possibly assessments. Most of the funds left over after claims are paid are funneled back as dividends or premium rebates. Aetna Life & Casualty is an example of a stock company, and Mutual of Omaha is an example of a mutual company. Over 90 percent of all insurance in the United States is sold by either stock or mutual insurance companies.

Two other types of insurers are fraternal societies and associations of insurers. **Fraternal societies** are groups formed for social and benevolent purposes that also offer low-cost insurance to their members. The two largest of these societies are the Aid Association for Lutherans (AAL) and the Lutheran Brotherhood. Almost a third of all Lutherans—some 2.3 million—are insured with these two fraternals.[3] Rates are kept low by the large market, the very low mortality rate, and the lowest policy lapse rate in the industry.

**TABLE 21-1  Mortality table for males and females through age fifty.***

| Age | Male Deaths per 1,000 | Expectation of Life (years) | Female Deaths per 1,000 | Expectation of Life (years) |
|---|---|---|---|---|
| 0 | 13.37 | 70.2 | 10.58 | 77.8 |
| 1 | 1.01 | 70.1 | 0.71 | 77.6 |
| 2 | 0.75 | 69.2 | 0.56 | 76.7 |
| 3 | 0.59 | 68.3 | 0.46 | 75.7 |
| 4 | 0.49 | 67.3 | 0.38 | 74.8 |
| 5 | 0.43 | 66.3 | 0.33 | 73.8 |
| 6 | 0.40 | 65.4 | 0.29 | 72.8 |
| 7 | 0.37 | 64.4 | 0.26 | 71.8 |
| 8 | 0.33 | 63.4 | 0.23 | 70.8 |
| 9 | 0.28 | 62.4 | 0.21 | 69.9 |
| 10 | 0.24 | 61.5 | 0.19 | 68.9 |
| 11 | 0.24 | 60.5 | 0.18 | 67.9 |
| 12 | 0.33 | 59.5 | 0.21 | 66.9 |
| 13 | 0.51 | 58.5 | 0.26 | 65.9 |
| 14 | 0.77 | 57.5 | 0.34 | 64.9 |
| 15 | 1.06 | 56.6 | 0.44 | 64.0 |
| 16 | 1.33 | 55.6 | 0.52 | 63.0 |
| 17 | 1.55 | 54.7 | 0.58 | 62.0 |
| 18 | 1.69 | 53.8 | 0.61 | 61.1 |
| 19 | 1.78 | 52.9 | 0.61 | 60.1 |
| 20 | 1.85 | 52.0 | 0.61 | 59.1 |
| 21 | 1.93 | 51.1 | 0.61 | 58.2 |
| 22 | 1.96 | 50.2 | 0.61 | 57.2 |
| 23 | 1.93 | 49.3 | 0.61 | 56.2 |
| 24 | 1.87 | 48.4 | 0.62 | 55.3 |
| 25 | 1.79 | 47.5 | 0.62 | 54.3 |
| 26 | 1.72 | 46.5 | 0.62 | 53.3 |
| 27 | 1.66 | 45.5 | 0.62 | 52.4 |
| 28 | 1.62 | 44.7 | 0.64 | 51.4 |
| 29 | 1.61 | 43.8 | 0.66 | 50.4 |
| 30 | 1.60 | 42.8 | 0.69 | 49.5 |
| 31 | 1.60 | 41.9 | 0.72 | 48.5 |
| 32 | 1.63 | 41.0 | 0.76 | 47.5 |
| 33 | 1.68 | 40.0 | 0.80 | 46.6 |
| 34 | 1.76 | 39.1 | 0.85 | 45.6 |
| 35 | 1.86 | 38.2 | 0.90 | 44.6 |
| 36 | 1.99 | 37.2 | 0.98 | 43.7 |
| 37 | 2.13 | 36.3 | 1.07 | 42.7 |
| 38 | 2.29 | 35.4 | 1.19 | 41.8 |
| 39 | 2.47 | 34.5 | 1.33 | 40.8 |
| 40 | 2.68 | 33.6 | 1.49 | 39.9 |
| 41 | 2.93 | 32.6 | 1.66 | 38.9 |
| 42 | 3.22 | 31.7 | 1.85 | 38.0 |
| 43 | 3.58 | 30.8 | 2.06 | 37.1 |
| 44 | 3.99 | 29.9 | 2.28 | 36.1 |
| 45 | 4.44 | 29.1 | 2.52 | 35.2 |
| 46 | 4.93 | 28.2 | 2.78 | 34.3 |
| 47 | 5.48 | 27.3 | 3.06 | 33.4 |
| 48 | 6.08 | 26.5 | 3.34 | 32.5 |
| 49 | 6.73 | 25.6 | 3.65 | 31.6 |
| 50 | 7.46 | 24.8 | 3.98 | 30.7 |

*The numbers in this table are for white males and females. For blacks and others, the number of expected deaths per 1,000 is somewhat higher, and the expectation of life is somewhat lower.

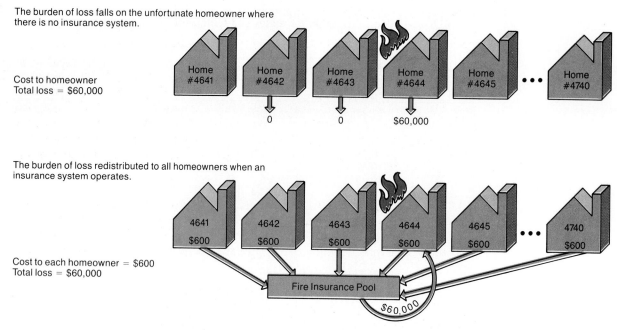

The burden of loss falls on the unfortunate homeowner where there is no insurance system.

Cost to homeowner
Total loss = $60,000

The burden of loss redistributed to all homeowners when an insurance system operates.

Cost to each homeowner = $600
Total loss = $60,000

**Figure 21-1** Insurance redistributes the costs of losses. [Adapted from Mark S. Dorfman, *Introduction to Insurance* (Englewood Cliffs, N.J.: Prentice-Hall, 1978), p. 5. © 1978 Prentice-Hall, Inc.]

Since insurance is based on the law of large numbers, when the numbers are small and the chances of loss enormous, one insurer can't handle all the risk alone. Therefore, a group of insurers like Lloyd's of London may form an association for that purpose. Or a corporation like General Re will specialize in assuming the risks originally underwritten by other insurers.

## Government Insurers

The principal types of government insurance coverage are Social Security, workers' compensation, and unemployment compensation.

▲ **Social Security** Social Security provides insurance protection to workers and their families. Coverage under Old Age, Survivors, Disability, and Health Insurance comes simply from being part of the labor market, and most occupations are covered. However, military personnel, police, and railroad employees are covered under other programs. Over 90 percent of the gainfully employed in the United States are covered under OASDHI.

The insured employee's *retirement benefit* is effective at age sixty-five. However, employees can elect to retire at age sixty-two at a reduced benefit. The spouse of the retiree is entitled to a benefit of 50 percent if he or she is sixty-five or over or if there is a dependent child under age eighteen. The maximum benefit that can be paid to an individual and dependents or survivors is related to the insured employee's average monthly earnings.

Individual employees are also eligible for cash *disability benefits*, which continue as long as the disability exists. Monthly benefits are also payable to their dependents.

▲ **Workers' Compensation** Although not paid by the government in most states, **workers' compensation** is required by law. All employers must provide medical and income benefits to employees injured or disabled on the job as well as income to survivors of employees whose death is job-related, regardless of fault. Medical benefits provide unlimited medical and hospital care, and the injured worker is also paid cash income benefits during temporary or permanent total disability. In most states, employers may insure with a private insurer or qualify as self-insurers; the other states have workers' compensation funds; some states have both. Special maintenance benefits to encourage disabled workers to engage in a rehabilitation program are available and often required.

▲ **Unemployment Compensation** Each state creates and administers its own **unemployment compensation** program which provides weekly income benefits to unemployed workers. The firm bears the burden of the risk by means of premiums. However, management can reduce its cost by stabilizing its em-

## Stability.

A corporation like Gen Re will specialize in assuming the risks originally underwritten by other insurers.

ployment and preventing payment of unjustified benefits. Certain occupations, such as agriculture, domestic service, and casual labor, are excluded, as well as the self-employed.

The amount of the weekly benefit payment is usually about half to two-thirds of the worker's full-time weekly pay. A waiting period for eligibility, typically one week, is generally prescribed. The maximum number of weeks benefits can be paid ranges from twenty to thirty-six but may be (and often has been) extended by Congress during severe recessions.

## TYPES OF INSURANCE

**Objective 4**

**The different kinds of property and liability insurance affecting business.**

Many types of insurance are needed by both business firms and individuals. For purposes of discussion, they can be classified as either property and liability or personal. Personal insurance, in turn, can be classified as either life or health. Figure 21-2 summarizes the types of insurance provided by the private insurance system.

### Property and Liability Insurance

**Property and liability insurance** provides protection against loss of, or damage to, property itself and against any liability caused by owning the property. A **property loss** is a financial loss resulting from fire, theft, vandalism, or other

**Figure 21-2** Branches of the private insurance system.

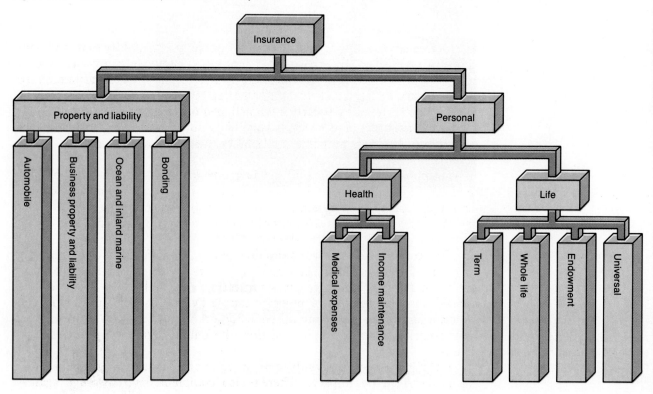

Property insurance provides protection against storm damage.

destructive damage to personal or business property. A **liability loss** is a financial loss suffered when a person's or business's property causes damage or injury to another person. Examples would be injury or death of another caused by your automobile, shock to a customer caused by a product you sold, or a broken arm suffered by someone who slipped on your icy doorstep.

The usual types of property and liability insurance affecting businesses are automobile, business property and liability, marine, and bonding.

▲ **Automobile Insurance** A major source of liability risk for a business or family is the automobile. It's also a major property risk because it can be damaged, destroyed, or stolen. Further, it's a major personal risk because its use may cause the death or injury of a key executive, client, guest, or family member.

One can buy a personal automobile policy, which combines liability insurance, health insurance, and property insurance in one policy. The part providing *liability coverage* gives protection against liability for injury or damage to other persons or property caused by the insured, an employee, a client, a family member, and others while driving the insured's car—if they have permission to do so. In addition, the liability coverage provides legal defense.

*Collision coverage* pays the cost of repair or replacement if the insured's car is damaged by impact. There's also *comprehensive coverage* against

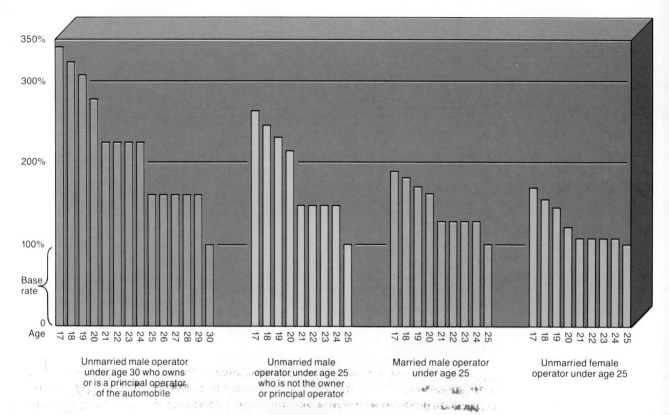

**Figure 21-3** Rating surcharges on young drivers. [Adapted from Emmett J. Vaughn, *Fundamentals of Risk and Insurance*, 3rd ed. (New York: John Wiley & Sons, 1982), p. 505. © 1982 John Wiley & Sons, Inc. Reprinted by permission of John Wiley & Sons, Inc.]

damage to the covered automobile caused by a host of perils other than collision, for example, theft, explosion, earthquake, windstorm, hail, flood, and fire.

*Medical payments coverage,* a form of health insurance, pays the insured for reasonable and necessary medical expenses incurred as the result of an accident.

*Uninsured motorist coverage* will pay the insured or a member of his or her family if another driver is legally liable to the insured for bodily injury caused by an automobile accident but has no liability insurance and cannot pay or is a hit-and-run driver and cannot be found.

In some twenty-five states, there are **no-fault laws,** which limit the insured's right to sue or be sued. Such laws usually provide a minimum amount of loss that must be reached before one party can sue another party in connection with loss covered by automobile insurance. The purpose of the laws is to limit litigation to large losses. As you might imagine, no-fault is vigorously opposed by trial lawyers.

Rates for automobile insurance are usually based on factors such as age, sex, marital status, place of residence, and driving record. As shown in Figure 21-3, young unmarried males pay the highest rates, young married males next, and then young unmarried females.

Do you think these rates discriminate against young people, especially males? As you can see from Table 21-2, drivers under age thirty are involved in a disproportionately high number of traffic accidents and fatal accidents. Drivers in that age group made up only 33.7 percent of the U.S. motoring population in 1981, yet they accounted for 50.7 percent of all drivers involved in accidents and 50.3 percent of all drivers in fatal accidents. The highest involvement in fatal accidents was among drivers aged twenty to twenty-four (78 per 100,000 drivers).

Is this discrimination or merely differential costs based on the laws of probability?

Lower rates are provided for young people with good grades and those who have had driver education, as well as for people who don't drink. State Farm, for instance, gives a 10 percent reduction in premium to those with a passing score in a driver education course and also to high school juniors and above with a "B" average the previous period.

**Business Property and Liability Insurance** Since most companies can't withstand huge losses from physical damage to their facilities, lenders (mortgagees) insist on their having insurance—fire insurance, flood insurance where applicable, and title insurance—against these risks, usually on an actual cash value basis, sometimes on a replacement basis.

**TABLE 21-2  Motor vehicle accidents by age of drivers.**

| Age Group | Number of Drivers | % of Total Drivers | % of Drivers, All Accidents | % of Drivers, Fatal Accidents |
|---|---|---|---|---|
| Under 20 | 14,500,000 | 9.8 | 16.0 | 14.6 |
| 20–24 | 17,600,000 | 11.9 | 20.0 | 21.1 |
| 25–29 | 17,800,000 | +12.0 | +14.7 | +14.6 |
| 30–34 | 17,000,000 | 11.5  33.7 | 12.0  50.7 | 12.6  50.3 |
| 35–39 | 14,100,000 | 9.5 | 7.3 | 7.1 |
| 40–44 | 11,800,000 | 8.0 | 6.7 | 7.1 |
| 45–49 | 11,600,000 | 7.8 | 5.3 | 5.2 |
| 50–54 | 11,800,000 | 8.0 | 4.0 | 4.2 |
| 55–59 | 10,200,000 | 6.9 | 4.4 | 3.8 |
| 60–64 | 7,700,000 | 5.2 | 3.3 | 3.4 |
| 65–69 | 6,500,000 | 4.4 | 3.3 | 2.3 |
| 70–74 | 4,400,000 | 3.0 | 1.0 | 1.7 |
| 75 and over | 3,000,000 | 2.0 | 2.0 | 2.3 |
| Total | 148,000,000 | 100.0 | 100.0 | 100.0 |

SOURCE: Adapted by permission from *Insurance Statistics: A Pocket-Size Summary Selected Data Property/ Casualty Insurance, 1983 Edition* (New York: Insurance Information Institute, 1983).

Most basic policies combine property and liability insurance with a small amount of health and hospital insurance for visitors and employees. The coverages take care of the building, other structures, personal property, loss of use, personal liability, and medical payments to others. Some of the perils typically covered are fire, lightning, windstorm, hail, explosion, riot or civil commotion, aircraft, vehicles, smoke, vandalism, theft, sprinkler system malfunction, and glass breakage. As home computers used for business normally aren't covered by such policies, Columbia National General Agency in Columbia, Ohio, introduced a policy in 1983 that covers home computers regardless of their use.[4] The insurer pays the amount of the actual loss sustained and the expenses necessary for the business to resume normal operations when covered damage interrupts the business or stops rental income because the premises are not in rentable condition.

The insured can purchase a **flood insurance** policy from the National Flood Insurance Association if the building is in an area approved for the program. It covers losses that result directly from river, stream, coastal, and lakeshore flooding.

A **title insurance** policy protects the insured against loss caused by a defect in the property's title that existed at the time the policy was issued. If you were to buy a house, you'd take out title insurance to protect yourself in case someone else later claimed to own it.

Special policies protect insured business property against losses from burglary, robbery, and theft. Also covered are losses caused by employee dishonesty, such as embezzlement, inventory shortages, and fraud. Often called *invisible crime*, these situations require special coverage and handling. For example, in 1983, an employee of Cartier, the swank New York jeweler, made off with about $500,000 in gems. Employees in a J. C. Penney store in Lafayette, Indiana, forged store merchandise refund slips with names of people selected at random from the phone book.[5] For this reason, most firms need blanket policies covering staff members and conspiracies with outsiders.

**Public liability insurance** provides for the insurer to pay all sums—up to the policy's legal limits—for which the insured becomes legally liable because of property damage or personal injury. For example, if a passenger gets hurt at an airport's baggage recovery area, the airport's insurer will often pay medical and other expenses. Often, automobiles, aircraft, boats away from premises, workers' compensation, and professional liability are excluded, as they may be covered by separate liability policies.

**Product liability insurance** is designed to protect companies against claims of injury or damages resulting from the use of their products. But even that insurance protection may not be sufficient to cover the claims. For example, Manville Corporation, the largest producer of asbestos in the Western world, filed for voluntary bankruptcy when faced with 52,000 potential lawsuits expected to cost about $2 billion.[6] It now plans to stop producing asbestos.

**Professional liability insurance** provides that the insurer will pay damages due to injury caused by the insured (or any person for whose acts or omissions the insured is legally responsible) in rendering—or failing to render—professional services. It's available for professionals such as physicians and surgeons, accountants, architects, lawyers, real estate brokers, and insurance agents. The policy also provides legal defense against alleged malpractice.

▲ **Marine Insurance** One of the oldest forms of insurance protection is **ocean marine insurance,** which originated with the ancient Greeks and Romans. It provides protection against the perils of the seas—men-of-war, fire, pirates, and all other perils that damage ships and goods afloat. **Inland marine insurance,** an outgrowth of ocean marine insurance, provides protection for all goods in transit.

▲ **Bonding** **Bonding** is a unique form of insurance that is a legitimate part of a business's casualty protection. It represents an agreement among three different parties: (1) the bonding company, (2) the employer, and (3) a third party. The two major types of bonding are fidelity bonding and surety bonding.

With a **fidelity bond,** the bonding company agrees to pay the employer for losses caused by employee dishonesty. Bank employees, cashiers, company treasurers, and others who handle cash in performing their jobs are often bonded. Figure 21-4 shows how this type of bonding operates.

On the basis of money lost by U.S. business, who do you think is Public Enemy Number 1? It could be the white-collar criminal, for the U.S. Chamber of Commerce estimates annual losses from employee theft, kickbacks, and bribes at $40 billion or more.[7] Other estimates range up to $200 billion. In 1981, insurance claims covered only about 10 percent or less of these losses.

**Figure 21-4** How fidelity and surety bonds operate. [Adapted from Mark S. Dorfman, *Introduction to Insurance* (Englewood Cliffs, N.J.: Prentice-Hall, 1978), p. 42. © 1978 Prentice-Hall, Inc.]

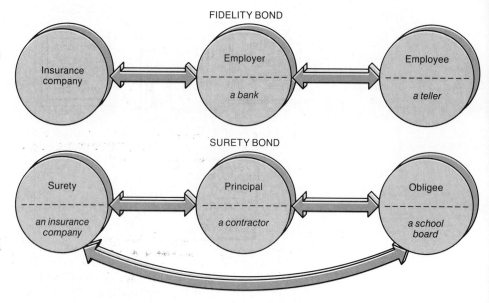

With a **surety bond**, the bonding company (or surety) guarantees the performance of the second party (the principal) to the third party (the obligee). (See Figure 21-4.) Surety bonds are often used for construction projects. For example, contractors are required to post a bond before they are awarded a contract to build a building, a dam, or a bridge. If the work isn't completed satisfactorily or when promised, the obligee—the person or organization that commissioned the job—may obtain compensation from the bonding company. Other firms that must be bonded are exterminators, public warehouses, and handlers of toxic wastes and hazardous materials.

## Health Insurance

**Objective 5**

**How health insurance provides medical coverage and income maintenance.**

Over 1 million workers are out sick every day, and more than 330 million workdays are lost each year because of health-related causes. This problem costs business billions of dollars in lost productivity and medical expenses—in addition to affecting employees' well-being and income. Health insurance provides protection against the risk of medical expenses and loss of income. The major types of health insurance programs are medical expense coverage and income maintenance.

**Medical Expense Coverage** The basic forms of medical expense protection are hospital, surgery, and other medical insurance. *Hospital insurance* covers the insured, as well as the spouse and unmarried children, if any. *Surgical insurance* benefits are usually paid according to a schedule of surgical procedures. The maximum benefit for each type of operation covered is specified. Other *medical insurance* covers all or part of doctors' fees for hospital, office, or home visits—other than for surgical services.

Medical expense benefits may be provided on a valued or a reimbursement basis. When they are provided on a *valued basis*, the insurer agrees to pay a specific amount of money, such as $100 a week, while the insured is hospitalized. The insured may use the money to pay the hospital or to replace lost

income. Coverage on a *reimbursement basis* provides payment for loss, such as hospital expenses, within specified limits and for specified causes. For example, the insured, while hospitalized, could pay a maximum of $100 a day for hospital room and board, submit a bill to the insurer, and be reimbursed.

The rising costs of health care and health insurance have led to increasing pressure for a national health insurance program. For the pros and cons, see the Business Debate on page 576.

**Income Maintenance** In addition to workers' compensation and Social Security programs, there are **disability income contracts,** which provide limited income while the insured is unable to work.

## Life Insurance

**Objective 6**

The different types of life insurance policies that are available.

**Life insurance,** another frequent employee benefit, provides protection against the following contingencies: (1) when a person dies before the end of his or her income-earning years, and (2) when a person lives beyond the income-earning years but has less or no income. In both cases, life insurance can provide a safety net. In the first case, insurance provides dependents with a replacement income, as well as supplying funds for death expenses such as estate taxes, legal fees, and burial costs. In the second case, insurance provides the insured with a replacement income.

Life insurance is based on pooling the risks of many into a group, accumulating a fund from the group members' premiums (which are based on a mortality table like Table 21-1), and paying losses from this fund. **A mortality table** is based on the past experience of a large number of policyholders and is used to predict the number of persons at each age who will die in a given year.

**Individual and Group Policies** Life insurance is bought on either an individual or a group basis. When life insurance is bought by individuals, a medical examination is usually required, premiums tend to be higher, and, of course, they must be paid regularly by the insured. **Group life insurance** is a nearly universal fringe benefit for employees in the United States. Since the

Surety bonds are often used for construction projects such as bridge building.

# Business Debate

## Do We Need a National Health Plan?

Critics of our current health care system have proposed a national health insurance program as a solution. Some approaches that have been suggested are (1) the social insurance approach, (2) incentive-stimulated or mandated private insurance, and (3) catastrophe coverage.

The *social insurance* approach would be government-run and tax-financed, similar to Medicare. A universal system would be funded by payroll taxes and general revenues and administered by a federal agency.

The *incentive-stimulated or mandated private insurance* approach would consist of a comprehensive form of voluntary insurance, with government incentives to induce employers, employees, and individuals to purchase private insurance that would conform to legislated standards. Alternatively, the program could require mandatory health insurance purchased from private insurers.

The *catastrophe coverage* approach would consist of a program designed to pay benefits, through a government-administered and -financed program, only to persons who incurred prohibitively high health care expenses.

Those *in favor of a national health insurance plan* cite as reasons the following deficiencies in our present health care system:

1. *Rapidly rising health care costs.* Costs are skyrocketing, seemingly out of control. The absolute level of health costs and their escalation from year to year are both serious problems.
2. *Ineffective health delivery arrangements.* The supply of health services is insufficient and poorly distributed, making health care inefficient and inaccessible to some people.
3. *Inadequacy of private insurance.* Private health insurance covers about 85 percent of the civilian population under sixty-five but pays only a third of the health expenditures of those covered.
4. *Inadequacy of health care services for residents of rural and inner-city ghetto areas and other poor people.* Although U.S. medical research is among the most advanced in the world, and although many of our hospitals are the best equipped in the world, the United States has been slipping behind other nations in the key indices of national health. Other countries spend a smaller percentage of their gross national product on health services than our 7+ percent, and in return they get better medical care, lower infant mortality rates, longer life expectancy, and fewer people dying during their productive years.

Those who *oppose a national health insurance plan* offer the following reasons:

1. The federal government is already encroaching too much on the health care area.
2. Present government health care programs result in the offices of physicians, dentists, and other professionals being clogged with people who have only minor ailments—or none at all.
3. Overburdening health professionals would result in a deterioration of health care.
4. Such a plan would be horrendously expensive and would place an unbearable financial burden on employed people.
5. National health insurance is an idea whose time is past, at least until inflation and persistent budget deficits are solved.

*What do you think?*

insured acquires it by being a member of a group, such as a firm, labor union, or professional association, an examination is not required. Generally, it's term insurance (see below), and the employer pays at least part of the premium. Group life insurance accounts for almost half of all life insurance in force in the United States.

The basic types of life insurance contracts are term, whole life, endowment, and universal. The contracts vary as to amount of premium paid, protection received, and savings accumulated.

**Term Life Insurance** Term life insurance is protection for only a specified period, with no accumulated savings value at the end of that period. In fact, some people have called it "death insurance," since it's worthless unless the insured dies. If an insurer issues a one-year life insurance policy on the insured's life, it promises to pay the face amount of the policy if the insured dies during the one-year term. The length of the term varies, with policies ranging from those with one-year terms to those that are effective until age sixty-five or seventy. The most common terms are five, ten, fifteen, and twenty years, and there's often an option to renew. The primary advantage of term is its low cost during youth and middle age, when large amounts of insurance are most needed.

**Whole Life Insurance** Whole life insurance provides for payment on the insured's death regardless of when it occurs. It's considered permanent insurance because the policy stays in force as long as the premiums are paid. In whole life policies, the cash value can also provide a policy loan or monthly income payments to the insured who retires.

**Endowment Insurance** Endowment insurance provides for payment of the face amount of the policy in the event of the insured's death during a specified period or for payment of the full face amount at the end of this period if the insured is still living. It may be regarded as a scheduled savings program. Some endowment policies are designed to mature at a specified age—fifty-five, sixty, or sixty-five. Others are written for a designated period—ten, fifteen, or twenty years.

**Universal Life Insurance** A controversial new type of insurance is universal life (see the Business Debate on pages 578 and 579). Universal life insurance is a combination of term insurance and tax-free investment income. A small portion of the first-year premium pays for the term insurance. The remainder of the cash from premiums is invested in medium- and short-term securities rather than the traditional long-term investments of life insurers. The income on this savings component is tax-free. Interest on the cash value is geared to current market rates—11 percent in 1982—but subject to a minimum, such as 4 percent. The insured can add funds to the savings component as long as the face amount of the term insurance is higher than the policy's cash value. The insured may borrow against the cash value and also make withdrawals from it without terminating the contract and without a tax penalty. In effect, the premiums, cash values, and level of protection can be adjusted during the policy term to meet the insured's changing life needs.

# *Business Debate*

## Universal Life Insurance: White Knight or Edsel of the Insurance Business?

To certain insurance authorities, universal life insurance *is a white knight* for the following reasons:

1. Death benefits, including cash value, are considered life insurance proceeds and are excluded from the beneficiary's gross income.
2. The insured does not receive the cash value and thus no income tax is incurred unless funds in excess of premiums are withdrawn.
3. State regulators are willing to accept such innovative new products if they benefit consumers.
4. A few companies have indexed their current invest-

ment rate to the ninety-day U.S. T bill discount rate and have guaranteed that index.
5. Insurers must be able to show competitive rates of return, which universal life policies offer.
6. Universal life insurance is likely to replace most traditional life insurance forms except term insurance. It will probably account for 90 percent of all nonterm life insurance sales by 1990.
7. Several agents who sell universal life report that most calls on prospects have resulted in a sale, especially to high-income clients, including self-employed professionals and firms with ten to fifty employees.

## ⩘ LEARNING OBJECTIVES REVISITED

1. *What risk and risk management entail.*

   Risk is pervasive in any firm and involves property and personnel, marketing, finance, production, and the environment. The purpose of risk management is to conserve a firm's earning power and assets by minimizing the financial effect of accidental losses. Speculative business risks, such as the possibility that a given firm will be unprofitable, are uninsurable. But pure risk is insurable.

2. *The three fundamental principles of insurance.*

   The three fundamentals of insurance are insurable interest, insurable risk, and the law of large numbers. No one can be insured unless there is an insurable interest—that is, unless he or she would suffer financially if a loss occurred. An insurable risk meets four conditions: (1) reasonable predictability of losses, (2) broad geographic distribution of risk, (3) determinability of loss and its extent, and (4) occurrence of an accidental loss

8. The use of computers and computer printouts has induced an increasing number of prospects and clients to come to the agents' offices to conduct business. Clients are kept actively interested in their insurance programs because the cost of every component of the policy is presented in a printout.
9. The key features for consumers are universal life insurance's flexibility and high cash accumulations. Its tax-deferred rates offset the higher, non-tax-deferred interest yielded by other investments.

To other authorities, universal life *is an Edsel,* for the following reasons:

1. Regular insurance agents tend to be hostile toward universal life policies because they believe the policies reduce the agent's income, complicate the sale, and create rate competition that will reduce company loyalty. Agents fear universal life insurance will replace the whole life insurance they have in force and lessen renewal accounts.
2. Agents believe that universal life insurance benefits the company and not them or their clients.
3. Buyers of insurance are asked to reshuffle their unbundled benefits to and fro as their life situation changes, and agents aren't going to do this for free or even for a small service fee.

4. Universal life insurance is a threat to established life insurance companies, whose investment returns may be reduced by higher yields to policyholders.
5. Many companies are afraid that policyholders will cancel existing whole life policies in favor of universal life policies, and their losses could run into the millions.
6. Some major insurance companies are lobbying intensively with the IRS to have favorable tax rulings on universal life insurance changed.
7. The number of insurance agents (about 250,000) could drop dramatically. Agents who pocket first-year commissions of 55 percent or more on whole life sales won't be able to survive if universal life insurance cuts into their market. The commissions on universal life insurance are low—only slightly higher than commissions on term life insurance.
8. Stockbrokers may be more at home selling universal life insurance than life insurance agents are.

*What do you think?*

Sources: Based on John F. Fritz, "The White Knight of the Insurance Business," *Best's Review, Life/Health Insurance Edition* 82 (February 1982):10, 114–16; and Alvin Vogel, "The Edsel of the Insurance Business," Ibid., pp. 11–12.

beyond the insured's control. According to the law of large numbers, as the number of cases increases, the risk of something happening to one of the units decreases.

3. *The different types of private and government insurers.*

Both private insurers and government agencies sell insurance. Private insurers are mostly stock companies or mutual companies. Stock companies are organized to make a profit for themselves and their stockholders, who are the owners. Mutual companies are owned by the policyholders and are run principally for their benefit. Fraternal organizations and associations also insure people.

Government-required insurance includes Social Security, which provides retirement, survivorship, and disability benefits, as well as unemployment compensation. Also, workers' compensation statutes require employers to provide medical and income benefits to employees disabled on the job, as well as income to survivors of employees whose death is job-related.

4. *The different kinds of property and liability insurance affecting business.*

Property and liability insurance provides protection against loss of, or to, property itself and against a liability caused by owning the property. An automobile policy combines liability insurance, health insurance, and property insurance. Collision coverage pays the cost of repair or replacement if the insured's car is damaged by impact. Comprehensive coverage provides protection against damage to the covered automobile caused by perils such as fire, flood, theft, and explosion. Differential rates are based on variables such as age, sex, marital status, place of residence, type of car, and driving record.

Business policies combine property and liability insurance with medical insurance for visitors and employees. Buildings, personal property, loss of use, personal liability, and medical payments to others are covered. A title insurance policy protects the insured against loss caused by a title defect existing at the time the policy was issued.

Public liability insurance pays for claims against the insured for damages due to bodily injury, property damage, or personal injury caused by a specified occurrence. Product liability insurance is designed to protect firms against claims for injury or damage resulting from the use of their products. And professional liability insurance is available to protect professionals against financial loss resulting from their professional actions.

Marine insurance provides protection against perils of the seas—men-of-war, fire, pirates, and other perils that damage the ship and goods, both on the ocean and in transit on rivers, canals, and coastal waters.

In a fidelity bond, the bonding company agrees to pay the employer for losses caused by employees' dishonesty. In a surety bond, the bonding company guarantees the performance of the second party (principal) to the third party (obligee).

5. *How health insurance provides medical coverage and income maintenance.*

The basic forms of medical expense protection provided as employee benefits are hospital, surgery, and medical insurance. Benefits may be provided on a valued or reimbursed basis. Health insurance can also provide disability income while the insured is unable to work.

6. *The different types of life insurance policies that are available.*

Two major contingencies provided for by life insurance are (1) a person's death during the income-earning years and (2) a person's living beyond the income-earning years but having no income. The basic types of life insurance are term, whole life, endowment, and universal life, offered as individual or group policies. Term insurance is protection for a specified period, say five, ten, fifteen, or twenty years. Whole life insurance is permanent, providing for payment upon the insured's death whenever it occurs. Endowment insurance provides for payment of the policy's face value upon the insured's death if the insured dies within a certain period, or at the end of that period if the insured is still living. Universal life insurance is a combination of term insurance and tax-free investment income.

# ⬛ IMPORTANT TERMS

As an extra review of the chapter, try defining the following terms. If you have trouble with any of them, refer to the page listed.

risk management *560*
pure risk *560*
speculative risk *560*
self-insurance *561*
insurance *561*
insurable interest *562*
insurable risk *563*
law of large numbers *564*
stock companies *564*
mutual companies *564*
fraternal societies *564*
workers' compensation *567*
unemployment
  compensation *567*
property and liability
  insurance *568*
property loss *568*
liability loss *569*
no-fault laws *570*
flood insurance *572*

title insurance *572*
public liability insurance *572*
product liability insurance *572*
professional liability
  insurance *572*
ocean marine insurance *573*
inland marine insurance *573*
bonding *573*
fidelity bond *573*
surety bond *574*
health insurance *574*
disability income contracts *575*
life insurance *575*
mortality table *575*
group life insurance *575*
term life insurance *577*
whole life insurance *577*
endowment insurance *577*
universal life insurance *577*

# ⬛ REVIEW QUESTIONS

1. Distinguish between the two types of risk and discuss their insurability.
2. How does a business cope with risk?
3. What are the three fundamental principles of insurance? Explain each.
4. What are the major types of private insurance companies?
5. How does the government provide insurance?
6. Describe the major automobile insurance coverages.
7. Describe the principal coverages of the basic business owner's liability policy.
8. Describe the principal coverages of health insurance.
9. What are the major contingencies for which life insurance provides protection?
10. Describe the basic life insurance contracts.

# ⬛ DISCUSSION QUESTIONS

1. A speaker on insurance stated: "All business risks are insurable. There is no risk against which some insurer will not protect the insured." Do you agree with this statement? Why or why not?
2. How did the principles of insurance operate after the eruptions of the Mount St. Helens volcano?

3. Should the function of risk management be performed in a small firm? Why or why not?

4. Do you think there's a case for a national health plan? Explain.

5. Is the need for liability insurance increasing or decreasing? Why?

6. How do you appraise the future of universal life insurance?

7. What kind of risk is involved when the space shuttle flies?

8. What if an atomic bomb were accidentally launched by some country, and it exploded over New York City? Would any survivors or their heirs be able to collect insurance? Why or why not?

## ⬧ CASE 21-1  Sotheby's and the Case of the Missing Diamond

Sotheby's is one of the oldest and most respected auction galleries in the world. Headquartered in London, it has branch galleries in various cities, including New York. A major theft from an auction house is one of the worst things that can happen to it, for it undermines the trust placed in it by owners of the valuable artifacts it handles. Therefore, imagine the consternation at Sotheby's New York gallery when a 9.58-carat, nearly flawless, rare pink diamond came up missing in early 1983. The gem, owned by a group of Japanese businessmen, was estimated to be worth more than half a million dollars.

What happened? No one seems to know. In addition to the usual armed guards, the diamond had been protected by video cameras that snapped a picture of it every ten seconds. Nevertheless, when a potential customer asked to examine it more closely the day before the auction, a cheaper diamond, apparently coated with pink nail polish, was found in its place. The FBI believes the switch was made when a "few very special clients" had briefly examined it. According to one FBI spokesman, "It was a very special job."

### Case Questions

1. What kind of risk was involved?
2. Does the theft meet the criteria of insurability? Why or why not?
3. What kind of insurance company would cover such a loss?

## ⬧ CASE 21-2  Fixed-Fee Standards for Medicare

There are large variations in what hospitals in different regions of the United States—and even various hospitals in the same area—charge for treating Medicare patients with the same illness. For instance, in 1982, the Department of Health and Human Services (HHS) paid anywhere from $1,500 to $9,000 for treatment of Medicare patients' heart attacks.[8] The reason for the discrepancy was that Medicare paid whatever the hospitals charged. And the hospitals charged for the tests, treatments, and number of days in the hospital that the doctors prescribed.

In an effort to bring down such costs, HHS tried an experiment in New Jersey whereby hospitals were paid a fixed amount for each patient depending on which of 467 standard diagnoses the

doctor came up with. That payment didn't vary, whether the patient stayed three days or three weeks. The hospitals stood to gain if they could treat the patient for less than the fixed fee, since they could keep the difference as profit.

In late 1982, HHS termed the New Jersey experiment a success and said it intended to expand the system nationwide for the almost 30 million elderly and disabled Medicare recipients. It estimated that the $56 billion annual Medicare cost would rise to $110 billion by 1987 if something drastic weren't done to economize.

Many hospitals and doctors oppose the new program because it would tend to weaken the doctor-patient and the doctor-hospital relationship. Also, it might tempt some hospitals to specialize

in higher-priced diagnoses, as the others might be unprofitable.  A hospital would have to accept the set fee as payment in full in order to participate in Medicare.

### Case Questions

1. Do you think this system would provide adequate incentives for hospitals to economize?  Explain.
2. Would it tend to lower patient care standards?  Why?
3. What alternatives do you suggest for lowering health care costs?

# DIGGING DEEPER

## Careers in Finance, Insurance, and Real Estate

Financing, a basic business function, is crucial to the success of any size or type of business. People interested in this field will find great challenges and good employment prospects, since there are career opportunities in small businesses, giant multinational firms, and a wide variety of financial institutions. Also, real estate—the one irreplaceable commodity—tends to increase in price over time as it becomes scarce. Its sale and the sale of insurance are good sources of jobs.

### What Finance Jobs Require

Those engaged in finance deal not only with numbers but also with human relations and contacts. Business services are expected to grow rapidly into the 1990s and beyond, and financial services are expected to grow faster than services as a whole, with employment in this career area increasing 30 percent or more. The fastest growth is expected in banks and credit agencies. Banking and consumer credit are service businesses, and they require individuals who are willing to render personal service. Jobs will be available in four major groups: (1) banking, (2) consumer credit, (3) corporate finance, and (4) securities.

### Banking

Generally, the college graduate enters a bank as a *trainee*. After completing a training program, the employee becomes a *bank officer* (see details in Table VI-1).

Many large banks, with accounts located throughout the world, employ *international bank officers*, who are responsible for maintaining the balance of those accounts and determining the bank's foreign exchange position. They also determine at what price currency can be purchased or sold and sell foreign exchange drafts.

There are several levels of *managers* in banks. The job description of bank *operations manager* is found in Table VI-1. Operations, the largest department, is primarily composed of cler-

ical employees such as tellers, bookkeepers, data-processing operators, and customer service representatives.

Career opportunities exist with the Federal Reserve banks and their branches. Also, there are *bank examiners* who conduct internal audits of banks and their branches.

### Consumer Credit

Consumer credit is a rapidly growing area that has bountiful job opportunities. Most forms of consumer credit are classified as either (1) noninstallment credit, which involves a bill that is paid in one payment, or (2) installment credit, which involves bills that are paid in two or more installments. Most job opportunities are related to the latter type of credit. Consumer finance and sales finance companies are typical employers. *Consumer credit counselors* interview customers to gather credit information, explain to customers arrangements for making payments and complete supporting papers. A *credit officer* makes the decision to extend credit. Individuals are employed in *collections* to monitor payments. *Credit managers* may be in charge of (1) credit departments of stores, (2) credit unions, (3) the loan department of a savings and loan association, (4) the consumer loan department of a bank, or (5) consumer or sales finance companies. The job of credit manager is described in Table VI-1.

### Corporate Finance

Corporate finance is another significant source of employment possibilities. The chief financial executive is usually called the *vice-president of finance*. This executive participates with other key executives in developing company policies and implementing financial policies within the business. The trend is for corporations to hire professional financial managers who have moved laterally from one position in financial management to another in a number of industries. The

584

vice-president, the treasurer, and the controller are important in implementing effective financial management. The *treasurer* acquires funds and administers and protects them. The *controller* manages accounting and other information systems, conducts financial planning, and complies with the requirements of tax and regulatory agencies.

The responsibilities of a *financial analyst* include analyzing overall financial operations, policies, or problems of the firm and preparing reports making specific recommendations to its management. Often this position is filled by someone with an MBA.

Another area experiencing a demand for personnel is *financial public relations.* Responsibilities include financial publicity, stockholder correspondence, preparation of financial reports, planning annual stockholders' meetings, and working with security analysts.

## Securities

The securities industry is involved in buying and selling stocks, bonds, or shares in mutual funds. Four basic functional areas are sales, trading, underwriting, and research.

Securities salespersons are called *registered representatives* or *stockbrokers*, and both individual investors and large institutions work through them. This job is described in Table VI-1. *Investment counselors* work for themselves, alone or in groups. They are also called money managers or financial planners.

*Floor brokers* spend their day on the trading floor of the New York or American Stock Exchange, filling their own investment firm's buy and sell orders and developing an inventory of particular securities. They specialize by type of security. Some traders deal in commodity futures at the Chicago Board of Trade.

*Investment bankers* are underwriters; they underwrite, or finance, the sale of a corporation's securities to the public by purchasing the securities and then selling them on the market. Only top-level professionals are employed as investment bankers.

*Securities research and analysis* is important in the sale, trading, and underwriting of securities. Analysts provide investment advice. Most of them specialize by industry.

## What Insurance Jobs Require

A variety of career opportunities are available in the insurance industry, which is growing in importance because of our increasing population. In addition to dealing with sales, investment, underwriting, and claims, insurers are now becoming involved with rehabilitating the injured, product safety, industrial hygiene, accident prevention, and consumer education. More than half of all insurance industry employees hold professional, managerial, or technical jobs.

Positions unique to this industry are *actuaries*, *agents* and *brokers*, *field representatives*, *underwriters*, *claims examiners and adjusters*, and risk managers. Most of these jobs are described in Table VI-1. A *risk manager* is a loss prevention and insurance specialist, usually employed by a firm outside the insurance industry. Table VI-2 shows some specific career opportunities in the life and health insurance industries and their minimum education and training requirements. Property and liability underwriters are usually located in regional offices in major metropolitan areas. Life underwriters have offices in a few large areas such as New York, Chicago, Philadelphia, Hartford (Connecticut), Dallas, and San Francisco.

## What Real Estate Jobs Require

Even though real estate was hard hit by recession and high mortgage interest rates in the early 1980s, the field has fine potential. It should grow in importance with increases in population and in the number of residence, commercial, and industrial properties.

The job titles of *real estate agent* and *broker* are covered in Table VI-1.

**TABLE VI-1   Selected careers in finance, insurance, and real estate.**

| Job Title | Job Description | Education and Training | Salaries ( Beginner / Experienced ) | Outlook to 1990 |
|---|---|---|---|---|
| Bank clerks | Sort checks, total debit and credit slips, prepare monthly statements for depositors, and use office machines. | High school diploma. Associate degree. | $6,750–$8,300 | Employment is expected to grow faster than the average for all occupations. |
| Bank tellers | Cash checks and process deposits or withdrawals.  In larger banks, may sell savings bonds or accept customers' payments for utilities.  May keep records for customer loans. | High school diploma. Associate degree. | $6,750–$8,300 <br><br> $8,850–$11,950 | Employment is expected to grow faster than the average for all occupations. |
| Collection workers | Keep delinquent and bad debts to a minimum.  Persuade people to pay their unpaid bills.  May arrange new payment schedules, advise customers with financial problems, and repossess automobiles and furniture not paid for. | High school diploma. Associate degree. | $9,000 <br> $12,000–$15,000 | Employment is expected to grow about as fast as the average for all occupations. |
| Bank officers and managers | Must have broad knowledge of business activities. | College degree is usually required for management trainees. These positions are also filled by promoting outstanding bank clerks or tellers. | $19,100 <br><br> $46,000–$61,000 at banks with at least $10,000,000 in deposits | Employment is expected to grow faster than the average for all occupations. |
| President | Directs total bank operations. | | | |
| Vice-presidents | Act as general managers or are in charge of bank departments. | | | |
| Controller | Is responsible for all bank property. | | | |
| Loan officers | Evaluate the credit and collateral of individuals and businesses applying for loans. | | | |
| Trust officers | Must understand each account before funds are invested. | | | |

**TABLE VI-1  Selected careers in finance, insurance, and real estate.**—*continued*

| Job Title | Job Description | Education and Training | Salaries (Beginner Experienced) | Outlook to 1990 |
|---|---|---|---|---|
| Operations managers | Plan, coordinate, and control the workflow, update systems and structure for adminis-trative efficiency. | | $22,800–$34,000 | |
| Credit managers | In extending commer-cial credit, analyze detailed financial re-ports submitted by applicants, interview company representa-tives, review credit agency reports to de-termine the firm's record in paying debts.  In extending consumer credit to individuals, conduct personal interviews and review credit bu-reau and bank reports that provide informa-tion about applicants. | College degree is be-coming increasingly important for entry-level jobs.  Newly hired workers usually begin as management trainees. | $19,100<br><br>$22,000–$28,000 | Employment is ex-pected to grow more slowly than the aver-age for all occupa-tions. |
| Securities sales workers | Explain the meanings of stock market terms and trading practices, offer financial coun-seling, devise an indi-vidual financial port-folio for the client, and offer advice in the purchase or sale of a particular secu-rity.  Relay orders through the firm's office to the floor of securities exchange or over-the-counter mar-ket.  May specialize in certain kinds of securities. | A college degree is becoming increasingly important because these individuals must be well in-formed about eco-nomic conditions and trends. | $16,160<br><br>For serving individual investors, $40,000; for serving institutional accounts, $88,000 | The number is ex-pected to grow faster than the average for all occupations.  The demand fluctuates as the economy expands and contracts. |
| Actuaries | Design insurance and pension plans and make sure that they are maintained on a sound financial basis. Assemble and analyze statistics to calculate probabilities of death, sickness, injury, disa-bility, and other haz-ards.  Determine the expected insured loss. | Bachelor's degree with a major in mathematics or sta-tistics, or a degree in actuarial science. Examinations are of-fered by professional actuarial societies. | $13,000, or $17,000 if a special training course has been com-pleted<br><br>$21,000–$52,000 | Employment is ex-pected to grow faster than the average for all occupations. |

**TABLE VI-1  Selected careers in finance, insurance, and real estate.**—*continued*

| Job Title | Job Description | Education and Training | Salaries ( Beginner Experienced ) | Outlook to 1990 |
|---|---|---|---|---|
| Insurance agents and brokers | Help select the right policy for the insured's needs. Sell policies that provide financial protection against expected losses. Plan for the financial security of individuals, families, and businesses. Advise about insurance protection and help policyholders obtain settlements of insurance claims. | Many insurers prefer college graduates. Newly hired workers usually have at least a high school diploma or associate degree, potential or proven sales ability, or a record of success in other types of work. | $14,400–$16,200  $22,000–$40,000; some over $100,000 | Employment is expected to grow about as fast as the average for all occupations. Because of group and mail sales, employment may not keep pace with the rising level of insurance sales. |
| Claims representatives | Investigate claims, negotiate settlements with policyholders, and authorize payments. Some work with all lines of insurance; others specialize in claims from fire damage, automobile damage, workers' compensation loss, and so forth. | A growing number of companies prefer college graduates. | $16,900–$19,100  For senior adjusters, $22,000 | Employment is expected to grow faster than the average for all occupations. |
| Underwriters | Appraise and select risks that their companies will insure. Analyze information in insurance applications, reports from loss consultants, medical reports, and actuarial studies. May outline the terms of the contract. Frequently correspond about policy cancellations. Usually specialize in one category of insurance; e.g., life, health, or property and liability. | Most large companies seek college graduates who have a degree in liberal arts or business administration. Continuing education is necessary for advancement. | $17,000  $25,000 | Employment is expected to rise about as fast as the average for all occupations. |

**TABLE VI-1  Selected careers in finance, insurance, and real estate.**—*Continued*

| Job Title | Job Description | Education and Training | Salaries (Beginner Experienced) | Outlook to 1990 |
|---|---|---|---|---|
| Real estate agents and brokers | Should have a thorough knowledge of the housing market in their community. Must know which neighborhoods will suit their clients' lifestyles and budgets, local zoning and tax laws, and where to obtain financing for the purchases. Act as intermediary between buyer and seller. | Many large realty firms seek college graduates. | Agents' and brokers' median, $14,700–$29,000 | Employment is expected to grow faster than the average for all occupations. |

SOURCES: U.S. Department of Labor, *Occupational Outlook Handbook, 1982–1983* (Washington, D.C.: U.S. Government Printing Office, April 1982) and *1980–1981* (Washington, D.C.: U.S. Government Printing Office, April 1980); College Placement Council, *CPC Salary Survey, Summer Supplement* (Bethlehem, Pa.: CPC, 1983), pp. 2–5; and Steven D. Ross, "The 12 Top Money-Making Careers of the '80s," *Business Week's Guide to Careers* 1 (Spring 1983):9.

**TABLE VI-2  Job positions in insurance and their minimum education and training requirements.**

| Position | High School Diploma Necessary | College Degree Desirable* | College Degree Necessary | Previous Business Experience Desirable | Advanced Degree or Special Training Desirable Prior to Application | Advanced Degree or Special Training Necessary Prior to Application |
|---|---|---|---|---|---|---|
| Actuary | ✔ | | ✔ | | | ✔ |
| Agent | ✔ | ✔ | | ✔ | | |
| Home office underwriter | ✔ | ✔ | | | | |
| Investment analyst | ✔ | | ✔ | | ✔ | |
| Claims administrator | ✔ | ✔ | | | | |
| Auditor | ✔ | ✔ | | ✔ | | |
| Accountant | ✔ | ✔ | | | ✔ | |
| Computer programmer | ✔ | ✔ | | | | ✔ |
| Systems analyst | ✔ | | ✔ | | | ✔ |
| Data processor | ✔ | | | | | ✔ |
| Computer console operator | ✔ | | | | | ✔ |
| Personnel administrator | ✔ | ✔ | | | | |
| Librarian | ✔ | | ✔ | | ✔ | |
| Advertising and public relations specialist | ✔ | ✔ | | ✔ | | |
| Lawyer | ✔ | | ✔ | | | ✔ |
| Secretary | ✔ | ✔ | | | ✔ | |
| Stenographer, clerk, typist, mailroom personnel | ✔ | | | | | |

SOURCE: *Career Opportunities for You in Life and Health Insurance* (Washington, D.C.: Education and Community Services, American Council of Life Insurance, Health Insurance Institute), p. 18.

*Including two-year courses

# PART VII

## THE WORLD OF BUSINESS

The world of business is constantly growing, and its dimensions are always expanding. The national business system is only a part of the international business community, without which the U.S. business system couldn't exist. Chapter 22 discusses international business and shows its effects on the domestic system.

Private business, driven by the private enterprise system, doesn't exist in a vacuum either. Instead, it operates in, is controlled by, and contributes to the legal and governmental system. Therefore, Chapter 23 covers the legal and governmental environment.

Finally, what happens in today's business world affects future business activities and your place in that future. So, in Chapter 24, we explore your future in business.

# 22

# International Business

*Time and space cannot be discarded, nor can we throw off the circumstance that we are citizens of the world.*

Heywood Broun

*Every individual, every organization, has to sustain a conversation with the rest of the world.*

Morris L. West

**Learning Objectives**

After studying the material in this chapter, you will understand:

1. What international business is, including exports and imports.
2. Some of the more important international trade concepts, including comparative advantage, balance of trade, balance of payments, and exchange rate.
3. Which are the world's key trading nations.
4. What multinational corporations are, and some of the current leaders.
5. The more important natural and imposed barriers to international trade.
6. The efforts being made to remove trade barriers and improve international trade.

**In This Chapter**

What Is International Business?
Some Important Concepts
The World's Key Trading Nations
The World's Leading Multinational Corporations
Barriers to International Trade
Efforts to Improve International Trade

592

## CLARK COPY REALLY GOES INTERNATIONAL

In April 1982, David beat Goliath in the world photocopy business. Clark Copy International Corporation, a small, five-year-old company making paper copiers in a cramped plant near Chicago, beat out the industry's world leaders—Minolta, Olympia, Sharp, and Xerox—for a lucrative contract with China. It signed a twenty-year agreement in Peking to sell the People's Republic of China 1,000 CMC 2000 plain-paper (untreated paper) copiers and parts for another 5,000 machines which the Chinese will assemble. This first phase of the contract is expected to bring Clark $5.5 million of revenue.

Under the second phase of the agreement, Clark will train 1,600 Chinese technicians, who will manufacture 200,000 CMC 2000 copiers and other Clark products for domestic and export sales in a new plant in Kweilin in South China. Clark—which will be a full partner with the Chinese—will help lay out and set up the plant. This phase will bring Clark approximately $60 million.

Clark was the smallest bidder participating in the eighteen months of negotiations between the Chinese and German, U.S., and Japanese conglomerates, including giants like IBM and Xerox.

How did Clark do it? According to the company's fifty-six-year-old founder and president, Otto A. Clark, a Slovak who emigrated to the United States in 1950, it wasn't a fluke. "You can't do business in China on a simple buy and sell basis, like most multinationals do," he said. "Instead, you have to establish a close human relationship and a commitment to stay." That human relationship was established with the assistance of David Yao, Clark's Far East representative. Yao was born in Shanghai and speaks Chinese. Yao and Clark went to China eight times to negotiate, including the closing with China's National Bureau of Instrumentation Industries. It also didn't hurt that the Chinese disliked even dealing with the Japanese, let alone using their copiers, because of their invasion and occupation of China during World War II. Finally, the larger firms had done poorly with low-cost, plain-paper copiers. So the real deciding factors were simply the quality and price of Clark's CMC 2000 and the personal relationship.

We've spent most of our time in this book talking about the workings of U.S. businesses of various shapes and sizes. By now, you should have a pretty good idea of what makes a business run internally. And occasionally we've talked about international influences such as Japanese excellence and foreign franchises. But there's literally a whole world out there for business to deal with. Pepsi is sold in many hard-to-deal-with countries, including the Soviet Union; McDonald's, with 350 fast-food outlets, is Japan's largest restaurant chain; American Motors is building its Jeeps in China; and scores of Boeing's 757 jetliners will fly for British, Brazilian, and Costa Rican airlines. You may drive a Toyota or Nissan, drink Beck's beer, eat Familia cereal, or carry a Sony portable radio. They're all evidence of international business.

## WHAT IS INTERNATIONAL BUSINESS?

**Objective 1**

**What international business is, including exports and imports.**

Successful managers in foreign trade were once seen as "shrewd Yankee traders" who used their sales or showmanship abilities to "exploit the natives" in undeveloped nations. But today's international managers have to be diplomats. There are many complex variables that should be considered by an international business firm, the host nation, and the governments involved. And the idea of exploiting the economy of another country for the benefit of the home country has changed to the present philosophy of mutual benefit to the participating countries. Today's international business firm is expected to contribute to the host nation's economic growth as well as to produce a profit for the owner's business.

From 1970 to 1982, direct U.S. investment abroad almost tripled—from $75.5 billion to $221.3 billion.[1] One job in every eight in the United States depends on exports. You can see from these figures that international operations are becoming increasingly important to the nation, to individual firms, and to future managers. Probably half of you will work in companies having at least something to do with international business. And if you're a business major, your school probably requires that you have some exposure to the international aspects of your courses.

There are two faces to international business: **exports,** or sales to other nations, and **imports,** or purchases from other nations.

### Exports

As various parts of our economy mature—that is, as industries become able to produce more than we can consume—our businesses look for customers in world markets. For example, U.S. farmers, who account for only about 3 percent of our work force, not only can feed all of us but also have large enough surpluses to export to other nations.

Some of the reasons why U.S. firms expand into international operations are:

1. The U.S. firm usually can obtain a higher percentage of earnings from foreign operations than from local activities. Usually demand is greater and competition is less in foreign markets, resulting in higher profits.

2. There is an effective demand abroad for many U.S.-made goods. The agricultural products, computers, and airplanes we export help pay for our imported cars, cameras, and music systems.
3. U.S. investments can benefit the host country by providing the capital and technology needed to produce economic development in the country. Our export of hybrid seeds, fertilizers, pesticides, and machines has helped many Asian countries develop their "green revolution," or improved agriculture.

Economic considerations and political factors have caused people all over the world to strive for a higher standard of living. This trend, in turn, creates a demand for U.S. goods, which leads to high U.S. earnings. Also, a strong dollar tends to encourage Americans to import non-U.S. goods and to travel to other countries. International business increases the volume of internal business activities in addition to being profitable for those firms engaged in the international activities. Table 22-1 shows the importance of foreign operations to some selected U.S. corporations, and Table 22-2 shows the major products exported from, and imported into, the United States in 1983.

> Notice how important foreign operations are to Allied Chemical. While only 16 percent of its assets are in other countries, and 24 percent of its sales are abroad, 86 percent of its profits come from those activities. See FYI on page 597 for one of the problems this heavy investment in overseas assets has caused Exxon.

During most of its history, the United States has exported raw materials and industrial and consumer finished goods, since it had the advantage of both technology and productivity. However, as the United States matured economically, plants and technology became antiquated, labor costs increased, and

**TABLE 22-1  Effects of foreign operations on major U.S. firms, 1982.**

| Firm | FOREIGN OPERATIONS AS % OF TOTAL | | |
| --- | --- | --- | --- |
| | Sales | Earnings | Net Assets |
| IBM | 45 | 41 | 42 |
| Coca-Cola | 43 | 60 | 32 |
| Nabisco | 36 | 31 | 44 |
| Johnson & Johnson | 43 | 52 | 43 |
| Pfizer | 53 | 49 | 56 |
| Allied Chemical | 24 | 86 | 16 |
| General Electric | 20 | 26 | 25 |
| Texas Instruments | 31 | 44 | 34 |
| Hewlett Packard | 46 | 40 | 32 |
| 3M | 38 | 34 | 32 |
| Union Carbide | 33 | 42 | 30 |
| McDermott | 37 | 42 | 43 |

SOURCE: Extracted from "BI's Profitability Survey," *Business International*, July 29, August 5, September 16, October 28, November 11, November 25, December 2, and December 16, 1983.

**TABLE 22-2** **Primary items exported from, and imported into, the United States in 1983.**

| Items Exported | Value (in $ Billion) | Items Imported | Value (in $ Billion) |
|---|---|---|---|
| Grains | $15.2 | Petroleum products | $54.3 |
| Motor vehicles | $14.6 | Motor vehicles | $29.8 |
| Aircraft | $12.2 | Telecommunications | |
| Office machines and data | | equipment | $11.6 |
| processing | $11.7 | Clothing | $10.3 |
| Specialized industrial machinery | $9.1 | Non-ferrous metals | $7.5 |
| Power-generating machinery | $8.7 | Iron and steel | $7.4 |

SOURCE: U.S. Department of Commerce.

government regulations complicated the productive process. The net result has been a declining advantage in the world marketplace and a movement of U.S. capital into less developed countries to gain the advantage of a lower cost of production. Yet there continue to be some areas where U.S. businesses have a competitive advantage.

1. Improved seeds and technology and mechanization have made U.S. agriculture the most efficient in the world. There continues to be a strong demand for our agricultural commodities from other nations of the world, including the Soviet Union and mainland China. For instance, at least one out of three bushels of corn grown near Garden City, Kansas, and soybeans harvested around McLean, Illinois, is shipped each year to Japan, Spain, or the Soviet Union.[2]

2. Because of their knowledge of the technology of petroleum exploration and development, U.S. energy companies have been able to market their services and gain proprietary interest in areas of the free world having undeveloped stocks of petroleum reserves (see Table 22-1). For example, Red Adair of Houston, Texas, the world's most renowned firefighter, is called in whenever there's an oil well fire anywhere in the noncommunist world. He has an expertise that no one else has. And Exxon and Shell, in a competitive bidding process in 1983, won the right to drill for oil off the coast of China as joint-venture partners.[3]

3. Engineering know-how has been exported in the form of contracts to design and supervise the construction of modern industrial plants and processes. On occasion, as those facilities have started production, they've been able to produce products and parts more efficiently than their U.S. counterparts.

4. U.S. military, commercial, and general aviation aircraft have enjoyed a favorable reception in international markets. Recently, though, foreign competition has appeared to threaten the U.S. position. An example is the European "air bus" that's been purchased by some U.S. airlines. However, jumbo jets such as the Boeing 747, Lockheed L-1011, and McDonnell-Douglas DC 10 still seem to predominate in international air service.

5. Generally, we don't think of managerial expertise as marketable, but it has been demonstrated to be so. Some U.S. companies have a variety of overseas contracts to staff, manage, service, and maintain operational projects. Also, other countries come here to learn from us. Most of Japan's vaunted

## FYI

### The Fateful Decision of Exxon Corporation and China Light & Power Company

In 1983, Exxon Corporation and its Hong Kong partner, China Light & Power Company, had to make a difficult and fateful decision—whether or not to commit $750 million to finish the final two units of Castle Peak B, a four-unit power station.

Great Britain's lease on Hong Kong's New Territories, where the power station is located, expires in 1997, and the colony's political future is quite uncertain. Exxon, Hong Kong's largest foreign investor, showed faith in Hong Kong's future when it and China Light committed $1.65 billion to build the first two units of the $2.4 billion plant. Those units won't be completed until 1987, and the total project isn't due to be completed until 1990—just seven years before the lease is up. Moreover, the loans for the project won't be repaid until the year 2002, five years after the lease deadline.

There were many political factors to consider, as well as the purely economic ones. Could profits, which have been consistent and predictable under British regulation, be repatriated after 1997 if the lease isn't renewed? Would the company and its plant be nationalized? Also, Exxon was one of thirty-two foreign energy companies bidding for drilling rights in China-controlled areas around Hong Kong, and Beijing government officials would probably react negatively if Exxon caused financial panic by pulling out of the power project. China Light was already supplying electricity to some neighboring districts across the Chinese border and had offered to invest in a nuclear project in China.

In May 1983, Exxon decided to go ahead and invest its share—$450 million—and China Light soon did the same.

Sources: Based on information from Esso Eastern, Inc.; "The Fateful Decision That Exxon Must Make," *Business Week*, January 31, 1983, pp. 40–41; and others.

management expertise was learned in our universities after World War II. And now, even China is trying to learn from us: in 1983, Nanjing Telecommunications Works, a government-owned company, bought a 19 percent interest in Santec Corporation, a U.S. maker of computer printers. The stated purpose was to "give them an inside view of American business."[4]

6. The know-how of U.S. banking and financial institutions has enabled them to compete successfully in international financial activities. A number

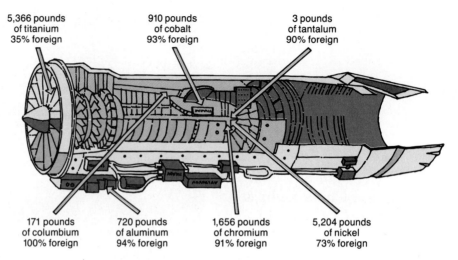

5,366 pounds
of titanium
35% foreign

910 pounds
of cobalt
93% foreign

3 pounds
of tantalum
90% foreign

171 pounds
of columbium
100% foreign

720 pounds
of aluminum
94% foreign

1,656 pounds
of chromium
91% foreign

5,204 pounds
of nickel
73% foreign

Note: Metals indicated are used in more than one place in engine.

**Figure 22-1** Imported metals in F-15 and F-16 jet fighters. (Adapted from Kenneth R. Sheets, "America's Gap in Strategic Minerals," *U.S.News & World Report*, February 8, 1982, p. 59.)

of these financial institutions have established branch offices in cities throughout the world, including Zurich, Brussels, Hong Kong, London, Tokyo, Berlin, and Paris.

> Why do you think Otto Clark wanted to enter the Chinese copier market? Was it to help the Chinese people to have a better standard of living? Would he have been allowed to enter the market if his operations weren't going to create jobs and improve performance? Would he have done it if it didn't promise him a profit?

## Imports

As big, complex, and varied as the U.S. economy is, it can't produce all the goods and services it needs. Instead, we're becoming increasingly dependent on other countries for many of our wants—and necessities. As you can see from Figure 22-1, most of the metals required for the engines of our jet fighters come from abroad. Table 22-3 shows how reliant we are on others for goods.

As the productive capacity of other nations grows, they seek U.S. markets and, since world trade is a two-way street, we buy their goods—even if we also produce the products they sell. Figure 22-2 shows the major countries we trade with, including our exports to them and their exports to us. Table 22-3 shows the main items we imported in 1983.

Thus we see foreign goods flooding U.S. markets at the same time that some of our companies are suffering a lack of customers. For example, foreign-made automobiles, cameras, television sets, stereos, radios, apparel, shoes, calculators, and home computers are being found in growing numbers.

**TABLE 22-3 Primary items imported by the United States, 1981.**

| Primary Imports | Value of Imports (in $ Million) |
|---|---|
| Petroleum | 78.5 |
| Motor vehicle parts | 27.4 |
| Iron and steel | 12.1 |
| Electrical machinery parts | 9.4 |
| TV, radio, and sound products | 9.2 |
| Clothing | 8.0 |
| Nonferrous metals | 7.1 |
| Natural gas | 5.8 |
| Chemicals | 5.6 |
| Special-purpose machinery | 5.3 |

SOURCE: Bureau of the Census, *Statistical Abstract of the United States* (Washington, D.C.: U.S. Government Printing Office, 1984), pp. 842–843.

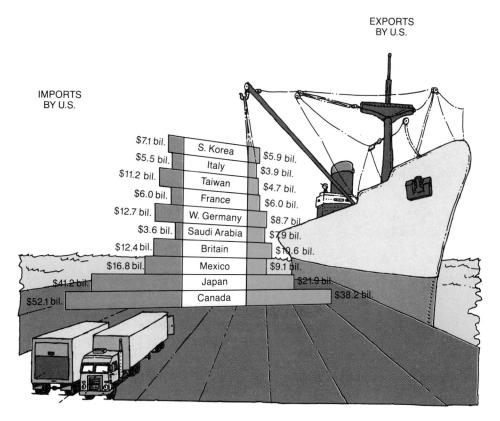

**Figure 22-2** America's top trading partners. (Data from U.S. Department of Commerce.)

IMPORTS BY U.S.

EXPORTS BY U.S.

| | | |
|---|---|---|
| $7.1 bil. | S. Korea | $5.9 bil. |
| $5.5 bil. | Italy | $3.9 bil. |
| $11.2 bil. | Taiwan | $4.7 bil. |
| $6.0 bil. | France | $6.0 bil. |
| $12.7 bil. | W. Germany | $8.7 bil. |
| $3.6 bil. | Saudi Arabia | $7.9 bil. |
| $12.4 bil. | Britain | $10.6 bil. |
| $16.8 bil. | Mexico | $9.1 bil. |
| $41.2 bil. | Japan | $21.9 bil. |
| $52.1 bil. | Canada | $38.2 bil. |

## SOME IMPORTANT CONCEPTS

Trading on an international basis introduces some new terms and concepts into business language. The most important of these are the law of comparative advantage, balance of trade, balance of payments, and exchange rate.

## Law of Comparative Advantage

**Objective 2**

Some of the more important international trade concepts, including comparative advantage, balance of trade, balance of payments, and exchange rate.

Countries export some products and import others because it's more efficient to operate that way, just as it's cheaper for a talented carpenter to concentrate on building and use the income he receives to buy the things he needs from other people. Economists call this the **law of comparative advantage,** which means that some countries can produce certain goods more cheaply than other countries because their workers have special skills—or will work for lower wages—or because the countries have access to more, better, or cheaper materials.

For example, the Australian climate, terrain, and vegetation are ideal for raising sheep, so Australia exports large quantities of high-grade wool. Hong Kong has large numbers of Chinese who are skilled tailors, so it exports low-priced, tailor-made men's suits. Taiwan has many highly skilled craftspeople and technicians, so it produces radios, television sets, and other electronic products for export. Japanese workers are educated, trained, and skilled, as well as highly motivated, so they turn out excellent cameras, radios, tape recorders, and music systems. Canada's climate is ideal for wheat, which it ships to Argentina, which, in turn, is a low-cost producer of meat—especially beef—exports. Saudi Arabia, Iraq, Iran, Nigeria, England, Mexico, Venezuela, and other countries sit atop large petroleum deposits. South Africa has most of the commercial-quality diamonds in the world. Spain has olives and Toledo steel. South Korea and the Philippines make excellent low-cost clothing, and Italy's leather goods are in great demand.

But a country may lose its comparative advantage because of declining resources, increasing production costs, or newer technology developed elsewhere. For example, Switzerland, with limited resources and surrounded by often unfriendly competitors, had developed highly skilled and motivated craftspeople to manufacture compact, high-unit-value products such as music boxes and watches. But because of the increasing demand for electronic watches, which were developed as a by-product of the U.S. space program, the market share of Swiss watchmakers declined from 44 percent in 1970 to 28 percent in 1980. The Japanese share during the same period increased from 9.5 to 30 percent.[5]

## Balance of Trade

A nation's **balance of trade** is the relationship between the value of its exports and the value of its imports. When the amount of exports exceeds the amount of imports, the country has a favorable balance of trade, since more money comes in than goes out. If its imports exceed its exports, it has an unfavorable balance of trade, since it must ship money out to pay for the import surplus. That's what happened to U.S. trade from 1967 to 1983. Exports increased 547 percent, but imports escalated by 910 percent.[6] Thus, the final deficit in merchandise trade for all of 1983 was over $70 billion, a very unfavorable balance of trade.[7]

## Balance of Payments

The balance of trade affects a nation's **balance of payments,** which is the relationship between flows of money into and out of the country. When there's an

# *Profile*

## Sam Ayoub: Citizen of the World

In late 1983, Coca-Cola Company lowered its internal earnings projections for the year. The reasons, according to Sam Ayoub, Coke's senior executive vice-president and chief financial officer at the time, were problems in Latin America and the "continued strength of the dollar." He emphasized that, while the company's many businesses were still quite profitable, Coca-Cola was running into selling problems because of the "unrealistically high levels" of the dollar in hard-currency countries. Also, the problems of the overvalued dollar, into which all of Coke's financial results were translated, reduced the company's second-half consolidated net earnings between $13 million and $15 million.

Sam Ayoub is an Egyptian by birth and an American by residence, but a world citizen by occupation. He joined Coca-Cola in 1959, came up through its international division, and was made chief financial officer in 1981. From that position, he supervises 400 employees.

In discussions with Ayoub, you get a sense of brilliance, especially in his quick recall and his command of tremendous amounts of technical information. But the overriding impression is one of a sensitive, emotional person who relies heavily on intuition. "My foreign currency is right here," he'll say, patting his stomach. "I rely heavily on my gut feelings." Of course, he also gets hourly updates on major currency exchange rates, as well as economic, social, and political information from financial managers in the field. His phone rings all day long, and every day at 4 A.M. he receives a call at home about how the European markets are doing so that he'll have a jump on the situation when he arrives at the office. Finally, he travels extensively in the 155 countries where Coke operates, talking with the firm's local bottlers and receiving inside information about local politics and economic conditions.

Not only is it important to predict what another currency is going to do—it's also important to predict timing of corrective action. Ayoub made a $2.6 million profit trading $30 million of German marks in late 1981 when the mark advanced as expected. But earlier in the year, he lost $1 million on $30 million of Japanese yen when the yen rose more slowly than expected. "I was right on what happened, but wrong on the time," he lamented.

Source: Based on the following articles from *The Wall Street Journal:* Jody Long, "By Trusting Intuition, Educated Guesses, Coke Capitalizes on Exchange-Rate Shifts," September 3, 1983, p. 17; and Eric Morgenthaler, "Coca-Cola Lowers '83 Profit Projections, Cites Latin American Woes, Strong Dollar," September 8, 1983, p. 10. Reprinted by permission of *The Wall Street Journal,* © Dow Jones & Company, Inc. 1983. All Rights Reserved. Also based on personal discussions with Mr. Ayoub.

unfavorable balance of trade, there's often an unfavorable balance of payments. If the trade balance is favorable, there will often be a favorable balance of payments.

However, other activities, such as banking, communications, data processing, transportation, military shipments, and profits of companies operating in foreign countries, affect the balance of payments. For example, the United States had a $17 billion unfavorable balance of payments in 1983, in addition to its unfavorable balance of trade at the time.[8]

### Exchange Rate

Trade among two or more countries is complicated by the fact that each country has its own currency. Therefore, when a firm in one country sells goods to a firm in a second country, the agreed-upon price must be converted from one currency to another. The rate at which the money of one country is exchanged for that of another country is its **exchange rate.** This rate is important because it influences how much a nation can import or export. For example, when the rate for the dollar is high, as it was in 1982 and 1983, U.S. goods like Coca-Cola (see the Profile on page 601) become more expensive and difficult to sell abroad. But goods from other countries become relatively cheaper, and more are imported. The reverse is true when the dollar's rate declines.

The exchange rate can be either a **floating exchange rate**, which varies with market conditions, or a **controlled exchange rate,** arbitrarily set by the country itself. The latter may have little relation to the actual value of the currency. For example, U.S. tourists in Moscow in April 1962 had to pay $1.10 for a ruble at the official exchanges. Yet they could buy a ruble for as little as $0.20 in the streets. Thus a fur hat could cost as much as $110 or as little as $20, depending on where one exchanged dollars for rubles.

## THE WORLD'S KEY TRADING NATIONS

**Objective 3**

**Which are the world's key trading nations.**

Ten countries account for 61 percent of the world's exports. In general, the more industrialized nations, such as Germany, the United States, Japan, France, the United Kingdom, Italy, the Soviet Union, the Netherlands, and Canada, are leading exporters because their exports are high-value manufactured products. **Industrial nations** are those that import raw materials and export finished goods, especially manufactured products. A **developing nation,** or newly industrialized country, has relatively little manufacturing, and its people have a low standard of living. As natural resources become scarce and increase in price, they can enhance the value of a developing nation's exports. Thus, with the energy shortage of the 1970s, Saudi Arabia, a developing nation, became one of the top ten exporters and is now becoming an industrial nation. Some other developing nations that are emerging as industrial nations are South Korea, Spain, and Taiwan.

# THE WORLD'S LEADING MULTINATIONAL CORPORATIONS

**Objective 4**

**What multinational corporations are, and some of the current leaders.**

A multinational corporation (MNC) is one that operates on an international scale. It moves capital, skills, know-how, goods and services, and other resources to various nations in order to make a profit for the owners, often helping the other countries at the same time.

Multinational corporations are more than just giant economic units. In many cases, they are nearly a form of government, richer and more powerful than some of the countries in which they operate. For example, in a typical year, the combined sales of Exxon, General Motors, and Royal Dutch/Shell Group (see Table 22-4) exceed the gross national product (GNP) of most of the industrial nations of the world.

MNCs are citizens of, operate in, own property in, and pay taxes to many countries. Yet they have goals and objectives of their own—which may be contrary to those of the nations they serve. MNCs are praised by some people as providers of advanced technology and contributors to a better way of life. Others say they're just another form of imperialism, exploiting people in un-

**TABLE 22-4  The world's twenty-five largest industrial corporations.**

| RANK | | COMPANY | HEADQUARTERS | SALES $000 | NET INCOME $000 |
|------|------|---------|--------------|------------|-----------------|
| '82 | '81 | | | | |
| 1 | 1 | Exxon | New York | 97,172,523 | 4,185,932 |
| 2 | 2 | Royal Dutch/Shell Group | The Hague/London | 83,759,375 | 3,486,694 |
| 3 | 4 | General Motors | Detroit | 60,025,600 | 962,700 |
| 4 | 3 | Mobil | New York | 59,946,000 | 1,380,000 |
| 5 | 6 | British Petroleum | London | 51,322,452 | 1,245,623 |
| 6 | 5 | Texaco | Harrison, N.Y. | 46,986,000 | 1,281,000 |
| 7 | 8 | Ford Motor | Dearborn, Mich. | 37,067,200 | (657,800) |
| 8 | 11 | International Business Machines | Armonk, N.Y. | 34,364,000 | 4,409,000 |
| 9 | 7 | Standard Oil of California | San Francisco | 34,362,000 | 1,377,000 |
| 10 | 16 | E. I. du Pont de Nemours | Wilmington, Del. | 33,331,000 | 894,000 |
| 11 | 12 | Gulf Oil | Pittsburgh | 28,427,000 | 900,000 |
| 12 | 9 | Standard Oil (Ind.) | Chicago | 28,073,000 | 1,826,000 |
| 13 | 10 | ENI | Rome | 27,505,858 | (1,206,970) |
| 14 | 14 | General Electric | Fairfield, Conn. | 26,500,000 | 1,817,000 |
| 15 | 13 | Atlantic Richfield | Los Angeles | 26,462,150 | 1,676,078 |
| 16 | • | IRI | Rome | 24,815,296 | N.A. |
| 17 | 15 | Unilever | London/Rotterdam | 23,120,471 | 659,550 |
| 18 | 18 | Shell Oil | Houston | 20,062,000 | 1,605,000 |
| 19 | 17 | Française des Pétroles | Paris | 20,029,197 | (80,595) |
| 20 | 23 | Petrobrás (Petróleo Brasileiro) | Rio de Janeiro | 19,004,999 | 579,170 |
| 21 | 44 | U.S. Steel | Pittsburgh | 18,375,000 | (361,000) |
| 22 | 41 | Occidental Petroleum | Los Angeles | 18,212,226 | 155,602 |
| 23 | 20 | Elf-Aquitaine | Paris | 17,785,313 | 536,336 |
| 24 | 31 | Siemens | Munich | 16,962,630 | 279,794 |
| 25 | 29 | Nissan Motor | Yokohama (Japan) | 16,465,167 | 444,462 |

SOURCE: Reprinted from Michael McFadden and Ann Goodman, "The International 500: The Fortune Directory of the Largest Industrial Corporations Outside the U.S.," *Fortune*, August 22, 1983, pp. 170–171. © 1983 Time, Inc. All rights reserved.

derdeveloped economies. Still, a University of Pennsylvania study found that MNCs are generally better citizens than similar companies operating solely within a nation's borders.[9] They generally follow voluntary guidelines on international labor relations and enhance economic growth and employment.

> Notice that Table 22-1 shows that over half the net assets of Pfizer are outside the United States. Also note that over half the net earnings of three of the twelve firms come from foreign operations. Why do you think this is true? Do you think these operations help or hurt the economies where they operate? Do you think that Exxon's operations are helpful or harmful to the people of Hong Kong?

## BARRIERS TO INTERNATIONAL TRADE

**Objective 5**

**The more important natural and imposed barriers to international trade.**

International trade is carried out by private companies, government trading agencies, and nonprofit organizations. The varied nature of these groups and the ideological differences generated tend to limit such trade. For example, there's little chance for trade between free-enterprise firms in the United States and the highly regulated and controlled state-owned organizations in the communist states of North Korea and Albania. In addition, there are many **trade barriers** that restrict the ability or willingness of groups to sell to one another in foreign markets. These can be classified as natural barriers, tariff barriers, and other artificial, or imposed, barriers.

### Natural Barriers

Even if one country can produce a product more cheaply than another country, that comparative advantage may be lost because of the cost of *transporting* it to the second country. For example, the distances from Europe to Southeast Asia are a major factor in the cost of goods shipped between these markets. Also, natural terrain, such as the mountains around Switzerland, may form barriers. Air transport has lessened the physical effect of these barriers, but not the cost factor.

*Language* acts as a natural barrier. For instance, Esso Standard Eastern had to withdraw the "Put a tiger in your tank" sales campaign from East Pakistan, because the people thought of the tiger more as a vicious animal than as a cute cartoon character. English is fairly well established as the language of business communication, but many nationalities, such as the French, resent that fact and give preference to businesspeople willing to use their language.

*Sociocultural factors* can be a barrier for businesses entering a foreign market. Mattel found that Barbie dolls, for instance, left the Japanese cold because the dolls didn't conform to Japanese standards of beauty. But with dark eyes, darker blond hair, less bust, and shorter legs, Barbie became a Japanese craze.

*Customs* and tradition limit trade. Since the Japanese are very reluctant to say no to a guest, visiting salespeople are often fooled into believing they've made a sale, only to have the reservations come out later. And the pride of many Spaniards limits their trading with someone of lower status.

*Religious conflict,* such as that between Islam and Hinduism on the Indo-Pakistan subcontinent, Christianity and Islam in Lebanon, and Catholicism and Protestantism in Northern Ireland, is a limiting factor. Religious conflict was one of the many reasons why DeLorean Motor Company failed near Belfast.

The U.S. *measuring system* conflicts with the metric system used in many countries. Our appliances are produced for 110-volt, 60 cycle, alternating current (AC) systems and outlets that differ from the 115–120 volt, 50 cycle, AC systems or the 220-volt, direct current (DC) systems in many other countries. Also, the *quality standards* of our products are often considerably lower than those in other countries and must be upgraded if we are to compete, a challenging but not impossible task. One U.S. company that did so successfully is Webco Lumber Company. In 1981, one of Webco Lumber Company's sawmills was closed and the other was working only half-time because U.S. housing construction was practically at a standstill. At the same time, the Japanese demand for lumber was booming and supply was low. This seemed like a perfect situation, but Japan's standards and specifications were exceedingly high. So Barbara Webb, Webco's president, and her brother, its sales manager, secretary, and treasurer, went to Japan with a trade mission, learned what the Japanese wanted, and returned home to start producing according to those needs. They changed the type of wood being harvested, cut it to different lengths (13.12 feet instead of 12, 14, or 16 feet), and planed it to much finer tolerances—all under the tough scrutiny of the buyer's U.S. and Japanese inspectors. The company survived with the help of the Japanese orders.[10]

### Tariff Barriers

**Tariffs** are duties or taxes imposed by a government on imported or exported goods. Tariffs serve two purposes: (1) **revenue tariffs** are imposed to generate tax revenue, and (2) **protective tariffs** are set to discourage imports. Only rarely are protective tariffs imposed on exports, and then only to protect a very scarce resource.

Since the purpose of revenue tariffs is to raise money, they're set at that point—usually a low one—where the most goods will be sold and consequently the most money will be raised. Protective tariffs, however, are set so high that they discourage imports. The tariff is usually the difference between the foreign price and the local price.

In 1982, 214,000 heavy motorcycles were sold in the United States. Only one U.S. firm, Harley-Davidson, with a scant 2,500 workers, produced the megabikes, which it sold for $4,200 to $8,600. The Japanese equivalents sold for around $1,500 less. Consequently, there were only 32,000 U.S. and over 180,000 Japanese motorcycles sold in the United States in 1982. So, in early 1983, President Reagan imposed a 49.4 percent tariff on all imported motorcycles after the first 6,000, which were taxed at the old 4.4 percent rate.[11] The new rate will drop to 14.4 percent in 1987, after Harley-Davidson has had ample time to recover from the 1981–1983 recession.

## Other Imposed Barriers

Firms often become involved in political, legal, moral, and ethical controversies. For example, the products of Nestlé, the giant Swiss food firm that does

96 percent of its business in other countries, were boycotted worldwide by church, education, and health groups from 1977 to early 1984. The boycotters claimed that Nestlé's advertising for its infant milk formula, a best-seller in many Third World countries, had weaned mothers away from breastfeeding, causing poor families to buy an unneeded product with money that should have been spent on necessities. It was further charged that impure water and improper mixing of the formula (caused by ignorance, illiteracy, or false economy) led to infant mortality or malnutrition. Nestlé denied the charges and, in fact, won a libel suit against a Swiss group for publishing a pamphlet entitled *Nestlé Kills Babies.* But it did eventually comply with worldwide marketing codes and agreed to teach foreign mothers the pros and cons of bottle feeding.[12]

Some of the nontariff trade barriers erected by governments include embargoes, import and export quotas, exchange controls, standards and specifications, sanctions against dumping, and "buy national" campaigns. Custom procedures, government purchasing policies, tax controls, and subsidies also are barriers to trade.

**Embargoes**  An **embargo** is an outright prohibition of the import or export of certain products. An embargo may be for *military reasons*—to build up or maintain defense industries or to prevent weapons going to a certain country. For example, in order to remain neutral, we embargoed arms sales to the new state of Israel in the late 1940s.

Certain products are prohibited for *health or sanitary reasons*, as when Japan embargoed oranges from California during the "medfly" scare of the early 1980s. The United States prohibits the import of certain birds and animals to prevent the spread of disease.

*Moral reasons* are the grounds for embargoing cocaine, heroin, and other harmful substances. There are also embargoes for outright *political reasons*, such as the United Nations embargo of sales to, or purchases from, white-controlled Rhodesia before it became Zimbabwe. Most nations also embargo the export of national art treasures and archeological artifacts, as well as endangered animal species.

**Quotas**  An **import quota** places a limit on the amount of a product that can be brought into a country. An **export quota** specifies how much of a product can be shipped out. The quota may be absolute, so that when the quantity is reached, no more can enter, or it may be combined with a stiff tariff on all units over that amount. The U.S. tariff on imported motorcycles is an example of the latter method: The first 6,000 to enter have a 4.4 percent tariff, and all others bear a 49.4 percent rate.

Quotas, especially export quotas, can be voluntary. In early 1981, Japan agreed to "voluntarily" limit its export of cars to the United States to 1.68 million units annually. Japan agreed to this restriction in order to prevent the U.S. Congress from passing "buy national" legislation (see below).[13]

**Exchange Controls**  Governments use exchange controls to restrict the availability of their currency to foreigners. For example, Pakistan had several different exchange rates during the late 1960s when it was trying to develop its economy. The most favorable rate was for importing industrial goods to be used in producing goods locally. The most unfavorable rate was for importing

luxury goods, such as cars. The exchange rate more than doubled the cost of the luxury goods.

**Standards and Specifications** The standards and specifications for products sold in a given country may be valid ones—like the Japanese requirements for building materials discussed in the Webco Lumber case. However, standards can also be manipulated to hinder or restrict imports of a given product. For example, U.S. baseball bat manufacturers claim that Japanese standards are designed to keep out U.S.-made bats, especially aluminum ones.

**Sanctions Against Dumping** Sanctions are a form of coercion against unpopular or illegal actions of another party. **Dumping** involves shipping substantial amounts of a product to another country at prices below the full cost of producing it or significantly below the selling price in the home or competitive market. In 1982, for instance, the European Economic Community (EEC) spent $7 billion to subsidize the sale of its surplus grain around the world. After protesting this dumping for six months, the United States sold 1 million tons of wheat flour to Egypt for $160 a ton, which was $100 below the price in the United States.[14] The EEC protested to the General Agreement on Tariffs and Trade Tribunal.

**"Buy National" Campaigns** "Buy national" (or local) campaigns encourage customers to show their patriotism by buying local goods. Sometimes, such regulations even require that government purchasing agents buy products made in the home country, if they're available. Alternatively, the government might subsidize the use of local products. For example, when Japanese imports' share of the U.S. market for automobiles reached 22 percent in the early 1980s, the United Auto Workers union pressured a congressional committee into passing "local content" legislation requiring that up to 90 percent of the price of cars sold in the United States be for local parts and labor. The full House of Representatives passed the measure in late 1983.[15] It seems that a desire for protectionism is growing in the United States, at least according to a 1983 Gallup poll for *Newsweek*.

Campaigns encourage customers to show their patriotism by buying domestic goods.

## EFFORTS TO IMPROVE INTERNATIONAL TRADE

**Objective 6**

**The efforts being made to remove trade barriers and improve international trade.**

It might seem that so far we've emphasized things nations do to *discourage* business with one another. While there's a good deal of debate about the extent to which international trade should be controlled (see the Business Debate on page 610), no country can get along without such trade. Therefore, most governments in the free world actually try to *encourage*, improve, or facilitate it. Table 22-5 summarizes some of the most important institutions and organizations encouraging trade between the United States and other countries.

### At Home

There are several institutions and policies that are designed primarily to improve U.S. foreign trade. In general, they're designed to spur exports.

▲ **Foreign Trade Zones** Foreign trade zones (FTZs) are areas in the United States that are treated as foreign territory as far as international business is concerned. Foreign goods can be imported into these areas without payment of U.S. duties. The goods can then be sold and shipped from the zone to other countries duty-free. Or the goods can be worked on and then shipped out of the FTZ into the United States, where duty is imposed.

The primary advantage of FTZs is that they provide jobs for U.S. workers and markets for U.S. goods. Work that would otherwise be done in other countries is done here by Americans, using U.S. materials. There are now ninety-seven such zones in the United States, doing $7 billion of business and creating nearly 29,000 jobs (see Figure 22-3). They're located in areas such as New York, at the Brooklyn Navy Yard; New Orleans; Del Rio, Texas; and Port Everglades, Florida. One zone is a 320-acre site in Mount Olive, New Jersey. A Japanese firm, Seiko Corporation of America, has set up a manufacturing and distribution center there, and the German automaker BMW plans to build its largest parts distribution plant on the site.[16]

**TABLE 22-5**  **Institutions and policies that foster foreign trade.**

| Institution | Purpose |
|---|---|
| 1. Foreign Trade Zones | 1. Areas into which goods can be imported without being subject to customs duties or quotas. Often, the imported materials are manufactured into finished products. If re-exported, they are not subject to any tariffs. If they enter into domestic commerce, they are subject to regular tariffs. |
| 2. The Export-Import Bank (Exim-bank) | 2. Created by the U.S. government to reduce domestic unemployment. Makes loans to exporters who cannot secure financing through private sources and to foreign countries who use the funds to buy American-made goods. |
| 3. The Foreign Credit Insurance Association (FCIA) | 3. A firm can buy insurance from FCIA to cover political risk (such as expropriation and loss due to war). Comprehensive coverage can be bought to cover business risks (such as credit default). The exporter can also buy insurance coverage on credit sales to foreign customers. |
| 4. The International Bank for Reconstruction and Development (World Bank) | 4. Furthers the economic development of member nations by making loans to them, either directly by using its own funds, or indirectly by borrowing from member countries. |
| 5. The International Monetary Fund (IMF) | 5. Eliminates trade barriers and promotes financial cooperation among member countries. Enables them to cope better with balance of payments problems. Thus, if firms in Peru wish to buy from American firms but Peru lacks American dollars, Peru can borrow American dollars from the IMF. It pays the loan back in gold or the currency it receives through its dealing with other countries. |
| 6. The General Agreement on Tariffs and Trade (GATT) | 6. Negotiated by member nations to improve trade relations through reductions and elimination of tariff and other barriers. |
| 7. The International Development Association (IDA) | 7. Affiliated with the World Bank. Makes loans to private businesses and to member countries of the World Bank. Similar organizations make loans to governments and firms in certain country groupings. The Inter-American Development Association, for example, is for countries belonging to the Organization of American States. |
| 8. The International Finance Corporation (IFC) | 8. Affiliated with the World Bank. Makes loans to private businesses when they cannot obtain loans from more conventional sources. |
| 9. Domestic International Sales Corporation (DISC) | 9. American firms can form tax-shelter subsidiaries (DISCs) to handle their export sales. The purpose is to spur exports and encourage American firms to enter the export market. A firm can defer some of its taxes on export earnings by establishing a DISC. |
| 10. Overseas Private Investment Corporation (OPIC) | 10. Offers insurance to American firms that operate overseas. Covers loss due to expropriation, damage caused by war, revolution, or insurrection, and inability to convert local currencies into U.S. dollars. |

SOURCE: From John A. Reinecke and William F. Schoell, *Introduction to Business: A Contemporary View*, 4th ed. (Newton, Mass.: Allyn and Bacon, Inc., 1983), pp. 542–543. Copyright © 1983 by Allyn and Bacon, Inc. Reprinted with permission.

▲ **Financial Institutions**  The Export-Import Bank (Eximbank) makes loans to U.S. exporters and foreign buyers of U.S. imports if private financing isn't available. The Foreign Credit Insurance Association (FCIA) and the Overseas Private Investment Corporation (OPIC) offer insurance to firms to cover risks

# Business Debate

## Should We Have a Protectionist Industrial Policy?

In December 1982, the U.S. House of Representatives took two steps toward establishing a policy of protecting U.S. industry from foreign competition by keeping out imports. First, the House added an amendment to the $30 billion highway improvement bill requiring that only U.S.-made goods be used for the projects it finances. On the same day, the House Rules Committee approved a bill that would require that 90 percent of the parts and labor in automobiles sold in the United States be U.S.-made.

In effect, these bills would keep out foreign-made automobiles and road materials and lead to a protectionist battle between nations. The arguments *in favor* of a protectionist industrial policy are:

1. The older "smokestack" industries, such as steel, autos, and clothing, are having to make painful cuts in production—and employment—because of foreign competition. They should be subsidized and protected.
2. The emerging high-tech industries fear that they'll be unable to compete with overseas competitors. They, too, would have an easier time if competitive products were kept out.
3. Other governments, notably those of France, Germany, and Japan, nurture new industries and protect old ones with subsidies and by permitting monopolies. These policies, together with government underwriting of commercial research and development, have led these countries to have increased shares in foreign markets and large export balances. Why shouldn't we do the same?

4. Jobs must be protected at all costs, even if it means abandoning free trade.[17]

The arguments *against* such a policy are:

1. U.S. producers have brought on themselves the pain caused by the entry of lower-priced goods into the U.S. market. They've failed to keep labor costs in line, they haven't accurately identified and catered to the needs of their customers, and they haven't modernized their plants and equipment quickly enough.
2. Protecting inefficient industries now would only postpone the need for corrective action.
3. This protection would involve long-range planning by the government, resulting in more interference with business.
4. Most of the help given by foreign governments occurred during the decades before 1975 when world trade was expanding rapidly, and the trade of those countries would have risen whether or not governments had helped. That time is now past, and such help would probably fail if we tried it.
5. Such a policy would put the government in the position of deciding which industries would grow and which would die—a function which should be left to the free enterprise system.
6. Around 80 percent of our new manufacturing jobs from 1977 to 1980 were related to exports, especially in industries emphasizing efficiency, quality, and innovation.

*What do you think?*

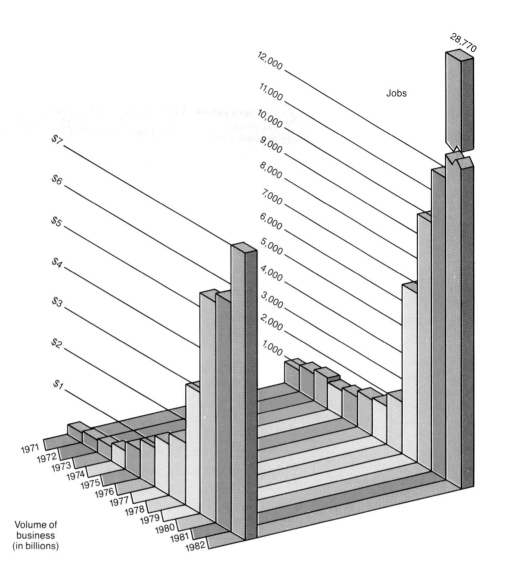

**Figure 22-3** Jobs and volume of business provided by FTZs. (Data from *USA Today*, December 23, 1983, p. 1-B; and National Association of Foreign Trade Zones.)

that private insurers can't handle. U.S. exporters also form tax-sheltered subsidiaries called **domestic international sales corporations (DISCs)** in order to defer some taxes on export sales.

### Worldwide

Recognizing the importance of having international trade flowing as freely as possible, most nations have cooperated to set up institutions and policies for this purpose.

**The General Agreement on Tariffs and Trade** The General Agreement on Tariffs and Trade (GATT) is an international agreement in which member nations committed themselves to trying to reduce trade barriers. Since 1948, GATT has sponsored several rounds of negotiations to cut tariffs on thousands of products and remove many nontariff barriers to trade. In the series of talks from 1975 to 1979, called the Tokyo Round, tariffs were reduced nearly a third

on about 6,000 products. In the Geneva Round (1982–1983) participants discussed adopting rules on service exports, such as engineering, construction, and high-tech services, which weren't covered by GATT rules on merchandise exports.[18] However, no action was taken.

**Financial Institutions** The International Bank for Reconstruction and Development (called the World Bank) borrows money from the more prosperous nations and lends it—at very favorable rates—to the governments of needy nations so they can develop their industries. Its affiliates, the International Finance Corporation (IFC) and the International Development Association (IDA), make loans to private businesses when funds aren't available elsewhere. The International Monetary Fund (IMF) tries to promote financial cooperation by improving the balance of payments of member countries through making scarce currencies available.

## LEARNING OBJECTIVES REVISITED

1. *What international business is, including exports and imports.*

   As various parts of an economy mature, businesses expand outward into international trade. The two faces of international business are exports and imports. Firms engage in international exporting to obtain higher earnings, as well as to provide host countries with the capital and technology needed for economic development. Imports fill needs that nations can't fill for themselves.

2. *Some of the more important international trade concepts, including comparative advantage, balance of trade, balance of payments, and exchange rate.*

   According to the law of comparative advantage, some countries can produce certain goods more efficiently and cheaply than others. A nation's balance of trade is favorable when it exports more goods than it imports; it is unfavorable when imports exceed exports. Goods in international business must be paid for, so when more goods are imported than exported, there is an unfavorable balance of payments. One currency must be exchanged for another when goods are shipped between countries, so an exchange rate must be worked out between the countries.

3. *Which are the world's key trading nations.*

   The world's important exporters—Germany, the United States, Japan, France, the United Kingdom, Italy, the Soviet Union, the Netherlands, Canada, and Saudi Arabia—are industrial or newly industrialized nations.

4. *What multinational corporations are, and some of the current leaders.*

   A multinational corporation (MNC) is one that operates on an international scale, regardless of where its headquarters is. MNCs are more than just giant business firms, for they tend to have social and even political effects as well as economic ones. They have been found to be generally good citizens of the countries where they operate.

5. *The more important natural and imposed barriers to international trade.*

In addition to natural barriers to trade, such as those created by distance, terrain, languages, sociocultural factors, customs, religious conflicts, measuring systems, and quality standards, there are barriers imposed by governments. The most important of these are tariffs, embargoes, import and export quotas, exchange controls, standards, sanctions against dumping, and "buy national" campaigns.

6. *The efforts being made to remove trade barriers and improve international trade.*

In an effort to overcome trade barriers, governments have established foreign trade zones; low-cost loans, subsidies, insurance, and guarantees; and international agreements. The most prominent of these agreements are the General Agreement on Tariffs and Trade (GATT) and the agreements creating the International Bank for Reconstruction and Development (the World Bank) and the International Monetary Fund (IMF). GATT has been quite effective in reducing tariffs and other restrictions on the free flow of trade.

## IMPORTANT TERMS

extra review of the chapter, try defining the following terms. If you have
le with any of them, refer to the page listed.

| | |
|---|---|
| rts  594 | trade barriers  604 |
| orts  594 | tariffs  605 |
| of comparative | revenue tariffs  605 |
| vantage  600 | protective tariffs  605 |
| nce of trade  600 | embargo  606 |
| nce of payments  600 | import quota  606 |
| range rate  602 | export quota  606 |
| ting exchange rate  602 | dumping  607 |
| trolled exchange rate  602 | foreign trade zones (FTZs)  608 |
| ustrial nations  602 | domestic international sales |
| eloping nation  602 | corporations (DISCs)  611 |
| ltinational corporation | |
| MNC)  603 | |

. Why is international business important to an economy?
. Why do nations (a) export? (b) import?
3. Name some key U.S. exports.
4. What is the law of comparative advantage?
5. Contrast balance of trade and balance of payments.
6. What are the world's key trading nations, and why are they leaders?
7. How do multinational corporations operate?
8. How would you explain some of the natural barriers to trade?
9. What are some of the imposed barriers to trade?

Flo Lucente - 3ʳᵈ Per.

wrong - ~~IIII~~ ~~IIII~~ ~~IIII~~ IIII = -2 /-40

appearance - 1 -2 } -40

45 /45

10. What are some of the reasons for restricting international trade?
11. What is the difference between a revenue tariff and a protective tariff?
12. What are some of the more important approaches to improving trade?

## ⬈ DISCUSSION QUESTIONS

1. How can a nation with an unfavorable balance of trade still have a favorable balance of payments?
2. Describe how changes in the value of the dollar affect imports and exports.
3. Do you think multinational corporations are helpful or harmful to developing economies? Explain.
4. Should the United States protect businesses, such as Harley-Davidson, from foreign competitors that produce goods at a lower cost? Why or why not?
5. Why do governments encourage international business?
6. How might a U.S. firm use a foreign trade zone in the United States?

## ⬈ CASE 22-1   Japanese Cigarette Exports

Japan Tobacco Corporation has a government monopoly on the sale of cigarettes in that country, as imports are priced 40 percent higher than local brands. But the monopoly has a problem. The Japanese smoked about 315 billion cigarettes in 1982, only 1 percent more than in 1981. Japan Tobacco had to do something—its domestic market was stabilizing, and U.S. trade negotiators had won concessions so that U.S. imports would probably capture up to 1.5 percent of the local market.

Japan hasn't the comparative advantage over other countries in tobacco that it has in music equipment, photographic supplies, and automobiles. Also, the company had almost no export experience.

Japan Tobacco set up a subsidiary in 1984 to specialize in exports. The North American, South American, and European markets have been growing much more slowly than those in Southeast Asia, the Middle East, and Africa.

### Case Questions

1. Assume that Japan Tobacco had asked you to serve as a consultant to help the firm try to compete successfully in other markets. What would your advice to them have been?
2. Research what actually happened.

## ⬈ CASE 22-2   To Move or Not to Move?[19]

John S. Chamberlin, chairman and chief executive officer of Lenox, Inc., of Lawrenceville, New Jersey, was asked what the hardest decision he'd had to make as a manager was. He answered that it was one he made as an executive with General Electric in the early 1970s. Although the decision had to be approved by GE's board, he had to make a recommendation and defend it.

GE had been manufacturing clock-radios and table radios in Utica, New York, for several years. The workers and townspeople considered the GE operations a permanent fixture. But the company had started to lose its market share because its AM-FM clock-radios were selling for about $29.95 each, while a comparable Japanese brand sold for about $9.95.

Based on tough economic realities, Chamberlin had two alternatives: remain in Utica or move operations to Singapore. There were about 2,000 workers employed in Utica. Labor costs for the U.S. workers were about $5 an hour, while the cost for workers in Singapore would be about $0.50 an hour. If the operation left Utica, the workers would have to be laid off, since there was nowhere in the company to transfer them.

### Case Questions

1. What do you think Chamberlin recommended?
2. Can you think of any alternatives besides the two mentioned?

# 23

# The Legal and Governmental Environment

*No man shall be judged except by the legal judgment of his peers or the law of the land.*

Magna Carta

*Our Constitution is in actual operation; everything appears to promise that it will last; but in this world nothing is certain but death and taxes.*

Benjamin Franklin

## Learning Objectives

After studying the material in this chapter, you will understand:

1. The basic legal foundations upon which the U.S. business system is built.
2. What business law is and the types of laws it encompasses.
3. How the U.S. judicial system operates.
4. The many roles played by the U.S. government.
5. The effects of government regulation on business.
6. The effects of pressure for deregulation.
7. How the U.S. tax system functions and its effects on business.

## In This Chapter

Understanding the U.S. Legal System
What Is Business Law?
Understanding the Judicial System
Understanding the Government's Role

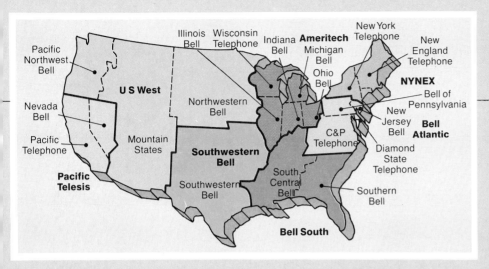

For most of its history, the business of the American Telephone and Telegraph Company (AT&T) was easily defined: *providing telephone service,* aiming to create one universally accessible telephone network. Because it was a legal monopoly, its activities were closely regulated. But, as telephone lines began carrying signals for television, computer data, and other forms of communication, the firm's business changed to *telecommunications.* And regulation began to hurt "Ma Bell." Its activities in the newer areas were still restricted, while those of competitors weren't. With the breakup of AT&T in 1982, its business changed again to include new markets for communications and information. This change occurred because of advances in technology and new government policies reducing regulation. The company is now in the business of *transporting and managing information,* and most of its activities are regulated to the same extent as those of other private businesses.

The pressure to break AT&T up began to build in 1968, when the U.S. Supreme Court let non-AT&T equipment be connected to the Bell system. The next year, the cracks in the system widened, as the Federal Communication Commission (FCC) gave MCI the right to hook its long-distance network into AT&T's local phone systems. Then, in 1974, the final blow fell: The Justice Department filed an antitrust suit against AT&T. The settlement of that suit in 1982 meant that on January 1, 1984, AT&T became a new type of business. The company—which could no longer use the Bell name—retained its long-distance network, its manufacturing arm (Western Electric Company), and Bell Labs. But, in return for giving up its twenty-two local operating companies—now operating as part of seven regional holding companies—AT&T was allowed to move into the closely related business of transporting and managing information and to compete with established information-processing and -managing firms, such as IBM. The new competitive atmosphere was fine. But the cost of the breakup (just to AT&T, and not to the twenty-two operating companies) was estimated to be $1.9 billion, over $60 million of which was spent just to change the corporate logo—twice. Another $4.8 billion was written off in 1983 for obsolete equipment.

What effect will the breakup have on AT&T in the long run? According to Chairman Charles L. Brown, who thought the breakup was a mistake but won wide praise for his part in seeing it through: "While we're facing a couple of hard years of adjustment, there's every reason for confidence in the future." One reason for those hard years was a series of lawsuits between AT&T and the new operating companies. The operating companies sued for the right to use the prestigious Bell name, and won—*after* AT&T had spent $30 million familiarizing the public with the new name of its marketing subsidiary now renamed AT&T Information Systems.

A business is involved in a legal and governmental environment that sets rules and regulations for activities from choosing a form of business to paying taxes or possibly even being broken up, as AT&T was. There's no question about the broad impact this environment has. Throughout this book, we've talked about government paperwork, laws protecting consumers, and business's social responsibility. In this chapter, we'll spend more time looking behind those examples—at the body of business law and at the government's overall influence on business.

## UNDERSTANDING THE U.S. LEGAL SYSTEM

**Objective 1**

**The basic legal foundations upon which the U.S. business system is built.**

It seems that people and institutions seek to resolve many of their problems through legal action rather than by other methods. A lot of people feel there ought to be a law to solve every problem. For instance, when the Great Salt Lake threatened to flood parts of Utah in 1979, the legislature passed a law forbidding the lake to rise higher than 4,202 feet above mean sea level.[1]

Before looking at laws that apply to business problems, let's see how the legal system as a whole works. Many of the legal theories and concepts now used in the United States have grown out of the Roman legal system and the British system of common law. **Common law** is the body of the law arising from judicial decisions based on unwritten laws (customs or usages) that are generally accepted by the people. Much of this basic legal system has now been converted into **statute law,** which consists of the laws that have been passed by federal, state, and local legislative groups.

Although the U.S. legal system is often criticized for its burdensome imperfections, it has many built-in safeguards. Probably the most basic concept of the legal system is the **rule of law,** which means that everyone is equal under the law. The United States has a government of laws, not of individuals, and everyone, regardless of status or position, must obey those laws.

A second principle is that all laws must be based on *the federal or a state constitution.* In the states, the regulation of business is based on the use of police power. Not nearly as severe as it sounds, **police power** is the right of state authorities to use the forces of the state to promote the general welfare of its citizens. The interstate commerce clause of the U.S. Constitution gives Congress the right to "regulate Commerce with foreign nations, and among the several States."

A third principle is that the system operates under **due process,** which means that everyone is entitled to his or her day in court, and that legal procedures must be applied under conditions of decency and fairness. These rights are guaranteed by the Sixth and Fourteenth amendments to the U.S. Constitution. A fourth basic protection is that a person is *presumed to be innocent until proven guilty.*

A fifth concept, and one of the most difficult for people in other countries to understand, involves the *multiple levels of government* in the United States. According to the Tenth Amendment of the Constitution, "The powers not delegated to the United States . . . are reserved to the [individual] States." Then, within the states, there are units such as counties, parishes, and townships, and smaller units such as cities and towns. Therefore, there are at least four levels of relatively uncoordinated government—federal, state, county, and local—and all of them regulate business to some extent.

A sixth concept is the **separation of powers,** by which the making, administering, and interpreting of laws are separated into three distinct branches of government. The **legislative branch**—the U.S. Congress, a state legislature, or a town or county council—passes legislation in the form of laws or statutes. The **executive branch**—the president, a governor, the president of a county commission, or a mayor—enforces the laws through regulatory agencies and decrees. The **judicial branch**—the courts—interprets the laws.

## WHAT IS BUSINESS LAW?

**Objective 2**

**What business law is and the types of laws it encompasses.**

Like most business and economic subjects, the legal system can be studied from many different viewpoints. But whatever the approaches, some method must be used to classify laws into groups. Before we look at what business law is, we will begin by stating what it *isn't.*

**Criminal law** is concerned with punishing individuals who commit illegal acts against society (for example, a firm that bribes a government official in order to get a contract). On the other hand, **civil law** tries to resolve problems or differences between individuals or groups of individuals, or to settle grievances by requiring monetary compensation to those who've been harmed. Occasionally, it's difficult to separate the two types of law, as in the case of Ford's exploding Pinto (see FYI on page 42), which was tried as a criminal rather than a civil suit. This case was significant in the area of product liability since, if the decision had gone against Ford, it would have changed the legal system.

Business law has usually been taught in programs that stress legal issues that apply to business and its activities. But now teachers, students, and the general public are also sensitive to problems of safety, environmental pollution, equal employment opportunity, labor-management relations, consumerism, trusts and monopolies, price fixing, and security regulations. Prospective business owners and managers don't need a law degree, but they do need to understand how to deal with the legal aspects of these problems. Table 23-1 summarizes some of the sources of business laws. It will give you an idea of why there are so many laws, and why they're so complex and often contradictory.

> Notice that all three *branches* of government (four, counting regulatory agencies) can be said to make laws. What effects does this complex system have on business? Does it make obeying the law more difficult?

### Contracts

The law of contracts deals with legal business relationships resulting from agreements among two or more individuals or businesses. A **contract** is an agreement between two parties, be they individuals or groups, that is enforced by law. A contract may be valid and enforceable whether it is oral or written. Without contracts there could be no business as we know it, for contract law affects almost all business operations.

**TABLE 23-1  Bases and sources of laws affecting business.**

| Government Level | Basis of Laws | Statutory Acts | Executive Decrees | Regulations (Administrative Laws) | Court Decrees |
|---|---|---|---|---|---|
| | | SOURCES AND FORMS OF LAWS | | | |
| Federal | United States Constitution, as amended | Legislation passed by Congress | Executive orders of the President, as authorized by congressional statute or the Constitution | Issued by federal regulatory agencies, as authorized by Congress | Based on court decisions and interpretations of laws, orders, and regulations |
| State | Constitution, as amended | Legislation passed by legislatures | Orders issued by the governor, as authorized by the legislature or constitution | Issued by state regulatory agencies, as authorized by the legislature | Same as above |
| County | Charter | Legislation passed by the county's legislative body | Orders of the chief executive officer, as authorized by legislative act or the county's legislative body | Issued by county regulatory agencies, as authorized by the state legislature and county governing body | Same as above |
| City | Charter | Acts of state legislature or ordinances passed by city council or board of aldermen | Orders of the chief executive officer, as authorized by legislative act or city ordinance | Issued by city regulatory agencies, as authorized by state legislature and city governing body | Same as above |

A classic example of a contract dispute was the battle that took place in early 1984, when both Pennzoil Company and Texaco tried to buy Getty Oil Company, a privately held company, in one of the biggest corporate takeovers in U.S. history.[2] Pennzoil made a certified offer of $110 per share for 20 percent of Getty's shares to Gordon Getty, the youngest surviving son of Getty's founder, J. Paul Getty. Gordon Getty heads the Sarah C. Getty Trust, which owns 40.2 percent of all shares. Texaco offered $125 per share to Getty's board of directors for the 12 percent of the stock owned by the J. Paul Getty Museum and all other shares. Gordon Getty and Getty Oil's management and board had been battling for months over who ran the company—the board, the Sarah C. Getty Trust, or the J. Paul Getty Museum. The Texaco offer was given preference over the Pennzoil offer, and accepted. The total price was $9.9 billion. We'll see below how all of this is interpreted in terms of contract law.

For a contract to be legal in the United States, the following conditions must be met:

1. Both parties must be legally competent to act. This means not only being of sound mind but also being the authorized representative of a group or corporation. Notice that Gordon Getty and the Sarah C. Getty Trust were judged *not* to represent Getty Oil.
2. The agreement must not involve illegal actions or promises. The

mobster who puts out a "contract" on someone he wants killed couldn't, of course, take such a contract into a court of law. But Pennzoil and Texaco were both taking perfectly legal actions.

3. A valid offer to enter into an agreement must be made by one party in a serious manner, not in jest. Both Pennzoil and Texaco made serious offers. The offer may be explicit—the automobile salesperson may offer to sell you the Super Deluxe Whizbang for $9,000 plus your old car—or it may be implicit—a retailer marks a videotape recorder on the shelf "$499.99."

4. The second party must voluntarily accept this offer equally seriously, without duress (physical force or other compulsion) or "undue influence." The Getty board did accept the Texaco offer voluntarily, without duress.

5. Each party must promise the other some form of **consideration,** which is something of value, such as money, services, goods, or the surrender of some legal right. Texaco promised money in return for ownership, in the form of stock, of Getty.

6. The contract must be in a legal form, even if oral, but it may really be quite simple (see Figure 23-1 for an example). It must contain all the elements of the contract—the identity of the two parties, offer, consideration, and acceptance—but little more.

### Sales

Laws affecting sales are really part of contract law, except that many of the millions of sales contracts casually entered into each day are oral or implied. While both goods and services are sold, sales law covers only the sale of goods.

**Figure 23-1** A simple contract.

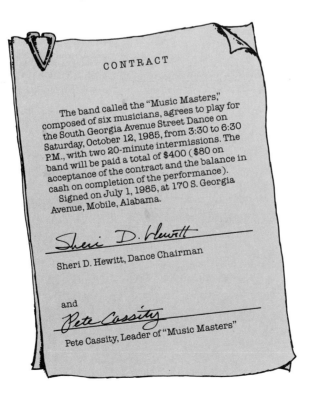

CONTRACT

The band called the "Music Masters," composed of six musicians, agrees to play for the South Georgia Avenue Street Dance on Saturday, October 12, 1985, from 3:30 to 6:30 P.M., with two 20-minute intermissions. The band will be paid a total of $400 ($80 on acceptance of the contract and the balance in cash on completion of the performance). Signed on July 1, 1985, at 170 S. Georgia Avenue, Mobile, Alabama.

*Sheri D. Hewitt*

Sheri D. Hewitt, Dance Chairman

and

*Pete Cassity*

Pete Cassity, Leader of "Music Masters"

This body of business law evolved from early English laws based on the customs and practices of merchants in their relationships with customers. There were special courts to enforce these laws. Most of these laws came into our system through common law but later were incorporated into the Uniform Commercial Code (UCC), which provides uniformity in all aspects of commercial law, including sales. (The UCC will be discussed later in this chapter.)

▲ **Warranties**  A **warranty** is a representation made to the buyer by the seller regarding the quality and performance of a product. It may be expressed or implied. **Express warranties** are specific representations made by the seller regarding the product. They often come in the form of warranty cards to be completed and returned by the buyer. **Implied warranties** are those legally imposed on the seller. Unless implied warranties are disclaimed, in writing, by the seller, they are automatically applied. The law of warranties for sales transactions is set forth in the UCC.

▲ **Product Liability**  A frequent and serious problem these days is product liability. An ever-present question facing sellers is "How safe *should* the product be?" Much attention is now being focused on the design of products and quality control to ensure product safety. Of course, if all possible safety precautions were built into all products and their production, they'd be prohibitively expensive—and sometimes impossible to use. Thus the degree of safety required depends on the product. For example, the proper functioning of a pacemaker is a matter of life and death, so each one must be perfect. On the other hand, a defective ballpoint pen may present only a minor inconvenience.

## Property

Property law involves the rights and duties resulting from the *ownership or use* of personal or real property. Contract, sales, and other types of law apply to the *transfer* of property. **Personal property** is anything of value, aside from land, that can be owned or used by an individual. **Real property** is land or anything attached more or less permanently to land, such as a house, factory, research laboratory, or oil well.

Personal property may be **tangible property**—that is, some material good or product such as a car, stereo, or clothing—or it may be **intangible property**—that is, something whose ownership is represented by a written document, such as a share of stock or a deposit slip. Personal property also includes patents, copyrights, and trademarks. The transfer of personal property is usually achieved by conveying the **title,** or the legal right to possess and use it, from one party to another. When this isn't done, use of the property constitutes fraud.

The ownership of real property is usually transferred by means of a **deed,** which is a written document used by the owner of real property to convey it to another owner. However, the use of property may be made possible by a **lease,** which is a written agreement permitting the use of property by someone other than the owner for a limited period of time.

## Agency

The law of agency is based on common law principles, as formalized in statute law and legal decisions. The term **agency** describes the legal relationship be-

tween two parties, the principal and the agent, when they agree that the agent will act as a representative of the principal. The **principal** is the person who wants to do something legally but is unwilling or unable to do it personally. The **agent** is the person or company employed to act on behalf of the other person. All types of business transactions, and many personal ones, involve agency. Directors, officers, and sales personnel act as agents for a corporation. For instance, the board of Getty Oil acted as an agent for the owners. Partners act as agents for each other, and most professional athletes, actors, artists, writers, and musicians have agents. Heisman Trophy winner Mike Rozier's agent, Mike Trope, signed a $3 million contract for him with the USFL's Pittsburgh Maulers, apparently without notifying his principal, who denied to the press that he had signed such a contract. (Later, Rozier accepted the contract, but fired the agent!)

### Negotiable Instruments

Special laws deal with the legal rules involved in buying, owning, and selling negotiable instruments. A **negotiable instrument** is some form of financial document, such as a check, bank draft, or certificate of deposit, that's transferable from one party to another. The law requires that negotiable instruments be written, not oral; signed by the maker; good for the promise of a given sum of money; and payable when endorsed by the payee.

### Torts

Laws concerning torts cover the responsibilities and obligations of people involved in business dealings other than those already discussed. A **tort** is an act by one party, not covered by criminal law, that results in injury to a second party's person, property, or reputation, for which the second party is legally entitled to some form of compensation. The laws of torts tend to provide for the performance of duties and compensation for physical, mental, or economic injuries resulting from faulty products or actions of employees. This usually involves some form of economic restitution (monetary payment) for damages or loss incurred.

For example, in 1975, a Miami, Florida, jury awarded a paralyzed high school football player a $5.3 million judgment against Riddell, Inc., a maker of football helmets. Now 14 percent of the cost of Riddell's helmets is due to insurance, lawsuits, and settlements.[3] In another tort case, a man who tried to commit suicide by throwing himself in front of an oncoming Metropolitan (New York) Transit Authority subway train won a $650,000 settlement because the train's operator "demonstrated negligence."[4]

### Bankruptcy

Under **bankruptcy** law, people or businesses can petition the courts for relief from debts they can't repay, and are relieved of the obligation to pay. There are two types of bankruptcy, voluntary and involuntary. **Voluntary bankruptcy** occurs when a debtor files an application with a court claiming that debts exceed assets and asks to be declared bankrupt. When one or more creditors file the bankruptcy petition, it's called **involuntary bankruptcy.** The Bankruptcy Reform Act, passed in 1978, provides for quick and efficient handling of such cases. Under its Chapter 11, there's a provision for reorganizing the

bankrupt business, whether the bankruptcy petition is filed voluntarily or involuntarily. Thus the firm can continue to operate while its debts are being repaid. If the business is so far gone that it can't keep operating, Chapter 7 provides a procedure for liquidating it.

In one of the most celebrated bankruptcy cases, Manville Corporation, with a net worth of $1 billion, filed for Chapter 11 bankruptcy in 1982. In that case, which is still pending, Manville claimed that, with 16,000 suits filed by victims of asbestos-related diseases and with potential liabilities of $2 billion, it would soon be insolvent. The firm asked that the 16,000 suits be brought into bankruptcy court, where they could all be dealt with at the same time.[5]

### The Uniform Commercial Code

Laws affecting business vary greatly from state to state. Therefore, an effort has been made to draft a set of uniform model statutes to be used in all fifty states in business and commercial transactions of businesses and individuals. It's called the **Uniform Commercial Code (UCC)** and contains regulations pertaining to sales, bills of lading (used in shipping), financial transactions—including transfer of investment securities—and personal property. It's in use in all the states except Louisiana, which still has some laws based on the Code Napoléon, the French civil code that's been in effect there since before the Louisiana Purchase.

## UNDERSTANDING THE JUDICIAL SYSTEM

**Objective 3**

**How the U.S. judicial system operates.**

Laws operate through people and institutions and become effective only when applied and enforced by them. Thus the impact of a given law depends on how the law is interpreted and enforced. This is done by the **judicial system,** which consists of the lawmaking and law-interpreting people and institutions of the nation, including lawyers, judges, juries, review court judges, and their support personnel. The judicial system is responsible for interpreting laws and the administrative orders, guidelines, and decisions of regulatory agencies. Yet the courts also "make" laws through their decisions.

The judicial system is composed of many courts at different levels of government, from the city to the county, state, and national levels. Each level also has many layers, because the courts are arranged so that the decisions of lower-level courts are subject to appeal to a higher-level court. Yet the process must finally end—as it frequently does—at the U.S. Supreme Court, which has the final authority to say whether a given law or activity is legal as far as the Constitution is concerned (see the Profile on p. 626).

## UNDERSTANDING THE GOVERNMENT'S ROLE

**Objective 4**

**The many roles played by the U.S. government.**

Over a century ago, the U.S. legal environment often permitted large businesses to use the government almost as a partner in their ventures. The development of the railroads followed this pattern, and shippers and receivers wound up being exploited by the railroad owners. Railroads' abuses of their

monopoly position moved Congress to set up the Interstate Commerce Commission (ICC) in 1888 to regulate railroad operations. The Standard Oil Company and its owner, John D. Rockefeller, also misused power by unfairly driving out competition and overcharging customers. These abuses, and similar actions by other firms, led to the passage of the first antitrust legislation (the Sherman Antitrust Act) in 1890, which was strengthened in 1954. Since then, the government's role has become larger, so that it now influences, directly or indirectly, almost every business decision made by owners and managers.

> Who do you think is the major purchaser of the goods and services produced by U.S. business firms? Who's the largest employer in the country?

First, as shown in Chapter 1, the government, through the legal and judicial systems just covered, makes the free enterprise system possible.

Second, the U.S. government is the nation's *chief financial executive,* raising and collecting taxes (around 22 percent of the nation's total production of goods and services), providing and regulating the supply of money, giving subsidies and tax breaks, lending money, spending money, purchasing materials, and guaranteeing private and business loans.

Third, it's the *chief industrialist-employer* in the country. It owns more real estate, constructs and maintains more buildings, borrows more money, purchases more goods and services, and employs more people than any other organization in the free world. Each year, the government hires about 5 million people for military and civilian positions. It also provides retirement pay to about 42 million people and other benefits to many millions of others.

Fourth, it's the nation's *chief regulator.* As will be shown in the next section, there are fifty-four major federal agencies, each with annual budgets of over $6 million regulating industries, controlling imports and exports, and enforcing health, safety, and environmental rules.

## Government Regulation of Business

**Objective 5**

**The effects of government regulation on business.**

The state and federal governments regulate everything from the air we breathe, the medical care we receive, and the food we eat to our travel to and from other countries. For example, there are about 41,000 regulations, stemming from 200 laws and 111 precedent-setting court cases, affecting the production and sale of a hamburger. These add about $0.08 to $0.11 to its cost. Similarly, there are 310 separate regulations, covering forty pages of federal documents, governing what goes into a pizza (see FYI on page 628). When the milk lobby pressured the U.S. Department of Agriculture to require more cheese in pizza in 1983, over 4,700 letters were received by April 1983—mostly protesting the rule.[6] Until recently, federal energy policies were enforced by eleven different agencies. And one medium-sized trucking firm, which operates in all but a few states, must file 2,310 state forms and 52 federal ones every year.

These examples begin to tell you why it's so difficult for businesspeople to conform to today's legal requirements. Most owners, managers, and employees are willing to accept and obey "the law." Yet they find it difficult to do so

## *Profile*

**Sandra Day O'Connor: FWOTSC**

In a news article, the *New York Times* referred to the "nine men" of SCOTUS (Supreme Court of the United States). In a sharp letter to the editor, published in the October 12, 1983, edition, Justice Sandra Day O'Connor wrote:

> According to the information available to me, and which I assumed was generally available, for over two years now

SCOTUS has not consisted of nine men. If you have any contradictory information, I would be grateful if you would forward it as I am sure that POTUS (president of the United States), the SCOTUS and the undersigned would be most interested in seeing it.

(Signed) FWOTSC (for First Woman of the Supreme Court)

because of conflicts over what "the law" really is and because of the cost involved in time, effort, and money.

▲ **Regulatory Agencies**  In theory, a regulatory agency is more flexible and sensitive to the needs of society than Congress can be, since less time is needed for an agency to develop and issue new regulations than for Congress to enact new legislation. It's also assumed that agencies will be less sensitive to political pressure. Experience, however, doesn't seem to justify this theory. It's been claimed, for example, that (1) agencies tend to perpetuate themselves through bureaucratic empires; (2) they tend to become insensitive to the needs and well-being of society; and (3) on occasion, their findings may be arbitrary or may protect their own security or that of the industry they're supposed to regulate. FYI on pages 630 and 631 shows some of the more important regulatory bodies and their duties.

There are at least three areas of general concern relating to government regulation of business, all with economic consequences. The first problem is

Realizing that Justice O'Connor isn't a woman to be treated lightly, the *Times* soon ran an apology on its editorial page.

This incident tells you a lot about the wit and fighting spirit of the first woman to break into the nation's most exclusive men's club. She's brought a different voice to its ranks.

When Justice O'Connor was appointed the 102nd Supreme Court Justice by President Reagan, she became an instant media sensation. Today, hers is turning out to be one of the Reagan administration's wisest appointments. But in her early days as a lawyer, O'Connor had to scramble to survive. She started her first law practice in the late 1950s at a Phoenix, Arizona, shopping center where her clientele consisted mainly of people wandering through the mall. Her opinions and dissents show that O'Connor hasn't forgotten her roots. A former state legislator, she has consistently defended the states' prerogatives; a former trial judge, she moved to end incessant appeals by convicted defendants. She says it's time for state judges to get some respect.

Justice O'Connor redeemed herself in the eyes of some feminists when she cast the decisive vote in a decision outlawing public-employee pension plans that discriminate by sex. However, she joined with four other Justices to prevent the new rule from being made retroactive. Thus the new rule is applicable only to future payments into pension plans. Because of her stand on abortion, right-to-life groups bitterly complained that the Reagan administration

had sold them out with the appointment of Sandra O'Connor. But she strongly dissented from a majority decision that struck down a variety of local laws restricting a woman's right to end her pregnancy. Her reasoning wasn't based on her own personal views of what's right and wrong but on the dictates of court precedents.

Although Justice O'Connor's stands are sometimes undefined when measured on the basis of jurisprudence, her social position couldn't be clearer. Sandra and John O'Connor are on the "A" list of Washington hostesses and have their pick of parties. She plays tennis weekly and is looking forward to seeing her life return to normal. However, as the first woman Justice, this capable judge may find that those normal days are gone forever.

Sources: "Had to 'Scramble' in Early Days," *Mobile Register*, October 24, 1983, p. 15-A; Aric Press, "The Court's New Tough Guy," *Newsweek*, June 21, 1982, pp. 69–70; "Sizing Up Ms. Justice," *Newsweek*, July 18, 1983, p. 57; "Justice O'Connor Lauded on N.Y. Times Letter," *Mobile Press-Register*, October 15, 1983, p. 4-A; and Daniel B. Moskowitz, "How the Supreme Court Is Redistributing Power," *Business Week*, July 18, 1983, p. 55.

the *difficulty of understanding some of the regulations,* as well as the confusing, and often contradictory, nature of some laws and regulations. For example, the Civil Rights Act of 1964 prohibited separate toilets for men and women employees. The Occupational Safety and Health of 1970, on the other hand, required that there be separate facilities.

A second problem is the *enormous amount of paperwork* involved in preparing and handling the reports needed to comply with government regulations and in maintaining the records needed to satisfy the regulators. The *Armed Forces Journal* reported in 1981 that two contractors—Bell Helicopter and Hughes Helicopter—had submitted 2.8 tons of paper proposals for a small Army targeting helicopter that will weigh only about 1.5 tons at take-off. A single copy of one proposal weighed ninety-nine pounds; the other weighed seventy-four pounds.[7]

A third problem is the *difficulty and cost of complying with the regulations.* The costs are greater than just the administrative expenses; bringing operations into compliance with the regulations is also expensive.

## *FYI*

### A Pizza with the Works—Including 310 Regulations

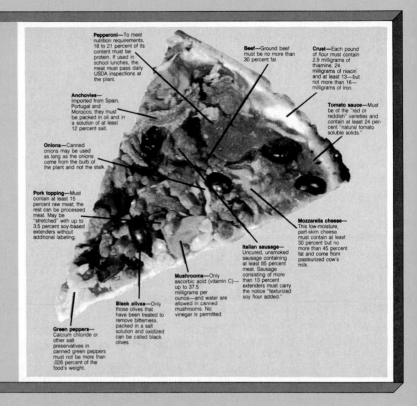

**Pepperoni**—To meet nutrition requirements, 18 to 21 percent of its content must be protein. If used in school lunches, the meat must pass daily USDA inspections at the plant.

**Anchovies**—Imported from Spain, Portugal and Morocco, they must be packed in oil and in a solution of at least 12 percent salt.

**Onions**—Canned onions may be used as long as the onions come from the bulb of the plant and not the stalk.

**Pork topping**—Must contain at least 15 percent raw meat; the rest can be processed meat. May be "stretched" with up to 3.5 percent soy-based extenders without additional labeling.

**Green peppers**—Calcium chloride or other salt preservatives in canned green peppers must not be more than .026 percent of the food's weight.

**Black olives**—Only those olives that have been treated to remove bitterness, packed in a salt solution and oxidized can be called black olives.

**Mushrooms**—Only ascorbic acid (vitamin C) up to 37.5 milligrams per ounce—and water are allowed in canned mushrooms. No vinegar is permitted.

**Italian sausage**—Uncured, unsmoked sausage containing at least 85 percent meat. Sausage consisting of more than 13 percent extenders must carry the notice "texturized soy flour added."

**Mozzarella cheese**—This low-moisture, part-skim cheese must contain at least 30 percent but no more than 45 percent fat and come from pasteurized cow's milk.

**Tomato sauce**—Must be of the "red or reddish" varieties and contain at least 24 percent "natural tomato soluble solids."

**Beef**—Ground beef must be no more than 30 percent fat

**Crust**—Each pound of flour must contain 2.9 milligrams of thiamine, 24 milligrams of niacin and at least 13—but not more than 16—milligrams of iron.

When it comes to snacks, few foods can rival pizza in popularity.

Since New York City restaurants first offered the tangy pies in 1936, pizza has grown into a booming, $6-billion-a-year business.

Last year, Americans gobbled up more than 1.5 billion pizzas at home, in schools and sporting arenas, and in the more than 20,000 restaurants that serve it. That breaks down to about seven pizzas for every man, woman and child in the U.S.

But along with the popularity have come scores of regulations from the Food and Drug Administration and the Department of Agriculture on the ingredients in what the government describes as "a bread-base meat food product with tomato sauce, cheese and meat topping."

In all, the rules governing what goes on a pizza and how those toppings can be described on labels and menus take up more than forty pages of federal documents, including some 310 separate regulations. Here's a sampling of just a few of those standards for a pizza—with everything.

▲ **Benefits of Regulation**   One difficult aspect of government regulation is determining whether the benefits of a regulation outweigh its cost.  Since there's no profit mechanism that measures this, as there is in private business, and since the costs and benefits themselves are hard to determine, estimates must be made.  Even with these measurement limitations, though, it's been shown that some regulations are truly cost-effective.  For example, air pollution regulations have provided economic benefits that far outweigh the costs of complying with them, according to the White House Council on Environmental Quality.[8]  The cost of meeting pollution standards for a year was about $13.1 billion, but it was estimated that about $22 billion in environmental damage was being prevented.  The panel also showed that air and water pollution were diminishing as a result of regulation.

▲ **Regulating Competition**   Another important benefit of government regulation is that the marketplace is kept relatively free from restrictive monopolistic influences.  The Federal Trade Commission (FTC), set up in 1914, enforces the laws designed to maintain relatively unrestricted competition, especially the Sherman Antitrust Act (1890), the Clayton Act (1914), and the Celler-Kefauver Act (1950).  These laws prohibit companies from entering into agreements to control trade through monopolistic actions.  Such actions would include one firm's buying out a competing firm, or entering into a joint venture, in order to decrease competition in that industry.  For example, Chrysler Corporation went to court to block the GM/Toyota joint venture to build 200,000 subcompact cars at a Fremont, California, plant after the FTC approved it.  Chrysler claimed the joint venture would let "the two strongest automobile companies in the world monopolize the small car market."[9]

Price fixing is also prohibited.  The Robinson-Patman Act (1936) outlaws price discrimination that can't be justified on the basis of quality or quantity differences, or that injures competition.  Thus, a store can't offer you a discount for trading with it, unless the same discount is offered to everyone in

# FYI

## An Army of Regulators

The Reagan administration is clamping down on federal rules, but an army of Uncle Sam's enforcers still polices the marketplace.

Some 324,000 government employees staff fifty-four regulatory agencies, despite the tighter budgets and personnel cuts of recent months. Among the major agencies:

### Consumer Product Safety Commission

Issues and enforces performance and safety standards for more than 10,000 products, including toys, lawn mowers, tools and clothing.

### Federal Trade Commission

Insures that firms compete fairly—without price fixing, deceptive advertising and other questionable practices.

### Food and Drug Administration

Inspects and tests drugs, cosmetics and food products before they are offered to the public.

### Environmental Protection Agency

Protects the nation's water and air by monitoring discharges and emissions from factories, sewer systems, other polluters.

### Occupational Safety and Health Administration

Investigates on-the-job accidents and enforces rules for protecting employees in some 3.5 million workplaces.

### Securities and Exchange Commission

Regulates trading in stocks and bonds and gathers financial information on firms.

### National Labor Relations Board

Oversees elections to determine whether workers want union representation and investigates employer-worker disputes.

### Equal Employment Opportunity Commission

Investigates complaints of discrimination in hiring or promotion of workers on the basis of race, sex, physical handicap, or age.

### Federal Communications Commission

Grants operating licenses for radio and TV stations and citizens'-band radio owners. It also oversees interstate telephone operations, including rates on long-distance calls, and sets standards for cable TV and communications satellites.

### Drug Enforcement Administration

Controls legal distribution and sale of narcotics and dangerous drugs and hunts down traffickers in illicit drugs.

### Federal Aviation Administration

Spells out what kinds of aircraft may be used for commercial and personal flying and sets standards for airline maintenance, air-traffic control and pilot fitness.

**Federal Deposit Insurance Corporation**

Insures the deposits held by banks belonging to the Federal Reserve System and establishes standards for the proper operation of financial institutions.

**National Highway Traffic Safety Administration**

Sets rules for fuel efficiency and safety standards for bumpers, seat belts, tires and other features.

**Interstate Commerce Commission**

Establishes railroad and truck rates, investigates complaints against carriers and oversees mergers of transportation companies.

**Federal Home Loan Bank Board**

Regulates the federally chartered savings and loan associations and insures the deposits held by member S&L's through its Federal Savings and Loan Insurance Corporation.

**U.S. Forest Service**

Regulates the cutting of timber on federal lands and provides national leadership in forestry.

**Immigration and Naturalization Service**

Controls the flow of newcomers into the U.S. and enforces rules for citizenship.

**Nuclear Regulatory Commission**

Issues licenses for nuclear power plants, sets standards for plant construction and supervises the disposal of nuclear wastes.

**Food Safety and Quality Service**

Certifies the wholesomeness, grade and quality of meats, poultry and fresh fruits and vegetables.

**Patent and Trademark Office**

Protects the rights of inventors and producers of new goods and services and prevents infringement upon established products.

Source: Adapted from "The Ever Present Hand of Government," *U.S.News & World Report,* April 26, 1982, p. 44. Reprinted from *U.S.News & World Report;* Copyright, 1982, U.S.News & World Report, Inc.

your demographic group—such as senior citizens. It can, though, offer a discount for cash or to anyone who buys a dozen furnace filters at once, as a local hardware store does.

## Pressure for Deregulation

**Objective 6**

**The effects of pressure for deregulation.**

The pressure for greater regulation seems to be diminishing, at least from the general public. Instead, there now seems to be a move toward deregulation.

President Reagan's election in 1980 was evidence of this movement. He campaigned on the promise of general and thorough deregulation throughout the federal government. The main agencies and practices he sought to deregulate are shown in Table 23-2. But there had already been extensive steps toward deregulation going back to 1968 (see Figure 23-2). Deregulation of the transportation and financial industries by Congress had begun under President Carter—with the airlines in 1978 and trucking and railroads in 1980.

Now, U.S. business is undergoing its first redirection toward competition in 100 years. The results are striking. Deregulation is boosting the economy

**TABLE 23-2   Reagan's regulatory hit list.**

| Agency | Action |
|---|---|
| Environmental Protection Agency | Move away from technology-forcing standards, such as smokestack scrubbers for all coal-fired plants, toward performance standards |
| Occupational Safety & Health Administration | Emphasize personal-protection devices rather than costly engineering controls to achieve workplace safety |
| Consumer Product Safety Commission | Emphasize dangerous-product warnings over product regulation |
| Food & Drug Administration | Review the law that prohibits food additives that may cause cancer—no matter how low the risk |
| Agriculture Dept. | Ease meat-labeling requirements |
| National Highway Traffic Safety Administration | Postpone rule requiring air bags or passive seat belts in autos |
| Energy Dept. | Relax requirements for utilities and industry to convert to coal power |
| Interior Dept. | Accelerate leasing of mineral and energy resources on federal land |
| Nuclear Regulatory Commission | Streamline licensing of nuclear power plants |
| Securities & Exchange Commission | Prosecute major offenders vigorously rather than file numerous cases now often settled out of court |
| Urban Mass Transportation Administration | Review requirement that subways and buses be fully accessible to the handicapped |
| Federal Energy Regulatory Commission | Speed up decontrol of natural gas |
| Equal Employment Opportunity Commission | Look for case-by-case discriminatory practices rather than seek industrywide patterns of discrimination |

SOURCE: From "Deregulation: A Fast Start for the Reagan Strategy." Reprinted from the March 9, 1981 issue of *Business Week* by special permission, © 1981 by McGraw-Hill, Inc., p. 63.

by encouraging innovation, increasing productivity, reducing prices, and revitalizing three basic industries—finance, telecommunications, and transportation. The cost to small investors of buying stock is now 60 percent below that charged by old-line brokerage firms; long-distance airline fares (adjusted for inflation) have gone down nearly 50 percent in seven years; many trucking rates have skidded 30 percent (in real terms) since 1980; and the costs of standard telephones dropped by a third from 1982 to 1983.[10]

One of the most drastic changes in over half a century occurred with the deregulation of the financial area. In 1979, the federal government began to gradually remove the ceiling on interest rates so that other financial institutions could compete effectively with banks, which had a competitive advan-

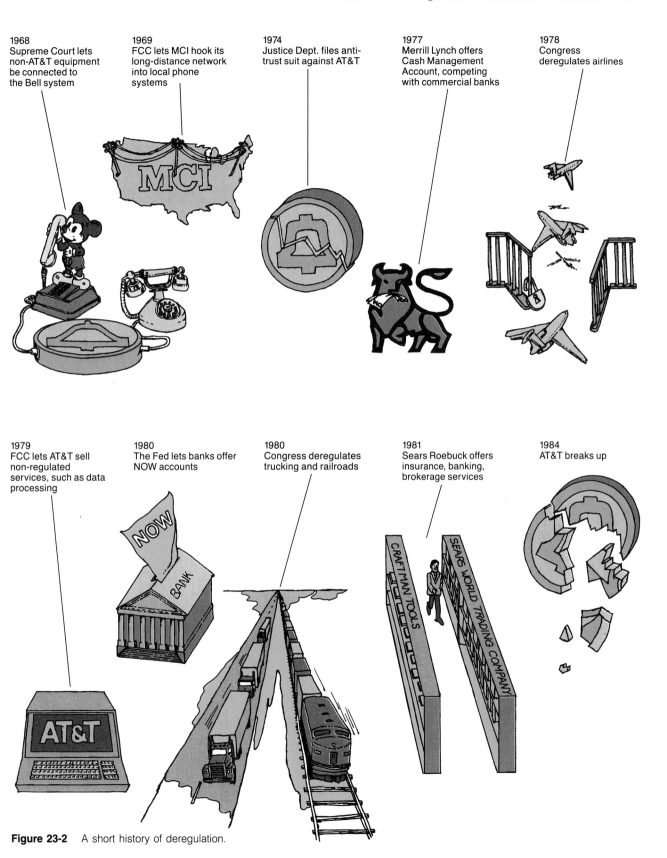

1968
Supreme Court lets non-AT&T equipment be connected to the Bell system

1969
FCC lets MCI hook its long-distance network into local phone systems

1974
Justice Dept. files anti-trust suit against AT&T

1977
Merrill Lynch offers Cash Management Account, competing with commercial banks

1978
Congress deregulates airlines

1979
FCC lets AT&T sell non-regulated services, such as data processing

1980
The Fed lets banks offer NOW accounts

1980
Congress deregulates trucking and railroads

1981
Sears Roebuck offers insurance, banking, brokerage services

1984
AT&T breaks up

**Figure 23-2**   A short history of deregulation.

tage. This phaseout, which will be completed in 1986, is revolutionizing the financial area, as was shown in Chapter 18.

In early 1981, President Reagan lifted all regulations over the supply and price of gasoline, and natural gas is in the process of being deregulated. These deregulation efforts have been quite effective in reducing prices and increasing employment. The original efforts toward deregulation of oil and gas were announced by President Carter in April 1979. From then until June 1981, the average employment in the oil and gas industries increased by about 6,600 jobs per month, while employment in coal mining and other energy companies was growing very little.[11]

In keeping with the philosophy of deregulation, existing regulations have been quietly phased out, modified, or not enforced. Extensive economic analysis is now required by the Office of Management and Budget before a new regulation is adopted, in order to ensure that it's needed and that its potential benefits to society outweigh its potential costs.[12] After two years of reform, the number of pages in the *Federal Register* (where proposed regulations are printed) had been cut by one-third; federal paperwork requirements for 1981 were reduced by 200 million person-hours; and reductions in excessive regulations saved industry $10 billion in one-time investment costs and $6 billion in annually recurring costs.[13]

Of course, there have been many short-term costs of deregulation. Wages are falling in some formerly regulated firms in the airline and trucking industries; more than 300 trucking firms have gone bankrupt; some smaller airlines failed, Continental Airlines is in Chapter 11 bankruptcy, and others, such as Eastern and Republic, are struggling to survive.[14] Yet fourteen new airlines have been formed since 1978, and one of them—People Express—is the fastest-growing airline in history. And 10,000 new, small trucking operators are in business as a result of deregulation.

Now there's growing pressure to *re*regulate the airlines, as shown in the Business Debate on page 635. *Fortune* reports that, largely because of problems in the Environmental Protection Agency (EPA) and airline bankruptcies, many Americans feel that deregulation has had undesirable side effects. As a result, the "voice of reregulation is ringing loud and clear these days, and would-be reregulators have a lot going for them."[15]

## The Tax System

**Objective 7**

How the U.S. tax system functions and its effects on business.

As Benjamin Franklin said, "nothing is certain but death and taxes." No one denies the truth of that. **Taxes,** or the charges levied by a government on persons and organizations subject to the jurisdiction of that government, are inevitable. Therefore, we'll try to explain how the government's tax system affects business.

The theory underlying taxation is simple enough. The government uses its power to tax in order to have funds to spend on essential goods and services. In the past, it's been considered desirable to have taxes levied according to the *ability of the payer to pay,* not according to the value of the benefits used. Thus the federal income tax is imposed directly on companies and individuals to raise the funds needed to meet the nation's regular budgetary needs. In general, the amount paid varies according to the ability to pay.

A consideration that's now becoming more important, though, is the *consequences of the tax*—that is, the effects a tax will have on the national econ-

# Business Debate

## Should Regulations Be Reimposed on Airlines?

In May 1982, Braniff International filed for bankruptcy; in 1984 Continental was operating under Chapter 11 bankruptcy, and Eastern, Republic, and others were having financial difficulties. Many observers such as airline consumer groups and airline employees—including pilots and high-level managers—blamed these problems on the dismantling of the Civil Aeronautics Board, which permitted airlines to compete freely in fares, routes, and schedules. (The carriers still had to obey the Federal Aviation Administration safety rules.) Now there's pressure from several groups to reregulate the airlines. For instance, one bill would require "stabilizing" air fares.

The arguments *for* reimposing regulations are:

1. Deregulation has forced carriers into self-destructive competition, causing the industry to be inefficient and unhealthy. Airlines can't handle the increased competitive pressure to set routes, rates, and schedules that are complex and interrelated with those of other airlines.
2. The large seating capacity of the jumbo jets and the long lead times between observation of a need for new planes to serve increased demand and delivery of these planes results in overcapacity.
3. Overcapacity and high fixed costs force airlines to engage in uneconomic price cutting to increase the number of passengers, even if that means taking them away from other lines.
4. The rush of more carriers into large central airports to reach popular markets has caused congestion and safety hazards because the controllers are unable to control the traffic.
5. While increased competition has reduced fares on popular, heavily traveled routes, deregulation has increased fares on routes abandoned by the major carriers.

The arguments *against* reimposing regulations are:

1. Deregulation has permitted each company to "do its own thing" and succeed or fail on its own. (By 1984, Braniff was reorganized and operating on a limited scale with new owners.)
2. Newer and more customer-oriented lines, such as People Express (see Case 20-1), have entered the industry with lower fares, frequent-traveler benefits, more convenient routes and schedules, smaller and more fuel-efficient planes, and smaller, more motivated and versatile staffs.
3. The benefits of deregulation, such as more logical routing and convenient scheduling, far outweigh the inevitable disadvantages, such as the failure of lines with poor management and high overhead expenses.
4. Factors other than deregulation, such as high fuel and labor costs, the 1981 air controllers' strike, the deep recession, and high interest rates, have caused some of the airlines' problems.
5. Many new commuter airlines are serving the communities abandoned by the major carriers.

*What do you think?*

Sources: For additional information, see "Letters to the Editor: Airline Deregulation Is Clipping Carriers' Wings," *Wall Street Journal,* May 24, 1982, p. 23; John D. Williams, "Aerial Counterattack: Major Airlines, Stung by the Competition of No-Frills Carriers, Are Fighting Back," *Wall Street Journal,* March 1, 1983, p. 56; John Brecher, "A Proud Bird Loses Its Wings," *Newsweek,* October 3, 1983, pp. 71–72; Cindy Skrzycki, "Airlines in Turbulence and More to Come," *U.S. News & World Report,* October 10, 1983, pp. 33–34; "Behind the High-Flying People Express Airline," *USA Today,* January 6–8, 1984, p. 3-D; and "Early Braniff Passengers Exceed Carrier Forecast," *Aviation Week and Space Technology* (April 23, 1984), p. 49.

**TABLE 23-3  Taxes on business.**\*

| Kind of Tax | Taxpayer | Point of Collection | Collecting Agency |
| --- | --- | --- | --- |
| Corporate income tax | Corporations | Tax collectors | Internal Revenue Service<br>State revenue departments<br>City tax collectors |
| Corporate franchise tax<br>(on capital stock) | Corporations | Tax collectors | States |
| Excess profits tax | Businesses | District IRS office | Internal Revenue Service |
| Undistributed profits tax | Corporations | District IRS office | Internal Revenue Service |
| Customs duties | Corporations | Customs agents | U.S. Customs Service |
| Excise taxes | Businesses<br>Customers | Utility companies<br>Wholesale distributors<br>Tax collectors | Internal Revenue Service<br>State revenue departments |
| Motor fuel taxes | Businesses | Wholesale distributors | Internal Revenue Service<br>State revenue departments |
| Highway use tax | Motor transport<br>businesses | Interstate Commerce<br>Commission | Interstate Commerce<br>Commission |
| Unemployment compensation | Employers | Internal Revenue Service | Internal Revenue Service |
| Licenses, permits | Businesses | Tax collectors | City tax collectors<br>State revenue departments<br>CAB, ICC, FCC, etc. |
| Old Age, Survivors,<br>Disability, and Hospital<br>Insurance (OASDHI) | Employers<br>Employees | Businesses | Internal Revenue Service |
| Sales and use taxes | Customers | Businesses | City and state revenue<br>departments |
| Property tax | Businesses | Local tax collectors | City and county tax<br>collectors |
| Inventory or floor tax | Businesses | Local and state tax<br>collectors | County and state tax<br>collectors |
| Public utility taxes | Utility companies | City, county, and state<br>tax collectors | City, county, and state<br>tax collectors |

\*This table applies to direct taxes only; the shifting of taxes from the point of collection backward or forward isn't considered.

omy. An example is the so-called windfall profits tax levied on the "un-earned" profits that energy companies made when gasoline prices were deregulated. The stated purposes of the tax, which the companies passed on to consumers through higher gasoline prices, were (1) to reduce gasoline consumption and (2) to provide funds for energy research.

When the term *tax system* is used, it usually refers to all the federal, state, and local systems. However, each of these systems has at least two parts. The first part is the system for determining what the taxes will be and who will pay them. The processes involved are enacting tax legislation, imposing the tax, and determining the liability for each individual or institution. The second

part is the system for collecting the taxes. Only the first part will be covered in this text.

▲ **Who Pays?** For our purposes, taxes can be either indirect or direct. **Indirect taxes** are paid not by the person or firm against which they're levied, but by someone else. Since indirect taxes are part of the cost of doing business, they must either be added to the price of the firm's goods or services or be shifted backward to the persons or firms who produced the goods or services. For example, the owner of a building containing a retail shop pays the property tax to the tax collector, but the amount of the tax is included in the rent paid by the retailer to the owner. In turn, the retailer includes the tax in the price that a customer pays for the goods or services being sold.

**Direct taxes** are paid directly to the taxing authority by the person or business against which they're levied. For example, as indicated earlier, you pay tax on your income although your employer may withhold it and send it to the tax collector for you. Similarly, when you buy something you pay the sales tax, where required, even though the retailer collects it and sends it to the tax collector.

Table 23-3 gives an overview of selected taxes on businesses. It shows the kind of tax, the taxpayer, the point of collection, and the governmental unit collecting the tax.

▲ **How Taxes Affect Business** Business owners and managers are interested in the tax system for several reasons. First, the administrative cost of being a tax collector for the government is becoming burdensome. As shown in Table 23-3, it's the responsibility of business to collect several taxes for the government by withholding the taxes from employees' paychecks or by adding the tax (sales or use taxes) to the purchase price of the goods or services purchased by the customer. This procedure becomes very expensive in terms of people, time, and money. The added burden in time and costs resulting from the necessity of maintaining the required records and preparing the periodic reports adds further to the cost of business operations.

## ▲ LEARNING OBJECTIVES REVISITED

1. *The basic legal foundations upon which the U.S. business system is built.*

   The U.S. legal system is based on the principles of (1) the rule of law, (2) a constitution, (3) due process, (4) presumption of innocence, (5) multiple levels of government, and (6) separation of powers. The two basic bodies of law are common law and statute law.

2. *What business law is and the types of laws it encompasses.*

   The main types of business laws deal with contracts, sales, property, agency, negotiable instruments, torts, and bankruptcy. Most states have now adopted the Uniform Commercial Code, which was designed to make business laws in all the states uniform.

3. *How the U.S. judicial system operates.*

   The judicial system is made up of lawyers, judges, review court judges, juries, and their support personnel. There are separate courts at different levels of government. The highest court is the U.S. Supreme Court,

which makes the final decision as to whether or not a law or action is constitutional.

4. *The many roles played by the U.S. government.*

The U.S. government plays several roles as far as business is concerned. It makes the free enterprise system possible through its legal and judicial systems. It also serves as the nation's chief financial executive, industrialist-employer, and regulator.

5. *The effects of government regulation on business.*

The federal and state governments regulate practically all aspects of business. Most managers try to comply with government regulations but find it difficult to do so because of the large number and great complexity of the rules. Also, many rules are confusing and contradictory. Finally, compliance requires tremendous amounts of paperwork and is quite costly. But there are many benefits of regulation. For example, antitrust laws help encourage competition by regulating monopolies.

6. *The effects of pressure for deregulation.*

Considerable deregulation is now going on, especially in the transportation and financial industries. Deregulation is revolutionizing those industries and leading to increased competition, which may or may not be in the customers' best interest.

7. *How the U.S. tax system functions and its effects on business.*

The tax system is composed of two parts, the system for determining who pays what amount of what taxes and the system for collecting the taxes. Indirect taxes are paid by someone other than the person against whom they're levied. Direct taxes are paid directly to the taxing authorities by the person who owes the tax. Business is very interested in the tax system because of the increasing tax rates, the cost of being a tax collector, and the burden and cost of keeping records for taxes.

## ⛰ IMPORTANT TERMS

As an extra review of the chapter, try defining the following terms. If you have trouble with any of them, refer to the page listed.

| | |
|---|---|
| common law  *618* | consideration  *621* |
| statute law  *618* | warranty  *622* |
| rule of law  *618* | express warranties  *622* |
| police power  *618* | implied warranties  *622* |
| due process  *618* | personal property  *622* |
| separation of powers  *619* | real property  *622* |
| legislative branch  *619* | tangible property  *622* |
| executive branch  *619* | intangible property  *622* |
| judicial branch  *619* | title  *622* |
| criminal law  *619* | deed  *622* |
| civil law  *619* | lease  *622* |
| contract  *619* | agency  *622* |

## ⬟ REVIEW QUESTIONS

1. Outline the foundations of the U.S. legal system.
2. What does each of the following types of law involve?
   a. Law of contracts
   b. Law of sales
   c. Law of property
   d. Law of agency
   e. Law of negotiable instruments
   f. Law of bankruptcy
3. Distinguish:
   a. Common law and statute law
   b. The legislative, executive, and judicial branches of government
   c. Criminal law and civil law
   d. Personal property and real property
   e. A deed and a lease
   f. Direct and indirect taxes
4. What conditions must be met for a contract to be legal?
5. What roles does the U.S. government play in our economy?
6. Name the areas of business affected by deregulation since 1968.
7. Why is business so interested in the tax system?  Explain.

## ⬟ DISCUSSION QUESTIONS

1. Why do you think the state of Louisiana doesn't accept the Uniform Commercial Code?
2. Which of the government's roles do you think it performs well?  poorly?
3. Do you think there is (a) too much, (b) too little, or (c) just the right amount of government regulation of business?  Explain.
4. How would you suggest improving the U.S. regulatory system?
5. Do you think regulations should be reimposed on airlines?  Why or why not?

## ⬟ CASE 23-1   Conrail: Public or Private Ownership?

Consolidated Rail Corporation (Conrail) is a group of several northeastern railroads that the U.S. Department of Transportation has owned since 1976, when it took them over to prevent their demise. After losing money for four years, Conrail made meager operating profits in 1981 and 1982. But

because of factors like the cost-cutting measures instituted by L. Stanley Crane, its chairman, Conrail made a profit of $275 million in 1983, over 50 percent more than in 1982. The profits resulted from reducing the number of employees, cutting the salaries of those who remained, and eliminating many unprofitable routes.

Five different proposals have been made regarding Conrail's future. First, the Department wants to sell Conrail quickly to a private railroad in order to "get the government out of the railroad business." In mid-1983, the Santa Fe Railway seemed to be interested in buying Conrail, but it later merged with Southern Pacific. Some other lines being courted by the Transportation Department were CSX Corporation, Norfolk Southern Corporation, and Alleghany Corporation.

Second, Goldman, Sachs & Company, the investment banking firm that Conrail retained, wants to make a public offering of the stock so that anyone who wants to can buy the railroad.

Third, the road's employees, who make 12 percent less than other railroad union members, want to buy Conrail but don't have the needed cash.

They say their sacrifices have contributed to its profitability, so they should benefit through ownership. They threaten to withdraw their wage concessions during 1984 labor negotiations if anyone else gets ownership of the line. Transportation officials are opposed to such a buyout, for they claim it would put the line back into debt and weaken its chances of remaining solvent.

Fourth, the U.S. Railway Association (USRA), which Congress created to be Conrail's banker, wants to refrain from selling for two more years, to give Crane time to make the line more profitable by cutting 10,000 more workers and 1,000 more miles of track. Then, it claims, Conrail would command a premium price in a public offering because of a better profit history.

Finally, some members of Congress want Congress simply to keep Conrail.

By June 1984, Conrail was such a "hot property" that there were four potential buyers. These were CSX, Norfolk Southern, Conrail employees, and Alleghany Corporation—which promised to keep the line in its same form rather than selling off parts of it.[16] Sixteen bids were finally received.

### Case Questions

1. Do you think the U.S. government should "get out of the railroad business"? Why or why not?
2. What would you suggest be done with Conrail? Why?
3. How do you explain the position of the parties involved? the investment banker? the employees? the Transportation Department? the USRA?

## ⏛ CASE 23-2   Hands Across the Sea—Building Cars

In February 1983, Toyota, the largest Japanese automaker, and General Motors (GM), the world's largest auto firm, signed a twelve-year agreement to form a joint venture to manufacture 200,000 subcompact cars each year in GM's idle Fremont, California, plant. The new car would benefit from Japanese expertise in car design and manufacture and GM's marketing expertise. GM would have firsthand access to Toyota's production and management knowledge; Toyota would escape some of the protectionist pressures now growing in the United States.

But criticisms of the deal ran rampant. Ford Motor Company and Chrysler complained to the Federal Trade Commission, which must approve the agreement, that it could lead to price fixing and collusion. As indicated earlier, Chrysler went to court to keep the world's strongest auto firms from monopolizing the small car market. The U.S. House of Representatives' Judiciary Committee held hearings to see if the venture would violate Section 7 of the Clayton Act, and permanently change competitive relationships among companies in the auto industry. The Clayton Act says that "no corporation engaged in commerce shall acquire . . . any part of the assets of another corpo-

ration engaged in commerce, where . . . the effects of such acquisition may be substantially to lessen competition or to tend to create a monopoly." Nevertheless, the FTC approved the venture in the spring of 1984.[17]

The potential partners claimed the venture would create 12,000 new U.S. jobs overall. But critics claimed it could jeopardize the jobs of up to 50,000 workers if GM's Chevette were to go out of production.

### Case Questions

1. Do you think this arrangement would lead to price fixing, collusion, and reduced competition? Explain.
2. What do you think the Federal Trade Commission should do—approve or disapprove the deal? Why?
3. Why do you think Chrysler and Ford really complained?

# 24

# Your Future in Business

*To be what we are, and to become what we are capable of becoming, is the only end of life.*
Robert Louis Stevenson

*Prediction is very difficult, especially about the future.*
Niels Bohr

*No amount of sophistication is going to allay the fact that all your knowledge is about the past and all your decisions are about the future.*
Ian H. Wilson

## Learning Objectives

After studying the material in this chapter, you will understand:

1. How to plot a career strategy.
2. The life-cycle stages of career growth.
3. How to go after your first permanent job.
4. Some of the kinds of change that will affect you in the business world of the future.
5. New developments you can expect in some selected industries.

## In This Chapter

Plotting Your Career Strategy
The Career Life Cycle
The First Job
Facing a Changing World
The Future of Work

# NISSAN — TENNESSEE
*Factory of the Future*

In Smyrna, Tennessee, a group of workers is coming face to face with the working world of the twenty-first century in a $500 million, ultramodern plant built by Nissan Motor Manufacturing Corporation, U.S.A. The operations of the 3.2-million-square-foot plant may offer a preview of two threats with which U.S. management and workers must come to grips in the future: advancing automation and global competition.

When the new plant started assembling Nissan pickup trucks in June 1983, it was one of the most highly automated automobile plants and had one of the most highly skilled work forces in the United States. Its 220 computerized robots do the most difficult and tedious tasks, while its 2,000 highly trained and motivated production employees—called "manufacturing technicians"—operate and maintain the plant's complex equipment and machinery.

On the assumption that "you can teach workers a job, but not attitudes," the firm was highly selective in its hiring. There were 130,000 applicants for the 2,000 jobs, and those tentatively selected went through numerous interviews and up to 360 hours of preemployment training—without compensation—before being hired. All the employees were given hundreds of hours of training in general skills, like decision making, responsibility, care of equipment, quality and efficiency, and how to view their jobs and supervisors within the company's philosophy of "loving and trusting your fellow workers." The owners had found from experience that multiskilled workers are not only more productive but also more content than traditionally trained and specialized assembly-line workers. In addition, about one in six trainees, including 128 hourly workers, went to Japan for extended on-the-job training in Nissan plants. One critical lesson they all learned was to be team players and "members of the family."

The Smyrna managers essentially told UAW union organizers not to apply from the very start. The employees receive good wages and benefits and are fairly treated, so there's no need for a third party to negotiate for them. According to some employees, "Workers have to have trust, and Nissan hasn't given us any reason to distrust. We intend to work here for life." Still, the UAW, with 300,000 members out of work, is trying to organize the workers. Unlike some Japanese firms, the plant isn't guaranteeing its employees lifetime employment. Instead, Nissan's president, a retired Ford executive, told them, "You can make your own lifetime employment by doing a good job and helping to keep the company strong."

Throughout this book, we've attempted to keep reality firmly in mind. And your reality will include not only school and family, but pursuit of a meaningful career. Whether or not you've been reading the Digging Deeper career sections at the end of each part of this book, you've probably learned quite a bit about the business environment where you presently work or will work in the future. Now it's time for us to equip you with some tools for pursuing that work—and with a forecast: How will the work world change for you during your career life cycle? How likely is it that you'll be embraced by a company like Nissan?

## PLOTTING YOUR CAREER STRATEGY

**Objective 1**

**How to plot a career strategy.**

Assuming that you want a career in business, what's the best way to pursue it? One good way is to plot out a career strategy and follow it through in seeking your first meaningful job. "You will be what you resolve to be," begins a practical book on career development.[1] This simple observation is quite true. When you resolve to reach a certain position, you'll begin to prepare to achieve that objective. You'll read about the position and study the courses leading to it. Your spouse, children, parents, friends, teachers, and mentors will help you reach your goal. You may change your goal as you progress, but you'll have a strategy to follow.

There are some fairly well defined steps to follow in narrowing down a career strategy. Regardless of how it's actually formulated, a career strategy should consider at least the following:[2]

1. *Your opportunities.* The things you *might* do.
2. *Your competencies and resources.* A list of abilities, time, money, skills, and the aid you can expect from others will help you determine what you *can* do.
3. *Your ambitions and hopes.* What you *want* to do.
4. *Your obligations.* The moral, emotional, and financial obligations you owe to your family and other groups to which you belong will determine what you *ought* to do.
5. *Your personal values.* The things you believe in will largely dictate what you are *willing or unwilling* to do.

You should set realistic dates for completing specific phases of your career strategy, along with specific criteria for measuring progress. Make these measurements of career objectives (time limitations, job titles, and actual rewards) specific, and it will be easier to determine whether or not you've achieved them.

### Opportunities

"If you don't know where you're going, you'll probably end up somewhere else" is the theme of a book with some sound principles to guide you in searching for options and opportunities.[3] In considering your options, you shouldn't forget the technological, economic, political, and sociocultural environments in which you live.

Undoubtedly, new businesses and jobs will develop for technological reasons, as we'll see later. Some questions you might ask about the economic

environment are: What kinds of resources (skills, values, and abilities) are in demand in the economy? What's the current, short-run, and long-run extent of this demand? What areas of the economy—such as manufacturing, finance, and services—are most likely to use these resources? What's the reward for someone with these resources? What costs will be involved in upgrading present skills? The political environment, including present, pending, and probable legislation, also affects career decisions. New opportunities are available for women, minorities, the handicapped, and older workers in the present sociocultural environment, as was shown in Chapter 9.

## Competencies and Resources

Next, you should determine the strengths you can build on and weaknesses you can overcome. A good match of your strengths with crucial factors needed for success in a given job should lead to success. Some questions to consider are: Which tasks do I perform well? What are my distinctive competencies?

Probably the future will demand a different set of competencies, but the basic ones—such as the ability to communicate well orally and in writing, to analyze rationally, to work well with people, and to plan in a systematic and orderly way—will still be important. Therefore, you should make an effort to overcome, or at least diminish, any weaknesses, while searching for competencies to emphasize. There are various testing services that can indicate which of your abilities need improvement.

Some other key questions to ask yourself are: Can my strengths be utilized in a variety of situations or only in limited areas? How mobile am I? Am I limiting myself to a certain location? How well do I manage myself? Do I set measurable standards of performance to be met in reaching objectives? Do I seek performance feedback in order to determine how well I'm doing?

A part of identifying one's abilities is going through a self-analysis. Knowing your talents and vocational interests well will help you determine the type of work that suits you best. There are a number of practical things you can do to learn more about yourself. You can begin your analysis by answering the first part of the Quiz on p. 646. Although this information will provide only a rough outline, it does give you a concrete basis for locating specific career options in the labor market.[4] Then go on with the rest of the Quiz, to narrow your options further.

## Ambitions and Hopes

It's easy enough to dream of fame and fortune, but you should be realistic, too. What would you *really* like to do or become? What are you willing to sacrifice to achieve your dreams? Do you want to become an entrepreneur and found a company for your children and grandchildren? Do you want to be a top executive in someone else's business? Or would you be satisfied with some other position?

## Obligations

We usually try to live up to the expectations of other people, for they help us to satisfy some of our needs and to develop a sense of identity and self-worth. Therefore, those people deserve some of our time, energy, and other resources.

# *Quiz*

## A Career Self-Analysis

**Part I**

1. What major projects, hobbies, and activities have I engaged in in the past few years? (Identify those activities that gave you the most satisfaction and most nearly matched your talents and interests.)
2. What are my favorite activities—in order of preference? (Relate them to specific skills you have.)
3. Have I consulted my campus career counselors? (Most schools have counseling services offering career planning.)
4. Have I obtained advice from my professors or my supervisor at work? (Ask for their honest assessment of your strengths and limitations. Be prepared not to be hurt when a true assessment is given.)

**Part II**

1. Make a list of twenty-five activities you like to do, even though some may seem insignificant. You may like to hunt, play sports, work on cars, cook, read books, and so on.
2. Separately, list twenty-five skills you have that produce good results—what you do that causes others to compliment you. This might result in a list that includes singing, sewing, making others feel relaxed, handling children, and so on.
3. Select the top five activities and skills from your answers to 1 and 2, and make a grid with horizontal and vertical categories. This gives you twenty-five different possible categories. Select ten.
4. On ten separate sheets, list three or four jobs that could fit into each category. For example, if you like indoor plants and feel that one thing you do well is grow plants, jobs to consider might be working in a nursery, owning a plant shop, becoming a horticulturist, etc.
5. Grade each job from A to C, with A for those giving you the maximum degree of satisfaction and C for those giving you the least satisfaction. Then rank each in terms of practicality, such as additional education that may be required, the probability of finding such a position, financial considerations, and so on. Ask yourself, "Am I willing to take the necessary action to get such a job?" If not, eliminate if from consideration.

Source for Part II: Tom Jackson, *Guerilla Tactics in the Job Market* (New York: Bantam Books, 1978).

For instance, your family might want you to return home to help run the family business. Or one of your parents may need you to help him or her physically or financially. Remember that you need not plan to accomplish all of your desired goals on the job; some can be achieved at home or elsewhere.

### Personal Values

Although talents, interests, ambitions, hopes, and obligations are important in the choice of a career, personal values must also be considered. **Values** are the relative worth or importance we place on people, ideas, or events. These greatly influence the choice of what we want to do because the work we do also affects the way we feel about ourselves.[5] Some key questions to ask are: What is my personal concept of success, and how important is it to me to achieve it? How much risk am I willing to take? What's the basis of my values? Do I believe in the work ethic or in a more leisurely approach? The work ethic is a principle emphasizing hard and diligent work, thrift, frugality, and dedication to work as a life interest.

## THE CAREER LIFE CYCLE

**Objective 2**

**The life-cycle stages of career growth.**

Many career goals can't be achieved without long years of preparation and effort, through formal education, job training, and job experience. And people make career-related decisions at different stages of their working lives. Although people differ in their career experiences and the timing of changes, they generally progress through an orderly sequence of developmental stages. Figure 24-1 shows a model of one such **career life cycle.** In essence, it shows that different types of decisions affecting one's career tend to be made at different ages.[6]

### Teens and Twenties

The teens and twenties are a time of experimentation, of trying on new roles to see how they fit. Yet it's at this sensitive time of exploration that we make the basic decisions that will shape the rest of our career lives—all the more reason to evaluate the choices carefully.

Some of you are in this stage and have already decided or will soon decide (1) whether or not to obtain a college degree; (2) whether or not to obtain

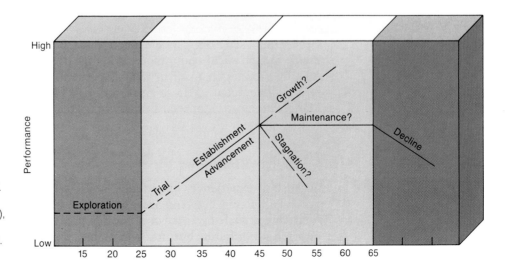

**Figure 24-1** The career life cycle. [Adapted from *Careers in Organizations*, by Douglas T. Hall (Glenview, Ill.: Scott, Foresman and Company, 1976), p. 57. Copyright © 1976 by Scott, Foresman and Company. Reprinted by permission.]

a graduate degree; (3) whether to work for a small company or a large one; (4) whether to be an owner-manager of a company or to work for someone else; (5) whether to work in accounting, finance, marketing, personnel, production, or some other functional area; and (6) whether to adopt the work ethic or pursue a more relaxed lifestyle.

### Thirties

As people reach the landmark of age thirty, they begin to take stock of earlier choices to see how closely reality matches the goals they set for themselves. As a result, people in their thirties make many important decisions about their jobs, work satisfaction, and advancement possibilities. At this point, they usually decide whether to stay with the same employer or to look elsewhere. It's in the mid-thirties that many people—such as Pam McAllister Johnson (see the Profile on page 649)—begin to have a "midlife crisis."

Sam Baker had worked as a paint salesman in the paint department of a department store while attending high school. For the next five years he worked for several paint stores. Then he decided he wanted something better out of life, so he enrolled in the night program at a local university and earned a degree in marketing. He became a sales representative and later national sales manager for the paint manufacturer whose product he had once sold in stores. At age thirty-eight, he started his own paint and decorating store.

In general, it's advisable to stay with the same firm as long as one is learning and growing. The person who changes jobs frequently is accepted and respected if the reason for the changes is personal development rather than dissatisfaction with the jobs. On the other hand, one shouldn't be a "floater," changing jobs every year, because employers are reluctant to hire people they can't expect to stay. In fact, most of your tryout job changing could be done by the time you're thirty. After that, frequent shifts might give people the impression that you don't know how to handle responsibility or tough times.[7]

### Forties

In their forties—the usual time for midlife crises—many people become dissatisfied and bored with their jobs as well as with their lives. This tendency is unfortunate, for a new career becomes more difficult to start each year after age forty. On the other hand, those years can be a time of maximum achievement if one emphasizes one's assets, such as leadership, experience, reliability, judgment, and physical endurance. But this still can be a good time to consider making a career change. In 1977, 9 percent of those aged thirty-five to forty-four and 5 percent of those aged forty-five to fifty-four changed occupations.[8] Many women enter or reenter the work force when they are in their forties (see FYI on p. 650).

### From Fifty to Sixty-Five

Because of experience, knowledge, and confidence, many people reach their peak of efficiency between ages fifty and sixty-five. Most people have attained their career goals by this time. Some, however, may want or need to seek a new job—a difficult, but not impossible, task. The assets mentioned for the previous age group also apply here, and some of them become even more valua-

## *Profile*

### Pam Johnson: It's Never Too Late

Pam McAllister Johnson made history as the first black woman publisher of a leading white daily newspaper. The paper, the *Ithaca Journal,* has a circulation of 20,400 and is a sturdy link in the eighty-five-newspaper Gannett chain.

Sturdy in her own right, Johnson was taught by a neighborhood couple—her role models—to have a "very, very strong self-concept." She was made to believe that she could be anything and do anything she wanted to. Although she received much of her journalism background from academia—she holds a Ph.D. in journalism and educational psychology from the University of Wisconsin—Johnson had also been a reporter and a radio and television interviewer/announcer.

Johnson considers herself a real go-getter. So when a midlife crisis hit at age thirty-five, while she was teaching journalism, she knew that she had to make a career change. What may have triggered the crisis was her completion of a Mini-Sabbatical for Minority Journalism Faculty Members program sponsored by the American Society of Newspaper Editors and funded by the Gannett Foundation. As part of the program, she'd explored newspaper business management at the *Patriot Ledger* in Quincy, Massachusetts. Knowing that journalism was the area she wanted to be involved in, she began to think seriously about where her career was going.

She left her teaching position at Norfolk State College, in Virginia, to join Gannett Corporation as a general executive at the Bridgewater, New Jersey, *Courier-News.* Attracted to the Gannett Corporation because its philosophy meshed with her own go-getter attitude, Johnson soon moved up the ladder to the position of assistant to the publisher of the *Ithaca Journal* and then became its publisher in November 1981.

People who know her say that Pam Johnson is a highly motivated, intelligent person with a gift for understanding and working with people. A well-organized, high-energy person, Johnson adheres to a very strict schedule. For example, since becoming publisher at Ithaca, she's advanced press start-up time by an hour and a half.

Even at home, her philosophy is much the same. She and her husband Don, director of Cornell University's Equal Employment Opportunity Office, try to encourage their two children—Dawn and Jason—"to learn everything you can and think positively."

Sources: Marilyn Zeitlin, "Ms. Publisher," *US,* September 28, 1982, pp. 71–72; Margaret Genovese, "Pam McAllister Johnson: Her 'Midlife Crisis' Is Resolved by Appointment as a Publisher," *Presstime,* August 1982, p. 23; "Woman Named Newspaper Publisher," *Epoch,* March/April 1982, pp. 42–43; and correspondence with Pam McAllister Johnson.

*FYI*

**Creative Alternatives for Women:
Helping with Reentry**

During the past few years, organizations like Creative Alternatives for Women (located in Jenkintown, Pennsylvania) have given women like Ruth Sugerman the chance to embark on second careers after years of absence from the job market.

For twenty years, Ruth Sugerman was a homemaker, raised four children, and was active in community service. Then, at age forty-three, she decided to reenter the job market. Anticipating the problems she might run into after such a time lapse, she approached Creative Alternatives for Women.

Creative Alternatives for Women and other reentry organizations make women aware of resources they didn't know they had. Having as their chief clientele women from ages thirty-five to forty-five, these organizations are geared toward helping women develop confidence in themselves. Workshops are arranged in which the women identify their interests, gain knowledge about how businesses work, and get instruction in job hunting. Most of these workshops require women to conduct interviews to gain information on their particular field of interest. This maneuver forces them to communicate with others in the business world. Then internships follow—from three to six months, often salaried. These internships include special projects at the preprofessional and managerial levels. (No internships in file clerking are offered!) Interns gain valuable information on how to interact with one's boss—the dos and don'ts.

These programs have been very successful in placing at least half their graduates in such professions as marketing research, public relations, and banking. Twenty years after she received her master's degree in the field of psychology, Ruth Sugerman reentered the job market as a result of her internship with Educational Testing Service in Princeton, New Jersey. She served, appropriately enough, as a researcher for "Project Access," a study about aid to women returning to work. She was offered a permanent position with ETS as a full-time senior research assistant.

Sources: Based on Erik Larson, "Firms Providing Business Internships Lure Middle-Aged Women Looking for Careers," *The Wall Street Journal*, September 2, 1981, p. 23. Reprinted by permission of *The Wall Street Journal*, © Dow Jones & Company, Inc. 1981. All Rights Reserved. Also based on correspondence with Educational Testing Service and Creative Alternatives for Women.

ble with increasing age. In fact, many people take on a second career at this time, turn a hobby into a business, establish or buy a business, or go into teaching or consulting. For instance, Charles Jackson, controller of a large independent firm, took all the tax courses offered at a local university and some by correspondence. As he outgrew his job, the owner set him up as a tax consultant, with himself as Jackson's first client.

A women's reentry workshop.

### Over Sixty-Five

It isn't a foregone conclusion that age sixty-five marks the end of a career. In fact, many people choose not to retire at that age. Numerous executives have obtained fine positions even in their seventies. Health is the major factor: people who are vigorous and in good health may continue working, while others may seek early retirement or retire at age sixty-five.

## THE FIRST JOB

**Objective 3**

**How to go after your first permanent job.**

It almost goes without saying that choosing your first permanent job is important to your career development. In looking for that job, you will start with some idea of your chosen **occupation**—that is, the main activity you will engage in during your lifetime, probably some kind of gainful employment. But you may make your first-job decision primarily on the basis of a company rather than a chosen occupation.

### Choosing a Company

Some people simply seize upon the most promising local opportunity and proceed to make the most of it. In choosing the company for which to work, however, you should look toward the future, both your future in the company and its future in business. You should consider management excellence, reputation, financial soundness, growth record, innovation in new product development, location, and people. Information concerning these criteria can be obtained from local customers of the company, bankers, the company's annual report, and Dun and Bradstreet reports.[9]

You should also think about how well a given employment opportunity will fit in with your career plans and whether your lifestyle will fit in with the

company culture. After all, over a third of your waking time will be spent there. For example, the IBM culture at one time demanded that its male representatives wear white, oxford-cloth, button-down shirts; subdued ties; standard-issue corporate cordovan shoes; and the proverbial blue suit. This particular culture is much more relaxed now, but you can see the potential impact a company's atmosphere can have.

> Which do you prefer: small town or big city? pressure or lack of pressure on the job? access to a large number of cultural opportunities or fewer distractions? a highly structured business or a less structured one? (You may not know the answers to all of these questions until you've experienced some of the alternatives. These are some of the things you'll learn during your career life cycle.)

### Choosing a Job

The factors that are usually important to college graduates in choosing their first job are opportunities for advancement, the chance to do something important and get recognition for it, responsibility, a chance to use special abilities, opportunities for challenge and creativity, and a high salary.[10]

Here are two career tips about what to do on that first job. First, you should know how your job is related to others at the same or higher levels. You need this knowledge in order to plot a strategy for advancement within the company and to design a self-development program that will prepare you for promotion.

Second, you may find a wide discrepancy between what the boss thinks his or her job is and what you think it is. Therefore, be aware of what the boss considers his or her job to be. Such considerations will provide a perspective for setting your own ambitions. Ask yourself: Do I want to be doing what the boss is doing? What are the basic ideas and policies of the company? Can I honestly endorse them and carry them out? If the answers to these questions are negative, then start looking for another position. Table 24-1 shows some other important characteristics of a good job.

## FACING A CHANGING WORLD

**Objective 4**

**Some of the kinds of change that will affect you in the business world of the future.**

To be sure, change is the essence of progress, growth, and development. That's true both for your career and for the whole business world. Nothing remains constant for long; everything and everyone must adapt to changing situations and environments. But the changes occurring today in the world of business are so large and complex and coming so rapidly that they threaten to overwhelm us if we don't try to understand what's happening and prepare to cope with it.

### Organizational Changes

As early as 1971, John Mee of Indiana University predicted that by the year 2000, decision making and planning would be decentralized to lower manage-

**TABLE 24-1 Characteristics of a good job.**

1. *Direct feedback.* There should be opportunities for frequent, direct, and nonsupervisory feedback on how well one is doing.
2. *A client relationship.* Employees should be responsible to, and relate to, those who are affected by what the employees do.
3. *A natural module of work.* The work should be in units with a definite beginning and end.
4. *Personal accountability.* Employees should be responsible for the end results of only the work for which they have adequate authority.
5. *Decision making and other control.* Employees should be able to make decisions and control the resources needed, including setting priorities and scheduling work.
6. *Demand for each individual's unique expertise.* The job should provide opportunities for workers to grow and develop specific and unique knowledge and skills.

SOURCE: R. Lathrop, *Who's Hiring Who* (Berkeley, Calif.: Ten Speed Press, 1977).

ment levels to provide satisfaction and self-fulfillment to employees throughout the business.[11] A group of top business leaders and college professors reached a similar conclusion in 1979.[12] They also concluded that decision making would shift from the individual manager to the management team, and that companies would set up formal processes for consulting with all employees.

Probably the most specific forecast of future organizations was given by Dr. Steve Fuller, vice-president of human resources for GM, when he made these predictions in 1976:

1. Nonmanagerial employees will serve on boards of directors.
2. All employees will be salaried and time clocks eliminated.
3. Employment will be guaranteed from the date of becoming a permanent employee to the time of retirement.
4. Employees in operating departments will work as teams, scheduling their own work and approving plant changes and modifications.
5. Supervisors will be elected by—and their actions will be subject to the approval of—the people they supervise.
6. The employee teams will determine who will be laid off when it becomes necessary to do so (for employees without lifetime protection).
7. Sabbaticals for educational and development purposes will be granted to employees who desire them.
8. Yearly surveys will be made to determine employee attitudes and behavior.
9. Bonuses for executives will be based partly on employee attitudes.[13]

These changes may sound extreme, but many are now in effect in one or more U.S. organizations.

Did you notice how similar these predictions are to the way management works at the new Nissan plant?

# *Profile*

## John Naisbitt: Calling the Trends

John Naisbitt, professional trend watcher and head of the Naisbitt Group of Washington, D.C., believes that "Trends, like horses, are easier to ride in the direction they are already going." He tries to predict these trends and shares his predictions with anyone who'll listen—and pay as much as $15,000 a year to receive them.

Naisbitt's theory is that trends begin as local events and can't be observed in places like Chicago, Los Angeles, New York, and Washington. From reading 125,000 items a month, trivial and otherwise, in 6,000 newspapers, Naisbitt and his associates predict the future. They've studied a total of two million articles in the last twelve years. Naisbitt packages the product of his discernment into speeches, seminars, and printed matter for nearly seventy corporate clients, including AT&T, General Electric, United Technologies, Sears, and Westinghouse. He delivers broad social, economic, and political predictions.

Naisbitt seems to be successful, for he predicted the end of mandatory retirement a year before it was legislated, the decline of nuclear power well before the Three Mile Island accident, and the failure of the Equal Rights Amendment four years before time ran out on it.

He's also developed a list of "megatrends," such as the end of the United States' reign as the world's industrial leader. The U.S. economy is now based on the creation and distribution of information rather than on industry. To Naisbitt, though, the most important megatrend is decentralization—the shift of power from the federal government to states and cities and from great corporations to smaller, more entrepreneurial ones.

Another trend he sees is that technological advances won't be accepted by the public unless they're counterbalanced with human responses; that is, "high tech" needs "high touch." Thus, as we embrace computers, we also rebel against them by sending handwritten memos and letters. One bank has capitalized on the idea of having its automatic tellers display friendly banter on the screen.

Are Naisbitt's trends real predictors of the future? Only time will tell, but they're intriguing to study and watch.

---

Sources: Based on Bill Abrams, "Ten Trends That Will Transform Our Lives," *The Wall Street Journal*, October 22, 1982, p. 28; and *The Wall Street Journal*, September 30, 1982, p. 52. Reprinted by permission of *The Wall Street Journal*, © Dow Jones & Company, Inc. 1982. All Rights Reserved. Also based on John Naisbitt, *Megatrends: Ten New Directions Transforming Our Lives* (New York: Warner Books, 1982); Ken Jackson, "Computer Written Out," *Tulsa Daily World*, March 17, 1983, p. A-1; and others.

### Environmental Changes

Alvin Toffler, futurist and author of *Future Shock*, predicted in *The Third Wave* that future managers would be evaluated by many criteria, not just productivity, sales, and profits.[14] Toffler said that managers would be appraised on the basis of how well they handled environmental, ethical, informational, political, and social factors. Moreover, he believes, the emphasis will shift from "bigger is better" to "the most appropriate size" for social units, including businesses.

John Naisbitt (see the Profile on page 654) has identified several trends that will transform our lives. The most important of these trends are:

1. Labor unions and representative democracy are becoming obsolete.
2. In their personal lives, people are relying less on institutions and more on themselves.
3. The flow of power in society is changing from "top → down" to "bottom → up."
4. In spite of small personal and business computers that permit individuals to work at home, most people are still working in offices because they "want to be with people." Indeed, technological innovations, such as cable TV banking and shopping, won't succeed unless they provide for some form of human response.
5. Aging midwestern and northeastern industrial cities and states are losing out, as economic opportunities go to those in the South and West.
6. The United States is no longer the self-sufficient, independent industrial leader of the world but is now part of a global economic system.
7. Businesses involved in the generation, transmission, interpretation, and storage of information are replacing the traditional smokestack industries, such as automobiles, steel, and textiles.
8. Giant conglomerates' merging with, or acquiring, other large companies is like "the mating of dinosaurs," since smaller, more innovative and creative businesses will replace them.[15]

As an example of this last point, seventeen of the fifty largest corporations listed by *Fortune* magazine in its 1960 issue were no longer anywhere in the top fifty in 1980.[16]

### Work Force Changes

As a result of changing economic conditions, ethical considerations, and life-styles, as well as affirmative action programs, the future work force will be quite different from today's. In general, it will be a more diverse group than it is now (see Chapter 9). Employees will be more affluent, more mobile, more technically and professionally oriented, and more demanding of time off from work. Workers will be older and better educated (or at least have more years of formal schooling), and there will be more women and minorities, at least in the technical, professional, and managerial ranks.

Increased education and training will lead to increased productivity and earnings for those who can establish themselves in the workplace. These same higher education and skill levels will cause more turnover and greater mobility, as workers at these levels will find many employment opportuni-

ties. To deal with greater worker independence, management will have to discover and use new motivational techniques.

On the other hand, there will be fewer employment opportunities for the millions of uneducated, unskilled, and inexperienced workers, especially young people and minorities. Many of these *unemployed* will become *unemployables*—or individuals unable to get a job because they lack the needed education, skill, training, and experience. And the higher levels of education may lead to alienation and frustration among college students without entry-level skills who are equally unable to get jobs, or must work at jobs below their educational level.

> Did you notice how Nissan's management, in order to motivate employees, trained them to have multiple skills and participate more in the company's activities?

## Technological Changes

Since change can either give a company a competitive edge or make it go bankrupt, managers of the future must devote considerable time, money, and personnel to preparing for technological change through research and development of new products, services, and processes. Large firms usually have the resources and organization to prepare for technological change, so the future may be less of a threat to them. Yet even big companies can't avoid or prevent change. In fact, the record is very clear: firms that lead at first in technological developments tend to lose out later when further advancements are made. General Electric, RCA, and Sylvania were once leaders in vacuum tubes. Yet they lost out to newer and more innovative firms when transistor technology revolutionized the industry.

Smaller firms must depend on the owner or on outside research systems, such as universities or research organizations, for new ideas. They usually concentrate on innovations in a smaller area and thus often react more quickly to changes as they occur than larger firms would. The development of so many new companies in the electronics industry is an example of such innovation. Wang, a smaller firm, overtook giant IBM, which had at first dominated the word processing field. Then Compucorp, a small Los Angeles firm, also upstaged IBM in the word processing area when it produced a 1-million-word electronic dictionary to catch and correct misspelled words. In the future, such small firms will rely even more on outside sources, and noncompeting firms may form cooperative research organizations to develop new products and processes.

> Test yourself. Before reading any further, jot down the *new industries* that have become commercially feasible just since the United States entered World War II in 1941. Then think of the *new products* and/or *processes* that have become available just in your own lifetime.

As new industries and products are developed, changes in production processes or operations are necessary. New developments in one industry (computers, say) will also bring about change in other industries and production processes. A few examples of changes of this nature have been:

1. Substitution of transistors for tubes and silicon chips for transistors.
2. Use of computers to design products, control processes, and even design other computers.
3. Use of laser beams for printing.
4. Use of biological processes to reduce waste chemicals discharged into rivers.
5. Use of robots in manufacturing, the office, and the home.

Some technological developments predicted in 1970 for the year 2000 were:

1. Automatic language translators.
2. Controlled affective relationships and sleep.
3. Human hibernation for extended periods.
4. Artificial elements to replace human organs.
5. Reliable weather forecasts and control.
6. Entirely new energy sources.
7. Undersea farming and mining.
8. Use of robots in homes and the service industries.[17]

The fact that many of these have already been achieved in fifteen years should tell us something about the rate of technological change!

## Coping with Change

There are two ways managers can cope with expected future changes. They can *react to them*, or—preferably—they can *anticipate and plan for them.*

In the reactive process, management keeps the business as steady as possible by solving problems as they arise. Managers adapt, step by step, on a piecemeal basis, to problems and issues, with little planning or preparation. This process isn't very effective in dealing with "threats" to the organization, but it is often used for solving routine, current, and visible problems. However, dealing with problems in this way can be disastrous over a period of time.

Swift, a meatpacking firm started in 1855, became a leader in its field by concentrating its operations in Chicago. It pioneered in slaughtering and shipping dressed carcasses to market instead of shipping live cattle. Yet its position was taken over by Iowa Meat Processors (IMP), which, in 1960, started building plants near the western feedlots. IMP's system was to cut the carcasses into smaller pieces, put them in boxes, and ship them to supermarkets, where the final slicing was done for the customer. The savings in labor and shipping costs achieved by this method soon made Swift's strategy obsolete, as it reacted to change rather than planning for it.[18]

**Planned change** involves anticipating changes in the external and internal environments and using deliberate actions to make those changes more favorable to the business. Managers set out to change things by setting a new course rather than correcting the current one. Dealing with change is like playing a video game where the target changes and new foes zoom in from all sides. To

succeed, the player of the game—or a business—must develop sensitive reflexes and the ability to anticipate challenges and make fast, rational decisions.

AT&T, anticipating the information explosion, as well as the technological revolution in telecommunications, poured untold amounts into basic and applied research. Because of its innovative technical leadership, it was more than ready to face its competition technologically. It also rearranged its organizational structure, marketing strategy, and managerial philosophy so as to survive and grow in a competitive environment. AT&T used planned change. But then came its breakup, which had to be completed by 1984. Because of its plans for change, AT&T was able to make the unprecedented adjustment with less disruption than might be expected.

## THE FUTURE OF WORK

**Objective 5**

New developments you can expect in some selected industries.

Now let's see what's happening and is expected to happen in the near future to a few selected industries. First, we'll discuss a few of the older and more traditional businesses, such as foods, communications, and transportation. Then we'll look at some of the new industries, such as electronics and services, to show how the trends will affect you in your career in business.

### Agribusiness

When we talk about food these days, we're really talking about **agribusiness,** or all the activities involved in producing, distributing, and financing food products. Agribusiness has more in common with large-scale manufacturing than with the small family farms of the past.

The acceptance of frozen foods (including complete meals), freeze-dried items, exotic fruits, ethnic foods, specialty foods for different age groups, diet foods, natural foods, and so forth has been surprisingly quick and enthusiastic. As a result, many more innovations are on the way.

Rising labor costs have made it necessary to substitute machines for people in harvesting and processing food. As a result, new strains of fruits and vegetables have been developed that can be planted, nurtured, harvested, and processed cheaply and effectively by mechanical means. An example is a variety of tomato developed especially for canning. While not as tasty when eaten raw as the vine-ripened kind, it's uniform in shape, size, texture, and color and is quite satisfactory for eating when processed.

There will continue to be an increase in demand for foods whose preparation requires a minimum of time and effort. And new specialized production methods such as trout and catfish "farming," hydroponics (growing plants in special solutions without soil as a mechanical support), and mariculture (growing food in the sea or other natural bodies of water) also will increase in importance.

New outlets for food distribution include super-supermarkets, quality supermarkets, and convenience markets. **Super-supermarkets,** with their bakeries and delicatessens in addition to the usual products, are designed and stocked to attract customers back to home cooking and away from fast-food outlets. **Quality supermarkets** sell better-quality produce and better-quality, cut-to-order meats and offer their customers a variety of personal services.

They appeal to a selected affluent clientele. And convenience markets seem to be here to stay. In the years ahead, the recent trend of selling gasoline as well as food, drugs, and cosmetic items at convenience markets will probably continue.

## Communications

Communications have progressed from private messenger to glass fiber transmission (see Figure 24-2). Advances in electronics technology have made new systems and forms of communication available. In addition, the quality of communication has improved. Advances in satellite transmission and other information systems promise to create many new business opportunities.

The use of satellites will produce many economies in the cost of operations. There are now over 275 communications satellites orbiting the earth, most of them with twenty-four transponders, the devices that receive electronic signals and retransmit them to earth. That gives you an idea of the almost infinite possibilities for communication. RCA, for instance, held an

**Figure 24-2**   Developments in communication.

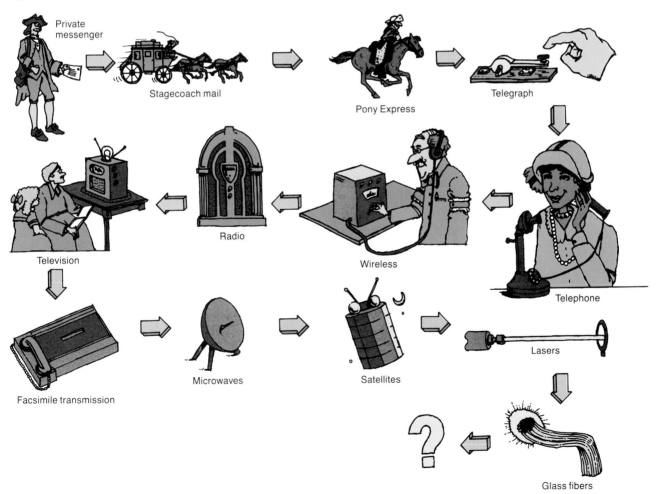

Private messenger

Stagecoach mail

Pony Express

Telegraph

Television

Radio

Wireless

Telephone

Facsimile transmission

Microwaves

Satellites

Lasers

Glass fibers

auction at a prestigious gallery to sell seven transponders on a satellite not scheduled to be in orbit for another two months. The transponders were in such demand that RCA received an average of $14.4 million for a seven-year lease on each one.[19] These satellites now provide practically unlimited communication possibilities.

The production and installation of telephonic equipment in the United States is expected to continue to grow with the development of new technology, such as fiber optics, solid state lasers, and computerized switching systems, and as AT&T's twenty-two operating divisions are reorganized and expand. The Federal Communications Commission's encouragement of competition in long-distance communication has brought additional firms into competition with AT&T. The FCC recently decided to allow independent firms to sell a broad range of services, including Wide Area Telephone Service (WATS) and teleconferencing (the connection of people in several offices, even in different cities, by telephone and/or TV). Within nine months, more than 100 new telephone companies had been federally licensed.[20] As these companies expand in number and size, the cost of service will be reduced. The cost of local service is expected to increase considerably now that the operating companies have been separated from AT&T, as this service was subsidized by profits from long-distance service. The expansion in this field has been very rapid.

Of course, television has been one of the major factors in U.S. business, communications, entertainment, and culture for a long time. Over 85 million homes have at least one TV set, more than half of them have two or more sets, over 85 percent have color sets, and over 30 percent are hooked up to cable. Yet the three networks now share only around 80 percent of prime-time evening viewing,[21] primarily because of satellite transmission, videocassettes, videodiscs, video games, home shopping and banking, videotapes for learning and motivation, cable TV, and privately owned satellite-receiving dishes. Between 30,000 and 40,000 consumers now have their own dishes to receive free programs on more than fifty channels from the satellites.

The popularity of these new TV technologies is growing at a dizzying pace, threatening regular TV, the movie theater business, and book publishing. Of course, these affected industries are fighting back in an effort to save their business. The Deerpath 2 cinema in Lake Forest, Illinois, calls itself "the theater of the future." In addition to its regular movie, it offers soundproof viewing rooms for toddlers, a room with a big-screen TV set, high-quality projection equipment, and good-quality food.

Publishing and television are becoming more dependent on each other in an effort to cope with future changes. Television has long broadcast shows based on books—for example, "Roots," "Shōgun," "Masada," "The Winds of War," and "The Thorn Birds"—but now books and shows are being produced together. For example, *Cosmos*, the popular PBS science show, was conceived and developed as both a book and a TV series. Richard Simmons, the diet guru, was spotted as a guest on *General Hospital*. Because of his hyperactive approach to dieting exhibited on the show, he was asked by Warner Books to write a book, which became a best-seller and a popular TV series.

### Transportation

As technology has advanced and needs have changed, the transportation industry has responded with new and varied vehicles and systems of transportation.

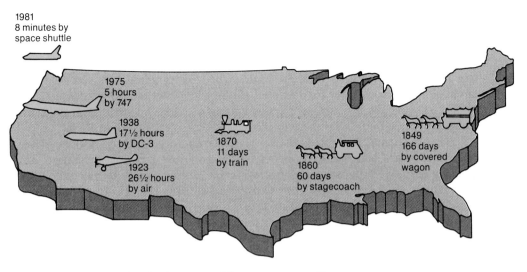

1981
8 minutes by
space shuttle

1975
5 hours
by 747

1938
17½ hours
by DC-3

1923
26½ hours
by air

1870
11 days
by train

1860
60 days
by stagecoach

1849
166 days
by covered
wagon

**Figure 24-3**   How long has it taken to travel from coast to coast?

Consequently, the time required to travel from coast to coast has been compressed dramatically (see Figure 24-3).

▲ **Effects of Energy**   A nation's economic development is dependent on the quality of its transportation system.  In the past, private vehicles, such as cars and trucks, have been the primary means of transportation, but when and if the energy and economic situations worsen, public transit systems will have to be accepted as an alternative.  More emphasis will be placed on mass transportation in the future.  Buses will probably continue to serve both commuters and long-distance travelers.  Rapid rail systems may be able to serve larger metropolitan areas.  For example, the rapid transit system built by the city of San Diego at its own expense is proving quite popular as a fast and inexpensive way for tourists to travel to and from Juarez, Mexico.  Feasibility studies are now being made on building a similar system between Los Angeles and Las Vegas.

Railroads may be used more for moving people and freight, especially if the fast French, West German, and Japanese trains can be adapted to U.S. needs.  The Budd Company, a Michigan-based subsidiary of the West German firm Thyssen, is planning to offer "maglevs"—magnetically levitated trains—in the United States.  These 250-mph trains float gently on magnetic fields, pulled along on the crest of an electromagnetic wave.  Such a train has already reached 320 mph on a test track in Japan, and maglevs are also being tested in Germany.[22]

Airlines are seeking more fuel-efficient aircraft that can be used more frequently because they require less repair and maintenance.  Regular passenger and freight travel in space is quite possible in your lifetime.  In fact, approximately 100 people per day are already signing up with the National Aeronautics and Space Administration to travel on one of the space shuttles.  Cargo space in the shuttles has already been contracted for by private industry through 1986.

▲ **The U.S. Auto Industry**   The U.S. auto industry is in trouble because of past and present abuses by management, labor, and government.  Until the late

1970s, U.S. automakers prospered because they produced a big car, which Americans wanted and other countries couldn't provide. But employee earnings and benefits outstripped productivity, leading to prohibitive costs; management became complacent and ignored consumer desires, especially the desire for quality and fuel efficiency; and the government imposed stringent environmental and safety regulations. These and other factors increased costs until U.S. cars couldn't compete with foreign ones. So, between 1978 and early 1982, 600,000 U.S. jobs were lost, out of a total of 1.9 million.[23]

But U.S. firms are fighting back. Management is becoming more effective, and workers are being more cooperative, giving up many costly benefits and forming employee involvement groups. Ford Motor Company has over 1,000 such groups at its sixty-eight U.S. plants. In addition, the government is being more realistic in its rules and regulations. More importantly, automakers are giving the public what it wants—safe, fuel-efficient cars and good service. Chrysler now provides a 50,000-mile, five-year warranty and practically trouble-free operation. Advertisements boast that all you should have to pay for is gas and periodic maintenance.

## Electronics

According to one computer executive, "If you were born before 1965, . . . you're going to be out of it."[24] "It" means the new electronic revolution sweeping the country.

▲ **The Industry** The electronics industry is, in essence, still in its infancy. Yet, with a continued flow of highly sophisticated technological advances from research and development, the size, complexity, and variety of firms and products in the industry are expected to increase at an explosive rate. The greatest growth potential seems to be in computers for home, office, industrial, and scientific applications.

The technological advances of the past two decades have increased the capability and capacity of computers. Also, the prices of computer hardware and software have declined sharply, making computers economically feasible for an ever-increasing number of businesses and individuals.

▲ **Home Computers** It's anticipated that by the late 1980s the market for home or personal computers will be one of the most successful segments of the computer market. Personal computers, video games, and hand-held electronic games based on a computer-like microprocessor have been very well received.

Home computers are capable of such activities as doing school homework, transmitting written documents, controlling appliances through built-in decoders, and providing a one-stop shopping center in your home. You can already check references from data banks (for a fee), shop for real estate, and do banking at home via computers. In 1982, the Knight-Ridder newspapers introduced in-home shopping and electronic banking to over 5,000 South Florida homes.[25] These services are offered through Viewtron, an electronic home information service that operates through regular cable lines and TV sets.

Even more significantly, personal computers are making their presence felt in formerly mainframe-oriented companies. Their low cost and high power make them potent money-makers for industries using computer-aided design and manufacture. Personal computers are now being used for tasks formerly reserved for mainframes.

The electronic revolution.

Using a home information system to shop.

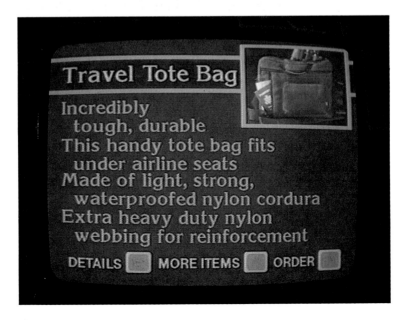

### Service Industries

The proportion of the U.S. work force providing services has grown from 50 percent to over 70 percent in the last three decades, so service industries will be one of the most important parts of the national economy in the future. No matter what happens to the economy in the late 1980s and 1990s, hundreds of thousands of new firms, and millions of old ones, will continue to provide accounting, consulting, banking, legal, medical, educational, credit, repair, dry cleaning, and other services to individuals, business, industry, and government agencies.

During the last decade, there was a net increase of nearly 20 million jobs in the United States. Nearly nine out of ten of these jobs were in service industries, and over two-thirds of them were in firms with fewer than twenty employees.[26] Many large firms, including manufacturers and retailers, hire smaller firms to perform service-type activities. For example, most banks, office buildings, and professional organizations have outside firms do their maintenance and custodial duties, and temporary employees are supplied by firms such as Kelly Services and Norrell Services, Inc.

Often, those who have a need for services aren't even aware of their need until it's called to their attention. But, as new service needs are recognized, new businesses spring up to fill them. Until the mid-1950s, most private citizens in the United States—except the very wealthy—calculated their own income taxes, while businesses had a staff to do theirs. But as both incomes and taxes increased, Henry and Richard Block of Kansas City developed a lucrative nationwide chain of offices to prepare income tax returns for individuals at all economic levels.

## ⬠ LEARNING OBJECTIVES REVISITED

1. *How to plot a career strategy.*

   In choosing a career, one must develop a career strategy by identifying one's opportunities, competencies and resources, ambitions and hopes, obligations to other people and groups, and personal values.

2. *The life-cycle stages of career growth.*

   People make different career-related decisions at different ages. In general, as people mature, they expand their career goals and seek more meaningful work. In their teens and twenties, people make educational and job entry decisions; in their thirties, they make decisions about changing jobs, work satisfaction, and advancement possibilities; people may become dissatisfied during their forties and change careers; workers are at their peak efficiency from age fifty to age sixty-five; although many people retire, some people continue working after age sixty-five.

3. *How to go after your first permanent job.*

   In seeking your first permanent job, it is important that you decide which is more important—the company or the job. Some characteristics of a good job are (1) direct feedback on performance; (2) a client relationship; (3) a natural module of work; (4) personal accountability; (5) decision-making opportunities; and (6) demand for your unique expertise.

4. *Some of the kinds of change that will affect you in the business world of the future.*

   Organizational changes in the future may include more decentralized and shared decision making. Environmental change will involve more self-sufficiency, more global concerns, an information explosion, and growth of small business. The work force will become more diverse and better educated. Technological change will involve research and development of new products, services, and processes. Managers can cope with these changes best not by reacting to them but by anticipating them.

5. *New developments you can expect in some selected industries.*

   Agribusiness, communications, transportation, electronics, and services will be areas of dramatic change and growth in the future.

## ⌂ IMPORTANT TERMS

As an extra review of the chapter, try defining the following terms. If you have trouble with any of them, refer to the page listed.

| | |
|---|---|
| values  *647* | agribusiness  *658* |
| career life cycle  *647* | super-supermarkets  *658* |
| occupation  *651* | quality supermarkets  *658* |
| planned change  *657* | |

## ⌂ REVIEW QUESTIONS

1. What are the five steps in developing a career strategy? Describe each.
2. What is the relationship between a career strategy, a career, and an occupation?
3. What are some of the career-related decisions one would make (a) in the teens and twenties? (b) in the thirties? (c) in the forties? (d) between age fifty and age sixty-five? (e) after age sixty-five?
4. What are some of the factors to be considered by college graduates choosing their first job?
5. Summarize the organizational, environmental, work force, and technological changes predicted for the future of business.
6. How can managers cope with change?

## ⌂ DISCUSSION QUESTIONS

1. What do you think might hinder you from "being what you resolve to be"?
2. Describe your career strategy, including the five key steps and your answers to the Quiz on p. 646.
3. Where are you in your career life cycle? Where are your parents?
4. Which should be chosen first—the company or the job itself? Why?
5. What social, economic, cultural, and technological factors in the environment should you consider as you plan your future in business?

6. Which of the organizational changes predicted by Steve Fuller have already happened?

7. Do the numerous predictions made in this chapter have any common threads? If so, what are they?

8. What new industries and products did you name as having arisen since the beginning of World War II? in your lifetime?

## ⬙ CASE 24-1   Education's Payoff: Is It Worth It?

According to a study reported by the U.S. Census Bureau in early 1983, a bachelor's degree was estimated to be worth about $329,000 (in 1981 dollars) to an eighteen-year-old man, and $142,000 to an eighteen-year-old woman. That's the extra amount they could expect to earn in a lifetime if they went on to get a college degree instead of being satisfied with only a high school diploma.

A male high school graduate could expect to earn $861,000; the amount increased to $1,190,000 if he went on to get the undergraduate college degree. But a man who didn't complete high school could expect to earn only $601,000. For women, the figures were only $211,000 without the high school diploma, $381,000 with it, and $523,000 with the bachelor's degree.

Bruce Chapman, census director at the time, cautioned against using the figures to prove salary discrimination, since they covered all individuals, whether they worked full time, part time, or not at all. Also, the study didn't consider breaks in employment service, and women have tended to break work service more than men. In fact, a break in employment service was shown to hurt men more than women. A two- to four-year break in work experience reduced earnings by 13 percent for women and 21 percent for men. A five-year or longer break lowered earnings 19 percent for women and 29 percent for men.

Finally, the report indicated that the average woman works for twenty-eight years, while for men the figure is thirty-eight.

### Case Questions

1. Do you think it's worth four years of your time and effort to earn the extra $142,000 or $329,000? Why or why not?

2. Do you think these differences between men and women in earnings and years worked will remain true in your lifetime? Why or why not?

## ⬙ CASE 24-2   Robots: Will They Replace Human Workers?

There were estimated to be between 8,700 and 15,000 relatively simple, computer-controlled machines—commonly called robots—installed in U.S. companies in early 1984. This number was expected to increase from 35 to 45 percent annually for the next ten years. Thus there would be over 200,000 of these steel-collar workers by 1994, and they'd be much more sophisticated and complex.

The 1984 machines weren't cheap: they cost around $25,000 to $80,000 apiece to buy and about $5 an hour to operate. But they did the work of employees who weren't cheap either. Employee earnings (including benefits) ran from $10 to $20 an

hour. Also, the robots improved quality and productivity, cut labor costs, could work practically around the clock (without overtime pay), were able to work safely in dangerous environments, and could be "trained" quickly and cheaply (by programming) to do new jobs effectively. The pressure was great to replace people with machines. Also, there was the danger of "silent firings," as firms closed because they couldn't compete with foreign producers if they didn't automate.

However, growth in service, information and communications, health care, electronics, transportation, banking and finance, and other industries was expected to continue, and the ability of

robots to fill jobs in these fields was uncertain. Also, jobs were being created to "feed and care for" the new workers. The design, production, installation, and maintenance of robots was expected to create as many jobs for humans as the robots themselves would take away. It was further predicted that, during their lifetime, half the students in college in the 1980s would probably work in jobs that don't even exist now.

**Case Questions**

1. Do you believe that use of robots will lead to a reduction in the total number of employees needed during the next decade? Why or why not?

2. What factors do you see in today's environment that could lead to even greater use of robots than was estimated in this case?

3. What can you do to prevent yourself from being replaced by a robot?

# DIGGING DEEPER:

 Careers in International Business and Business Law

Many interesting and rewarding career opportunities are available in international business and business law.

## What International Business Jobs Require

Import and export employees buy and sell raw materials and finished products between U.S. firms and foreign firms. They may specialize in either importing or exporting. Some individuals are also employed in the foreign trade departments of large firms.

The job of the *export manager* is described in Table VII-1. Orders from foreign customers are processed by *export sales managers*, who make contracts and arrange shipping details, and *export credit managers*, who review the customers' financial status and arrange credit terms. For import functions, the larger firm usually employs a *support manager*, whose job is also described in Table VII-1.

Some firms don't employ their own import and export workers. Instead, they use the services of *export brokers*, who sell the firm's products abroad for a commission, or *import merchants*, who sell products from foreign countries in the United States. A firm may also sell its products to *export commission house brokers*, speculators who buy domestic products outright and then sell them in foreign countries.

## What Business Law Jobs Require

A heavy proportion of most law firms' revenues is derived from business-related transactions entered into by their attorneys. Some such transactions are described in Table VII-1.

A private research firm predicts that the job market for attorneys will remain healthy, especially in small towns and suburban areas, during the 1990s. However, at the national meeting of the American Bar Association in 1983, many members were concerned about the tremendous number of graduates from law schools and the glut that might develop.

**TABLE VII-1  Selected careers in international business and business law.**

| Job Title | Job Description | Education and Training | Salaries ( Beginner / Experienced ) | Outlook to 1990 |
|---|---|---|---|---|
| Export managers | Responsible for the overall management of a firm's export activities. Supervise the activities of *foreign sales representatives*, who live and work abroad. | Bachelor's degree is preferred. | $17,800<br><br>For international sales manager, $52,000 | Employment is expected to grow faster than the average for all occupations. |
| Support managers | Purchase foreign products or raw materials. Supervise the work of *buyers*, who live and work in foreign countries. | Bachelor's degree is preferred. | $17,800–$45,000 | Employment is expected to grow faster than the average for all occupations. |
| Lawyers | Engage in business-related functions such as making patent applications, drawing up business contracts, preparing tax returns, and settling labor disputes. Take on regulatory tasks in areas of transportation and energy conservation. Interpret laws, rules, and regulations for business. Counsel clients concerning legal rights and obligations. | LL.B. degree and admission to bar. | $10,000–$35,000<br><br>Over $60,000 up to $100,000–$250,000 | Employment is expected to grow faster than the average for all occupations. |

SOURCES: U.S. Department of Labor, *Occupational Outlook Handbook*, 1982–1983 (Washington, D.C.: U.S. Government Printing Office, April 1982) and 1980–1981 (Washington, D.C.: U.S. Government Printing Office, April 1980); College Placement Council, *CPC Salary Survey, Summer Supplement* (Bethlehem, Pa.: CPC, 1983), pp. 2–5; and Steven D. Ross, "The 12 Top Money-Making Careers of the '80s," *Business Week's Guide to Careers* 1 (Spring 1983): 9.

# Notes

## Chapter 1

*Opening case:* Based on various sources, including "Outer-Space Entrepreneurs," *Time*, September 20, 1982, p. 19; "A Giant Step for Capitalism," *Newsweek*, September 20, 1982, p. 64; "Free Enterprise Goes into Space," *U.S. News & World Report*, September 20, 1982, p. 12; and Stephen Harrigan, "Mr. Hannah's Rocket," *Texas Monthly*, November 1982.

[1] Quoted by Gerald L. Phillippe, chairman of the board, General Electric Company, in an address to the National Association of Manufacturers, December 8, 1967.

[2] Manufacturers earn 5 percent; supermarkets, from ½ to 1½ percent.

[3] Linda K. Lanier, "Wealth—'I Could Care Less,'" *U.S. News & World Report*, May 31, 1982, p. 59.

[4] "Supersonic Delivery," *Time*, September 28, 1981, p. 71; and "Federal Express Wants to Deliver in Space," *Business Week*, July 4, 1983, p. 42.

[5] See "The Rise and Fall of Diamonds," *Business Week*, June 7, 1982, p. 10.

[6] Michael D. McIntyre, *Economic Roots: A Saga of the American Economy* (Wesson, Miss.: Copiah-Lincoln Junior College, Business Division, 1977).

[7] John J. Putman, "A Different Communism: Hungary's New Way," *National Geographic* 163 (February 1983):225–61.

[8] David Brand, "Russia's Private Farms Show State-Run Ones How to Raise Output," *Wall Street Journal*, March 23, 1981, p. 1.

[9] "China's New Leap Forward: Free Enterprise," *U.S. News & World Report*, March 23, 1981, p. 1.

[10] Vigor Keung Fung, "China Will Allow Individual Foreigners to Buy Stock in a Domestic Corp.," *Wall Street Journal*, June 28, 1983, p. 39.

[11] *Wall Street Journal*, July 15, 1981, p. 26. See also Linda S. Lichter, S. Robert Lichter, and Stanley Rothman, "How Show Business Shows Business," *Human Events*, February 26, 1983, p. 11.

[12] U.S. Department of Commerce, Bureau of the Census, *Statistical Abstract of the United States* (Washington, D.C.: Government Printing Office, 1983), p. 103.

[13] Pat Ordovensky, "USA Adults Mean Business When Returning to School," *USA Today*, December 15, 1983, p. 3A.

[14] Computed from *Enrollment Trends with Minority Data, 1978–79* (St. Louis: American Assembly of Collegiate Schools of Business, 1980).

[15] Ellie McGrath, "Head High, Chin Up, Eyes Clear," *Time*, June 28, 1982, pp. 56–57; and Lucia Solorzano, "Liberal Arts Colleges Bow to the Future," *U.S. News & World Report*, May 23, 1983, p. 67.

[16] *Wall Street Journal*, February 19, 1980, p. 1.

[17] *Human Events*, April 23, 1983, p. 13.

## Chapter 2

*Opening case:* Based on "A Bitter Pill for Aspirin Makers," *Business Week*, July 5, 1982, p. 78; Dennis Kneale, "Remedy Ruckus: Tylenol, the Painkiller, Gives Rivals Headache in Stores and in Courts," *Wall Street Journal*, September 2, 1982, p. 1; "Lessons That Emerge from Tylenol Disaster," *U.S. News & World Report*, October 18, 1982, pp. 67–68; Michael Waldholz, "Johnson & Johnson to Bring Back Tylenol, Says It Is Committed to Rebuilding Name," *Wall Street Journal*, November 12, 1982, p. 2; Michael Waldholz, "Speedy Recovery: Tylenol Regains Most of No. 1 Market Share, Amazing Doomsayers," *Wall Street Journal*, December 29, 1982, pp. 1, 6; and "J&J Will Pay Dearly to Cure Tylenol," *Business Week*, November 29, 1982, p. 37.

[1] See *IBM Stockholders' Second Quarter Report, 1982*, p. 9, for further details.

[2] *Wall Street Journal*, January 26, 1979, p. 1.

[3] John M. Leger, "'Socially Responsible' Funds Pique Interest, but Results Often Have Been Unimpressive," *Wall Street Journal*, November 18, 1982, p. 33.

[4] Milton Friedman, *Capitalism and Freedom* (Chicago: University of Chicago Press, 1962), p. 133.

[5] U.S. Congress, Subcommittee of the Joint Committee on the Economic Report, *Hearings on Profits* (testimony of C. E. Wilson of General Electric), 80th Cong., December 1949.

[6] *Dodge* v. *Ford Motor Company*, 204 Mich. 459 (1919).

[7] Much of this material is based on Fred Luthans and Richard M. Hodgetts, *Social Issues in Business* (New York: Macmillan, 1972); and Daniel A. Wren, *The Evolution of Management Thought*, 2nd ed. (New York: John Wiley & Sons, 1979).

[8] See Leon C. Megginson, *Personnel: A Behavioral Approach to Management*, 2nd ed. (Homewood, Ill.: Richard D. Irwin, 1972), p. 80.

[9] See letters in *New York Times*, August 25, 1918, and *New York Herald*, October 1, 1918.

[10] Upton Sinclair, *The Jungle* (1906; rep. ed., Cambridge, Mass.: R. Bentley, 1972).

[11] Robert Hay and Ed Gray, "Social Responsibilities of Management," *Academy of Management Journal* 17 (March 1974):142.

[12] *U.S. News & World Report*, May 30, 1983, p. 12.

[13] Susan Dentzer and Renee Michael, "They Shall Overcome," *Newsweek*, May 23, 1983, p. 60.

[14] Thomas Oliver, "The Coke-PUSH Pact: 1 Year Later," *Atlanta Journal–Atlanta Constitution*, August 15, 1982, p. 1-E; and "A Minority Stake in Coke," *Business Week*, August 1, 1983, p. 32.

[15] "Technology Is Opening More Jobs for the Deaf," *Business Week*, May 9, 1983, pp. 134–35.

[16] *Business Week*, May 20, 1982, pp. 96–104.

[17] "Fish Stories and Empty Offices," *Time*, April 11, 1983, p. 18.

[18] "The NRC Puts the Heat on Nuclear Power," *Business Week*, May 23, 1983, pp. 51–52.

[19] "Dow's Dioxin Program: New Studies to Reassure the Public," *Chemical & Engineering News*, June 6, 1983, p. 8.

[20] *Parade*, June 12, 1983, p. 17.

[21] "Library in Tulsa Due Computer Center," *Tulsa World*, May 21, 1982, p. 8-A.

[22] "The Struggle to Go to the Head of the Class," *Business Week*, June 20, 1983, p. 68.

[23] Jennifer B. Hull, "Defense Contracts Stir Some Student Protests on College Campuses," *Wall Street Journal*, May 20, 1983, p. 1.

[24] Robert Johnson, "Aetna Sets Out to 'Do Good' for Chicago but Ends Up in Fight with Neighborhood," *Wall Street Journal*, December 6, 1982, p. 25.

[25] *Wall Street Journal*, May 5, 1983, p. 1.

[26] Milton Moskowitz, Michael Katz, and Robert Levering, eds., *Everybody's Business* (New York: Harper & Row, 1980), pp. 688–89.

[27] Larry Margasak, "Boeing Admits Guilt in Payments Case: Fined $400,000," *Mobile Register*, July 1, 1982, p. 6E.

[28] Jim Drinkhall, "Hitachi Case's Last Defendant Has Plea of No Contest Accepted by Federal Judge," *Wall Street Journal*, May 16, 1983, p. 6; and "Defendant Is Facing Fine of $7,500 in Case on IBM Trade Secrets," *Wall Street Journal*, June 17, 1982, p. 8.

[29] Daniel Hertzberg and Daniel Machalaba, "Harcourt's Use of Pensions Is Criticized," *Wall Street Journal*, May 25, 1983, p. 33.

[30] Daniel Hertzberg, "More Firms Issuing Stock to Pensions," *Wall Street Journal*, June 2, 1983, p. 33.

[31] Brooks Jackson and Edward Pound, "Legislative Lucre: Fees for Congressmen from Interest Groups Doubled in Past Year," *Wall Street Journal*, July 28, 1983, pp. 1, 14.

[32] Howard Rosenberg, "Sex and Snooty Behavior Sell: Are TV Ads Going Too Far?" *Tulsa World*, March 18, 1983, p. 2-E.

[33] "Did Rivals Play Fair with Sir Freddie?" *Business Week*, April 18, 1983, pp. 35–36; and John Brecher, "Did They Gang Up on Laker?" *Newsweek*, August 1, 1983, p. 54.

[34] Charles Kaiser, "Is Secret Taping Ethical?" *Newsweek*, June 27, 1983, p. 79.

[35] *Washington Vantage Point* (Washington, D.C.: American Society of Personnel Administration, July 1979).

[36] "Four-Way Test" Copyright 1946 by Rotary International.

[37] Carolyn Ashburn, "Deaf People in Mobile Protest Lack of Captioned CBS Shows," *Mobile Register*, May 20, 1982, p. 2C.

[38] All names have been changed.

## Chapter 3

*Opening case:* Based on William M. Bulkeley, "Inventor Kloss Trying for the Fourth Time to Turn His Ideas into a Healthy Business," *Wall Street Journal*, April 16, 1982, pp. 31, 44; "Millionaire by Design," *Dun's Review* 104 (December 1974):12, 13, 16, 90, 92; and correspondence with Kloss Video.

[1] Stephen P. Morin, "Fans Are Baffled by 'Coup de Team' of Boston Red Sox," *Wall Street Journal*, June 8, 1983, p. 20; and "Red Sox Takeover Mixed," *Mobile Register*, August 11, 1983, p. 6B.

[2] Irving Wallace, David Wallechinsky, and Amy Wallace, "From Rags to Riches," *Parade*, March 20, 1983, p. 21.

[3] "New Businesses in Some States Have Less Red Tape to Fight," *Wall Street Journal*, June 7, 1983, p. 33.

[4] All names have been changed.

[5] Thomas F. O'Boyle, "Laid Low by Recession, Big Steel Companies Consider Major Change," *Wall Street Journal*, May 27, 1983, p. 16; O'Boyle, "U.S. Steel's Venture Talks Seen Snagged on Cash Amount British Steel Must Invest," *Wall Street Jour-*

*nal*, June 27, 1983, p. 4; and "Time Runs Out for Steel," *Business Week*, June 13, 1983, pp. 83–84.

## Chapter 4

*Opening case:* Reprinted by permission from Micki Van Deventer, "Game Brings Profit, Honor," *Tulsa Daily World*, May 2, 1982, pp. G-1–G-5. Also based on "Game Earns Pretty Pente for Inventor," *Tulsa Daily World*, July 3, 1983, p. A-9; and other sources, including information from the company.

[1] *The State of Small Business: A Report of the President* (Washington, D.C.: Government Printing Office, March 1983), pp. 6, 53.

[2] *ABC Evening News*, April 7, 1983.

[3] Lawrence Rout, "Many Big-Company Executives Leaving for More Responsibility in Smaller Firms," *Wall Street Journal*, March 13, 1981, pp. 25, 31.

[4] W. B. Barnes, *First Semi-Annual Report of the Small Business Administration* (Washington, D.C.: Small Business Administration, January 31, 1954), p. 7.

[5] From *Meeting the Special Problems of Small Businesses* (New York: Committee for Economic Development, 1974), p. 14. Copyright 1974, Committee for Economic Development. Used with permission.

[6] *The State of Small Business* (1983), p. 28.

[7] *ABC Evening News*, April 7, 1983.

[8] U.S. Small Business Administration, *The State of Small Business: A Report to the President* (Washington, D.C.: Government Printing Office, 1982), p. 89.

[9] *The State of Small Business* (1983), p. 37.

[10] Dean Rotbart, "Starting a Business Separates the Men from Boys, Usually," *Wall Street Journal*, August 18, 1981, p. 1.

[11] *The State of Small Business* (1983), p. 54.

[12] Letter from Smith's Bakery, January 18, 1980.

[13] Steve Mufson, "Tough Oil Man: Amerada Hess Chief Keeps Controls Tight, Emphasizes Marketing," *Wall Street Journal*, January 11, 1983, p. 1.

[14] Carol Deegan, "Owning a Business Is the Sure Way to the Top," Associated Press article, February 11, 1979.

[15] *Wall Street Journal*, January 22, 1980, p. 1.

[16] *Wall Street Journal*, April 19, 1982, p. 23.

[17] *The State of Small Business* (1983), p. 28.

[18] Arthur Levitt, Jr., "Small Business Discovers Its Strengths," *Business Week*, March 10, 1980, p. 23.

[19] Michael Doan and Walter S. Wingo, "The Famine Is Over for Small Business," *U.S. News & World Report*, July 4, 1983, p. 55.

[20] See Curtis E. Tate, Jr. et al., *Successful Small Business Management*, 3rd ed. (Plano, Tex.: Business Publications, 1982), pp. 25–28, for further details.

[21] See Joel Katkin and Don Gevirtz, "Business Entrepreneurs: Festering Anger over Economic Plight," *Tulsa World*, January 23, 1983, p. I-1.

[22] Tate et al., pp. 35–37.

[23] *The State of Small Business* (1983), p. 112.

[24] *Wall Street Journal*, May 5, 1983, p. 1.

[25] *The State of Small Business* (1983), p. 112.

[26] His name has been changed.

[27] See *Working Woman*, September 1978, pp. 17ff., for further details.

## Chapter 5

*Opening case:* Based on correspondence with company officials, interviews with store managers, and published sources, including Guy S. Miller, "Pizza Hut's New Sales Strategy: Faster Service, Expanded Menus," *Wall Street Journal*, November 20, 1980, p. 29; "The Man Who McDonaldized Burger King," *Business Week*, October 8, 1979, pp. 132, 136; "Pizza Hut Tries a New

Recipe for Success," *Business Week*, January 18, 1982, pp. 87–88; and Janet Guyon, "Pepsi Is Losing Fast-Food Whiz to Chart House," *Wall Street Journal*, May 13, 1983, p. 4.

[1] Amal Nag, "Auto Dealers Say They're Bypassed in Sales to Fleet Buyers and Move to Halt Practice," *Wall Street Journal*, June 21, 1983, p. 37.

[2] "A New Hamburger Chain Built on Hindsight," *Business Week*, September 20, 1976, p. 101.

[3] Clemens P. Work, "As Franchising Spreads Far Afield," *U.S. News & World Report*, December 6, 1982, p. 51.

[4] U.S. Department of Commerce, Bureau of Industrial Economics, *Franchising in the Economy, 1980–1982* (Washington, D.C.: Government Printing Office, 1982), pp. 29–32; and miscellaneous bulletins.

[5] "A Franchise Investment in Every Pot," *Business Week*, April 12, 1982, p. 114.

[6] Frederic M. Biddle, "Franchising's New Frontier," *Boston Globe*, June 28, 1983, pp. 45, 50.

[7] Work, p. 51.

[8] Robert E. Wiegand, "Buying into Market Control," *Harvard Business Review* 58 (November-December 1980):147.

[9] Work, p. 50.

[10] Sanford L. Jacobs, "Operating a Franchise Often Pays, but Demands on Buyer Are Great," *Wall Street Journal*, November 3, 1980, p. 33.

[11] These ideas are based on information from the National Association of Franchised Businessmen, 1404 New York Avenue NW, Washington, D.C. 20005.

[12] Based on various sources, including "Burger King Converts to Pepsi from Coke in 3,200 Restaurants," *Wall Street Journal*, June 14, 1983, p. 6; "Pepsi Joins the Whopper," *Business Week*, June 27, 1983, p. 36; and radio, TV, and newspaper reports.

[13] Based on various sources, especially Nancy Ann Rathbun, "Franchising Wave of the '80s," *Nation's Business* 70 (March 1982):82–86; and "A Franchise Investment in Every Pot," *Business Week*, April 12, 1982, pp. 113–14.

**Digging Deeper: Careers in Business**

[1] "How Much Is a Degree Worth? $329,000," *Tulsa World*, March 14, 1983, p. B-6.

**Chapter 6**

*Opening case:* From various sources, including Amanda Bennett, "President Iacocca? No, But in Detroit It Sounds Plausible," *Wall Street Journal*, June 28, 1982, p. 1; Tom Nicholson and James C. Jones, "Iacocca Shifts into High," *Newsweek*, February 14, 1983, p. 64; and David Abodaher, *Iacocca* (New York: Macmillan, 1983).

[1] "Did Rivals Play Fair with Sir Freddie?" *Business Week*, April 18, 1983, pp. 35–36.

[2] Based on John M. Ivancevich, James H. Donnelly, Jr., and James L. Gibson, *Managing for Performance* (Dallas, Tex.: Business Publications, 1980), pp. 60–67.

[3] Edwin E. Ghiselli, *Explorations in Managerial Talent* (Pacific Palisades, Calif.: Goodyear Publishing, 1971).

[4] Based on R. L. Katz, "Skills of an Effective Administrator," *Harvard Business Review* 52 (September-October 1974):80–102; and Henry Mintzberg, *The Nature of Managerial Work* (New York: Harper & Row, 1973), pp. 188–93.

[5] Joel Dreyfuss, "Handing Down the Old Hands' Wisdom," *Fortune*, June 13, 1983, pp. 97–104.

[6] David B. Richardson, "Answer to Ailing Industry: Overhaul at the Very Top," *U.S. News & World Report*, January 17, 1983, p. 37.

[7] Robert N. McMurry, "What to Do About Executives Who Can't Delegate and Won't Decide," in *Business/Management 81/82*, ed. Joseph G. Mattingly, Jr. (Guilford, Conn.: Dushkin Publishing Group, 1981), pp. 110–11.

[8] K. M. Chrysler, "What It's Like to Run Biggest U.S. Companies," *U.S. News & World Report*, October 20, 1980, p. 83.

**Chapter 7**

*Opening case:* Hal Lancaster, "Baseball's Big Hit: Los Angeles Dodgers, Again Seeking Pennant, Keep On Winning Fans," *Wall Street Journal*, October 5, 1978, p. 1. Adapted by permission of *The Wall Street Journal*, © Dow Jones & Company, Inc. 1978. All Rights Reserved. Also based on Red Smith, "Of God, Baseball, and Dodger Blue," *New York Times*, March 14, 1979, p. D-21; and others.

[1] Gerald C. Lubenow, "The Silicon Valley Style," *Newsweek*, June 8, 1981, p. 80.

[2] Peter Drucker, "We Have Become a Society of Organizations," *Wall Street Journal*, January 9, 1978, p. 12.

[3] Kathleen Day, "Costly Misses: Success Tales Have Flip Side," *USA Today*, June 30, 1983, p. 1B.

[4] Lubenow, p. 80.

[5] Ibid.

[6] John Koten, "Iacocca Says He Will Stay at Chrysler," *Wall Street Journal*, July 11, 1983, pp. 21, 31.

[7] "Behind the Exodus at National Semiconductor," *Business Week*, September 21, 1981, p. 95.

[8] Lubenow, p. 80.

[9] "Why Procter & Gamble Is Playing It Even Tougher," *Business Week*, July 18, 1983, p. 186.

[10] "Zapped: Losses and Layoffs at Atari," *Time*, June 13, 1983, p. 50.

[11] "When Marketing Takes Over at R. J. Reynolds," *Business Week*, November 13, 1978, p. 82.

[12] Kenneth R. Sheets, "Incentive Has a Lot to Do with Performance," *U.S. News & World Report*, October 27, 1980, p. 86.

[13] Laura Landro, "Highflier's Fall: How Headlines of 1982 Led to 1983's Doldrums for Warner and Atari," *Wall Street Journal*, July 25, 1983, p. 1.

**Chapter 8**

*Opening case:* "White Consolidated's New Appliance Punch," *Business Week*, May 7, 1979, pp. 94–98; Milton Moskowitz, Michael Katz, and Robert Levering, eds., *Everybody's Business: An Almanac* (New York: Harper & Row, 1980), pp. 191–93; and Lisa Miller Mesdag, "The Appliance Boom Begins," *Fortune*, July 25, 1983, pp. 52–57.

[1] Monroe W. Karmin, "Industry: Lean, Mean and Ready for Recovery," *U.S. News & World Report*, May 9, 1983, pp. 141–42.

[2] Charles P. Alexander, "The New Economy," *Time*, May 30, 1983, p. 63.

[3] Ernest Conine, "Industrial Robot Race Under Way," *Tulsa World*, January 24, 1982, p. 2.

[4] Hidehiro Tanakadate, "The Robots Are Coming and Japan Leads the Way," *U.S. News & World Report*, January 18, 1982, p. 47.

[5] Carol Hymowitz, "High-Tech Track: Manufacturers Press Automating to Survive, But Results Are Mixed," *Wall Street Journal*, April 11, 1983, p. 1.

[6] Jeffery L. Sheler, "A Tale of Two Worlds in Tennessee," *U.S. News & World Report*, December 20, 1982, pp. 84–85; and correspondence with company officials.

[7] Michael Doan, "How 7 Firms Have Bucked the Tide," *U.S. News & World Report*, November 23, 1981, p. 60.

[8] Norman Gall, "Close the Door, They Come in the Window," *Forbes*, February 15, 1980, p. 18.

[9] Erik Calonius, "Factory Magic: In a Plant in Memphis, Japanese Firm Shows How to Attain Quality," *Wall Street Journal*, April 23, 1983, p. 19.

[10] "Mexico: U.S. Computer Makers Rush to Set Up Plants," *Business Week*, May 17, 1982, p. 45.

[11] Calonius, p. 19.

[12] Young, p. 23.

[13] John Koten, "Auto Makers Have Trouble with 'Kanban,'" *Wall Street Journal*, May 7, 1982, p. 35.

[14] Since the critical path is the longer one, in this instance it is Path B, which takes 30 (6 + 4 + 6 + 6 + 1 + 1 + 1 + 3 + 1 + 1) weeks, while Path A takes only 28 (4 + 4 + 6 + 6 + 2 + 1 + 3 + 1 + 1) weeks. A delay in operations on Path A of two weeks or less is therefore not critical to prompt completion of the project.

[15] "Gunk Grounds the Second Shuttle," *Time*, November 16, 1981, p. 58.

[16] Hymowitz, p. 1.

[17] All names have been changed.

## Chapter 9

*Opening case:* Based on company reports and literature, as well as Janet Guyon, "'Family Feeling' at Delta Creates Loyal Workers," *Wall Street Journal*, July 7, 1980, pp. 2, 13; "Airline Woes Catch Up with Delta," *Business Week*, November 8, 1982, pp. 131–34; and *ABC Evening News*, December 15, 1982.

[1] M. R. Weisbord, "Management in Crisis," *Conference Board Record* 7 (February 1970):13.

[2] "High-Tech Industry Turns to Retirees," *INC.* 4 (April 1982):20.

[3] *Wall Street Journal*, July 14, 1981, p. 1.

[4] Ibid., September 15, 1981, p. 1.

[5] Edward P. Dear, "Computer Job Matching Now and Tomorrow," *Personnel* 47 (May–June 1970):57–63.

[6] Paul Sheibar, "A Simple Selection System Called Jobmatch," *Personnel Journal* 58 (January 1979):26–30, 56.

[7] Earl R. Gomersall and M. Scott Myers, "Breakthrough in On-the-Job Training," *Harvard Business Review* 44 (July-August 1966):62–71.

[8] John W. Buckley, "Programmed Instruction in Industrial Training," *California Management Review* 10 (Winter 1967):71–79.

[9] Arthur J. Fraser and James G. Sucey, "Two Experiments in Programmed Learning," *Training Directors* 16 (February 1962):9–13.

[10] "TV Teachers Training Plant Bosses Statewide," *Business Week*, August 29, 1964, pp. 64–66.

[11] H. H. Meyer and W. B. Walker, "A Study of Factors Relating to the Effectiveness of a Performance Appraisal Program," *Personnel Psychology* 14 (August 1961):291–98.

[12] "Why Procter & Gamble Is Playing It Even Tougher," *Business Week*, July 18, 1983, p. 179.

[13] Tom Bailey, "Industrial Outplacement at Goodyear: Part I. The Company's Position," *Personnel Administrator* 25 (March 1980):42ff.

[14] *ABC World News Tonight*, August 9, 1983.

[15] "Behind the UPS Mystique: Puritanism and Productivity," *Business Week*, June 6, 1983, p. 66.

[16] Donald Lambro, "New Positive OSHA Attitude Aids U.S. Businesses," *Human Events*, February 11, 1984, p. 9.

[17] All names have been changed.

[18] All names have been changed.

## Chapter 10

*Opening case:* Company name has been changed. Adapted from
*Human Resources: Cases and Concepts* by Leon C. Megginson, © 1978 by Harcourt Brace Jovanovich, Inc. Reprinted by permission of the publisher.

[1] "Can Don Lennox Save Harvester?" *Business Week*, August 15, 1983, p. 82.

[2] For more details, see Frederick W. Taylor, "What Is Scientific Management?" in *Classics in Management*, ed. Harwood F. Merrill (New York: American Management Association, 1960), pp. 78ff.

[3] See F. J. Roethlisberger and W. J. Dickson, *Management and the Worker* (Cambridge, Mass.: Harvard University Press, 1939), for a description of these studies.

[4] *Wall Street Journal*, October 19, 1982, p. 1.

[5] See Robert L. Kahn, "Productivity and Job Satisfaction," *Personnel Psychology* 13 (Autumn 1960):275–87.

[6] Abraham H. Maslow, "A Theory of Human Motivation," *Psychological Review* 50 (July 1943):370–96.

[7] For an analysis of the reasons for failure, see Erwin L. Malone, "The Non-Linear Systems Experiment in Participative Management," *Journal of Business of the University of Chicago* 48 (January 1975):52–64.

[8] For details, see Raymond E. Miles, "Human Relations or Human Resources?" *Harvard Business Review* 43 (July-August 1965):148–63.

[9] See Richard T. Pascale and Anthony G. Athos, *The Art of Japanese Management: Application to American Executives* (New York: Simon and Schuster, 1981).

[10] In the 1920s, IBM had a company songbook with lyrics such as: "Our voices swell in admiration,/Of T. J. Watson proudly sing./He'll ever be our inspiration,/To him our voices loudly ring." See Milton Moskowitz, Michael Katz, and Robert Levering, eds., *Everybody's Business: An Almanac* (New York: Harper & Row, 1980), p. 439 for further details.

[11] *CBS Morning News*, Labor Day program, September 5, 1983.

[12] "Behind the UPS Mystique: Puritanism and Productivity," *Business Week*, June 6, 1983, p. 67.

[13] Edgar F. Huse, "Do Zero Defects Programs Really Motivate Workers?" *Personnel* 43 (March–April 1966):5–11.

[14] David Reed, "Detroit Faces the Sun: A New Day Dawns for the Motor City," *Reader's Digest*, September 1983, p. 172.

[15] "As You Were Saying—The Number One Problem," *Personnel Journal* 45 (April 1966):237–38.

[16] Reed, pp. 89–165.

[17] "Behind the UPS Mystique," p. 69.

[18] "At Radio Shack, Six-Day Weeks and Six-Figure Bonuses," *Business Week*, September 12, 1983, p. 95.

[19] Tracy Kidder, *The Soul of a New Machine* (New York: Avon Books, 1981), p. 291.

[20] These needs were introduced by A. H. Maslow in *Motivation and Personality* (New York: Harper & Bros., 1954) and modified by Douglas McGregor in *The Human Side of Enterprise* (New York: McGraw-Hill, 1960). This is the generally accepted grouping and classification of these needs.

[21] Adapted from McGregor, *The Human Side of Enterprise*, pp. 35–37.

[22] Frederick Herzberg et al., *The Motivation to Work*, 2nd ed. (New York: John Wiley & Sons, 1959). You should be aware that teachers and journalists accept this theory more than practicing managers and employees.

[23] "Can Don Lennox Save Harvester?" p. 82.

[24] Reed, p. 157.

[25] "You Have to Bend and Stretch a Little to Keep Your Job," *Business Week*, August 29, 1983, p. 56.

[26] From *Management Methods Magazine*, © 1952 by Management Magazines, Inc.

[27] Reprinted by permission from Leon C. Megginson, *Personnel: A Behavioral Approach to Administration*, 2nd ed. (Home-

wood, Ill.: Richard D. Irwin, Inc., 1972), pp. 687–88. © 1972 Richard D. Irwin, Inc.

## Chapter 11

*Opening case:* For more details and greater understanding of this quite complex case, see "Caterpillar: Sticking to Basics to Stay Competitive," *Business Week*, May 4, 1981, pp. 74–80; "At Caterpillar, Both Sides May Bend," *Business Week*, December 13, 1982, p. 28; "What's Pushing Caterpillar to Settle," *Business Week*, March 14, 1983, p. 28; Harlan S. Byrne, "UAW Bargainers Agree to Submit Offer of Caterpillar to Vote by Full Membership," *Wall Street Journal*, April 20, 1983, p. 7; Byrne, "Caterpillar Well Positioned to Recover as the UAW Ratifies 37-Month Contract," *Wall Street Journal*, April 25, 1983, p. 10; "A Strike-Weary Caterpillar Knuckles Under," *Business Week*, May 2, 1983, pp. 30–31; and "Cat Purrs," *Time*, May 9, 1983, p. 67.

[1] John S. DeMott, "Labor's Unhappy Birthday," *Time*, November 16, 1981, p. 124.

[2] "A Decade of U.S. Leadership—The Long View," *U.S. News & World Report*, May 23, 1983, p. 53; and "Institutions That Affect the Nation," *U.S. News & World Report*, May 14, 1984, p. 50.

[3] Harry Anderson, "The Rise and Fall of Big Labor," *Newsweek*, September 5, 1983, p. 50.

[4] Jeffery L. Sheler, "Unions Still Find South a Tough Row to Hoe," *U.S. News & World Report*, June 21, 1982, p. 62.

[5] Joseph Kraft, "Then I Must Have Been Misinformed," *Mobile Register*, September 13, 1983, p. 4-A.

[6] Philip Revzin, "British Unions to Resume Talks with the Tories," *Wall Street Journal*, September 7, 1983, p. 34.

[7] "A Spark of Militancy in the Land of Loyalty," *Business Week*, September 5, 1983, pp. 96–98.

[8] "Unions Break Out of a Political Tailspin," *U.S. News & World Report*, November 15, 1982, p. 80.

[9] "More Unions Brandish Money as a Weapon," *Business Week*, February 26, 1979, p. 47.

[10] See Trevor Armbrister, "When the Mob Runs a Union," *Reader's Digest*, September 1983, pp. 140–44, for an example of such corruption.

[11] These hearings were called Senator McClellan's Senate Select Committee on Improper Activities in the Labor and Management Field. Senator John F. Kennedy was a member, and his brother, Robert, was general counsel. The TV coverage of the hearings publicized Kennedy and helped propel him into the presidency.

[12] "Belabored: A Litany of Woes," *Time*, May 2, 1983, p. 59.

[13] Myron Magnet, "Phelps Dodge's Lonely Stand," *Fortune*, August 22, 1983, pp. 106–10.

[14] Anderson, p. 51.

[15] About 32 percent of all public workers belong to labor organizations. See Joann S. Lublin, "The Air Strike's Effect on Organized Labor," *Wall Street Journal*, August 18, 1981, p. 22.

[16] Amanda Bennett, "Salaried Staff at GM Flirts with Union," *Wall Street Journal*, August 18, 1982, p. 29.

[17] *Wall Street Journal*, April 22, 1980, p. 1.

[18] George Gallup, "Union Backing at All-Time Low," *Mobile Register*, September 17, 1981, p. 7-B.

### Digging Deeper: Careers in Human Resources Management

[1] See Nicholas Basta, "Human Resources Managers," *Business Week's Guide to Careers* I (Fall/Winter 1983), p. 11, for further details.

## Chapter 12

*Opening case:* Based on Gail Bronson, "Baby Food It Is, But Gerber Wants Teen-Agers to Think of It as Dessert," *The Wall Street Journal*, July 1, 1981, p. 29. Adapted by permission of *The Wall Street Journal*, © Dow Jones and Company, Inc. 1981. All Rights Reserved.

[1] Theodore Levitt, "Marketing Myopia," *Harvard Business Review* 38 (July-August 1960):45–46.

[2] U.S. Department of Commerce, Small Business Administration, *Personal Qualities Needed to Manage a Store*, by Irving Schwartz (Washington, D.C.: Government Printing Office, 1970), Small Marketing Aids, No. 145.

[3] "Ma Bell Dresses Up," *Wall Street Journal*, April 28, 1982, p. 31.

[4] "GM Takes On the Japanese," *Newsweek*, May 11, 1981, p. 56.

[5] "Hershey: Joining with Friendly to Diversify Away from Chocolate," *Business Week*, January 29, 1979, pp. 118–19.

[6] "Less Mickey Mouse: Disney to Shift Target of Some Parks, Movies to Teen-Agers, Adults," *Wall Street Journal*, January 26, 1979, p. 1.

[7] *Wall Street Journal*, October 14, 1982, p. 1.

[8] "Sears' Strategic About-Face," *Business Week*, January 8, 1979, pp. 80–83.

[9] Steve Huntley, "The Gold Mine in Pampered 'Gourmet Babies,'" *U.S. News & World Report*, p. 52.

[10] "Who Would Smoke Cigarettes Overloaded with Tar, Nicotine?" *Wall Street Journal*, March 20, 1979, p. 1.

[11] "Brother Types Its Way into U.S. Offices," *Business Week*, December 6, 1982, p. 53.

[12] "Labor Letter," *Wall Street Journal*, October 5, 1982, p. 1.

[13] *Wall Street Journal*, January 11, 1979, p. 1.

[14] Laura Landro and James A. White, "Computer Firms Push Prices Down, Try to Improve Marketing Tactics," *Wall Street Journal*, April 29, 1983, p. 35.

[15] See Bill Abrams, "People Appreciate Good Ads, An Agency Survey Concludes," *Wall Street Journal*, April 28, 1983, p. 33.

[16] See Earl C. Gottschalk, Jr., "Hotel Industry Seems to Be Baffled on How to Please Businesswomen," *Wall Street Journal*, June 15, 1983, p. 31.

[17] "How Levi's Is Helping Lee Sell More Jeans," *Business Week*, May 23, 1983, p. 46.

[18] Milton Moskowitz, Michael Katz, and Robert Levering, eds., *Everybody's Business: An Almanac* (New York: Harper & Row, 1980), p. 17.

[19] Ralph Nader, "The Flawed Corvair," *Christian Science Monitor*, June 6, 1980, p. 22.

[20] Robert Garfield, "Coffeehouses to Club Rooms," *USA Today*, December 23, 1983.

[21] "Older Persons Growing Force in Retail Sales," *AARP News Bulletin* 25 (February 1984):2; Robert Garfield, "Marketers Discover U.S.A.'s Over 40 Customers," *USA Today*, December 14, 1983, p. 3B; and U.S. Department of Commerce Bulletins.

## Chapter 13

*Opening case:* Based on "How to Serve with the Big Racket," *World Tennis*, August 1981, p. 51; Walter McQuade, "Prince Triumphant," *Fortune*, February 22, 1982, pp. 84ff; *Tennis*, February 1983, pp. 10–11; and others.

[1] "Survey Finds 67% of New Products Succeed," *Marketing News* 8 (February 1980):1.

[2] "Listening to the Voice of the Marketplace," *Business Week*, February 21, 1983, pp. 90, 94.

[3] "Slowdown Predicted in Products," *Tulsa World*, May 30, 1982, p. G-5.

[4] "[Carson] Wins 'Here's Johnny' Court Battle," *Mobile Register*, February 2, 1983, p. 5-D.

[5] Harold S. Gorschman, "New Dimensions in Unhidden Persuasion," in *Marketing Update*, ed. Harold W. Berkman (Du-

buque, Iowa: Kendall Hunt Publishing, 1977), p. 331.

[6] *Wall Street Journal*, May 13, 1982, p. 37.

[7] "No-Frills Food: New Power for the Supermarkets," *Business Week*, March 23, 1981, p. 70; see also Meg Cox, "Grocery Specials: Food Stores with Few Services Spring Up to Lure Increasingly Frugal Consumers," *Wall Street Journal*, January 23, 1981, p. 42.

[8] Alan Freeman, "Levi Unit Tries to Give Jeans Limited Appeal," *Wall Street Journal*, August 17, 1981, p. 33.

[9] "Pricing Strategy in an Inflation Economy," *Business Week*, April 6, 1974, pp. 42–46.

## Chapter 14

*Opening case:* Based on Bill Abrams, "Seven-Up Stirs a Fizz As Ads Stress Lack of Artificial Flavors," *The Wall Street Journal*, May 24, 1983, p. 7. Adapted by permission of *The Wall Street Journal*, © Dow Jones & Company, Inc. 1983. All Rights Reserved. Ewart Rouse, "Seven-Up Again Stirs Industry Ire," *Tulsa World*, May 31, 1983, p. B-7; "Another Hardball Campaign from Seven-Up," *Business Week*, June 6, 1983, p. 30; John Greenwald, "A Hot Fight over Cold Drinks," *Time*, May 16, 1983, pp. 52–53; and others.

[1] "RCA's Biggest Gamble Ever," *Business Week*, March 9, 1981, p. 79.

[2] *Wall Street Journal*, March 11, 1982, p. 27.

[3] Rod Townley, "Cola Pizza Wars: No Hitting Below the (Money) Belt," *TV Guide*, August 7, 1982, pp. 18–20; and "A Burger Battle—With Everything," *U.S. News & World Report*, November 8, 1982, p. 76.

[4] Bill Abrams, "Some New Ads May Rekindle Burger Battle," *Wall Street Journal*, March 4, 1983, pp. 25, 30.

[5] Bill Abrams, "Despite Progress, *USA Today* Finding Advertisers Skeptical," *Wall Street Journal*, September 22, 1983, p. 33.

[6] It is now the third largest daily circulating newspaper in the United States.

[7] *Tulsa World*, February 28, 1983, p. 5-A.

[8] *Wall Street Journal*, March 24, 1983, p. 35.

[9] "Beauty Pays," *Parade*, February 10, 1980, p. 6.

[10] "Look to the Stars for Sales Pitches," *Advertising Age*, March 26, 1981, pp. S-20–21; and John Love, "Stars for Sale—If Price Is Right," *Parade*, November 11, 1979, pp. 23–25.

[11] *Reader's Digest*, November 1983, p. 13.

[12] "Mail-Order Buying," *Consumer Reports* 48 (October 1983):514–21.

[13] *Wall Street Journal*, April 19, 1982, p. 23.

[14] *U.S. News & World Report*, April 11, 1983, p. 7.

[15] Irwin Ross, "J. Walter Thompson," *Fortune*, October 1970, pp. 102–5.

[16] *Wall Street Journal*, May 26, 1983, p. 33.

[17] "Chatty Robot Sparked Design Firm's Success," *INC.* 4 (April 1982):18.

[18] ORC Marketing Index, August 1982, cited by Martin Sloane, "The Supermarket Shopper," *Mobile Press-Register*, January 23, 1983, p. 13-D (United Feature Syndicate, Inc.).

[19] See also Michael Waldholz, "Bold Bid to Return Tylenol to Homes Is Called Risky by Marketing Experts," *Wall Street Journal*, November 15, 1982, p. 14.

[20] "Why Marlon Brando Passed the Milk Duds to George C. Scott," *Wall Street Journal*, May 24, 1982, p. 1.

[21] "Labor Letter," *Wall Street Journal*, May 4, 1982, p. 1.

[22] Based on "Candidate Puts Election in the Bag," *Tulsa World*, April 22, 1978, p. 22. Used by permission of The Associated Press.

[23] Adapted by permission from Martin Zook, "Tulsa Ad Agencies Come of Age," *Tulsa World*, May 9, 1982, p. G-1.

[24] Based on *The Wall Street Journal*, April 15, 1982, p. 23.

## Chapter 15

*Opening case: Who's Who in America*, 1914–1915; Milton Moskowitz, Michael Katz, and Robert Levering, eds., *Everybody's Business: An Almanac* (New York: Harper & Row, 1980), pp. 308–14; Ann M. Morrison, "Sears' Overdue Retailing Revival," *Fortune*, April 4, 1983, pp. 133–37; "The Synergy Begins to Work for Sears' Financial Supermarket," *Business Week*, June 13, 1983, pp. 116–17; Thomas J. Lueck, "Sears Roebuck to Open 45 Stores This Year to Sell Computers, Other Electronic Items," *Wall Street Journal*, February 10, 1982, p. 2; *Wall Street Journal*, February 10, 1984, pp. 1, 16; and others.

[1] Dean Rothbart, "Emergence of the Savvy Consumer Forces Some Painful Rethinking by Supermarkets," *Wall Street Journal*, September 29, 1980, p. 33.

[2] "Top Direct Marketers," *USA Today*, May 18, 1984, p. 1B.

[3] *Wall Street Journal*, December 17, 1982, p. 1.

[4] Based on Claudia Ricci, "Counter Strategy: Woolworth Defeated in Discounting, Aims at Specialty Stores," *The Wall Street Journal*, November 3, 1982, pp. 1 and 21. Reprinted by permission of *The Wall Street Journal*, © Dow Jones & Company, Inc. 1982. All Rights Reserved. Also based on "Is Woolworth Too Late in Upgrading Woolco?" *Business Week*, December 28, 1981, pp. 51–52; John Brecher, "Woolworth Wakes Up—At Last," *Newsweek*, June 27, 1983, p. 74; and "Woolworth Is Still Rummaging for a Retail Strategy," *Business Week*, June 6, 1983, pp. 82–83.

[5] Based on Claudia Ricci, "Penney to Spend Over $1 Billion on 450 Stores," *The Wall Street Journal*, February 1, 1983, p. 5; and Claudia Ricci, "J. C. Penney Goes After Affluent Shoppers, But Store's New Image May Be Hard to Sell," *The Wall Street Journal*, February 15, 1983, p. 35. Reprinted by permission of *The Wall Street Journal*, © Dow Jones & Company, Inc. 1983. All Rights Reserved. Also based on "Penney Targets New Markets," *Tulsa World*, May 8, 1983, p. G-7; and Susan Dentzer, "J. C. Penney Goes Back to Basics," *Newsweek*, February 14, 1983, p. 69.

### Digging Deeper: Careers in Marketing

[1] Pamela G. Hollis, "Market Is Wide Open for Marketing Executives," in "Careers '84," *New York Times National Employment Report*, October 16, 1983, p. 19.

## Chapter 16

*Opening case:* Based on IBM annual reports for 1979–1982; Susan Chace, "With 'Peanut,' IBM Plans Attack on Low-Priced Computer Market," *Wall Street Journal*, January 18, 1983, p. 33; George Anders, "IBM's New Line Likely to Shake Up the Market for Personal Computers," *Wall Street Journal*, October 13, 1981, p. 21; "The Computer Blitz on TV," *Business Week*, March 14, 1983, pp. 56–57; Peter D. Petre, "Meet the Lean New IBM," *Fortune*, June 13, 1983, pp. 68–82; John Greenwald, "The Colossus That Works," *Time*, July 11, 1983, pp. 44–54; and Peter Hall, "What It's Like to Work for IBM," *Business Week's Guide to Careers* 1 (Fall/Winter 1983):80–83.

[1] Susan Everly-Douze, "U.S. Edge Threatened in Race for Computers," *Tulsa World*, April 24, 1983, p. A-1.

[2] Manuel Schiffres, "Behind the Shakeout in Personal Computers," *U.S. News & World Report*, June 27, 1983, p. 59.

[3] "The Coming Shakeout in Personal Computers," *Business Week*, November 22, 1982, pp. 72–73.

[4] The National Inventors' Hall of Fame gives this honor to George R. Stibitz of Bell Laboratories for his closet-sized digital computer, invented in 1937. It took thirty seconds to divide two eight-digit numbers. He also developed the first programmable computer during World War II. See "Inven-

tors: Changing Tomorrow," *USA Today*, February 11, 1983, p. 3-B, for more details.

[5] Tracy Kidder, *The Soul of a New Machine* (New York: Avon Books, 1981), p. 13.

[6] Charles P. Alexander, "The Chips Are Flying Again," *Time*, September 19, 1983, p. 72.

[7] "Computers: A Crash Plan to Foil Japan," *U.S. News & World Report*, May 30, 1983, p. 8.

[8] William D. Marbach, "The Race to Build a Supercomputer," *Newsweek*, July 4, 1983, pp. 58–64; Susan Everly-Douze, "U.S. Edge Threatened in Race for Computers," *Tulsa World*, April 24, 1983, pp. A-1, A-4; and Stanley N. Wellborn, "U.S., Japan Square Off over Supercomputers," *U.S. News & World Report*, July 11, 1983, pp. 46–47.

[9] For one of the clearest and best explanations of what computers are, how they operate, what they can do, how they're being used, what to consider when buying one, and where and how to buy one, see "Computers: Should You Take One into Your Home?" *Consumer Reports* 48 (September 1983):461–88.

[10] See "Computers, Part 2," *Consumer Reports* 48 (October 1983):531–51, for an excellent discussion of output devices.

[11] Stephen Solomon, "Whiz Kids! Striking It Rich in Software," *Science Digest*, October 1982, p. 55.

[12] Ibid., p. 58.

[13] *Wall Street Journal*, June 17, 1983, p. 29.

[14] "Bed and Keyboard," *Time*, May 16, 1983, p. 63.

## Chapter 17

*Opening case:* Tandy Corporation annual reports; Milton Moskowitz, Michael Katz, and Robert Levering, eds., *Everybody's Business: An Almanac* (New York: Harper & Row, 1980), pp. 331–34; "Tandy Corp. Aims to Get Some Respect," *Business Week*, September 12, 1983, pp. 94–101; and others.

[1] Michael Doan, "How 7 Firms Have Bucked the Tide," *U.S. News & World Report*, November 23, 1981, p. 60.

[2] "Quaker Sheds Poor Performers," *Business Week*, May 9, 1983, p. 42.

[3] Paul Blustein, "Phantom Ads: How the JWT Agency Miscounted $24 Million of TV Commercials," *Wall Street Journal*, March 30, 1982, pp. 1, 20.

[4] Brenton R. Schlender, "Fall from Glory: Datapoint Kept Trying to Set Profit Records Until the Bubble Burst," *Wall Street Journal*, May 27, 1982, pp. 1, 23.

[5] Margaret Loeb, "High Joblessness Forcing Hospital in Alabama to Trim Emergency Care," *Wall Street Journal*, February 10, 1983, p. 33.

[6] "Indigent Care Losses Still Mounting at USA Medical Center," *Mobile Register*, January 28, 1983, p. A-14.

[7] "USAMC Audit, Deficit Discussed by Trethaway," *Mobile Register*, January 28, 1983, p. A-14.

### Digging Deeper: Careers in Data Processing and Accounting

[1] According to Fox-Morris Personnel Consultants, Philadelphia, Pa. See Beth Brody, "Programmers, Engineers Top Employers' Most-Wanted Lists," *USA Today*, December 28, 1983, p. 3-B, for details.

## Chapter 18

*Opening case:* Based on the following articles from *The Wall Street Journal*: Julie Salamon, "Bank of America, Continental Illinois, Chase Join 23 Others in Teller Network," April 4, 1982, p. 20; and Julie Salamon, "Citicorp Trying to Enter Insurance Sector Via Units in Delaware, South Dakota," February 9, 1983, p. 7. Reprinted by permission of *The Wall Street Journal*, © Dow Jones & Company, Inc. 1982, 1983. All Rights Reserved.

Also based on Edward E. Scharff, "The Savings Revolution," *Time*, June 8, 1981, pp. 58–69; "Citicorp," *Everybody's Business: An Almanac*, Milton Moskowitz, Michael Katz, and Robert Levering, eds. (New York: Harper & Row, 1980), p. 457; and "Citibank's Back Door to a Mutual Fund," *Business Week*, March 7, 1983, p. 68.

[1] "History According to Salt," *Time*, March 15, 1982, p. 68.

[2] Otto Friedrich, "F.D.R.'s Disputed Legacy," *Time*, February 1, 1982, p. 33.

[3] Mark J. Flannery, "Deposit Insurance Creates a Need for Bank Regulation," *Business Review* (Federal Reserve Bank of Philadelphia), January 1982.

[4] Federal Reserve Bank of Philadelphia, *The Hats the Federal Reserve Wears*, November 1980.

[5] The required reserve varies with the size of a bank's deposits. For example, in late 1982, banks with less than $2 million of demand deposits had to keep 7 percent of those deposits on reserve, while banks with over $400 million had to keep 16½ percent on reserve (*Federal Reserve Bulletin*, August 1982, p. A8).

[6] "The Crash of 1929," *Newsweek*, October 22, 1979, pp. 40–41.

[7] Orin Kramer, "Winning Strategies for Interstate Banking," *Fortune*, September 19, 1983, p. 104.

[8] Patricia M. Schersel, "Revolution in Banking: Has It Gone Too Far?" *U.S. News & World Report*, May 16, 1983, pp. 69–71.

[9] Scharff, p. 59.

[10] "Now Banks Turn to a Hard Sales Pitch," *Business Week*, September 21, 1981, p. 82.

[11] Based on the following articles from *The Wall Street Journal*: Julie Salamon, "Idealism Gives Way to Laws of Business as First Women's Bank Heads for Recovery," August 26, 1981, p. 25; and Tom Herman, "First Women's Bank of New York Faces Financial Struggle," January 25, 1980, p. 33. Reprinted by permission of *The Wall Street Journal*, © Dow Jones & Company, Inc. 1980, 1981. All Rights Reserved. Also based on "Problems and Solutions for First Women's Bank," *Business Week*, October 9, 1978, p. 130; and others.

[12] "The New Sears," *Business Week*, November 16, 1981, p. 142; "Selling Socks and Stocks," *Time*, August 2, 1982, p. 51; "How They Manage the New Financial Supermarkets," *Business Week*, December 20, 1982, p. 50; and Alexander L. Taylor III, "Scrambling for New Customers," *Time*, May 2, 1983, p. 58.

## Chapter 19

*Opening case:* "The 50 Largest U.S. Industrial Corporations," *Fortune*, May 3, 1982, pp. 260–61; Charles Alexander, "Tough Times for the Exxon Tiger," *Time*, August 2, 1982, p. 58; "Why Things Aren't Going Right for Exxon," *Business Week*, June 7, 1982, pp. 88–93; "What's Wrong at Exxon Enterprises," *Business Week*, August 24, 1981; pp. 87–90; "Synfuels Get Pushed Further into the Future," *Business Week*, May 17, 1982, pp. 30–31; "Colorado Boom Town After the Bust," *Newsweek*, May 30, 1983, pp. 14–15; and Sheri Poe Bernard, "Hope Lingers in Boom Gone Bust," *USA Today*, January 11, 1984, p. 6-A.

[1] "California Set to Issue IOU's to Pay Its Debts," *Wall Street Journal*, February 16, 1983, p. 5.

[2] Heywood Klein, "Financial Officers Often in Demand as Companies Seek Cost-Cutters," *Wall Street Journal*, November 22, 1982, p. 33.

[3] "The Fateful Decision That Exxon Must Make," *Business Week*, January 31, 1983, pp. 40–41.

[4] Sanford L. Jacobs, "Small Clothing Manufacturer Fighting to Survive Recession," *Wall Street Journal*, November 29, 1982, p. 23.

[5] G. Christian Hill, "Concerns Deep in Debt and Those That Aren't Fare Very Differently," *Wall Street Journal*, April 30, 1982, p. 1.

[6] "More Debt, More Short-Term Pressure," *Business Week*, March 1, 1982, p. 52.

[7] Randall Smith, "Detroit Center Seen Avoiding a Foreclosure," *Wall Street Journal*, February 24, 1983, p. 4.

[8] Ibid.

[9] Hill, p. 29.

[10] Stephen J. Sansweet, "MGM Film Gives Small Investors a Chance to Share in Rising Cost of Making Movies," *Wall Street Journal*, August 13, 1981, p. 21.

[11] Janice Castro, "How to Make a Cool Half-Billion," *Time*, March 14, 1983, p. 68.

[12] "Behind the Shakeup at Occidental Petroleum," *Business Week*, July 11, 1983, pp. 78–79.

[13] Hill, p. 29.

[14] "Can Chrysler Keep Its Comeback Rolling?" *Business Week*, February 14, 1983, p. 132.

## Chapter 20

*Opening case:* Reprinted by permission from "At the Exchange: 'Controlled Pandemonium'," *Time*, October 22, 1979, p. 13. Copyright 1979 Time Inc. All rights reserved. Also adapted from Christopher Lindsay, AP Business Writer, "Wall Street Traders Miss Lunch, But Not Much Else On Busiest Day," *Jackson (MS) Daily News*, August 19, 1982, p. 7-C. Used by permission of The Associated Press.

[1] *Business Week*, November 29, 1982, p. 20.

[2] *Wall Street Journal*, November 15, 1982, p. 54.

[3] "The Big Money Professionals Are Running Scared," *Business Week*, December 27, 1982, p. 73.

[4] *You and the Investment World* (New York: The New York Stock Exchange, Inc., 1979), p. 14; and "Putting the Big Board Out to Pasture," *Newsweek*, October 3, 1983, p. 78.

[5] In December 1983, 88.3 million shares of 2,032 issues were traded on the NYSE. "Two Weeks of Trading Days," *USA Today*, December 16, 1983, p. 8-B. See also "Putting the Big Board Out to Pasture."

[6] In December 1983, 6.42 million shares of 819 issues were traded on the AMEX. "Two Weeks of Trading Days"; and "Putting the Big Board Out to Pasture."

[7] In December 1983, 65.85 million shares of 3,979 stock issues were traded in these exchanges. "Two Weeks of Trading Days."

[8] "Putting the Big Board Out to Pasture."

[9] *Wall Street Journal*, December 12, 1983, p. 54.

[10] "Bopped: Its Underwriters Assess Apple," *Fortune*, October 31, 1983, p. 10.

[11] "Cause for Cheer: Chrysler Is Back in the Money," *Time*, March 7, 1983, p. 67.

[12] Based on several sources, including "Is People Express Stock Flying Too High?" *Business Week*, May 30, 1983, pp. 79, 82; Harry Anderson, "Newark to London for $149," *Newsweek*, June 6, 1983, pp. 76–77; John Skow, "People Expressing Themselves," *Time*, July 25, 1983, p. 44; and others.

[13] From several sources, including "Welcome Back," *Time*, December 12, 1983, p. 55.

## Chapter 21

*Opening case:* Based on Timothy Green, "If You Name It, Lloyd's of London May Well Risk It," *Smithsonian* 11 (March 1981):80–89; "Wide-Ranging Scandal Rocks Lloyd's of London," *Tulsa World*, October 3, 1982, p. G-7; and William S. Cowles, "Premium Return: Despite Disasters, Profits Up at Lloyd's of London," *Clarion-Ledger & Jackson* (Miss) *Daily News*, February 26, 1984, p. 12G.

[1] Thomas Petzinger, Jr., and Heywood Klein, "Haunted Hotel: Building Snags Dogged the Kansas City Hyatt That Collapsed in 1981," *Wall Street Journal*, October 8, 1982, p. 1.

[2] "Citibank's Test of Paying to See Tellers Doesn't Pay," *Wall Street Journal*, May 26, 1983, p. 6.

[3] Thomas Baker, "You'll Never Walk Alone," *Forbes*, September 14, 1981, pp. 46, 51, 55.

[4] *Wall Street Journal*, May 5, 1983, p. 1.

[5] David Pauly and Marilyn Achiron, "Stealing from the Boss," *Newsweek*, December 26, 1983, p. 78.

[6] "Federal Action Sought as Product Liability Litigation Soars," *Tulsa World*, October 8, 1982, p. 14-A.

[7] Charles W. Patchen, "Accountant's Admonitions," *Tulsa World*, September 12, 1982, p. G-3.

[8] Harry Schwartz, "Can the U.S. Make Hospital Costs Go Down?" *Wall Street Journal*, November 2, 1982, p. 28.

**Digging Deeper: Careers in Finance, Insurance, and Real Estate**

[1] According to the Bureau of Labor Statistics, the number of jobs in finance (including real estate) should increase 1.5 million by 1993.

## Chapter 22

*Opening case:* Based on John Curley, "Small Firm Outmaneuvers Big-Time Rivals in Winning Copier Sales from the Chinese," *The Wall Street Journal*, April 26, 1982, p. 29. Reprinted by permission of *The Wall Street Journal*, © Dow Jones & Company, Inc. 1982. All Rights Reserved. Also based on various sources, including "Clark Copier Challenges the Giants," *Inc.* 4 (June 1982):45; "Tiny Copier Maker Taking a Big Step in Deal with China," *New York Times*, April 26, 1982, p. D-4; and correspondence with Clark Copy International Corporation.

[1] U.S. Department of Commerce, *Survey of Current Business* (Washington, D.C.: U.S. Government Printing Office, August 1983), p. 24.

[2] Tad Szulc, "Is Your Job Secure?" *Parade Magazine*, May 22, 1983, p. 18.

[3] Bill Paul, "Exxon, Shell Win Drilling Rights Offshore China," *Wall Street Journal*, August 28, 1983, p. 29.

[4] William M. Bulkeley, "China Seeks to Learn Management Skills of Capitalism in New Hampshire Town," *Wall Street Journal*, July 7, 1983, p. 8.

[5] "Switzerland: The Top Watchmakers May Be Synchronizing," *Business Week*, June 15, 1981, p. 52.

[6] Bulletin issued by U.S. Department of Commerce, March 1984.

[7] Richard Alm and John Collins, "Now in Prospect: A $100 Billion Trade Gap," *U.S. News & World Report*, April 9, 1984, pp. 56–57.

[8] U.S. Department of Commerce, *Survey of Current Business*, p. 24.

[9] *USA Today*, December 19, 1983, p. 1-B.

[10] Erik Larson, "Logging Sales: Small Mill Survives by Setting Its Blades for Export to Japan," *Wall Street Journal*, May 7, 1982, pp. 1, 14.

[11] William F. Buckley, Jr., "Bike Surrender," *Mobile Register*, April 17, 1983, p. 4; Art Pine, "Stiff Motorcycle Duties Aimed at Spurring Japan into Aiding the Ailing U.S. Industry," *Wall Street Journal*, April 4, 1983, p. 23; and "Helping the Hogs," *Time*, April 11, 1983, p. 74.

[12] Milton Moskowitz, Michael Katz, and Robert Levering, eds., *Everybody's Business: An Almanac* (New York: Harper & Row, 1980), p. 61; and "Nestle Boycotters Say Their Campaign Is Over," *Boston Globe*, January 27, 1984.

[13] Amal Nag, "Import Limits Don't Restrain Japanese Profits," *Wall Street Journal*, April 28, 1983, p. 30.

[14] Michael Doan, "The Cutthroat Battle for World Food Sales," *U.S. News & World Report*, September 5, 1983, p. 38.

[15] "Domestic Content: Payoff to Labor," *Human Events*, November 19, 1983, pp. 3–4.

[16] Lorianne Cichowski, "Trade Zones: Growing in Popularity," *USA Today*, December 23, 1983, pp. 1-B, 2-B.

[17] According to the Congressional Budget Office and the Reagan administration, abandoning free trade would lead to "no net increase in employment, but a likely drop." See Hodding Carter III, "Democrats Reach for Protectionist Snake Oil," *Wall Street Journal*, December 9, 1982, p. 29.

[18] *USA Today*, October 20, 1983, p. 1-B.

[19] Based on "My Toughest Business Decision Was . . . ," *Wall Street Journal*, February 14, 1983, p. 16.

## Chapter 23

*Opening case:* From various sources, but primarily from information provided by the "old" AT&T.

[1] Ken Wells, "Spreading Out: As Utah's Great Salt Lake Keeps Getting Greater, State Attempts to Determine What to Do About It," *Wall Street Journal*, March 29, 1983, p. 58.

[2] AP story in the *Mobile Press-Register*, January 7, 1983, p. 6-D; and other sources.

[3] "The Devils in the Product Liability Laws," *Business Week*, February 12, 1979, p. 73.

[4] *Fortune*, January 23, 1984, p. 31.

[5] Anna Cifelli, "Management by Bankruptcy," *Fortune*, October 31, 1983, pp. 69–70.

[6] Johanna Neuman, "Pizza Rule: Matter of Cheese and Dough," *USA Today*, April 16, 1984, p. 8A.

[7] "Asides," *Wall Street Journal*, May 8, 1981, p. 26.

[8] *Wall Street Journal*, January 26, 1979, p. 1.

[9] Paul Eisenstein, "Chrysler May Go to Court over GM Pact," *USA Today*, December 23, 1983, p. 1-B.

[10] "Special Report: Deregulating America," *Business Week*, November 28, 1983, pp. 80–92.

[11] "What Oil Decontrol Did for the Job Market," *Business Week*, June 29, 1981, p. 16.

[12] See Janice R. Long, Lois R. Ember, and David J. Hanson, "Federal Deregulation Efforts Get Mixed Reviews," *Chemical & Engineering News* 60 (May 19, 1982):13–17, for results.

[13] "Deregulation's Lost Momentum," *The Morgan Guaranty Trust Survey*, June 1983, p. 7.

[14] See "A Painful Transition for the Transport Industry," *Business Week*, November 28, 1983, pp. 83, 86; John S. DeMott, "Bitter, Deadly Dogfights," *Time*, October 10, 1983, pp. 44–45; and Andy O'Connell, "Continental, Eastern Focus of Airline Woes," AP article in *Mobile Register*, September 30, 1983, p. 23-A.

[15] Anna Cifelli, "Here Come the Reregulators," *Fortune*, January 9, 1984, pp. 123–25.

[16] "Conrail Bidding Heats Up," *USA Today*, June 1, 1984, p. 1B.

[17] Several sources, including "The All-American Car Is Fading," *Business Week*, March 12, 1984, pp. 88–95.

## Chapter 24

*Opening case:* Based on Jeffery L. Sheler, "A Tale of Two Worlds in Tennessee," *U.S. News & World Report*, December 20, 1982, pp. 84–85; Daniel Pauly, "Nissan Takes on the UAW," *Newsweek*, February 21, 1983, p. 64; CBS's *60 Minutes*, May 1, 1983; "Nissan's Tennessee Startup," *Business Week*, July 4, 1983, p. 44; and correspondence with Nissan's management.

[1] John Shingleton and Robert Bao, *College to Career* (New York: McGraw-Hill, 1977).

[2] Based on Andrew H. Souerwine, *Career Strategies* (New York: AMACOM, 1978), pp. vii–viii; and C. G. Moore, *The Career Game* (New York: National Institute of Career Planning, 1976). The latter book leads the reader through the steps in career decision making and provides much practical information on how to market oneself to prospective employers.

[3] D. P. Campbell, *If You Don't Know Where You're Going, You'll Probably End Up Somewhere Else* (Niles, Ill.: Argus Communications, 1974).

[4] See Curtis E. Tate et al., *Successful Small Business Management*, 3rd ed. (Dallas: Business Publications, 1982), pp. 38–43, for an extensive self-analysis that you can perform if you would like to go into business for yourself.

[5] For more about this subject, see Studs Terkel, *Working* (New York: Avon Books, 1975).

[6] See Kae Chung and Leon Megginson, *Organizational Behavior* (New York: Harper & Row, 1981), pp. 529–48, for further discussion.

[7] Darrell Gifford, "When to Leave Job Is Part of Career Planning," *Tulsa World*, March 30, 1983, p. B-2.

[8] John Griffin, "Midlife Career Change," *Occupational Outlook Quarterly* 25 (Spring 1981):2–4.

[9] See Tom Jackson, *Guerilla Tactics in the Job Market* (New York: Bantam Books, 1978), for information on locating hidden job markets.

[10] See Edgar H. Schein, "How to Break In the College Graduate," *Harvard Business Review* 42 (November-December 1964):68–76.

[11] John Mee, "Speculation About Human Organizations in the 21st Century," *Business Horizons* 14 (February 1971):16.

[12] "Management in the XXI Century," an Arden House Colloquium, November 12–14, 1979 (AACSB-EFMD), p. 27.

[13] Leon C. Megginson, Donald C. Mosley, and Paul H. Pietri, Jr., *Management: Concepts and Applications* (New York: Harper & Row, 1983), p. 571.

[14] Alvin Toffler, *The Third Wave* (New York: Morrow, 1980).

[15] John Naisbitt, *Megatrends: Ten New Directions Transforming Our Lives* (New York: Warner, 1982).

[16] Paul Ingrassia, "Corporations: A Perilous Life at the Top," *Wall Street Journal*, February 5, 1981, p. 8.

[17] Daniel D. Roman, "Technological Forecasting in the Decision Process," *Academy of Management Journal* 13 (June 1970):127–38.

[18] Ingrassia, p. 8.

[19] Neil Hickey, "The 'Birds' Are Taking Off," *TV Guide*, February 20, 1982, pp. 17–22.

[20] Jody Long, "A New Breed of Phone Firm Starts to Grow," *Wall Street Journal*, April 29, 1982, p. 31.

[21] "Nielsen Says Viewing at All-Time High; Networks' Down," *TV Guide*, April 10, 1982, p. A-3.

[22] Dennis Overbye, "U.S. Firm Dreams of 'Maglev' Trains Used in Europe, Japan," *Tulsa World*, March 21, 1982, p. 14-H.

[23] "Can Detroit Ever Come Back?" *U.S. News & World Report*, March 8, 1982, pp. 45–48.

[24] Frederic Golden, "Here Come the Microkids," *Time*, May 3, 1982, pp. 52–56. This article has excellent material about the new electronic generation.

[25] "Knight-Ridder Readies System for Banking, Shopping at Home," *Adweek*, March 15, 1982, p. 16.

[26] Susan Chace, "Scientists Are Laboring at Making Computers Think for Themselves," *Wall Street Journal*, March 29, 1983, pp. 1, 22.

# Credits

**PART I**     **xxxiv** (top) © Steve Dunwell, 1981; **xxxiv** (bottom) Dan McCoy/Rainbow; **1** (left) Kevin Horan/Picture Group; **1** (right) L. H. Jawitz/The Image Bank

**Chapter 1**     **3** Ben Weaver/Camera 5; **8** David Burnett/Contact; **11** Courtesy Levi Strauss & Company; **12** Courtesy Levi Strauss & Company; **18** Leonard Freed/Magnum Photos, Inc.; **23** © 1981 Gahan Wilson; **24** Jim Argo/Picture Group; **26** Neal Preston/Camera 5

**Chapter 2**     **33** Courtesy McNeil Consumer Products Company. Photograph by Martucci Studio; **35** Courtesy General Motors Corporation; **36** Robert Phillips/The Image Bank; **42** UPI/Bettmann Archive; **44** © Jim Pickerell, 1980; **45** Courtesy The Coca-Cola Company; **46** Bo Rader/Picture Group; **49** Drawing by Dana Fradon; © 1977 The New Yorker Magazine, Inc.

**Chapter 3**     **59** © Steve Hansen; **67** Dennis Brack/Black Star; **69** (top) Don Smetzer/Click/Chicago; **69** (center) © Jerry Howard/Positive Images; **69** (bottom) Brian Seed/Click/Chicago; **73** Reprinted by permission. © 1979 NEA, Inc. **75** Bill Campbell/Picture Group; **76** © Steve Hansen; **81** Courtesy Ford Motor Company.

**Chapter 4**     **89** Courtesy Pente Games, Inc.; **95** Don Smetzer/Click/Chicago; **96** © David R. Frazier; **98** Courtesy Korey, Kay & Partners; **104** Courtesy Snugli, Inc.

**Chapter 5**     **113** Pizza Hut and the Pizza Hut logo are registered trademarks of Pizza Hut, Inc. Photo courtesy of Pizza Hut, Inc., international headquarters, Wichita, Kansas; **119** © Rick Friedman, 1984; **120** Courtesy Kemmons Wilson Companies; **121** Shepard Sherbell/Picture Group; **122** Courtesy Kentucky Fried Chicken; **127** Margarite Bradley/Positive Images; **130** Rachel Ritchie/Picture Group

**PART II**     **140** (top) Tom Tracy/Black Star; **140** (bottom) Dan McCoy/Rainbow; **141** (left) Stan-Pak/International Stock Photo; **141** (right) Gabe Palmer/The Image Bank

**Chapter 6**     **143** Ted Thai/SYGMA; **149** Courtesy Service Master; **157** (top) © 1982 Peter Menzel; **157** (center) Gabe Palmer/The Image Bank; **157** (bottom) John Lund/Phototake; **159** Reprinted by permission of the publisher, from *Personnel*, November–December 1967 © 1967 by American Management Associations, Inc. New York, page 24. All rights reserved

**Chapter 7**     **167** Doug Bruce/Picture Group; **169** Courtesy 3M Company; **173** Courtesy McDonnell Douglas Corporation; **184** *Sally Forth* by Greg Howard © 1982 Field Enterprises, Inc. Courtesy News America Syndicate

**Chapter 8**     **195** Courtesy White Consolidated Industries; **199** Courtesy McDonnell Douglas Corporation; **203** Courtesy Burger King Corporation; **207** Dick Durrance/Woodfin Camp & Associates; **211** Adapted by permission from Curtis E. Tate, Jr., Leon C. Megginson, Charles R. Scott, Jr., and Lyle R. Trueblood, *Successful Small Business Management*, 3rd ed. (Plano Tex.: Business Publications, Inc., 1982), pp 294–300. © 1982 Business Publications, Inc.; **212** Reprinted from *The Saturday Evening Post* © 1950. Courtesy The Curtis Publishing Company; **214** Courtesy General Electric Information Services Company; **216** Courtesy the Brooklyn Museum

**PART III**     **230** (top) Chuck Place; **230** (bottom) Kevin Horan/Picture Group; **231** (left) Mark Antman/Phototake; **231** (right) Gabe Palmer/The Image Bank

**Chapter 9**     **234** Photo provided by Delta Airlines, Inc.; **235** Reproduced with permission of AT&T; **240** Courtesy Burger King Corporation; **241** © Brent Jones, 1982; **248** Photograph by Merrill Worthington courtesy Xerox Corporation; **253** Photo courtesy Mike Levy and Mary Partridge

**Chapter 10**     **261** Mark Perlstein/Black Star; **263** Courtesy AT&T Technologies; **268** Shelly Katz/Black Star; **272** Jerry Wachter/*Sports Illustrated*; **275** Courtesy Sperry Corporation

**Chapter 11**     **285** Kevin Horan/Picture Group; **288** Courtesy United Auto Workers; **291** International Museum of Photography at George Eastman House; **299** Ira Wyman/Sygma; **304** Kevin Horan/Picture Group

**PART IV**     **314** (top) John Lund/Phototake; **314** (bottom) Tom Campbell/West Light; **315** (left) © Dick Luria, 1983; **315** (right) Courtesy The Coca-Cola Company

**Chapter 12**    **317** Courtesy Gerber Products Company; **330, 331** Courtesy Buick Motors Division; **333** Courtesy Ford Motor Company; **334** Paul Poplis/Click, Chicago

**Chapter 13**    **343** Prince Manufacturing, Inc.; **346** (left) LLT. Rhodes/ATOZ Images; **346** (right) © Dick Luria Photography, Inc.; **347** Mercedes-Benz of North America, Inc.; **348** Johnson Products Co., Inc.; **350** Courtesy The Gillette Company; **352** © 1981 by NEA, Inc. Reprinted by permission of NEA; **353** Rick Friedman © 1984; **354** Courtesy Coleco Industries

**Chapter 14**    **369** The Seven-Up Company; **372** (left) Campbell Soup Company; **372** (right) Whirlpool Corporation; **373** Whitman's Chocolates; **375** American Gas Association; **376** Shell Oil Company; **380** Remington Products; **382** Herman J. KokoJan/Black Star; **383** Billy Grimes/Black Star

**Chapter 15**    **395** Kevin Horan/Picture Group; **399** Kuppenheimer Manufacturing Company, Inc.; **406** J. C. Penney Company; **407** Terry Hourigan/TIME Magazine; **408** Ben Weaver/Camera 5; **409** Timothy A. Murphy, U.S. News and World Report; **410** Drawing by Chas. Addams; © 1978 The New Yorker Magazine, Inc.; **414** Donald L. Miller; **415** Chuck O'Rear/West Light

**PART V**    **424** (top) David Wagner/Phototake; **424** (bottom) Carol Lee/ATOZ Images; **425** (left) Dan McCoy/Rainbow; **425** (right) Andrew Popper/Picture Group

**Chapter 16**    **427** John Marmaras/Woodfin Camp; **429** Photo courtesy Fairchild Camera and Instrument Corporation; **431** Chuck O'Rear/West Light; **432** Diana Walker/Gamma-Liaison; **434** Photo courtesy Sperry Corporation; **435** International Business Machines Corporation; **439** Photo courtesy Hewlett-Packard Company; **441** Universal Press Syndicate. © 1982 by G. B. Trudeau; **442** Photo courtesy Sperry Corporation

**Chapter 17**    **453** Photo courtesy Radio Shack, A Division of Tandy Corporation; **456** Reprinted by permission: Tribune Company Syndicate, Inc.; **457** (right) Rick Mansfield/Picture Group; **457** (center) Jerry Howard/Positive Images; **457** (left) Jim Pickerell/Click, Chicago; **458** Photo courtesy Main Hurdman/KMG; **461** Michael Patrick/Picture Group

**PART VI**    **482** (top) Gabe Palmer/The Image Bank; **482** (bottom) Burt Glinn/Magnum Photos; **483** (left) Chuck O'Rear/West Light; **483** (right) © Dick Luria, 1982

**Chapter 18**    **485** Kathleen Foster/Black Star; **494** Dennis Brack/Black Star

**Chapter 19**    **509** Duane Howell/The Denver Post; **513** From the Wall Street Journal—Permission, Cartoon Features Syndicate; **517** Ted Thai/Sygma; **522** Reprinted courtesy GMAC, 767 Fifth Avenue, New York, N.Y. 10153; **524** Reprinted by permission of American Telephone and Telegraph Company, 195 Broadway, New York, NY. 10017; **525** Ben Weaver/Camera 5

**Chapter 20**    **533** Andy Levin/Black Star; **540** (left) New York Stock Exchange Archives; **540** (right) Jim Pickerell; **542** Merrill Lynch, Pierce Fenner & Smith, Inc.; **544** Lee Lorenz cartoon reproduced by permission of Newcomb Capital Corporation

**Chapter 21**    **559** Lloyd's of London; **562** P. Tatiner/Gamma-Liaison; **567** Reproduced with permission from General Re Corporation; **569** Pam Price/Picture Group; **573** From the Wall Street Journal—Permission, Cartoon Features Syndicate; **575** Joe Outland

**PART VII**    **590** (top) Gregory Edwards/International Stock Photo; **590** (bottom) John Lund/Phototake; **591** (left) Harry Redl/Black Star; **591** (right) Jim Argo/Picture Group

**Chapter 22**    **593** Clark Copy International Corporation; **597** Photo courtesy China Light and Power Company; **601** Coca-Cola Company; **607** Brent Jones/ATOZ Images; **608** Reprinted by permission of NEA, Inc.

**Chapter 23**    **626** Tom Zimberoff/Sygma; **629** Reprinted by permission: Tribune Company Syndicate, Inc.

**Chapter 24**    **643** Dana P. Thomas/Gamma-Liaison; **649** 1982 James Stillings; **651** Camilla Smith/Rainbow; **654** Jamie Phillips; **663** (top) Shepard Sherbell/Picture Group; **663** (middle) Edgar Roskis/Gamma-Liaison; **663** (bottom) Rick Browne/Picture Group

# Glossary

**Accounting** System of principles and techniques used to record, classify, summarize, and interpret financial information. (*454*)

**Accounting equation** The basic accounting principle that Assets = Liabilities + Owners' Equity. (*459*)

**Accounts** One of accounting's storage units, in which the financial elements are classified and recorded. (*460*)

**Administrative management** *See* Top management.

**Administrative skills** Ability to establish and follow procedures, process paperwork, and manage expenditures. (*156*)

**Advertising** Any paid form of nonpersonal sales or promotion. (*371*)

**Advertising media** The different means, devices, or vehicles through which advertisers reach their audience. (*375*)

**Affirmative action programs (AAPs)** Plans for actively seeking out members of protected groups, hiring them, training and developing them, and moving them into better positions in the firm. (*43, 241*)

**AFL-CIO** The combined union of the American Federation of Labor and the Congress of Industrial Organizations, which merged in 1955. (*292*)

**Agency** Legal relationship between two parties in which they agree that one will act as a representative of the other. (*23*)

**Agency shop** Agreement under which all employees must pay union dues even if they choose not to join the union. (*293*)

**Agent** 1. A wholesaler's, retailer's, or manufacturer's representative who does not take title to goods but brings buyers and sellers together. (*400*) 2. Person or company employed to act on behalf of another person. (*23*)

**Agribusiness** All the activities involved in producing, distributing, and financing food products. (*658*)

**American Federation of Labor (AFL)** A major national craft union, formed in 1886 and led by Samuel Gompers. (*290*)

**Analytic process** Production process in which a raw material is broken down or separated to form a variety of outputs. (*197*)

**Applications software** Program giving a computer specific instructions for a given job. (*440*)

**Apprenticeship training** Teaching of job skills that require an extended period of practice and experience. (*247*)

**Approach** The second step in the sales process, in which the salesperson tries to win the prospect's attention and interest. (*385*)

**Arbitration** Method of dispute settlement in which a neutral outsider weighs the arguments of union and management and makes a binding decision. (*298*)

**Articles of incorporation** Information required by individual states before a company may incorporate. (*73*)

**Asset** Anything of value owned by a business or individual. (*459*) *See also* Current assets; Fixed assets.

**Auditing** Review of a firm's accounting system, operations, and accounting records, to determine their reliability and accuracy. (*456*)

**Authority** The right to do something or to have someone else do it. (*144*)

**Automatic teller machines (ATMs)** Electronic devices that serve bank customers' needs twenty-four hours a day. (*503*)

**Automation** The use of a mechanized system with the ability to automatically run and adjust itself to continuous operations as planned and programmed. (*206*)

**Bait-and-switch** Unethical variation on loss leaders in which a customer is pressured into buying a more expensive item. (*364*) *See also* Loss leaders.

**Balance of payments** The relationship between flows of money into and out of a nation. (*600*)

**Balance of trade** Relationship between the value of a nation's exports and the value of its imports. (*600*)

**Balance sheet** Financial statement showing the status of a firm's assets, liabilities, and owners' equity at one point in time. (*464*)

**Bankruptcy** Petition to court by people or business asking for relief from payment of debts. (*623*) *See also* Involuntary bankruptcy; Voluntary bankruptcy.

**Barter** Trading things for other things. (*486*)

**BASIC** Beginners All-Purpose Symbolic Instruction Code. Computer language noted for its clarity and simplicity; used in most small business systems. (*442*)

**Batch processing** Method of data processing in which groups of records are processed in batches. (*444*)

**Bear market** Stock market condition in which all stock prices tend to drop. (*543*)

**Benefits** *See* Employee benefits.

**Birdybacking** Mode of transportation in which truck trailers are loaded onto airplanes. (*416*)

**Blacklisting** Management's listing the names of union troublemakers to prevent them from being rehired; made illegal by the Norris–La Guardia Act of 1932. (*293*)

**Blue-sky laws** State legislation designed to protect the public from unscrupulous securities dealers. (*541*)

**Board of directors** Governing body of a corporation, elected by the stockholders and responsible for appointing the corporate officers. (*75*)

**Body language** Transmission of a message without the use of speech or formal language. (*275*)

**Bond indenture** Legal contract detailing all provisions of a bond issue. (*537*)

**Bonding** Insurance protecting employers and individuals against losses to, or caused by, a third party. (*573*) *See also* Fidelity bond; Surety bond.

**Bonds** Corporate IOUs agreeing to pay the face amount at a specified time in the future. (*521*) *See also* Debenture bonds; Mortgage bonds.

**Bookkeeping** The clerical side of accounting; recording the data of financial transactions. (*455*)

**Boycott** Attempt by a union to persuade the public not to purchase the employer's product or service. (*299*)

**Brand** Name, term, design, sign, symbol, or combination of these used to identify and distinguish a company's products. (353)

**Breakeven point** The level of sales, at a given price, that will cover total variable and fixed costs. (360)

**Bribery** Offering something of value to a person to influence his or her judgment or conduct. (50)

**Broker** *See* Agent.

**Bull market** Stock market condition in which all stock prices tend to move up. (543)

**Business** The activities of individuals or groups who are involved in developing, producing, and distributing the goods and services needed to satisfy other people's needs or desires. (4)

**Business cycle** The roller-coaster pattern an economy takes as it moves through chronological stages of growth, decline, and recovery. (19)

**Business ethics** The standards used to judge the rightness or wrongness of a business's relations to others. (50)

**Business plan** A document covering all aspects of business, beginning with the objectives of the business. (105)

**Business selling** Personal selling to businesses and institutions rather than to individuals. (384)

**Bylaws** Rules governing the formation, management, and operations of a corporation. (73)

**Bytes** Units for measuring number of characters in computer memory. (443)

**Capital** All the human-produced items, such as tools, machinery, and buildings, used to produce and distribute other goods and services. (12)

**Capital gain (loss)** Increase or decrease in a stock's market value. (544) *See also* Market value.

**Capitalism** An economic system based on the private ownership of resources, in which individuals have the right to make choices about how to use their resources. (16)

**Career life cycle** Progression through stages of career development as one ages. (647)

**Cash discount** Discount offered to customers who pay promptly or with cash. (364) *See also* Discount.

**Cash flow** The amount of money coming in from all sources and the amount going out for all purposes. (510)

**Catalog showroom** Retailer that sells merchandise at low prices because of lower display, sales, and service costs. (407)

**Cathode ray tube (CRT)** Video screen displaying data on hand in computer memory. (439)

**Centralization** Concentration of authority in the hands of higher managers. (186)

**Central processing unit (CPU)** The controller for a computer system, containing all logic and arithmetic circuitry. (439)

**Certificates of deposit** Savings instruments that tie up deposits for longer periods of time and pay higher interest than traditional savings accounts. (489)

**Certified public accountant (CPA)** Public accountant who has completed accounting training and passed a uniform exam prepared by the AICPA. (456)

**Channels of distribution** The different paths that goods pass through in moving from the producer to the consumer. (396)

**Chief executive officer (CEO)** Top-ranking corporate officer, who may be president of the company, chairperson of the board, or both. (77)

**Chip** *See* Integrated circuit.

**Civil law** Law concerned with resolving problems or differences by means of monetary compensation. (619)

**Close** Critical step in the sales process in which the salesperson asks the prospect for an order. (385)

**Closed shop** Agreement under which all prospective employees must be members of the union before they can be hired; made illegal by the Taft-Hartley Act of 1947. (293)

**Closing** Price paid for a given stock in the last trade of the day. (552)

**Coaching** Training of managerial personnel in which superiors provide guidance to their subordinates in the course of their regular job performance. (249)

**COBOL** *CO*mmon *B*usiness-*O*riented *L*anguage. Computer language approximating normal business English, used for business applications. (442)

**Code of ethics** Formal statement that serves as a guide to action in problems involving ethical questions. (52)

**Collective bargaining** Mutual obligation of the employer and employee representatives to meet at reasonable times and places and to confer in good faith over terms and conditions of employment. (298)

**Commercial bank** Privately owned, profit-seeking corporation organized to serve individuals' and businesses' financial needs. (487)

**Commercial paper** A short-term, unsecured IOU from a corporation, usually repaid within 270 days. (491)

**Commodities** Equity investment area involving raw materials such as cattle or soybeans. (546)

**Common law** Body of law arising from judicial decisions based on unwritten laws. (618)

**Common stock** Certificate of ownership in a corporation that entitles its owner to receive dividends and to vote. (75)

**Communication** The transmission of meaning and understanding from a person or group to another person or group. (272)

**Communism** An economic system based on the principles that (1) all factors of production, including labor, are either owned or controlled by the state, and (2) each person produces according to ability but shares in the economic benefits according to need. (17)

**Comparative advertising** A form of persuasive advertising in which two or more products—mentioned by name—are compared in terms of quality. (372)

**Compensation** Employees' financial reward for past performance and incentive to future performance. Takes the form of wages, salary, incentive wages, profit-sharing, and employee benefits. (251)

**Competition** Rivalry among similar businesses for a share of the same consumer dollars. (16)

**Competitive edge** A quality that sets a firm apart from, and gives it an advantage over, its competitors. (321)

**Computer** An electronic device that can perform computations, or process data, without the intervention of a human being. (428)

**Computer system** Collection of all the devices a computer needs to input, process, output, and store data. (436)

**Computer terminal** Keyboard from which data can be entered directly into computer memory. (438)

**Conceptual skills** The mental ability to sift, analyze, and draw conclusions from information, without becoming immersed in details. (155)

**Conglomerate** The result of a merger of two or more corporations that operate in entirely different, unrelated industries. (78) *See also* Merger.

**Congress of Industrial Organizations (CIO)** A group of unions within the AFL, composed of all the workers in different industries. They broke away from the AFL in 1938, and then became part of the AFL-CIO in 1955. (291)

**Conservation** The most effective use of resources, considering society's present and future needs. (47)

**Consideration** Something of value promised by both parties to a contract. (621)

**Consumer goods** Products that are used by the consumer or

household that buys them and that call for no further commercial processing. (345)

**Consumerism** The organized efforts of independent, government, and business groups to protect consumers from undesirable effects resulting from poorly designed and produced products. (41)

**Consumer markets** Individuals or households that purchase goods and services for their own use. (324)

**Continuous process** Production process in which production runs for a long time, making the same product over and over. (198)

**Contract** Agreement between two parties that is enforced by law. (619)

**Controlled exchange rate** Exchange rate arbitrarily set by a country. (602) *See also* Exchange rate.

**Controlling** The management function that involves following up on planned performance by measuring and correcting it as necessary. (155)

**Convenience goods** Products sold to the consumer whose shopping time is limited and who buys them often, routinely, quickly, and in any store that carries them. (345)

**Convenience stores** Small supermarkets that offer late-hour shopping seven days a week in exchange for higher prices and limited selection. (407)

**Convertible bonds** Fixed-rate bonds that entitle their holders to trade them in for common stock. (537)

**Cooperative** A business enterprise owned by and operated for the benefit of those it serves, whose income is distributed to shareholders according to their participation. (81)

**Corporate charter** Official document issued by an individual state, based on the articles of incorporation and contingent on payment of fees, which establishes a corporation. (73)

**Corporate officers** Top management of a corporation, elected by the board of directors and responsible for directing day-to-day activities of the company. (76)

**Corporation** An "artificial being, invisible, intangible, and existing only in contemplation of the law." Form of business that has many of the duties, rights, and powers of people who run a business, including issuing and selling stock. (66)

**Coupons** Advertising inserts or package enclosures used to reduce the price of an established product and to promote new or different products. (388)

**Craft unions** Labor unions composed of workers in a specific skill, craft, or trade. (290)

**Credit unions** Financial institutions, formed by people with a common interest, place of employment, or occupation, which make low-interest loans and offer high interest rates on deposits. (489)

**Criminal law** Law concerned with punishing perpetrators of illegal acts. (619)

**Critical path** In a PERT chart, the longest sequence of operations or steps, whose prompt completion is necessary for the whole project to be done on time. (218)

**Current assets** Assets that are used or sold in less than a year. (466)

**Current liabilities** Debts that must be repaid within one year. (466)

**Data processing** Routine use of a computer to manipulate data and other types of information. (429)

**Debenture bonds** Unsecured bonds, backed only by the reputation of the issuing organization. (521)

**Debit card** Banking customer's plastic access card to automatic teller machines and electronic funds transfer. (503)

**Debt financing** Long-term financing method based on borrowing. (521)

**Decentralization** The division and sharing of authority, through delegation, among managers at lower levels in the organization. (186)

**Decision making** Conscious selection of an effective course of action from among two or more available alternatives, in order to reach an objective. (158)

**Deed** Written document used to convey real property to another owner. (622)

**Delegation** Giving another person the right to use a part of one's authority. (150)

**Demand** The desire for a good or service, given sufficient buying power and the willingness of consumers to use that buying power. (14)

**Demand deposits** Checking accounts. (488)

**Departmentation** Division of work into operating units on the basis of the similarity or importance of the work or the abilities and preferences of the workers. (174) *See also* Functional; Process; Product; and Territorial departmentation.

**Department store** Retailer consisting of several different departments located together under one roof in order to achieve economies in buying, service, promotion, and control. (404)

**Deposit insurance** A guarantee by the Federal Deposit Insurance Corporation (FDIC) on deposits at banks and S&Ls. (491)

**Developing nation** Nation with relatively little manufacturing and a low standard of living. (602)

**Direct mail** Advertising by catalogs, letters, folders, pamphlets, handbills, and postcards. (381)

**Direct retailer** A retailer that sells directly to the customer, by telephone, mail, or personal visits. (407)

**Direct taxes** Taxes paid directly by the person or business against which they are levied. (23)

**Disability income contracts** Income maintenance agreements for an insured person who is unable to work. (575)

**Discipline** Any action intended to correct wrong behavior and train the individual to perform correctly. (250)

**Discount** Reduction in price offered by a seller to a buyer. (364) *See also* specific discounts.

**Discount rate** The interest rate charged by the Federal Reserve on loans to member banks. (500)

**Discount stores** High-volume, low-price retailers that feature national-brand merchandise and convenience. (405)

**Disk drive** Device that can read data from disks. (438)

**Diskette** *See* Floppy disk; Magnetic disk.

**Disk pack** Stack of eleven hard disks used for storing data in large amounts. (440)

**Dispatching** Production control step that involves issuing the required paperwork to make sure that materials, tools, machines, and workers are brought together at the right time and place, and that production proceeds according to schedule. (215)

**Distribution centers** Warehouses that serve a regional market, consolidate large shipments, process orders, and maintain a full line of products for customer distribution. (411)

**Distribution strategy** Marketing decisions about the physical distribution of goods and the selection of marketing channels. (336)

**Diversified portfolio** Strategy of investing in more than one company and industry. (546)

**Division of labor** *See* Specialization.

**Domestic international sales corporations (DISCs)** Tax-sheltered subsidiaries for U.S. exporters. (611)

**Double-entry system** System of bookkeeping that requires that each transaction be recorded in two places, to keep the accounting equation in balance. (459) *See also* Accounting equation.

**Dow Jones Industrial Average (DJIA)** Composite index of overall stock market performance. (546)

**Due process** The legal principle that everyone is entitled to a day in court, under fair legal procedures. (23)

**Dumping** Shipping substantial amounts of a product to another country at prices below the full cost of producing it or significantly below the selling price in the home or competitive market. (607)

**Durable goods** Products whose physical qualities and uses permit them to last a relatively long time. (344)

**Earnings per share (EPS)** The amount of profit a company earns for each share of stock. (552)

**Ecology** The relationship between living things—especially people—and their environment. (46)

**Economic resources** The means, or inputs into the production process, used by businesses to produce goods and services. Usually categorized as land, labor, capital, and entrepreneurship. Also called *factors of production.* (10)

**Economics** The study of how scarce resources are allocated to satisfy human wants. (10)

**Effectiveness** Doing whatever needs to be done to achieve objectives. (144)

**Efficiency** Doing something in the best possible way, so that there are minimal wasted resources. (144)

**Electronic funds transfer (EFT)** Transfer of money through a computerized electronic system. (503)

**Embargo** Outright prohibition of the import or export of certain products. (606)

**Employee benefits** Form of pay over and above regularly paid wages or salaries. (254)

**Employee referral** An employee's suggesting a friend or relative to fill a position that is or soon will be vacant. (242)

**Employer associations** Groups of companies that join together to negotiate with unions instead of doing so individually. (302)

**Endowment insurance** Life insurance that provides for payment of the face amount in the event of the insured's death during a specified period, or for full payment if the insured is still living at the end of this period. (577)

**Entrepreneurs** Innovative owner-managers who create some new product or service or suggest a better way of using existing products or services. (5)

**Equal employment opportunity** All employment opportunities are equally available to minorities, women, Vietnam veterans, and older and disabled workers. (41)

**Equilibrium price** Price at which the amount of a product demanded just equals the available supply of that product. (359)

**Equity financing** Long-term financing method based on selling part interests in a firm. (521)

**Esteem needs** In Abraham Maslow's hierarchy, the need for self-respect, the respect of others, job status, the prestige of position, recognition, and ego satisfaction. (268)

**Ethics, code of** *See* Code of ethics.

**Exchange** The marketing function of buying and selling. (318)

**Exchange rate** The rate at which the money of one country is exchanged for that of another country. (602) *See also* Controlled exchange rate; Floating exchange rate.

**Exclusive distribution** Market coverage in which a single dealer is given the exclusive right to sell an item in a specified area. (403)

**Executive branch** The part of government that enforces laws through regulatory agencies and decrees. (619)

**Expenses** The cost of doing business. (468)

**Export quota** Limit set on the amount of a product that can be shipped out of a country. (606)

**Exports** Sales to other nations. (594)

**Express warranties** Specific representations made by the seller regarding the product. (23) *See also* Warranty.

**Extinction pricing** Pricing a new product far below cost to eliminate competition before raising prices to normal levels. (362)

**Facilitation** The marketing function of financing, risk taking, standardizing and grading, and researching. (318)

**Factor** *See* Factoring company.

**Factoring company (factor)** Financial institution that buys a business's accounts receivable after deducting a percentage as its fee. (491)

**Factors of production** *See* Economic resources. (10)

**Factory outlets** Retailers that sell products directly from the factory to consumers, usually at a substantial discount. (407)

**Featherbedding** Union practice of keeping workers on the payroll even when they do no work; made illegal by the Taft-Hartley Act of 1947. (293)

**Federal Reserve System (FRS)** The nation's central banking system, which creates and controls the money supply. (492)

**Feedback** In the communication cycle, the final step in which a response of some type from the receiver shows the sender that the idea has been received. (274)

**Fidelity bond** Agreement protecting an employer from losses due to employee dishonesty. (573)

**Financial accounting** Accounting used to develop financial information needed by those outside the firm, as well as by owners and managers. (454)

**Financial institutions** Businesses that distribute or deal in money and financial affairs. (487)

**Financial management** The business function of effectively raising and using funds. (510)

**First-line management** *See* Supervisory management.

**Fishybacking** Mode of transportation in which railroad cars or truck trailers are loaded onto water carriers. (415)

**Fixed assets** Relatively permanent investments that a firm intends to keep for long periods of time in order to produce income. (466)

**Fixed costs** Business costs that remain the same regardless of the amount of production, such as property taxes. (361)

**Flextime** A work arrangement in which employees schedule their own hours for starting and stopping work around a core of required hours. (277)

**Floating exchange rate** Exchange rate that varies with market conditions. (602) *See also* Exchange rate.

**Flood insurance** Insurance against losses resulting from river, stream, coastal, and lakeshore flooding. (572)

**Floppy disks** Thin, flexible, mylar disks that can contain up to 1.5 million characters. (440)

**Follow-up** Postsale activities designed to obtain and maintain repeat customers. (386)

**Foreign trade zones (FTZs)** Duty-free areas in the United States that are treated as foreign territory with respect to international business. (608)

**Formal organizations** The sum of clearly defined relationships, channels of communication, and responsibilities resulting from the delegation of authority from one organization level to another. (170)

**Form utility** The change of raw materials into a product or service that satisfies the customer's needs. (197) *See also* Utility.

**FORTRAN** *FOR*mula *TRAN*slation. Computer language developed for scientific uses. (442)

**Four P's** The product, price, promotion, and placement components of the marketing mix. (336) *See also* Marketing mix.

**Fractional reserve system** Requirement that banks keep a cer-

tain percentage of each demand deposit on reserve to meet withdrawal demands. (498)

**Franchise** Exclusive arrangement that enables a private owner to conduct business using the name, operating guidelines, and distinguishing features of the parent company. (114)

**Franchisee** Local independent businessperson who contracts with a franchise owner to operate the franchise locally or regionally. (114)

**Franchisor** National or regional company that owns a franchise's name, distinguishing features, and operating rights. (114)

**Fraternal societies** Groups formed for social and benevolent purposes that also offer low-cost insurance to their members. (564)

**Free enterprise system** An economic system in which businesses are organized, owned, operated, and controlled by private individuals, who have the right to a profit (or must suffer the loss) from operations. (5)

**Fringe benefits** *See* Employee benefits.

**Functional authority** A specialist's right to oversee lower-level personnel involved in that specialty, regardless of where the personnel are in the organization. (186)

**Functional departmentation** The process of putting together in one unit those activities needed to perform the same business function, such as production, marketing, or finance. (177) *See also* Departmentation.

**Gantt charts** Production control tools that graphically measure all production steps performed, the time each is supposed to take, and the time each actually takes. (217)

**General construction firms** Firms that build residences, commercial and industrial buildings, government offices and installations, and other structures. (91)

**General obligation bonds** Government debt securities fully backed by the issuing body's power to assess and collect taxes. (538)

**General partners** Co-owners of a partnership who have all the benefits as well as the liabilities of the partnership. (64)

**Generic products** Slightly lower-quality, lower-cost goods that have no brand indication. (353)

**Government-owned corporations** Federal, state, or local businesses operated for the public welfare, and whose shares are all government-owned. (68)

**Grade label** Product label specifying the quality level of a good. (355)

**Grapevine** Communication system used by the informal organization to relay news outside and around formal communication channels. (172)

**Grievance** Formal complaint to management about working conditions or terms of employment. (298)

**Gross national product (GNP)** The monetary value of all the final goods and services produced by a nation in one year. (9)

**Group life insurance** Fringe benefit providing life insurance to all members of a group or organization. (515)

**Handicapped person** Anyone with a physical or mental disability that substantially restricts major normal activities such as walking, seeing, speaking, or learning. (44)

**Hardware** The physical components of a computer system. (437)

**Hawthorne studies** Series of motivation studies, conducted at the Hawthorne plant of Western Electric, to determine the effect of the environment on productivity. The experiments demonstrated that a sense of recognition may be more motivating than more material factors. (263)

**Headhunters** Executive search firms that actively seek managers for given positions in business. (242)

**Health insurance** Insurance against the risk of unplanned medical expenses and loss of income. (574)

**Hierarchy of needs** Abraham Maslow's theory of five levels of needs: physiological, safety and security, social, esteem, and self-actualization. (267) *See also* specific needs.

**Horizontal mergers** Purchases by a corporation of smaller competitors. (78)

**Human relations** The process of getting both managers and employees to *want* to strive for organizational goals and objectives, through motivation and communication. (262)

**Human relations skills** The ability to understand other people and to interact effectively with others. (156)

**Human resources philosophy** Philosophy that workers should be treated with dignity and respect, but their output is an economic resource that must be cost effective. (264)

**Hygiene factors** In Frederick Herzberg's two-factor theory, job factors that cause dissatisfaction if they are absent, yet do not motivate if they are present. (271)

**Implied warranties** Warranties that are legally imposed on the seller unless disclaimed in writing by the seller. (23) *See also* Warranty.

**Import quota** Limit set on the amount of a product that can be brought into a country. (606)

**Imports** Purchases from other nations. (594)

**Impulse goods** Products bought on sight to satisfy a strong momentary need. (345)

**Incentive wage** Earnings directly related to the amount produced or sold by the employee. (254)

**Income statement** Financial statement showing the status of a firm's revenues, expenses, and profits over a period of time. (464)

**Indirect taxes** Taxes paid, not by the person or firm against which they are levied, but by someone else. (637)

**Industrial goods** Products used by businesses to produce other goods or to provide services. (346)

**Industrial markets** Firms that buy goods for resale and firms or institutions that buy goods and services to use in performing their operations. (324)

**Industrial nations** Nations that import raw materials and export finished manufactured products. (602)

**Industrial unions** Labor unions composed of workers in the same industry. (291)

**Inflation** An increase in prices over a period of time, usually during a peak in the business cycle. (22)

**Informal leaders** Workers with no formal authority who nevertheless have great influence because their fellow workers respect them and look to them for leadership. (172)

**Informal organizations** Spontaneous natural groups of employees who share channels of communication and personal relationships not shown in any formal organization chart or manual. (172)

**Informational advertising** Advertising that tells what a product is or does. Used in the introduction stage of a product. (372)

**Injunction** Court order prohibiting a person or group from carrying out given actions, such as a strike or boycott, that would cause irreparable damage. (302)

**Inland marine insurance** Insurance protecting goods in transit on rivers, canals, and coastal waters. (573)

**Institutional advertising** Advertising used to create a favorable impression or goodwill for a business or industry in general. (371)

**Insurable interest** Principle of insurance stating that, in order to be insured, one must stand to suffer financially when a loss occurs. (562)

**Insurable risk** Risk filling four conditions of insurability: (1) predictable losses; (2) broad geographical spread; (3) ability to determine when a loss has occurred and its extent; (4) accidental loss. (563)

**Insurance** Risk transfer in which an insurance company

agrees, for a fee, to pay an individual or organization an agreed-upon sum of money for a given loss. *(21)*

**Intangible property** Ownership represented by a written document. *(561)*

**Integrated circuit** Miniaturized silicon electronic component that replaced multiple components. *(434)*

**Intensive distribution** Broad market coverage in which as many distribution channels and outlets are used as is possible. *(402)*

**Interest** The price of capital. *(13)*

**Intermediaries** The units or institutions in the channel of distribution that either take title to goods or negotiate a sale as an agent or broker for the producer. *(396)*

**Intermediate management** *See* Middle management.

**Intermittent process** Production process involving short production runs, where the machines are often stopped and started or changed to make a different product or to serve different customers. *(199)*

**International markets** Buyers of goods and services from other countries. *(324)*

**Internship training** Training program in which selected students, who are enrolled in a regular academic program, work for a company for a limited time to gain employment experience. *(248)*

**Inventory** All of a production organization's raw materials, supplies, and parts, as well as finished products not currently being stored, moved, used, or sold. *(213)*

**Investment bank** Financial institution that buys and resells corporate securities for a profit. *(490)*

**Involuntary bankruptcy** Bankruptcy in which creditors file the bankruptcy petition. *(623)* *See also* Bankruptcy.

**Job analysis** Process used to determine what each job is and what is required to perform it effectively. *(237)*

**Job description** List of a job's duties, responsibilities, and working conditions. *(237)*

**Job enrichment** Giving employees greater authority and responsibility over their jobs as the best way to motivate them. *(277)*

**Job rotation** The training process whereby young managers learn various operating procedures by temporarily performing in many different jobs. *(249)*

**Job specification** A job description along with statements of mental, physical, educational, experience, and other qualifications required of a person to successfully perform the job. *(237)*

**Joint venture** Temporary partnership formed to carry out a specific business activity. *(64)*

**Judicial branch** The part of government that interprets laws; the courts. *(619)*

**Judicial system** The lawmaking and law-interpreting people and institutions of a nation. *(624)*

**Just-in-time (JIT) production system** A hand-to-mouth method of buying parts and materials in very small quantities just in time for use, with minimum storage, in order to save on storage and carrying costs. *(214)*

**Keypunch** Typewriterlike machine that punches cards for computer input. *(438)*

**Knights of Labor** The first national U.S. labor union, formed in 1869 by several craft unions. *(290)*

**Labor** All human physical and mental effort. *(12)*

**Labor relations** All interactions and relationships between management and its employees in which a union is concerned. *(286)*

**Labor union** An organization of workers banded together to achieve economic goals, especially improved wages, hours, and working conditions. *(286)*

**Laissez faire** The philosophy that government's involvement in business should be as little as possible. *(16)*

**Land** All the natural resources occurring on, in, and under the earth's surface, such as timber, petroleum, iron ore, sand, and gravel. *(10)*

**Law of comparative advantage** Principle that some countries can produce certain goods more efficiently and cheaply than others can. *(600)*

**Law of demand** Economic principle stating that if price goes down, the quantity demanded goes up, and if price goes up, the quantity demanded goes down. *(14)* *See also* Demand.

**Law of large numbers** As the number of individual cases increases, the risk of something unpleasant happening to one of them decreases. *(21)*

**Law of supply** Economic principle stating that if price goes up, the quantity supplied goes up, and if price goes down, the quantity supplied goes down. *(15)* *See also* Supply.

**Layout** The way in which a production facility's walls, partitions, machines, tools, equipment, offices, and aisles are arranged. *(212)*

**Leaders** Those who inspire others to follow them to achieve agreed-upon goals. *(151)*

**Leadership** The ability to induce another person to work toward a specific goal. *(151)*

**Leading** Directing, guiding, supervising, and motivating subordinates to perform their duties and responsibilities. *(151)*

**Lease** Written agreement permitting use of property by someone other than the owner. *(622)*

**Legislative branch** Those parts of government that pass laws and statutes. *(619)*

**Leverage** The use of borrowed money to make more money. *(515)*

**Liability** Anything owned by a business or individual. *(459)*

**Liability loss** Financial loss suffered when property causes damage or injury to another person. *(569)*

**Life insurance** Insurance against death before retirement and loss of income after retirement. *(575)*

**Limited partners** Co-owners of a partnership whose participation is restricted to certain agreed-upon aspects of the business and whose liability is limited to the amount they invest. *(64)*

**Line authority** A manager's right to tell subordinates what to do and then see than they do it. *(185)*

**Line of credit** A given amount that a firm can borrow without making a new request. *(520)*

**Liquid assets** *See* Current assets.

**Liquidity** Having readily available cash to meet expenses as they come due. *(516)*

**Lockout** Management response to a strike in which the company closes its premises to employees in order to win its own demands. *(302)*

**Logistics** The process of managing the storage and physical movement of goods from producers to users. *(410)*

**Long-term liabilities** Loans to be repaid in the future, with a regular interest charge on the money used. *(466)*

**Long-term sources of funds** Sources of funds that are used for needs lasting longer than one year, to be paid off in periods longer than one year. *(521)*

**Loss leaders** Pricing a product very low to attract customers into the store to buy other, more profitable items. *(364)* *See also* Discount.

**M-1** Definition of money, including coins, currency, and checking accounts. *(487)*

**Machine language** A binary code in which all letters and numbers are represented in terms of only two different digits. *(441)*

**Magnetic disk** Magnetized metal or mylar platter on which data can be recorded or stored for computer input. *(438)*

**Magnetic tape** Magnetized mylar tape on which data can be

recorded or stored for computer input. (438)

**Main computer storage** Location in a computer's processor where data and programs are kept. (439)

**Mainframe** Full-scale computer with large memory storage and complex capabilities. (429)

**Management** The process of working through people to achieve objectives by means of effective decision making and efficient allocation of scarce resources. Also an individual, an occupational group, or a discipline of study. (144)

**Management by objectives (MBO)** Technique in which managers and their subordinates jointly set objectives, which they then are motivated to achieve. (149)

**Management information systems (MIS)** Computer data systems that maintain a comprehensive master file of all data relating to each subject. (447)

**Managerial accounting** Accounting used inside the firm, which provides management with financial information to be used in decision making. (454)

**Manufacturers' agents and brokers** Representatives of one or a few manufacturers, who follow the terms set by the manufacturers. (403) *See also* Agent.

**Manufacturers' sales offices and branches** Wholesalers owned and managed by large manufacturers. (403)

**Manufacturing firms** Firms that use raw materials and semi-finished parts to produce finished goods. (91)

**Margin requirement** The percentage of securities' prices, controlled by the Federal Reserve, that must be paid in cash. (502)

**Market** People (including governments and institutions) who have the necessary authority, purchasing power, and willingness to buy a good or service. (323)

**Market approach** Pricing technique in which a company sets its prices in terms of current market prices for similar products or services. (361)

**Market characteristics** Population, age, income, and regional patterns that affect marketing strategies. (325)

**Marketing** Determination of customers' needs and wants, development of goods and services to satisfy those needs and wants, and then delivery of those goods and services to the customer. (318)

**Marketing concept** The belief that a business must attempt to determine and satisfy the desires and needs of customers in order to make a profit. (321)

**Marketing mix** The combination and blending of product, price, promotion, and distribution decisions into an overall marketing strategy designed to satisfy chosen customers. (337)

**Marketing research** The systematic gathering, recording, and analysis of data about problems related to the marketing of goods and services. (332)

**Marketing strategy** Overall plan for developing the marketing process to reach a firm's objectives. (336)

**Market positioning** Placing a product in the market so as to convey a desired image and to make the product attractive. (330)

**Market segmentation** Division of the total market into groups with similar characteristics. (329)

**Market value** Current price at which a stock is being bought and sold. (536)

**Markup** The difference between the cost of an item and its selling price. (360)

**Markup percentage** A product's markup divided by its production cost. (360) *See also* Markup.

**Mass-merchandising shopping chains** Huge retail organizations with high sales volume and many outlets, which may own all or part of their manufacturers. (405)

**Materials management** Assurance that the required materials are available when needed at each stage of the production process. (213)

**Matrix organization** Form of organization in which employees simultaneously report to their regular functional manager *and* to a project manager. (179)

**Mechanization** The process of using machines to do work otherwise handled by people or animals. (205)

**Mediation** Method of dispute settlement in which an outsider meets (jointly or separately) with union and management representatives to try to find an acceptable solution to the problem. (298)

**Merchant wholesalers** Wholesalers who take title to and possession of the items they buy from producers to sell to retailers, industrial users, or other large-scale buyers. (403)

**Merger** Purchase of one business by a similar business in which the purchasing company retains its independence and dominance. (78)

**Microcomputer** Small computer in a single unit that houses all memory, processing circuits, wiring, and some input-output devices. (429)

**Microprocessor** Miniaturized computer processor stored on a silicon chip. (435)

**Middle management** The level of management responsible for lower levels in a firm, such as a department within a division. (145)

**Minicomputer** Smaller computer system with the power of a mainframe. (429) *See also* Mainframe.

**Mission** Long-term vision of what an organization is trying to become. (147)

**Missionary selling** Personal selling done to develop goodwill and demand for a new product. (384) *See also* Business selling.

**Mixed capitalism** An economic system based on the principles of pure capitalism, but limited by government involvement. (16) *See also* Capitalism.

**Monetary system** The use of a common unit of exchange throughout a society. (486)

**Money** Anything generally accepted as a medium of exchange, a store of value, and a measure of value. (486)

**Money market funds** Investments pooling money to buy short-term securities such as commercial paper and Treasury bills. (546)

**Mortality table** Summary of data on past policyholders, used to predict the number of persons at each age who will die in a given year. (575)

**Mortgage bonds** Bonds that are secured by a pledge of specific assets of the corporation. (521)

**Mortgage loan** Secured loan against which the borrower has pledged real estate or some other fixed asset. (521)

**Motivation** The process by which managers bring out the best in their subordinates by giving them reasons to perform better. (265)

**Motivators** In Frederick Herzberg's two-factor theory, job factors that positively encourage employees to perform effectively. (271)

**Motive** A drive, impulse, or desire that directs a person to seek to satisfy a need and moves the person toward a goal. (265)

**Multinational corporation (MNC)** Corporation that operates on an international scale. (603)

**Mutual companies** Nonprofit private insurers owned by policyholders. (21)

**Mutual funds** Investments by mutual investment companies that pool money to buy a wide range of stocks and bonds. (546)

**NASDAQ** National Association of Security Dealers Automated Quotation system, a computerized communication

system developed in the 1970s to tie the OTC market to-gether. (540)

**National Labor Relations Board (NLRB)** The five-person judi-cial body charged with enforcing labor legislation. (295)

**Near money** Securities a corporation buys with excess funds in order to earn income until the funds are needed. (516)

**Needs** Inner cravings that people try to satisfy by outward be-havior. (267)

**Negotiable instrument** Financial document, such as a check, that is transferable from one party to another. (623)

**Negotiable order of withdrawal (NOW) account** A checking account that pays interest but requires a minimum bal-ance. (489)

**Net income** The result of deducting expenses from revenues. (469)

**Networking** The transmission of information on job leads and of mutual support via informal business contacts. (245)

**No-fault laws** Automobile insurance laws in twenty-five states that limit the insured's right to sue or be sued. (570)

**Nondurable goods** Products whose physical qualities and uses cause them to be used quickly or for only a few times. (345)

**Nonprofit corporations** Service institutions, such as universi-ties or hospitals, that are incorporated in order to gain lim-ited liability. (68)

**No-par stock** Stock with no given value. (534)

**Objectives** Translation of a firm's mission into workable day-to-day goals. (148)

**Occupation** The main activity a person engages in during his or her lifetime. (651)

**Ocean marine insurance** Insurance protecting ships and goods against perils of the seas. (573)

**Odd pricing** Setting a price at an odd amount, such as $3.97, that is more appealing to customers. (362)

**Off-price store** Discount store that sells high-quality, usually high-priced name brands at 30 to 80 percent off the stated price. (405)

**On-line processing** Method of data processing in which the user communicates directly with the computer and re-ceives immediate feedback. (444)

**On-the-job training (OJT)** Training of new employees in which they perform regular work duties under the supervision and guidance of an experienced worker or instructor. (247)

**Open market operations** Methods, determined monthly by the Federal Reserve, for controlling the money supply by buy-ing and selling securities on the open market. (502)

**Operations** *See* Production.

**Organization** A group of people striving together to reach a common goal and bound together by a set of understood authority-responsibility relationships. (168)

**Organization charts** Graphic representations of the authority-responsibility relationships among members of a formal organization. (171)

**Organization manuals** Written documents describing formal authority-responsibility relationships, the functions of op-erating units, and job procedures. (172)

**Organizing** The management function of dividing tasks among work groups and assigning each group to a manager who has the necessary authority and responsibility. (149)

**Orientation** A new employee's introduction to the company—either a simple introduction to present employees or a lengthy process of filling the employee in on company his-tory, policies, procedures, and benefits. (247)

**Outdoor advertising** Advertising by billboards, signs, and other advertising spaces. (381)

**Outplacement** Counseling, financial assistance, and help in finding new jobs that a company provides for its terminated employees. (251)

**Outside directors** Executives from companies or nonprofit foundations outside the corporation who serve on the board of directors. (75)

**Over-the-counter (OTC) market** Network of securities dealers operating outside of the organized exchanges. (540)

**Owners' equity** Net worth of a firm after all debts have been taken into account. (459)

**Ownership utility** Arranging for the transfer of title to the goods from seller to buyer. (320) *See also* Utility.

**Packaging** The external presentation of a product, as in a wrap-per, box, bag, or bottle. (356)

**Parent company** Corporation that owns most or all of another corporation's stock. (78)

**Partnership** Form of business owned and operated by two or more co-owners, one of whom must be a general partner. (63) *See also* General partners.

**Partnership agreement** Contract for formation of a partnership, spelling out how profits will be shared, circumstances for admitting new partners, how the partnership will cease, and so on. (64)

**Par value** Dollar amount printed on the face of each stock cer-tificate. (534)

**Penetration pricing** Pricing a new product relatively low to allow the company to achieve broad market acceptance and to gain a large market share before increasing prices later. (362)

**P-E ratio** Comparison of a stock's closing price with the com-pany's earnings per share of stock. (552)

**Performance appraisal** Process an employer uses to determine whether an employee is doing the job as intended. (250)

**Personal distribution ads** Handbills, shopping newspapers, and other advertisements distributed by hand. (381)

**Personal property** Anything of value, aside from land, that can be owned or used by an individual. (622)

**Personal selling** Sales presentation made directly to a potential customer by a salesperson. (384)

**Personnel management** The process of recruiting, selecting, training, developing, evaluating, compensating, and pro-tecting the health and safety of employees. (234)

**Personnel planning** All the activities carried out by both per-sonnel and operating managers in order to provide the right types and numbers of employees to reach a firm's objec-tives. (236)

**Persuasive advertising** Advertising that tries to improve a product's competitive edge. Used in the growth and early maturity stages of a product. (372)

**PERT (Program Evaluation and Review Technique)** Graphic production scheduling and control tool that enumerates, in linked sequence, all the tasks in a production process. (218)

**Physical distribution** All business activities that are concerned with storing and transporting finished inventories or raw materials so that they arrive at the proper place, at the right time, in the desired condition. (318, 410)

**Physiological needs** In Abraham Maslow's hierarchy, the low-est level of needs, including respiration, elimination, food, drink, sex, and sleep. (267)

**Picketing** Employees walking back and forth outside their place of employment, usually carrying signs, in order to in-form the public of the reasons for a dispute. (298)

**Piggybacking** Mode of transportation in which specially de-signed truck trailers are loaded onto flat railroad cars. (415)

**Place utility** Providing a product or service to customers at a convenient location. (320) *See also* Utility.

**Planned change** Anticipation of changes in the environment and use of deliberate actions to make those changes more favorable. (657)

**Planned progression** Blueprinted path of promotion for trainee managers. (*249*)

**Planning** The management function that involves selecting, and deciding how to achieve, future courses of action for the firm as a whole and for each of its subunits. (*146*)

**Point-of-purchase (POP) advertising** Displays designed to reflect a store's image, feature products, or promote a service. (*386*)

**Police power** The right of state authorities to use the forces of the state to promote the general welfare of its citizens. (*618*)

**Policy manuals** Written documents explaining basic personnel activities and company policies on working hours, absences, and so on. (*172*)

**Pollution** The destruction or contamination of the natural environment. (*47*)

**Portfolio** *See* Diversified portfolio.

**Preemptive right** Common stockholders' right to purchase a proportionate share of any new stock issue. (*536*)

**Preferred stock** Certificate of ownership in a corporation that entitles its holder to receive a fixed dividend before any profits are paid to common stockholders. (*75*)

**Premium** Price higher than a bond's face value. (*554*)

**Presentation** The third step in the sales process, in which the salesperson informs the prospect of how the product or service fills his or her wants or needs. (*385*)

**Price leadership** Situation in which all the firms in an industry follow the pricing practices of one dominant company. (*361*)

**Price lining** Setting prices around a few specific pricing points rather than pricing each item individually. (*362*)

**Pricing objectives** Long-term goals a firm hopes to achieve through its pricing policies and procedures. (*357*)

**Pricing strategy** Marketing decisions for setting profitable and justified prices. (*336*)

**Primary boycott** Boycott in which a union encourages, or tries to force, its own members and others not to buy from the offending employer. (*299*) *See also* Boycott.

**Prime rate** Lowest commercial interest rate available at a particular time and place. (*487*)

**Principal** In the legal relationship of agency, the person who wants to do something legally but is unwilling or unable to do it personally. (*623*) *See also* Agency.

**Printer** High-speed, typewriterlike device for printing computer output. (*439*)

**Private (house) brand** A wholesaler's or retailer's own brand. (*353*) *See also* Brand.

**Private corporations** Corporations with few owners, whose shares are not traded on the open market. (*68*)

**Private employment agencies** Organizations that charge a fee to either the employer or the employee for finding an acceptable employee for a given position. (*242*)

**Private enterprise** Private ownership of resources and of the businesses that use them. (*16*)

**Private ownership** Business ownership by individuals operating alone or in a group. (*60*)

**Process departmentation** The process of putting together in one unit all activities involving the same operating process. (*177*) *See also* Departmentation.

**Process layout** A production arrangement in which machines are grouped together according to the type of work they do. (*212*)

**Product advertising** Nonpersonal selling of specific products or services. (*371*)

**Product departmentation** The process of placing all work activities related to specific product lines in separate operating units. (*177*) *See also* Departmentation.

**Product differentiation** Making a firm's goods or services distinguishable from those of other companies. (*330*)

**Production** The use of human, physical, and financial resources to produce products or services. (*196*)

**Production and operations management** The management of production operations through planning the use of resources, organizing the use of facilities, and controlling the efficiency of the operation. (*204*)

**Production capacity** Amount of goods or services the facilities can handle during a period of time. (*208*)

**Production chain** The series of production processes that includes all activities from gathering of raw materials to the delivery of the final product or service. (*202*)

**Production concept** The assumption that anything produced that is of reasonable quality and price can be sold. (*320*)

**Production control** System for coordinating people, machines, and materials in order to reach objectives. (*215*)

**Production process** The process of converting economic inputs into useful outputs. (*197*)

**Productivity** 1. The ability of a nation's work force to produce goods, as measured in units of work per unit of time. (*23*) 2. The amount of goods or services produced by one worker in a given period of time. (*196*)

**Product layout** Production arrangement in which work stations are arranged according to the sequence of operations on a given product. (*212*)

**Product liability insurance** Insurance against claims of injury or damages resulting from the use of a company's products. (*572*)

**Product life cycle** A series of increases and decreases in sales and profits of a product, including the stages of introduction, growth, maturity, and decline. (*350*)

**Product planning** Marketing decisions about package design, branding, trademarks, copyrights, warranties, and new product development. (*336*)

**Professional corporations (P.C.)** Form of incorporation popular among doctors and lawyers as a means of limiting liability and reducing taxes. (*68*)

**Professional liability insurance** Insurance covering professionals for injuries they might cause during the performance of professional services. (*572*)

**Profit** Income received, minus the costs of operating the business. (*5*)

**Profit motive** The desire to make a profit as a reward for taking the risks of running a business. (*5*) *See also* Profit.

**Profit-sharing plan** Employees' receipt of a given percentage of the firm's profits as extra income. (*254*)

**Program** The set of instructions given to a computer. (*440*)

**Programmed instruction** Training technique in which material to be learned is presented in sequential order by means of a TV monitor, film, programmed book, or computer. Learners may not proceed beyond a given point until they have demonstrated mastery of the preceding information. (*248*)

**Project organization** Form of organization in which independent teams from different departments are brought together for a limited time, to complete a specific project. (*179*)

**Promoting** Moving an employee from a lower-level job to a higher-level one, usually with a higher salary, a new job title, and added duties and responsibilities. (*240*)

**Promotion** The process of informing, persuading, and influencing customers in their decisions about purchasing products or services. (*370*)

**Promotional strategy** Marketing decisions involving personal selling, advertising, and sales promotion. (*336*)

**Promotion mix** The best combination of promotional methods. (*370*)

**Property and liability insurance** Insurance against loss of, or

damage to, property itself and against liabilities resulting from ownership. (568)

**Property loss** Financial loss resulting from destructive damage to property. (568)

**Prospecting** The first step in the sales process, which involves identifying and qualifying potential customers. (385)

**Prospectus** Registration statement required of any company making a securities offer. (541)

**Protective tariffs** Tariffs set to discourage imports and, rarely, exports. (605) See also Tariffs.

**Proxy** Document, signed by a stock's owner, that permits the person named on it to vote the owner's shares of stock. (75)

**Public accountants** Accountants independent of a firm who offer their services to the general public. (456)

**Public corporations** Large corporations whose stock is publicly bought and sold. (68)

**Public employment agencies** Organizations that try to match employee qualifications and job needs as part of a public service. (243)

**Publicity** Any nonpaid information concerning an organization and its products or personnel that appears in any published or oral medium. (388)

**Public liability insurance** Insurance that provides that the insurer will pay all sums, up to the legal limits, for which the insured business becomes liable because of bodily injury, property damage, or personal injury. (572)

**Public ownership** Form of business ownership in which some level of government owns and operates a company for the public's benefit. (61)

**Public warehouses** Independently owned facilities where goods are stored, usually in large quantities, while waiting to be sold or used. They often specialize in handling certain products such as furniture or refrigerated goods. (410)

**Punched cards** Means of computer input in which holes are punched to correspond to characters. (438)

**Pure risk** Uncertainty as to whether there will occur some unpredictable event that can only result in loss. (560)

**Quality control** The production control process designed to ensure that the quality produced is the same as that planned for. (219)

**Quality control circle (QCC)** A group, consisting of the supervisor and workers in a unit, which meets to discuss the quality desired and ways of achieving that level of quality. (219)

**Quality supermarkets** Supermarkets that offer better-quality goods and personal service. (658)

**Quantity discount** Discount offered to buyers who order large quantities of goods. (364) See also Discount.

**Quasi-public corporations** Businesses owned partly by the government and partly by private investors. (68)

**Quota** See Export quota; Import quota.

**Real property** Land or anything attached permanently to land. (622)

**Recession** The low point in a business cycle; consumption and production are at their lowest ebb. (19)

**Recruitment** Reaching out to attract the required number of people with the right abilities to fill available jobs. (241)

**Recycling** The reprocessing of used items for further use. (47)

**Reminder advertising** Advertising that attempts to keep a product's name before the public, and that is used to rejuvenate the product during later stages of the life cycle. (373)

**Rent** The price of using land. (10)

**Reserve requirement** The percentage of deposits that banks must hold in reserve. (498)

**Responsibility** Accountability for performance of assigned duties, by oneself or by subordinates. (144)

**Retailers** Firms or people who obtain goods from wholesalers, brokers, and agents and sell them to the ultimate consumer for personal, nonbusiness use. (91, 404)

**Retail selling** Personal selling that takes place primarily in department or specialty stores. (384)

**Revenue bonds** State or municipal debt securities issued to finance a specific project and backed by that project's success. (538)

**Revenues** Income from sales of products or services. (468)

**Revenue tariffs** Tariffs imposed to generate tax revenue. (22) See also Tariffs.

**Reverse discrimination** Situation in which it is charged that a more qualified or senior person is denied an opportunity because of guarantees given to members of a legally protected group who may not be as well qualified or have as much seniority. (52)

**Right-to-work laws** State legislation giving employees the right to join or refuse to join a union without being fired. (293)

**Risk** See Pure risk; Speculative risk.

**Risk management** The process of conserving the earning power and assets of a firm by minimizing the financial effects of accidental losses. (560)

**Routing** Production control step that determines operations required, the best sequence in which to perform tasks, the machines and tasks used, and the paperwork. (215)

**Rule of law** The legal principle that everyone is equal under the law. (618)

**Safety and security needs** In Abraham Maslow's hierarchy, the need for protection from the environment, as through shelter, regular income, and clothing, or from danger, as through the police. (268)

**Salary** Fixed earnings received by the week, month, or year, usually paid to higher-level employees. (254)

**Sales promotion** Specialized activities—other than personal selling, advertising, and publicity—designed to help transfer ownership and move goods from manufacturer to customer more effectively. Includes displays, specialty advertising, trade shows, coupons and trading stamps, and sales contests. (386)

**Savings and loan associations (S&Ls)** Financial institutions that pay higher rates of interest and invest in the housing industry. (489)

**Savings banks** Financial institutions common in the Northeast that operate much like savings and loan associations. (489)

**Savings bond** U.S. government debt security with a relatively low face value. (537)

**Scabs** See Strikebreakers.

**Scientific management** Frederick W. Taylor's managerial approach that emphasized the scientific determination of jobs; selection, training, and motivation of employees; and the separation of management and nonmanagement duties. (262)

**Seasonal discount** Discount offered on seasonal products that are bought out of season. (364) See also Discount.

**Seat** Membership in a major stock exchange which must be bought and approved. (539)

**Secondary boycott** Boycott aimed at outside firms dealing with the employer. (299) See also Boycott.

**Secured loan** Loan made on the condition that an item of value be pledged as security. (487)

**Securities** Issued obligations from an organization to provide a stated or expected return on investment. (534)

**Securities markets** Exchanges that provide investors with a convenient means of buying and selling their securities. (534)

**Selection** Choosing a specific person from among other qualified applicants to fill a vacant position. (243)

**Selective distribution** Market coverage in which dealers and outlets are screened to select a limited number of better outlets. (403)

**Self-actualization needs** In Abraham Maslow's hierarchy, the highest level of needs, for self-development, self-expression, achievement, creativity, and self-fulfillment. (268)

**Self-insurance** Funds set aside by a firm to meet unpredictable losses. (561)

**Separation of powers** Separation of the making, administering, and interpreting of laws into three distinct branches of government. (619) *See also* specific branches.

**Service businesses** Businesses that perform essential, specialized, and often technical services for customers, businesses, and institutions. (91)

**Service corporations (S.C.)** *See* Professional corporations.

**Shopping goods** Infrequently purchased products found in only a few stores and bought after comparison shopping. (345)

**Short-term sources of funds** Sources of funds that are used for short-term needs and that must be paid off within one year. (578)

**Skimming pricing** Pricing a new product relatively high in order to make quick, high profits before the price is gradually lowered. (362)

**Small business** Business that is independently owned and operated and that is not dominant in its field of operation. (90)

**Social audit** Formal procedure for evaluating and reporting on actions with social implications. (52)

**Socialism** An economic system based on government control of all primary industries. (17)

**Social needs** In Abraham Maslow's hierarchy, the need for association and interaction with others, for love, friendship, belongingness, and acceptance. (268)

**Social responsibility** A firm's obligation to set policies, make decisions, and follow courses of action that are desirable in terms of the values and objectives of society. (34)

**Software** Programs and languages used with a computer. (437)

**Sole proprietorship** Form of business owned and operated by one person. (61)

**Span of control** *See* Span of management.

**Span of management** The number of people a given manager supervises directly. (188)

**Specialization** The principle that the most efficient way to do something is for each person to do what he or she is most capable of doing, rather than doing everything. (169)

**Specialty advertising** Items of little value that are imprinted with an advertiser's name or logo. (387)

**Specialty goods** Products bought infrequently, often at exclusive outlets, and after a special effort by the consumer. (345)

**Specialty stores** Retailers that specialize in a particular type of merchandise. (405)

**Speculative risk** Uncertainty as to whether a voluntarily undertaken activity will result in a gain or a loss. (560)

**Staff authority** A staff specialist's right to give advice to a superior. A staff specialist cannot order anyone to carry out that advice. (186)

**Staffing** The management function that involves recruiting, selecting, training, and developing people to fill the jobs that are created through organizing. (150)

**Stagflation** Stagnant economic growth coupled with inflation. (22) *See also* Inflation.

**Standard & Poor's 500 Composite Index** Index of stock market performance that uses a broad group of industrial, transportation, utility, and financial stocks. (547)

**Statement of changes in financial position** Financial statement that focuses on the flow of funds into and out of a business. (464)

**Statute law** Body of laws passed by legislative groups. (618)

**Steward** *See* Union steward.

**Stock companies** Private insurers designed to make a profit for themselves and for their stockholders. (564)

**Stockholders** Ultimate owners of a corporation, with that ownership defined by their purchase of shares in the company. (74)

**Strategic planning** Identifying the long-range mission of an organization and determining objectives and appropriate strategies for achieving it. (147)

**Strike** The withholding of employee services from an employer in order to win certain demands. (298)

**Strikebreakers (Scabs)** Workers who cross the picket line to work during a strike. (302)

**Subchapter S corporation** Corporation with twenty-five or fewer owners. Corporate profits or losses flow straight to owners, who then pay income taxes at individual rates. (70)

**Subsidiary** Corporation whose stock is mostly or completely owned by another corporation. (78)

**Supermarkets** Large-scale self-service food stores laid out by department. (407) *See also* Quality supermarkets; Super-supermarkets.

**Super-supermarkets** Supermarkets featuring fresh baked goods and delicatessens. (658)

**Supervisory management** The level of management responsible for operations of the narrowest organizational units. (145)

**Supply** The desire and effort of producers to satisfy consumer demands, given the willingness and ability of producers to provide goods and services. (15)

**Surety bond** Agreement in which the bonding company guarantees the performance of a second party to a third party. (574)

**Sweetheart contracts** Agreements by corrupt labor leaders to give concessions to management at the expense of employees, in exchange for bribes. (292)

**Synthetic process** Production process in which two or more inputs are mixed or assembled to form one or a very few outputs. (197)

**Systems software** Set of instructions built into a computer to control its inner workings. (440)

**Tangible property** Owned material good or product. (622)

**Target market** The specific group of customers, as defined by factors like age, education, occupation, economic status, and location, toward which a firm directs its marketing efforts. (328)

**Tariffs** Duties or taxes imposed by a government on imported or exported goods. (22) *See also* Protective tariffs; Revenue tariffs.

**Taxes** Charges levied by a government on persons and organizations subject to the jurisdiction of the government. (634) *See also* Direct taxes; Indirect taxes.

**Technical selling** Business selling aimed at convincing a potential customer's technical staff of the superiority of a company's products. (384) *See also* Business selling.

**Technical skills** Ability to understand and perform effectively processes, practices, or techniques appropriate to the job. (156)

**Term life insurance** Life insurance for only a specified period, with no savings value at the end of that period. (21)

**Territorial departmentation** The process of putting all the activities that take place in a certain geographic location in the same operating unit. (177) *See also* Departmentation.

**Theory X and Theory Y** Douglas McGregor's theory of two basic assumptions managers make about their subordinates. Theory X assumes that employees are motivated

only by lower-level needs; Theory Y assumes that they are motivated by higher-level needs. *(270)*

**Time deposits**  Savings accounts and certificates of deposit that earn interest and are left with a bank for a stated period of time. *(488)*

**Time utility**  Having a product or service available when consumers want to buy it. *(320) See also* Utility.

**Time (day) wages**  Hourly earnings received in a check at the end of the week, usually paid to lower-level employees. *(252)*

**Title**  Legal right to possess and use property. *(622)*

**Title insurance**  Insurance against loss caused by a previous defect in a property's title. *(572)*

**Top management**  The level of management with overall responsibility and ultimate authority for the whole organization. *(145)*

**Tort**  Act that results in injury to another, for which the injured is legally entitled to some form of compensation. *(623)*

**Trade barriers**  Factors that restrict the ability or willingness of groups to sell to one another in foreign markets. *(604)*

**Trade credit**  Credit extended to a business by its suppliers. *(579)*

**Trade discount**  Discount given to an intermediary by a producer. *(364) See also* Discount.

**Trademark**  A brand that has been given legal protection so that only its owner has the right to use it. *(353) See also* Brand.

**Trading stamps**  A bonus given by retailers, based on the amount of purchase, which customers may redeem for additional merchandise. *(388)*

**Training**  *See* Apprenticeship; Internship; On-the-job training; Vestibule training.

**Transferring**  Moving employees from less desirable or less rewarding jobs in the company to others that better satisfy their and the company's needs. *(238)*

**Transistor**  Electronic device for transferring an electrical current across a resistor. *(434)*

**Transportation advertising**  Posters and placards on buses, taxis, railway cars, and subways. *(381)*

**Transportation modes**  The methods used to take people and products from place to place. *(411)*

**Treasury bills (T bills)**  U.S. government debt securities with $10,000 minimum face values and maturities of less than one year. *(537)*

**Treasury bonds**  U.S. government debt securities with $5,000 minimum face values and maturities of up to twenty-five years. *(538)*

**Treasury notes**  U.S. government debt securities with $5,000 minimum face values and maturities of up to ten years. *(538)*

**Trial close**  Preliminary to the close in the sales process, a step designed to determine whether the prospect is really interested in buying. *(386) See also* Close.

**Trust**  Arrangement in which a designated person or institution takes legal possession of personal assets and manages them for the benefit of those who created the trust or for some other designated person. *(80)*

**Trust company**  Financial institution that safeguards individuals' estates or the interests of a company's bond holders. *(491)*

**Trustee**  Trust company appointed by corporation to protect bond holders' interests. *(491)*

**Two-factor theory**  Frederick Herzberg's theory of motivation, based on factors called motivators and hygiene (maintenance) factors. *(271) See also* individual factors.

**Unemployment compensation**  State-run programs providing weekly income benefits to unemployed workers. *(567)*

**Uniform Commercial Code (UCC)**  Code containing regulations pertaining to commercial transactions of businesses and individuals. *(624)*

**Union label**  Label indicating that a manufacturer's product is union-made. *(300)*

**Union shop**  Agreement under which all employees must join the union within a specified period or be fired. *(293)*

**Union steward**  Local union representative. *(298)*

**Universal life insurance**  New type of life insurance that combines term insurance and tax-free investment income. *(577)*

**Universal product code (UPC)**  Bar code that can be scanned and read by computerized checkout stations at supermarkets and other stores. *(355)*

**Unlimited liability**  Business condition in which an owner or owners are responsible for all of the debts of the business. *(63)*

**Upgrading**  Educating, training, or developing present employees to perform the same job better, as changing circumstances demand. *(238)*

**Utility**  The ability of a good or service to satisfy the wants or needs of consumers. *(197) See also* specific utilities.

**Values**  Relative worth or importance placed on people, ideas, or events. *(647)*

**Variable costs**  Business costs that increase directly with production increases, such as materials or parts. *(361)*

**Venture capital**  Money invested in risky new or struggling companies by investment specialists who expect to receive a fast, above-average rate of return. *(108)*

**Vertical mergers**  Purchases by a corporation of other firms that are either suppliers or customers for materials or services of the acquiring firm. *(78)*

**Vestibule training**  Training under simulated work conditions, in an area near the production area that is furnished with equipment like that which employees will be using. *(247)*

**Voluntary bankruptcy**  Bankruptcy in which debtor files the bankruptcy petition. *(623) See also* Bankruptcy.

**Wages**  The compensation employees are paid for their effort. *(12) See also* Time (day) wages.

**Warehouses**  *See* Public warehouses.

**Warranty**  Representation made to the buyer by the seller regarding the quality and performance of a product. *(622) See also* specific warranties.

**Wheel of retailing**  The concept used to describe retailing's state of continual change, as new enterprises grow and are replaced by other new enterprises. *(409)*

**Whole life insurance**  Life insurance providing payment upon the insured's death, regardless of when it may occur, as well as a source of cash-value savings. *(21)*

**Wholesalers**  People or firms that buy finished products from manufacturers and other producers and sell them to retailers, other wholesalers, industries, and government agencies, but rarely to the ultimate consumer. *(91, 403)*

**Word processing**  Using a computer system with letter-quality printer to type, edit, check spelling in, and correct material before sending it to the printer. *(446)*

**Workers' compensation**  Requirement that all employers provide medical and income benefits to employees disabled on the job and to their survivors, in the case of a job-related injury or death. *(567)*

**Work ethic**  Principle emphasizing hard and diligent work, thrift, frugality, and productivity. *(40, 24)*

**Working capital**  A firm's investment in short-term assets, such as cash, short-term securities, accounts receivable, and inventories. *(100)*

**Yellow-dog contracts**  Contracts forbidding employees to join a union, often forced on them by management; made illegal by the Norris–La Guardia Act of 1932. *(293)*

# Suggested Readings

## Chapter 1

CATTERSON, DON. "When U.S. Industry Took the Lead." *Business Week*, October 5, 1981, pp. 14ff.

CLARK, LINDLEY H., JR. "Service Revolution: Too Much Too Soon." *Wall Street Journal*, April 13, 1982, p. 35.

FRIEDMAN, MILTON, and ROSE FRIEDMAN. *Free to Choose.* New York: Harcourt-Brace-Jovanovich, 1980.

JOHNSON, MARGUERITE. "China: Certain Measures of Capitalism." *Time*, April 4, 1983, p. 49.

LOUIS, ARTHUR M. *The Tycoons.* New York: Simon and Schuster, 1981. "Sagas of Five Who Made It." *Time*, February 5, 1982, pp 43–44.

SIMON, WILLIAM E. *A Time for Truth.* New York: Reader's Digest Press/McGraw-Hill, 1978.

TAYLOR, ALEXANDER L., III. "Striking It Rich." *Time*, February 15, 1982, pp 36–42.

"When a Daughter Takes Over the Family Business." *Business Week*, March 29, 1982, pp 172–75.

## Chapter 2

ACKERMAN, ROBERT W. "How Companies Respond to Social Demands." *Harvard Business Review* 51 (July-August 1973):88–98.

BUEHLER, VERNON, and Y. K. SHETTY. "Managerial Response to Social Responsibility Challenge." *Academy of Management Journal* 19 (1976):66–78.

DIBACCO, THOMAS V. "Business Ethics: A View from the Cloister." *Wall Street Journal*, June 10, 1982, p. 30.

"The FTC's Miller Puts His Faith in the Free Market." *Business Week*, June 27, 1983, pp. 66, 70.

GARMENT, SUZANNE. "Toxic-Liability Bills Plant a Time Bomb of Entitlement Costs." *Wall Street Journal*, June 3, 1983, p. 20.

GOTTSCHALK, EARL C., JR. "Firms Hiring New Type of Manager to Study Issues, Emerging Troubles." *Wall Street Journal*, June 10, 1982, pp. 33, 36.

HOLMES, SANDRA. "Corporate Social Performance: Past and Present Areas of Commitment." *Academy of Management Journal* 20 (1977):433–38.

STEINER, GEORGE A., and J. F. STEINER. *Business, Government and Society.* 3rd ed. New York: Random House, 1980. See especially Part 3, pp. 75–217.

WILLIAMS, WALTER. *The State Against Blacks.* New York: New Press, McGraw-Hill, 1982.

ZENISEK, THOMAS J. "Corporate Social Responsibility: A Conceptualization Based on Organizational Literature." *Academy of Mangement Review* 4 (1979):365.

## Chapter 3

CARRINGTON, TIM. "The Annual Nightmare: Meeting with the Shareholders." *Wall Street Journal*, May 9, 1983, p. 30.

HUGHES, KATHLEEN A. "In Mergers, Manners Can Matter a Lot." *Wall Street Journal*, October 4, 1982, p. 35.

HUGHEY, ANN. "More U.S. and Japanese Companies Decide to Operate Joint Ventures." *Wall Street Journal*, May 10, 1983, p. 37.

"J. Peter Grace: Building a New Company Wall Street Ignores." *Business Week*, October 5, 1981, pp. 80–90.

LANDRO, LAURA. "If You Have Always Wanted to Be in Pictures, Partnerships Offer the Chance, but with Risks." *Wall Street Journal*, May 23, 1983, p. 60.

LOUIS, ARTHUR M. "The Bottom Line on Ten Big Mergers." *Fortune*, May 3, 1982, pp. 84–85.

PAULY, DAVID, and HOPE LAMPERT. "The Urge to Unmerge." *Newsweek*, May 2, 1983, p. 70.

SHELLENBERGER, SUE. "Shakeout Begins for Cooperatives As Slump, Competition Take Toll." *Wall Street Journal*, May 17, 1982, p. 33.

WHISLER, THOMAS L. "Some Do's and Don't's for Directors." *Wall Street Journal*, March 21, 1983, p. 20.

WORK, CLEMENS P. "When Merger Mania Gets Too Hot." *U.S. News & World Report*, October 4, 1982, p. 67.

———. "The Merger Drive Goes into Reverse." *U.S. News & World Report*, May 2, 1983, pp. 55–56.

## Chapter 4

The Small Business Administration produces a variety of helpful booklets for people who already run or want to start a small business. These booklets can be obtained from the Superintendent of Documents, U.S. Government Printing Office, Washington, D.C. 20402. Here are ten of the most popular:

*Managing for Profits*, stock number 045-000-00005-2

*Strengthening Small Business Management*, 045-000-00114-8

*An Employee Suggestion System for Small Companies*, 045-000-00020-6

*Human Relations in Small Business*, 045-000-00036-2

*Improving Material Handling in Small Business*, 045-000-00041-9

*Profitable Community Relations for Small Business*, 045-000-00033-8

*Small Business and Government Research and Development*, 045-000-00130-1

*Insurance and Risk Management for Small Business*, 045-000-00037-1

*Selecting Advertising Media: A Guide for Small Business*, 045-000-00154-7

*Financial Control by Time-Absorption Analysis*, 045-000-00134-2

Other suggested readings are:

BULKELEY, WILLIAM L. "The Attractions of Starting a New Venture Prove Irresistible to Some Entrepreneurs." *Wall Street Journal*, June 9, 1981, p. 56.

COX, MEG. "In a Quest for Security, More Employees Set Up

Private Little Ventures." *Wall Street Journal,* September 15, 1981, p. 1.

DiBacco, Thomas V. "Time to Begin Celebrations for Horatio Alger." *Wall Street Journal,* December 31, 1981, p. 6.

Graham, Roberta. "Small Business Beset, Bothered and Beleaguered by Five Big Problems." *Nation's Business* 68 (February 1980):22–31.

———. "The Small Business Report That Tried." *Nation's Business* 68 (June 1980):43–45.

Merwin, R. F. "Does Your Firm Need Outsiders on the Inside?" *Nation's Business* 70 (February 1982):73–79.

"The New Entrepreneurs." *Business Week,* April 18, 1983, pp. 78–82.

Rotbart, Dean. "Husband-and-Wife High-Tech Businesses Start Springing Up As the Industry Booms." *Wall Street Journal,* September 17, 1982, p. 25.

"When Wives Run the Family Business." *Business Week,* January 17, 1983, pp. 118, 121.


## Chapter 5

Chrietelmeir, Jack. *Franchising.* Columbus, Ohio: Ohio Distributive Education Materials.

Finn, Richard P. *Your Fortune in Franchising.* Chicago: Contemporary Books, 1979.

*Franchise Opportunities.* Revised edition. New York: Drake Publishers, 1978.

Henward, Debanks, III, and William Ginalski. *The Franchise Option.* Phoenix, Ariz.: Franchise Group Publishers, 1979.

Seltz, David. *Franchising: Proven Techniques for Rapid Company Expansion and Market Dominance.* New York: McGraw-Hill, 1980.

Tate, Curtis, et al. *Successful Small Business Management.* 3rd ed. Plano, Tex.: Business Publications, 1982. Chapter 24.

U.S. Department of Commerce. *Franchise Opportunities Handbook.* Washington, D.C.: Government Printing Office, 1979. (Contains names, addresses, descriptions of approximately 800 franchise companies.)

———. *Franchising in the Economy, 1981–1983.* Washington, D.C.: Government Printing Office, 1983.


## Chapter 6

Adizes, Ichak. "Once Again and for the Last (?) Time: What IS Management?" In *How to Solve the Mismanagement Crisis.* Homewood, Ill.: Dow Jones–Irwin, 1979.

Athos, Anthony G. *The Art of Japanese Management.* New York: Simon & Schuster, 1981.

Brown, David S. "The Changing Roles and Functions of the Manager." *Management Quarterly* 23 (Summer 1982):7–13.

"A Call for Vision in Managing Technology." *Business Week,* May 24, 1982, pp. 24–33.

Dreyfuss, Joel. "Handing Down the Old Hands' Wisdom." *Fortune,* June 13, 1983, pp. 97–104.

Kotter, John P. "What Effective Managers Really Do." *Harvard Business Review* 60 (November-December 1982):156–57.

Larson, Erik. "Why Are Some Managers Top Performers? A Researcher Picks Out 16 Characteristics." *Wall Street Journal,* January 21, 1983, p. 17.

Lubenow, Gerald C. "The Silicon Valley Style." *Newsweek,* June 8, 1981, pp. 80–83.

Mintzberg, Henry. *The Nature of Managerial Work.* New York: Harper & Row, 1973.

"My Toughest Business Decision Was . . . ." *Wall Street Journal,* February 14, 1983, p. 16.

"A New Era for Management." *Business Week,* April 25, 1983, pp. 50–86.

Ouchi, William G. *Theory Z: How American Business Can Meet the Japanese Challenge.* New York: Avon Books, 1981.

Peters, Thomas J., and Robert H. Waterman, Jr. *In Search of Excellence: Lessons from America's Best-Run Companies.* New York: Harper & Row, 1983.

Reid, Robert D. "A Practical Guide to Using Your Time More Efficiently." *Wall Street Journal,* January 24, 1983, p. 22.

Richardson, David B. "Answer to Ailing Industry: Overhaul at the Very Top." *U.S. News & World Report,* January 17, 1983, pp. 37–39.


## Chapter 7

Cole, Benjamin M. "As Business Copes with 'White-Collar Bloat.'" *U.S. News & World Report,* May 2, 1983, pp. 69–70.

"Corporate Culture." *Business Week,* October 27, 1980, pp. 148–60.

Drucker, Peter. "We Have Become a Society of Organizations." *Wall Street Journal,* January 9, 1978, p. 12.

Jacobs, Sanford L. "A Boss's Most Crucial Decision Often Is to Let Others Decide." *Wall Street Journal,* July 27, 1981, p. 19.

Patton, Arch. "Industry's Misguided Shift to Staff Jobs." *Business Week,* April 5, 1982, pp. 12, 15.

Petre, Peter D. "Meet the Lean, Mean New IMB." *Fortune,* June 13, 1983, pp. 68–82.

Tomasko, Robert M. "Subbing Division, Line Work for Corporate Staff." *Wall Street Journal,* March 28, 1983.

"Why Procter & Gamble Is Playing It Even Tougher." *Business Week,* July 18, 1983, pp. 176–86.


## Chapter 8

Bylinsky, Gene. "The Race to the Automatic Factory." *Fortune,* February 21, 1983, pp. 52–59.

Faflick, Philip. "Here Come the Robots." *Time,* March 7, 1983, pp. 76–77.

Foster, Richard N. "A Call for Vision in Managing Technology." *Business Week,* May 24, 1982, pp. 24–33.

Halberstam, David. "The Quiet Revolution: Robots Enter Our Lives." *Parade,* April 10, 1983, pp. 17–20.

Koten, John. "Further Auto-Plant Closings Likely As Capacity Far Exceeds Production." *Wall Street Journal,* November 24, 1982, p. 29.

Lublin, Joann S. "Steel-Collar Jobs: As Robot Age Arrives, Labor Seeks Protection Against Loss of Work." *Wall Street Journal,* October 26, 1981, pp. 1, 25.

"Quality: The U.S. Drive to Catch Up." *Business Week,* November 1, 1982, pp. 66–80.

Saga, Ichiro. "Japan's Robots Produce Problems for Workers." *Wall Street Journal,* February 28, 1983, p. 21.

Schonberger, Richard J. "A Revolutionary Way to Streamline the Factory." *Wall Street Journal,* November 15, 1982, p. 28.

Waters, Craig R. "There's a Robot in Your Future." *INC.* 4 (June 1982):64–67.

White, George, et al. "A Drive to Put Quality Back into U.S. Goods." *U.S. News & World Report,* September 20, 1982, pp. 49–50.

"Will the Slide Kill Quality Circles?" *Business Week,* January 11, 1982, pp. 108–9.


## Chapter 9

Barthel, Joan. "Network Newswomen Explain: Why There Are Still No Female Dan Rathers." *TV Guide,* August 6, 1983, p. 10.

Buss, Dale D. "High-Tech Track: Retraining of Workers for Automated Plants Gets Off to Slow Start." *Wall Street Journal*, April 13, 1983, pp. 1, 17.

"Can You Afford to Retire?" *Newsweek*, June 1, 1981, pp. 24–25.

Clark, Lindley H., Jr. "Service Revolution: Too Much Too Soon?" *Wall Street Journal*, April, 13, 1982, p. 35.

"The Crisis in Social Security." *Newsweek*, June 1, 1981, pp. 25–27.

"A Fight over the Freedom to Fire." *Business Week*, September 20, 1982, p. 116.

"Flexible Work Hours Gather Momentum." *U.S. News & World Report*, September 28, 1981, pp. 76–77.

Freund, William C. "The Looming Impact of Population Changes." *Wall Street Journal*, April 6, 1982, p. 34.

Hildreth, James M. "Social Security Pitting Old Against Young." *U.S. News & World Report*, May 2, 1983, p. 64.

"How Executives See Women in Management." *Business Week*, June 28, 1982, p. 10.

"It's Getting Harder to Make a Firing Stick." *Business Week*, June 27, 1983, pp. 104–5.

Larson, Erik. "Why Do Some People Outperform Others? Psychologist Picks Out Six Characteristics." *Wall Street Journal*, January 13, 1982, p. 33.

Lublin, Joann. "Effects of 'Baby Bust' Are Shrinking Ranks of Younger Workers." *Wall Street Journal*, September 10, 1981, pp. 1, 23.

Mills, David. "Program to Employ Minorities Is Criticized As It Drifts Toward Aiding Middle Class." *Wall Street Journal*, July 28, 1983, p. 21.

Ohmae, Kenichi. "Steel Collar Workers: The Lessons from Japan." *Wall Street Journal*, February 26, 1982, p. 26.

Scheler, Jeffery, and William D. Hartley. "When Women Take Over as Bosses." *U.S. News & World Report*, March 22, 1982, pp. 77–80.

Schwimmer, Lawrence D. "Women Executives: What Holds So Many Back?" *U.S. News & World Report*, February 8, 1982, p. 63–64.

Waldholz, Michael. "'Cafeteria' Benefits Plans Let Employees Fill Their Plates, Then Pay with Tax-Free Dollars." *Wall Street Journal*, May 9, 1983, p. 58.

Wall, Jerry L., and H. M. Shatshat. "Controversy over the Issue of Mandatory Retirement." *Personnel Administrator* 26 (October 1981):25–30, 45.

Wermiel, Stephen. "Court Orders That Shield Minorities from Layoffs Generate Bitterness." *Wall Street Journal*, March 23, 1983, pp. 1, 42.

## Chapter 10

Alber, Antoine F. "How (and How Not) to Approach Job Enrichment." *Personnel Journal* 58 (December 1979):837–41.

Arch, J. "How Effective Speaking Bolsters Your Career Rise." *Marketing Times* 27 (March-April 1980):33–34.

"Behind the UPS Mystique: Puritanism and Productivity." *Business Week*, June 6, 1983, pp. 66–73.

Bralove, Mary. "Taking the Boss at His Word May Turn Out to Be a Big Mistake at a Lot of Companies." *Wall Street Journal*, June 4, 1982, p. 29.

Cook, David T. "The 'Idol' Job: Meeting Problems Is All Part of It." *Christian Science Monitor*, April 26, 1982, p. 15.

Fay, P. P., and D. N. Beach. "Management by Objectives Evaluated." *Personnel Journal* 53 (October 1974):767–69.

"How Bosses Get People to Work Harder." *U.S. News & World Report*, January 29, 1979, pp. 63–64.

Kidder, Tracy. *The Soul of a New Machine*. New York: Avon Books, 1981.

Leslie, Stuart W. *Boss Kettering*. New York: Columbia University Press, 1983.

"Short Work Week for Some." *Personnel Administrator* 24 (October 1979):45.

## Chapter 11

Anderson, Harry. "The Rise and Fall of Big Labor." *Newsweek*, September 5, 1983, pp. 50–54.

Barth, Peter S. "The New Mood in Labor-Management Relations." *Wall Street Journal*, April 6, 1982, p. 34.

Cangemi, Joseph P., et al. "Differences Between Pro-Union and Pro-Company Employees." *Personnel Journal* 55 (September 1976):451ff.

Greenberger, Robert S. "AFL-CIO's Big Organizing Drive in the Sun Belt Runs into Problems." *Wall Street Journal*, November 16, 1982, p. 35.

Kassalow, Everett M. "Occupational Functions of Trade Unionism in the United States." *White-Collar Report*, January 9, 1961, pp. 7ff.

Lublin, Joann S. "Steel-Collar Jobs: As Robot Age Arrives, Labor Seeks Protection Against Loss of Work." *Wall Street Journal*, October 26, 1981, pp. 1, 25.

Main, Jeremy. "How to Be a Better Negotiator." *Fortune*, September 19, 1983, pp. 141–46.

Megginson, Leon C. *Personnel Management: A Human Resources Approach*. 4th ed. Homewood, Ill.: Irwin, 1981, pp. 500–24.

Reed, David. "Detroit Faces the Rising Sun: A New Day Dawns for the Motor City." *Reader's Digest*, September 1983, pp. 89–94, 153–72.

Schnapp, John B. "The '82 Auto Negotiations: Last Hurrah?" *Wall Street Journal*, December 3, 1981, p. 28.

Sheler, Jeffery L. "Unions Still Find South a Tough Row to Hoe," *U.S. News & World Report*, June 21, 1982, pp. 62–63.

## Chapter 12

Bloom, Paul N., and William D. Novelli. "Problems and Challenges in Social Marketing." *Journal of Marketing* vol. 45 (Spring 1981):79–88.

Curley, John. "Some Think a 'Baby Boom' Spending Spree Could Lead to Strong Economic Recovery." *Wall Street Journal*, January 24, 1983, p. 25.

"It's Consumers Who Really Rule the Roost." *U.S. News & World Report*, April 16, 1982, pp. 36–37.

"Learning to Think About Today's Mature Market." *Marketing Times* 26 (May-June 1979):27–29.

McBee, Susanna. "Lifestyle of the '80s: Anything Goes." *U.S. News & World Report*, August 1, 1983, pp. 45–48.

Nag, Amal. "Information Brokers Thrive by Helping Firms Get Facts." *Wall Street Journal*, July 7, 1981, p. 31.

"A Portrait of America." *Newsweek*, January 17, 1983, pp. 20–33.

Sanoff, Alvin P. "As Americans Cope with a Changing Population." *U.S. News & World Report*, August 9, 1982, pp. 26–28.

Shellenbarger, Sue. "Societal Shift: As More Women Take Jobs, They Affect Ads, Politics, Family Life." *Wall Street Journal*, June 29, 1982, pp. 1, 8.

Sowell, Thomas. *Ethnic America: A History*. New York: Basic Books, 1981.

Taylor, Ronald A. "Telephones' New Era: How Users Will Fare." *U.S. News & World Report*, March 14, 1983, pp. 71–72.

Toman, Barbara. "Department Stores Start Adding Seminars and Services to Attract Working Women." *Wall Street Journal*, July 19, 1982, p. 19.

## Chapter 13

ABRAMS, BILL. "Packaging Often Irks Buyers, But Firms Are Slow to Change." *Wall Street Journal*, January 28, 1982, p. 29.

BIRNBAUM, JEFFREY H. "Pricing of Productions Is Still an Art, Often Having Little Link to Costs." *Wall Street Journal*, November 25, 1981, pp. 29, 49.

CARLEY, WILLIAM M. "Laws Against 'Predatory Pricing' by Firms Are Being Relaxed in Many Court Rulings." *Wall Street Journal*, July 14, 1982, p. 54.

"Food: A Move Toward Higher-Margin Products." *Business Week*, January 8, 1979, pp. 46–50.

IBRAHIM, YOUSSEF M., and DAVID IGNATIUS. "Energy Switch: As Oil Use Declines, Experts See a Slowing in Price Increases." *Wall Street Journal*, January 27, 1982, pp. 1, 24.

JOHNSON, ROBERT. "Rebating Rises, But Unhappy Firms Can't Think of a Good Alternative." *Wall Street Journal*, December 9, 1982, p. 31.

KNEALE, DENNIS. "Makers of Designer Goods Starting to Crack Down on Counterfeiting." *Wall Street Journal*, June 28, 1982, p. 15.

"Listening to the Voice of the Marketplace." *Business Week*, February 21, 1983, pp. 90, 94.

"Supermarket Scanners Get Smarter." *Business Week*, August 17, 1981, pp. 88–91.

WHITE, GEORGE, et al. "A Drive to Put Quality Back into U.S. Goods." *U.S. News & World Report*, September 20, 1982, pp. 49–50.

"Why Detroit Can't Cut Prices." *Business Week*, March 1, 1982, pp. 110–11.

## Chapter 14

ABRAMS, BILL. "Firms Start Using Computers to Take the Place of Salesmen." *Wall Street Journal*, July 15, 1982, p. 31.

"Are Big Advertisers Turning Off TV?" *Wall Street Journal*, May 7, 1981, p. 29.

BRALOVE, MARY. "Advetising World's Portrayal of Women Is Starting to Shift." *Wall Street Journal*, October 28, 1982, p. 31.

COONEY, JOHN E. "Going Commercial: Cable Television Is Attracting More Ads; Sharply Focused Programs Are One Lure." *Wall Street Journal*, March 31, 1981, p. 56.

KESSLER, FELIX. "American TV Ads Look Bad to Some International Judges." *Wall Street Journal*, July 1, 1982, p. 19.

KNEALE, DENNIS. "Stations That Show Only Ads Attract a Lot of TV Watchers." *Wall Street Journal*, September 23, 1982, p. 33.

MACHALOBA, DANIEL. "More Magazines Aim for Affluent Readers, But Some Worry That Shakeout Is Coming." *Wall Street Journal*, October 4, 1982, p. 35.

"Magazines That Mirror Women's Success." *Business Week*, January 11, 1982, pp. 39–40.

PERRY, JAMES M. "The Power Brokers: A PR Man Uses Access to Influential People to Lure, Help Clients." *Wall Street Journal*, March 25, 1982, pp. 1, 20.

PETERSON, FRANKLYN, and JUDI KESSELMAN-TURKEL. "Catching Customers with Sweepstakes." *Fortune*, February 8, 1982, pp. 84ff.

SALMAN, SANDRA. "Marketing by Satellite in Europe." *New York Times*, August 18, 1982, p. D-9.

———. "[Advertising] Untouched by Human Hands." *New York Times*, August 16, 1982, p. D-9.

WALDHOLZ, MICHAEL. "Drug Firms Using Publicity to Popularize New Medicines." *Wall Street Journal*, July 22, 1982, p. 21.

"What It Takes to Succeed in $ALE$." *Nation's Business*, April 1982, pp. 42ff.

## Chapter 15

ABRAMS, BILL. "Electronic Shopping Awaiting Customer, Corporate Support." *Wall Street Journal*, June 16, 1983, p. 33.

"An Airline Ticket at the Corner Store." *Business Week*, December 27, 1982, p. 34.

CURLEY, JOHN. "Catalogs Are Getting Thin, Specialized." *Wall Street Journal*, September 13, 1982, p. 25.

———. "Payless Profits by Prompting Impulse Buys." *Wall Street Journal*, July 3, 1983, p. 33.

GALLESE, LIZ ROMAN. "The Cheese at Spag's Is Next to the Rugs—Over by Golf Balls." *Wall Street Journal*, January 28, 1983, pp. 1, 23.

MALONEY, LAWRENCE D. "Now It's the 'Stay-at-Home Society.'" *U.S. News & World Report*, June 28, 1982, pp. 64–66.

"No Frills Food: New Power for the Supermarkets." *Business Week*, March 23, 1981, pp. 70–80.

RICCI, CLAUDIA. "Discount Business Booms Pleasing Buyers, Irking Department Stores." *Wall Street Journal*, May 3, 1983, p. 35.

"Ringing Up Sales." *Time*, June 14, 1982, pp. 65–66.

"Round Two for Home Computer Makers." *Business Week*, September 19, 1983, pp. 93–95.

## Chapter 16

"Artificial Intelligence: The Second Computer Age Begins." *Business Week*, March 8, 1982, pp. 66–75.

BRALOVE, MARY. "Direct Data: Some Chief Executives Bypass, and Irk, Staffs in Getting Information." *Wall Street Journal*, January 12, 1983, pp. 1, 25.

BURNHAM, DAVID. *The Rise of the Computer State*. New York: Random House, 1983.

CHACE, SUSAN. "Silicon's Successor? Tomorrow's Computer May Reproduce Itself, Some Visionaries Think." *Wall Street Journal*, January 6, 1983, pp. 1, 14.

CHRISTIE, LINDA G., and JESS W. CURRY, JR. *The ABCs of Microcomputers: A Computer Literacy Primer*. Englewood Cliffs, N.J.: Prentice-Hall, 1983.

"The Coming Shakeout in Personal Computers." *Business Week*, November 22, 1982, pp. 72–83.

"Computer Security: What Can Be Done." *Business Week*, September 26, 1983, pp. 126–30.

"Computer Shock Hits the Office." *Business Week*, August 8, 1983, pp. 46–60.

EBY, SHEILA M. "Eight Problems a Computer Can't Solve." *INC.* 4 (March 1982):103–4.

EVANS, CHRISTOPHER. *The Making of the Micro—A History of the Computer*. Princeton, N.J.: Van Nostrand Reinhold, 1983.

FALVEY, JACK. "Don't Count Too Heavily on That Personal Computer." *Wall Street Journal*, August 15, 1983, p. 16.

GOLDFIELD, RANDY J. "Executive Terminals: Where They Pay and Where They Don't." *Administrative Management* 43 (January 1982):31ff.

"High-Tech Entrepreneurs Create a Silicon Valley in Taiwan." *Business Week*, August 1, 1983, pp. 34–37.

"How Computers Remake the Manager's Job." *Business Week*, April 25, 1983, pp. 68–70.

*How to Buy a Home Computer*. Washington, D.C.: Electronic Industries Association, 1983.

"How to Conquer Fear of Computers." *Business Week*, March 29, 1982, pp. 176–78.

HUBBARD, LINDA. "Keys to a Better Life." *Modern Maturity* 26 (June-July 1983):36–39.

KIDDER, TRACY. *The Soul of a New Machine*. New York: Avon Books, 1981.

MACOVSKY, SUSAN J. "Who Needs Home Computers?" *Money*, June 1980, pp. 108–9.

MALONEY, LAWRENCE. "A Nation That's Hooked on Computers." *U.S. News & World Report*, July 25, 1983, pp. 64–66.

NEIKIRK, BILL. "Do Students Need Computer Literacy?" *Tulsa World*, March 30, 1983, p. A-11.

PASZTOR, ANDY. "Expert Fights Fraudulent Use of Computers." *Wall Street Journal*, May 28, 1982, pp. 1, 22.

PHILLIPS, CAROLYN. "Campus Glitch: Universities in U.S. Are Losing Ground in Computer Education." *Wall Street Journal*, January 14, 1983, pp. 1, 15.

"The Spreading Danger of Computer Crime." *Business Week*, April 20, 1981, pp. 86–92.

"The Squeeze Begins in Personal Computers." *Business Week*, May 30, 1983, pp. 91, 95.

VAN HORN, RICHARD L. "Don't Expect Too Much from Your Computer System." *Wall Street Journal*, October 25, 1982, p. 24.

WARD, BERNIE. "The Computer Age: Where Will We Find the Talent?" *Sky*, March 1982, pp. 76–84.

### Chapter 17

BALDWIN, WILLIAM. "Productivity, American Style." *Forbes*, February 15, 1982, pp. 31ff.

GRANT, JOHN L. "Inflation's Full Impact on the Bottom Line." *Business Week*, February 7, 1983, p. 8.

GREENE, RICHARD. "The Check Is in the Mail." *Forbes*, March 1, 1982, pp. 100ff.

HERSHMAN, ARLENE. "New Game in Off-Balance Sheet Financing." *Dun's Business Month* 119 (February 1982):56–60.

HUDSON, RICHARD L. "Cooking the Books: SEC Charges Fudging of Corporate Figures Is a Growing Practice." *Wall Street Journal*, June 2, 1983, pp. 1, 24.

"Inflation Scoreboard: A Real Look At Earnings; 1982 Was a Dismal Year." *Business Week*, May 2, 1983, pp. 76–80.

KETCHUM, BRADFORD W., JR. "You and Your Accountant." *INC.* 4 (March 1982):81–90.

SHERN, STEPHANIE. "The Lively Life of an Accountant." *Business Week's Guide to Careers* 1 (Fall/Winter 1983):31–34.

"When National Debt Gets Out of Control." *U.S. News & World Report*, June 14, 1982, pp. 71–72.

### Chapter 18

ANDERSON, HARRY. "Is the Fed Flying Blind?" *Newsweek*, May 18, 1981, p. 87.

"Banking's Squeeze." *Business Week*, April 12, 1982, pp. 67–85.

BETTNER, JILL. "New Money-Market Deposit Accounts Will Spur Competition for Funds and Benefit Consumers." *Wall Street Journal*, November 15, 1982, p. 56.

CLARK, LINDLEY H., JR. "Make the Fed a Branch of the Treasury." *Wall Street Journal*, March 16, 1982, p. 29.

———. "Now Is the Time to Let the Federal Reserve Alone." *Wall Street Journal*, August 24, 1982, p. 31.

———. "The Fed Did Its Act and Nobody Clapped." *Wall Street Journal*, December 21, 1982, p. 27.

"Electronic Banking." *Business Week*, January 18, 1982, pp. 70–80.

FEDERAL RESERVE SYSTEM, BOARD OF GOVERNORS. *The Federal Reserve System: Purposes and Functions.* Washington, D.C.: Government Printing Office, September 1974.

GARDNER, JUDITH B., and JOHN COLLINS. "Will Tax Cut Start a New Savings Surge?" *U.S. News & World Report*, July 12, 1982, pp. 70–71.

"International Banking: The Battle Heats Up." *Dun's Business Month* 119 (March 1982):100–102.

MALABRE, ALFRED L., JR. "Tracking a Trend: Interest Rates Often Continue Edging Down Long After Recession Ends, Recovery Begins." *Wall Street Journal*, November 18, 1982, p. 56.

METZ, TIM. "Merger Trend Among Banks and S&Ls Viewed as Chance for Small Investors, Not Professionals." *Wall Street Journal*, May 21, 1982, p. 33.

"New-Fashioned Thrift: Growing Variety in Insured Deposits." *Business Week*, December 28, 1981, pp. 138–40.

PAULY, DAVID. "How Safe Are Your Savings?" *Newsweek*, March 15, 1982, pp. 50–55.

QUINN, JANE BRYANT. "Your One-Stop Money Shop." *Newsweek*, July 19, 1982, p. 57.

SMITH, LEE. "Merrill Lynch's Latest Bombshell for Bankers." *Fortune*, April 19, 1982, pp. 57ff.

TANGORRA, JOANNE. "It's 9 A.M. Do You Know Where Your Cash Is?" *INC.* 4 (April 1982):48–50.

"Why New S&Ls Are Doing So Well." *Business Week*, June 7, 1982, pp. 96–98.

### Chapter 19

"Bonds and Beyond: Long Term Gets Tougher." *Business Week*, March 1, 1982, pp. 47–50.

FELDSTEIN, MARTIN. "America's New Savings Policy." *Wall Street Journal*, August 19, 1981, p. 28.

FORD, JOAN G. "A Dozen Ways to Borrow Money." *INC.* 3 (December 1981):75–80.

JACOBS, SANFORD L. "Venture Capital Conference Attracts Many Seeking Cash." *Wall Street Journal*, May 28, 1982, p. 19.

———. "SBA's Plan to Cut Loan Rates Generates Lots of Opposition." *Wall Street Journal*, October 26, 1981, p. 25.

MAMIS, ROBERT, and SUSAN E. CURRIER. "R&D Partnerships Come of Age." *INC.* 4 (March 1982):63–76.

"The Perilous Hunt for Financing." *Business Week*, March 1, 1982, pp. 44–45.

PHALON, RICHARD. "[The Venture Capital Business Is] Getting A Little Crowded." *Forbes*, February 15, 1982, pp. 51–52.

SALAMON, JULIE. "Bankers Who Step In If Loans Go Bad Reveal Lenders' Other Face." *Wall Street Journal*, April 2, 1982, pp. 1, 14.

"Short-Term Credit: Playing Easy to Get." *Business Week*, March 1, 1982, pp. 45–46.

"Venture Capital: The Game Gets Riskier." *Dun's Business Month* 119 (April 1982):68ff.

### Chapter 20

AMLING, FREDERICK, and WILLIAM G. GROMS. *Personal Financial Management.* Homewood, Ill.: Richard D. Irwin, 1982.

"Behind the Market's Wild Ride." *Business Week*, October 25, 1982, pp. 98–103.

COHEN, JEROME B., EDWARD ZINBARG, and ARTHUR ZEIKEL. *Investment Analysis and Portfolio Management.* 3rd ed. Homewood, Ill.: Richard D. Irwin, 1977.

ENGEL, LOUIS. *How To Buy Stocks.* 6th ed. New York: Bantam Books, 1977.

GREENLEAF, JAMES, RUTH FOSTER, and ROBERT PRINSKY. *Understanding Financial Data in the Wall Street Journal.* Princeton, N.J.: Dow Jones & Company, Education Service Bureau, 1982.

HARDY, C. COLBURN. *Dun and Bradstreet's Guide to $Your Investments$.* New York: Harper & Row, 1982.

LANG, LARRY R., and THOMAS GILLESPIE. *Strategy for Personal Finance.* 2nd ed. New York: McGraw-Hill, 1981.

"Mutual Funds Resurge." *Business Week*, March 31, 1980, pp. 68–78.

New York Stock Exchange. *You and the Investment World.* New York: NYSE, 1979.

*1983 Mutual Fund Fact Book.* Washington, D.C.: Investment Company Institute, 1983.

*What Every Investor Should Know.* Washington, D.C.: Securities and Exchange Commission, 1982.

Zweig, Martin E. *The ABC's of Market Forecasting.* New York: Dow Jones & Company, 1981.

## Chapter 21

Anderson, Harry, et al. "A $60 Million Vanishing Act." *Newsweek,* October 17, 1983, p. 79.

Christy, James. "Selling Insurance to Risk Managers." *National Insurance Buyer* 13 (September 1966):16.

"Federal Action Sought as Products Liability Litigation Soars." *Tulsa World,* October 8, 1982, p. 14-A.

Gest, Ted. "The Price Women Would Pay for Unisex Pensions." *U.S. News & World Report,* May 9, 1983, pp. 168–69.

———. "When Employees Turn into Thieves." *U.S. News & World Report,* September 26, 1983, pp. 79–80.

Kelly, Orr. "Where There's a Profit, There's a Spy." *U.S. News & World Report,* May 9, 1983, pp. 121–22.

Lublin, Joann S. "Feminists Plan Push for Bill Requiring Unisex Insurance." *Wall Street Journal,* June 3, 1983, p. 6.

Mack, Barbara. "A Prescription for Cutting Corporate Health Expenses." *Wall Street Journal,* July 18, 1983, p. 18.

"New Court Rulings That Raise the Risks for Insurers." *Business Week,* August 15, 1983, pp. 118–19.

"New Types of Life Insurance." *U.S. News & World Report,* September 5, 1983, p. 59.

"Pro and Con: Require Unisex Insurance Rates?" *U.S. News & World Report,* July 25, 1983, pp. 59–60.

Silverman, Elizabeth S. "Insurance Whose Value Can Soar." *Fortune,* July 11, 1983, pp. 155, 158.

Sullivan, Brian P. "Life Insurance Coverage Changing." *Tulsa World,* February 5, 1983, p. B-4.

Wermiel, Stephen. "Supreme Court Reaffirms It Won't Decide Who Is Liable for Asbestos-Injury Claims." *Wall Street Journal,* March 8, 1983, p. 12.

## Chapter 22

Brand, David. "Europeans Subsidized Soviet Pipeline Work Mainly to Save Jobs." *Wall Street Journal,* November 2, 1982, pp. 1, 24.

———. "In Western Europe, Some Countries Owe Big Sums to Foreigners." *Wall Street Journal,* December 14, 1982, pp. 1, 16.

Brooks, Geraldine. "Here's a Trade War That May Stretch Your Imagination." *Wall Street Journal,* September 9, 1983, pp. 1, 19.

Clutterbuck, David. "Breaking Through the Cultural Barrier." *International Management* 35 (December 1980):41–42.

Grover, Stephen. "Employees Start Looking Again at Jobs Abroad." *Wall Street Journal,* October 28, 1981, p. 22.

Kessler, Felix. "France Spends Billions on Goal of Becoming Leader in Technology." *Wall Street Journal,* September 14, 1982, pp. 1, 18.

Kneale, Dennis. "New Foreign Products Pour into U.S. Market in Increasing Numbers." *Wall Street Journal,* September 11, 1982, pp. 1, 25.

Lehner, Urban C. "The Japanese Market, Once Hostile to U.S., Is Opening to Imports." *Wall Street Journal,* May 12, 1982, pp. 1, 24.

"Living Standards—U.S. Still Ranks High." *U.S. News & World Report,* December 20, 1982, pp. 52–53.

Pascale, Richard Tanner, and Anthony G. Athos. *The Art of Japanese Management: Application to American Executives* (New York: Simon and Schuster, 1981).

Pine, Art. "Taiwan Seeks Move to High Technology; Plan Could Pose Threat to U.S. and Japan." *Wall Street Journal,* January 20, 1983, p. 46.

———. "Threat of a Trade War Rises As Recession Spurs Competition, Natives Impose Curbs." *Wall Street Journal,* November 17, 1982, p. 56.

———. "U.S. Plans Moves to Ease the Debt of Poor Nations." *Wall Street Journal,* February 7, 1983, p. 3.

Schlender, Brenton R. "U.S. Firms in Mexico Ride Out Disruptions in the Economy There." *Wall Street Journal,* November 26, 1982, pp. 1, 22.

Smith, Lee. "Cracks in the Japanese Work Ethic." *Fortune,* May 14, 1984, pp. 162–68.

Spivak, Jonathan. "Italian Socialists Try to Reduce State's Role in Running Industry." *Wall Street Journal,* September 23, 1982, pp. 1, 12.

Tyson, Laura D. "World Economic Outlook: The West Snaps Back, But the Socialist Bloc Stagnates." *Business Week,* May 24, 1982, pp. 166–84.

"Why Detroit Still Can't Get Going." *Business Week,* November 9, 1981, pp. 106–10.

## Chapter 23

Bernstein, Peter W., et al. "Will Uncle Sam Go Private?" *Fortune,* January 9, 1984, pp. 33–34.

Cifelli, Anna. "Here Come the Reregulators." *Fortune,* January 9, 1984, pp. 123–25.

———. "Rolling Back the Freedom to Manage." *Fortune,* January 9, 1984, pp. 90–94.

"Deregulation Will Take Bus Lines on a Rough Ride." *Business Week,* July 11, 1983, pp. 66, 68.

Hughey, Ann, and Eileen A. Powell. "Government-Waste Panel Eyes $60 Billion in Cost-Cutting, But Loud Dissent Expected." *Wall Street Journal,* April 4, 1983, p. 19.

Litan, Robert E., and William D. Nordhaus. *Reforming Federal Regulation.* New Haven: Yale University Press, 1984.

McBee, Susanna. "Reagan's Regulators—Their Fire Is Flickering." *U.S. News & World Report,* September 26, 1983, pp. 51–53.

"One Touch of Unity on Unitary Taxes." *Fortune,* January 23, 1984, p. 41.

"State Regulators Rush In Where Washington No Longer Treads." *Business Week,* September 19, 1983, pp. 124–31.

"A Stunning Challenge to the Sanctity of Contracts." *Business Week,* August 22, 1983, pp. 76–77.

Tolchin, Susan J., and Martin Tolchin. *Dismantling America.* Boston: Houghton Mifflin, 1983.

## Chapter 24

Abernathy, William J., Kim B. Clark, and Alan M. Kantrow. *Industrial Renaissance.* New York: Basic Books, 1982.

Bolles, Richard N. *What Color Is Your Parachute? A Practical Manual for Job Hunters and Career Changers.* Berkeley, Calif.: Ten Speed Press, 1979.

Borders, James. "Career Niches in the Coming Era: An Interview with Alvin Toffler." *The Black Collegian,* September/October 1983, pp. 112–115.

Bostwick, B. E. *Finding the Job You've Always Wanted.* New York: John Wiley and Sons, 1977.

Career Research Systems, Inc. *Career Opportunity Index.* Huntington Beach, Calif. Annual. (Each edition provides placement officials and individual applicants with (1) a six-month projection of each employer's anticipated openings, the typical requirements of the positions, and the benefits

offered, (2) a description of each employer, including products, services, financial history, facilities, etc., and (3) an occupational index matching an individual's background to needs of those employers using compatible experience and/or education.)

———. *Career Opportunity Update.* Huntington Beach, Calif. Semi-monthly. (Lists positions available in accounting and finance, administration and management, business specialists, clerical, computer science and data processing, manufacturing and production, overseas employment opportunities, sales and marketing, and other business positions. Companies and addresses are included.)

CHACE, SUSAN. "Mind Machines: Scientists Are Laboring at Making Computers Think for Themselves." *Wall Street Journal,* March 29, 1983, pp. 1, 22.

THE COLLEGE PLACEMENT COUNCIL, INC. *College Placement Annual.* Bethlehem, Pa.: The College Placement Council. (Counsel for the graduate; alphabetical listing of U.S. employers and U.S. government agencies; and employment indexes—occupational, geographical, and special employment categories. Provides information on the positions customarily offered to college graduates by principal employers.)

FOSTER, RICHARD N. "A Call for Vision in Managing Technology." *Business Week,* May 24, 1982, pp. 24–33.

FOUNDATION FOR STUDENT COMMUNICATIONS, INC. *Business Today.* Princeton, N.J.: Foundation for Student Communications. (Published three times during the academic year, for students by students.)

FOX, MARCIA R. *Put Your Degree to Work: A Career-Planning and Job-Hunting Guide for the New Professional.* New York: W. W. Norton, 1979.

HILLKIRK, JOHN. "Japan Stars at Gee-Whiz Hi-Tech Show." *USA Today,* January 9, 1984, pp. 1-A, 2-A.

JOHNSON, PATRICE. "Where the Jobs Are." *Black Enterprise,* February 1981, pp. 39–40.

LAWRENCE, PAUL R., and DAVIS DYER. *Renewing American Industry.* New York: Free Press, 1982.

PINE, ART. "Today May Appear Bleak But 1990 Looks Great." *Wall Street Journal,* May 29, 1982, p. 1.

PORT, OTIS. "Business in the Year 2001." *Business Week's Guide to Careers* 1 (Fall/Winter 1983):53–55.

"A Productivity Revolution in the Service Sector." *Business Week,* September 5, 1983, pp. 106–8.

"A Quantum Leap for Communications." *Business Week,* November 28, 1983, pp. 92–96.

RECER, PAUL. "Yankee Ingenuity: Ways It Will Change Your Life." *U.S. News & World Report,* June 8, 1981, pp. 64–66.

SCHMIDT, PEGGY J. *Making It on Your First Job: When You're Young, Inexperienced and Ambitious.* New York: Avon, 1981.

U.S. DEPARTMENT OF LABOR. *Occupational Outlook Handbook.* Washington, D.C.: U.S. Government Printing Office. (A major source of vocational information for more than 850 occupations and 30 industries. For each occupation, the handbook describes what workers do on the job, the training or education needed, earnings, advancement possibilities, and working conditions. Comments on the availability of jobs in the years ahead are also provided.)

UNIVERSITY COMMUNICATIONS, INC. *Business World—Men* and *Business World—Women.* Rahway, N.J.: University Communications. (A career magazine for college seniors, published in the fall and spring each year.)

"What the Next 50 Years Will Bring." *U.S. News & World Report,* May 9, 1983, pp. A-1, A-42.

"Year 2000: The Shape of Things to Come." *U.S. News & World Report,* April 26, 1982, pp. 58–59.

# Name and Company Index

# Subject Index